Distributism for Dorothy

Or

The Economy of Salvation and other Exhortations to Dethrone the Great God Mammon

by Father Lawrence C. Smith

Sacerdos vagus

Loreto Publications
Fitzwilliam, NH 03447
AD 2014

Dedicated to the Second Person
Of the Most Holy Trinity Incarnate
Jesus Christ

From the Novena to the Immaculate Conception

O Mother of the King of the universe, most perfect member of the human race, "our tainted nature's solitary boast," we turn to thee as mother, advocate, and Mediatrix. O Holy Mary, assist us in our present necessity. By thy Immaculate Conception, O Mary conceived without sin, we humbly beseech thee from the bottom of our hearts to intercede for us with thy Divine Son and ask that we be granted the favor for which we now plead... (State your intention here.*)

O Mary of the Immaculate Conception, Mother of Christ, thou hadst influence with thy Divine Son while upon this earth; thou hast the same influence now in heaven. Pray for us and obtain for us from Him the granting of our petition if it be the divine will. Amen.

*That the United States of America will recognize and obey the sovereignty of Jesus Christ our King, Our Lady and patroness, the Immaculate Conception our Queen, the primacy of St. Peter and his successors, and thus strive to bring about the triumph of the Blessed Virgin Mary's Immaculate Heart by the power of the Holy Ghost to bring us the mercy of our Lord Jesus Christ's Sacred Heart for the glory of God the Father. Amen.

Contents

Part One

Preface: "Distributism for Dorothy"

What follows in the next two-thirds of a ream of thoughts trying to get unjumbled is not an apologia for distributism. The intent is to emphasize the necessity of bringing back *sanctity*, as revealed by God and taught by the Catholic Church, to the heart of man's existence on earth. That is, the necessity of doing so for those who wish to have a life that does not simply cease (or more accurately, descend into the inferno—and stay there) when existence on earth ends. Distributism is, in the estimation of the author of the present collection, the best summation of what had once been the common sense of Christendom, which is to say what formerly was the set of assumptions of all who arranged their economic lives in keeping with their profession of faith within the Church founded by Jesus Christ on the Rock of St. Peter. Different names for, descriptions of, or perspectives on the same subject are possible, but the point is that man lives or dies, not by bread alone, but to the extent that he embraces the wood of the Cross—or not.

The title of this initial series of recollections is chosen for reasons wholly unrelated to what would be expected if economics were the only subject at hand. Three reasons especially recommended themselves to the author as he decided upon the title for this preface: 1) he likes alliteration 2) said title is reminiscent of titles of not entirely dissimilar works by G.B. Shaw () and Hilaire Belloc () and 3) at the conclusion of this preface are answers to a set of questions posed by a nice lady named "Dorothy". That is her real name, and if this work had not already been dedicated to the second person of the Most Holy Trinity incarnate, it would have been given to her. Dorothy, good Catholic that she is, does not mind being Miss First Runner-Up when the winner is Jesus.

That said, let us into the breach…

Karl Marx made the gross mistake of predicating his edifice of thought on all-out class struggle. Adam Smith's theories lead to the absurd assertion that self-interest motivates man's every economic action. Some contemporary Catholics posit their observation of the faith on the idea that as long as they attend the immemorial Mass, little heed need be given to how they earn their daily bread. Others aver that to earn one's daily bread is tantamount to a spiritual experience. All of these positions are wrong, if not actually all wrong. That's the problem with error, its love-hate relationship with the truth. Heresy courts orthodoxy seeking only a marriage of convenience; divorce is inevitable.

In the inimitable Latin of St. Thomas Aquinas: *Bonum est ex integra causa, malum ex quocumque defectu.* In the vulgar idiom of 21st century America, one might paraphrase that to mean, "Being a little wrong is like being a little pregnant—either you are or you aren't!" To be a bit more refined, we might put it thus: "That which is good is wholly good, the bad is so because of *any* defect." A miss is as good as a mile. Moral theology is a far more exact science than horseshoes, hand-grenades, or nuclear weapons.

Catholic faith is catholic in the realm of dogma. It is catholic in its transcendence of history. It is catholic in its ubiquity in geography. It is catholic in its applications to the multitudinous disciplines of human thought. *And it is catholic in its presence in the daily life of the home, which is the simple way of saying in the* **economy.**

Economics is not about nation states. Economics is not about money. Economics is not about production. Economics is not about consumption. Economics is about *justice*, in which man receives his due by first seeking to render God his due. The arena where just desserts are made, received, and enjoyed is the home. Tip O'Neill once said, "All politics is local." The corollary to that in ethics is, "All economics is domestic."

When one says *home*, one indeed means "homeland", but not exclusively. One means, primarily, the place where the hearth is warm and the heart is kept. Fundamentally and ultimately, however, reference is made to a different, a better, a permanent home. Our Lord referred to this place as *My Father's house.* Therein is found the many mansions where the children of God live forever. That house is established on the faith taught by the body of Christ, the Catholic Church, whose bedrock and visible head is St. Peter and his successors, the Popes. That house is built to attain the lofty height of being a house of prayer.

But since God is not a monomaniac, more goes on than just prayer. Mass is the focal point, source, means, and goal, of all that contributes to eternal life. An authentic devotion to that truth allows, encourages, and expects much more than just a Sunday experience. Three-score and ten is a matter of far more than merely 3,640 hours, give or take a few hours considering leap years and the length of Father's sermons. Thus, the economy of salvation is the home, the nation, the Church, the mind, the body, the soul, discipline, recreation, art, science—all that is human seeking the one true God. Distributism does the least bad job of providing a material context for such a vast undertaking.

It is Sunday, August 15th, 2004. Mr. Johnson has just gone to Mass at the local traditional chapel. He has returned home, where he is going to spend the rest of the day and late into the night finishing up the end-of-the-fiscal-year reports that have to be finished in the next ten business days. His wife and his children know that this two-week period in August every year is very stressful, and they are not to disturb him at all—no phone calls, no meals together, no squabbles over whose turn it is to get to play a video game. The family also knows that a similar period happens at tax time in late March. And, of course, the Christmas rush is a nightmare as well. Mr. Johnson hates his job, but it puts food on the table and supports his family.

It is Sunday, January 27th, 1996. The Super Bowl is being played today. Mr. Thomas and ten of his best buddies are skipping Mass to make a day of it. They're going to play a round of golf in the morning, get a pizza and beer for lunch at the local pub, and then spend the whole evening at the Thomas house watching the game. Mrs. Thomas makes him feel guilty about this every year. But it's just once a year. And he always confesses it the next week anyway, so what's the big deal?

It is Sunday, April 16th, 1950. Mr. Brown went to Mass a week ago. It was Easter. His wife made him go. Today he gets to sleep in. He gets to sleep in for the next eight months until the ol' battleaxe makes him go again for Christmas. She can be awful pushy when she wants to be.

It is Saturday, December 23rd, 1922. This is the last shopping weekend before Christmas. Mr. Green is opening early and closing late to take advantage of the booming business. He probably won't get home until after midnight, and then he'll be back first thing on Sunday to do the books. Mass just won't fit in.

The Jews down the street don't take Sunday off—or Saturday for that matter. If Mr. Green is going to stay in business and get ahead, a few things have to be sacrificed.

It is Tuesday, September 12th, 1816. Mr. Dillon is lying in bed dying. His frantic wife doesn't know what to do. There isn't a priest within a hundred miles. Her grandmother had always told her to pray for a holy death and to beg Our Lady to make sure a priest was nearby at the hour of death. Mrs. Dillon, sitting at the side of her husband's deathbed, cannot hear his labored breathing over the sound of the memory of her grandmother's sobs back in the old country begging her not to go to a foreign Godless land where there were no priests, no sacraments, and no faith—just savages, mosquitoes, and heretic protestants. With four small children and no money, Mrs. Dillon is thinking about leaving the Illinois Territory and going back to Europe after Mr. Dillon passes away.

It is the morning of October 5th, 1582. Monsieur Gilson doesn't care what that fool of a man Gregory XIII says. You can't rob a man of ten days of his life and walk off like nothing happened. This was just further proof to Monsieur Gilson that the Church was a gaggle of thieves and liars. Ever since his brief seminary days in his early adulthood he had told everyone who would listen for three minutes how far gone things were. Not that the English or the Germans had it right, but no self-respecting Frenchman would look to an Italian for sense and reason. The Mass and priest-craft and prayer and all were just that much idiocy to keep honest men down and keep fiends in power. Monsieur Gilson is not fooled by it all. His calendar is not going to move for anything or anyone.

It is Thursday, February 23rd, 1516. Father Luther has just finished celebrating Mass. He is fretting that he should have gone to Confession first. That is usually the first thought he has as he makes his thanksgiving after Mass each day. Of course, there are days when his confessor tells him that he should have gone to the sacrament much sooner, but Father Luther doesn't put much stock in that old man's old ideas about what constitutes sin. Father Luther doesn't know how much longer he can put up with his own interior doubts and the anger he feels toward his superiors.

It is Wednesday, January 1st, 1250. There was no Mass in the village this morning. The priest died two days ago in the outbreak of the plague that has been raging for two months. Most of the others who had died were buried by the priest and a few other brave souls. No one is there to bury the priest. Quite a few of the people still alive have said out loud that there is no reason to bury the damned anyway. If there were a God, they say, He wouldn't let so many innocent people die so horribly. And if there weren't a God, nothing but nothing, or hell itself, awaited them. Life with the plague is hell enough.

It is the end of the world, December 31st, 999. The Cathedral is filled to overflowing with people praying, dozens of Masses are being offered, and hundreds of people are in line to go to Confession. With only a few hours to live, everyone wants to get his life in order. The scene in one week will be quite different.

It is Thursday, March 24th, 33. Mass is not yet over, but one of the attendees has left already. He has some business to transact. Judas has a pressing appointment with the Jews. The profits from the exchange, he is sure, will go to a good use.

Ladies and gentlemen, sin and error were not invented in 1969, 1962, 1917, 1717, 1517, 900, or before dessert at the Last Supper.

Those who come from some kind of a Catholic background that allows them to adhere fervently to the immemorial teachings, practice, and worship preserved by the one true Church, have no fear that dancing girls will be at Mass on Sunday bringing the various and sundry items forward in the procession during the preparation of the altar and gifts. There will be no lector hectoring in some modern translation of English noted for its "inclusive" language style. And of all of those privileged to assist at the immemorial Mass of permanent tradition, only the priest will lay hands on the Blessed Sacrament, receiving no assistance from an army of "Extraordinary" Ministers of the Eucharist.

However, there a few other pressing problems among the people who attend chapels dedicated to preserving permanent Catholic traditions. There is a plague of Lexi—or whatever the plural of Lexus might be—infesting parking lots across the land. Parishioners face attack on a daily basis from gargantuan, soul-eating home-entertainment systems that have invaded their living rooms. Almost all of the men have succumbed to the allure of a seductress, resulting in their infidelity to the sacrament of Holy Matrimony through a very public and scandalous love affair with wage slavery. Everyone in the community docilely accepts oppression from their fellow citizens in the world by way of court-mandated, legislature-approved, and executive-enforced endorsement of divorce, sodomy, abortion, usury, and pornography. This state of affairs is so typical as to admit of no exceptions.

There is an urgent need to recognize that the *Novus Ordo Missae* is not just a liturgical rite, but a way of life. Thanks be to God, it is still possible to worship according to the constant mind of the Church. However, precious few live according to a thorough *sensus Catholicus,* and even fewer know what the ramifications for that would be today.

To put it very simply: it must be understood that this is decidedly *not* a Catholic world. It is not Catholic in its faith. It is not Catholic in its understanding of the family. It is not Catholic in its economics. It is not Catholic in its philosophy. It is not Catholic in its systems of government. It is not Catholic in its application of science. It is not Catholic in its recreation. It is not Catholic in its artistic aesthetic. It is not Catholic in its morality. It is not Catholic in how it educates the young. It is not Catholic in anything at all. Modernity is a completely, wholly, entirely non-Catholic, anti-Catholic, Catholic-hating world.

What even Catholics faithful to the Church's traditions of dogma and worship seldom understand properly is that the Catholic faith, expressed in the Mass, gave us Christendom, a Catholic culture; modernism and apostasy steeped in humanism and hedonism inform the *Novus Ordo Missae.* The strength of Western history was not a culture that supported the faith. Christendom's former strength was an unwavering faith that flowered in a wonderful culture. What ails the world today is not a horrible liturgy that has created a woeful society. The current mess is due to having a Godless and even demonic world that has given rise to a set of liturgical principles that have been brought to bear on worship.

What is needed to strengthen the Church today is the same as what was needed in Imperial Rome, barbaric Europe, the complacent Renaissance, the insanity of the protestant revolt, the chaos of the French Revolution, the terror of two World Wars, and the uncertainties of most folk during young adulthood: **Faith must come first!**

It is imperative to live the faith in everything, not just in the Mass on Sunday. A vibrant faith can heal a terminally ill culture. No culture in and of itself can produce authentic faith. This culture is actively hostile to the true faith. The ultimate goal is not to reproduce the culture of our fathers, but to receive, nurture, and hand down *the faith of our fathers.* The culture that springs from such a renewal will bear some resemblance to the past, but will also benefit from the fact that the Master of the house of God has treasures both new and old that he will bestow on his family.

Often it is said that what matters is the Mass. Even Vatican II acknowledges that the Mass must be the source and summit of the life of Catholics. What is needed today is a conviction to carry on the work of our fathers in the faith, particularly the martyr-saints. As they died in order to preserve the faith inviolate from sin, heresy, and apostasy, today's Catholics are called to live. The faithful must the Mass.

They must live for the Mass. They must live from the Mass. They must devote the entirety of life to making Christ all in all through worshipping him in his Mass, or else the faith will die as surely as it did for millions of people just before and after the Council. They must live true to the fullness of the faith in every aspect of life, or whatever of heart, mind, soul, and strength that is not given to God will die as surely as the Church has died out in Northern Africa, Western Europe, and most of the Americas. Eternal life depends on the whole of this earthly life being united to Jesus Christ in His perfect sacrifice on the cross: as He gives absolutely everything of Himself to the Church on Calvary through the Mass, the faithful are to give absolutely everything—government, work, recreation, families, homes, heart, mind, soul, and strength—to Him through the Mass.

Do not feel awkward for feeling out of sorts in reading thus far. Others before you have felt at sea among such sentiments. For instance:

> Dear Father,
>
> To the extent I am able, all your poems are appreciated. I very much liked "*Tuba Mirum*", and that you composed it while waiting for penitents in the confessional. As telling as the sound of a trumpet is the final couplet:
>
> This wondrous scene once more will come to pass
> as I ascend the altar at the Mass.
>
> Thank you very much for sending "Where Does the Remnant Live?" I think I understood a great deal of it. There are a

few questions: Could you elucidate a little on modern employment and modern politics? You have spoken on this but it is not clear. Did not saints come from families with sainted mothers and fathers who live much like us, with mother toiling at home and father going out to work to earn a living for his family? Did not kings who lived regally and did the lavish things kings do, become saints, while loving God and giving generously to the Church? All saints did not live an agrarian life. How do super-highways, condos, and IRAs "pose grave dangers to the sanctification of souls?" Condos are useful when the old family home becomes too large for the couple living in it and downsizing seems sensible. As you do, we must travel the freeways to get from place to place. You mention some of the great religious orders of the Church. Well and good, but are they not the shepherds of which Our Lord speaks and we, the sheep who follow in the particular vocation that is ours? . . . I believe my favorite lines are "We must be easy marks, vulnerable to the lions, the scoundrels, and the pagan who wants a handout without realizing that his only satisfaction—and our only gift—is Christ and Him crucified."

Could you and would you, Father, construct an imaginary "Joe Bloe," a guy right out of today's world here in America, and give us specifics as to how he might extricate himself from ordinary life as we know it, to live the Christ-life in the way you say we must? Take him through all those facets of his existence which you enumerate and move him from what we normally do, thinking it acceptable to God, to the changes he must make to live a truly Catholic life. If you could do that, perhaps we could understand exactly what you mean. Modernism in *e.g.* music, theater, or education, is easily understood, but other areas, some of which I have mentioned, are unclear.

Most of us are followers. Our Lord called us "the sheep." [author's deletion of an overly kind compliment]. May he sustain you.

With a prayer,

Dorothy

It is the task of the essays and articles in this book to attempt to clarify things for people like Dorothy. In case the reader has not the time in the next few minutes to examine three-hundred pages of explanation, the next several pages might sustain until sufficient time is available for a more thorough exploration. Thus, to answer Dorothy, and in so doing to provide a synopsis for things to come...

Joseph and Colleen Bloe live in Urbandale, Iowa. Their four grown children live in Minnesota, Hawaii, France, and Dubuque. Joseph is a recently retired insurance company middle-manager. Colleen began their married life working as a teacher, then stayed home when the children came along, went back to work when the youngest entered grade school, and now she is two or three years from her own retirement. Mr. and Mrs. Bloe are "old-timers" in their neighborhood—they have lived in their house for twenty-three years. The home in which they lived until several years after the last of their four children was born had been built by Colleen's grandfather in what used to be the country, but is now a strip mall on the outskirts of Des Moines. That mall prompted them to build the house in which they now live, but which they are seriously considering selling in favor of a smaller, cheaper condo.

Colleen is away for a long five-day weekend. Her dear cousin, born a mere two days before her, is very ill. Colleen is taking time off from work to visit her "other-sister", as she calls her. Joseph is left to fend for himself. He has lots of time on his hands and thoughts on his mind.

More than twenty years ago, Joseph had his mid-life crisis—he and his marriage both survived. Thus, he does not consider his current angst to be of the geriatric-adolescent sort. But he is doing a lot of thinking with Colleen away. Joseph is being plagued by thoughts of what might have been.

Many years ago, many more than when the mid-life crisis occurred, Joseph was a young man, a teenager, entering the seminary. It was an amazing time. He learned many things that have floated in the back of his mind for decades. This was the heady time before and during the Council. Lots of speculation about the nature of the Church, the role of the priest, and the status of the laity was in the press and in the classroom.

Joseph was not touched by any of that. He had as a spiritual director and professor a priest who was about 1800 years old, not quite apostolic, but close enough. Father Phillips was probably named after St. Philip the Deacon, who was in all likelihood Father Phillips' father's catechist.

Father Phillips taught Joseph. The Archbishop, the Rector, and the Academic Dean thought that Father Phillips was teaching philosophy. What Joseph discovered to his enduring delight was that Father Phillips had played his superiors a bait-and-switch. Joseph and his classmates learned not philosophy from Father Phillips. They learned a *love of wisdom!*

Lady Wisdom! She was their paramour. They wooed her. They quested in her honor. They slew dragons that menaced her. Father Phillips tried each of his students by fire, and those who overcame the ordeal, he knighted with the Sword of Truth! Joseph was privileged to be among those whose shoulders were so tapped.

But he also was among the fallen. Holy Orders was *the* Quest, and he was not up to the task. Torn between his budding love for Lady Wisdom and the allure of the world offered in the wake of the Council, Joseph succumbed to the wiles of modernity. Perhaps Colleen never realized how broken was the man she married five years after he left the seminary.

Joseph constantly fretted within himself about the direction his life had taken. It was not just his anxiety over whether he had failed God by refusing to fully pursue the priesthood. That was involved. But even more Joseph wondered about the "success" he had had in the world. He was not a millionaire or a captain of industry or a celebrity darling. His house was not quite paid off—nor were their two cars and the boat sitting in dry dock. When Colleen retired they would not starve, unless they *both* lived thirty more years.

It profits a man nothing to gain the world while losing his soul. A man can not serve two masters. Joseph Bloe felt that he had served no one. He feared that God was not pleased with him. His bosses were never terribly impressed. None of his family looked to him as a model to emulate. Even Joseph could not muster esteem for Joseph. Worse than trying to serve God *and* mammon was serving *neither* God nor mammon. It was to be vomited out of the mouth of the Lord for being lukewarm.

One nice thing about their suburban home was the deck over the back yard. Joseph grabbed the special box of stout beer that he kept aside for when he treated himself to his guilty pleasure of idling, drinking, smoking a pipe, and brooding. The deck was the perfect setting for his vices. No reminders of chores undone, no cops waiting to give tickets to fools behind the wheel, and no stern looks about making the living room smell like a saloon. In Joseph's mind, it was a pleasant trip from the salon to the saloon, but Colleen rarely was amused by his plays on words.

So Joseph retired to the private security of his redwood enclosure. Alone with his thoughts he started an examination of conscience according to the principles he learned so long ago from Father Phillips. Joseph was not only taking stock of his life, but of life itself.

Life on earth had not always been as it was in modern greater Des Moines. Joseph remembered his own father and the farm where he grew up in far northwestern Iowa, which was where his Dad grew up, which was where his Dad grew up. Joseph and his five brothers decided that none of their sons would be farm boys. His two sisters married farm boys who also refused to raise any more of the vermin.

Grandpa used to tell the boys about his childhood. The farm was like a little city all to itself. They grew what they ate, his mother and sisters spun and weaved, and the house and barn and the outbuildings were all built with nothing more than the manpower generated by the family itself. Going to town was a blue-moon event. There was not much they could afford there, few things that they really needed, it was hard to get there, and, frankly, Grandpa's Dad didn't like the looks of the folk who lived there.

In those days Grandpa and his brothers and sisters did not have to walk five miles through snow uphill both ways to get to school. Boys and girls learned their letters and numbers from mother. Father taught the boys the million-and-two things that a farmer had to be good at, and the girls learned the extra million things that mother took care of around the house. The older brothers and sisters took on some of the teaching responsibilities when they reached their teen years.

On Sundays all of the children would be drilled ruthlessly in their catechism by Father. They had no parish church back then, and Mass happened only infrequently when a mission priest was spared to visit the nether regions of Iowa. There were not a lot of Catholics in northwestern Iowa, and families had to learn and preserve the faith pretty much on their own. Grandpa's Dad made sure that his children knew how to get to heaven. Part of the lesson that they learned was the taste of hell they got if they answered a question incorrectly, incompletely, or less than immediately.

Joseph thought of his own catechesis as a child. He always loved the lives of the saints more than anything else. It seemed to him that between the Bible and the saints of God, you had all you needed to know about being Catholic. For reasons that remained unclear to Joseph even now, he was particularly drawn to royalty who became saints. Somehow kings and queens being that *good* struck

Joseph as being proof of what Jesus said about camels and the eyes of needles and the impossible being possible with God.

Later on in seminary, Father Phillips helped Joseph organize in his own mind how Europe was shaped by these royal saints, princes and princesses of the kingdom of heaven. Practically every European nation had a king or queen or both who attained great sanctity by insisting that their realms receive and practice the one true faith. Bavaria had St. Henry and St. Cunegunda. England had St. Edward the Confessor. Scotland had Queen St. Margaret. Portugal and Hungary each had a St. Elizabeth for a queen. St. Louis ruled France and received the Crown of Thorns for his efforts. St. Bridget gave great example and great wealth to the faithful in Sweden. Hungary can also claim King St. Stephen and Poland boasts St. Casimir. And quite a few other regal saints grace the local churches of Christendom.

Noblesse oblige meant for these holy men and women that the royal purple was to be set aside frequently in favor of the hairshirt, the penitent's tears, the alms required by the poor, the justice due to the oppressed, and the piety owed to God. They established the natural foundations for great nations and the supernatural foundations for the growing body of Christ. Cities sprang up near monasteries; universities were endowed within newly erected dioceses; and armies marched forward to protect the realm from invasion and the faith from heresy.

The sainted kings and queens of Europe left a legacy that can be measured in roads and architecture and enduring culture. They also humbly offered their gifts in creating a legacy of faithful souls around the world whose only measure is in the mind of God. Many have sought the wealth of bad monarchs; too few have begged the poverty of spirit for which good monarchs long. It has been decades since Europe has had a monarch with real power, but centuries since Europe has produced a monarch worthy of being raised to the altar of God. Precious few Catholic Prime Ministers or Presidents have had or seem likely to have a desire for *heroic* sanctity.

What his grandfather described and what Father Phillips helped to put in context were of a piece as far as Joseph was concerned. The family farm and the kingdom are differences in degree, not of kind. Each is a society, the family in small, the kingdom in large. Fathers and kings must protect and provide for the material and spiritual well being of their respective societies. Mothers and queens must nurture and nourish the bodies and souls in their care. Fathers as kings of the home castle would not get such a bad reception in the modern mind if kings had taken more seriously their role as fathers to their countries. A queen who does not understand her dignity as mother to her people will be as ineffective as a mother who does not teach her children to respect the sacred nature of the authority of mother and father in the home.

Within a kingdom, on a farm, and in the home it is possible to accomplish what is impossible by a secular constitutional democracy, in the city, and among the nomads of the modern economy. God makes things grow naturally where a people is united by the faith, in bringing forth the fruits of the earth, and in raising up children to praise God on earth and to share His glory in heaven. There is something real and organic about a kingdom that speaks to the heart much more profoundly than the synthetic reality that produces creatures like the Soviet Union or the European Union or the United States of America. A family knows who they are if they are Russian or Portuguese or Hawaiian. What does one call a citizen of what used to be the Soviet Union or will be the European Union or still is the United States—and what do those names *mean*? A "Soviet" is not a description of a human being, but a mechanism of a form of government. "European" denotes a continental land mass, not the identity of the flesh and blood who live thereon. And "American" can be applied equally to the residents of two different continents containing three-quarters of a billion people and dozens of nation states.

There used to be a common sense of nationality. Language, a monarch, and the faith made a people one, informed the people of their identity, and formed the people in a living culture. Modern nation states deny all three of those realities. International languages are not meant to bind nations together as sovereign equals, but to blur the distinctions between nations. Monarchs vanished with the passenger pigeon, replaced by governing entities wherein small groups of people are elected by large groups of people to rule over mammoth groups of people according to the dictates of what small groups of people wrote on pieces of paper. These pieces of paper and the people responsible for them forbid that faith of any kind be present as a principle to direct the laws governing people, to guide the morals of a people, or to check the hubris of the people.

Joseph stood up abruptly. He dumped the cold ashes from his pipe over the edge of the deck and filled his mug with more stout, slightly emptying it before sitting down again. For a minute he stopped thinking so as to catch his breath. Tamping new tobacco into the bowl was a welcome respite from his mental toil. Concepts can be every bit as exhausting to stack up as bales of hay.

That was what it was like when he worked. He never broke a sweat or a bone or any ground, but he came home a physical, emotional, and mental wreck every night. Cajoling salesmen, calming customers, and compromising with other managers was a far cry from his grandpa's descriptions of planting and harvest times, but Joseph thought his Dad always looked healthier at the end of the farm day than how he felt in what passes for rush hour in Des Moines.

For the life of him Joseph could not at that moment remember what he thought was so awful about growing up on the farm that made him frantic to move to the city, first as a seminarian and then as a husband and a father. He wondered about his own boys and why they stayed in town in spite of their constant complaints about what that entails. What was so awful about their parents that made all of his children want to live so far away from home?

Suddenly Joseph leapt from his chair again. He threw open the deck door and dashed into the house. So frenzied was his motion that he did not even notice the still smoking pipe in his mouth filling the living room, then the family room, then the hallway, then the basement stairwell with a delightful aroma grown only in Virginia. In seconds Joseph was through the house and down the stairs, rushing to a pile of boxes, and tearing through one of the most deeply buried. It did not take long for him to find what he was looking for. Putting the boxes back where he found them, minus a sheaf of papers held as firmly in his hand as his pipe in his teeth, Joseph then flew back up the stairs two steps at a time. Returning to his redwood throne he began to read:

Modernity: A Diagnosis of What Ails Us

A thesis never intended for publication or completion, by Father Scott Phillips

I. Introduction
Urban Renewal

Sion
The walls of cities once were havens
for unarmor'd man and helpless wife,
within which noble hearts, ne'er cravens,
serv'd their lords and prais'd the Lord of life.

Inside their walls both great and lowly
gave their all for fam'ly, king, and God;
to die for these made sinners holy
and the land, both graves and homestead's sod.

Babylon
No longer cities boast of mortar
pil'd against invading armies' might,
for now the foe is given quarter
in the streets, more dark by day than night.

What present threatens is not warfare
come from foreign soldiers' fill'd with lust,
but faceless neighbors for whose welfare
laws are built, protecting by distrust.

A love for strangers is the dearer
for the undefended city's souls
who lie beseig'd behind the mirror's
prison walls, whose locks bear keyless holes.

New Jerusalem
With New Jerusalem descending
will be power, light, and glory's weight
bestow'd upon the saints unending,
safe behind twelve open city gates.

At last the wall will more a window
be, but clean; and then horizon's ends
be seen—not own'd but here to borrow,
and forever there to share with friends.

Amen.

When New Jerusalem is established, when the former heaven and the former earth pass away, when all things are made new again, Eden and Sion will be surpassed, the Lord's own city will rule supreme, and the tree of life will flower in the midst of all. God will dwell with man and man will call on God as *Father.* Nothing will exist that could diminish, threaten, or mar the security of the heavenly city. All will be devoted to the worship of God, and He will share the fullness of His glory with all the elect. There will be one God, one people, and one home where only life, love, and peace are found.

'Til this comes to pass, the Kingdom is in our midst even now as the mystical Body of Christ, the Catholic Church, endeavors in the project of building the Kingdom according to the will of God, by grace of Christ crucified, in the power of the Holy Ghost mediated through the sacraments. There is far more to the Kingdom than human eyes now can see, but everything now in communion with Christ's Church, his Bride, will be present to enjoy beatitude when God's plan of salvation reaches fruition with the end of time. Indeed, the end of time, its proper purpose and goal, is the perfection of the saints, the submission of all creation to God the Father, and Christ the King of the universe being acclaimed as all in all by all.

The Book of the Apocalypse by St. John the Beloved tells us that the New Jerusalem is massive, beautiful, and impregnable. Those who dwell there with God in light are perfect, participate in the divine Sonship of Christ as reigning heirs with Him, and are united to God and one another in the unbreakable bonds of the Spirit of Love. All that is in the New Jerusalem is good, and all good shall be forever there. Outside the city is darkness and evil, sinners unrepentant, and death and the devil. What is outside the city can never enter in, 'tho' the gates stand open, for they are powerless to do so, *and they desire sin and separation from God.*

Earth serves as analogue to the New Jerusalem *and* the city of the damned. It is the proving ground where souls are tested in their worthiness of beatitude or perdition. This world is also the field of battle where the hosts of heaven under St. Michael the Archangel defend the divine honor against the powers and principalities doomed to utter and eternal defeat for their rebellion.

History experiences two aspects of the city of man, one in league with the devil, the other obedient to the will of God marching beneath the banner of Christ crucified. The world succumbs to the appetites of mere flesh and thereby comes under the devil's sway. The Church Militant joins with St. Michael and the good angels in allegiance to God. Hell does battle against Heaven even as men contend on earth allied with Christ or against Christ. There is no compromise possible, no treaty offered, no quarter given where these warring armies are in strife.

Eden offers no home to man. Cast out of Paradise, mankind is in the wilderness, exposed to physical want and the spiritual malice of the devil. Men have sought haven behind the walls of fortified cities from the threats posed by strife between tribes and nations, by material dearth, and by the chaos of the unredeemed world. Strong walls raised against foes, fertile farmlands surrounding them, and organized rule under a sovereign authority have been the hallmarks of civilization by which the city of man has sought to overcome the ravages of original sin. The city stands as a symbol of man's ascendancy over mere animals; it is his citadel against enemies both material and spiritual; and it is the mark of identity prized by those privileged to possess the title "citizen".

No earthly city, however, is equal to the task of mounting a continuing, focused, and effective defense against the many enemies of mankind, the ultimate opponent being death. By war, by murder, by disease, by mishap, by age, death comes to every man. The ultimate cause of death, sin, is the birthright of every child born of man and woman, of flesh and blood, of mortal will. No wall, no army, no rule has ever brought death to bay.

This is seen in the tragic irony of the modern city. Where cities once gave haven to populations fleeing hunger, disaster, or invasion; where cities once stood as emblems of pride and accomplishment; where cities once were the home where a man was amongst his own family and familiars; the modern city is a veritable prison. Teeming masses languish within cities without productive work, basic human hygiene, or hope of material improvement. Those neither very wealthy nor very poor flee the city, while the impoverished remain behind incapable of escape, and the rich enjoy an otherworldly existence unlike anything attainable by the middle class or conceivable to the poor. Strangers surround the inhabitants of cities, danger walks the streets, and armed force is directed at the citizenry rather than at marauding hordes from foreign lands. Once the ideal of mystics, the boast of kings, or the dream of engineers and statesmen, the city has become a nightmare for its residents, a source of embarrassment for governments, and an unbearable burden to the resources and spirit of those who cling to the memory of better hopes. Perversely, cities and their problems continue to grow; and where a central city might be shrinking, still the urban area of which it is the hub explodes in size and population.

For a brief moment in human history, it seemed that a city had been built that would satisfy all of man's wants. Milk and honey flowed in the lands around it. A philosopher-king wrote poetry and sang and danced while effecting his just rule. God Himself dwelt in the midst of its citadel, calling the people His own, delighting in them and their praises, and blessing the works of their hands. Alas! Sion stands no more, cast down in its pride, condemned for its faithlessness, doomed to exile for having abdicated the right to be a people bound as one under God.

A people who were not a people became a people, but then lost their nation and their national identity. What makes a people *one*? Who decides to bring them together? How do they maintain a common patrimony? Why should other people recognize them, respect them, or reject them?

In the case of the Jews, it is all about God. He chose, He gathered, He commanded, He loved, and He punished. Abram was called from pagan stock. Moses guided the people whom God raised from Abraham's seed. Saul was chosen to lead the nation when they were unsatisfied to have God as king.

Saul, the first king of the Jews after the Jews rejected God as King, was rejected by God for his unrighteousness. God then anointed David to be the new king, calling him *son*, and promising to give his people an eternal kingship. But David's immediate descendants were unfaithful and led the people in idolatry. God took from them both their king and their kingdom, allowing them to be ruled by foreign powers much like they had been oppressed in Egypt by Pharaoh. Eventually they were in the thrall of Rome and many had become enslaved to sinful passions, giving in to the practices of the pagans who surrounded and ruled them. From pagan stock to deliverance from slavery to divine anointing, the Chosen People delivered themselves back to slavery and thence to a virtually pagan state. Yet God did not abandon them, nor did He forget His promise to establish an eternal realm and undying kingship.

Jeremiah (31:31–34) prophesied that the sins of Israel would be forgiven and that the very hearts of the people would be inscribed with the divine Law. Stone tablets—and stony hearts—would be replaced by flesh infused with the Breath of God. Ezekiel (34:11–16) foretold that the wandering sheep of Israel would no more be guided by faithless shepherds, and a faithful flock would take the place of the wayward sheep. God Himself would shepherd His people. St. John (10:1–18; 1:1–18) relates that Jesus is the Son of God, the King to come, the Good Shepherd who knows and is known by His sheep. No longer would lying wolves attack the sheepfold, nor would the sheep succumb to the seduction of the wolves' lies. Our Lord also reveals in St. John's Apocalypse (21:1–4, 22-27; 22:1–5) that in the new Kingdom, God will once again dwell with men, His people will be His sons, and nothing will ever again imperil His children.

Since the Ascension, men have cooperated with God's plan to greater or lesser degrees, with varying results depending on their degree of cooperation. Catholics have expressed their faith through national identity and ethnicity, obeying God thereby, and receiving blessing and divine favor. Sinful Catholics and non-Catholics have established nations hostile or indifferent to the Faith, and thus have sown apostasy, depravity, and fratricide among men. A people joined together to manifest and spread the one, true Faith will find their natural identity preserved and elevated. Faithless people ignorant of, or excommunicated from, the Church will discover dissension in their midst, use force to impose a false peace, and lose a proper sense of human dignity capable of pursuing common purpose or agreeing on the nature of good and evil.

The final fruit of original sin is the loss of knowledge of God, the loss of the knowledge of the difference between good and evil, and an ignorance of a means to life wholly preserved from death. Nations founded in apostasy or in ignorance of Christ are powerless to avoid the full measure of the wages of original sin: moral depravity, human degradation, and eternal death. Without the light of the Faith, man is plunged into darkness inescapable.

Supernatural grace is necessary for a nation to be pleasing to God and to be of worth to man. Such grace is built on a multitude of natural blessings from God. Perhaps the most obvious natural element of a national identity is language. Hawaii is the place where the people speak Hawaiian, Denmark is where Danish is spoken, and Arabia where Arabic is the *lingua franca*. Babel demonstrates that the division of languages brought the division of peoples, but sin results in division even among peoples of a common language. Where faith does not forbid the use of forked tongues, tongues will fork to divide people or divided peoples will use forked tongues against each other.

A world war was fought, in part, because one group of German speakers in Germany decided that users of that language in the Sudetenland, Poland, and Austria, among many other places, should belong in one sovereign German-speaking nation, whether they wanted to be or not. Cultural battles are waged between the native English speakers on either side of the border between Canada and the United States, with the Canadians mostly on the losing side, seeming to be a cultural colony or suburb or wholly-owned subsidiary of America. China and Taiwan have not come to blows—yet—but neither has their sharing of the Chinese language forged a sense of national unity between them.

Converse to the phenomenon of a common language failing to create a single nationality out of two nations is that of a single nation divided internally by two languages. Flemish-speaking Walloons lose little love for their French-speaking brother Belgians. The Québecquoi would prefer that English and its speakers in the rest of Canada would allow them to dwell at peace alone in a French-speaking enclave sovereign unto itself. Spaniards must ask themselves every now and then why they are so insistent that the obscure, rugged, and exotic Basque region should remain attached to a nation with which all agree Basque-speakers have nothing in common except physical proximity. Language by itself has insufficient power either to forge or to dissolve a nation's identity.

Military might can force together, for a time, people who would otherwise desire permanent separation from, if not subjugation of, the others. Ideology backed by military force created the France of the Revolution, preserved the American "union" under Lincoln, and sustained the Soviet Union until it collapsed beneath the weight of its Gallic internal contradictions and the refusal by Gorbachev to apply Lincoln's solution to the Slavic problem. Babylonian, Egyptian, Persian, Roman, Chinese, Aztec, and British emperors have discovered the challenges, wealth, and futility of building empires from disparate peoples.

Efforts to bind as one the many different aspects of human culture evident in human history have ranged from the sublime to the ridiculous to the tragicomic. Hellas did not succeed, although its profound influence is felt even to the present. Maximilian was taken seriously by none other than himself, with the possible exception of his wife. Napoleon inspired armies, symphonies, and contempt, seemingly invincible in the field, yet doomed almost from the start by the limitations besetting him from politics, military vagaries, and his own ego. Coca Cola has conquered for America in lands her armies will never see.

The one means to bring many together into a real unity that has real hope to succeed is the one means forbidden by modernity. Holy Mother Church would call all mankind her children, but most men prefer to be orphans. Be it a lukewarm lip service to faith or a specious separation of the state from the Church or an outright atheism, not one nation in the modern world admits that Christ is King, Sovereign not only over believers, but over all men, all nations. Rather than dwell together as one sharing a single faith that enriches diverse cultures, modern men chase a chimera falsely promising to preserve the cultures that multinational corporations dissolve, to make peace among the cultures whose profound differences multiculturalism exaggerates, and to synthesize as one the cultures that are informed by multitudinous faiths in a multiplicity of gods. All the while *Homo modernus* shouts, "Peace! Peace!" as he denies the meaning of peace, the source of peace, the Prince of Peace.

If one Faith, one Baptism, one Lord, one Church, is acknowledged, then one people can be formed. This is so even if many nationalities are involved. The mystical Body of Christ has many members through which the fullness of truth can be expressed. A variety of nations in agreement on one Church can live together and be mutually supportive. A variety of faiths in false gods can never be one, will agree on nothing, and will seek only mutual destruction.

Alas! man is rarely put off by the irrational or the impossible.

Modern man has reached something of a consensus about God: He does not exist. Perhaps a few individuals here or there, or even a few hundred million scattered around the world, still believe in Him, but the universal agreement on which almost all men act is that *collectively* we operate on the premise that there is no God sovereign over the universe. If indeed He is out there somewhere, He has no vote or voice in modern democracies.

Instead, modern men have elected a demigod to worship. Some call it the euro, some adore the almighty dollar, but all pay homage—and high interest rates—to mammon. There are myriad sects or rites given over to this false worship. Some revere consuming and owning things, others venerate raw power over people, and the cult of controlling thought possesses practically all of the high priests of the temple of secular humanism-materialism-rationalism—call it what you will, its name is Legion. Among the favored means of oblations in modern idolatry are usury, sexual license, and the murder of innocents. It is no accident that the stock-in-trade of modern irreligion consists largely of the sins that cry to heaven for vengeance.

Very likely it would come as a surprise to most people to realize that the European Union, the North Atlantic Treaty Organization, the Organization of Petroleum Exporting Countries, the World Bank and International Monetary Fund, and the International Olympic Committee all share a common goal. Each seeks in its own peculiar way to advance the hegemony of a few men over all men. C.S. Lewis asks in his book, *The Abolition of Man*, who and on what basis will decide how men are to live, which men will be allowed to survive, and what constitutes worth in a man. These pan-national entities hold billions—of people and of dollars—in their sway. They or their successors provide an answer to Lewis' extraordinary question.

The European Union destroys national sovereignty as it pertains to government structure. NATO destroys national sovereignty as it pertains to military security. OPEC destroys national sovereignty as it pertains to issues of trade. The IMF and World Bank destroy national sovereignty as it pertains to finance, debt, and currency. The Olympic "movement" combines a bread-and-circus mentality with big business and a pseudo-religious mythos to bring nations to war on playing fields while refraining from disputes on matters of meaning.

Yes, that is an oversimplification. For the purposes of this argument this oversimplification is sufficient to illustrate how the average nation-state is accepting the premise that *none* can feed itself, fuel itself, protect itself, fund itself, or define itself. Nations that attempt any kind of self sufficiency are bombed (Iraq), tariffed (the United States), refused existence (Israel), embargoed (Cuba), culturally colonized (everyone by America), morally assaulted (Ireland and Malta by the EU), or isolated into irrelevancy (the Vatican by itself).

There are *no* good guys in this, as Psalm 13 says:

> The fool hath said in his heart:
> There is no God.
> They are corrupt and are become abominable in their ways:
> There is none that doth good, no, not one.
> The Lord hath looked down from Heaven
> Upon the children of men,
> To see if there be any that understand
> And seek God.
> They are all gone aside; they are
> Become unprofitable together:
> There is none that doth good, no, not one.

All modernity has conspired in apostasy by the wretched principle of denying God's kingdom pride of place over the state. Or to put it perhaps more palatably to modern ears, the state has been set adrift with no place for it within the Church. A foolish, lamentable, diabolic inversion has taken place: from an acknowledgement of God's Kingdom reigning over all and man's states finding a home in God's many mansions, we have devolved to seeking one world-encompassing state within which national sovereignty, individual conscience, and Christ the King will receive toleration without recognition.

Brothers, this is not the shape of things to come. This hellish future is *now.* Already our governments, corporations, and wealthy individuals operate along transnational lines. Legal jurisdictions, commercial incorporations, and citizenship already assume entities occupying multiple national residencies. Throughout the fabric of modern life runs the thread of understanding that legal and business interests span the globe, but faith in God stops at the lip service he is paid.

We have come to this pass along a path stretching back eight centuries. Ironically, the first salvo of mammon's increasingly successful rebellion against the perfect society of the Church was launched during the zenith of Christendom in the thirteenth century. The *Magna Carta* established the unintended precedent that a monarch could be bullied in law. At each step since then the very concept of authority has been attacked with the aim of limiting all authority. Christ has been the victim throughout, for all authority is His. To undermine authority is to attack Christ. The process begun in the *Magna Carta* of negotiating the rights of sovereignty and monarchy has culminated in the regicide of Christ the King. The separation of the state from the Church, so dear to modern man's concept of freedom, is an eerie echo of that bellowing shout from nearly two-thousand years ago: *We have no king but Caesar!*

Within three centuries of the *Magna Carta,* Christ was attacked directly in the person of His Vicar. *Sola Scriptura* assaults the spiritual rule of Christ the King as His temporal rule is challenged by separating governance from divine law. Democracies elected to be under no king and to have no God above the sovereignty of the people; Luther wanted no regent of the supreme monarch over him. The anarchy of democracy is the result of several centuries of dilution of the acceptance of God's ultimate sovereignty invested in any governmental form, particularly in a monarchy. The revolting protestants of the sixteenth century contributed to that anarchy and to the weakening of the Church universal by the rejection of absolute truth regarding salvation. Christ's sovereignty is rejected on the natural level by states whose notion of sovereignty is self-created; He is rejected on the supernatural level by heretics and apostates whose notion of salvation acknowledges no concrete connection between the will of God and the actions of man.

Christ in His kingship and Christ in His Body the Church received wholesale rejection in the atheistic Constitution of the United States of America.

England's barons kept the faith but imperiled the state. Luther's minions found succor in thrones but denied the throne of Peter. America wanted no king, including Christ, and no church, including Christ's own Body. At present, the United States of America has the dubious distinction of being the longest-lived nation ever to exist entirely without an acknowledgement of some kind of divine suzerainty.

This may be remedied eventually by the Charter of the United Nations, of which the United States is a signatory and a permanent member of its governing Security Council. It seems that protestantism believes that individual men determine truth, while democracy asserts that collectives of individuals determine truth; but the UN is predicated on the notion that collections of nations are the final arbiters of truth. Man's truths come not from God nor from the individual nor from the sovereign nation, but from the world convened in New York City to render judgment, at last, on Pilate's age-old query, "What is truth?" The United States demonstrates how to synthesize a nation from nothing, the euro proves that currency can be synthesized from nothing, and the United Nations is sure that global sovereignty and economy can be synthesized from nothing as well. All that is necessary is for the interested parties to be convinced to *believe* in nothing.

Vatican II has given permission for this final abomination to occur. *Dignitatis Humanae* gives free rein to religious liberty. *Lumen Gentium* allows for the efficacy of grace totally independent of the Church. The new catechism and innumerable papal statements and encyclicals from Pope John Paul make it abundantly clear that modern Churchmen do not believe that the Church is necessary for salvation. Christ was dethroned by democracy, excommunicated by Luther, exiled by the U.S. Constitution, and ignored by the UN Charter; now He appears to have abdicated by the words and actions of his own vicar!!

What is needed is not fear, but trust. Among the three permanent things that last, the modern world is most in need of supernatural Hope. Let us consider the good as it comes from God, as it is assailed by man, and as it can be—and *will* be—re-established by and in the Church. Those who trust in the Lord will know His goodness in the land of the living. In trust in the Lord's goodness abides certain hope.

II. When Saints and Sages Rule

Moderns tend to think that as things are now, they ever have been and always will be. This is a curious irony given the fact that with the exception of the culture shaped by apostasy and modernism, all human cultures really were the matter of centuries if not millennia of unchanging stability. Sovereignty did not fluctuate except by military conquest, a man's sons would follow their father's profession, a family resided on the land for generations.

Contemporary lifestyles assume that personal mobility is a virtue as it regards place of residency, employment, and conjugal relations. Technology requires personality shifts, upheavals in labor forces, and the revamping of legal codes on an almost annual basis. Immigration, refugee movement, and international business commuting have resulted in countries losing their ethnic focus and in individuals denying a specific racial, national, or ethnic identity. But somehow in the midst of this dizzying flux, modern man has convinced himself that such a state is normal, typical, and constant, indeed, modern man considers himself the measure by which the human is judged. As he is now, all men wanted to be, or strove to be, or assumed they were. We have lived to see most interesting times.

Americans have exercised a sovereignty over themselves, the natural law, and being itself unparalleled in human history. Diversity is the hallmark of the novel rule gripping this nation. Liberals, conservatives, protestants, Catholics, pagans, Jews, the rich, the poor, native-born North Americans, and immigrants from the world's four corners are in absolute agreement: *of the people, by the people, and for the people* need not and should not defer or refer to physical realities, moral verities, or divine commandment. The government of the United States is answerable only to itself, a prerogative once held only by God.

Of course, loud and unceasing vitriol is spilled by various interests begging to differ with their enemies of the moment (who tomorrow, you can be sure, will be embraced as allies of longstanding) over just who has the right to pull the levers of power and set the agenda for the next assault on the moral law, social custom, economic common sense, or all of the above. What few people seem to notice is that no matter how embittered a given battle might be while it is waged, a surprisingly short time is necessary for the warring parties to abandon their strife and laud the latest novelty as a human necessity recognized by all men since before Adam. Who argues anymore about the gold standard? Where is the neanderthal who takes exception to women voting? How can anyone suggest with a straight face that stores should be closed on Sunday?

It is the very fluidity that emboldens purveyors of change for the sake of change. Sure, they say, this new thing is a stretch for you, but so was desegregation a challenge for your grandparents. The temporary foes of whatever modernist depravity is under consideration veritably wilt at the prospect of impeding progress, of being reactionary, of seeming behind the times changed at the whim of the winds of carnal appetites, intellectual sloth, and spiritual hubris. The spirit of the age presents as a *fait accompli* the notion that then was always wrong and now is forever right. Timid and undependable defenders of timeless Truth bow to the inevitability of their current defeat in much the same manner as their fathers capitulated to modern errors, with one exception—the sons are much quicker to surrender than were their sires.

And then to join in the revolution. If you can't beat them, be them! We are not seeing noble struggles in which the vanquished vanish. No, the conquered today will conquer tomorrow on the side of their conquerors. These are not struggles over lands and thrones and seaports, but conflicts with the end of possessing the opponents' very *souls*. After all, our battle is not with flesh and blood, but with powers and principalities, and the spoils of this war are the hearts, minds, and *souls* of the defeated converted to the lifestyle, mindset, and *faith* of the victors.

All-out war in ancient times meant looting the town, burning the buildings, and killing or enslaving the inhabitants—and then going home. Most warriors were lovers, not fighters. They fought viciously because they loved honor, life, and home. Fighting was a means to securing those things (and some booty to boot). Exile was one of the harshest punishments of antiquity, surpassed if at all only by enslavement or death. Occupying a conquered foe was seen by the men in arms as a lesser form of exile.

With the advent of modernity giving rise to the Roman empire (!), things changed. Empire ceased to mean subject peoples paying tribute to their conquerors. Citizenship became, at least in part, a legal reality, not just an ethnicity or accident of birth. Losing in war no longer meant merely to lose one's life. One lost one's identity…

Father Phillips' great-nephew and namesake, Father Phillips, took about as many prisoners as the original. Joseph had gotten a hold of this paper when he heard that Father Phillips, a son of one of Joseph's classmates at seminary who was the nephew of the elder Father Phillips, had been killed in a car accident. Evidently, Father Phillips the younger was working on this piece when he died. It was the content, not the subtitle, which was meant to be prophetic.

When Joseph had begun his examination, the sun had just begun to climb past noon. Now the day was well on its way to evening, still quite bright out, but the hours left to this day were numbered by the fingers of one hand. Joseph did not mind. He could think by starlight as well as by daystar light. Or again, his native irresolution could be reinforced in the dark with no less success than the waywardness of his days.

That, Joseph was increasingly convinced, had been his lifelong problem. He disliked the farm, not because it was dislikeable, but because his older brothers told him it was no fun. He soured on seminary and the priesthood, not because he felt no call, but because everything and everyone around him—except Father Phillips—was calling into question the very nature of the priesthood. He raised four boys to loathe the idea of country living and to be constantly discontent in the city, not because his own experience in the country had been bad or that he had ever really given the city a chance, but because he had nothing else to offer them. He had never embraced a *summum bonum,* so the best he could give his sons was a sense that nothing was quite good enough. But he never told them to keep looking, or what to look for, or why it might be worth looking. How could he? He did not know himself—nor did he know anything other than his own self-ignorance.

Joseph had no sense of direction in his life. The roads he had driven, the promotions he had sought, the investments that provided his retirement income were never *meant* for anything. Interstate 35 connected Kansas City and Minneapolis by way of Des Moines. Why? Anyone who has visited Minnesota and Missouri knows that it is not worth a six-hour drive through Iowa to see either. What was the point of becoming district vice president for sales of an insurance company? His customers never wanted to use his product, he tried to dissuade the customers who needed his product from using it, and his success depended to a great extent upon laws that coerced the public to buy his product whether they wanted to or not. His company and his retirement portfolio prospered not because their capital was employed in enriching the world with useful products, but because they were rather shrewd at choosing the issuers of stock certificates most adept at producing more stock certificates.

In this the last third or so of his life, Joseph could point to nothing of lasting value created by ten hours a day in the office, forty-thousand miles a year on the road, and twenty-six years rising slowly to the middle ranks of a multi-national conglomerate. He had not even the memories of individual days that could be described as enjoyable for their own sake. No fellow citizen could point to Joseph and his profession and say with gratitude that life was improved for everyone because of their strenuous efforts.

Some men consigned themselves to this kind of meaningless existence for the sake of the family. Joseph had not seen his second son in ten years, and the four boys had not all been in the same room together in around twenty years. Was that what was supposed to be produced by the life that Joseph had led—and taught them to lead?

Here was another bone of contention in Joseph's internal conflict. Father Phillips had waxed rhapsodic and vehement in his endorsement of what is now called homeschooling. Back then Father just called it handing down the truth. This is what the Church meant by tradition. What the Pope and the bishops in union with him were responsible for giving to the whole world, parents bore the obligation of ensuring was received in their own homes. Joseph was shamed more than Colleen was ever going to know that his own wife was a professional teacher of other women's children. Colleen, as a faithful union member, constantly advocated smaller class sizes of fifteen to twenty pupils. It never dawned on her, and Joseph never raised the subject, that they had a class of four which they exported to become members of classes of thirty.

Where had they gone wrong, gone so, so wrong?

Joseph put down his pipe and his mug and got down on his knees. He prayed the *Memorare.* He invoked his patron, the foster-father of the Son of God. He called on his guardian angel, St. Philomena, and Father Phillips. He begged for an answer, for some answers.

And his prayers were heard.

Joseph stood again. He retrieved his pipe and emptied it overboard once more. For a few moments he stared into the darkening distance of the late afternoon sky. He went to take a drink from his mug, only to discover that it was empty. How had that happened? Joseph wondered, amused and irked. He sat back down to fill both his pint and his pipe and to allow his mind to fill with the fruit of his answered prayers.

Faith must come first! Such a simple concept expressed in such a simple sentence. Joseph could hear Father Phillips even now repeating it again and again as he lectured on history on politics on economics on morality on culture on philosophy on sitting around and properly doing nothing. ***Faith must come first!***

Indeed, it must, but Joseph was keenly aware at the moment that he had not put the Faith first for most of his adult life. He and Colleen had not thought in those terms for their marriage. They had not raised their boys with that in mind. Certainly the many children they prevented after their youngest was born were not testaments to the Bloe family's faith in Christ and His Church. And no one ever pretended that the insurance business had anything to do with faith—except in the conviction that horrible things were just about to happen and usury was the only way to defend oneself. "In God we trust" was an insufficient safeguard for the cash of the insurance man. His money was in the care of compound interest and quarterly dividends.

Joseph got up from his seat, slowly this time, but still with his smoking pipe between his teeth. He went back inside the house. In the gathering gloom he felt his way to the master bedroom. Joseph went to his side of the bed and picked up from the nightstand the Bible that served as a shelf for his glasses each night. With the book in hand, he returned to the deck.

Tucked inside the back cover, just after God cursed all who dared add to or subtract from Sacred Writ, was a yellowed sheet of paper. Joseph grinned at his own handwriting, unchanged after so many years. The page had the hastily recorded notes that he had made during one of his first spiritual direction sessions with Father Phillips. They were rules intended both to ease the transition of the new seminarian from the world into the life of the priest, and to offer the priest advice that would help his parishioners in but not of the world. At the time that Joseph was preparing to leave the seminary, Father Phillips went back over them with him. Father Phillips, extremely disappointed with Joseph's decision, wanted the young man to have some means to preserve his faith against a hostile world. With just barely enough light to see by, he read:

> *A few simple principles for the spiritual life:*
> 1) Daily prayer (daily Mass is the supreme example of this)
> 2) Weekly Confession and Sunday Mass [Holy Days]
> 3) A monthly day of recollection
> 4) Annual retreat

Daily prayer must include the Rosary (fifteen decades), mental prayer, and spiritual reading (especially from the Bible). The writings of St. Theresa of Avila on mental prayer are must reading and re-reading. Of course, the cleric prays the

Divine Office throughout the day. This is a laudable practice for the laity who are able to do so, even if only a portion of the Divine Office, or the Little Office of the Blessed Virgin Mary.

Visit Our Lord in the Blessed Sacrament whenever you possibly can. Everyone should arrive at Mass early enough to spend ample time in prayer with Him before the Sacrifice begins. This goes double for the priest. Jesus is the source *par excellence* of the spiritual life. No one advances in sanctity without spending lots of time with Him. Do not expect to enjoy an eternity with Jesus if you find spending extra time with Jesus unpleasant, unfair, or uninviting. Get used to spending lots of time with Jesus so that spending eternity with Him will be a pleasant experience of Heaven being just like earth.

Structure in your life is a must. The monks have it right. Work is done to support prayer, not prayer to support work. Thus, plan your day as a day of prayer in which you take time periodically to do a little work when needed.

When you leave home, adhere to your normal daily schedule. Do not allow exceptions to your life of prayer to become the rule. Your life of prayer is the rule to which you allow occasional exceptions for your duties in the world. This is the mindset that must be cultivated from the first, not so as to make you irresponsible toward your daily duties, but to remind you of their context and the reason for which they are undertaken. You should begrudge the world every moment it takes away from your time spent with God. Your life should be a reminder to people in the world to seek time with God—and thus be judged worthy to spend eternity with God.

Your only goal is to spend eternity with God, without exception; loving Him with your whole heart, whole mind, whole soul, and whole strength is the only way to accomplish that goal. Your whole heart, whole mind, whole soul, and whole strength requires you to want to spend your whole life, every minute of it, with God. If that is not at least your desire on earth, you have no hope of achieving it when this life is over. If you do not *want* to spend all of your time with God on earth, you do not *want* to spend all of your eternity with Him in heaven.

God makes allowances for your need to attend to secular duties, but the Saint directs those chores toward God and finds them endurable only insofar as they can lead to beatitude. "Seek ye first, therefore, God and his righteousness, and all these things shall be added unto you!" Anything that can not be made to assist in the endeavor of gaining Heaven is happily cast aside by the saint. "Go, sell all, give to the poor, and come, follow me!" Saint Jean-Marie Baptiste Vianney said, "Anything that can not be offered to God is wasted!"

Set a bedtime for yourself based on when you need to rise in the morning. Determine the times throughout the day at which you will pray. Give thought to the intentions for which you will offer your frequent prayers. Be definite about the types of prayers that you will engage each day. Write all of these things down and look at the list at the end of each day as part of your examination of conscience. Once all of this is in place, then insert the other activities of the day into your calendar. You will find that little time is left over to do unnecessary things—like television, idle gossip, newspapers, trash novels, and trips to the fetid cinema—but you will have more than enough time, and desire, for truly worthwhile things. Please do not approach getting to Heaven with less fervor, single-mindedness, and tenacity than athletes seek gold medals, or bankers seek millions, or sinners seek hell.

For your nightly examination of conscience, use the Ten Commandments, the Six Commandments of the Church, and the Two Great Commandments of Our Lord as your basis for answering these four questions:

1) Where has God offered His grace to me today?
2) Where has God received my cooperation with His grace today?
3) Where has God been denied my cooperation with His grace today? (This becomes the matter for your next Confession.)
4) Where does God desire me to make use of His grace tomorrow?

Remember, God knows you better than you do. He is the one offended by your sins. Ask Him what most bothers Him about you. Sin is all about you—thinking of ourselves is what gets us into trouble in the first place, it is the source of sin. Our desire for God's mercy must not be about us, but about Him. Do not make the examination of conscience or Confession yet another example of our self-centeredness. Make it about God and His will, His will to be merciful, His will to love us. Your worst sins are not the ones that bother you most or cause you the most embarrassment; your worst sins are those that offend God the most and contributed most to the Cross of His Son. Look to Him to know the difference. Specifically, invoke God the Holy Ghost in this task. All knowledge comes to man from the Spirit of God; knowing God and knowing yourself requires you to seek knowledge from the Spirit who knows all of God and all of men. The more you gain knowledge in the Spirit, the more that what bothers God will bother you—and you'll stop doing it!

Keep Our Lord, Our Lady, and the saints ever on your lips. Make little aspirations throughout the day: "Jesus! Mary! Joseph!" "My Jesus, mercy!" "Immaculate Heart of Mary, pray for us, now and at the hour of our death!" "O Mary, conceived without sin, pray for us who have recourse to Thee!" "Glory be to the Father, and to the Son, and to the Holy Ghost!" "O Sacred Heart of Jesus, make my heart like unto Thine!" Love the things of Heaven and their Lord in life on earth, and the Lord of Love will judge you to be a welcome participant in life with Him in heaven forever and ever. Amen.

Joseph was ashamed at how quickly after he left Father Phillips' influence he had dropped any pretence of trying to live according to these principles. By the time he met Colleen several years after seminary, she had no hint that piety had any place in his day. Sunday Mass two or three times a month was what they taught their sons made them "good" Catholics. And, of course, the "Catholic" school at which Colleen taught and which their sons attended disabused all involved of any need for regular Confession. That was all "old school". It did not take long before Joseph stopped biting his tongue when such things were said in his presence, and when it healed, he lent his tongue to spreading the good news of freedom from guilt.

Step one, then, for Joseph as he decided to repair his ramshackle life was to get a spiritual life. Boy, this was going to be hard. Colleen would probably start looking for a doctor willing to prescribe Prozac or something for him. He determined that he would apply himself to a new structure of discipline in his own life for thirty solid days, and then break the news to Colleen—she was going to join him!

Which provided the segue to step two. Colleen did not need to work two or three more years. She already was committed to the current academic year, so in fairness to everyone, she needed to finish it out. But Joseph was certain that a big chunk of what was necessary was for the two of them to reshape the way they approached their domestic economy.

He was going to sell one of the cars. Colleen could drive to school each day. Joseph would walk wherever he needed to go and wait until the evening if he needed the car for any reason. If push came to shove, he could drive Colleen to school in the morning on the odd days that he might need transportation when her car would otherwise be sitting in the parking lot collecting snow, graffiti, or high temperatures depending on the season: summer, winter, or football.

That would be just this year, anyway. Because next summer they were going to move. He and Colleen were already agreed upon the idea of moving when she retired. They were thinking of a condo in Florida, or some kind of controlled community for "active" retirees. Joseph had a better idea.

With their two pensions, his stock, and the sale of their house, they had more than enough money to live on and to buy a smaller place in which to live. Buying something in Iowa would be far cheaper and stretch their household dollar farther than going to the sunbelt. But Des Moines and Iowa City were the two most popular and most expensive places to live in the state. So Joseph decided to go where it was a buyer's market—Buffalo!

Several years ago he had visited a friend there and was charmed by the sign that read, "Welcome to Buffalo, Iowa: Scott County's oldest city!" It was clean, safe, and affordable. He and Colleen could buy an acreage near town, plant a garden, save a fortune on property taxes and mortgage payments, and he even had a name for the new homestead: *Breezy Acres, by J. & C. Bloe.* A man is allowed to be corny when he is pushing seventy.

They needed to cook more at home. It was high time that they entertained one another rather than spending so much time and money buying their entertainment on the town. He and Colleen really had not talked in years. They became strangers long ago, during his midlife crisis. Joseph worried that these ideas might be a bit too strange for her to handle at this late date.

But was life meant to be just a constant struggle to get money so as to pay taxes and usurers? Was man's only purpose to support the military-industrial complex and receive high-tech bread-and-circuses in exchange? If he wanted to assert his freedom of religion, that was fine so long as he did not interpret that to mean freedom from the rule of people who condone the slaughter of infants, who never utter the Holy Name in any way other than blasphemies, and who insist on their right to make your private business smoke-free while you have no right to make a public school pornography-free. Surely Colleen could understand the stakes, couldn't she?

Well, Joseph was going to try. Next weekend he would treat Colleen to a romantic car drive on county roads out to Omaha. They would have a nice stay in a hotel, do dinner and a show of some kind, and then attend the Latin Mass on Sunday morning before heading back to Des Moines. When they moved to the other side of the state, they would have to spend their weekend getaways in Peoria for the Mass there. Maybe he was going to have to bring Colleen up to speed sooner than in a month's time.

The other thing Joseph was going to do was to invite all four of the boys and their families to visit early next year to celebrate Christmas together as a family reunion. Most of the cousins had never met each other. Joseph would have to telephone the sons living in France and Hawaii, but he was going to drive to Dubuque and the Twin Cities next week to invite the other two in person. He and Colleen could afford to help any of them who pleaded poverty. It seemed to Joseph that he was responsible for explaining to his sons what he was coming to understand so that maybe, just maybe, they might understand sooner than he did. And possibly raise their children better than he and Colleen had raised theirs. Ouch.

Father Phillips was fond of saying that it was always about the cross, all about the cross, and the cross hurts. Joseph was anticipating quite a bit of pain in the offing. No one was going to understand this. They would say that it won't work and that nothing would change and that the world is just too big to take on by one man.

True, perhaps, but Joseph realized that his life was not working at present. If he was going to be miserable anyway, he should at least be allowed to live with himself without the shame of giving up. He was not trying to change the world, just himself and his family. One little house and a couple dozen people were not too much for one man to whip into shape. Could one man, his wife, four sons, and ten grandchildren really be that disruptive of the *status quo*? Would mammon really see them as such a threat? Why would anyone fear the effort toward sanctity, the attempt at poverty, and the desire for real love in the family of just one simple, average Joe Bloe?

Joseph got down on his knees again. He had no Rosary—he'd have to go out and get one first thing tomorrow—but he had fingers, the Rosary God provides at the factory. Sighing deeply, contentedly, determinedly, he began:

In nomine Patris, et Filii, et Spiritus Sancti. Amen.

Credo in Deum, *Patrem Omnipotentem, Creatorem caeli et terrae; et in Jesum Christum, Filium eius unicum, Dominum nostrum, qui conceptus est de Spiritu Sancto, natus ex Maria Virgine, passus sub Pontio Pilato, crucifixus, mortuus, et sepultus; descendit ad infernos; tertia die resurrexit a mortuis; ascendit ad caelos; sedet ad dexteram Dei Patris omnipotentis; inde venturus est iudicare vivos et mortuos. Credo in Spiritum Sanctum, sanctam Ecclesiam Catholicam, Sanctorum communionem, remissionem peccatorum, carnis resurrectionem, et vitam aeternam. Amen.*

Pater noster, *qui es in caelis, sanctificetur nomen tuum. Adveniat regnum tuum. Fiat voluntas tua, sicut in caelo et in terra. Panem nostrum cotidianum da nobis hodie, et dimmite nobis debita nostra, sicut et nos dimittimus debitoribus nostris. Et ne nos inducas in tentationem, sed libera nos a malo. Amen.*

Ave Maria, *gratia plena Dominus tecum; benedicta tu in mulieribus, et benedictus fructus ventris tui, Iesu. Sancta Maria, Mater Dei, ora pro nobis peccatoribus, nunc et in hora mortis nostrae. Amen.*

Gloria Patri, et Filio, et Spiritui Sancto! *Sicut erat in principio, et nunc, et semper, et in saecula saeculorum. Amen.*

O, mi Jesu, *indulge peccata nostra. Conserva nos ad igne infernum. Duc omnes ad caeli gloriam, praecipue tua misericordia indigentes.*

Salve Regina! *Mater misericordiae, vita, dulcedo, et spes nostra, salve! Ad te clamamus, exules filii Hevae. Ad te suspiramus, gementes et flentes in hac lacrimarum valle. Eia ergo, advocata nostra, illos tuos misericordes oculos ad nos converte. Et Iesum benedictum fructum ventris tui nobis post hoc exsilium ostende. O clemens, O* *pia, O dulcis, Virgo Maria! Ora pro nobis sancta Dei Genetrix, ut digni efficiamur promissionibus Christi. Amen*

In nomine Patris, et Filii, et Spiritus Sancti. Amen

...I have always thought the only salvation for our civilization is in going back; not so much going back to former conditions as going back to first principles.
– G.K. Chesterton, *The Illustrated London News*, 25 May 1929

Bad News for Modern Man

Notes from an Inmate of Prison Earth—An Honest Assessment for the Stout of Heart

Fifty dollars is all I have ever received for any of my articles, essays, or whatnots. That was about five years ago. Not a dime before, not a penny since. About six years ago, three of my poems were chosen as winners in a small contest, for which I received a check for six dollars, two dollars per prize. So, my grand total of remuneration for my artistic, philosophic, and polemic efforts comes to fifty-six dollars U.S. Don't laugh—rendered in pounds sterling or euros it's even more pathetic.

This does not bother me. I write because I have something on my mind that I want to get off of my chest. If others are foolish enough to pay for it, so much the better. Perhaps it is a comfort to the world to know that such foolishness has happened but rarely. If others are dumb enough actually to print my rantings, that is just an indication that insanity indeed can be contagious. My spread of infection more than counterbalances the aforementioned lack of folly among editors and comptrollers of periodicals and other publications.

An instance of the virulence of the contagion of which I am a carrier is the recent request from a friend to allow some of my writings to be posted on his website. Several friends have asked this sort of thing over the years. In addition, no fewer than five periodicals have had me as a regular contributor, *gratis*, to their pages at various times in the last decade.

While mulling in my mind whether or not I wanted to mount the effort needed to compile the sort of things this friend might find worthy of cyber-space, that is, meritorious of being given room on the web, it occurred to me that this particular friend actually makes some money from his site. He wants me to provide content for which he will be compensated by his readers. It then dawned on me that the same has been the case for my diocesan newspaper, local newspapers for which I have written in parishes where I have been assigned, and the handful of conservative and traditional papers and magazines that have featured what passes for thought from me. No one has gotten rich off of me, but all of these entities have *infinitely* more money pass through their hands due to their publishing activities than I receive for my contributions thereto. Even a penny is infinitely more than a nothing.

Now, it is not lost on me that costs must be covered, salaries paid, and proper postage affixed. I do not begrudge these people making a living. It just happened that this morning it popped into my head that what I have always done for fun, for interest, or for the purpose of disturbing the consciences of my fellow men, is undertaken by others for monetary gain. Maybe they do not gain much by way of cash, true, but I assist them more toward accomplishing that end than any of them have shown a desire to aid my attempts at pleasure, intellectual stimulation, and/or inflicting my afflictions and discomfiting the conformable.

Priests are more than well fed, adequately housed, and easily garbed. It does not come into my mind to refuse to write something for someone when I am asked. It is yet further from my mind to expect that they will pay me. It is as far from my mind as a geocentrist is from a heliocentrist in their worlds-view to think to *ask* to be paid for my writing. Besides, what I print on paper is worth just as much as what the Federal Reserve prints on paper.

What hit me in considering my friend's request was that he and many in my acquaintance loathe what they must do in order to get by in the world. They do not want jobs, mortgages, and property taxes/income taxes/sales taxes infesting their lives. Quite a few of them mount some kind of money-making venture or wage-slavery so as to get the prince of this world and his minions off their backs, allowing them two or three minutes a week to love their wives, play with their children, and think two thoughts back to back.

It was in contemplating this reality, not with a small amount of pity, that I had what the trite and modern would call an "Aha!" moment. Buddhists and new-agers might term it a small enlightenment. For me, it seemed more a realization of just how bad things are. This is a relief. I'm glad to know that I am not so crazy as not to recognize insanity when it assaults me. This it has been doing for almost forty years, and for most of that time I have made others mad by calling the mad world mad. The more I call it what it is, the more I see it for what it is. *This place, ladies and gentlemen, is a loony bin.*

For those of you yet only partially convinced, let me try to lessen your insanity by demonstrating the ubiquity of insanity in our lives. Only the blind, willfully insane, and comatose will fail to understand. Only the demented will fault me. Only the devil's own will argue with me.

1) *Moderns Can Not Feed Themselves: Money does not grow on trees, but food does!*

Until roughly 1950, most Americans lived on farms or in rural towns. For three-quarters of our country's history, most of the, ahem, citizens, I use that word under the duress of not having just one word that can encompass *slave-subject-felon*, grew food, ate food that they grew, and sold food that they grew that they could not eat. Included with that number were the tradesmen and laborers who directly supported food-growing and food-selling activities.

Since the middle of the just ended and benighted twentieth century of unhappy memory, things have changed. For the period from about 1950 until about 1980, most Americans called a city home. A shift occurred in the last two decades or so in which suburbia overtook urbia, resulting in most Americans moving back in the direction of the country, while bringing all of the amenities of the city with them. Where farms and farmers once flourished, one now can find pavement, malls, and high crime statistics. Replacing the quaint customs of barn-raising, hay-baling, and skinny dipping in the local water hole is an epidemic of methamphetamine labs, drunken hot-rodding, and fallow land making a "profit" by dint of the government paying the (corporate) farmer not to farm.

Most Americans do not know where their next meal is going to come from. No, there is not a famine o'er the land. This ignorance is from the fact that most American meals are pre-packaged, highly processed, ready-to-eat travesties; or expensively advertised, really fattening, barely nutritious fast-food; or chemically-engineered, industrially produced, largely tasteless offerings from Agri, Inc. Twinkies do not fit into one of the four food groups; Big Macs, Buckets of Original Recipe, and Thirty-Minute-Delivery guarantees do not have their corollaries in memories of Sunday dinner at Grandma's; and Mother Nature never intended tomatoes to be available year-round. The average American lives a life of thrilling spontaneity, wondering in what neon shade his next bottle of catsup will be, which summer blockbuster will be served with his oversized fries, and how much more he will pay for his wine to cover the litigation costs over copyright infringement alleged by the blush-grape-growing region of South Madagascar against the pastel-grape-growing region of Old Prussia.

Mystery meat is not the only mystery in Americans' quest for sustenance. Not only does one have difficulty knowing what one is eating, whence it came, and who created it, but one is in a constant dither about whether or not and how much one should eat of any given food. Coffee drinking both hurts the heart *and* increases intellectual acuity—bad for the heart, good for the head. Fat contributes to high blood pressure *but* a high-fat/low-carb diet helps with weight loss, which in turn reduces high blood pressure—bad for the heart, good for the hips which is good for the heart. Leafy green vegetables should be eaten in greater quantities *unless* they are doused with chemical pesticides that might cause cancer, in which case one should eat organically grown produce, but that costs more, so one might not be able to eat as much of them, leading to cancer anyway and expensive chemotherapy treatments that one can not afford unless one gives up food, which is typically fatal—cancer costs lives but fighting cancer costs bucks, and without bucks no one can live in this topsy-turvy world.

It is distressing to realize that poor people eat poorly because affordable food is generally less nutritious. The poor disproportionately patronize fast food establishments where the food is notorious for its lack of nutritive value. To increase the earning power of poor people, entry-level positions are created in fast food establishments. In order to provide these jobs, marketing campaigns are mounted to increase the attractiveness of fast food, usually by offering larger or free servings. Poor people are especially attracted by these campaigns because their food dollar can be stretched further. Fast food establishments do quite well for their bottom lines, and thus are able to hire more poor people at entry-level positions.

Until it is seen how sick and fat people are becoming because of their horribly unhealthy diets. Fast-food establishments will be taken to task for their marketing schemes and for their veritably poisonous menus. The lawsuits shut down quite a few restaurants. Closed restaurants fire entry-level employees. Fired employees are poor. The poor are left with little money with which to purchase any food, healthy or un.

Government and industry attempt job-training programs. Food stamps and welfare checks are doled out. Schools have their curricula beefed up. Small businesses are encouraged. Tax incentives are given to women and minorities to go into the service sector or middlemen retail ventures. Surplus food is given away. Charitable organizations open up food pantries. Supermarkets, restaurants, and food processors are begged not to throw away unsaleable food, but to donate it instead to the needy. All in an effort to find work for people so that they can find food for themselves, or just to hand the food to the helpless. ***Thus far it has not occurred to anyone in the modernist world that having people farm for themselves is perhaps the most efficient way to get food to the hungry.***

2) *Moderns Can Not House Themselves: Don't buy a house for the family to live in if buying the house kills the family!*

Houses generally are built of wood, stone, brick, or in combinations thereof. Houses generally are built on lots slightly bigger than the houses themselves, allowing in most instances space for but a modest yard. Houses generally are built to ward off the ill effects of the elements, to provide security for the dwellers therein, and to promote a sense of happiness and wellbeing.

As well, houses generally are built for the occupants to use for, on average these days, five years. Houses generally are built for the profit of developers, construction companies, and banks. Houses generally are built at a cost that results in the buyer spending thirty years paying off the principal and the interest and the total they pay usually amounts to three times or more what the original principal was. Houses generally are built with the idea in mind that the debtor will leverage his debt into a larger house one day, or that he will utilize the "equity" in the home to enter into greater indebtedness as the years go by. Houses generally are built as part of the engine driving a boom economy. Houses generally are not built when the economy goes bust.

Another way in which houses generally are not built is by their occupants. Most home "owners" do not know the first thing about drywall and laying foundations. Houses generally are not built for the use of people who will do much more with them than sleep in them and argue over them in divorce proceedings. Houses generally are built for use by people who spend a third of the day at work or school, an eighth of their waking hours in various modes of transportation, a quarter of the day in some kind of "recreational" activity more often than not involving inordinate attention being given to lights dancing across a screen of some sort, and the bulk of any remaining time complaining about all of the things that need to be done around the house that never seem to get done. Additionally, these people who have mortgaged themselves to an enormous debt for the house, who work ridiculously long hours to service the debt for the house and to meet life's other pressing needs, and who point to their "dream home" with great pride and a sense of accomplishment long before the bank surrenders title to them—these people go to malls, amusement parks, and wilderness areas because home is so boring.

Some people in human history have had the novel idea of building houses in the country. There they build their dream homes themselves, according to their specific needs and abilities, not according to a developer's set of variations on a theme. These houses are situated on land that is ample enough to offer an acreage for growing food, space for children to run about in, and for untamed environs where animals, creeks, and curious humans can roam about unfettered.

Houses built under these conditions are not subject to a tyranny known in the United States of America as the property tax. Productive land might well have a levy placed on the produce, but none of the inhabitants of places where such houses are welcome would dare think that land can be taxed just for being landed on by a house and family. A house constructed in these circumstances is considered the property of its builder, who is not to be reduced to being the renting tenant of a government entity in perpetuity.

And as the property of their builders, these houses are at the disposal of said builders. If one of them would like to add a room, he may do so without consulting the local owners' association. If one of them would like to drain a marsh so as to plant corn, he may do so without asking the permission of a government bureaucrat in charge of wetlands, deserts, and the oppression of citizens. If one of them would like to stay in the house his whole life and hand it down to his eldest son to hand to his eldest son, then he may do so without worrying that the exercise of the absurdity of eminent domain will result in his back forty becoming the fast lane on the new highway to MegaMall USA. If one of them would like to build his house in such a way that it would require his three older boys to take turns carrying Grandma up and down three flights of stairs to and from her bedroom each day, he may do so and his sons should thank him in his dotage for teaching them to honor their elders and to be conscientious in performing the corporal works of mercy.

Boredom is not allowed in houses built to these specifications. The land needs care. The buildings need maintenance. The people need not look far to see the next thing that needs doing. One of the delightful things that will need doing on a regular basis will be the spontaneous decision, over which no one has veto except one's own common sense, to do absolutely nothing right now.

What is allowed in these houses and their environs is their full use. Hunting and fishing need no permits. Campfires can not be forbidden. Cottage industry carries no regulation. The castle's king, the husband/father, has no royal oversight commission empowered by his fellow kings from their neighboring castles—nor does he exercise such interference in their domains.

There are historians who can tell tales of a time when the peasantry abode in such circumstances. It will be pointed out that vermin frequently shared space with families—much like the lice that run through third grade classrooms in our day or the legendary sewer rats of New York City terrorizing the inattentive or the gads of termites fumigated every five years in posh suburban homes near Los Angeles. It is a fact that the average medieval peasant lived in what would now be called a hovel, resembling in most respects the public housing available in big cities throughout the United States—with the major difference being that the medieval peasant owned his hovel and could not be put out of it. Marauding hordes might beset a medieval village from time to time, true, but there was never a knight on every street corner inspecting each passing donkey cart for hemlock or eye-of-newt—gang graffiti, the highway patrol, and home (in)security systems attest to a different reality in the twenty-first century. Peasants were indeed bound to the land, but they also knew nothing of RIFS, outsourcing, or chapter 11 reorganization.

Modernity is rather unimaginative. Suggestions that our society might return to the medieval understanding of property rights is met with an instantaneous dismissal as if such would mean a return to medieval understanding of indoor plumbing. The medieval man would not have balked at modern notions of "home improvement". It is very sad that modern man thinks that not owning, not using, and not building his own home is an improvement. Such modern ideas of "progress" are to any but the modern mind unimaginable.

Exile was among the worst of nightmares for the medieval man. To lose one's home, family, and friends was to lose one's identity, one's very self. The little boy growing up in the modern suburban dream home dreams of the day when he can finally escape and be on his own in an apartment in the big city. The little girl growing up in the modern dream home in the big city dreams of the day when she can finally have a family in the suburbs. The woman commuting from the suburban dream home to her office tower downtown dreams of the promotion, coupled with alimony, that will allow her to move her two children and herself to a condo uptown. The man out of work and living in an apartment complex has dreams of selling his suburban dream home so as to move the ex and the two kids to a cheaper place and ease his support payments. When one has no home, one likely will have no family, no friends, and no sense of self to lose.

3) *Moderns Can Not Dress Themselves: Trust not the cravings of an impure heart!*

Few have commented on the power exerted by women over the ages by virtue of the old saying "clothes make the man". This is less an issue of clothes making the man than of the woman making the clothes. From infancy, women dress men to suit their tastes. It is Mommy who chooses Junior's jump suit. It is Mom who sewed his first pair of pants or brought him clothes shopping before kindergarten. It is fear of underwhelming the girls in the sophomore class that prompts Junior to have Big Sis show him which jeans to buy at the mall. His lovely bride picks out the wedding tux, vetoes the striped-and-polka-dotted tie he wanted to wear to the office, and burns those old jeans that are so yesterday's cool. And she will have Grandma knit a new jump suit for Junior just like the one in Junior's baby pictures that make him look *so* adorable.

Feminists, however, are abdicating almost all of the power that women once wielded over the closet. Women do not sew. Women are at the mercy of designers and department stores when it comes to sizes and styles available for themselves, their children, and the men for whom they shop. Women dress like men—either looking like slobs in the home, or mimicking men in the corporate boardroom where they claim to want to bring a feminizing element to humanize business. Women dress not like ladies, but like ladies of the evening when it comes to socializing, and then wonder why men treat them like so much flesh whose only purpose is for the pleasure of men, free to discard any woman—girlfriend, wife, or mistress—when something fresher comes along.

When women did sew, they chose the fabrics, designs, colors, and styles of the clothing for everyone in the family. The one exception to this would be tailored men's suits, which change their overall appearance about as often as the moon changes its mind about which side should face the earth. Now that women do not sew, they, and everyone else, must buy clothes. Clothes, as with all other consumables these days, are made to the order of mega-corporations. These corporations are dominated by men. These men decide what "decisions" are available for women to make when dressing themselves and dressing their men.

A slight tangent is necessary here. The kind of men making these choices are *not* the kind of men that would satisfy most women. The fashion "industry" is not noted for its emphasis on the masculine. This would not be remarkable were women to dominate fashion as they dominate nursing. What should concern more people than it does is the fact that America is being dressed by men whose primal urges tend in directions that healthy people would find disturbing, distasteful, and disoriented.

Here is a slightly different tangent to the tangent. The mega-corporations producing the clothes no longer sewn by women do so in most unwomanly ways. Slave labor makes production costs very low and profit margins very high, while doing little or nothing to reduce retail costs. A large proportion of the slaves laboring for these corporations are children. Women in America buy clothes for their children made by other women's children whose monthly income would be insufficient to purchase a pair of shoes. The ability to make such purchases, rather than the necessity of providing such items herself, makes it possible for the American mother to be away from her family and at work (although this work is no longer in the American garment and textile industry, now virtually extinct). This is a reality she does not share with the Third World slave mothers because their children are just a few benches down in the same sweat shop, happy that the family has attained full employment.

Women are told that they should aspire to be mathematicians and scientists. In happier, healthier days of Western civilization, a far higher proportion of women excelled at dressmaking and sewing—highly skilled arts—than their husbands were able to find success as rocket scientists or doctors. Women are encouraged to go into business and politics. They often pursue careers in business wherein they appeal to women's homemaking skills; in politics they frequently emphasize the importance of the home and family; and in both instances they miss the irony that they no longer nurture their own nurturing skills and hire some other mother to mother their children. Women in the workplace and in government are supposedly the repositories of a mystical feminine key to universal beatitude. They discard the very things most readily recognizable as feminine—dress, homemaking skills, and empathy—in favor of participating in the very things that destroyed the traditional husband and father—unprincipled competition, displaced priorities, and exile from the home. Blurring the line between men and women has not brought a more feminine touch to commerce nor a stronger masculine presence in the home, but has dehumanized most aspects of modern public life and has all but crippled the modern family.

"Dressing for success" has come to mean that women wear pants-suits and that men have forgotten how to put—or keep—their pants on. Women now see men as competitors and men see women as threats. Women have ceased to look to men as providers and companions while men no longer seek wives for themselves or mothers for their children. Women are replacing men in office suites and the corridors of power and men have absented themselves from the home and the responsibilities of fatherhood. "Unisex" does not mean that sex roles are interchangeable; it means that one of the sexes, the female, has come to usurp the position of the other, the male, and the male has taken advantage of the situation to be as demanding as the female has become. Women are demanding a right to help rule the world. Men are demanding the right to live in a world without rules.

This is a world without real men or real women. Females now lack husbands, fathers, and helpmates, having instead bosses, employees, and clients. Males now lack wives, mothers, and helpmates, having instead one-night stands, mistresses, and old girlfriends. Children are thus taught never to grow up, continuing the childish insistence on having one's own way in imitation of the females in their lives, or continuing the childish insistence on instant gratification in imitation of the males in their lives. Somehow, this does not seem what St. Paul had in mind in Galatians 3:26-29 or in Ephesians 5:22-24.

4) *Moderns Can Not Rule Themselves: When majority rule descends into mob justice, how does one overthrow the tyrant?*

This is a free country. Russia is now a free country. China is on the way to being a free country. Things are so free in Sweden as to make it a libertarians' paradise. Canada has recently codified in law certain practices which render our neighbors to the north a veritable libertines' paradise.

What do these and so many countries around the world have in common bringing them such wonderful freedoms? Democracy! And where there is no democracy, there is Free Trade! Even China now recognizes private property! The Age of Aquarius must be just around the corner!

Kings quickly become tyrants, we are told. Aristocracy is by definition unjust, it is preached. And heaven help the nation afflicted with a theocracy governed by priests! None but the citizen has the right to rule. Democracy, of the people, by the people, for the people, must reign.

It is the common man wherein wisdom truly resides. The sagacity of the common folk is unsurpassed by academe. If one seeks common sense, one should look no further than in the community. Elites are selfish where they are not being unjust. Only in the mob, I mean, in the majority are rights to be found and preserved.

In our infinite collective wisdom we have discerned the justice of finding and preserving the right to commit child murder. Attempts to limit the most outrageous forms of abortion are underway, but little is done to insist that abortion is *absolutely* forbidden by divine Law. The piecemeal approach to legislation that would reduce the number of abortions or make obtaining an abortion more difficult leaves in place the fundamental *demonic* principle that a child's life may be destroyed by his mother.

Common sense, as wielded by the common man, has determined that sodomy should be illegal. However, several governmental units have extended to practitioners of unnatural acts the same legal privileges that are properly the domain of Holy Matrimony. This has been done repeatedly in the name of the citizens of this country without any consistent, broad-based, or effective opposition from voters. Further efforts in this depraved direction are promised and inevitable. Provision in American jurisprudence for the allowance of sins that cry to heaven for vengeance is part of a larger assault against Holy Matrimony that includes self-abuse, fornication, contraception, and divorce.

Mr. and Ms. J.Q. Public have decided to make God *illegal.* Legislators, executives, and judges have colluded in passing, enforcing, and interpreting laws that result in the elimination of an acknowledgement that God is sovereign over all creation, including the United States of America. Either through direct legislation that attacks the Faith, or through appointing judges known to be hostile to the Faith, or through a legal positivism condemned by the Faith, the people of this country have countenanced a power grab in their name, deposing God as the ultimate Lawgiver and Judge, and placing in His stead the sinful mandates of mankind.

We the people of this country have irrational priorities. Fiscal concerns, entertainment activities, and immoral behavior can move citizens to recall officials, boycott corporations, and/or demand the passage of laws at odds with reason and sanctity. However, the fact that 4,000 children are murdered daily through legalized abortion causes barely a stir in the public debate, private consciences, or the activity of the Catholic Church. Sixty million Catholic Americans, given three decades to do so, have been utterly impotent to recall one sitting governor or President *because* he favors child murder. No outcry is heard from bishops and priests about the decadent morality that permits sodomites to form curricula offered to children, *even in Catholic schools.* Businesses such as the Walt Disney Corporation feel no pressure from Catholics to alter their policies about immoral content in movies, music, and television. The National Education Association with around two million members is more effective in advancing its agenda than is the Catholic Church claiming more than thirty times that many members.

Concerned citizens seem unconcerned that the politician kissing their babies today would have helped them kill those babies before, or as, they were born. The lips that made the promise to make abortions available to every mother are the same lips we let kiss our babies. Those same lips assure us that he has our best interests at heart, that he cares about the future of our babies, that we have the right to kill every baby to come if we so desire.

What happens, then, if one of the plain Janes or simple Joes would like to run for and hold elective office at the state or national level and bring some *real* common sense to governance? S/he has no money. S/he has no name recognition nor money to gain access to the advertising by which s/he could increase name recognition. The media charging those large amounts for advertising would sponsor news reports criticizing Jane or Joe for lacking practical experience or sophistication or expertise. Laws, drafted by incumbents of the two major parties, make it difficult for anyone without a major-party affiliation to get on the ballot.

Then, of course, there is the problem of plain Jane's and simple Joe's fellows in the unwashed masses. They will be dubious that either has much of a chance of actually winning. The bulk of the electorate does not vote anyway. Those who do stubbornly cling to their party affiliations, and overwhelmingly reelect incumbents at every level. And no one pays much attention to the fact that practically every politician who wins office to serve in Washington, D.C., either goes in or comes out a millionaire several times over, in a rather significant contrast to the hordes back home in their tract houses, minimum-wage jobs, and children in public schools.

If Jane or Joe wants to win, one of the major parties must be embraced. To embrace party politics is to toe the party line. Toeing the party line will mean that "some day", when enough power is had to effect real changes, never comes, because the party only lets those have power who will keep things unchanged. Both parties draw the line at controversy—elective politics these days are a tweedledee/tweedledum affair. Do you want abortion on demand or just up until the third trimester? The populace wants it that way, never wasting a vote on that insignificant third-party candidate who "has some good ideas, but he has no chance of winning". "Throw the bums out!" always means the other guy's bums—*my* bums are great.

American citizens are admonished that small steps are necessary to make changes. Roe vs. Wade puts the lie to that. The American electorate is told that given time, decent candidates will use the system to make changes. Indeed, things have changed, from anti-sodomy laws on the books in every state in the Union fifty years ago, to the United States Supreme Court last year striking down as unconstitutional Texas' anti-sodomy law. Americans are encouraged to be patient as little by little the moral center of the nation shifts, which it in fact has. No-fault divorce, the Patriot Act, and interference with home-schooling families demonstrate that Americans *en masse* are more than willing to permit the dissolution of the family, to allow the government to trample on individuals' rights, and to condone the seizure of children from their homes for state indoctrination of them in mores opposed by their parents. As is always the case with conservatism, what is occurring is not a repeal of the liberal revolution, but its codification and the window-dressing necessary to make it look respectable. Abortion remains legal, sodomy is now formalized, and divorce is commonplace among the commoners, I mean, citizens.

The issue of the issues is an international phenomenon. Most Americans claim that abortion is a bad idea, but no serious challenge to it has been mounted in thirty-one years. It is unlikely that the average Russian is happy with the organized crime pervading the country as a law unto itself, but Russian law pretends that graft, bribes, and intimidation do not affect government in the least. China and Sweden share the curious trait of their respective inhabitants possessing very little by way of private property, though such ownership is perfectly legal in both countries. In China, there simply is not much produced for the Chinese to possess, almost everything of worth being exported; in Sweden, the taxman takes so much for the state that next to nothing is left over for the citizens.

Abortion is bad, but it's not going anywhere. Crime is despicable, but it is dangerous to attack it. We're not rich, but we're fed. What can one person do about such big issues? The government says they're OK, so who am I to object? You can't fight city hall. All politicians are corrupt. No one pays any attention to the little guy, anyway.

It is the common man wherein wisdom truly resides. The sagacity of the common folk is unsurpassed by academe. If one seeks common sense, one should look no further than in the community. Elites are selfish where they are not being unjust. Only in the mob, I mean, in the majority are rights to be found and preserved.

I stand corrected. It is only in the mob, I mean, in the majority that rights are to be neglected and relinquished. The people have spoken: it's just the way of the world...

5) Moderns Can Not Teach Themselves: Children should not be taught by people who do not teach their own children!

Poor celibate priests are to be pitied because we can not marry and have babies. The joys of parenthood are denied presbyters by the oppressive patriarchs of the Catholic Church, presbyters to a man and men to a man. A Catholic priest might suffer from feelings of inadequacy and disappointment when reaching midlife without some kind of patrimony to whom to pass on his genes, his wisdom, his personality quirks.

Moms and Dads, on the other hand, have the blessing of having as many children as they want, one or two at the most. Families have the invaluable gift of youthful energy and curiosity filling the home, except for the eight to ten hours each day that they are in daycare while the parents are at work. Married couples have the opportunity to share with the next generation all of the wonders and insights gleaned over the years, an opportunity promptly turned over to the public schools.

Perhaps you have noticed the hullabaloo over the last decade or so about the possibility of computers making it possible for employees to earn their slave wages at home via the internet. Along those same lines, maybe you have heard the breathless reports this last year that internet commerce, by which people shop at home, now constitutes almost five percent of the entire behemoth that is the American economy. If you, unlike me, do not live your life with your head in the cultural sand, then you are surely aware that various digital technologies now permit your living room to be turned into a home theatre thanks to the DVD, plasma televisions, and a plethora of content providers including cable, satellite, and fiber optics.

One would think that the prospect of working at home, shopping at home, and going to movies at home would portend the resurgence of other home activities. But, as our friends the French say, *Mais non, mon ami!* Americans are not flocking back to their dining rooms for family meals. There is not a shortage of front porches available for the latest McMansions. Caller ID features, answering machines, and cell phones multiplying *ad nauseam* are not a sign that Americans have taken to cocooning from the madding crowd in the comfort of their parlors, dens, and rec rooms.

Many would assert that the option of being at home or of being on the go is the blessing of modern technology. These proponents of man mechanized would aver that it is a token of a newfound freedom that one can choose either to work late into the night, or to interact with one's children from the supermarket, or to record a favorite television program without commercials, or all of the above. Modernity has seemingly solved the problem of being in two places at once by bringing thousands of places into the home, the auto, or the symphony concert during the slow movement.

Such freedom is oddly lacking in one rather particular, prominent, and profound area of modern American life. For reasons I wish did not so readily lend themselves to conspiracy theories, Americans of a singularly broad variety are against people bringing the education of their children into the homes of their children. Homeschooling has become the contemporary version of the family in the fifties without a car, the family in the seventies without cable, the family in the nineties without a divorce. A bizarre peer pressure is being applied to get people to do things that are definitely unnecessary and arguably lethal, such as going into debt for transportation, importing moral pollution into the family room, rending asunder what even God is incapable of destroying, and exposing one's offspring to the secondhand irresponsibility of the parents who send their children to the average public, private, or parochial school.

This is even more strikingly strange when one considers the explosion of materials available for the rare occasion of couples wishing to conceive, bear to term, and raise children. One can serenade a tot *in utero* with the melodies of Mozart, acclimate her budding genius to mathematics in the crib, and prepare his major league career shortly after his first step with the help of thousands of dollars' worth of home educational supplies easily had at Walmart, FAO Schwarz, or eBay, depending on your socioeconomic-technologic abilities. Loving, caring, materialistic parents will find support in catalogues, tax breaks, and the neighbors' competition in the task of readying their little ones to rush out into the world to be just like everyone else in the name of freedom, individuality, and self-assertion.

Other parents, however, are decidedly left out in the cold when they decide that they know best when it comes to forming their children more perfectly in the image and likeness of God as the Lord has commanded us to do. It is not only the sneers of employees of the sundry educational special interests besetting the society that pose obstacles to parents who desire to school their children themselves. Mothers who teach in the home must endure the pitying gaze of their sisters in the womanhood who can not fathom why any modern, liberated woman would prefer her own flesh and blood to the blood and guts of the corporate board room. Fathers heading families where the children are not primarily, but *solely,* in the care of their parents find it necessary to learn how to fend off attacks from government bureaucracies, interference from directors of religious education, and parish priests reluctant to offer the sacraments to children who have not been subjected to the whims of persons of whom parents do not approve. Children who are schooled in the home must overcome the disadvantage of...

Would someone please tell me what the disadvantage of raising, educating, and loving your own children would be?!?

Perhaps some parents object to the idea of their children being deprived of the chance to learn gang sign language. Maybe it is the case that there are parents who wish to be grandparents so badly that they will try anything, including exposing their kindergartners to "health" classes that amount to how-to courses in conceiving babies. It could be, I suppose, that the hearts growing fonder from prolonged absences demonstrate their parental affection by increasing those absences so that the children will experience that much more love when they see Mommy and Daddy for their half-hour of "quality time" before bed on alternating Tuesdays and Thursdays. Possibly parents are succumbing to peer pressure: since step-Mom and Dad Jones get to be wage slaves and have no means to work productively from the home, it is only fair that Mom and step-Dad Brown should be allowed to drop their blended family at the school bus stop with a group hug at the beginning of each day. Or, dash it all, it must be that public schools are just such swell places that the children are simply dying to get in—and out.

6) *Moderns Can Not Entertain Themselves: If you can not stand to spend time alone with yourself, do not inflict that company on anyone else!*

The most oppressive rule in that most oppressive of rule-making bodies is the Catholic Church's enforcement of God's Third Commandment: *Remember to keep holy the Sabbath.* This means that one may not do servile work on Sunday, including dashing off that little report left over from Friday needed for Monday's meeting. This means that Holy Days of Obligation are to be observed in the same manner as Sundays, including the prohibition of servile work, such as doing the week's shopping instead of going to Mass. This includes understanding that the Lord's Day is not an odd celestial phenomenon in which a rotation of the earth occurs within the fifty-nine minutes of the early Low Mass with Father's abbreviated sermon; but the acknowledgement that twenty-four hours do a day make. This means, on pain of mortal sin, that you will pray, you will rest, you will enjoy your family and yourself and not tucker yourself out on needless work and worry! What tyranny!

It is ironic to the point of hysteric bitter laughter that Holy Mother Church is accused of impinging on men's freedoms. She requires that at least one day in seven be spent in quiet, rest, recreation with the family, and communion with the All-Loving God. She has as one of her primary obligations the comforting of those whose lives are disordered, burdensome, and hopeless. Her highest law is that of charity, which commands that whatever a brother in need asks, for mind, body, or soul, must be given, at the risk of the selfish being damned for all eternity. She calls her children to imitate her Lord, who teaches that perfect love offers all of life and receives the reward of endless life, complete joy, and the vision of infinite glory.

This, however, does not satisfy the modern sophisticate. He would rather have his boss insist that he miss his daughter's fifth birthday so that he can play golf with the big client being wooed in New York. His equally sophisticated live-in mate, the mother of his daughter, is upset, not because her unhusband is missing their child's birthday party, but because she can't find a new job. She wants to quit her current job because the couple's two-week old "accident" can't get into daycare until he's three months old, and her boss won't give her paid leave to stay with the baby until he's older. Without the job they can't afford daycare, which they need so that she can work. And she's not thrilled with her boyfriend right now, not because he's going to New York to play golf on their child's birthday, but because he wants her to have her tubes tied but refuses to have a vasectomy. She thinks it only fair that both of them end up mutilated. He thinks that even though she might not want to bear more children, he might still want to make some with another woman some day. That part about another woman bothers her less than having him miss their daughter's fifth birthday. After all, she can always get another guy, but their daughter will only turn five once.

Other examples of liberated, freethinking modernism include the hordes of people walking around with wireless chains attached to their ears. Butlers to the king of England answered bells at odd times, in inconvenient moments, and for strange demands. This is considered servile and undignified in contemporary society. No self-respecting, twenty-first century empowered citizen would willingly stoop to such depths of servitude. Instead, in the middle of meals, a bell goes off and they leap to respond to whatever command issues forth on their text-messaging service. A different bell goes off, the opening strains of Beethoven's Fifth Symphony, for instance, and the modern freeman rushes to find out which out-of-state client desires him to leave the orchestra concert to discuss what was discussed in the conference call this afternoon. Yet another ring happens, and an emancipated denizen of modernity stops her friend in mid-sentence to speak on the telephone to the friend who isn't speaking to the friend that she is speaking to over coffee.

In the home, the family exercises a newfound freedom unknown before electricity. "Daddy, tell me a story." "Sure, sweety. Bring me the DVD box and let's choose a movie." "Mommy, sing me a song." "Of course, dear. Let Mommy find our favorite CD and pop it in the computer." "Big Brother, come and play with me." "Sure, squirt. Let's go downstairs and get out the video games."

Some demur and say that not everyone, for example, sings well, thus, recorded music is a real help for them. To this I respond, "Then stop doing anything for your children!" If only the best is good enough for little Jane and Joe, then they will hear nothing but the Chicago Symphony Orchestra for bedtime lullabies, Sir Lawrence Olivier must act out the Brothers Grimm on rainy days, and Julia Child will prepare their afternoon snacks. I am firmly convinced that every child believes that his Mommy's voice is the prettiest, her face the most beautiful, and her cooking the tastiest in the whole wide world! The only children who think otherwise were taught such lies by their own parents mouthing foolishness like, "I can't sing" or "I'm too fat" or "My cooking is awful".

A bizarre phenomenon is occurring in our day. Everyone mouths platitudes about family values, but when it is suggested that people actually spend time with their families unimpeded by electronic devices, admission fees, or interstate-highway travel, suddenly the members of the family bear a familial resemblance to a herd of deer staring down a pair of headlights on the aforementioned interstate. No one has anything to talk about with their loved ones. No one has any common interests with their loved ones. No one knows their loved ones—and everyone shows very little interest in curing their mutual ignorance.

Why not cook a meal from scratch together? How about a game of tag? Perhaps it would be fun to pop popcorn—in a skillet with oil on the stove!—and tell ghost stories in the dark. When was the last time you built a neighborhood of card houses? Wouldn't it be great if Mom, Dad, and the kids spent more time enjoying each other's company than in the company of ogres at work, bullies at school, and strangers in the living room?

7) *Moderns Can—and Do—Worship Themselves: Smart men think the world is governed by impersonal laws of physics; wise men know the world is governed by the law of Love!*

White-lab-coated men scurry to various archaeological dig sites or stoop over microscopes or squint into the eyepieces of giant telescopes intoning arcane dogmas, such as the tautology "survival of the fittest", or the oxymoronic "multiple infinities", or the *non sequitur* "with so many stars in the universe, life *must* exist on other planets besides earth". Their acolytes are bound to receive, embrace, and parrot these and myriad other like phrases on pain of losing research dollars, being denied tenure, and having the epithet "medieval" hurled at them in polite scientific journals and the popular press. The faithful place credence in the doctrine of trained skepticism, applying to all assumptions except their own a blistering demand for proof of first principles. No one seems interested in the question, "Why should materialism be the governing philosophy of modern science?" And with that in mind, "Why should science, and thus materialism, govern the life of man, who is *spirit* embodied?"

For some strange reason, actually in lack thereof, modern man prefers to live in a universe which is, in the estimation of many respected scientists, a random occurrence. Modern man finds comfort somehow in the idea that his own existence is the result of billions of years of flukes that resulted in his evolving. An origin in inorganic matter becoming so much mold transformed into giant ferns related somehow to jellyfish whose ancestors at some remove slithered through forests giving birth eventually to mouse-like beasties who one day ascended the trees who changed their minds and descended into subways, satisfies modern man's curiosity about whence he came. Whither all this leads is left unanswered—and by the rules set down by the randomness of physics, chemistry, and biology running the evolutionary processes, that curiosity is unanswerable. Men who rebel at the idea of obeying the dictates of divine commands humbly acquiesce when they are told that they must evolve or become extinct.

If pond scum can become a sequoia, who knows what man might evolve into?

I do! Evolution, if it is true, will result in man evolving into something *inhuman*! Proof of the moral truth of this is available in today's newspapers. The scientists tell me that the material proof of this is available in the human genome recently deciphered. My proof is a bit more accessible. And believable. And provable.

The modern Godless approach to science is a regression to pantheism. Man is deferring to the elements, to the matter of creation, to faceless forces, and assumes their incontrovertibility in making his laws, raising his children, and understanding himself and his plight in the universe. The ancients perhaps appealed to Zeus or to *fire* or to the All. Moderns do the same by different names, calling their gods DNA, or the nuclear weak force, or string theory. Ancients and moderns alike see themselves as the subject of fate and determinism and just dumb luck.

Impotence is the result. Moderns can not feed, house, clothe, rule, teach, or entertain themselves. Nor can they understand themselves. And, oddly enough in a worldview predicated on evolutionism, moderns can not change themselves. Hurtling down a road to who-knows-where, armed with all of the material might the latest science can offer, equipped with every kind of freedom that hubris can imagine, modern men are convinced that man does not change, that greed will rule his economics, that hate will rule his relations with other nations, that lust will rule his libido, that envy will rule his notions of self worth, that naked desire will rule his aesthetics, that despair will be his end.

An epidemic of depression sweeps modernity. Pills are prescribed. None seems inquisitive about the cause of the worldwide sadness besetting us. Oh, yes, people talk about overbearing mothers and distant fathers and repressive cultures and oppressive economics and being potty trained too early, but what the final cause of all that might be is unaddressed. There is plenty of food to go around, if we would but share it. Technology allows for ease in construction, transportation, and medicine which could relieve the physical suffering of virtually everyone on earth. The sun is as beautiful today as it was for St. Francis, swinging on a swing is as thrilling now as it was when Grandma was a girl, falling in love happens more often in real life than in the movies. So, what is missing? Why is there so little happiness?

Each man worships nothing or himself. There is no will to feed the hungry, to house the homeless, to clothe the naked. There is no will to rule one's own passions, to learn the true Faith, or to face the specter of the void that we have created in the very heart of the world made in our own image and likeness. A universe which is its own god has no god outside of itself, thus one must look within to see god. When modern man looks within himself, he sees a black hole, a vacuum, a pit. Nothing.

So he turns on the PC, takes another Prozac, and continues to refuse to pray.

This place, ladies and gentlemen, is a loony bin. But it is not filled with Napoleons, fruit bowls, or men from mars. It is the abode of the enraged, the frightened, and the suicidal.

Anyone care to join me in a jail break?

Father Smith, *Sacerdos vagus*

15 July 2004: St. Henry of Bavaria

Sensus Catholicus with Father Smith

May one advertise Viagra (if the ads are modest)? Is it possible to be modest in such an advertisement? There seems to be a legitimate use for the drug for couples having difficulty conceiving because of male impotency, isn't there? (PQ, Boise, ID)

Dear PQ and all Readers,

Perhaps you have seen the latest uproarious advertisement airing in prime time marketing the newest version of the primary product manufactured by Gravity, Inc.? As you motor home after a hard day at the office, you might look up, while stalled in traffic, to be startled by the daring billboard now in national distribution by the conglomerate that holds the copyright and patent for the most advanced model of that excellent innovation known by the trade-name *Property Tax*. And, of course, everyone is familiar with the radio campaign with endorsements from all of the nationally syndicated talk-show hosts extolling the wonders of Food-Shelter-Clothing.

Advertising comes in three basic designs: alerting you to the consequences of what will happen if you do what you may not (drink and drive, exceed the speed limit, fail to buckle up); cajoling you to do what you ought not (borrow money, tattoo your child, vote for crooks); or convincing you to do what you otherwise might not (eat at Joe's instead of Jack's, drink beer instead of wine, wear sandals instead of boots). All advertising works, to the extent that it does, because it is dealing with options. One can speed if he so chooses and he is willing to brave the ticket; one can elect not to mutilate his child's body, thereby condemning said offspring to ridicule amongst the "in" crowd at the local purveyor of indecency and illiteracy known as the school; and one can purchase footwear for comfort, for beauty, or for neither. Nothing absolutely obligatory needs be advertised—you will note the absence of promos from the Association to Increase Respiration (AIR).

Appetite and the passions are behind advertising, and such is also the driving force of American commerce. Appeals are made to lust, to gluttony, to fear, to pride, to envy, to sloth, to greed, to lust, to lust, to lust—did I mention lust? Sane people would not succumb to advertising. They would understand that advertising makes everything more expensive. For instance, pharmaceutical companies spend around 14% of their annual budgets on R&D and about 25% of their annual budgets on marketing, reaping a profit margin of about 17%. In modern economics it is less important to have a good product than to have a campaign calling the product good. Savvy customers would pay less attention to celebrity shills and more heed to the implications of planned obsolescence.

But an even better defense against advertising than saving money is the desire to save one's soul. Someone bent on sanctity will not fall for the gimmicks of advertising. My car drives just fine after 150,000 miles. New models with more leather and higher tech and bigger sticker prices can not convince me that my car, well maintained these last seven years, is suddenly unable to locomote from point A to point B. Detroit, however, counts on millions of people worrying about depreciation of trade-in value, CD-player capacity, and self-esteem to sell unneeded cars—while neglecting in its huge advertising campaigns to point out that GM and Ford make far more money on the interest paid on car loans than on the actual purchase of the cars. As automobile manufacturers, the biggest two of the Big Three are really big banks.

If buyers paid off their cars in four or five years, kept the cars for another five years, and each month saved the money that used to go to car payments, they could buy new cars with cash when their old cars finally gave out, thereby saving thousands in interest payments, reducing their exposure to avarice and envy, and frightening the beejeebies out of the car makers, banks, and oil companies. Car makers, and every other business, count on the fact that customers are not actually customers, but *consumers*. Car owners are not interested in owning the car or in reliable transportation as such. They have image in mind; they do not understand the devastation of compound interest and chronic debt; and they have not learned the spiritual virtue of being satisfied with sufficiency rather than being anxious over what the next guy has that they *must* have next. Salesmen know that their commission depends on the weakness of their marks, I mean, of their clients. There is little profit to be made among the spiritually poor, regardless of how much money they might have in the keeping of usurers.

But what of the appropriateness of the advertising of certain chemicals to facilitate that which should not be discussed in print? If indeed said product is of help for a medical condition that prevents the accomplishment of the primary good of Holy Matrimony—which is *never* mentioned in the ads—then use of the product is licit. It is unfortunate, unseemly, and unspeakable how the actual advertising is entirely about pursuing fleeting pleasures as a kind of *summum bonum* without which life loses meaning.

However, it might well be that difficulty in obeying God's first commandment to mankind could be aided by medicine. A doctor who discovers what such medicines might be, by way of public advertising, is a specialist who goes by the technical name of *quack.* A patient who continues to rely on the skills of a doctor who receives his continuing education from his patients' exposure to the idiot box will soon contract the fearful illness known in the medical field as *death.* The *JAMA*, *The Lancet,* and *Popular Science* agree: a billboard in center field does not constitute a peer-reviewed study.

Do not go to doctors who depend on drug companies' advertising to stay on top of the latest advances in their discipline. Find a doctor who delights in reading the best research concerning his patients' recurring conditions. Ask your doctor how often he visits medical libraries versus time spent in front of the boob tube. A doctor who is not committed to learning as much as possible about what his colleagues are developing as options for treatment is to be trusted no more than a priest who does not pray *all* of his Office *every* day. Would you want a confessor who picked up his best spiritual advice on *Oprah*?

Ecclesiasticus 38:1–15 has some wonderful advice about the esteem with which doctors should be held. Ask your doctor if he is familiar with that passage. A doctor's office sporting a framed copy of that text would be immensely more comforting than one in which the Hippocratic Oath is proudly displayed. Hippocrates admonished: "*Do no harm!*" Jesus son of Sirach explains of the physician that *he was created by the most high, and all healing is from God!* Hippocrates sets a fairly low bar in comparison.

The product in question is not advertised because doctors do not know about such things. Any competent GP, much less a specialist, would have access to information on the subject without needing recourse to thirty-second spots during drive time. Its manufacturers are not endeavoring to strengthen the conjugal bond. What is used in its promotion is an emphasis on gratification in the act with absolutely no reference whatsoever to the purpose of the act.

These people are not interested in health or in holiness. They are unabashedly engaged in inciting people to unleash their passions, to place a premium on physical pleasure, to reduce society's threshold for the discussion of such delicate matters—and to make a buck. Frankly, it is astonishing that the spouses of the celebrity spokesmen for such products are able to show themselves in public. It is astonishing that the celebrity spokesmen can show themselves in public. It is astonishing that the public agrees to listen to descriptions of such unmentionable topics in public.

While one is inquiring into the frequency of one's doctor's use of the window-on-hell, the patient would do well to examine his own (ab)use of the demon box. Couch potatoes are not the healthiest specimens of human vigor. It could be, in at least some instances, that conjugal difficulties are a matter of plain old being out of shape. Getting up from the divan and diving into an exercise regimen might not correct the problem *per se,* but certainly both physical and spiritual health would improve. This should be a goal with or without having prescriptions filled.

Blessed is the man that hath not slipped by a word out of his mouth and is not pricked with the remorse of sin. Happy is he that hath had no sadness of mind, and who is not fallen from his hope. Riches are not comely for a covetous man and a niggard. And what should an envious man do with gold? He that gathereth together by wrongdoing his own soul, gathereth for others: and another will squander away his goods in rioting. He that is evil to himself, to whom will he be good? And he shall not take pleasure in his goods...The eye of the covetous man is insatiable in his portion of iniquity: he will not be satisfied till he consume his own soul, drying it up. An evil eye is toward evil things: and he shall not have his fill of bread, but shall be needy and pensive at his own table. My son, if thou have any thing, do good to thyself, and offer to God worthy offerings... Give and take, and justify thy soul. Before thy death work justice: for in hell there is no finding food. — Ecclesiasticus 14:1-17.

God bless you,
Father Smith

26 August 2004: Pope St. Zephyrinus

Reflections on Belloc's *On Usury*

This is the house that debt built.

These are the cards that make up the house that debt built.

Here are the banks that issue the cards that make up the house that debt built.

We are the spendthrifts who beg from the banks that issue the cards that make up the house that debt built.

There is the interest that's paid by the spendthrifts who beg from the banks that issue the cards that make up the house that debt built.

Here is more interest on top of the interest that's paid by the spendthrifts who beg from the banks that issue the cards that make up the house that debt built.

But wait! More interest is owed over interest on top of the interest that's paid by the spendthrifts who beg from the banks that issue the cards that make up the house that debt built.

That's the default that must come when more interest is owed over interest on top of the interest that's paid by the spendthrifts who beg from the banks that issue the cards that make up the house that debt built.

Here's the recession that's caused by defaults that must come when more interest is owed over interest on top of the interest that's paid by the spendthrifts who beg from the banks that issue the cards that make up the house that debt built.

Where is the money to end the recession that's caused by defaults that must come when more interest is owed over interest on top of the interest that's paid by the spendthrifts who beg from the banks that issue the cards that make up the house that debt built?

It's not in the cards that collapsed on the banks that issued the cards to spendthrifts on credit who lost all their jobs that came from the companies that owe to the banks more interest o'er interest on top of the interest that now they can't pay 'cause recession stops spendthrifts from working and begging but not from defaulting and frightening their banks who foreclose on the companies who fire the spendthrifts who get no more credit from banks, no more lending to dead beats and blue chips unless and until the Fed raises their interest by raising the interest that's paid to the banks who at last will proclaim the recession is over and start to rebuild the house of their dreams by issuing cards that bring on new debt for spendthrifts like us excited to hear that all is forgiven…so we can come home!

Brother, can you spare a dime?

The latter half of the Chesterbelloc is the leading thinker in the cause of distributism. (I am annoyed that the moronic spell check in my computer does not know how to spell *distributism*.) It was while reading Chesterton's wonderful, *The Outline of Sanity*—a definite *must* read—that I became aware of this. I have read probably ten books by Chesterton for each of Belloc's with which I am familiar. To date I have read two by Belloc, *The Great Heresies* and *Essays of a Catholic*. It is in one of the essays from the latter book that I wish here to rejoice, although each and all merit praise.

When I was in seminary, a popular phrase used by our pastoral counseling professor (yes, such things exist outside of nightmares) was, "Insanity is doing the same thing repeatedly and expecting different results each time." This was propounded as a means to illustrate to disturbed souls that Shakespearean truism, "The fault, dear Brutus, lies not in our stars, but in ourselves." Chesterton's *Outline* is a brilliant description of this, as well as a remedy.

Belloc's *On Usury* demonstrates how the mechanism of usury is the economic equivalent of the serpent devouring its own tail. Frankly, his indictment of modern finance points to the conclusion that the United States is the pinnacle of a monstrous pyramid-scheme fraud. The wonder is not that we have been foolish—and greedy—enough to buy into the scam; the wonder is that any of us manage to stave off bankruptcy.

Such may yet be our common destiny. The recent debacles at Enron (the largest bankruptcy in U.S. history) and K-Mart (the largest retail bankruptcy ever) threaten to become the norm. What is still ignored, to the peril of all things mammon, is that Amazon.com (the largest e-trade enterprise) and Walmart (the largest retailer on earth) point to identical fates.

Both Amazon.com and Walmart remain successful at what K-Mart and Enron failed to do. All four of these companies became behemoths without producing one product, lacking any tangible assets unique to themselves, and banking on a mix of marketing and market manipulation to increase profits. K-Mart and Enron failed spectacularly at this; Amazon.com has just barely managed its first-ever profitable quarter (while awash in two-billion dollars of debt); and Walmart is now the world's largest corporation as calculated by annual revenue.

Does it not worry anyone else that none of these companies actually makes anything? Most of the American economy is consumer-driven retailing, and most Americans work in the so-called "service" so-called "industry". Where does our money come from? Why are we paid for doing whatever it is we are doing? What do we have to show for our absurdly long work week?

Some would argue that ideas, software, and marketing are the new American "cash crops". The problem with these is that they can be mimicked, stolen, and readily replaced. If you build widgets, your widget can be proved yours, unique, and state-of-the-art. If you sell corn, no one can counterfeit your commodity, and you can eat it even if no one else will. If you manufacture vaccines, no one will wait to buy it until your competitors come out with next year's model.

But ask the recording "industry" how they feel about MP3 technology. Or discern the difference between a sandwich at the Bovine-Patty Sovereign and one from the Celtic Auric Vaults. Or explain the purchase of expensive clothing with a logo (manufactured by slave labor) in favor of inexpensive clothing without a logo (manufactured by slave labor).

Throughout the 1990s the American workforce was congratulated on leaps in productivity, information was designated an essential just below air and above nutrition, and investors laughed at being chided for "irrational exuberance" in running stock prices through the roof. This is odd. Nay, insane.

Manufacturing tanked in the United States as a procession of factories moved to the Third World—so what is now produced by all of our vaunted productivity? Our glut of information is inflicted by way of computer (one of the culprits in the phantom productivity increase), but no one has explained why a billion bits of inaccessible information on the computer improves life more than a thousand well-written words in pen on paper. As for stock prices, it has yet to be made clear where the wealth of K-Mart and Enron came from, why it was accepted as legal tender while it supposedly existed, and where it is now.

So far as I can make out, it was all on paper. Seems to me that a stockholder who gets back his original investment has lost nothing but time, a false sense of security, and perilous pride. Since our ultimate home is eternity, all of those "losses" can be transformed into real, profound gains.

I am afraid, however, Belloc's diagnosis and Chesterton's prescription notwithstanding, what ails us will not be recognized by the bulk of us for the disease that it is. Modern materialist man is more likely to take the hemlock of "the hair of the dog" than to swallow the bitter pill of sanity. This culture is addicted to debt; an unpleasant reality of addiction is the preference for self-destructive pleasure over self-improving pain. Play money and playing with money feel good, though they are bad for us, so we insist on an endless play time that can not work. Sacrifice and discipline feel bad, though they are good for us, but few of us will admit the need to do real work before we go out to play.

In a mad world, the sane *seem* crazy. In a mad world, the insane ***are*** crazy. Ours is to choose the madness disdained by the mad!

Let us not be in debt. Let us buy from need from those who make—and let us be among the makers more than of the consumers. Let us measure our wealth less in things had than in gifts shared. Let us put a stop to the insanity, not by forcing sanity on the mad, but by joyfully offering a vision of the bliss possible only to the sane. It's such a crazy idea that it might appeal even to the terminally insane.

Father Smith

5 February 2002, St. Agatha
Jesus Christ, Prince of Peace
Clinton, Iowa

Father Smith Presents a Layman's Explanation of Usury

Usury is not, as assumed erroneously by the uncritical, the charging of excessive interest. Usury is the unjust imposition of debt, frequently involving excessive interest, in which "wealth" is created without true labor and often without the fruits of labor attached to it. To illustrate, here are two scenarios, the first licit, the second usurious:

1) Mr. Jones is a farmer. He wants to plant an extra crop of barley this year. He does not have seed or money to purchase the seed. Mr. Brown lends him $100 for that purpose. At harvest, Mr. Jones has a yield worth $350. Mr. Brown receives $225, which represents his principle plus a 125% profit on his investment, 50% of the total profits. Even though 125% seems to be a high return, it is just because he incurred the risk and Mr. Jones still receives a fair share of the increase of real property. Mr. Jones now has $100 for next year's crop and $25 for his costs of living as well. You will notice that the return on the investment is based on the ***profit*** made.

2) Mr. Jones is a farmer. He wants to plant an extra crop of barley this year. He does not have seed or money to purchase the seed. Mr. Brown lends him $100 for that purpose. Half-way through the growing season, a plague of locusts descends and devours the whole crop. Mr. Brown demands that Mr. Jones pay back the $100 principle plus $8.50 in interest. Mr. Jones mortgages his house to raise the money to pay back Mr. Brown, but now Mr. Jones has

no crop this year, no money for seed for next year, and his house is mortgaged for thirty years at 6% interest, resulting in payments over the life of the mortgage that will be several times the amount of the initial principle. Mr. Jones eventually gets out of farming and takes a job in the tech sector to be able to pay his mortgage, buy health insurance, and put food on the table. He also will need extra money for property taxes since in selling the farm to a developer, the land on which his house sits increases in value ten-fold and the tax rate rises commensurately.

Basically, usury is making something out of nothing. This is impossible unless you are God, and I know that you are not God. Usury is based on the idea of generating capital, not on generating real property, real products, or real wealth. Money exchanged at usury demands an increased return no matter what the circumstances of the investment might be. It is just to gain a return on an investment that yields a profit, but unjust to demand a return on an investment that either loses money or, more importantly, generates no wealth whatsoever. Houses, cars, meals bought at restaurants do not generate income. To demand interest on money lent to purchase those things is unjust regardless of how low that interest might be. Conversely, a fair return on a truly successful investment might result in a very high rate of interest paid back, but it is fair given the increase of wealth that occurred.

Food, shelter, and clothing are necessities. If someone is in need of these things and can not provide them for himself, Christian charity demands that they be given to him. If he is later in a position to be able to pay back the generosity, justice requires him to pay back the actual cost of the charity, no more. A spirit of generosity might result in the charity case offering more as a sign of gratitude, but the creditor is not just in demanding that extra.

In business, risk is involved in investing. To make an investment (such as lending money to a family for a home) that generates no wealth—and involves no risk—does not entitle the creditor to a profit. When Mr. Jones buys a house, the bank is guaranteed to receive back its principle, plus many times more than that in interest. If, God forbid, he defaults on the loan, the bank keeps whatever Mr. Jones already paid in principle and interest, *and* gets the house to boot, which it can turn around and sell to someone else at yet higher interest rates. This is utterly unjust.

Houses do not generate income. When you buy your house, you will discover that it does not grow tennis courts in a year, a gazebo after five years, and a swimming pool when a decade has elapsed. Your property taxes, however, continue to increase because the government assumes that property values will go up as your neighborhood becomes increasingly fashionable with your presence there. The government assumes that this makes you wealthier, thus, able to pay higher taxes. This "wealth", however, only comes if you sell your house at a profit or take out another mortgage on it. If you sell your house at a profit, you will need to buy a more expensive house (and mortgage) in order to avoid disastrous capital gains taxes. If you mortgage your house again, far from having greater wealth, *you will be deeper in debt.*

According to modern economics, your home loan translates into home equity which translates into more wealth for you. That same loan represents wealth for the bank, which claims your loan as an income-generating source of wealth. The government claims that wealth is increased because you are a homeowner, the bank is making a profit, and tax revenues increase. Supposedly, you are wealthier because you have borrowed money, the bank is wealthier because it has lent money, and the government taxes all of this new wealth. Your increase of wealth is based on the hope that you can sell your house to the next man at a profit, the bank's increase in wealth is based on the necessity of your employment generating more income than your debt burden can consume, and the government counts each loan, each interest payment, and each paycheck as part of a growing economy.

But this is all smoke and mirrors. All of this "wealth" is based on debt. The original loan, say $100,000, comes from the bank out of other peoples' accounts. They are making interest on their savings accounts. The bank then lends their money to you, charging higher interest from you than it is paying to its depositors. The same $100,000 is claimed by the depositors at the bank, the bank itself, and you through your mortgage.

Now you must service the interest on the loan, pay back the principle, pay taxes, maintain the house, feed your family, and take care of all the other costs of living. You must have a job which pays enough cash to make all of this happen. The company for which you work borrows heavily to make payroll, buy its own stock, pay taxes, and service interest on said loans. Since most of the American economy is no longer propelled by manufacturing but is based upon the "service industry", the dollar is not backed by gold, and debt is several times higher than the worth of the annual economy; all of this financial activity is based on "wealth" on paper. "Money in the bank" is not in the bank, it is not backed by gold, and it is not generated by production. It is almost entirely a matter of interest compounding for no other reason than that investors expect every investment to yield a high return.

This is obviously insane. Not all investments yield returns. Those that do will not yield enough to cover those that fail. What is happening is an enormous pyramid scheme where the idea is to get your money out at the highest profit before the thing collapses.

The stock market from 2000 on, Enron, and now Parmalat, are just the latest and biggest examples of what usury does. In each of those instances, "wealth" was used to purchase real property. Eventually it became evident that the "wealth" never existed. Overnight, billions of dollars just vanished. Many people count as "wealth" the fact that they hold stock or are creditors of large corporations. When stock prices plunge or companies go bankrupt, the real money that was invested is destroyed along with the unreal companies or investment vehicles that produced no wealth except on paper, or at least much less wealth than was represented on paper. And, of course, money is only so much paper.

Fundamentally, a just economy is predicated on everyone making a living by producing a necessary product or service. An increase in wealth needs to be an increase in real property. And everything needs to be motivated by a love of God, expression of holy poverty, and the sanctification of man's activities in keeping with the Kingdom of Heaven. Usury (a.k.a. modern capitalism), communism, and socialism are materialistic, avaricious, and atheistic. Not only do they not give God His due, they make it impossible for men to receive their due. The love of money is the root of all evil; the love of money is at the root of the modern economy. What do you suppose that makes the modern economy? Hmmmm...?

Father Smith,
Sacerdos vagus

5 January 2004
The Vigil of our Lord's Epiphany

Money Does Grow on Trees

It is made of paper, after all.

In the aftermath of Christmas, the biggest binge of buying of the consumerist year, it is convenient to reflect on just what money is. At rock bottom, it is paper. Yes, it has pretty pictures, colorful inks, historic scenes, but it is just so much paper. With some cotton fiber, if I remember correctly. And fancy holograms and what-nots nowadays.

But a ream by any other name would shred as fine…

A friend has directed me to a website called Norfed.com, the internet venue of the National Organization for the Repeal of the Federal Reserve Act and the Internal Revenue Service. Their desire is to get Americans to assert their sovereignty by participating in an alternative monetary system. Rather than dealing with the Federal Reserve Notes—dollar bills of various denominations—issued under the patronage of the United States Government, Norfed would have us circulate what it calls "Liberty Dollars".

These are certificates attesting to the existence of a certain amount of silver which, I suppose, but could not be sure of from their explanation, could be redeemed on demand. The idea is that the Liberty Dollar has an objective worth, based on the tangible value of a precious metal, in this case, silver. Normal dollar bills commit the unforgivable sin against civil liberty of having no concrete value, nor a consistent means to measure its worth. Norfed refers to modern money as fiat currency. I share with them their concern over a merely human item being invested with a divine potency.

There is, however, a set of difficulties in the philosophical position of Norfed and their ilk in the world that is no different from the mammon-and-moloch-worshipping denizens of the American body politic. They are correct in their identification of the symptoms which plague us, but their diagnosis is wrong, indeed, their prescription will exacerbate the condition. Secularism and a naïve, blind patriotism are the least of their problems. Norfed, the government, and modernity at large do not understand the true nature of wealth, nor do they have a proper appreciation of property.

Gold and silver are property, but they are not wealth. They do have limited and restricted practicality in a narrow field of human activity, most of them luxuries, but the majority of men can live from cradle to grave without them and never miss them. Objectively speaking, they are no more "valuable" than a Stradivarius violin, Babe Ruth's baseball bat, or a ten-thousand dollar bill. Any worth attached to them is arbitrary, subjective, and wholly dependent on the mutual agreement of the parties involved. If you are a philatelist, certain postage stamps will move you to offer pounds of silver for them, and more if they have never been used; if you are a tree-hugger, no amount of gold tonnage will convince you that mailing letters is worth the loss of one termite-ridden Joshua tree, especially if it is useless for any purpose other than hugging it and the termites themselves are a threatened species.

True *wealth* consists of those things upon which man's very life depends: food, shelter, clothing—and salvation. Money might be a convenient conveyance to exchange for material sustenance, but in itself it is entirely without use to man. In a manner of speaking, money is entirely worthless because by definition it is a medium that the spender is willing to part with. Money is worth less to its owner than anything for which the owner finally divests himself of the money. If the money were truly worth anything, one would part with it no more than with air, water, or bread. By this measure, even barter systems deal with items for trade that the trader deems worth less than that for which he trades. All currency is based on the idea of giving something that one finds expendable, or of which there exists a surplus, for something that one finds invaluable, or that is in short supply. It goes without saying that cash is of even less value in the eyes of God.

Advocates of the Liberty Dollar and like alternative currencies are doing the precisely same thing for which they excoriate the Federal Reserve. They assign a value to a thing of worth, not according to its value in the hands of the possessor thereof, but in terms of a commodity in the keeping of an elite who produce neither the thing by which value is measured, nor the thing whose worth is being measured thereby. You will notice that the federal government neither operates the banks of the Federal Reserve system whence comes our cash, nor does it produce the goods and services it taxes in order to force the exchange of said notes for its own benefit (which benefit is money to intrude ever further into the lives of the peasantry, I mean, citizenry). Those who mint coinage do not create gold or silver, nor do they show much interest in growing food, building houses, or weaving cloth. People with money want to *buy* things, not make things.

In the happier days of kings, the monarch had lands like any other nobleman by which he was expected to provide for his reign; if his lands did not produce sufficiently, he had to tax and borrow like any other of his class. The medieval ideal was that the king's primary income came from his working land; inadequacies were made up for by set taxes and borrowing (without usury). Custom and tradition forbade the king from raising taxes beyond historic levels, inflation was unheard of, usury was (and is) mortally sinful.

Our federal government does have productive lands and incomes from some fees, but the overwhelming majority of its money comes from taxes, first and last, with borrowing everywhere in between. The money that it borrows is paid back by further taxing the populace. This costs the serfs, I mean citizens, twice: first in competing with the government for loans at usury, resulting in higher interest rates for everyone; and, second, in paying the taxes that pay for the loans that require higher interest payments that necessitate higher taxes that further depress the economy that is weakened yet more by a need for borrowing that drives up interest rates that causes the government to raise taxes, *ad infinitum, ad nauseam*...

Be *very* careful of middlemen. Liberty Dollars, Federal Reserve Notes, and mutual funds are predicated on someone holding the silver, or the levers on interest rates, or the telephone sending the buy and sell orders. That someone is not you, nor is it the person from whom you buy things with Liberty Dollars, Greenbacks, or equity from your second mortgage. Whoever holds the silver, the Fed, or Chase-Manhattan is the one getting "rich" off of those whose only wealth is on paper.

Hug a tree if you love money.

Speculation is behind all monetary exchanges. Gold and silver change hands not because of their objective worth, but because speculators are convinced that they will increase in worth. They will increase in worth because of speculation. The fluctuations of the dollar's worth versus precious metals in the 1970s cited by the Norfed site, were caused and worsened by gross manipulation of the markets, particularly in the case of silver by the Hunt brothers of Texas.

Precious metals can be manipulated with the same ease as money. In good times a bushel of corn is worth, say, an ounce of silver. Famine does not change the need for food, but commodity speculation banks on that constant need to demand more silver. That silver is of worth to them only insofar as they can demand other goods for it. The farmers' *greed* drives up the "value" of silver; the speculator's *greed* makes the procurement of corn more difficult without more silver; the family's *need* makes them desperate to get more silver in order to get even a small amount of corn. They might well sell themselves into slavery to survive.

Farmers wanting more silver does not change the worth of corn to the family. Speculators demanding more interest on lending their silver does not change the worth of the corn to the family. The only thing of value to the family is the corn, but the farmers and the speculators are most pleased by, and find the most value in, the family's dearth. The realization of this dynamic at work has given rise to the modern phenomenon of dealing in shortages, and creating them if necessary. This in turn has led to a modern slavery wherein families are mortgaged for thirty years to their house payments, fifty years to an employer, and a lifetime to the taxman. What is needed here is not more silver for the family or lower interest rates or even more corn; what is lacking is the spiritual virtue of *charity*.

Lest any think that farmers are here undeservedly singled out for greed, it must be remembered that the capital that provided the funding for the industrial revolution came in no small measure from the landed gentry of England. Farmers as the holders of the greatest wealth were replaced by industrialists. Turnabout being fair play, industry made possible the amazing technological advances of the twentieth century, and it is the manufacturing sector in our economy that is hurt the most by that shift in the global shape of things that came. At present even high-tech is limping along and none can say if it will recover or what might come in its stead. You will notice that at each step along this trail of tears of economic misery, I mean history, the moneylenders wielding the rod of usury have been present, have prospered, and have set the terms for what constitutes success.

But in the world, under the rule of mammon, bereft of fealty to Christ the King, what ends up being of value is not human labor nor the produce of the land nor, ironically, the money that purchases both. What ends up having the highest value, greatest power, supreme sovereignty is *control* of the money supply (it is not for nothing that Alan Greenspan, responsible for controlling America's money supply, is called the most powerful man in the world). Money measured in cash or precious metals or loans is immaterial (literally, and in regard to the philosophical principle at hand). The issue is that a synthetic, unnatural, capricious set of strictures is placed on human commerce.

Some would say that the shortage of corn in the above-mentioned scenario accounts for the shifting values experienced. That makes sense only in a Godless, faithless society. People *need* food. Raising prices does not change that fact. Raising prices will cheapen human life. Raising prices will make *some* people "wealthier" than they might otherwise have been, but it will make *more* people *deader* than they might otherwise have been—death to the body through famine, death to the mind through relativism, or death to the soul through apostasy and heresy. Higher costs for many result in artificial wealth for a few, but they feed no one, shelter no one, and clothe no one.

Money, precious metal, and human labor have no objective, absolute value. Attempting to base an economic system on them will create nothing but gross injustice. As one's whims, appetites, and crop yields change, one will coddle, torture, or ignore human beings accordingly. Liberty Dollars divorced from Catholicism produce no more freedom than Federal Reserve Notes in a state separated from the Church. Any freedom experienced is of the kind mentioned in the Norfed site: illusory, and the worst form of enslavement.

The only solution to what ails man is a two-fold affirmation of the divine order of things. On a natural level, men must be free to own property, earn a living by the labor of their own hands, and produce tangible, necessary goods for society. On the supernatural level, all men must be Catholic. The first level is essential to the maintenance of life on earth. The higher level is essential to ordering earthly life to its proper end of eternal life. Without Catholicism, there is no motivation (doing God's will), means (Christ and him crucified), and medium (his body, the Church), for man to be anything but inhuman, unjust, and unkind to his fellow man and to himself.

Do not forget: the love of money is the root of all evil. (1 Tim. 6:10) The measure with which you measure will be measured back to you. (Mt. 7:2) You can not serve God and Mammon. (Lk. 16:13) Liberty does not come from a love of money or metal or mammon. Freedom is to know, love, and serve God in this life so as to be happy with him forever in heaven!

Father Smith
Sacerdos vagus
19 December 2003: Ember Friday

Leaping into the Handbasket Bound for Hell

[Gerald M.] Levin, who provided plenty of access to the authors of all three of the books on the [AOL-Time Warner] merger, does not come off well in any of them, but he reserved his flakiest comments for Munk: "It's absolutely true that I plotted the departure of Nick Nicholas after working with him for twenty years." Levin told her about the palace coup that got him the top job at Time Warner in 1992. "And I don't have justifications for it other than that I'm a strange person." He did cite Albert Camus by way of explanation. As he explained to Munk in another context, his own philosophy was rooted in what he learned from Camus: "That we impute meaning and purpose to things that are totally adventitious or accidental; that there is no God; that there just is; that there's no life after death." Fine for grad school, and probably true, but not exactly suited to the boardroom.—Adam Liptak, "The Making and Taking of AOL-Time Warner", *New York Times, 18 January 2004*

Where and how does one begin when everything around him is ending?

The above quote is a sign of the times, a portent of the dissolution of all things. It is not necessary to go into detail about the substance of the article whence the quote came. The writer is waxing indignant that there are greedy people operating in corporate America—imagine that!

None but the delusional believed that the "wealth" with which AOL "purchased" Time Warner existed anywhere but in the dreams of stock options dancing in the heads of the major players. Of course, in 2000 and 2001, much of Wall

Street and Main Street was delusional, caught in the grip of what the primary inmate guarding the insane asylum known as capitalism, Alan Greenspan, called "irrational exuberance". A media goliath was formed worth dozens of billions of dollars, only to be brought down (in stock price, that is) by the David of reality rearing its ugly head, namely, that businesses are expected to post profits at some point, and actually producing a product is not a bad idea, either. AOL was (is) so woefully inadequate at profits and production that its very name is now expunged from the Time Warner corporate identity. It is perhaps only a matter of time before Time Warner sells its purchaser to one of its competitors—for a sizeable quantity of stock options and a business plan to be named later.

But the best story involved in this story is the reporting thereof. Read the quote again. I'll wait a few minutes to give you a chance.

Do you see the problem? If not, you, too, can be a part of the parade to perdition. For those of you who caught the absurdity, please be patient with your slower fellows as I attempt to illustrate what is contributing to the destruction of mankind in our day.

Fine for grad school, and probably true, but not exactly suited for the boardroom. That might as well be the epitaph of modernity. The barons of capitalism run this country (into the ground). They do so without reference to God or to Our Lord and Savior, Jesus Christ, or to His body, the Catholic Church. Their willing minions, sometimes known as wage slaves, blithely play along and sell themselves to the bidder who is least likely to fire them before they get a chance to refinance their mortgages. What's good for GM is good for America, or maybe the new *summum bonum* is Walmart, or perhaps Microsoft.

At any rate, the writer in the offending article says that the boardroom, the habitat of the captains of industry, the masters of our destiny, is not a place suited for the expression of what he considers to be "probably true". This probable truth, that there is no meaning, purpose, God, or afterlife, just an amorphous "is", evidently can satisfy graduate students, treacherous friends, and newspaper reporters, but is to be disdained by men responsible for trillions of dollars and billions of people.

It does not seem to occur to many people that if there is no meaning, no purpose, no God, and no afterlife, then there is also no such thing as good or evil. There just *is*. Whatever *is* is. Bill Clinton, eat your heart out!

Which leads one to wonder why, then, must anyone get upset over a few billion dollars changing hands among our corporate keepers? If there is no right or wrong, no God, no meaning, and no purpose, just an *is* happily being whatever an *is* can be, then no one needs to complain, no one needs to attempt correction, none needs to hesitate to rip off stock holders whenever one lacks justification beyond being "a strange person". It should surprise no one that a self-described strange person, capable of betraying a business associate of twenty years' standing, would feel few if any qualms about gambling with billions of dollars of other people's money, playing fast and loose with thousands of people's livelihoods, and walking away after it all, satisfied that his ego has been gratified.

For if the truth is that there is no meaning, no purpose, no God, and no afterlife, one should not hold one's breath seeking virtue in the boardroom. There is a quaint old idea among us moralists that truth is a virtue. The reporter in the *New York Times* story tells us that truth has no place in the boardroom, or, to put it quaintly, that virtue has no place in the boardroom. It would be foolhardy, then, to think that a room full of people lacking virtue, disdaining truth, are going to be champions of fair play, the little guy, or, indeed, honesty.

It could be my mistake, however. Perhaps the writer is saying that there is no place in the boardroom for such grievous relativism and nihilism. Could it be that he is suggesting that a better truth to be employed in the boardroom would be God and His greater glory in all things? It would be amusing to believe so, but one would need to be delusional to the point of looking for wealth in stock markets and non-productive "industries". Delusional people are rarely amused or amusing, for which reason they are called in better English, *mad.*

Minds should be boggled at the challenge of explaining how a reporter goes from averring that eternal life, meaning, purpose, and God are expendable realities for the boardroom, to then asserting that the tycoons inhabiting said boardrooms should respond to a sense of responsibility to someone beyond themselves. *Why* should they? Lacking judgment, meaning, purpose, and an all-powerful God, one is left with only the court system and federal prisons for ultimate protection. Anyone with a modicum of consciousness is aware that hard time is rarely done by "white-collar" criminals. And on top of that, what was done to and at AOL-Time Warner broke no human laws and, given the premise at hand, there being no God, no divine laws were broken, either.

What is sauce for the goose is sauce for the gander. Corporate America has convinced Americans that a business approach to all things—government, families, even the Church—is the most efficient, reasonable, and mutually agreeable means to maintaining social order. The loss of meaning, purpose, God, and the afterlife from the boardroom, it would seem, would result in a concomitant and parallel denial of such in the business savvy politics exercised in Washington, DC, and in statehouses around the country; in the personal economies of individuals and families throughout the land; and among those congregations fond of the modernist aphorism, "No margin, no mission".

Partisan gridlock, divorce, and the plummeting of numbers of people attending any kind of religious activity on a regular basis strongly suggest that meaninglessness, purposelessness, Godlessness, and hopelessness are endemic among us. This writer is at a loss as to how one keeps a "truth" of the magnitude that God, meaning, purpose, and the afterlife do not exist from invading simply every aspect of one's life. Admitting that "truth" is not seen as problematic by the modern mind. Acting on that truth seems to have become something of a reflex in the modern person. If indeed one can expunge that "truth" from the boardroom, and, presumably, from government, the home, and religious entities, one would think that some kind of improvement would result.

Two questions come to mind, then. First, do Americans indeed believe that God gives purpose and meaning to man, and can be trusted to provide for him after this life is over? And, second, if they do indeed believe that He is provident, loving, and involved, what sign can modern Americans offer that they are *acting* on that belief?

AOL-Time Warner, the war in Iraq, abortion, divorce, sodomy, and blind consumerism seem to indicate that American conviction lies more along the lines of Camus, Levin, and the *Times* reporter, than in keeping with Christ and Him crucified. How does one convince a culture, so far gone, to go back the other way? What can one do to convince his fellows of the peril of their ends when they do not think there is any end beyond "there just is"?

Father Smith
Sacerdos vagus

18 January 2004
The Feast of the Chair of St. Peter at Rome

An Epilogue to Belloc's *Europe and the Faith*

Hilaire Belloc summarizes the lynchpin by which the disaster of the "reformation" was able to establish a lasting foothold within the European heartland of the faith as the "Defection of Britain". This defection of an ancient Roman province from the fold of the true flock of Christ into heresy provided a voice, stability, and prestige to what might otherwise have been a more or less short-lived insurrection by disordered, disaffected, disjointed malcontents. Belloc describes a tripartite complex of phenomena that comprise the dynamic which largely explains how such a defection, unique in Christendom, could have occurred.

This complex was the interaction between wealthy men, whose faith ran tributary to material lusts; an open commerce of ideas decreasingly subject to an arbiter exercising authority in the name of objective truth; and a fetish for government as the medium of absolute power in all things temporal, spilling over into things eternal. Wealth and power more than error served to give motivation to those who became the servants of rebellion within the Church. Ultimately, however, it was not wealth and power that survived the ignominious period when sons of the Church foully shunned their mother. The wealthy and the powerful eventually made war on one another as they had against Truth and His Chosen, the Church, Peter's Barque. Error became sovereign in the hearts of foolish men who thought to usurp the authority of God's Kingdom and its Vicar on earth, the Pope.

It is readily evident that the so-called "reform" of the revolutionaries produced not renewal, but anarchy. The body—of truth, of doctrine, of Christ—which they abandoned, was replaced by something not reshaped, but misshapen. Rejecting the dogmas and formulas of the immemorial faith, they brought forth doubt and formlessness to cloud men's minds. The hundreds, nay, thousands of pretenders to be the authentic Church of Christ are separate incarnations of a shared condemnation: a house divided against itself can not stand. The various protestant sects can not stand: against the Catholic Church, to face the truth, or to endure the teachings and company of their fellows in rebellion.

Nigh on a half of a millennium has transpired since Luther's revolt. Mother Church has continued to stave off the attacks from without: error in doctrine, secularism, indifferentism, materialism, and persecution. This last half century, however, has exposed a longer process in which she seems to be succumbing to destruction from within.

Pope St. Pius x gave definition to the most pernicious of these perils by his condemnation of modernism in *Pascendi Dominici Gregis* and *Lamentabili Sane.* This was perhaps the high point, certainly the crystallization, of a succession of papal rebukes of encroaching errors within the Church dating back to the eighteenth century. St. Pius endeavored to make a definitive end to the modernist complex of heresies by imposing the Oath Against Modernism on all holding any teaching or pastoral positions within the Church.

Pope Leo XIII attempted, as had Pope Pius IX, to shield the Church from the ill-disguised malice of various nation-states. The mid-to-late nineteenth century until the early twentieth century was a period of "cold war" between the Church and secular governments. No quarter was asked, or given, as the Church refused the overtures of various secular powers to cooperate in the expanding hegemony of earthly rule denying reference to divine sovereignty.

Pope Leo also delineated a Catholic vision of society where material sufficiency is not an end in itself, but a means toward eternal beatitude. Through the still untried principles of the encyclical *Rerum Novarum*, Pope Leo gave the world an alternative to a warped communist *mercy* that would offer justice to the poor by impoverishing all; and a twisted capitalist *liberty* offering all an equal opportunity to defraud, oppress, and exploit their neighbors—or themselves to be so abused. *Rerum Novarum* presented a Catholic *via tertia* that allows communal security and personal sufficiency, *i.e.,* a commonweal securely founded on the creativity, initiative, and sanctity of men seeking God's will.

Here, at the threshold of the twenty-first century, only the blind, self-deluded, or pitifully ignorant fail to see how the efforts of Pius ix, Leo xiii, and Pius x are being unraveled. The modernist demand for the magisterium to have an open mind regarding error has resulted in the faithful being subjected to an open sewer of heresy, immorality, and apostasy. Cold war between God's sovereign on earth, the pope, and the princes of the world (all too often in league with the prince of the world, satan), has given way to a *détente* in which the Holy See appeases demands for the Church to acquiesce in the passage of immoral laws, covert persecution of the faithful, and the outright denial of a place for God and His rule in the world. The few who dared dream that a just society might be effected by men of the true faith, now share in the common nightmare of wealth absurdly mal-distributed, greed vaunted as virtue, and poverty misunderstood as synonymous with impoverishment.

Indeed, the three elements of the dynamic that led to the defection of Britain, and, thus, the entrenchment of protestant error, undue wealth, unreined skeptical speculation, and untrammeled secular power; are now fully visible and at work in Rome and throughout the Church. So dire are the current circumstances that Catholics, lay and clergy, are angered at authentic doctrine and insistent on embracing protestant untruth. If Britain's defection made possible protestantism's grip on modernity, what will come to pass should the forces that brought about Britain's apostasy be allowed to run their course within Rome?

St. Matthew 16:16–18 is solace to all. There is no cause for fear; what is needed is trust. Christ our Lord has promised that Peter shall stand, that his Bride is inviolable, that hell is utterly defeated.

The question for each and all also comes from the mouth of Our Lord: "Will you leave me as well?" (St. John 6:68). Many—the eastern schismatics, protestants, Mohammedans, Jews, the worldly—have turned their backs on Jesus, on salvation. There is but one legitimate response to Christ's question—Peter's: "Lord, to whom shall we go? Thou hast the words of eternal life!" (St. John 6:69–72).

That word has its fullness only within Catholicism. Problems within the Church have no solution outside of the Church. Her enemies, within or without, are vanquished only by the deposit of the indefectible faith found only within the unchanging Church. Members of the body might be cut off, but the body united with its head shall ever perdure in truth.

Certitude of Christ and the Church's final victory notwithstanding, integrity requires an honest appraisal of where we stand *vis a vis* the historic forces conspiring against orthodoxy. Britain's defection was unprecedented, thus, few might have foreseen it, understood the gravity of its occurrence, or found adequate voice to convince their fellows of the peril. Five centuries subsequent, Britain's failure offers the Church an invaluable lesson in the nature of this dynamic, how it proceeds, and where hope of staving off a second, far worse, disaster lies.

A hardly exhaustive list of the error current in minds within the Church would include men such as Descartes, Kant, and Hegel, all of whom have a continuing, profound affect on modern(ist) thought. To that list should be added Darwin, Freud, and Marx, whose mistaken notions or the mistakes of whose followers have caused untold misery to mankind. More recently the likes of Teilhard, Rahner, and Bugnini have more directly protestantized Catholic morality, thinking, and worship.

Academic freedom is a bizarre principle by which the Catholic academy is admonished to admit thinkers demonstrably in error and frequently explicitly at war with the Church. The filth in the electronic media, the abandonment of the Index, and the refusal of proper authority to condemn heterodoxy are an outgrowth of four centuries of licentious philosophical speculation, laxity in devotional life, and desire for popular, rather than divine, approval. Led by the community of the intelligentsia—rather than seeking the Communion of Saints—clergy and laity have ceased to think in Catholic categories and, instead, have made gods of their bellies, their loins, or their egos.

Error as such is not the motivation in these men and their followers, willing or unwitting as they may be. Man must have reason or go mad. *Modernism provides a matrix, somewhat internally consistent, that allows sufficient rational justification for* ***aberrant behavior, the true goal of this enterprise.***

These people do not intend to think badly, they insist on doing bad. It is not their minds that are deceived, but their wills that have been darkened by the willful abandonment of the faith. It is faith alone that illuminates the heart so as to ensure the mind follows the right direction; refusing the faith, these men fall into the clutches of sin, and seek not to be justified sinners through repentance, but to justify their obstinacy in sin.

Homosexuality, contraception, divorce, self abuse, abortion, cohabitation, and fornication (among adults and children) are the manifestations of consciences formed by persistent sinners. Modernism is the system by which sinners make sense of disordered lives. It attempts to give rational form to the chaos of sensualism. If this list seems heavily weighted toward sins of the flesh, it is not because such appeals to the minds of those decrying error, but because such sins are the masters of those who propound error. It is a (mill)stone's throw from the abominations and depravities approved at present in the world, and the eventual demand that all license be allowed.

Already there are calls to permit the violation of children, the use of animals for carnal purposes, and "marriages" between three or more parties. The unthought capable of enshrining in law the absurdity of "no-fault" divorce, the perversity of homosexual unions, and the unspeakably evil act of abortion, is incapable of forbidding any sin of whatever magnitude on any grounds. Make no mistake: the desire of the propagators of errors is not to mislead the gullible into a false estimation of sanctity and the *telos* of the human being; they desire only that none forbid them whatever earthly appetite in which their lust, gluttony, hatred, apathy, impiety, avarice or pride wishes to indulge at any given moment.

Not unrelated to the phenomenon of error-rationalized immorality is the astonishing wealth of the Church. Since the Second World War the Church has become a middle-class entity. Though surely the Third World has seen the majority of the numerical growth for the Church, it has been the Western industrial (now technological) world that has had an inordinate influence on the thought, morality, and rituals of the universal Church. "Liberation" theology is imported from Europe into Latin America. "Gay rights" is not an issue indigenous to Africa. The outlawed Church in China is not agonizing over women's ordinations.

Much of what passes for theological controversy among the disaffected in the Church is predicated on the leisure necessary to invent problems. Agrarian societies dependent on human labor will not look kindly on the sterility born of homosexuality, contraception, and easy divorce. Those who brave bullets in the Sudan to celebrate Mass will not be terribly concerned about "inclusive" language. Interestingly, the so-called vocations "crisis" has been markedly less felt in areas of the world where opportunities for self-indulgent material excess do not exist.

It is the hallmark of the wealthy to attend more to luxuries than to basics. Americans are more concerned with the price of gas than about the fact that corporations are systematically monopolizing the food supply-and-distribution mechanism of the economy. The French expend more energy resisting the encroachments of English on their language than on teaching the classical literature of Latin which gave birth to their language. Western middle-class Catholics are equally apathetic about attending Sunday Mass, believing in transubstantiation, and electing legislators who sanction millions of child murders each year. Modernism dissolves the traditional standard by which priorities can be ordered. Material wealth establishes the most forceful appetite as the new standard for setting priorities.

Wealthy, middle-class Catholics the world over, far the most influential force in the Church, have a negligible appetite for sanctity. Attaining Heaven and avoiding hell are not among their hungers. What moves the materially endowed is the acquisition of more material wealth and the (vain) pursuit of happiness thereby. The poor merely want enough; the rich want to have it all.

This body of souls within the Church sees her teachings not as a means to their desires, but as obstacles thereto. These people have amassed their wealth by removing obstacles to their desired ends. Part of the dynamic by which they live comfortably is to define an obstacle to their desires as being a personal enemy. Holy Mother Church is in the eyes of many of her children an enemy, even *the* enemy. It is morally licit to go to war against a mortal enemy, thus destroying him; ergo, it is a moral good in the eyes of the wealthy, modernist Catholic to attack and destroy the Church as she is—and to refashion it as a means conducive to materialist and modernist ends.

When one is at war, one seeks allies. An ever ready and willing adversary of Holy Mother Church is the world. Satan is the prince of the world. By enlisting the aid of the world against the Church, some of her children have leagued themselves with the devil. In fact, in this is seen that the ancient struggle of the Church against the world is part and parcel of the war between Heaven and hell, of the absolute denial of satan's temptations by Christ the Lord. ("For our struggle is not against enemies of blood and flesh, but against the powers and principalities, against the cosmic powers of the present darkness, against the spiritual forces of evil…"—Ephesians 6:12.) The Church must utterly reject the world. In doing so, she not only lights the way to Christ, preserving and proclaiming truth to the nations, but she shares in Christ's triumph over satan.

Nonsensical constructions such as "separation of Church and state" are a lamentable indication that not all of the children of the Church would fight for her. The astounding and shameful silence of the faithful on the matter of abortion is *de facto* submission to the tyranny of sin. State usurpation of parents' roles by way of the policies that govern public education is an open attack by Caesar against the things of God.

All of this would be an unimaginable terror if imposed by an alien, military power. The shock and scandal inherent in how the Church now interacts with the world is that the ubiquitous confiscation of the Catholic patrimony by the state is largely unresisted. Most of this phenomenon occurs in nations that fancy themselves democratic, representative, popularly elected, and/or republican. Catholics suffer the distortion of their faith not only willingly, but joyfully. In many instances Catholics lead the way—e.g., in the United States Congress—voting to kill babies, licensing indecency, oppressing Catholic schools.

"You can't fight city hall" is an American truism. Alongside of this is heard, "You can't legislate morality." In the same breath often is declared, "You can't impose your religion on others."

This mentality (can't-can't-can't) means that the populace are not citizens, but slaves. Human interaction is not a concourse of equals sharing justice, but a mob restrained by force and fear of force. Jesus Christ is not God but a liar in exhorting His Apostles to "teach the nations, baptizing them in the name of the Father and of the Son and of the Holy Ghost!" (St. Matthew 28:19) Such are the direct results of immersion in error, materialism, and deifying temporal powers. Such is not of God; it is unmistakably, undeniably, unremittingly of the devil.

There is a cogent argument that the South had constitutional grounds for its secession. Some would argue that the sovereign majesty of England could take the realm out of the Church just as lawfully as Clovis brought all of Gaul into the Church. Both of these principles rely on the notion that what a man has done a man can undo.

Nothing of the kind applies to divine truth. The Church herself, parishioners, priests, and popes alike, can no more deny eternal truths in doctrine, morals, or worship than a man can change the fact of the father who conceived him and the mother who bore him. The Church is not an institution of human origin. The Church is the Body of Christ begotten of water and the Holy Spirit ("...born, not of blood or the will of the flesh or the will of man, but of God"— St. John 1:13). No power exists to alter who she is, to change her nature, to rescind the divine mandate to preach nothing but Christ and Him crucified.

Belloc did not live to see the defection of Britain become the motive force of Catholics around the world. He did, however, foresee the implications of error wherever it might lie. At present Catholics seem loath to apply to the Church the honest analysis Belloc applied to history. None knew in the sixteenth century where the road to disaster on which Europe embarked would lead. None now can pretend not to know what lies in wait for those who continue to tread that road. As Belloc predicted, "Europe [indeed, all the earth] will return to the faith or...perish."

Thou art Peter, and on this rock I shall build my church, and the gates of hell shall not prevail against it! (St. Matthew 16:18)

Without the gates of the city are dogs and sorcerers and fornicators and murderers and idolaters and every one that makes and loves lies. (Apoc. 22:15)

Blessed are they that wash their robes in the Blood of the Lamb: that they may have a right to the tree of life and may enter in by the gates into the city! (Apoc. 22:14)

Father Lawrence C. Smith
13 March 2002

(visiting) St. Joseph Rectory
Pilot Grove, Missouri

Re-establishing Christendom I: In the Faithful Heart

15 August 2005: The Feast of the Assumption of the Blessed Virgin Mary

Deo gratias! Alleluia! Jubilate Deo, omnis terra! This day made by the Lord is one of great rejoicing. Our Lady, the Queen of Heaven and earth, the Mother of God, the Blessed Virgin Mary is come into the fullness of glory. God our Father, Jesus Christ our Savior, and the Holy Ghost our Life now welcome home the Daughter of Sion, the Font of Grace, the Spouse of Love. We are pleased by divine indulgence to be on hand to join in this Feast of victory by humility over pride, Our radiant Mother's triumphant Assumption into heaven!

Let us contemplate and celebrate this wondrous truth through the lens of Our Lady's Immaculate Heart, the Heart of a faithful Daughter, the Heart of a generous Mother, the Heart of a devoted Wife. Today is the Feast of the Holy Family reunion, in which the Father is pleased to acknowledge his truest Daughter, wherein the Son is delighted to reward his devoted Mother, and through which the Holy Ghost exalts his beloved Bride. And, too, it is the satisfaction of the profound desire of the Handmaid of the Lord to embrace once more and forever her chaste companion on earth, St. Joseph, and to renew and to receive the perfection of the bond she has known since her very conception with her divine Son. Her loyal subjects, the Angels and Archangels, Thrones and Powers and

Virtues, Dominions and Principalities, all the Cherubim and Seraphim, thunderously praise God with unimaginable *Hosannas!* for the incredible gift He has given them of their majestic Queen. The Saints of the Church Triumphant give her thanks for bestowing on them the bounty of graces flowing from the Cross of Christ; the Poor Souls of the Church Suffering in Purgatory look on with longing as she stands before the Throne as the promise of Mercy pledged and fulfilled to those who rush to stand by her at the foot of the Cross of Christ; and we her children in the Church Militant on earth kneel in humble awe at the realization of the tremendous spectacle of her beautiful foot crushing the head of satan by the power of the victory won beneath the Cross of Christ.

Deo gratias! Alleluia! Jubilate Deo, omnis terra! our Father's house's many mansions are now adorned with the glory of the Lady who is their Mistress. Our Savior, who has prepared a place for each of His elect, bestows upon His most steadfast, most deserving, most blessed disciple pride of place as being the very dwelling of Him whom the heavens can not contain. The Holy Ghost receives her who received His fullness of grace, He accepts for eternity the body and soul of her who accepted the sweet yoke of bearing the Body-Blood-Soul-and-Divinity of Life Himself, and he hearkens to the prayers of her who served as man's advocate on His behalf in moving heaven's King to serve His subjects the miraculous wine that served as the sign of the blood which serves to transform sinners into Saints.

Where Mary goes, all her faithful children hope to follow. She believed and so conceived her Lord within her spotless womb. She trusted and did not despair at the humiliation of Calvary. She loves and thus reigns with the Triune Love who made the heavens and the earth. We must believe as we approach the sublime Presence who desires to fill us through our communion with Him. We must trust as we take up each day the crosses imposed upon us by the world, the flesh, and the devil, so that we may participate in the victory of Him who humbled death, conquered sin, and cast out the prince of this world. We must love our neighbor and our enemy for the sake of God alone if we are to be made perfect as our Father is perfect, holy as He is holy, divine by grace as He is divine by nature.

Deo gratias! Alleluia! Jubilate Deo, omnis terra! On this great festive day we share in the exaltation of the Blessed Virgin Mary. The separation she felt when St. Joseph died in the blessed presence of his mother and his Savior is now healed. The sorrow she endured when she stood as witness to the immolation of her Son on the cross is transformed into glory as she beholds Him reigning from His eternal throne. Having served the divine omnipotence of God the Father throughout her life on earth, willing only what He wills, asking only that which pleases Him, doing nothing but what gives Him glory and brings salvation to the world, Our Lady now reigns with Him wielding His omnipotence through the power of her perfectly efficacious prayer.

We benefit in unimaginable ways from the divine favor showered on the Queen of Heaven and earth. St. Joseph prays that we receive the benefit of the holy death which God granted him in the presence of Jesus and Mary. Our Lord daily renews His immolation on Calvary through His immolation in the Holy Sacrifice of the Mass, so that we are privileged to stand beneath the true cross in faithful witness beside Our Mother. Our Father in Heaven refuses nothing to us when we beg His grace through the intercession of Mary, in whom the fullness of God's grace is pleased to dwell. All the good that Heaven has to give is given to Mary, for she has embraced Jesus Christ in His fullness, Body-Blood-Soul-and-Divinity. All the good that earth can think to ask for is given through Mary, for she is the gate through which passes God Incarnate, Jesus Christ.

In this Feast of the Assumption of the Blessed Virgin Mary, we see the union of the perfection of Heaven and the perfection of earth. God in His perfection is united with His perfect creature. He who wills that the whole of the human heart, the whole of the human soul, the whole of the human mind, and the whole of human strength be given Him in love by each of the persons who desires to be called His child, receives in Heaven as He did on earth the unsullied will of the Mother of God, the brilliant sanctity of the lowly Handmaid of the Lord, the pure contemplation of the Seat of Wisdom, and the stainless desire of the Immaculate Conception. Our beloved Lady is set before us as the sign of the perfection of what we are to be in Christ, and as the beacon of hope that the promises of God indeed reach perfection in His creatures. Generous with the generosity of God, the Blessed Virgin Mary desires for us the beatitude begun in her on earth and brought to perfection on this glorious day in Heaven.

If we are to succeed in obeying the will of God and receiving the reward whose fullness is given to the Mother of God, then we must do as she has done. Love that shuns the world with the whole heart, the whole soul, the whole mind, and the whole strength, must be given instead to God the Father in obedience, to God the Son in humility, and to God the Holy Ghost with all the piety possible in the whole of our hearts, souls, minds, and strength reflecting the very love of God Himself. Nothing may be left out of the offer of ourselves which we make to God, for He has offered all of himself without exception for our sake. Divine justice finds its perfection in the human soul willing to give as God gives, wholly, humbly, and sacrificially.

This sublime call was answered and fulfilled by Our Lady as she served as the heart of the Holy Family at Nazareth. She persevered in faith by exposing her Mother's Heart to the seven swords of sorrow prophesied to her by St. Simeon, in which she was wounded with the sufferings of Christ as only a mother can experience. Her Heart now lies open to us so that, by her prayers, our hearts' desire to be at peace with Our Lord can be made known through our faith in Christ crucified, our hope in the resurrection in which He has proceeded us, and our love by which the glory of Christ in Heaven is shared even now on earth.

How might we accomplish our Father's will in imitation of our Mother? Seven words will suffice to describe the labor that lies before us***: Go home. Slow down. Be quiet. Now!***

Lest any be foolish enough to succumb to the temptation of interpreting those directions to mean that Mass is over, please keep in mind that Mass is where the faithful are most at home. It is in the Mass that time not only slows, but stops entirely so that eternity may enter into us and we may enter into eternity. In the Mass we experience the silence that will suffuse Heaven just before the sound of the last trumpet heralding the Judgment on the world which leads to the final triumph of the Kingdom of God. Even now we are blessed and privileged to be on hand for this exquisite reality, the ultimate reality where the world is entirely thrust aside and only God and that which gives Him glory is present.

Such is to be the desire of the whole of our lives: to do nothing but give God glory and to be sanctified by His merciful grace. We are meant to leave the hostile world behind us after we have entered through the waters of Baptism into the sanctuary of the Church. As Jesus came unto his own and His own knew Him not, we understand that we, too, are exiles among those who will not welcome us. We have here no abiding place, but Jesus has gone before us to prepare a place for us in His Father's house. That house is the Church, and the Church is our home on earth as it is in Heaven.

Thus, on earth, we must ever be endeavoring to ***Go home!*** The houses where we live with our families are but temporary dwellings to shelter us as we endeavor to spend as much time as possible in our true home, the House of God. Everything about our lives in the secular society is to be directed toward the ideal of sustaining our lives of prayer, our striving for sanctity, our journey to Heaven. We eat in order to preserve these mortal bodies long enough for them to benefit from receiving the immortal Body of Christ. We maintain our houses so that we can share love with our brothers whom we can see, the love commanded by the God we can not see in our houses on earth, but whom we hope to see in His House in Heaven. We dress modestly at all times in order to preserve and express the blazing purity given us at Baptism and with which we wish to be clothed in the glory of Heaven.

Our Lady dwells in Heaven for eternity in the presence of Him with whom she dwelt during her time on earth. Jesus Christ was at the center of the home of the Holy Family in Nazareth. He is meant to be at the center of the homes we have established around us. First and foremost in making this happen is the necessity of spending time with Jesus in His Eucharistic presence. Our home life should be centered around the time we spend in keeping holy the Lord's Day before, during, and after Mass. Our home life should be structured in such a way as to make it possible to visit Our Lord in the Blessed Sacrament during the week on a regular basis. Our home life should be so wedded to loving Our Lord present in the tabernacle that visitors to our homes will experience there a fundamental difference from the houses of unbelievers or of those weak in faith, because of the constant prayer taking place in our homes. Our houses are to bear a profound resemblance to the house of prayer which is the church building.

One of the most noticeable attributes of a church building where Our Lord is reserved in the Blessed Sacrament and given due honor by the faithful, is the silence that pervades the building. A house of prayer is to be a house of silence. The real Presence of Christ in the Blessed Sacrament demands a real quiet in the hearts of the people who come to adore Him, and a real quiet in the physical building where their worship takes place.

The quiet in the hearts of the faithful who come to adore the Lord must be fostered in a sense of quiet within their own homes. Those homes must allow for frequent reminders of the presence of Our Lord within the hearts of his faithful disciples. This is accomplished by fathers and mothers establishing a pattern of prayer in their family life. Days should begin with prayer: the morning offering, acts of Faith, Hope, and Charity, and appeals to Guardian Angels. Each meal should be preceded and followed by prayers of thanksgiving. The Angelus at least once a day is the quintessentially Catholic means of reminding us of the truth of the Incarnation of Christ. No family will ever be holy without reflecting on the life of Christ through the eyes of His Mother by faithful and fervent recitation of the Rosary every day. Before goodnight kisses are given and received, there should be prayers and blessings, an examination of conscience and act of contrition, and a commendation to Our Lord of all that the day brought and of the soul about to endure death's symbol in sleep.

The Cross of Calvary is at the very heart of everything that it means to be Catholic. The Mass is the means by which the Cross of Calvary is made present now. Reception of the Holy Eucharist is the consummation of our act of faith in the power of Christ crucified to forgive and destroy sin in us, to save us from everlasting death, and to bestow upon us eternal life.

Catholic families, then, must place the Cross of Calvary at the very heart of everything they endeavor on earth. Daily and Sunday Mass are the structuring principle of the rhythm of life in a Catholic home. Preparation for the reception of Holy Communion for the Catholic family is a matter of ongoing prayer, frequent and thorough Confession, and time spent in adoration before the Blessed Sacrament in the tabernacle. Fathers, as the head of Catholic families, must examine every aspect of their domestic life in light of the question, "How does this activity, purchase, conversation, book, or friendship flow from, and lead to, the perfection in this family of the merits of grace won for us by Christ on the cross and experienced so perfectly by Jesus, Mary, and Joseph?" Mothers as the heart of Catholic families must nurture the peace of their homes in light of the question, "How does this activity, purchase, conversation, book, or friendship lend itself to the expression of the sacrificial love given by Christ on the cross and shared so perfectly between Jesus, Mary, and Joseph?"

When a family is resolved to live in such a way, there will be a balance in their home wherein peals of laughter will happily reside next to a tangible silence bespeaking peace in the hearts of each member of the family yearning to be shared with all the members of the family. Families intent on imitating the sanctity of the Holy Family of Jesus, Mary, and Joseph, will cultivate frequent periods of silence wherein they can listen to the will of God the Father whispering in their hearts, they can hear the assurances of God the Son urging them to trust Him as they obey the Father, and they can pay heed to God the Holy Ghost speaking on their behalf the prayers to the Father which words are powerless to express, but which find their ultimate articulation in the silence of the divine. That silence will in turn bear fruit in family relationships where each person is desirous to hear the needs of all in the family, and each person is willing to sacrifice his own comforts in order to offer selfless love to the flesh and blood relatives made yet closer to him by the Faith, Hope, and Charity binding them together in the larger family of the house of God.

Accomplishing these ideals requires a commitment manifested by Jesus Himself in the words, "Did you not know that I must be about my Father's business?" This business has nothing to do with the busy-ness criticized by St. Paul as being the work of busybodies. No, it is the business of laboring for Food of which the world knows nothing. It is the business of storing up treasure in Heaven free from the assaults of time, moths, and rust. It is the business of attending to the better part, seeking the one needful thing, and resting confidently in the knowledge thus had that it can never be taken away. Our Lady evidenced this toil when she pondered within her heart the mysteries revealed to her at her Son's Birth, in finding Him in His Father's house about His Father's business, and standing with Him unafraid as they together battled satan and won the victory of Calvary.

Quiet can not come to a heart ignorant of prayer and distracted by unnecessary and frivolous diversions. Quiet can not come to a home where anxiety about the things of this passing world erodes trust in the King of the world that will never end. Quiet can not come to a family if the father and mother do not heed the example of the simple and humble work of St. Joseph, the piety radiating from the Blessed Virgin Mary, and the zeal for His Father's house which Jesus brought to the home at Nazareth. All given to the glory of God means that nothing can be accepted which would detract attention from that highest good. Souls wedded to serving this proper end of holy religion will not allow within their hearts, their homes, or their loved ones any desire that breeds frenzied dissatisfaction or any people who disrupt the pursuit of sanctity or any thing that can not be used for the greater glory of God.

Thus, if as Our Lord teaches even eyes, hands, and feet should be abandoned if they impede progress toward Heaven, how much more so should the internet, movies, immodest clothing, television and radio, adversarial athletics, oppressive employment, and impious persons be removed from family life. Eyes, hands, and feet are gifts from God. Modern media and entertainment are very windows on hell, piping the sewage of perdition into the hearts and minds of their victims. Avaricious commerce and Godless government destroy family stability and erect false gods that blind the intellect, bind the will, and enslave mankind to depraved passions. Games have ceased to be sources of enjoyment and have become instead gladiatorial combats waged by children to enflame pride in their hearts, encouraged by parents seeking self-fulfillment through the degradation of their children's innocence, and transformed into multibillion-dollar corporations fueling hatred, violence, and disregard for the duties owed the home, the dignity of the human person, and the worship of God at Sunday Mass and Holy Days. An absurd tolerance warps social mores so that families who school their children in the home are held in suspicion, but the highest respect and the highest offices are given to fiends who butcher children in the womb, who attack the principles given in the natural law and taught by Holy Mother Church, and who blaspheme our Blessed Mother, the Saints of Heaven, and God Himself. Families who would be holy must eliminate all such from their midst, they must denounce it to whomever defends depravity, and they must be willing to suffer at the hands of the faithless whatever crosses come their way because of the faith in the Cross of Christ manifested in the sanctity of their homes.

Our Lady assumed into Heaven is the triumph of the heroism of humility. She counted herself and the world as nothing in her pursuit of the will of God. The Blessed Virgin delighted in nothing except contemplating her Lord in prayer, serving her Lord in sacrifice, and loving her Lord with all her heart, with all her soul, with all her mind, and with all her strength. Far from needing to gouge out an eye or chop off a hand or dismember a foot, Mary Immaculate beholds the Beatific Vision in all of its splendor, she sings the glory of her Savior, she is the sweetest fragrance of human love desired by God, she reigns from the throne nearest her divine Son, she magnifies the Lord with every fiber of her being. The triumph of the Immaculate Heart of Mary on earth is certain for she has ascended on high where her will for our salvation is at one with the will of God to bring souls to Heaven.

Let us now, today and every day, renew the consecration of our hearts to the protection and guidance of Our Lady's Immaculate Heart. Let us dedicate our families and our homes to the mission of sanctity given its finest expression in the home of Nazareth where the Immaculate Heart of Mary beat in perfect tandem with the Sacred Heart of the Son of God, her own Son. And let us seek the peace which this world can not give by dwelling ever in our homes in keeping with the silence, the prayer, and the tranquility of our Father's House, where He has prepared a place for us forever in Heaven.

Father Smith

Holy Family House, Silver Cliff, Wisconsin

Re-establishing Christendom II: In the Homes of Holy Families

Introductory Apologies

You must accept your cross; if you bear it courageously, it will bear you to heaven! – St. Jean-Marie Baptiste Vianney

Jacob is sorry. It is his fault that this is before you. Many months ago Jacob asked me to put together suggestions for activities suitable for family recreation. The fact that this mound of words awaits your wading through it is a result of my honoring his request. Once more is demonstrated the prudence of careful consideration of one's desires lest they be granted.

Jacob is sorry. As noted just above, he asked me for this many months ago. I thought I had responded within days of his petition. Jacob insists that I merely showered on him a lofty *excursus* on the nature of engaging home life in a healthy fashion. He is sorry to have had to exercise so much patience, only to have the present far-longer treatise delivered as a consequence of relying on me for guidance. It is also lamentable that my poor memory, which failed to satisfy his need in a more timely manner, did not succeed in preserving him from the infliction of this very involved solution to his simple problem.

Jacob is sorry. Now that the months have gone by, the ink is spilled, and my work in this regard is complete, he has the dreary duty of doing something with, about, and in spite of it all. Some of the readers, innocent of any responsibility for the production of this compendium, are perhaps familiar with the story of the woman whose home harbored a mouse. To rid her house of the mouse, she procured a cat. To rid herself of the mangy, noisy cat, she obtained a dog.

To rid herself of the flea-ridden, ill-tempered dog, she took in a wolf. To rid herself of the ravenous, unmanageable wolf, she unleashed a lion. To rid herself of the man-eating, petunia-disturbing lion, she engaged an elephant. To rid herself of the unwieldy, home-wrecking elephant, she invited back the cute little mouse. Jacob may decide that, after reading what lies ahead, this unfamiliar set of cures is more trouble than the disease to which he has grown accustomed.

On the off chance that he and my other poor readers are willing to try anything, including listening to me, to improve their efforts at obeying God, sanctifying the family, and thus contributing to a better society, I offer these thoughts with my apologies. I do not pretend to have exhausted the subject. Although theology is engaged herein, this is by no means a scholarly work. It is to be hoped that the teachings of Holy Mother Church are not done violence by my effort, yet none should attach any of her authority to what I confess is no more than a collection of my opinions on how to apply her wisdom. And, of course, anything unhelpful may be ignored, cast aside, ridiculed, held in contempt, and consigned to the bottom of the birdcage without offense or notice being taken by the admittedly fallible author of these contents.

My prayer is that Jacob will accept my apology to him for putting words in his mouth regarding the apologies which served as prelude to this sorry excuse for intelligent discourse. I beg that as a token of my contrition, he and his sweet wife, Bethany, accept this feeble attempt at assistance in dedication to them and their happily growing family. Please pray that the power of the Holy Ghost amend my faults through enlightening the minds of my readers open to His grace. Beseech, please, St. Joseph, the head of the Holy Family, to guard the homes of all Catholics from the assaults of this fallen world. Seek the guidance of the Blessed Virgin Mary, our Mother and the Heart of the Holy Family, as she crushes the head of satan and brings back to the safety of her mantle the children who have wandered from the example given so perfectly at Nazareth. And may our Lord Jesus Christ, the joy, the purpose, and the creator of the Holy Family bring peace, salvation, and eternal life to every Catholic family of the Church Militant, to the glory of God the Father, now and forever. Amen.

Several years ago, I taught an introductory-level course in theology to undergraduates at a Catholic college. The students were assigned, among many other things, to read Josef Pieper's essay, *Leisure, the Basis of Culture.* It is my custom whenever I teach at whatever level to complete the same assignments which I give my students at the same time they are doing the work. This keeps me honest as a teacher in ensuring that I continue to engage the subject matter, resist repeating myself (from sloth as opposed to repetition mothering learning), avoid growing stale, and preclude complaints from the students that they can not do my assignments on top of all of their other pressing duties. I place myself in the same boat with my students with the admonishment that the boat is the best place to be if one does not want to have to choose between sinking and swimming. Of course, as the final arbiter of the grades, I have my hand alone on the wheel. I do the work that the students do, but the students are not permitted to do the work that I do. I might be fair, but I am no fool. OK, I might be a fool, but I'm not crazy.

Anyway, the students having read Pieper were then obliged to write a summary of his thesis. I, too, wrote a summary. Below I reproduce in its entirety my version of that assignment. It will serve as a theoretical foundation for the later portions of this work, which will be far more concrete in nature. But, as every good philosopher knows, form does not follow function, but matter follows form. *Logos* precedes *Fiat.* Or, less philosophically and more clearly, *read the instructions before you assemble the bookcase...*

A Succession of Not-So Random Thoughts on the Subject of Work and Leisure

It is unlikely that either G.K. Chesterton or Hilaire Belloc was familiar with the writings of Josef Pieper. I am not sure, but I think it equally unlikely that Pieper would have considered himself a distributist. All three, however, are in utter agreement that the mercantile mindset of modernity is such that the human person stands little chance of being respected or even preserved when in conflict with the profit motive.

Both Belloc and Chesterton understood that there were practical difficulties to be confronted when attempting to merge the economics of distributism with the realities of men in disagreement on matters of faith. The philosophy of Pieper, very much in keeping with Thomism, provides a basis for describing the desired goals of economic man in the abstract. From such abstractions it can be hoped that tangible results can be achieved.

Pieper relates in his essay, *Leisure, the Basis of Culture,* the imbalance between the servile arts (the functional) and the liberal arts (the free) within modern Western civilization. This is not an attempt to pit the human activities of sustaining life and enriching life against one another. Quite to the contrary, Pieper is attempting to illustrate how vital each sphere of human endeavor is to the fulfillment of the whole human person.

"Servile" is not intended to devalue the worth of labor. What is meant is that such activity is for the *service* of a greater good. Work is not to be an end in itself. It is necessary for the human person to determine goals for existence and then to establish the best practical means of reaching them. The servile arts contribute to satisfying the demand for practical efforts to reach goals that transcend descriptions of "practical" and "impractical".

An old saying can demonstrate this point: "Man eats to live, he does not live to eat." It is fitting and proper for life that people seek food. It is a distortion of the human condition when life becomes, on the one hand, an impoverished struggle for minimal nutrition, or, on the other hand, the hedonistic consumption of delicacies costing far more than the worth of the nutritional value they provide. In both dearth and wealth it is possible to warp a servile activity in such a way that the good of the human person suffers.

Lacking a means of identifying what constitutes a life lived well, humanity easily falls into the trap of making quotidian affairs the whole of human existence. There needs to be some notion of the transcendent in the mores of society in order for that society to be able to avoid sinking into animalistic savagery or Epicurean decadence. In simpler terms, men are neither beasts seeking only food and reproduction, nor are they angels without need of the goods of the material world.

Pieper suggests that the rush of late-twentieth century Western civilization toward work as sole good stems in large part from an inability to define and agree upon transcendent reality. Modern philosophy has placed much less emphasis on spiritual matters and is suspicious of claims that absolute knowledge is possible. With this the case, empiricism has become the major means of verifying reality. Work is eminently suited for quantification and, thus, increasingly has been advanced as the best measure of the quality of a human life.

This is in stark contrast to the classical view of human existence which accepts that the material world is in communication with a discernible spiritual order. Pieper sees leisure as the foundation of the human person's ability to sustain contact with an overarching *raison d'etre*. It is not possible for that which is merely physical to meet the needs of that which is spiritual in nature, therefore, it is necessary for human fulfillment that time be available to search out and experience spiritual reality.

Leisure is more than rest and relaxation, although they contribute to its attainment. The human at leisure is doing more than just getting the physical energy to do more work. He is setting about finding those things within himself, within the human race, and within the whole world that will accomplish a fuller understanding of his place in the universe.

The fruits of this search might be borne by the creation of art, the establishment of political systems, or the simple interactions between persons. Liberal arts are so called because they are free in their pursuit, in the means by which they are perfected, and in the arenas where they can be brought to bear. The liberal arts are not dependent upon some greater good for their justification, but are ends in themselves—at least provisionally.

When a person is at leisure there is a sense of timelessness at work. The benefits stemming from leisure are themselves outside of a temporal nature. A poem, a piece of music, a mother rocking her baby, or the discussions within a theology course are not predicated on how much time is needed to make them, nor are they concerned with how long they will be functional. It is sufficient that the endeavor is undertaken.

It is in leisure that the human person finds those things that make life worth living, rather than those things by which someone makes his living. When the age-old question is asked, "What is the meaning of life?" the best responses come not from the world of work, but from the realm of leisure. Life finds purpose not so much in what is produced as in the motivation that makes production desirable.

The peril to modernity is the increasing willingness of men of all stripes—professors, politicians, priests, and ordinary people—to reach the conclusion that there is no ultimate purpose of life. There is a growing desire amongst men to reduce the description of a good life to eating, drinking, and making merry. A life lived well is almost the stuff of fantasy.

There is certainly an alternative to this nihilism, as both history in the concrete and philosophy in the abstract can demonstrate, but whether or not that alternative is *desired* by the mass of men remains to be seen. At present quiet desperation is all the rage. But if we decide not to be satisfied with unchanging change, if we learn to appreciate leisure as more than fruitful boredom, we might just discover that more and better awaits man. We might discover changeless truth, the eternal God, and, God willing, man himself.

It is vital to understanding the human person that one engages the entire breadth of man's experience. Neither can one know man by merely looking at the things he produces; nor can man know himself without recourse to productive work, if for no other reason than that he will starve to death before learning anything of worth. Productive work and creative leisure are differences that require distinctions to avoid being turned into different forms of slavery. It is in their being distinguished one from the other that they become essential means to man's fulfilling his purpose in life.

A means of contrasting work with leisure is in attempting to provide adequate compensation for the products from the respective activities. Truck drivers can calculate mileage, the price of gas, maintenance costs, and the amount of time on the road in order to ask a fair living wage. This calculus means absolutely nothing when applied to activities such as child rearing, listening to the problems of a friend, or devoting a life to finding a cure for cancer. Work implies pay; leisure is done because it should be done.

Where a society loses—or abandons—such an understanding of the interrelationship between work and leisure, two fundamental problems arise. First, there is the very real danger that people will become bound to lives without rest. Work as the sole or highest good becomes slavery in the end. People in salaried positions in today's service industry often complain that they are expected to put in several times more hours at work than hourly employees, without the benefit of overtime pay. This is understood to be a condition for advancement within the business world. There also is a point, quickly reached, when pay is inadequate to compensate for *mandatory* overtime. No amount of money can buy a life's time.

What modern economists call either the work ethic proper to the managerial class, or the "benefits package" of the laborer class, involves the use of coercion to get work out of supposedly free men. Management staff who refuse to do the extra work will be passed over for promotion. Wage earners can be fired for refusing overtime. The full weight of the law allows this ubiquitous practice of forced labor. Earlier in American history it went by a different name: *slavery.*

The second and more insidious evil that is visited upon a society incapable or unwilling to properly value and balance work and leisure, is the deception that certain kinds of frivolity are the same as healthy leisure. Television, gambling, spectator sports, video games, and shopping are examples of how modern Americans spend their unscheduled time seeking leisure without gaining perspective on their own lives. Asked to define leisure, people frequently will respond with these sorts of activities. Asked to explain the motivations behind their life choices, many if not most are reduced to saying, "It feels right," or "It's just what I do," or "I don't know."

Work is helpful because it provides the basis for seeking further good. Leisure is meant to help the person seek the greatest good. Much of what passes for leisure in modern society not only fails to assist a person in this search, it is completely ignorant that such is even a valid question. Leisure that is incapable of leading beyond the concerns of everyday life ultimately becomes merely an escape and a waste of time.

Provisionally, leisure is seen as an end in itself. When leisure is pursued well, there comes a realization that it, too, points beyond itself. What is lacking in the values of modern Western civilization is an admission that something other than man is the measure of man. The idea that God is dead is no longer reserved to the nihilists, but has entered into debates on the U.S. Constitution, astronomy, and biology. Leisure without a moral compass sinks back into mere work insofar as there remains an inability to see outside the limits of the material world.

For leisure to work (ha, ha) it is necessary to orient its pursuit toward the spiritual underpinnings that make leisure different from work. It is in the timeless, priceless, spiritual quality of leisure that the distinction from work lies. Leisure itself, then, must move in the direction of the eternal, boundless, and divine.

The person of God must become the ultimate object of the search for leisure. One who would become free of the shackles of mortality, who is desirous of the perfection of leisure, needs to wrestle with the foundational issue of faith. Where faith exists, man has hope to be in communion with the source of the spiritual basis for leisure. Without faith, there is no spiritual reality to be engaged, hence no spiritual rationale for leisure. At that point, only work, only mortality is available as the end of human life.

Belloc did a fine job of describing the effort necessary to prevent the servile state from imposing a genteel slavery on mankind. He failed, however, to convey the importance of a point made by Chesterton in *The Everlasting Man:* "Even those dry pendants who think that ethics depend on economics must admit that economics depend on existence. And any number of normal doubts and day-dreams are about existence; not about how we can live, but about why we do. And the proof of it is simple—as simple as suicide."

Distributism was rejected in the early twentieth century in part because of Belloc's theoretical lacuna about *why* man is to live, and in part because of Chesterton's charming inability to be practical. But distributism still offers a tremendous opportunity to wed work and leisure. Particularly in its agricultural aspects it holds the promise of man finding in his daily activity a vitality, a sense of purposefulness, and a freedom unimaginable to the wage slave.

It is the work done in the home and for the family that comes closest to combining the material necessities of life on earth with the transcendent meaning of life that is a gift from God. At home, through work, and in leisure, man can discover the truth of Him who said, "In my Father's House, there are many mansions," and "My yoke is sweet, and my burden light."

What follows is my response to a request to aid a family in finding good recreational activities and doing them well. Leisure can not happen without reference to labor. Labor must have leisure to provide it direction. All work and no play make Jack a dull boy, true, but also true is the wisdom of St. Jean-Marie Baptiste Vianney: *Like the saints, let us be very zealous in fulfilling our duties; let the devil never find us doing nothing, lest we should yield to temptation.* What St. Jean said about work, *Do your work, not in order to grow rich or to win the approval of men, but for God's sake,* has a real application to recreation as well.

Structure, Pacing, Scheduling: Martha and Mary

At the beginning of the day, I endeavor to unite myself closely with Jesus Christ, and then I do the next thing, with the thought of this union in mind.—St. Jean-Marie Baptiste Vianney

Boring is good. Boring is good, that is, when boring means predictability, stability, and intentionality. Boring is good when one flies across the Atlantic on a jet airplane. One does not wish to have his pilot over-stimulated by masked men, low fuel, or sweet dreams. A boring roller coaster is something of an oxymoron, but a boring home life should be something of a redundancy.

Every time the "Fasten Seat Belts" lights go on, everyone on board is relying on the laws of physics remaining boring. That is, they want the predictable lift that comes with acceleration and flaps in the right position. They want the stable relationship between thrust and gravity. No one wants to hear the exclamation "Oops!" from the cockpit, followed by nervous laughter. It is also desirable that the rotation of the earth maintain its constancy so that England stays in place and the flight does not unaccountably come to an end in the Alps.

Certainly it is true that the boring elements of jet travel provide excitement for those unaccustomed to such marvels. Small children, poor people, and homebodies have few opportunities to partake of the commonplaces of the jet set. Thus, if they are given the chance to be hurled at dizzying speeds, miles above the ground, surrounded by large people and canned air, then they likely will experience something of a thrill. That being said, the most jaded business frequent-flyer does not appreciate such sentiments in the maintenance crew, the designing engineers, or air traffic controllers. Needless to say, not many first-time travelers would be comforted at the thought that the man at the wheel was so light-headed and fearful of heights as to require Dramamine by the fistful.

Getting out of bed does not strike many people as the adventure of a lifetime. For those unfortunates plagued by such cynicism, an antidote to their calloused sense of *joie de vivre* might be had in considering the concept of the "heroic minute". That is the instant of coming to consciousness after a restful night's sleep, resolving to begin the day, and leaping from bed. It is a fact that all of the most invigorating and edifying experiences of all of human history have occurred after the participants abandoned the reclined position. Outside of the occurrence of mystic visions in a small number of Saints, all of the best examples of God's will for man's salvation unfolded in the lives of people who bothered to wake up in the morning.

No, no one sings "Alleluia!" at the prospect of brushing his teeth, true. But no one can expect anything any more lively while remaining in a somnambulant stupor in his jammies. Labor supports the life of leisure. Alertness makes possible the life of labor. Before one may play, one must work. Before one can work, one must wake.

Upon waking, many extraordinary delights can be had. There is the wonder of the sunrise or the sweetness of an April rain. Birds might be singing or perhaps the ocean waves lap the sands of the backyard. Some people have the perfect spouse, that is, a wife or husband who rises yet earlier to put the coffee on. And, joy of joys, there are teeth to brush! (If you doubt the intensity of this pleasure, talk to someone who fishes his molars out of a glass every morning.)

Children offer Moms and Dads incentive to get up every day. Who knows what amazing things the little ones will do on a given day, what insights they will glean from the example of their parents, what needs being satisfied will confirm Mom and Dad as heroes of the universe in the sight of those trusting eyes? Each day is an opportunity for Moms and Dads to gather more proof for their families and neighbors of the unparalleled perfection present in their progeny, of which all the rest of mankind has been deprived until the very now. Ain't life grand! And what kind of life would it be without fluffing the pillows, smoothing the quilt, and getting first dibs on the hot water in the shower?

There are, of course, unimaginative souls who are not convinced by this description. These scenes depict not peace, security, and affection, but tedium, paralysis, and imprisonment. For them, perhaps, it would be better that, rather than a pleasant ascent to consciousness at 5:30am, the excitement of fire engines at 1:30am jolted them to panicked attention. Instead of the refreshing sound of water in the basin, they would prefer the silence beseeched by the aftermath of that fifth martini. And there are sure to be wags who brag that they get their best work done late at night, but other wags might point out that such a time and such circumstances are not the best for being able to recognize the color of one's wife's eyes or the sounds of one's children's voices or the consequences of missed opportunities dying, not in the dead of night, but at sunup, while the children play in the yard, and when the wife wants to hear sweet nothings after dinner and before bed.

One might be spared the sound of fire engines at 1:30am if one does not forget to turn off the oven left on after the midnight snack. Fifth martinis can not cause hangovers when the nightcap is something one wears or is merely the second glass of wine with dinner. And who but a vampire, a denizen of the devil in hell, would wish to describe himself as a "night person"? Night is when Judas betrayed Our Lord. Night is when the fiercest animals stalk their victims. Night is what Grandma meant when she scolded, "Nothing good ever happened after 9pm!"

The key to the good life, the life of goodness, the life lived well, is getting off to a good start at the start of the day. To start the day well it is necessary to get to bed at a decent hour. Bedtimes are not just for children. Moms and Dads need them, too. If you ever wonder why children are so much cuter than adults, remember that children usually get more rest than grownups. It's not for nothing that it is called *beauty* rest.

Bedtime is determined by the time that one must get up in the morning. The time at which one must get up in the morning (translation for really persnickety grammarians: *The time up at which one must get in the morning*) is determined by obeying the will of God. The will of God is that all of man's life is to be guided by prayer. The supreme prayer is the Mass. Thus, one rises in time to prepare for Mass, one goes to bed at an hour that allows for sufficient rest to be able to rise to prepare for Mass.

If daily Mass is seventy-nine miles away in another state and a December blizzard raged overnight, then one must get to bed at 5:45PM the previous evening in order to be able to rise at 1:45am, make a morning offering with the family, wash and dress the children, clear the driveway, and be on the road by 4:15am for the 7am Mass.

Okay, I admit, that's the plan for the advanced, canonized Saint-track family. For the rest of us for whom Purgatory is still too good—but we'll take it!—one endeavors to live in a community where daily Mass is more readily available. Preparation for Mass includes a morning offering, Acts of Faith, Hope, and Charity, and any of the many prayers composed to dispose the laity to a worthy participation in the Sacrifice and reception of Holy Communion. Your fellow attendees at Mass would also appreciate some basic hygiene beforehand.

So, for instance, if your daily Mass is at 7am, it is a good idea to have everyone out of bed by about 5:30am. This should permit ample time for prayer first, followed by hygienic necessities, followed by a quiet, prayerful trip (walk?!) to Mass. Give or take an hour, depending on age and health, eight hours of sleep is a typical amount. That means, then, getting to bed the night before by 9:30pm. Small children need more sleep and should be in bed earlier.

After Mass, time should be given for a fervent thanksgiving. Most missals have very good prayers for both preparation for and thanksgiving after Mass. These can be prayed either individually or as a family. Please refrain, however, from offering your family preparatory or thanksgiving prayers within the nave of the church. Father promises when he visits your home not to preach in your living room if you promise not to conduct the louder portions of your family life while others attempt to pray before the Blessed Sacrament.

In addition to one's morning prayers and Mass, other prayers and devotions should be spread throughout the day. The monks got it right. Life is one long prayer, with brief interruptions allowed for work from time to time. One works to support one's prayer; one does not pray to improve one's work, except insofar as working better will help one to pray better. Each home, just like the home at Nazareth given to poverty, chastity, and obedience, is meant to be a small religious community. The rhythm of prayer in our homes guides all of the other activities of our lives. Prayer gives form to the life lived in pursuit, not of excitement, but of sanctity.

It is assumed by the author at this point that the Marthas and Marys in various families are now glaring at each other, ready to do battle about practicality versus perfection. It is eminently practical to seek perfection. Perfection can not be had without some practicality. So long as the practice involved is sanctity and the perfection bears good fruit in the practice of an orderly life, there really is no conflict here. Tension, to be sure, but no conflict.

Dom Prosper Guéranger in his stupendous magnum opus, *The Liturgical Year,* tells of St. Francis de Sales instructing St. Jane Frances de Chantal to, "Do all things without haste, gently, as do the Angels; follow the guidance of the divine movements, and be supple to grace; God wills us to be like little children." I am frightfully unafraid to embellish the words of my betters. St. Francis is telling St. Frances, in effect, to do nothing: do nothing hurriedly, do nothing without introspection, do nothing other than what God wants, when He wants, as He wants, because He wants. This is not a matter of fast or slow, much or little, significant or unnoticed; this is all about absolute submission to the will of God. Fool is he who thinks that such absolute submission is reserved for Saints or vowed religious or priests only. Absolute submission to God, with the love of one's *whole* heart, *whole* soul, *whole* mind, and *whole* strength, is commanded for everyone with a rational soul united to a material body. This means you!

Chores I: Prayers, Devotions, Eucharistic Piety

In the Sacraments, it is God Himself who comes to annihilate our enemy. The devil, seeing Him in our hearts, throws himself despairingly into the bottomless pit; which explains why he does all that he can to draw us away from them, or to make us receive them badly.

– St. Jean-Marie Baptiste Vianney

Jesus knew that His teachings would meet with opposition. He declared that some would demand, "Physician, heal thyself!" The events of Easter Sunday should have silenced the naysayers. Alas! cleansing lepers, casting out demons, and raising the dead convinced none of the cold-hearted. They did not believe when He raised someone from the dead, nor when He rose from the dead.

There are perhaps some who, upon reading thus far, would be tempted to demand of me, "Father, have you ever changed a diaper?!" It has occurred to me that a soul or two might consider my suggestions up to this point a bit pie-in-the-sky. Anyone who has ever served me banana cream or blueberry knows that the sky is no place that I wish my pie to be served. The Kingdom of Heaven is at hand!

If God is capable of pardoning sins; triumphing over the world, the flesh, and the devil; of being incarnate, suffering, dying, rising on the third day, and re-presenting His Passion on Calvary every day in the Mass; of making the likes of liars like St. Peter, murderers like St. Paul, wantons like St. Mary Magdalene and St. Augustine of Hippo, innocents like St. Aloysius and St. Thérèse the Little Flower, and unknowns like St. Philomena saints in glory, then He is up to the task of waking us on time through the prayers of St. Vitus, preserving our purity through the intercession of St. Thomas Aquinas, warding off temptation by the protection of our Guardian Angels, teaching us eternal truth through the proclamations of St. Pius x, and making us his brothers through the Divine Maternity of the Blessed Virgin Mary. All things, even my salvation, are possible with God. If we can put a man on the moon, then we can put our trust in God.

Loving God with one's whole heart, whole soul, whole mind, and whole strength is a full-time occupation. Other occupations that preoccupy daily life must defer to this one needful thing, the better part, the business of Heaven. Being about our Father's business means spending time, lots of it, in our Father's house of prayer. The many mansions of His House are designed to provide a place for the houses here on earth where we spend our time in prayer yearning for the presence of our Father looking forward to an eternity spent in that same presence. If all the drudgeries of the home, the daily grind of the office, and the pressures of modern life seem to make it impossible to attend to our true work, then we are to do all in our power to remove those obstacles to cooperation with divine grace. If we are to find a place prepared for us by Jesus in His Father's House, then we must find time to give pride of place to Him and His Father to make a home with us in our houses on earth. Do not expect to enjoy eternity with someone with whom you found spending a few minutes on earth distasteful, inconvenient, or not worth the time and effort.

Slow down.

No, slow down more than that.

Even slower.

Time is not a renewable resource. There is no substitute for it. Every moment given to something or someone other than God is irretrievably lost. Forever. Better planning, a three-day weekend, and the best minds of science are impotent before the impossibility of gaining back a second lost in the world, to sin, or by inattention. Your glory in Heaven, if not entirely forfeited by infidelity on earth, is diminished to whatever extent your *whole* heart, *whole* soul, *whole* mind, and *whole* strength do not seek the greater glory of God in *all* things. Just what part of ***all*** don't you understand?

Well, if you're like me, the better part. Prayer does not come to us naturally. Practicing the presence of God takes practice. It takes grace. We also require the aid of the Holy Ghost who "helpeth our infirmity, for we know not what we should pray for as we ought: but the Spirit Himself asketh for us with unspeakable groanings."

God is not a bully. God is a gentleman. If we do not wish to spend time or eternity with him, we are free to go elsewhere. After life, the only where else we can go than heaven is hell. This life on earth devoid of prayer will be a foretaste of hell. The newspapers bear this out. Our homes should not be a part of the list that includes schools, government laws, and commercial establishments where the name of Jesus, invocation of the Most Holy Trinity, due reverence to the Blessed Virgin Mary and the Saints, and filial affection for Holy Mother Church and the Holy Father the Pope are not welcome, rarely witnessed, and seen as embarrassing superstitions.

The pace of the day is set by the prayer of the day. As one prays more, the day slows more. As one prays less, the day goes faster. Fast-paced days accomplish more for mammon. Slow-paced days build up treasure in the Kingdom of Heaven. What is accomplished for mammon bears absolutely no good fruit. Treasure fit for Heaven does a world of good for those in the world but not of the world—and it helps the world become less worldly.

Too oft we practical types are willing to sacrifice time spent in prayer in order to meet the demands of mammon. Far rarer are those occasions when we will let mammon go to the devil so that we can make a sacrifice of praise to Our Lord. Every now and then it would be good to pause to consider what it means to assume that mammon is less forgiving than God. Were this to be true, then we should be loath to indenture ourselves to such a harsh taskmaster. If it is mistaken in some respect, then we might wish to re-evaluate our attitude.

God is indeed more forgiving than mammon. He tolerates indifference, inattentiveness, and frailty, pardoning our sins of omission as readily as a mother will kiss a skinned knee. Mammon, on the other hand, audits tardy tax returns, docks wages of employees late for work, and fires tens of thousands of wage slaves whenever the god "free market" demands. Mammon's punishments are as fleeting as an eight-hour day, more or less with overtime. Offending God, though, trying His patience past its breaking point, results in penalties of a bit lengthier nature. And being "fired" by God is a lot more painful then getting fired by your boss.

Beset by the flesh, the world, and the devil, we sinners have very few places where we can safely place our trust. Our senses betray us with desires that are physically, as well as spiritually, destructive. The prevailing culture confuses us into believing lies to be true, thereby convincing us that somehow good can come from obeying the dictates of our appetites. Satan has his way with us whenever we give into his temptations and choose to prefer pleasure to health and sanctity, lies over truth, and infernal tyranny instead of heavenly freedom.

Let me say that a bit more simply. Original sin has rendered our bodies, minds, and wills defective. We see things in distortion, we are numb to things that should stimulate us, we feel desire to embrace things that should repulse us, we pay heed to noise as if it were music, we cover our ears to the sweet sound of piety, we demand bites from forbidden fruit, we are inured to the stench of death in the Godless life we pursue. And on top of that, we justify, rationalize, and philosophize ourselves into the conviction that if it feels good it is good; that genes have more to say about choices than the common sense God gave to turnips; that a collection of people enslaved to lethal desires are qualified to determine how best to make the world a fit place for human beings to find happiness. But, wait! There's more! All the while our bodies twist reality into a mad dash for ever more physical pleasure and our twisted minds argue against any suggestion that restraint of the body is a noble and human goal, we insist that the ways of righteousness are unfair and unfree, but that liberty is to be had in obeying the demands of a society built around the motto, *Non serviam!*

Hmmm…Perhaps I am still a bit unclear. Let's try it this way: Folks, stomachs can't think! Thinking requires more than merely parroting advertising slogans and the cant out of political parties! And the devil does not like you, he does not want your happiness, and anyone who does not look to God as the absolute ruler of the universe wants what the devil wants, namely, to hate you and to see you unhappy!

Myopic eyes tell the brain that the world is fuzzy and that there is no car in the next lane that you want to swerve into. The brain that accepts the data of myopic eyes assumes that you can safely swerve, and if you bump into anything, you won't be hurt by the fuzzy, soft objects all around you. People with wills untrained to correct bad thinking based on erroneous data go ahead and swerve into the SUV passing them on the right at eighty-five miles per hour.

People sitting at intersections might get rather impatient if the little old lady at the head of the line doesn't leap on the gas the instant that the light changes from red to green. It might seem reasonable to the tattooed, hemp-smoking biker babe to get really ticked off after three seconds have elapsed. Perhaps the pistol in her pocket will wake Granny up.

Doing what comes naturally is a beautiful way to live a life, according to the society fond of family planning, intact dilation and extraction, and euthanasia. So, when Mr. Brown and Mrs. Jones exchange meaningful glances across the bar, who (besides Mrs. Brown and Mr. Jones) can blame them for feeling that spark that calls from the depths of each of their impassioned hearts through their soulful eyes? None but a stone-hearted ogre would begrudge them the next four hours spent in a rented room.

Ahem... Senses are not infallible. Even correct data are useless without proper interpretation. Understanding what one senses accomplishes little where the use of sensory and rational faculties do not lead to acting on a good decision. We encounter the world through our senses. Our minds sort through the information gained thereby. The will is then engaged to persevere in doing that which is good based on what is known to be true. Sometimes the mind must correct the senses. Sometimes the will must override the passions. Sometimes the senses strengthen the resolve of the will. Sometimes the mind revolts against a weak will. Sometimes the will insists on pursuing a good beyond the capacity of the senses to perceive or of the mind to comprehend.

He who does not see, does not know; he who does not know, does not love; he who does not love God, loves himself, and at the same time loves his pleasures.—St. Jean-Marie Baptiste Vianney

Just because you are hungry does not mean that you have to eat this very instant. Just because you think someone insulted you does not mean that you have to belt him one. Just because you are afraid to lose your job does not mean that you need to miss Mass on the Feast of All Saints, even if the Department of Maintaining Slavery, I mean, the unemployment insurance officials declare that it is a just termination.

Prayer is how the senses are healed of the infirmities inherent in fallen flesh. Prayer is how the intellect is enlightened to overcome the concupiscence of the flesh and the ill effects of original sin. Prayer is how the will is emboldened to resist lies, the passions, and assaults from the devil and his human minions. Without the help of God, we are victims of the world, the flesh, and the devil, by which our senses, our sense, and our sensibility become the instruments of our own destruction. Prayer brings down the graces which repair what is damaged, resist that which attacks, and impel the heart to do that which is best.

Even more and even better, prayer is how the human will overcomes temptation, seeks the will of God, and becomes united with the divine will. Saints at prayer learn to deny the wants of the world, the flesh, and the devil. Saints at prayer learn to want the will of God. Saints at prayer learn to want with the will of God. Such is the progress from the purgative to the illuminative into the unitive stage of the spiritual life.

Prayer gives form to the material of life. It is the primary labor of the life lived in consonance with the will of God. Prayer is the rest given to the good laborer. Prayer fulfills and transcends the labor of this life and crowns with peace the desire of the soul for holy rest. Prayer is the labor done by love. Prayer is the labor that is done for the beloved. Prayer is the labor done alongside the beloved. Prayer as union with the beloved is the desire of love.

And, of course, the supreme prayer, the perfect prayer is the Mass. It is in the Mass that all which must be done is accomplished: God is glorified and man is sanctified. Martha is happy to work very hard at a worthy labor for her beloved, and Mary is happy to contemplate the fruits of this labor with her beloved. Martha and Mary agree that we are not to do nothing but prayer, but that we are to do nothing without prayer. Yet, love finds that the more one prays, the more one wants to pray. The more one prays, the less one wants to do anything other than pray. Eventually the lover of prayer, the lover at prayer, will seek to remove everything in life that is an obstacle to prayer, a distraction from prayer, or forbidden by prayer.

Families in love with prayer, who share their love through prayer, who love to pray together, will set aside ample time to pray their daily Rosary, to attend daily Mass, to pray the Stations of the Cross (they're not just for Lent anymore!), to visit the Blessed Sacrament and make a holy hour as a family, to be on hand for the parish's weekly Benediction, to recite various litanies for Saints' Feasts and during appropriate seasons, to read the Bible as an aid to all of their devotions. Parents will give their children prayer cards of the Saints as gifts, having their children pray them for one another as they grow up (and praying the prayers to and for the children before they learn to read). Statues and images of Our Lady and the patron saints of the family will adorn the walls and flat surfaces of the house, being the occasion of frequent invocations of their heavenly assistance. The home will have an altar wherein the Sacred Heart of Jesus and the Immaculate Heart of Mary are enshrined as proof of the family's consecration to them. Prayer will guide such families before, during, and after all family activities, and prayer will be the primary activity of the family.

Chores II: Housekeeping.

It is God's will that on Sundays we should occupy ourselves only with what has to do with His service and the salvation of our souls. By doing so, we draw down blessings on our work during the week.

—St. Jean-Marie Baptiste Vianney

Whoa! Whoa! Whoa, Father!

It is obvious that I have never changed a diaper, isn't it?

Skeptics are going to be asking, "How in heaven's name is anything to be accomplished in a family like this, that makes the Carthusians look like beatniks?"

Practical people will say that this emphasis (obsession?) on prayer is impractical. *Au contraire, mes frères*! Prayer is the most practical of all practices.

Take changing diapers (please). Moms and Dads, why do you change diapers? *Because the babies are crying.* Wrong. *Because the babies smell bad.* Wrong. *Because Father Smith won't do it for us.* Right, but wrong.

You change diapers because your love of God results in loving your babies. If you stop loving God, you will stop changing your babies' diapers. If you stop praying you will stop loving God. If you stop praying, you will stop changing your babies' diapers.

Well, Father, lots of unbelievers or weak Catholics who don't pray still change their babies' diapers and love them.

That is true. You can find individual parents who somehow find it possible to ignore God but to love the two-point-seven children they deign to bring to term. However, if you look across time and around a society you will find that where a significant minority or, God forbid, a majority of parents abandon true worship, there is a pronounced increase in the refusal to diaper babies, to conceive babies, to marry before having babies, to stay married after having babies, to engage in natural relations capable of conceiving babies, to allow the babies to live long enough to need diapers. A culture that comes to hate God will eventually hate its children. Not praying is deadly to the bodies and souls of babies and their faithless parents.

If you want babies' diapers to be changed, you need to pray. You need to pray to have babies. You need to pray to be able to provide diapers. You need to pray to love your babies enough to want to work to provide diapers, and to love your babies enough to take on a task as thankless and messy as changing babies' diapers is by definition. Diaper-changing is not for the faint of heart. A fair amount of fortitude is necessary. Fortitude is a gift of the Holy Ghost, granted in the Sacrament of Confirmation and maintained and increased through prayer, which, again, is the work of the Holy Ghost, who frowns on those who ignore Him through their refusal to pray to Him and by His power.

But for those parents who do pray, who do love God, who do love their babies, who love to change their babies' diapers, more is wanted. Those parents will want their babies to grow out of diapers, to grow to love their parents, and to grow to love God and to grow in their love of God. Parents who want to love their children will want their children to love their parents and to love God their Father. Thus, loving parents will want their children to learn to pray. They will want their children to learn to pray from them, with them, and for them.

A delightful fringe benefit of learning to pray and learning thereby to love, is that children so raised will learn to love to take out the garbage, wash the dishes, make their beds, do their homework, play properly with their brothers and sisters, dust the furniture, and mow the lawn almost as much as Mom and Dad loved changing diapers. People who love God know that they must love their neighbors as themselves. The very first neighbors given everyone are their families. The first recipients of the grace of obeying God's command to love Him above all things, expressed by love of neighbor, is the family for whom each member happily will do whatever labor is needed in the home to make it possible to get back to the business of praying, so as to increase and experience that love of God and love of neighbor.

Children need chores. No, not just because Mom and Dad want to take it easy. Children need chores as a means to grow in humility, to express their love for God and His gifts to them of their families, and as a real participation in making the homes where their families live a product of and a place for prayer. Where a family values prayer, they will value those things which make prayer possible, seeking the opportunities to accomplish them as well and as quickly as possible so as to have yet more opportunities to pray well and to pray often. Children need prayer, thus they need to do the chores by which the family's life of prayer is supported. If children are to grow up to teach their own children the value of prayer, they must learn as children how to go about establishing a home where prayer can happen.

Such a home has swept floors. It has clean linens. Windows are transparent. The roof does not leak. Snow is kept off of the sidewalk. Its inhabitants know their catechism. And smelly diapers receive prompt and loving attention.

There is a peril that wealthy families have in this vein. They can afford to pay others to do all of these things. Children raised under this condition might grow up without a proper appreciation of humility, service, and a grateful dependence on God for all things. Spoiled children make rotten children of God. Even where the means exist to hire others to do the housekeeping, families should insist on doing their own housework. Boredom never strikes where there are floors to be mopped, bathtubs to be scrubbed, and Rosaries to be prayed.

Families of limited means encounter a different peril. Bodies worked to the point of exhaustion mopping some other family's floor, picking their fruit, or increasing their capital will lack much spirit to pray a fifteen-decade Rosary at the end of a fifteen-hour day. Anxiety about paying the rent, fending off the rats, or purchasing medicine is relieved by prayer, but prayer requires relief from work before it can be offered by anxious hearts and tired bones.

Rather than employing the poor to clean the homes of the rich, the rich should employ their wealth to aid the poor in becoming owners of productive property. Rather than envying the rich their wealth, the poor should offer their wealth of suffering and privation to ease the peril of the camel-sized souls stuck outside the needle-sized gate of Heaven. The poor need the rich to show compassion on their material dearth. The rich need the poor to pity their spiritual destitution. Rich employers should close their businesses on Sundays and Holy Days so that their poor employees can go to Mass with their families and keep the Lord's Day holy. Families of poor employees and their rich counterparts need to take advantage of days off on Sundays and Holy Days to go to Mass and keep the Lord's Day holy. Poor and rich need to more highly esteem the treasures built up in Heaven by a life of prayer spent on earth.

Chores III: Feast Days, Anniversaries, Vacations

Never pass a day without thanking Jesus Christ for all He has done for you during your life.—St. Jean-Marie Baptiste Vianney

May 23rd, December 12th, March 17th, May 12th, and May 17th. August 10th, March 19th, December 27th, March 7th, August 11th. September 8th, October 7th, July 16th, December 8th, December 12th. December 25th, January 1st, July 1st, the last Sunday in October, the first Sunday after the first full moon after the first day of spring. Sunday, Monday, Tuesday, Wednesday, Thursday, Friday, Saturday.

I was baptized May 23rd (St. John Baptist de Rossi), received First Holy Communion December 12th (Our Lady of Guadalupe), was confirmed March 17th (St. Patrick), received diaconal Orders May 12th (Sts. Pancras, Nereus, Achilleus, and Domitilla), and received presbyteral Orders and celebrated my First Mass May 17th (St. Pascal Baylon and the Vigil of Pentecost). St. Lawrence was grilled on August 10th (nine months and two weeks before May 23rd). St. Joseph was born into Heaven on March 19th. St. John the Beloved was reunited with his best friend on December 27th. St. Thomas Aquinas entered glory on March 7th. St. Philomena overwhelmed pagan might through her virginal power on August 11th. The Blessed Virgin Mary, the Mother of God, was born on September 8th. She defeated satan in the Mohammedans on October 7th. Her Carmelite children especially exult on July 16th. The Immaculate Conception took flesh on December 8th. And the Empress of the universe is celebrated as the Empress of the Americas on December 12th (a day doubly blessed for yours truly). God was born on December 25th. He was circumcised on January 1st. The Blood first spilled at that Circumcision is adored in its fullness on July 1st. Jesus Christ is honored as King of the universe on the last Sunday of October. His glorious triumph over satan, sin, and death is lauded in Heaven and on earth the first Sunday after the first full moon after the first day of spring. All and each of these events contribute to the honor and glory of God as He is worshipped in spirit and in truth on every altar of the world where the Body-Blood-Soul-Divinity of Jesus Christ is offered to the Father every Sunday, Monday, Tuesday, Wednesday, Thursday, Friday, and Saturday in time, and for all eternity in Heaven.

Part of the excitement of the boredom of routine is the regularity of occasions on which to thrill with the joy of knowing the saving power of God. A day does not go by when He does not do something worth praising. In a family of, say, ten children with their Mom and Dad, there are more than a month's worth of days scattered throughout the year when they can give good reason for declaring feast days. Twelve Baptisms, twelve First Holy Communions, twelve Confirmations, and a wedding anniversary just for starters. Throw in twelve Name Day Feasts, twelve feasts of Confirmation patrons, the Guardian Angels, the patron Saint of the local parish, the Patron Saint of the local diocese, and the Feast of the Holy Family. Then there are the Feasts of the universal Church, a dozen smaller feasts of Our Lady, St. Joseph's two Feast Days, the Immaculate Conception and Our Lady of Guadalupe as the patronal Feasts for the United States, and all of the extra days of feasting on the various octaves involved with many of the great Feasts—*and* the entirety of the *Seasons* of Christmas and Easter. The family who is in circumstances which permit attending daily Mass is blessed to be beset by an embarrassment of riches.

But this is serious business. Confession is necessary to be properly disposed to all of the graces flowing so abundantly. Imagine, with so many Feasts popping up so frequently, how frequent must be the reception of the Sacrament of Penance to arrive at each festive day with one's wedding garment in good order. Then there are the family devotions maintained throughout the year in honor of the various Saints and the Mysteries revealed through the Faith. And, to enflesh the wonderful spiritual bounty present, there should be meals worthy of the name of *feast* to complement the spiritual banquets spread out by Holy Mother Church. And, of course, prayer, daily prayer, family prayer, individual prayer, prayer at church must happen ceaselessly as a response to and as a condition of all of this celebratory profundity.

Read *The Roman Martyrology* and a lives of the Saints every day so as to know who are the heavenly companions accompanying your family on the way from earth to the Kingdom of God. Ignore the silly, masonic activities around the fourth Thursday of November, the last Monday of May, and the first Monday of September, and instead gather family and loved ones for prayer, the Mass, and a meal at home to commemorate the glories of salvation history, both in the universal Church and in the particulars of your family life. Plan your family vacations around the octaves of Christmas, Easter, and Pentecost.

If you are an unfortunate in the bondage of wage slavery, when it comes time to beg days off from servile duress, consult the liturgical calendar and ask for a day or two on either side of any significant Feast Days, especially Holy Days of Obligation, that land during the work week. When you do take vacation time away from home, go where daily Mass is available and, instead of seeing some monument to American rejection of the social reign of Christ the King, visit the tomb of a Saint, e.g., St. Rose Philippine Duchesne in St. Charles, Missouri, or St. Elizabeth Ann Seton in Emmitsburg, Maryland, or the North American Martyrs in Auriesville, New York. Several other locales around the country boast the relics of holy men and women whose causes for canonization are underway. Pray in those places, both that the people in question might be raised to the altar in accordance with the will of God, and for their heavenly patronage to protect and sanctify your family.

Chores IV: Fasts, Lent and Advent, Retreats

In the morning we should behave towards God like an infant in his cradle. As soon as he opens his eyes, he looks quickly through the room to see his mother. When he sees her, he begins to smile. When he cannot see her, he cries.—St. Jean-Marie Baptiste Vianney

All work and no play makes Jack a dull boy. All play and no work leads to an early grave. The soul every bit as much as the body needs to rest. In between all of the joyous extravagances of the Church's frequent Feasts, we require regular and sincere fasts.

Saints are odd people. Where we typical sorts (notice, I say "typical", not "normal"—the Saints are normal, we are typical; there are more of us, but we should be more like their norm) flee pain and suffering, the Saints go looking for it. They have come to the wonderful realization taught by the science of the Faith that the Cross is what all of life is all about. The Cross is the new Tree of Life. If we are to live, we need to partake of its Fruit, the Body, Blood, Soul, and Divinity of Jesus Christ. The Saints are in love with Him, thus they seek Him where He is to be found, on the Cross. Would that we were as odd as they are, and that the Saints were as typical as they are normal.

Archbishop Fulton Sheen said in his reflections on the Stations of the Cross that "the Cross frightens more in its splinters than in its beams". At a distance the Cross looks imposing, fearful, dreadful. We shrink from proximity to it. What the Saints have learned, and what we would do well to learn from them, is that the nearer one comes to the Cross, the nearer one grows to Christ, both in being close enough to touch Him and in bearing His image on one's heart, soul, mind, and body. That is the image of love, and love is Cross-shaped.

If going to the Cross hurts, good! Pain should hurt. Bodies that don't feel pain when something painful happens are experiencing either poor circulation through the limbs, shock, paralysis, or death. It never ceases to amaze me how it never ceases to amaze me that sacrifices are unpleasant. I once said that God is full of surprises, like these:

The Son he sent;
the joy of Lent.

That blue can fly
in eyes and sky.

Wherever earth
has given birth

to fish in seas
or birds in trees.

The wet of rain
and crosses' pain.

Pain is the body's way of saying, "I'm still here!" If you hit your thumb with a hammer and you're not a leper but it doesn't hurt, there is something rather wrong going on. Unrepentant gluttons eat to the point of obesity and don't notice it—something is rather wrong here. Unrepentant fornicators contract gonorrhea, herpes, and AIDS, and think the cure lies in medications—something is rather wrong here. Unrepentant apostates think the Lord's Day belongs to them and spend it at the mall or on the golf course—something is rather wrong here.

By the same token, the conscience prompting us to seek penance and mortification is the soul's way of telling us that we aren't in hell. If you sin or if you claim to be perfect, and you don't go to Jesus on the Cross, there is something rather wrong going on. No pain, no gain goes for the spiritual exercises no less than for physical exercises. Marines say that pain is the feeling of weakness leaving the body; the Church might say that pain is the way to keep the Saint's soul from leaving the Body of Christ.

Sinners need Jesus and the Cross in order to be forgiven. Saints are kind enough not only to spend time with Jesus on the cross to atone for their sins, but for ours as well. Any of you who think that you are finished atoning for all of your sins, and that you have attained perfect sanctity, do the rest of us a favor and join Our Lady and Our Lord in doing what perfect souls do to express their sanctity and charity. The rest of us will happily accept the generous fruits of your efforts.

Well, Father, that's all well and good and nice and easy to say, but it sounds awfully hard to do. And painful, too, by the way.

Here is what I once said to someone else who wanted a bed of roses for a life:

At the risk of sounding flippant, I point out that roses also have thorns! Difficult as the gift may be, the thorn may be of more value than the bloom. St. Thérèse certainly recognized that the Little Flower had many thorns to endure, many weeds trying to choke her off, many droughts trying to wither her, many pests trying to devour her, many storms trying to uproot her—but perhaps I have taken the metaphor far enough.

At any rate, St. Thérèse embraced all of her little crosses lovingly because she acknowledged them as gifts from her Beloved. And her Beloved would never give her anything bad for her, anything unlovable, anything not to be grateful for. And she believed fervently that all of the challenges which she overcame made her more beautiful in the eyes of her Beloved. And she was sure that accepting all of her trials were sure-fire ways of pleasing her Beloved and making her way home to Him.

I strongly encourage you to ask the Little Flower to help you see the beauty attached to the thorn, the bloom rising above the stem. Also, along with the Apostles before the Sanhedrin, ask the grace to be able to "give thanks for being found worthy of ill treatment for the sake of the Name of Jesus". Those who endure their sufferings with and for Our Lord should "rejoice and be glad, for great is your reward in heaven!"

Remember that you are made in the image and likeness of God. This means not only that you look like God in the spirit, but that you look like God in how you perceive the world. It is not merely a matter of how you are seen, but of how you see; not just of how you look, but of that for which you seek. It is the nature of your search, the means by which you search, and the goal for which you search. Imago Dei *is man's being* AND *action—just like God!!!*

You see with the eyes of the Lord. The son resembles the father not only in how he looks to the world, but in his worldview. To have your Father's eyes is not just to look like Him, but to **see** *like Him, to learn to recognize what the Father reveals as good and true. That is the gift of the sons of God in the Faith: to see even as they are seen.*

Do not look at the Cross as do the faithless, with despair. Look on the Cross and see man's greatest and only hope. This is the love that St. Thérèse experienced in bearing all for Christ.

To shift the metaphor a bit, keep in mind that the thorn on the rose serves a wonderful purpose: to protect the blossom. The thorns you receive may well be God's call to you to suffer with Christ so as to win souls through your willingly embracing the trials others reject or can not bear.

St. Thérèse frequently offered her sufferings for missionaries spreading the Faith, walking another step in the midst of her consumption for the missionary consumed in the tropical heat. You may well be preserving a soul from disaster when you accept mortification and "misfortune" with the same charity with which Our Lord accepted the Cross. He saved those who could not save themselves. You can pray for those who need prayers—and pray instead of those who do not pray—through your patient endurance.

If you have not read St. Thérèse's autobiography, The Story of a Soul, *I strongly recommend you do so. If you have read it before, it sounds like now would be a time to refresh your memory. And one last thing: sometimes the best way to receive a rose is to give a rose. The rose that you give away is not yours to have, but the Beloved to whom you give it will make it yours to share. The blessing with which you bless will be measured back to you, full measure, pressed down, and overflowing. God is not outdone in generosity!*

I give my best advice when I steal from the saints. St. Jean-Marie Baptiste Vianney said, "The Saints did not complain." I am no Saint, but I quote them in my writings.

The cross needs to be a common thing, a typical thing, a normal thing in our daily lives. Praying the Stations of the Cross, the Sorrowful Mysteries of the Rosary, and the Gospel accounts of the Passion are immensely helpful in instilling in us a love for the Cross, a love of sacrificial love. Stopping whatever might be going on at 3pm and contemplating the terrible yet wonderful words, *Consummatum est!* is something else to do along the way of falling in love with the Cross. It is a good idea to extend the notion of taking up the cross each day and following Our Lord in love to keeping certain days of the week as penitential days, Wednesdays, Fridays, and/or Saturdays, for instance. Of course Advent and Lent lend themselves marvelously to a penitential way of life, being penitential seasons and all. Something else I once said was that it is

> ...*Advent always*, 'til the Time when times
> become no more, releasing claims on Past's
> iniquities, repenting Future's crimes.
>
> 'tis Christmas never while this world still lasts,
> where we will find no room within our hearts
> to offer Him whose Heart receives us all.
>
> Yet Easter ever fosters faith which starts
> us on the Way that rises o'er the fall,
> and lifts the craven soul above fear's pain.
>
> But yet a little longer Lent must be,
> for 'tho' First Sin is conquer'd, sins remain
> uncrucified upon an *x-mas* tree.
>
> We shan't the Truth of Advent grasp until
> we grow beyond the Crib and climb the Hill.

The cold of winter, the heat of summer, the muck of spring are built-in penances. If you live in southern California, meteorological perfection is your cross. Trust me, there definitely is such a thing as too much of a good thing when it comes to cloudless skies, mild temperatures, and palm trees. The only perfection that comes close to being complaint-free is autumn in deciduous forests, except for the fact of the winter that always ends them. But, anyway, mother nature gives us easy opportunities—like aging, the flu, and each other—to have things to offer up for atoning for own sins, making reparation for the horrid sins of the world, and to ease the sufferings and hasten the glory of the Poor Souls in Purgatory.

Keep in mind, also, that fasting as a means to sacrifice can mean more than not eating, although that is certainly to be embraced as well. In addition to keeping one's mouth closed at lunch, one might try a fast of keeping one's mouth closed rather than engaging in idle conversation. Instead of remaining fast asleep a full eight hours, one might fast from sleep by rising early to offer some extra prayers for the conversion of sinners.

I once suggested to a group for whom I was giving a spiritual conference to take up "Life in the Fast(ing) Lane". The idea was to designate each Saturday of the month as an occasion to fast from something in the home. For example, first Saturdays would be a Sleep Fast, in which on Friday night all stay up one hour later than usual in order to do an extended examination of conscience in preparation for going to Confession and Mass as part of fulfilling the Fatima Five First Saturdays devotion. Second Saturdays of the month would be a Talk Fast, in which little or nothing would be said for a predetermined period of the day, or even all day. Third Saturdays of the month would experience an Electric Fast, in which no electric appliances of any kind would be used. Fourth Saturdays of the month would be the day to Travel Fast, that is, to not travel at all, but to stay in the home and its grounds enjoying the company of one's family. The fifth Saturday when it occurs would be a Fast Fast on which to throw a feast, abstaining from abstaining for the day and perhaps inviting another family into the home to share in the joy of being redeemed in Christ crucified.

These are just suggestions. A few brains, a few minutes, and a few trials and errors will prompt a bunch of other possibilities to be attempted. The key is to get started. As Sam Gamgee quoted his Gaffer as saying, "It's the job that's never started that takes longest to finish!" You will not get to Easter without walking the *Via Dolorosa*. Earthly life can not get to Heaven until Heaven's life is embraced on earth.

Wait a second, Father. Your ignorance of diapers is showing again. Can you imagine trying to accomplish all of this with all of the other things that a family has to manage?

Yes, I can—priests grow up in families, not in ecclesial greenhouses. So I realize that it is a tall order, just like Archbishop Sheen said; "difficult from a distance". The closer you come to doing it right, the easier it will be to do it better. But, because I have seen how challenging it is for families to do all the doing that needs to be done, several years ago I put together a model for how a weekend retreat for the family might be engaged where the parents can't get away to do a retreat themselves, or the children are too young for it, or wage slavery or public brainwashing, I mean, public school will not allow. It looks like this:

The Holy Family Retreat

Overview: This is intended for participation by a family or a group of families. It is not necessary for a priest to be involved, but it is encouraged at least for the initial preparations.

Each member of the family must clear his calendar from Friday morning through Sunday evening. (If families enduring the curse of children in schools can get the children out of school for vacations, dentist appointments, and sporting events, they can get them excused to keep an appointment with God.) It would be most appropriate to choose a weekend wherein some significant Church Feast or family event is to be celebrated. These could include the Feast of the Holy Family during the Christmas season, the Easter Triduum, March 19 (Feast of St. Joseph, Spouse of the Blessed Virgin Mary), August 15 (Feast of the Assumption of Mary), March 25 (Feast of the Annunciation), a wedding anniversary, or other date holding some special meaning for a given family.

Do *not* make this a time of family vacation. The idea of the *Holy Family Retreat* is to engage in spiritual renewal, whereas vacation is for recreation and relaxation. Care should be taken to ensure that the family has both retreat time and vacation time scheduled separately each year. If you can't do both, skip the vacation.

Preparation for this retreat should include a habit of family prayer, individual prayer among the family members, regular assistance at Sunday Mass (and daily Mass where that is possible), and preparation for the Sacraments appropriate to each member of the family. Ongoing spiritual direction of individual family members would be a great asset, but not a necessity. Home life should be such that a pattern of eating meals together, conversing, recreating, praying, and socializing are a matter of course. If this does not already exist in the family structure, the retreat will aid the family in establishing them, but attention should be paid to continuing the work of building up the family once the retreat is over.

Only those chores necessary to be done on a daily basis should be part of the weekend. Any other chores should be done ahead of time or put off until the retreat is completed. Examples of daily chores acceptable during the retreat would include preparation of meals, washing dishes, making beds, and personal hygiene. Those which should be done before or after the retreat would include laundry, dusting, yard work, and any chore that would consume more than an hour of effort. The retreat is not a chance to catch up on housework or maintenance.

Every family member should make participation in the retreat a high priority. Time off from work and school should be arranged well in advance. Nothing short of illness should keep any member of the family from being a part of this experience.

Friday: *St. Joseph*
5am—Family Prayer: Dad leads all in the Our Father
Mom reads St. Matthew 11:25-30
Silent time
Morning Offering and other prayers
5:30am—6:30am: Quiet Time
6:30am: Breakfast Preparation
7:15am: Breakfast
9:30am: Family Walk
12:00 Noon Prayer: Dad leads all in Nicene Creed
Mom reads the Apocalypse 19:5-10
Silent time
Angelus and fifteen-decade Rosary
1:15pm: Lunch Preparation
2:00pm: Lunch
3:15pm: Dad leads Stations of the Cross
4:00pm: Quiet Time
5:30pm: Dinner Preparation
6:15pm: Dinner
7:pm: Family Recreation
8pm: Night Prayer: Dad leads all in three Hail Marys
Mom reads St. Luke 2:25-40
Children offer intercessions
8:30pm: Examination of Conscience and Bedtime

Saturday: *Blessed Virgin Mary*
5am—Family Prayer: Dad leads all in Our Father
Mom reads St. John 2:1-11
Silent time
Morning Offering and other prayers
5:30am—6:30am: Quiet Time

6:30am: Breakfast Preparation
7:15am: Breakfast
9:30am: Family Walk
12:00 Noon Prayer: Dad leads the Angelus and fifteen-decade Rosary
12:45pm: Lunch Preparation
1:30pm: Lunch
2:30pm: Mom & Dad lead examination of conscience
3:00pm: Family goes to church for Penance
4:00pm: Quiet Time
5:00pm: Dinner Preparation
6:15pm: Dinner
7:00pm: Recreation
8pm—Night Prayer: Dad leads all in three Hail Marys
Mom reads St. Luke 1:46-55
Children offer intercessions
8:30pm: Examination of Conscience and Bedtime

Sunday: *Jesus*
6am—Family Prayer: Dad leads all in Our Father
Mom reads St. Mark 14:22-25
Silent time
Morning Offering and other prayers
8:00am: Mass
9:45am: Breakfast Preparation
10:30am: Breakfast
12:00pm: Dad leads Angelus and fifteen-decade Rosary
12:30pm: Family Walk
2:00pm: Dinner preparation
5:00pm: Dinner
7:00pm: Recreation
8pm—Night Prayer: Dad leads all in three Hail Marys
Mom reads Genesis 1:26-31
Children offer intercessions
8:30pm: Examination of Conscience and Bedtime
Retreat Ends

Chores V: Visitors

"When I am about to talk to anybody," said a young village girl, "I picture to myself Jesus Christ and how gracious and friendly He was to everyone."—St. Jean-Marie Baptiste Vianney

A nifty thing happens whenever I visit a brother priest. Almost the very first thing we do is visit Our Lord in the Blessed Sacrament in the church—or, for some particularly blest rectories, right there in the house. Then he, the priest, shows me around: the altar, the sacristy, the confessional (which we frequently make use of for each other), the stained glass and statuary, and the parish hall. I rarely see the rectory rec room or how much shelf space is in the closets or how many gizmos are attached to the big-screen TV. God is good.

Sometimes when I visit lay people, there are other people already there or who arrive after me. Nervous smiles and inane small talk ensue. I do not expect to be taken to the family's private chapel where the Blessed Sacrament is reserved. It would be nice, however, to be told the name of the stranger staring at me, the odd man dressed all in black. And, I hazard to guess, the stranger would like to know my name and why I dress so unusually.

Please, people, when you are hosts in your home or if you bring guests to someone else's home, begin right away with introductions. Hospitality includes, among many other things, making guests feel welcome. It is hard to feel welcome when everyone in the room is still a stranger. Making oneself at home is difficult if one must refer to the other inhabitants of the home as "Hey you".

Train your children to answer the door. Countless times I have been greeted by short people on thresholds with eyes agape in wonderment and awe at the splendor of my visage. It seems to me a bit forward to stride across declaiming the right of entrance and seeking liquid refreshment without so much as a "Howdy do!" Instruct your little ones to say, "Good evening, Father. We are expecting you. Please come in. May I take your hat? Have a seat here where it's most comfortable. Mother and Father are finishing preparations for the evening. They send their greetings and will be here soon. We have water, pop, beer, wine, or tea. What would you like? Here is the life of St. Jean Vianney to browse while you wait. I will be right back."

Okay. If that actually happened, I might be a bit taken aback. But do your best to approximate it.

People visiting your home should receive the hospitality of the house. That means that you offer them what you have to give them. If they come to dinner and you normally eat bread and water on Fridays in Lent, they should not turn their noses up at it. (I admit that inviting someone to your home on a fast night would be a bit rude on your part, but I think you understand my point.) By the same token, if you are in the habit of praying before and after meals, as I'm sure you are, then do not be shy about doing so with your guests in attendance. You have a choice to make: deny your guest the right to have you apostatize in your own home, or deny your Lord in your house and risk never seeing the inside of His house. For those families who have the laudable habit of praying the Rosary after dinner, such would be a most edifying experience for one's house guests. We should give our guests the best we have to offer. There is nothing better than honoring Our Lord with the prayer given us by Our Lady. Your guests should feel honored to be a part of something so truly good.

On many occasions I have been asked by parents what to do about their children's little friends from down the street being raised by bad parents. It is appropriate to tell the wee one, "Mary may not visit you in your house, but you are welcome here when we let her invite you so long as you obey our family's rules." If little Hunter from down the block spews profanities, dresses like a midget harlot, and/or can not be entertained without the aid of the grid, Hollywood moguls, and software programmers, then some other family will need to be her savior, unless Hunter's Mom and live-in unDad allow you to correct her errant ways. Any of you who imagine that Mary might be permitted to visit Hunter under these circumstances are invited to pay me a visit for re-education at my dungeon spa for moronic parents.

Your home needs to be a place where you and your family enjoy spending lots of time. If it is not, do not be surprised that your guests make odd excuses to spend as little time there as possible. Before you ever invite anyone into your home, you need to make Jesus the primary resident therein. If He feels at home in your home, the only people who would not feel at home there are people you don't want there anyway. With Jesus at the center of your home, you will be able to offer your guests the same solicitude that you offer their brother Jesus, who will reward you and your family for showing Him hospitality through the kindness given your guests.

Having a comfortable home means having a home where everyone living there feels comfortable with family life. Your guests will feel out of place if your suggestion to pray the Rosary is met with audible sighs from your spouse and children. There will be embarrassment all around the table if you begin the thanksgiving after meals and no one knows the words, including you. If I come into one more home and see a TV before I am introduced to anyone, well, let's just say that I know how to make Holy Water and how to put it to good use—by the bucketful.

Holiday visits often coincide with Holy Days. It pains me greatly to hear Confessions from people telling me that they missed Sunday or Holy Day Masses because they felt uncomfortable inviting their out-of-town guests. Call me strange, but I feel uncomfortable inviting people into my home for days at a time who find it unpleasant to be around God. If the notion of a priest having Godless friends strikes you as disturbing, well and good; it should be almost as disturbing that the priest would have parishioners who keep Godless friends around. Do not maintain contact with people who shun contact with God and His Church. Visitors to your house should be willing to accept invitations to God's house—after all, your home is merely a small corner of His house. Whatever a faithless soul finds unpleasant in church, other than the Blessed Sacrament Himself, should be present in your home as well. Silence, prayer, and love belong in God's house and in His children's houses. Catholic families should be every bit as adamant about fidelity to Our Lord in their homes as they expect their priest to be when he is away from home.

There are times, of course, when you will find yourselves guests in others' homes. Be polite. Eat what is set before you. Compliment the cook, if not on the flavor, at least on the generosity of the meal. Send withering looks—full of promises of further retribution to be exacted once you are at home—to any of your children who dare to act anything other than monumentally grateful for every morsel set before them. If the family does not offer grace and thanksgiving out loud, instruct your children to bless their food silently and to give thanks afterwards. Your hosts will notice without you making mention of it. Should conversations veer in directions lacking discretion, change the topic with a lighthearted laugh and a firm sense of purpose. Should you discover that your hosts are quite different from your family in their life of faith, thank them at the earliest possible moment after dinner, assure them of your prayers, and get home ASAP, saying a decade of the Rosary for them during the trip home. Say a second decade for your family, thanking God for the gift of the faith, asking for the grace to persevere in the faith, and begging forgiveness for the many times when your own family fell short of the example of the Holy Family. And then, once home, spank the children who whined about any part of the rolled-turnip-casserole dinner you all just ate.

Remember, Jesus is not a visitor in your home. He is not the guest of honor in your home. Jesus is the Landlord, the Breadwinner, the central Resident in your home. You live there by His grace. Raise your children from infancy with this awareness. Rejoice in the warmth and affection you will be able to offer your actual visitors when they partake of the hospitality of Heaven within the home Jesus shares with you on earth. Rejoice that much more in realizing that sharing this wonderful home with Him on earth is the palest reflection of the home he desires to share with you forever in Heaven. When Jesus says, *Mi casa, Su casa!* He means it more than our frail minds can imagine. Try to convey that meaning to the neighbors whom you seek to love in your home. Trying oh-so-hard but failing to live up to Our Lord's impossibly high standard will be one of the greatest delights you can impart on your visitors. You'll have a nice time, too.

Playing: Games, Outings, Meals

Oh! how I love those words said the first thing in the morning: I will suffer everything this day for the Glory of God…nothing for the world or personal interest, all to please my Savior!

– St. Jean-Marie Baptiste Vianney

Jacob? Jacob? Jacob, are you still there?

This section is actually the *raison d'etre* of this whole endeavor. Jacob wanted ideas for fun and games for his family. Father Smith, a.k.a. Father Ogre, is such a stick-in-the-mud that he made all of you wade through a million words before getting to the good stuff. I trust that you all did read *every* word before coming to this point. If not, we will go no further until you read about your chores. I'm waiting…

…Three years later…

Okay. Now that our work is finished we can play! Yayyy! Anyone know any good games?

See, that's the problem that got us here in the first place. A lot of people don't know how to play simple games. Not the kind that take batteries, extension cords, and advanced degrees from MIT. You know the world is in *real* bad shape when people have to ask a *priest* of all things for ideas on how to have fun. When I decided to amass this *magnum opus*, it struck me that I'm the most exciting person I know. Thus, it would be really easy to answer Jacob's question about how to have fun. All I need to do is describe a typical day in my life. Just do what I do, folks, and you'll never know a dull moment. So, without further ado, here is a schema of my actual daily life of fun and games in the vineyard of the Lord:

ca. 8:30pm—Bedtime (this is actually a little later than I like, but I pray the Rosary every night at 8pm with the Lexow family)

ca. 3:30am—Waking (but I linger in sloth for a bit, mentally arranging the day, wondering where the night went)

4:00am—Rising (are we having fun yet?): this is when I pray my Morning Offering and several other devotional prayers

4:15am–4:45am—Hygiene: Make bed, brush teeth, shave, wash body, dress

4:45am–5:45am—Matins and Lauds

5:45am—Joyful and Sorrowful Mysteries of the Rosary, open chapel and prepare altar

6:45am—Mass

7:30am—Thanksgiving, Prime, Glorious Mysteries

8:00am—Correspondence (I confess—this is usually electronic in nature)

9:00am—Terce

9:30am–Noon—Study, writing, domestic stuff, various interruptions from around the country

Noon—Angelus and Sext

Noon:15—Lunch and spiritual reading

1pm–5pm—This period varies wildly depending on who needs what and where; today, for instance, I am writing this. If the devil stays away I am able to pray Nones at 3pm along with mental prayer. It is during this period that I am able to see people, go into town, see my confessor, attend to courses I am preparing and offering, get a little exercise, and/or whatever else is needful.

5:15pm—Vespers, personal devotions, quiet time/mental prayer

6:00pm—Supper

7:00pm—Relax a bit

8:00pm—Rosary and Compline

Now, catch your breath, everyone! If merely reading it leaves you so winded, imagine what the actual experience must be like! Keep in mind, I am a trained professional. Do not attempt this at home, especially with little children!!! Should any of you foolishly seek to inflict this regimen on a child, you stand in peril of hearing the two fatal words from him most to be feared by parents: *Nursing. Home.*

To avoid this fate I offer these following alternatives to the clerical state much better suited for the family with many children. Remembering all that has been said thus far about structure in life, prayer, and domestic chores, these more frivolous activities are possibilities for ways to glorify God through recreation. It is hard for me to fathom something more recreational than writing a sonnet or reading an ancient manuscript or praying Terce, but I am told that many people actually do find those diversions less than diverting. Go figure.

1) Take a hike! A long one. Walking is good. The body needs it. The mind can wander all the while. It can be done alone, in groups, by couples, in silence, chit-chatting about nothing in particular, raising profundities, offering a Rosary. Our Lord did a great deal of this: In Our Lady's arms to Egypt and to Nazareth, around Galilee, upon the *Via Dolorosa*, on the way to Emmaus, and beside the Saints on their way to Heaven. Families could do a whole lot worse than this.

2) Go fly a kite! When I was young and unattached, I made a habit of observing the first fair days of March each year by flying a kite. I was never good at it, but, boy, did I have a good time! One of the best days I remember from my youth is when my Dad took my two brothers, my sister, and me to a Davenport Parks and Recreation Department day-class on kite making. I did not learn to make kites well, but I learned that I loved the chance to do it badly. Long before I ever read G.K. Chesterton, I knew what he meant when he said, "Anything worth doing is worth doing badly."

3) Paper airplanes are even better than kites. Not as spectacular, but far more accessible. My brothers and sister and I used to experiment with different designs. Some of them flew straight ahead and swiftly. Others could do loop-the-loops. Many of them dropped like so much lightweight lead, but they were sweet to look at. We had models that required tape, others that were meant to have rips in the paper to change their aerodynamics, and some bordered on origami in the complexity of the folds necessary to make them flight worthy.

4) Poker was big in my house on Saturdays. No, silly, I didn't play. My Dad and his beer-drinking buddies took turns in each other's houses. But the fact that my Dad was one of the boys—they would call him "Chief", a term of endearment dating back to their high school days when my Dad was one of the Big Men on Campus—meant that there were always *cards* in a drawer in the kitchen. The kitchen table served as the poker table on the Saturdays when my Dad played host to his friends. At other times, those cards just sat in a drawer next to masking tape and screw drivers and barbecue tongs, begging to be built into houses! When we

built card houses, we bent, twisted, and marked the cards in such a way as to make them useless as poker decks. So my Dad would have to buy more cards. Which meant that we had more building materials. Which meant that we wrecked more decks. Which meant that Dad had to buy more cards. Which meant that we had more building materials. Before long, we weren't building card houses, but card *cities!* You simply have not lived until you have rebuilt Chicago after the great Fire of 1871 on a rainy day, preferably one involving severe thunderstorm warnings and a screened-in front porch. Ah, youth!

5) It's sundown on a February evening. Cover the windows with blankets. Turn out the lights. We're going to play hide-and-seek. You're it! If I have to explain further, there is no hope for you.

6) My mother was the queen of popcorn. Here my diaper-changing ignorance is going to surface again. Do they still make popcorn that understands what to do in a covered saucepan coated with butter on medium heat? My Mom used to make vats of the stuff. Anyone who does not think this is a game has never done the requisite shaking, listened to the percussion of grain on metal, and watched the top rise as the treasure spills out onto the stovetop. Then you get to shake salt on it, dump *melted* butter all over it, and start the next batch! The corollary to this late-winter activity was the late-autumn chore of doing the same thing *sans* melted butter and salt in preparation for strings to wrap around the Christmas tree. The needle and thread wielded by young hands "accidentally" and "lamentably" created many edible mistakes,

7) Pure water fights are not a matter of water quality but of ammunition. Buckets, balloons, and rubber hoses are the weapons of preference for purists. Where there is a need to make a purchase at a store—alas! for the loss of the likes of W.T. Grant, Turnstile, and Hester's "bug store" (that's a local, family, inside joke)—no cost in excess of coins that can be found in pants at the bottom of the closet, deep within cushions in the davenport, and pilfered from Mom's dresser top should be incurred. Spray bottles for misting Mom's potted plants or Tuesday ironing are bigger prizes than anything in the U.S. nuclear arsenal. My brothers and sister and I and our friends had several creeks available where our war games could be conducted, and flailing hands and arms could serve as defensive weapons of last resort. Lest any be foolish enough to think that such campaigns are mounted only after the midyear solstice, contemplate for a moment the effect of a garden hose on a backyard hill after the first good snowfall. Mother did and was not pleased with our pleasure.

8) Baseball, football, and basketball are fun only where there are no refs, no scoreboards (only the disputed reckoning of the combatants), no uniforms, no stands, and no rules, more or less—fouls are a matter of taste, for which there is no accounting, only arguments won by sheer decibelage. What kind of *game* demands participation fees, tickets, insurance waivers, doctors' physicals, cheerleaders, bands, painted yard lines, foul lines, or three-point lines? In Davenport we played a variant of baseball called "pickle", but, I am told, is called "hot box" or "base running" in other regions of the country. It takes only two bases, two basemen, a runner, and a front yard. One-on-one to one-hundred by ones was an endurance event my childhood best friend, Pat Kakert, and I used to play at Jefferson School Park from June through August—full court. Lafayette Park was the scene of epic battles of pick-up basketball played from before noon until just after sundown by scores of boys coming and going, shifting sides, and *teams* varying in size from two to ten. The Assumption High School Band used to play halftimes on Friday nights for the Knights at John O'Donnell Stadium. The same group of musicians would then gather on Saturday afternoon at Junge Park for a far more raucous game before repeating the pizza outing that is the obligatory end to all football contests. By the way, when Mr. Dugan tried to teach us soccer one day of junior high at Holy Trinity in 1977, we rebelled. He did not make that mistake again. I never touched another European "football" again until I subbed one day for the seminary team in 1996. Off-sides still makes no sense to me—or to the refs at the World Cup.

9) Pity the people who live where there is no spring to follow winter because there is no winter. They don't get to rake leaves and then pile them and then spend hours jumping in the piles and then stand around them as they burn giving the night a sample of the day it never gets to see. Those poor souls don't know the wonder of watching green metamorphose into hues no rainbow ever imagined. They also have no concept of what the Latins mean when they call spring *la primavera* or *les printemps.* There is a quality to the green of spring that shocks the sight every time it is seen for the first time no matter how many decades over the span of a life it is seen. Snowmelt on the bluffs of the Mississippi spawns thousands of little rivers looking for their father. Those miniature torrents can be dammed, splashed, or just followed downhill until there is no more street or there is a sewer grate, whichever comes first. March is the only time of year when icicles become popsicles. They're edible, don't you know. Certain houses in older neighborhoods unknown to suburbia but the very stuff of which Davenport-be-

low-the-hill is constructed are veritable icicle factories. Some creative sorts actually added sugar to them. Walking to and from school in the spring is a frolic in itself as the hoarfrost of the morning gives way to the puddles of the afternoon, as the first kite breezes blow in March, as the first days fit for bike riding come, as the lilies-of-the-valley first peek out in May. One of the things we always used to do in the springtime was to make soap bubbles out of Ivory Liquid and use all manner of household items as bubble molds for blowing globes, globs, and other indescribable shapes occurring only for a moment, only with just the right air pressure, only now, alas, in memory. I feel the urge to run some water and squeeze a bottle just thinking about it.

10) I was the most pathetic Cub Scout in the world's most pathetic Scout Troop with the best Den Mother in history. Mrs. Martin hosted our lame meetings. We stumbled through the oath, begged forgiveness for not doing whatever project was necessary for whichever merit badge we weren't going to ever get, and then went sledding in the Martin's two-block long, downhill back yard (we did *not* feel the need or the courage to apply the garden hose to that mini-mountain). Having our fill of snow down our shirts, bent sleds, and bruised butts, we rushed back indoors to hot chocolate and chocolate chip cookies. I am sure that we met at times other than winter, but all I remember from my scouting days, my scouting six months I should say, is those winter romps and yummy goodies. The great part of this is that such joys can be recreated without the muss and fuss of sewing on patches or memorizing masonic pledges or feeling ashamed for feeling no shame at the Jamboree. Any Mom can bake, any child can sled, and any time of the year is fair game for child's play.

Picnics were always a favorite pastime of my Mom's family. Our regular haunt near, but outside of, town was Scott County Park. That's where there were the best trails through the woods (this is a bit of a play on words, my Mom's maiden name being "Woods"), horses available for riding, and a huge swimming pool. When Mom's nine brothers and sisters wanted to get together with their cousins from Fort Madison, Iowa, we would meet halfway in Muscatine, Iowa. There we would spend the day at Weed Park, which had a zoo, a great view of the Mississippi, and a swimming pool with the highest high-dive around. When we picnicked in town, we frequently went to Fejervary Park, which was also the site of our annual school picnic for Holy Trinity. Fejervary Park (not to be confused with Fejervary Health Care Center—by the way, the 'v' is pronounced as a 'w'—my first place of steady employment) had a children's zoo with burro rides, an infamous monkey exhibit, and, in my youth what was merely a swimming pool, but now, I understand, is an *aquatic center. La-di-dah.* You might sense from this list that my family was not unfond of swimming. We ate a lot on those picnics, too, always, of course, an hour at least before going swimming.

When I was growing up (those who know me well wonder if that part of the sentence should be framed in the past tense), our family spent a lot of time in conversation. Later in life, in high school and college, some of my friends were a bit surprised, if not nervous, at the freewheeling debates that would take place in our house. All subjects were fair game. I am not entirely a fan of the idea of children engaging in the conversations with adults—seeing children is far more pleasant than hearing children—but we were allowed to jump in and opine with the worst of our elders. The down side of this was an emphasis on winning debate points rather than ascertaining truth. The up side was the sharpening of wits, the improvement of vocabulary, and the love of thought that it engendered. If my family had applied the same verve to discussing the truths of the Faith that we offered to current events, I would be a Saint already.

One of the primary places where these all-out verbal wars took place was the dinner table. I come from a broken home. But one thing my imperfect parents taught well to their imperfect brood was how to behave at table. At an early age we were expected to know how to handle utensils, how to handle serving dishes, and how to handle an argument founded on a false premise.

It was during this time that I had the experiences that led to my principles of life: *It is impossible to overdress; fashion is not always in good taste, but good taste is always in fashion; and ditch-digging clothes are forbidden at five-star restaurants, but formalwear can not be banned from ditches.* As a student in Catholic schools from age five to thirty-two, I became accustomed to dressing for dinner, for class, for mowing the lawn. Some have asked if I now own a pajama cassock. I'm not saying, but I will say that I did not own a pair of jeans until I was a sophomore in high school, purchasing them with my own money from the aforementioned part-time job at Fejervary Health Care Center. They were worn only on weekends. John Steinbeck once had a character say something to the effect that "you have to be very rich to dress like a slob." I think he had my Mom as a ghostwriter.

A central element in this education was eating whatever was put in front of us on pain of never seeing another meal again. This was in harmony with the principle of following whatever conversation was raging. If you didn't like what was for dinner tonight, Mom was going to make something different tomorrow night because there weren't going to be any leftovers—right?! If you didn't like the current topic of conversation, that was fine because it was going to shift and shimmy in the next ten minutes anyway.

We were better behaved in restaurants. Mom and Dad took us out for meals on special occasions, birthdays, and on family vacations. (A quick aside: in my youth, "family vacation" *always* meant the annual family reunion on the second weekend of August—no national parks, amusement parks, or RV parks for the Smith family, just the city park in whichever city was hosting the reunion that year. We never flew, always drove. And every fifth year we went nowhere because the reunion was hosted in Davenport.) As children we were taught to use a menu, how to spread a napkin, proper etiquette for summoning a waiter, the fine art of calculating a tip, and the wonders of the Kiddy Kocktail. The rarity of these occurrences made them particularly special when they did happen. A corollary to the whole family eating out was the unexpected phenomenon at great intervals of Dad bringing home Sandee's hamburgers and shakes or Mr. Quick hamburgers and onion rings. Every now and then Dad took leave of his senses (oddly perfectly coinciding with nights when Mom didn't want to cook), and fed us enough fat and oil to clog our arteries to the age of a hundred and three, if we should live so long. I remember when Burger King still gave cardboard crowns just for the asking. Well, maybe Dad did have to pay for them. I really don't know—they just magically appeared from time to time.

That magical happenstance is a big part of what Moms and Dads should be trying to effect for their children. One need not spend a bunch of money or travel far to make a special occasion for a child. Parents should plan before conceiving their first child how the discipline of the house is going to be maintained. Remember, "discipline" is different from "punishment". Punishment is what happens when things go wrong. Discipline is what is necessary to keep things going right. Thus, planning discipline in the home means knowing when the prayers are going to be prayed, when bedtime will be, when it will be time to get up, what the chores are, when they will be accomplished and by whom, and what will happen if there is a failure or breakdown in the system.

But the real delight of being parents, the real delight of growing up in a home where sanctity is the main event of daily life, is what comes when everyone obeys the will of God, the will of Mom and Dad, and the will to love everyone nearby. The example I like to give is the third Tuesday of months without an 'r' in them. Mom and Dad should explain to the children very clearly what is expected of them. When things go wrong, correction is in order and often punishment is necessary. When Mom and Dad see things going right, they designate the third Tuesday of the months without an 'r' as the moment for rewards to be received. This is not a random occurrence, but a well-planned response to the merits earned by the children. Punishments should be spelled out in great, excruciating, vivid, minute, delicious detail before the fact; rewards should seem to be lightning from a blue sky to the children, but the ordinary progression of the nature of things to the parents.

It might be the day when ice cream sundaes come after dinner or everyone gets to go for a boat ride at the local lake or the chance to visit Grandma for milk and her world famous peanut butter cookies (grandmas love being in on this kind of surprise). The children should not know that something good is coming or when, only that good things come when they are good. When children grow up realizing that good behavior brings down wonders and thrills without being asked for, they will do all they can to be wonderfully good and thrillingly obedient to hasten the arrival of those delights without being asked twice to be good. Moms and Dads should wish to be able to mete out more rewards than punishments. They should establish a home life where the good is far better by way of joy than the bad obtains pain by way of punishment. A child growing up like this will not be surprised to find that divine providence has plans for his comfort, not affliction, and life on earth moving toward Heaven is a real swell place to spend his time.

Boring is good. A Mom and Dad who make it their life's work to provide structure, sanctity, and sanity to their children will be magnificently predictable in their expectations, in the daily activities arranged for their children, and in the way they engage the perils of the world. Excitement will come to the children in discovering anew each day how God will work in their lives, through the affairs of the family, in the deeper appreciation of the heavenly value given earthly things when they are given to the attainment of the Kingdom of Heaven. "Been there, done that" will not be part of the vocabulary of a saintly child when he considers things like the family Rosary, evening meals, All Saints' Day costume parties at church, learning to mow the grass the very first time, watching little sister receive her First Holy Communion, riding the pony at the state park, or the fact that these are meant to be foretastes of Heaven by virtue of the love wherewith they are shared. Heaven has nothing worldly in it. Those who would arrive in Heaven must live in the world in such a way that what pleases Heaven provides them their greatest pleasures. Nothing pleases Heaven more than seeing the Holy Family imitated in families striving to be holy.

Miscellaneous: Conversation, Singing, Hobbies, Written Words, the Art of Virtuously Doing Nothing

We must take care never to do anything before having said our Morning Prayers... The devil once declared that if he could have the first moment of the day, he was sure of all the rest.

—St. Jean-Marie Baptiste Vianney

But I say unto you that every idle word that men shall speak, they shall render an account for it in the Day of Judgment.—St. Matthew 12:36

That is one of Father Ogre's favorite sayings of Jesus. It also scares him to no end. I am not one given to remembering my own advice: two ears, one mouth—use them in proper proportion!

We all would do well to spend more time in silence. As I like to say, if you don't enjoy spending time quietly alone with yourself, please do not inflict that company on anyone else. Believe it or not, not every one of our thoughts or opinions merits immediate dissemination to all within earshot.

You should talk, Father.

That's exactly the kind of thing I mean.

Just because we think it doesn't mean that we should say it. And, by the way, an awful lot of what we think, once we say it, is described by those unfortunate to hear it as being singularly thoughtless, inconsiderate, and mindless. It's not a bad practice to think before speaking. It is a better practice to pause after thinking and before speaking. Even better is to pray before thinking before pausing before speaking. Slow-speaking, quiet types are often thought of as deep thinkers and people hang on every one of their few words. Loud-mouthed, non-stop boors have many poor souls doomed to hear them, but are rarely asked their opinion. Of course, I like balancing the old saying, *Still waters run deep*, with the equally ancient gnome, *A man of no words has expressed the extent of his wisdom.*

Try to make the first thing you say to someone something positive. This is especially easy if you just begin with a hearty, "Good morning!" Don't gossip. If Fred didn't tell you to tell Mildred what he said to George, even if it's just that water is wet and the sky is blue, keep the incredible news to yourself. Find topics of conversation that obey St. Paul's instructions to the Ephesians: *Say only the good things men need to hear.* Emphasize the good and the needful.

Preaching to the choir is boring—and I mean that in a *bad* way—to them and should be tedious to the preacher. When you are with like-minded folks, don't operate on the assumption that *great minds think alike.* Instead, fear and tremble on the way to salvation that *fools seldom differ.* Rather than regaling your friends with how wise all of you agree all of you are, encourage one another to work that much harder to know the good and live it better. Actually attempting to accomplish that worthy goal leaves little time to discuss how much *they*—and you know who *they* are—have gotten everything wrong.

The longer you live, the longer can be your romps down memory lane. Work on telling the same old stories in ways that bring out a different aspect of their mirth or wisdom or the personalities involved. Tell the same stories, but tell them in different ways. Not only will you prevent the rolling of the young folks' eyes at the eighteenth hearing, but you won't have to listen to yourself ask the nineteenth time, "Have I told this story before?" If you really consider the events of your life and continue to learn from your past lessons, the old news can offer new insights.

Ask others about their lives, especially older people. When you ask, don't ask yes-or-no questions. Don't say, "Grandpa, did you have fun as a little boy?" Ask instead, "Grandpa, what happened the day you turned thirteen, same age as me?" **Please, please, please** do not imitate the idiots who do media interviews, asking questions that would take three pages of print to transcribe. Ask open-ended questions that obviously wish to learn what others have to say rather than conveying your conviction that what you mean simply must be expressed for the salvation of the world. You will know that you are failing at this if the man whose hand you are shaking as you explain your desire to know how he feels about your latest profound insight into the political process, begins gnawing his own arm from his shoulder while you are giving the background to the question you want him to answer. Simply *never* say the words, "Now I've said enough about me—what do you think of me?"

When you run out of things to say, there is always a song worth singing! Beer helps improve everyone's voice, so if you're asked to sing but you think you can't sing, drink a couple, and then you'll be convinced that Caruso would have been jealous of you—and no one will ever ask you to sing again.

But seriously, singing is a good thing, done by Moms to babes in arms, done by Our Lord after the Last Supper, done in Heaven by the choirs of Angels and Saints for all eternity. As I like to say to children, get used to singing—that's what you'll be doing forever if you make it to Heaven. Encouragement of a profound kind can be found in the words of St. Augustine: *He who sings prays twice!* Another less lofty incentive is had by reminding God: *Lord, this is the voice you gave me; this is the voice you're going to get praised with!*

Learn to sing by teaching your children to sing. They don't know a good voice from a bad one at first, and by the time they know the difference, your voice will be much improved by much practice. A great help to this is to stop listening to recorded music. Electronic devices of various sorts have convinced us that only the perfect can entertain us. Wrong. Somehow song was heard, dance was danced, jokes were told before there ever was a gramophone, Rockefeller Center, or foul-mouthed TV special. It is bad enough that *they*—and you know who *they* are—have convinced everyone that they can't teach their children, walk a block, or grow a crop; don't let them tell you that you can't sing even if the shower is five rooms away.

A great hobby to support your singing is taking up the piano or other musical instrument. When you have family gatherings or other guests, a sing-along can be great fun. If your guests plead that they can't sing or don't know the songs, you teach them as readily as the fiends wish to teach your children the wonders of "alternative lifestyles" or the federal government wants to teach foreign countries the marvels of the "free" market system (which is neither inexpensive nor unrestricted nor liberating). My parents forced me to take up the cornet at the age of eight. I went on to master the tuba, more or less, and got a degree in music. Now I am a priest! No, I don't offer that progression as an example of things gone wrong, but of the applicability of such endeavors throughout life, regardless of what one's major duties might be. One does not pursue skills exclusively nor even primarily to make a living. One is to live one's life well and take on the skills that will improve one's chances for success as defined, not by mammon, but by Heaven.

So, one might take up philately or numismatics or iambic pentameter. Everyone knows what philately and numismatics are, but on the off chance that some of my readers are unfamiliar with how to measure feet and frame metaphor, I will demonstrate such with an example of my own avocational pursuit:

Quallington Carpenter

It almost seems upon a time before
a visit to thy dwelling I have made,
for not unlike thy sturdy, humble door
are many others' who have plied thy trade.

Hast thou a Son who learn'd in eager youth
to value ere the saw has bitten deep
the tree in bloom unknowing winter's ruth
at lacking tears as sweet as willows weep?
Do I remember right His Mother's face
within His own, reflecting naught of thine,
suffused with peace and filled with simple grace
whose sight distills the truth that gladdens wine?
My feet have never had the heart to roam,
yet only now my eyes have seen a home.

Hobbies are engaged not because you will find a publisher or will win a blue ribbon at the county fair or because anyone else even knows that you do it. Hobbies are those little delights that are first had alone and then shared with an understanding friend or two. Hobbies are something that everyone should have, but that should not be shared with everyone. You don't need to know where Quallington is or what prompted me to rhapsodize its local carpenter. I don't ask people why they collect Nativity Scenes from around the world. It is enough that one gains enjoyment and peace. It is asking too much to want everyone else to be as thrilled about it as you, but it is nice to find one other soul silly enough to like what you love. What you find interesting may not interest anyone else, but it will help you to be a more interesting person, one who is capable of being *interested* in others, knowing how deep is the human craving to find a sympathetic heart and ear.

An offshoot of the lost-and-fine art of conversation and of the treat which is singing, is the written word. No, you don't have to take up sonnets, craft charming short stories, or pen the great American novel. It would be neat, however, if more people put down the computer and took up the ballpoint, or, as I prefer, the fountain pen and wrote letters that require philatelist's stock in trade purchased with that which makes a numismatist's heart go pit-a-pat. Write your grandmother a letter and mail it. See, I do speak English.

People who paint, who write poems, who send letters, who hum tunefully, or who have a generous ear understand the importance of doing nothing. One can not paint a landscape until one has *seen* it. There is no poem worth reading that was not first an unheard gasp within the heart. Mail from home takes time to arrive, and the answer to that treasured note does not come until after the silent waiting has happened. Whistling while you work is the compliment paid by attentive laborers to the birds that serenade them on the way to the office or field or factory. Many people just sit there and don't hear a word you are saying, but what a prize to have a friend who sits near and *listens* even to what you leave unsaid.

Remember back almost thirty pages ago. *Prayer is the labor of love, the labor that lovers share, the reward of those who labor at love.* Another word for prayer is contemplation. Prayer is the contemplation of the things of heaven. Art and the hobbies that contribute to it are the contemplation of things of the earth whose beauty, truth, and goodness comes from and leads to Heaven. The artist and the mystic need quiet and the opportunity to do the nothing which leisure seems to be. Once given that chance, they leap to work and seemingly effortlessly accomplish stupendous feats glorifying God and enriching man. Time to do nothing but contemplate on the way to productive labor comprises the moments of morning prayer, the Angelus, fast days, Advent and Lent, retreats, and that final reflection which is the prayer of commendation offered for the dying soul. From that nothing, God creates through man the worship in spirit and truth which is the Mass of the Church, the sanctity which binds the family in love, and the nature born on earth on which is built the grace which comes to fruition in Heaven. Creation *ex nihilo* is a divine prerogative which finds its proper reflection in the prayers of men adorning home life, lending beauty to the society, giving glory to the Author of all, our Father in Heaven.

Concluding Plea: Caritas super omnia!

There is hardly a day when we shall not be obliged to make some sacrifice to God, if we want not to displease Him and if we want to love Him.—St. Jean-Marie Baptiste Vianney

I am sorry that I had to write this. Oh, please don't misunderstand me. It has been quite an enjoyable romp for me. My sadness comes from the fact that we live in such a fractured world that it is necessary actually to explain how to enjoy God, His creation, and us His children. This has almost been like trying to tell a bird what to do with his wings, or a fish the value of gills, or a lily the difference between May and December. *For those with the Faith, no explanation is necessary; for those without the Faith, no explanation is possible.*

We live in a ruthlessly faithless world. The men of faith, therefore, need explanations. The necessity of this is not a matter of the grace denied, either by God in offering, or in men accepting. No, it is a matter of men receiving the gift without much by way of direction accompanying it. As the Eunuch said to St. Philip: *How can I understand unless some man shewest me?*

We have fully two generations who have grown to adulthood in a culture not only lacking the Faith, but attacking the Faith. What is before us is the task of re-establishing a Catholic culture based on the immemorial teachings of the Church, but now in a context far worse than the original pagan milieu of the time of the Acts of the Apostles. We are not dealing with pagans who never knew the Faith, but with apostates who were given the Faith and have willfully rejected the Faith. It is not easy to bring an apostate to repentance. History is of no help to us in showing how to re-establish a Catholic culture where one has been cast aside. This is an era utterly without precedent.

But spring still springs and birds still sing and the laughter of children still rings. God loves us. We are to love Him with our *whole* hearts, *whole* souls, *whole* minds, and *whole* strengths. Where there is love, there is life. Where there is life, there is hope. Where there is hope, there is joy, because we…

Hope in the Lord. One of the little graces that God is giving me as life as I have known it unravels, is a delightful sense of proportion, detachment, and trust. It has occurred to me on any number of occasions that there is no virtue involved in resisting temptations that are not happening. The hand of God is at work when temptation strikes and the sinner calls on the Lord to aid him in fending off the attacks of the devil.

In the same vein, while life goes well, one can not claim that one is placing trust entirely in the Lord. One might honestly say that he gives the Lord credit for the good that is happening, but it is not accurate to describe that situation as one requiring trust. Reliance on the Lord comes into play at all times, of course, but it is most in evidence and requires the greatest exercise of human will and faith in times of distress.

This means that the proof of the pudding of faith is tasting the bitter hurts that worldly life slings at us and insisting in the midst of it that the sweetness of the Cross is present (see St. Matthew 11:30). The will toward God's will demands that one does not pretend that the challenges of life on earth are irrelevant or insignificant, but that the Lord is more than a match for the worst that the world, the flesh, and the devil can throw at us. When the Lord comes through for us, part of our thanksgiving, paradoxically, is for the cross that made our faith so necessary. O happy fault of Adam that won for us so great a Redeemer! O joyful rent-payment-due when the paycheck is not coming that results in utter confidence in the God who saves!

Our hope in the Lord is not a groundless delusion in which we assume that nothing bad will ever happen. The theological virtue of hope, the grace from God that is hope, is founded on our own experience that God has preserved us in all the trials of our lives thus far. Even more, however, we know of hope because of what the Father did for the Son in the midst of the worst that has ever happened in the history of creation. When the Son was handed over to evil men in the service of satan, the Father glorified the Son's obedience on the Cross and raised Him in the power of the Spirit on the third day. The small crosses we bear in the image and imitation of our Savior's Cross result in the same exercise of the divine power, mercy, and love on our behalf on the last day.

It is not in spite of trials that we hope, but in the face of and because of trials that we hope. Hope is not in what is seen but in what is invisible. Hope exists not in what is unknown but in what is known. We do not see our salvation, but through faith we know and are certain that salvation has been won for us. We do not see the future manifestation of our salvation, but we have seen the fruits of salvation from the Cross Our Lord endured for us in time. Hope does not deny the reality of pain and suffering on earth, but lives in the confident expectation of the beatitude of Heaven. The hopeful neither lack reason to seek God's aid, nor do they lack reason to trust that He will be true.

Despair is the antithesis of hope, but it is also a sin against faith and charity. Despair denies what the faithful know, that God is faithful and keeps all of His promises. Despair refuses to reach out to the beloved, accusing the beloved of failing in His love. Despair is an act of the will, in which the faith experienced in history, and the charity promised as reward, are rejected in favor of the present danger. Rather than remember the mercies of the Lord from the past and the divine pledge of eternal joy, the despairing look only to what now assaults, believing only in the power of the world to oppress, the flesh to betray, and the devil to tempt and to destroy.

Pride and despair are close kin. The devil likes nothing better than to convince a soul that everything is about human suffering rather than about divine mercy. The devil frequently brings proud souls to despair by seducing them into the pleasures of the flesh, lust for power, and avarice for possessions, only to abandon those souls to the futility of their hardened hearts' desires, which have absolutely no power to satisfy human need. The proud soul begins by doubting the ability of God to bring him happiness, and ends with the certitude that nothing will bring him happiness.

Humility is essential to hope. First is the humility of God who places Himself at the disposal of those who hope in Him. Then is the reflection of the divine humility in the hearts of the hopeful when they call on the Name of the Lord, certain that where the man is incapable of saving himself, God can do all things for those who love Him as He has loved them. The union of the divine humility with its image in man's humility is the Cross of Christ, where God humbles Himself to accept the punishment of sinners and where sinners humbly admit their need for salvation from sin and death. Man's hope is Christ's Cross.

Thus it is imperative that we do not flee the trials and sufferings of this life, for it is in those very hardships that the Cross has the only opportunity to bring the graces of Faith, Hope, and Charity to the soul. The Cross is the sign of unseen Faith, wherein lies the proof that the Word of God does not abandon his own. The Cross is the sign of invisible Hope, wherein the Word of God is wholly given that God can be trusted to deliver His own from any attack the devil can mount. The Cross is the sign of the Love before all creation that has the power to repair what sin has marred, to remake what death has destroyed, to glorify what God has called *very good.*

Faith in God requires that we believe that on the cross we meet the Lord. Hope in the Lord requires that we act on the knowledge that through the Cross all can be forgiven, endured, and renewed. Love of God requires that we receive the Cross in the same spirit in which it is given—with the intention of offering all that can be offered in humility, trust, and generosity. As the Cross accompanied Jesus from Pilate to Calvary, so our crosses accompany us from Baptism 'til death. We eat the fruit of the Tree of Life, Jesus Christ crucified, in Holy Communion with Him in the Mass; in doing so we rise with Him who lives and reigns with the Father and the Holy Ghost, one God forever and ever. Amen!

ꕥ

At the risk of repeating myself, *Please pray the Holy Ghost enlighten our minds and hearts through his gifts of grace. Beseech, please, St. Joseph, the head of the Holy Family, to guard the homes of all Catholics from the assaults of this fallen world. Seek the guidance of the Blessed Virgin Mary, our mother and the heart of the Holy Family, as she crushes the head of satan and brings back to the safety of her mantle the children who have wandered from the example given so perfectly at Nazareth. And may our Lord Jesus Christ, the joy, the purpose, and the creator of the Holy Family bring peace, salvation, and eternal life to every Catholic family of the Church Militant, to the glory of God the Father, now and forever. Amen.*

Father Smith.
25 August 2005: St. Louis IX, King of France
Holy Family House, Silver Cliff, Wisconsin

For us as Catholics, the Distributive State (i.e., the state in which there are as many owners as possible) is not something which we discuss, but something we have to propagate and institute. No advance in social thought or social action is possible if we are seeking to prove to ourselves as a theory what we should be trying to realize as a fact.—Father Vincent McNabb, OP, *The Church and the Land*

Part Two

Introduction: A Skunk by any Other Name Still Stinks

In their foundational principles, capitalism and communism do not differ much in how they understand the nature of things. This is because they agree that things are the only things that matter. The political and economic systems adhering to either capitalism or communism are *always* rooted in materialism. Distinctions between how the various mechanisms play out are touted as differences by the partisans on each side, but in the end matter is all that matters to both the market and to the classless society. Bourgeois capitalist pigs and the red menace are equally averse to fulfilling the responsibility to conform the world of the flesh to the Kingdom of Heaven and, thus, are equally subject to the ultimate rule of the devil.

Karl Marx and Luke Skywalker have an odd thing in common—both have fathers of whom they should not be terribly proud. Karl Marx' Darth Vader is none other than Adam Smith. Were it not for the untrammeled capitalism in the name and at the behest of Adam Smith that roared through Europe generally and England particularly during the seventeenth and eighteenth centuries, there would have been no ogre for Karl Marx to inveigh against, no proletariat to pay him heed, nor a comfortable middle-class background safely from which to launch his revolution (from London, by the way) in the name of the unwashed masses in which he and his family shared no part. Keep in mind that Luke Skywalker obeyed his Jedi master no more than Darth Vader had obeyed his. Playing by the enemy's rules results in not only acting like the enemy, but also in becoming the enemy.

This comparison is no mere literary gimmick or exercise in anachronism. The much-vaunted "force" inspiring so many of the feebleminded to sing the praises of the stunted mythology of George Lucas' *Star Wars* series suffers from the same malady inherent in the *faux* debate between capitalists and communists, namely, the absence of an objective truth by which to define that which is good, to condemn that which is evil, and to distinguish that which is "light" from that which is "dark". George Lucas is not able to explain *why* Darth Vader should not destroy the rebellion, nor can Adam Smith explain *why* Karl Marx should not lead history's inexorable revolution against capital toward the workers' paradise. The "force" is merely all that is, and evil is part of what is; history is merely man's life through time, and capitalism is part of that life—for better or for worse depends not on the estimation of impersonal history, but on the personal experience of the individual man. No way out of this meaninglessness exists without an appeal to something absolutely outside of the categories in question. There is no final separation between one element of the "force", the light side, and another element of the same "force", the dark side; there is no final separation between one mode of materialism, capitalism, and its materialistic alter ego, communism.

Capitalism, communism, and science fiction comic books all deny Him who is outside, beyond, and transcendent of time, space, and the human mind. Godless economics, Godless politics, and Godless literature appeal to man's "better" angels in vain; if there is no God, there is no spirit, and if there is no spirit, there are no Angels. Man is on his own, which is just where materialists want him to be. Rules are only as good as the rule maker and are meant for the benefit of both the ruler and the ruled. God sets rules for His greater glory and for the sanctification of man. Fallen man, rejecting redemption in the Son of God and the Son of Mary, Jesus Christ, wants to eliminate that middle Man, electing instead to have man make his own rules. Godless commies no more than Godless democrats play by the rules made of the people, by the people, and for the people. The dirty little secret kept tightly behind the zipped lips of the powers-that-be within both communism and capitalism is that no one ever bothers to explain just *who* "the people" are. God, of course, wants His people to include every person on earth, both in terms of obeying His rules and by sharing in eternal rule with Him. Men, on the underhand, are a bit more exclusive.

"The people" in the average democracy are subject to the forces of "the market". "The market" has no face, obeys no man, and is never liable for malpractice. "The people" in the average communist workers' paradise are subject to the force applied by the thought and the arms of "the party". "The party" has no face, obeys no man, and is never liable for malpractice. Neither "the market" nor "the party" is on record as having brought even one man to eternal happiness. And although both "the market" and "the party" have slaughtered men by the millions, not one advocate of the "free" market has ever chosen freely to lay down his life for his friends in the name of "the market", nor has there ever been a selfless leader of the "peoples'" party willing to sacrifice his personal interests in favor of the larger interest of the people and at the expense of "the party".

Jesus Christ, God Incarnate, is the face of God in the flesh. He obeys not the whims of sinful man, but the divine truth of God the Father. He has laid down His life for enemies chained to sin so that their sins may be forgiven and they might become His friends. His face, witnessed by faith on earth, is the same face which is the very definition of eternal beatitude in Heaven. He "thought it not robbery to be equal to God, but emptied Himself, taking the form of a servant, being made in the likeness of men . . . becoming obedient unto death, even to the death of the cross." Neither capitalists nor communists are shy about rejecting this set of truths as their guide in pursuing ends entirely antithetical to the great command that man should "love the Lord thy God with thy whole heart, and with thy whole mind, and with thy whole soul, and with thy whole strength". Whether one is a ward of the state in the United States of America or a non-person in the Peoples' Republic of China, Jesus Christ is not acknowledged as Sovereign over the market, the party, or the nation's security.

This fact of life is a deadly reality. It leads to the death of the unborn, the ill, and the elderly. It has perpetrated the annihilation of Western civilization. It is wholly indifferent to the destruction of billions of human souls through unrepented mortal sins. The false masonic ideal of the "brotherhood of man" is upon us in the form of the whole world devoted to becoming more and more like Cain and silencing the blood of Abel crying out from the earth to God. But God hears all, and on the last day, none will avoid hearing His awful judgment. Cain received mercy after murdering his brother. Mankind at the end of time can expect nothing but justice when it is tried for the fratricide committed against bodies, souls, and the Son of God.

Worst things first: God is excised (Democracy is the deity it deserves)

The Fulang Gong in China is a recent poster-child for sensitive Westerners bewailing the lack of religious liberty within communist states. The ferocity of the government's prohibition against the members of the Fulang Gong publicly performing something as simple and peaceable as their aerobic meditation is reminiscent of the fervor with which the ACLU (The American Civil Liberties Union) attacks nativity scenes in city parks. What neither Mao's nor J. E. Hoover's philosophical descendents seem to understand, however, is that the same rationalization gives (il)legitimacy to the findings of both the Central Committee and of the Supreme Court. Communist men decided that the gods of the Fulang Gong should be forbidden a public platform; capitalist men decided that God Incarnate should be forbidden a public platform even as the majority of that public celebrates His Birth in time. Both sets of men, communist and capitalist, share a common atheism, equally hostile to the false gods and to the one, true God. Without God's rules, man rules. Men have ruled that the gods and God are unwelcome.

Religious liberty in the largest part of the former Union of Soviet Socialist Republics has taken the form of allowing all religions other than the Russian Orthodox schismatic church equal opportunity to be banned. Religious liberty in the formerly Catholic nation of France, once hailed as the eldest daughter of papal Rome, now means that all religions have the right to be excluded from displaying their distinctive garb in school settings. What moderns, either capitalist or communist, seem incapable of fathoming is that freedom of religion *never* means to practice whatever faith pleases you; but *always* means that you may not practice a faith displeasing to the faithless. Freedom of religion invariably devolves to freedom from religion and then to a religion-free state. Any who deny this fact are invited to *name one example of a nation that once held firmly to an official faith, which then abandoned that faith in the name of religious liberty, and now pursues a secular program which the formerly official faith would not find objectionable.* Religious liberty is merely a nice name for the more accurate term *apostasy.*

Canada and Sweden allow religious liberty. They also allow libertine practices among those who engage in the sin of Sodom. Where liberties conflict, priority is given to that liberty held most dear by the society, to that liberty which is deemed to be more important, more fundamental to the rights of man, and just more true. In both Canada and Sweden at this writing, various religionists are discovering that their liberty to express their firmly held religious belief that God finds sodomites abominable is considered an abomination by their ever so tolerant governments. Harsh penalties await ministers of different and conflicting faiths who agree with each other that man and woman are made for one another, but who have incurred the wrath of the all-powerful state begging to differ with this estimation. Men may bed with men in direct disobedience to God, according to the rule of man, but men may not disobey human caprice so as to submit themselves and their laws to divine rule. Curiously, communist countries are not quite so "advanced" in their take on sodomy; many still imprison and/or torture deviants guilty of this sin that cries to heaven for vengeance. The "virtue" of tolerance in the West on the subject of sodomy, supposedly illustrating yet another superiority of capitalist democracy over socialist communism, is akin to tolerating a tumor in one's brain as an enlightened statement about the ubiquity of the life force present in every life form.

There will surely be protestations against these incontrovertible truths from those who insist that with all their flaws, democracies such as capitalist America have kinder, gentler governments than communist regimes capable of imprisoning peaceful worshippers, banning religious symbols freely displayed by citizens, and torturing advocates of "alternative lifestyles". Let us set aside exceptions to this exceptional rule of the just such as what was done at Waco under the Clinton Administration in the 1990s,what the Supreme Court ruled in the early 1960s regarding school prayer, and what was experienced by the various sovereign Indian nations within United States territory during the last half of the nineteenth century at the hands of the United States Army. We will ignore as a mere aberration the conditions of black slaves imported to these shores as property according to the constitutionally-guaranteed right for Americans in the North and the South. Nothing will be said of the treatment given Catholic immigrants legally arriving in America, but denied work because of their religious background. And, of course, Americans of Japanese descent have nothing to complain about when remembering their ordeal in the wake of the perils facing the United States after Pearl Harbor—and other citizens, naturalized, second, or even third-generation, need never worry that their property, freedom, and lives will be forfeit without due process in time of national hysteria, I mean, national emergency.

But let us soberly consider a sobering fact: more citizens are incarcerated in the United States of America than in any other nation in the world. Of course, the United States has the third-largest population of any nation on earth at present, so in absolute numbers it is not remarkable that most other nations do not have the same quantity of inmates as the United States. However, America also has a higher proportion of prisoners in the penal system relative to the general population than either Russia or China, both countries with deep communist roots, and China having a population over three times greater than that of the United

States. What accounts for this sizeable group of men in bondage within the land of the free? How is it that America wins the dubious distinction of outperforming communist China and oppressive Russia in the practice of placing its citizens under armed guard?

Is it religious oppression of adherents to fanatical sects preaching problematic gospels of social upheaval? No. China is unparalleled in that respect. Could it be the case that Russia and others kill more than they imprison? Unprovable, though quite likely, but something else is at work. What then? America does not incarcerate because of the religious beliefs of criminals. America does not execute its criminals for their religious beliefs. *America has a huge prison population because its criminals have no religious beliefs.*

Hand it to the communists. They are honest. They hate God and they say so. If you say that you like God, they will throw you in jail. If you still like God after that, they will kill you. They make no apologies, offer no explanations, other than to say that God is not allowed. They got rid of God from their countries, and if you want to stand by God, then, by golly, they will get rid of you, too.

Americans, on the other hand, are hypocrites. We spew platitudes about religious liberty, and the pilgrim fathers seeking a land to practice their faiths freely, and in God we trust, and all that. Then we ban prayer from the schools and pass civil laws offensive to the divine law expressed in the natural law and self-censor ourselves so that businesses will not mention Christ at Christmas. After having given lip service to God and then silencing him in the schools, in the public square, and in the marketplace, we then are shocked to find that there are fiends among us who take us at our word. Our Godless rhetoric produces men who behave Godlessly!

So we put them in jail. By the busload. We preach incessantly that none needs adhere to any given faith. We legislate with the ideal in mind that no absolute norm exists for human behavior. We train our children to value diversity. So, some men act on the faith that they may help themselves to other men's property—and we imprison them. Other men follow the relative law that what feels good is good—and we imprison them. There is a diverse mode of thought among us that has decided that your life is worth less than the thirty-seven bucks in your pocket—and we imprison such freethinkers on death row for twenty years before finally getting around to killing them so that they will kick the bucket before their Social Security benefits would have kicked in.

Our government should be impeached. Not for high crimes and misdemeanors, but for malpractice. Having rid us of the scourge of God, our government has imposed on us the scourge of the Godless. Whether it is the fear of being mugged or the risk of having one's life savings wiped out in a multibillion-dollar pyramid scheme concocted by a "white-collar" crook or the danger inherent in turning over the levers of power to amoralists bent on violating the sixth and ninth Commandments, our nation has fallen into the hands of bandits. The fools who claimed that they could bring men more happiness apart from God should at least have the decency to admit that their Godless form of happiness bears a strange resemblance to what earlier and saner eras called misery. The fools who swallowed this lunacy should demand their tax money back, apologize to the children they have permitted to be warped by this childish refusal to obey authority, and then beg that divine authority to restore order, not at the point of a gun, but upon bended knees below bowed heads.

What few in the nation are willing to admit, however, is that our government is ourselves. As the wise wag once said, a democracy gets the government it deserves. The misery, insanity, and willfulness afflicting us is self-inflicted. Man can make a mess like this, but man unaided by grace can not clean up this kind of a mess. As long as God is denied any part in the governance of a nation, that nation will be ungovernable—the behavior of children in schools, of spouses in marriages, and of gangs on the streets is testimony to how the ungovernable will conduct themselves in the absence of external discipline and self-control.

Godless crooks are in jail because they are Godless. Godless governments are in power because Godless citizens put them there. Godless citizens are Godless because they have apostatized from the Catholic Church. Apostates who will not repent will get their wish—living a life in time on earth without God will result in an eternity in hell without God. If you do not want God to rule your country, you will find yourself under the rule of the Godless, now and forever. Whether in time or in eternity, the only alternative to the rule of God is being ruled by satan. Hence, the evil empire, Godless by definition, holds soil from the Atlantic to the Gobi, from Norway to the Veldt, from the Land of the Midnight Sun to the land of penguins, and from sea to shining sea. There is a prison without walls, a prison far larger than a whole continent, a prison from which there is no escape—and a Judgment from a Judge from whom there is no appeal. Obey any rule other than His, and discover the true meaning of justice. Obey Him and know mercy.

2. My belly and my god: Materialism as the measure of man

"Blessed are the poor." "The poor you will always have with you." "There is no man who hath left house or brethren or sisters or father or mother or children or lands, for my sake and for the Gospel, who shall not receive an hundred times as much, now in this time: houses and brethren and sisters and mothers and children and lands, with persecutions: and in the world to come life everlasting."

Jesus Christ, God in the flesh, said all of those things. Ordinary people with ordinary lives and ordinary attitudes about life heard Jesus say those things with their own ears. What they did not hear was the poor being cursed for their failure to be rich. God did not direct His hearers to seek wealth as the supreme blessing, and eradicating the poor as being the greatest service possible for man. The reward promised by the Lord Jesus did not omit reference to the ordinary reality of human suffering while in this world.

By way of warning, Jesus also said, "A rich man shall hardly enter into the Kingdom of Heaven." He explained that Dives received good things in his life, but after death was subject to unrelieved torment. The Son of God made it abundantly clear that the whole world is too small a paycheck for one's immortal soul.

Capitalism's insatiable lust for riches and communism's demand that a paradise for workers exist on earth, can only make sense in a universe bereft of God. If the highest good is the possession of material goods, then the disdain in which rich capitalists hold the poor and the crime of poverty punished by the communists are defensible attitudes and policies. If, on the other hand, ***God is,*** then no amount of labor to gain property and no extremity of effort to redistribute property is of ultimate worth. At best such labors and efforts may be used in the service of aiding men to gain a claim among the poor whose inheritance is the Kingdom of Heaven, and to assist nations in sharing their wealth so as to be counted among the peoples who shall enter the New Jerusalem on the Last Day. But the raw material of capitalists' capital and the communists' community property is the stuff of which moths make meals, rust devours, and time will utterly consume in its own end.

This is a harsh reality which, if confronted too directly, results in despair among those who have no spiritual lodestar. So in order to take their minds off being moth fodder, rust bait, and temporary workers of the most fleeting kind, capitalists and communists turn their attention to eating: filling their bellies with food and drink, filling their eyes with immodesty, filling their minds with lying philosophies, filling their hearts with passing passions based in the flesh, and filling their days with distractions from the inescapable horror of filling their graves with themselves. "Vanity of vanities, all is vanity and a chase after the wind" applies to whatever has no existence beyond this world and everything attached to it.

"Sin" is a word exiled from the speech of free marketers and party members alike. "Crime", however, is on the lips of legislators, secular moralists, and concerned citizens in whatever conversation pertains to the obstacles to rebuilding Eden in our day. Criminals in this mindset do not harm the soul or pose a threat to salvation; it is the body and the body politic which is to be safeguarded. Infractions against the social code, as opposed to the offenses against the divine majesty which constitute sin, are the ills to be remedied, the evils to be rooted out, and the injustice to be punished.

Contrary to the errors of the materialists, however, crime is not a symptom of poverty. Communists seek to eradicate poverty as a contradiction to socialist perfection, while capitalists excoriate the poor for having a lack of initiative, wanting in character, and simply being lazy. Communists and capitalists agree that the contrarian and the unmotivated will descend to lives predicated on harming true believers and the industrious. The poor are criminalized among communists as a threat to right thinking, and among capitalists as a drag on the juggernaut of the consumerist economy. In both instances, poverty is attacked as an evil to be ruthlessly expunged.

What each set of errors, capitalist or communist, fails to realize is that it is not poverty which leads to ill thinking or lethargy in production. The existence of poor men who grow up to be wise men and rich men who grow up to be embezzlers is proof positive that the material dearth of the home is not what determines moral fiber or worth to mankind. Yes, there are fools who are poor and philanthropists with the means to execute their beneficence, but neither the idiocy nor the largesse depends upon a material source. What the fiend lacks or the philanthropist possesses has nothing to do with property, and everything to do with the soul.

Extolling material sufficiency as an end in itself results in both the communist and capitalist systems ignoring the necessity of a spiritual component by which to direct the production and distribution of material goods. Without that component, i.e. , the true Faith of the Catholic Church, not only will production be stymied, as happens in socialist economies, and consumption become cancerous, as occurs in capitalist economies, but charity will wither, as is seen in the innumerable nations of the earth, neighborhoods of cities, and refugee camps in the middle of nowhere where homeless families starve in body and soul. Men without a transcendent *raison d'etre* will not labor with their life's blood for transitory goods; they will not hesitate to inflict suffering on other men who stand in the way of enjoying whatever material goods they do posses.

The fall of the Soviet Bloc occurred in large part because its economic system collapsed beneath the weight of material demands without a means of supply, and spiritual demands that none would acknowledge. The capitalist world is being consumed from within by a glut of material commodities utilized increasingly as impersonal means to exert power over persons who are ever on the edge of rioting in the schoolyard after lunch, in the streets after a sports team wins a championship or on the grounds of the courthouse when an unfavorable verdict is rendered. The communists could not keep control by starving their populations, while the capitalists are finding it ever harder to maintain control over a citizenry of addicts who are ravenous for bigger and bigger fixes.

Love of money motivates the capitalist. Love of the things that only money can buy motivates the communist. The root of capitalism's lust after capital and communism's lust after capital's harlot mother, the means of producing capital, is that which is the root of all evil, *i.e.*, the love of money. All economic systems demand capital as a means for pursuing the ends of what humans call good. Only materialism in its fraternal-twin guises of capitalism and communism pursues the means as an end in itself. Capitalism exists to produce ever more capital; communism exists to posses ever more control over the means that produce capital and its bastard offspring.

Industry, science, and market manipulation are employed by communist and capitalist alike in order to attain their common end of capital and the fruits of capital. Industry is developed so that more things might be produced. Science is advanced so that the production of things might be improved and increased. The market is controlled so that the production of things and things themselves might be more readily distributed with an eye toward creating more demand and/or dependence on things and their production. Whether it is a five-year plan of a soviet co-op or a multinational corporation's R&D budget, the end result desired is the same: to ensure that things are made, that the production of things increases, and that things do not lose their hold on the appetites of the men that use the things, make the things, and beg for more of the things.

Soviet Russia could legitimately propagandize about the surfeit of luxury cars on the streets of America while on the sidewalks alongside those streets homeless men looked at gutters as their commode. Americans could honestly critique the failures of the Soviet system by pointing to the state-of-the-art weapons systems deployed throughout Europe and Asia while Muscovites stood on line for hours at a time to buy bread. The things that either communism or capitalism produce in largest numbers and at the greatest profit or with the highest priority are rarely the things most conducive to human enrichment. Soviet unmanned space craft are quite a bit more reliable than the American space shuttle has proved to be, but the post-Soviet states know little about how to encourage private citizens to fend for themselves to produce the most basic of daily needs. American schools have few peers around the world in the achievement of generating athletes who will go on to become multimillionaires in professional sports, but few industrial countries are as embarrassed as is America at the dearth of high school graduates able to relate data pertaining to national history, to compute basic algebra equations, or to express themselves in a language other than their native tongue. And what truly unites nations East and West in the modern world is a refusal to see that regardless of scholastic aptitude, technological prowess, or commercial influence on popular culture, nothing is of any worth where the human person is reduced to a collection of physical demands, emotional appetites, and intellectual delusions predicated on defining human beings as merely physical, emotional, and mortal.

Where God is denied, the merely human provides no acceptable alternative. The loss of a sense of the spiritual is not compensated by overemphasizing the material. Without an absolute measure of that which is good and right and true, all human endeavors will decay into a disordered pursuit of the ephemeral, the unsatisfying, and the deadly. In fact, the inescapable conclusion to be reached by a materialist estimation of reality is that death is the ultimate reality. The death of God proclaimed by Friedrich Nietzsche was not imposed upon the Omnipotence. When men decided that God's condition was terminal, man was dealt a death sentence. God is wholly unaffected by the disease of apostasy, but men who succumb to this illness rarely recover. It remains to be seen if the remedy of repentance will be taken by either the apostates adhering to the atheism of the market or by the apostates who offer atheistic worship to the labor of the worker. Death is the only outcome when faith in the living God no longer lives in the hearts of men. Men who have no faith in God can not but lose the will to live and will end by dismissing the good of, having a disdain for, and being disgusted by life itself.

3. When you're tired of God, you're tired of life: Abortion for all ages

Communism as a political system depends upon socialism as an economic system. The two are inseparable. No communist state exists that is not a socialist economy; no socialist economy is wholly free of communist elements in the body politic. Few remember or admit that the Nazi government headed by Adolf Hitler was a socialist regime, the National *Socialists.* The fact that Stalin and Hitler hated one another, demons never get along, lulls most uncritical thinkers into the fallacy that the two despots held antithetical beliefs on matters of human governance. No, Virginia, there is no third way between the antipodes of Christ and antichrist. Hitler's socialists and Stalin's socialists did not get along because of a small adverbial distinction: Hitler wanted a socialism predicated on a pan-Germanic Aryan supremacy, which is to say *national* socialism; Stalin desired a socialist workers' paradise exported without heed of borders or nationality, that is, *international* socialism. Neither wanted free markets or capitalist magnates or private property or interests beyond socialism or obeisance paid to God almighty and His one true religion, Roman Catholicism.

Oddly enough, Franklin Delano Roosevelt did not disagree with this set of undesirables. Nor have any of his successors in the Oval Office these last sixty years. Nor was there much by way of opposition in the fifty or so years prior to the New Deal to the notion of materialist, modernist, and Godless government of men, by men, and for men. In the period that produced Lenin, Stalin, and Hitler, the United States of America imposed the Federal Reserve system, the federal income tax, the Social Security pension, and a foreign policy based on the exportation of the principles which produce such results, all at the expense of the preservation of states' rights, property rights, individual rights, and the rights of God and the freedom and exaltation of Holy Mother Church.

National Socialists manipulated borders and moved populations in order to establish the *lebensraum* demanded by the Aryan birthright. International socialists manipulated borders, moved populations, and erected puppet governments to guarantee the hegemony of the ideals at home in Moscow over all of Eastern Europe and most of Asia. The United States of America utilized the positivistic assertion of Manifest Destiny to eliminate American Indians as sovereigns over their ancient homelands; upheld the Constitutional provision of owning men as chattel to relocate millions of Africans to the New World to provide cheap labor, then violated Constitutional principles to force states to free the slaves; and interfered repeatedly in the affairs of governments throughout the Western Hemisphere from its intrusions into Mexico throughout the nineteenth century and continuing in America's unhelpful actions in Cuba, Chile, Argentina, Grenada, Panama, Nicaragua, and Haiti.

Hitler re-established Germany's military, modernized and rebuilt its industry, and projected its worldview and will far beyond its borders. The Soviets' militarism was second to none. They developed industry to support their military even at the expense of producing food for their large population, and gained influence in every country on earth by dint of their philosophical, economic, and sociological novelties in opposition to and contempt for Western civilization as nurtured in Christendom. America's military defeated Hitler's; its industry out-produced the communist world *in toto*; and Christ the King receives no more respect or obedience in the laws that come from Washington than from the tyranny that spewed from the Kremlin. The thousand-year reign of the Reich perdures in America; the errors of Russia are firmly embraced by Americans. Any who think that Our Lord Jesus Christ, the King of Heaven and earth, and Our Lady the Blessed Virgin Mary, the Queen of Heaven and earth, are any more pleased at the policies and actions of the United States than with the evil and errors of the Nazis or the Soviets is either delusional, ignorant, or imbued with the atheism that denies Our Lord and Our Lady.

Abortion, vivisection, forced sterilization, experimentation on unwitting human subjects, and euthanasia were part of the horrors of the Nazi era in Germany. Abortion, vivisection, forced sterilization, experimentation on unwitting human subjects, and euthanasia were part of the horrors of the Soviet Union. Abortion, vivisection, forced sterilization, experimentation on unwitting human subjects, and euthanasia were part of the horrors pursued by state and federal authorities in the United States during the period of Nazi ascendance and Soviet aggression. Abortion, vivisection, forced sterilization, experimentation on unwitting human subjects, and euthanasia are not repudiated *in principle* by the governments housed in Berlin, Moscow, or Washington here at the beginning of the twenty-first century. Abortion, vivisection, forced sterilization, experimentation on unwitting human subjects, and euthanasia are legal or tolerated in Germany, Russia, and the United States of America even now.

Through the penal system, medical research, and phantom rights within constitutional law, moderns in nations founded on either capitalist or communist ideologies have no problem taking innocent life, mutilating the healthy, sacrificing the weak to save the strong, embracing death in the pursuit of life, or committing self-murder as a means to assert self-dignity. Nothing within the tenets of capitalism or communism forbids such actions. Everything within communism and capitalism is meant to support the attainment of human willfulness regardless of its cost in human life. Capitalism and communism do not differ in the slightest detail in their refusal to accept a higher law from God to place restraints on the actions that men deem legal though the divine law calls them abominable. Inalienable rights to life, liberty, and the pursuit of happiness bereft of belief in God and His supreme law of love have unarguably resulted in a world made miserable by its misdefining of the nature of happiness; a veritable police state in which one's spouse and children, other citizens, and terrorists from points unknown are the enemies from which the government is incapable of protecting anyone except by depriving all of liberty by assuming everyone is a felon; and an ubiquitous attack on life in the womb, on life within weak bodies, and on life at its end in old age.

Why do materialists, whether communist or capitalist, who agree on so little, agree that babies can be aborted, sick and old people can be eliminated, and healthy people can be mutilated in obedience to a parent's will, the government's will, or their own will? The final cause that leads in this dance with death is disbelief in God. Materialists, socialists of whatever gradation toward communism or capitalism, serve a variety of efficient causes in the accomplishment of their common final cause of atheism. These efficient causes amount to differences in means, not ends. They are distinctions without differences.

Nazis killed people because they did not like them. It was eminently personal. Hitler did not like to share the earth with Jews, Catholics, blacks, sick people, and non-Aryans. So he had them offed. Since he was of the semi-divine race, he was able to execute his vicious will in the name of virtue. The Soviets in the forties and fifties and the Chinese today saw, and see, certain classes of weak, unproductive, disbelieving malcontents as a threat to the perfection of the workers' paradise, so the party decreed and decrees their destruction. Sometimes it is babes in the womb, sometimes it is girl babies outside of the womb, and always it is someone who is simply in the way, so they are removed. The communist attitude toward them is almost something of an afterthought: obstacles are not to be hated, but simply overcome. That attitude is seen by some as an improvement over Nazi hatred.

If indeed such an attitude is an improvement, its consummation is found in the anti-life ethos of the West, also known as the culture of death. Planned Parenthood kills babies—for a profit. Governments and research universities kill babies—for a profit. Adult children kill their enfeebled parents—for a profit. Spouses kill their incapacitated mates—for a profit. The despondent, the terminally ill, and the mistaken kill themselves—for a profit. "Profit" might be quarterly dividends, donations from true believers, scientific "advances", peace of mind, votes, an insurance policy, a house bequeathed in a will, the ability to remarry, or to escape from the demands that life places on beings with free will. Regardless of how "profit" is defined in this mindset, it has nothing whatsoever to do with that which pleases God. It is simply business. Nothing personal, Sir, it's just business. Death in the modern world is nothing but simply business as usual. There is no reference here to the Lord of life, to choosing life, to eternal life and its Author, God. life, on earth and in Heaven, is not the highest good. All is determined by a strange and fervent pursuit of the grave. Life is expendable and debatable, but absolute laws are passed to forbid any from standing in the way of sending someone prematurely to the tomb.

This universal acquiescence to death is not a personal vendetta. None claims to hate children. None admits to hating his dying mother. None suggests that the comatose patient is the object of contempt. All aver that love or at least compassion is operative. All protest a desire for nothing but what is best for everyone involved. Note that hatred of God, hatred of life, and a hatred for bearing one another's burdens are in no way disallowed by this impersonal approach to compassion, love, and dealing death. The "fetus" is not a person, the patient in a "persistent vegetative state" is not a person, the Creator of Heaven and earth is not a person. None of this desire for death should be taken personally, because the unborn, the dying, and the Lord of life are not to be regarded as persons. The only persons to be addressed are those whose wish is to rid themselves of the presence of the non-persons in the womb, in the ICU, in the Synagogue, in the Gulag, and on the throne of Heaven.

4. The Fifty-Percent Solution: Marriage is Made in Heaven. Divorce is Made in . . .

Hell is not displeased that man has decided that Holy Matrimony is no longer understood by man to be primarily for the begetting and raising of children for the glory of God. It would appear to be the case that most of mankind is not displeased by this paradigm shift in man's belief on the nature of the fundamental human society. If the primary fruit of marriage, children, and the subjects who effect marriage, adults, and the beneficiaries of the unconditional love nurtured in marriage, the aged, can be eliminated by abortion and euthanasia, then, of course, marriage itself can be eliminated by divorce, cohabitation, homosexuality, self-abuse, polyamory, contraception, and fornication. The popular stat is that half of the time, married couples find some excuse, though little reason, to terminate their unions. The other half of the time, married couples accept deadly divorce as a viable alternative should married life become unendurable. Rather than the divinely revealed *duty* to remain married, the capricious demand for the *right* to be divorced is defended by the state, by divorcing couples, and even by most couples who remain married. "The fifty-percent solution" ending half of all new marriages in divorce is a remedy concocted by the half-witted.

Life itself if not inviolate means that all manifestations of life are subject to destruction under whatever conditions are deemed acceptable by the self-appointed, non-divine arbiters of life. If babies can be killed, then old people can be killed. If babies can be killed in the search for cures for incurable illnesses, then victims of incurable illness can be killed when a cure is lacking. If the fruit of marriage is expendable, then marriage itself is expendable. Neither is life that flows from the married state an absolute necessity, nor is the married state as a way of life necessarily an absolute. Babies' future birthdays and future anniversaries of a marriage may both be terminated before they arrive. The infants' life may be ended before it reaches fruition and so may be the couple's life in common before it reaches its conclusion. Death may come to the bond before death parts husband and wife.

Divorce is the abortion of a person. The two-who-become-one is destroyed. Before man was comfortable with massacring babes in wombs, he had to get used to the idea of slaughtering wedded bliss in homes. Just as abortion is advocated as a means for freedom for men and women to pursue their personal desires, divorce is advocated as a means for society to pursue its desire that the state, not the family, be the indissoluble bond that forges unity among men. In fact, abortion is a means to this end of family bonds as dispensable aspects of human life and the absolute power of the state as indispensable to the experience of mankind. Killing babies is just another way that the Godless state accomplishes its desire to kill marriages and thus to kill families. Divorce kills a person and makes the killing of persons—the wedded couple, the couple's family, and the unborn, the ill, and the aged—palatable as an ordinary way of life for the society that accepts such atrocities. Divorce is part of the culture of death.

Abortion is the most extreme ill that breeds in the sterility of the family destroyed by divorce. Before abortion comes from divorce, another ill besets marriage with its deadly effects. The couple willing to kill their babies before they are born are willing to prevent those babies from being conceived. Abortion is the last resort of the contraceptive mentality. Most couples or individual women who elect to kill babies were quite comfortable with the idea of depriving their children of life before life could begin long before the decision to abort was made. The idea that human life does not begin until after birth is dependent upon the lie that human life is not worth beginning. Whether that beginning is prevented at conception or in the birth canal is moot once it is acceptable to believe that human life is better not to have been in the first place. The prophylactic is no less deadly to human bodies and the human spirit than is the saline solution or the forceps or the suction device. No one could kill a baby who exists who was not convinced that a baby should not exist in the first place. It is not at all rational for an aborting couple or individual to refuse to contracept a child; the contraceptive mentality can not in the least object to the conclusions reached by those who desire abortion on demand. If life is not an absolute good to be received regardless of the difficulties it might present, then ending that life before it begins at birth is no more to be refused than ending that life before it begins at conception. If life is a good that may not be deprived actively by abortion, then it is not to be denied through contraception, and is instead a good to be pursued actively in the conjugal act.

Objectivists, Democrats, Republicans, Anglicans, Lutherans, atheists, and communists all agree that what man has joined man may put asunder. They all agree that what man has joined is not accomplished by the irreversible will of God. There is no nation on earth that accepts divorce that has not come to embrace abortion. The few nations that held out against divorce were those that longest rejected abortion. Their acceptance of divorce in the civil law has led to at least a tolerance if not an encouragement of abortion in the laws of the state. Neither capitalism nor communism, not democracy or totalitarianism, no "high" church or "low" church has been equal to the task of keeping divorce on demand from leading to abortion on demand. None of the systems of modern thought is in the least committed to eliminating divorce as an ill that erodes social bonds and harms individuals. Quite the opposite, divorce is demanded as a right, celebrated as a matter of public policy, and in at least one case offered as the justification for a schism within Christendom leading to national apostasy and heresy.

The state is human society writ large. The family is human society expressed in its fundamental and essential unit. Human society can exist without the state, but is inconceivable without the family. The well-being of the state depends upon the health of the family. Divorce, contraception, and abortion are nothing less than suicidal policies pursued by both elements of human society, the state and the family. Where the state inflicts or tolerates divorce, contraception, and abortion on the family, there is an attack on the common good which should be resisted by every man who would not be a slave. Where the family surrenders to this attack or, God forbid, joins in this attack, not only will there be nothing left of the family, but the state itself will eventually cease to be. In its place will be anarchy, brute force, and the tyranny of sin and its wages, death.

This writer labors under the notion that whether the nation involved is Sweden or China or the United States, both the attack and the surrender described in the paragraph immediately preceding this one is very much underway. He is not averse to correction. That correction would need to explain the principles of communism or capitalism, in democracy or despotism, in atheism or religious indifferentism that forbid divorce, contraception, abortion, and their attendant destruction of the human family to the detriment and final destruction of human society. Said correction would be received as valid if even one example can be shown where a capitalist or communist, a democratic or totalitarian, humanist or ecumenical entity of any kind was able to advance its philosophy successfully without appeal to the divine absolute and still preserve human life in all stages, the inviolability of the family, and human liberty within the state. Please offer some indication that somewhere within modernity there is an *absolute* refusal to call innocent life dispensable, to see marriage as onerous, and the state as all-powerful.

As of this writing, the United States of America has enacted policies on a national level within the last two years that determine that sodomites may enter into the institution formerly known as matrimony, that caregivers may starve and dehydrate persons in their care with a will toward active euthanasia, and that the tax dollars paid by citizens to the federal government may be used to fund the destruction of infant children for the purposes of medical research. Stalin had no problem with *in utero* infanticide. Hitler did not balk at medical experiments on unwilling subjects and state-sanctioned starvation of non-persons. And now the United States Supreme Court in the case of *Lawrence vs. Texas* has officially condoned the sin of Sodom, declaring it a civil right. A sin that cries to Heaven for vengeance, on earth clamors for - and is granted - a marriage license.

Families whole, intact, and suffused with love echo the reality of the natural law, the authority of the Catholic Church, and the revelation of God's salvific will for the good of mankind. None in the family so devoted to truth and ultimate reality would desire anything that would result in diminution, harm, or destruction of the family. Members of the family might be persuaded to accept some of the principles or provisional goals of capitalism or communism, but would disavow them at the moment it became evident that such principles and goals were at enmity with the family, in denial of the natural law, disobedient to the Church, or offensive to the Divine Majesty. Because this frame of mind is the necessary condition of healthy family life, the family is beyond the pale according to the fiends who direct and populate the modern nation state. Whether in the name of the Constitution, the party, or the market, modern men will feel no compunction about sacrificing the interests of the family if they come into conflict with the self-interest of *homo divinus*. A holy family understands that the state, the economy, and social welfare are meant to nurture the home. The unholy minions of capitalism and communism demean the family as being merely elements in economics, as being as ephemeral as the walls of the houses in the subdivisions where they are confined, and as being ultimately expendable to the caprices of immorality, government policy, and whatever progress might mean tomorrow. Neither the communist nor the capitalist can pretend to conceive the family in the context of the Kingdom of God on earth destined for eternal life in Heaven; neither the communist nor the capitalist *desires* as motivation, method, or meaning for the conduct of life on earth the goal of living forever in Heaven.

Apologists for modernity and capitalism within the Catholic Church insist that capitalism is compatible with defined dogmas declared by the magisterium, with the tenets of natural law, and with the incontrovertible truths expressed in the divine positive law. Catholics such as this writer are insulted with the epithets of "socialist" or "unpatriotic" or "ignorant" for failing to see the good brought by modern democracy, for calling into question the nature of the supposed freedoms granted by governments elected through popular sovereignty without reference to Christ the King and His Vicar the Pope, and for insisting on a return to an understanding of human life predicated on the essential nature of the human family and divine worship to the happiness of man on earth and his beatitude in Heaven. This writer is waiting for an explanation of how the separation of the state from the Church has lent support to the absolute sanctity of life from conception to natural death. He desires to see proof that democratically elected governments and their citizens are committed to prohibiting divorce and the destruction of the family as mandated by God when He physically walked this earth two thousand years ago. Where is town life seen as dependent on, supportive of, and enriching to the agrarian norm that was operative throughout the whole world until the middle of the twentieth century, rejected simultaneously then by capitalist democracies and totalitarian communist states alike? If indeed there is a difference on the moral plane between capitalist consumption of goods and communist redistribution of goods, it is high time that man be given evidence of the existence of this singular truth which heretofore has been an amazingly well kept secret. Other than the fact that both communists and capitalists seek to produce as many material things as possible with the capitalists having far more success thereat, none has convincingly demonstrated that aught else separates the two systems in their impact on the understanding of the sanctity of human life, the controls placed on the conduct of human life, and the ultimate end of human life. In short, it needs to be shown whether and how communism and capitalism differ in their ability to make known the Kingdom of God at hand *now* and which, if either, is pursuing the same goals revealed by Jesus Christ, offered by the Holy Ghost, and taught within the immemorial doctrines of the Bride of Christ, the Catholic Church.

5. If only ignorance were bliss: Compulsory education

Many moderns would hear sinister overtones in the old Catholic axiom, "Give me your child for twelve years and he will be mine for life." To the progressive sophisticate of the contemporary age, such seems steeped in brainwashing and coercion. The fact that the Church taught the child to think for himself in accordance with the beliefs revealed by God is received with a large dollop of skepticism in today's freethinking minds. It is not admitted that education according to this bent producing the likes of St. Augustine, St. Thomas Aquinas, Dante, Shakespeare, Palestrina, Michelangelo, and Paschal is thus vindicated. Instead, the modern cynic would pretend that the accomplishments of such accomplished men were made in spite of, rather than because of, the cultural patrimony transmitted through the Catholic Church and their personal response to the Faith taught by the Apostles and their successors in the episcopate.

Setting aside the astronomical illiteracy rates, the metal detectors and armed guards, and the unwed pregnancies commonplace in the average big-city school in the United States of America at the dawn of the twenty-first century, one still is to be humored for wondering whether or not modernity can hold its own in a competition with antiquity in the task of producing men of letters, cultivating a culture enriching not only to the learned but to the simple, and recognizing and surviving its own vices. Keep in mind that George Washington was not taught in a public school nor was Karl Marx the product of an egalitarian university open to all regardless of ability to afford tuition. Many have commented on the alarming reality that modernity is living off of the capital inherited from its forebears in antiquity, that moderns, lacking principles to live by, have exhausted their principle and are consuming, not increasing, the capital. The question for the immediate future is whether or not the period since the end of Christendom has produced new principle, new principles, indeed, new capital, in the realm of ideas and ideals from which posterity may draw in the centuries to come.

St. Augustine writing against the Manicheans, St. Thomas' employment of the scholastic method of objections and responses, Paschal's need to demonstrate the rationality of the Faith all point to the fact that the Church has never enjoyed a monopoly on occupying the public platforms of the public discourse on truth. Catholic thinkers have always engaged atheists, heretics, and doubters honestly and openly. The very nature of that which Catholicism seeks to share and that which she must combat requires the ability to address that which falls outside of Catholic categories. The Catholic Church is catholic not only in its extent through history, through geography, and through political systems, but she is catholic in her applicability to every problem, proposed solution, and challenge—intellectual, emotional, physical, or spiritual—that has ever been part of the human experience. Not art, not science, not poetry, not government, not industry, not romance, not war, not death, not theory, not practice, not God Himself are outside of what the Catholic Church is able to engage in, expound upon, and educate about, for, to, and with her children.

When modern education declares that the Church and her Lord are off limits, practically all else must be jettisoned as well. None can pretend to understand the merits and demerits of Beethoven's *Missa Solemnis* without first appreciating what Christ established as the Mass for all time on Holy Thursday. Islam's threat to the West in the early twenty-first century makes no sense to anyone who does not study the origins of Islam in war, avarice, and Mahomet's unbelief in Jesus Christ and His Body the Catholic Church in the seventh century. The peculiar period of German history under the Nazis is an enigma without a key unless one gives heed to the rebellion of the Catholic priest Martin Luther four centuries before the rising of the Fuhrer. Dubbing the Woolworth's building in New York a "cathedral of commerce" is absurd when one has seen the light through the windows at Chartres, walked beneath the dome in Florence, paused in prayer on the piazza at St. Mark's in Venice, felt vertigo while contemplating the heights of the cathedral in Ulm, or touched the bronze foot of St. Peter in Rome. Pilgrims seeking to establish their shining city on the hill in New England would have known nothing of such imagery unless the Catholic Church had transmitted with authority the full canon of Sacred Scripture which the pilgrims held in a degraded state. The workers' paradise sought in the communist world owes much to the original paradise lost by the first Adam and restored by the second Adam on the Cross and through His Body, the Catholic Church—unless the workers' paradise denies the Father of both Adams, in which case something far different from paradisal bliss awaits party members in eternity.

It is a firmly held belief and teaching of the Catholic Church that the primary teachers of children are their parents. The ultimate goal of parental guidance of children is to make them fit for Heaven, or as everyone remembers from his catechism, *to know, love, and serve God in this life so as to be happy with Him forever in Heaven*. Within the Rite of Baptism, through a variety of authoritative encyclicals of the Popes, and Catholic common sense—*sensus Catholicus*—members of the Body of Christ are assured of, admonished to, and assisted in the fulfillment of their responsibility to foster the adopted children of God with the same solicitude and care with which the Blessed Virgin Mary and St. Joseph attended to the only-begotten Son of God. This is a truth rooted in the natural law, expressed in ecclesial law, and reflective of divine law. No human power has the authority to usurp parents' right to educate their children, and indeed, nature, the Church, and God Himself are powerless to rescind this law.

Collectivist Training Center 1515/b and P.S. 101 endeavor to do that which is impossible for God. Compulsory education in the modern world not only means that children must receive an education and that children must leave their homes to receive it, but that children must be educated in ways and in content foreign and repugnant to their parents. Communists used to have re-education centers to make sure that adults with ideas deviant from the approved norm would see the error of their ways and seek conformity—on pain of being reformed in the gulag instead. School boards in the United States simply ignore parents who object to the filth and foolishness being inflicted upon their children. Neither the Soviet Union offered, nor do most American parents seek, an alternative to the coerced indoctrination of the impressionable minds entrusted to them.

Soviet children and parents at least had the bad excuse that they would be slaughtered, disappeared, starved, or all of the above if they did not toe the party line. American parents subscribe to a system of government that allows for private and parochial schools (which cost additional tuition on top of the taxes for the public schools they find offensive), parent and citizen oversight of school boards, and an elective process designed to remove officials who fail to effect the will of the voters and taxpayers. Why, then, American parents docilely submit themselves and their children to a range of options veritably Stalinistic in its breadth is a question that defies rational explanation.

For most modern parents and children anywhere in the entire world today, it is inconceivable to the imagination that education means something other than an institutional setting wherein the parents are tolerated bill payers rather than at least active participants or, as was once the case, the central authority and provider of the educational process. Homes wherein children are discouraged or forbidden from being educated are taxed in perpetuity to force those children—and their children's great-grandchildren—to be brainwashed apart from their parents. Laxity in morals and manners, which would be severely punished by parents in those homes, is taught as objective good to their children in the schools by teachers about whom one wonders whether or not their own children are raised with such dearth of courtesy and common sense. The notion of good and evil is, simultaneously and oxymoronically, taught as a matter of relativity, allowing then for the teaching of laxity as an objective good.

Despair, drunkenness, and depravity swamped the communist world as a result, leading to its economic, though not ideological, dissolution. Despair, drunkenness, and depravity swamp the capitalist world, able to fend off economic dissolution so long as no one asks the dangerous question of what is produced by a "service" "industry" and how capital is generated when few citizens are engaged in the production of actual consumer goods for consumers who largely receive their income from jobs in the "service" "industry". Are third-world slave laborers producing in sufficient quantity to be able to supply the demands of service sector employees in the West, who buy the slave-produced wares that make the magnates rich, who then pay slave wages to their servants in the service sector who by their insatiable consumption perpetuate the slavery of their third-world counterparts? Ask employees, shareholders, and pensioners of K-Mart, Enron, WorldCom, Parmalat, Tyco, Global Crossing, United Airlines, and the Social Security Administration what they think. *Never* ask an accountant for an accurate rendering of a corporation's profits. *Never* rely on the accounting of a system—economic, philosophical, or theological—that explains away the sin of usury.

It is no accident that Soviet ideology pertaining to the state providing all for all citizens has become the "social safety net" in the capitalist West to hedge against the weaknesses of the free market system. It is no accident that the former Soviet Union is now counted among the world's democracies and that Maoist China has formally endorsed private property as an element within its communist ideal. Modern earth is now plagued with the inhuman ideology of the Soviets grafted on the Godless economics of the West. Your children are in school so that they may become accustomed to this foul reality and learn to like it, demand it, and defend it to the death—of its enemies—if need be. The fact that the Russians, the Chinese, and the Americans all subscribe to these perverse ideals while still remaining the most friendly of enemies should disturb anyone who prefers freedom to servitude, thought to propaganda, and the human condition to bestial and ignorant bliss.

Children throughout the world are being trained in the skills and indoctrinated in the ideas that will make their own servitude not only palatable but preferable to real freedom. Ultimate truth, immaterial reality, and God Himself are actively denied in the secular governments and educational systems of *every nation on earth*—with the alarming exception of the Mohammedans adhering to their false worship taught by their false prophet Mahomet in the name of their false god Allah. East and West ignore at their own peril the threat posed by their indifferentism's inability to confront Mohammedan fervor and furor. Without an appeal to absolute truth from the one true God, revealed in His Son Jesus Christ, through His Body the Catholic Church, mankind is vulnerable not only to the inhuman horrors of materialism, but to the demonic fury of the jihad. Servitude will be the final condition regardless of the form of apostasy embraced by what was formerly Christendom: either to succumb to the brute force of the scimitars from the mosques, or to bow to the brute force of mindless liars insisting that bread and circuses are the best that men can expect in this, their one and only life. Discovering that man has another way of true life, Christ and Him crucified, is the only hope for moderns. It will be far too late to repent when the dead learn the harsh lesson that a very different experience awaits the men who placed their faith in the hopeless and loveless promises of mammon on earth.

6. *Su casa, mi casa:* The myth of private property in modernity

Freed slaves rarely got their forty acres and a mule after the American Civil War, a.k.a. the War of Northern Aggression, better described as the Framers'

Hens Came Home to Roost War. Comrades in Soviet Russia and girl babies in Red China and wage earners the world over have never had promised much less obtained that much property for their own personal use—six feet by three feet by six feet is about all the real estate they will ever be able to call their own, though but briefly. The ancient wisdom expressed in the phrase, "You can't take it with you," has undergone a metamorphosis in modernity into, "You won't get any in the first place." Pretty much the only modern entity that can say "I got mine," is governments and the cabals that run them. Thems that gots from thems that's got not rule according to the principle, "It is better to give—a beating with a stick—than to receive—the short end of that stick."

Few imagine that Pemex, the Tokyo Post Office, and the Green Bay Packers share a great deal in common, *i.e.* , they are a lot alike and they have a sweetheart arrangement for doing their business. Pemex in oil, the Tokyo Post Office in banking, and the Green Bay Packers of the NFL in football are government-owned corporations, supported by taxes, which directly compete with private businesses. Green Bay, Wisconsin, makes millions from the Packers, the nation of Mexico reaps billions from Pemex, and the people of Japan have trillions tied up in the Tokyo Post Office. Pemex was created by a socialist seizure of oil fields, the Packers perdure as a shameless concession to the socialist demand of government provision of everything imaginable including entertainment, and the socialist-minded Tokyo Post Office is considering going private—which could well destroy most of its competition due to its sheer size, remaining socialist in act if not in fact.

Americans are taught as mother's milk the civic virtue of free enterprise—except when it comes to Amtrak. No one in the land of the free and the home of the brave would countenance a government destruction of legal businesses—unless the businesses operated to make a profit on alcohol in the 1920s. Red-blooded Yankees insist that monopolies bear bad blood for the economy—making allowance, of course, for the entity of which the New York Yankees is the wealthiest single franchise. Only the thought police, never our leaders obeying our sacred Constitution, would ever retroactively penalize corporations that benefited the federal government with hundreds of billions of tax dollars for decades—pay no attention to that tobacco-industry lawsuit settlement behind the curtain. And it is unthinkable that the objective, neutral, disinterested authority emanating from Washington and the various state capitols would ever allow foreign sovereigns to operate, at a profit, types of businesses that American citizens are forbidden to engage—all those Indian casinos along the interstate are either figments of your imagination or elaborate fundraisers for textbooks at the local elementary school, kinda like a numbers racket, I mean, a lottery would be if such things existed.

Bolshevists not only erected collectivist enterprises, they not only seized private enterprises, they not only destroyed private enterprise, they managed to sap the enterprising spirit of what had once been an energetic and prosperous people. Vladimir Putin now reigns over a population that found distasteful the mouthings of pseudo-democrats like Gorbachev and Yeltsin, finding satisfaction instead in the re-establishment of despotism beneath the direction of the KGB. Thuggery in Soviet Russia was presided over by the state; the new thuggery is a matter of the mob. Either way, Russians are producing much less than their lands or factories are capable of, live in fear, and become angry at the suggestion that they have not stumbled onto the best way to live a life.

In China today, there is an enormous reserve of foreign currency in the control of the government. The average citizen, especially in the rural regions, still lives a positively third-world existence, but it seems that change is on the way. Those reserves of foreign currency are allowing the Chinese to buy consumer items in quantities heretofore unthinkable in communist Asia—automobiles, modern media entertainment, IBM computers. No, not a PC here or there, but the entirety of IBM; Big Blue is going red. All of this activity of allowing private property in principle but discouraging its acquisition in practice, of producing private property with an end in mind of producing hard currency, and of acquiring private property to the detriment of private competitors of China, Inc., is a matter of the very public Peoples' Republic of China seeking to increase, not repent, socialism. Red China is managing to accomplish through market acumen what Stalin never dreamed possible with tanks and missiles: defeating America at its own game. And should China determine that America will not acquiesce to the weapons of interest rates and currency devaluations, they have tanks and missiles, too. IBM computers are handy to have around when computing targets for leveraged stock buyouts, commodities futures trading, and the annihilation of population centers on distant continents.

Graft and corruption were veritably synonymous with being a Soviet apparatchik. Little has changed since Russia exchanged a government that used the KGB to terrorize its citizens for a government run by a KGB agent whose citizens perpetrate, gladly tolerate, or seek to rationalize the terror of the mob. Business in the aftermath of the dissolution of communism has not diminished the inefficiency of socialism nor removed the shackles from people who might wish to pursue their livelihood without undue interference from malign authorities, threats from lawless thugs, or the still-present specter of being incarcerated and having one's goods confiscated for running afoul of the political and/or economic interests of the powers-that-be. Free enterprise has not brought freedom to Russia. The free market, to the extent that it operates at all in Russia, has not brought about discernible differences in the daily life of most of its citizens, does not seem to wish to acknowledge its essential impotence to establish justice without a set of philosophical principles that encompass more than the merely technical applications of economics, and receives but weak criticism from its free-market, democratic counterparts in the West.

This might be the case because no more than a Russian citizen can start a business without budgeting bribes as an operating expense can an American home "owner" with a house in an historic district choose the color of that house's exterior or the configuration of the walls in its interior without permission from bureaucrats. Americans might be loath to point fingers at the limited property rights of Russians when looking at what happens to private energy companies in the United States that desire to drill for oil offshore or to refine oil near urban centers or to reduce dependence on oil with nuclear power or coal mining. Neither Soviet nor post-Soviet Russia has risen to the levels of food production accomplished there under the Czars; nor can American farmers sell their produce for prices sufficient to sustain a family, relying instead on government subsidies to compensate them for land left intentionally fallow, to keep prices artificially low (at about the same levels as they stood a half century ago), and to enable gargantuan corporations the opportunity to become the only profitable players in agriculture. Serfs forced from the land under the Czars and forced back on the land by the Soviets were no worse off by way of property rights than are "owners" of real estate in jurisdictions throughout the United States who stand to lose their properties under various court rulings that allow the exercise of eminent domain to seize private property for the purpose of increasing tax revenues for government entities by selling that property to other private citizens for development. It would seem that the free market is not the overarching principle guiding these activities, nor the rights of citizens, nor a search for ultimate truth and justice, but instead the through line is a matter of the state invading the home, sacking industry, sapping initiative, and grabbing land for no other reason than that it can and no one can stop it. Strangely enough, this governmental hubris is witnessed in communist states like North Korea, capitalist states like Japan, democratic states like Canada, and transnational states like the European Union, despotic states all.

Any political or economic system that recognizes Jesus Christ and His Body the Catholic Church under His Vicar the Pope as its ultimate authority provides the individual with an appeal to justice entirely independent of human error and caprice. Systems in denial of this truth leave the individual vulnerable to whoever gets his hands on the levers of power. Communists and capitalists claim to do all they do in the name of and for the sake of the people. When it comes right down to it, however, if the people have a grievance against what the communists or the capitalists decree is for their own good, the people find themselves voiceless and powerless to sue the state, to remove the politicians unjustly wielding the power of the state, or to convince their fellows in society of the tyranny they have unwittingly and faithlessly inflicted on themselves. The man of faith subjected to injustice on earth can hope for justice and mercy before the throne of God on Judgment Day; the faithless man and the society he establishes refuses justice in this, the only life recognized, and the victims of injustice have no recourse other than to docilely submit or to rebel. Alas! rebels are what created this morass in the first place. Rebellion by the faithless against the faithless will achieve no more justice than was obtained when the faithless rebelled against the Faith. Without that Faith, man has no hope for justice. To paraphrase Hilaire Belloc, the nations must come to the Faith or the nations will perish.

7. Rendering unto Great Caesar's Ghost!: The state's claim of the right to tax everything

Throughout the twentieth century communists seized railroads, mines, farms, palaces, universities, churches, and lives in the name of the all-powerful state. That ubiquitous entity then went on to enforce its malign will on industry, agriculture, governance, education, religious expression, and the family. The result was depression, famine, despotism, error, atheism, and death. Russians have not stigmatized Stalin, the Chinese have not disavowed Mao, and Western intellectuals still cast in their lot with Castro. Not content with holding all the cards in terms of power, with keeping a stranglehold on the instruments of communicating truth, and beholding all opposition as fair game for destruction, the communist world has sought to increase its hold on the hearts of fools who refuse to come to grips with the commission of nigh on two-hundred million murders, the wanton annihilation of whole cultures, and the assault on God Himself in the desecration of altars and sacrileges against the Blessed Sacrament as the price to be paid for the brave new world created in the image and likeness of godless men who would make themselves gods.

When the English colonists revolted against King George III, the effective tax rate was well under twenty percent. The English subjects under the Crown of Elizabeth II at one point were subjected to tax rates approaching eighty percent. Rather than revolting against such injustice, the English wealthy took their wealth elsewhere.

For instance, tax exiles from England came to the United States. The home of that historic tax revolt of the eighteenth century received with open arms the separated brothers fleeing still more tyranny in the mother country. Where the colonists found twenty percent or less inflicted by a foreign power an onerous and outrageous burden, their descendants saw fit to tax themselves as much as fifty percent during a period of tax *relief* mounted in the 1980s.

Taxes have been described as one of the two sure things in life, the other being death. This is not true. Where death levies are placed against the dead through estate taxes, taxes themselves never die. Death is subject to taxes, but taxes are immune to death. Even at the time of this writing there is an existing tax on telephone service in the United States that was established, in time of war, to defray the costs of national defense. The tax was imposed as a temporary measure, to be lifted when hostilities ceased. Indeed, hostilities ceased in the Spanish-American War more than a century ago, but that "temporary" tax has not been repealed. Neither has Congress tried very hard to end that tax, nor has the citizenry risen up against it. The more things change, the more they stay the same—when it comes to taxes and their increase. What simply does not change is the capacity of some men to convince other men to harm themselves for the profit of rogues, liars, and politicians.

Real estate used to be understood as the condition for wealth. If one had land, one had a place to build one's house. If one had land, one had the materials available to build one's house oneself. If one had land, one had the means to feed oneself. If one had land, one had the resources to feed animals and raise crops suitable for providing clothing for oneself and one's family. It did not take much land for a man and his family to be self sufficient, enriching to his neighbors, and able to pay fixed taxes.

Wealth in the modern age has been redefined to mean income. This might come from wages, from interest on loans (productive or usurious), from stock investments, from one's own business in trade, or from a combination of all of these. Real estate is not eliminated from this mix, but is much reduced in its relative worth within the economy. The idea of being "land rich and cash poor" only has significance where income has usurped the place of real estate as the condition for wealth.

Many modern economists insist that this is a change for the better insofar as it allows for an immense increase in wealth and in the numbers of people with access to it. Land is a strictly finite quantity. Cash and the activities that produce it are virtually infinite in their potential for growth.

Virtual reality far predates the digital age.

This thirst for ever more "wealth" on paper is tenable as long as there is something tangible being produced on the land. Where industry declines and production of durable goods decreases, and where the agrarian way of life becomes unsustainable and the production of fungible goods no longer profitable in terms of producing cash, there is a profound probability that a crisis of some kind will arise. If there are not real goods backing up the cash in circulation, then paper money will become less valuable than the trees that made possible the printing of the currency—it is far easier to heat one's house by chopping down one's tree than by emptying one's wallet. The Soviet Union experienced frequent famines, largely self-inflicted through economic ineptitude and wishful thinking, because of an unwillingness to accept that nothing can replace actual production of goods for human consumption. The United States of America in the 1870s, the 1930s, and the 1970s discovered what happens to the value of cash when there is an imbalance between what is produced and what is available for consumption, an imbalance caused by speculators exhibiting economic ineptitude and wishful thinking. Enron is the poster child of the early twenty-first century for ineptitude wedded to wishful thinking out of sheer greed. The more things change…

Shifting the economy from a basis in real estate to a foundation on currency directly leads to the modern penchant for confiscatory taxes and the oppression they invariably bring. If the king wants to place a levy on the wheat you produce, he can take only so much before you die, before his granaries are full, and before the population rises up against him—depriving him of wheat to eat, a means to pay the soldiers to put down the peasantry, and, quite likely, the idiot head that prompted his tyranny in the first place. It simply is physically impossible to take forty, fifty, eighty percent of a landed estate—or a rundown hovel for that matter.

But when a man's wealth is tied up in stocks, bonds, certificates of deposit, savings accounts, and a weekly paycheck, it is only a small matter of manipulating numbers in a ledger, filing some forms, or making an electronic transfer to relieve him of as much of his "wealth" as the government desires. The Sheriff of Nottingham would stand in awe at the ability of the IRS to take from the rich and give to the richer. No income is too large or too small to be entirely free from the rapine of Uncle Sam and his relatives in parliaments, juntas, and peoples' assemblies around the world. No self-respecting man of the middle ages, be he a peasant or a duke, would have stood by as the king attempted to take a third of his wealth from him, his cattle, his barns, his house, his fields. Modern men meekly fill out their documents of self-incrimination and pray that the government will mercifully permit the family to retain two-thirds of their paycheck, a bit of tax-deferred retirement savings, and a small write-off for their indentured servitude to the bank holding their mortgage.

When the king's men came at tax time, they came understanding that the *productive* property being taxed belonged to the subjects and the king had a right only to a relatively small levy for the purpose of maintaining his just rule in the kingdom. Most high-tech serfs do not realize that the income they call their own is the property of the government. Federal Reserve notes—dollar bills—are promissory notes from the United States government to private bankers. When the government needs to pay on those notes, it will demand from the income earner whatever the government deems necessary to meet its obligations. The government borrows to put money in circulation, prints the money in circulation, owns the money in circulation, and determines the value of the money in circulation. It is a federal crime not only to counterfeit the government's money, but to destroy the government's money. No one, no matter how wealthy, not Bill Gates himself, has money to burn, because it is not his to burn, but the government's to take when, as, and in the amounts it pleases.

From this shift in the understanding of wealth has grown a subservience to government unknown in the pre-modern world. It used to be the case that a man could feed, house, and clothe his family at will, owing the government no more than a predetermined amount that likely was the same in absolute terms as was paid by his great-grandfather. In time of national emergency, the government had to make a case that an extraordinary levy was in order and convince the taxed population that its new demands were just, reasonable, and *temporary*. The former norm was that a man could go about his business and the government would have to explain its interference, if any, in his private affairs.

Now the man who would mind his own business will go to prison or suffer very heavy fines if he were to tell the IRS that it is none of its business how much a private citizen might be worth. Instead of the government receiving its funds through taxes based on readily understood principles obvious to all involved, now the government decides how much money it wants to spend, demands that money from the taxpayer, creates a positively Byzantine apparatus to calculate and collect the money owed by the taxpayer, and punishes the taxpayer if he fails to convince the government that his efforts at self-incrimination are satisfactory. No longer does the government have to present a case to justify its demands, but the citizen must present a case that the demands have been met. The burden of proof is not on the government to demonstrate that it is warranted in intruding into the lives of the citizens; the burden of proof is on the citizen to demonstrate that he has not hidden any aspect of his life from the scrutiny of the government. The modern citizen is burdened with regulation, ordinances, and taxes that the humblest peasant under the cruelest king would have believed deserved only by the foulest criminals and the damned in hell.

Whether it is one-hundred percent stolen by the communists or more than half coerced by the capitalists, property, wealth, and income are no longer understood as a fundamental right to the citizen, but instead are seen as the fair object of confiscation by government taxation. The industrialization, urbanization, and secularization of modernity have removed the only defense of the citizen against such government tyranny. Without the sufficiency that comes from feeding, housing, and clothing one's own family, the citizen is vulnerable to economic manipulation, political exploitation, and legalized injustice. Landed wealth provides a firm foothold from which the individual and the family can preserve the right to live according to the goods discerned in natural law, taught in the doctrines of the Catholic Church, and revealed in God's plan of salvation. Men without productive skills, political voice, economic acumen, land of their own, and the faith will ever be in fear of starvation, homelessness, oppression, imprisonment, and an unmourned death.

A healthy economy conducive to holiness possesses balance and proportion. There is a ruling class and a free citizenry whose rights the rulers defend. There is an active exchange between town and country, where raw materials are produced, skilled labor adds value, and all people may be enriched by the products thus made available. There is a mix of economic activities predicated not on the demands of some phantom market, but on the real needs of human beings, laboring on the land, performing skilled crafts, practicing professional disciplines, engaging in honest trade, and offering all aspects of their livelihood faithfully to God. There is a sense of social responsibility among the wealthy who offer assistance to the poor out of a sense of charity that lives in their hearts as a virtue before it takes on flesh as an alms. There is sympathy for the poor, free from the contempt that comes from hubris, and instead remembering the words of the greatest poor man ever to live, "Blessed are the poor in spirit: for theirs is the Kingdom of Heaven!" Such poverty is not the impoverishment inflicted by economic injustice, political tyranny, and faithless pride, but is a gift to be sought from God, who tells us that we are meant to be His sons, and He wishes us to call on Him as Father.

Conclusion: Ten Commandments or Ten Irrelevancies? God decides.

Aristotle could be adapted by St. Thomas Aquinas because truth is in no way foreign to God's revelation. Romanesque architecture was assimilated by the Roman Church while Roman mythology was rejected, because the buildings of Rome could house the truths of the Faith but there was no room for that truth to live alongside of pagan lies. Polyphony is not a repudiation of chant, but rather an extension and complement to it. Much that is not explicitly a matter of religious belief has been "baptized" by the Church without diminishing the deposit of Faith or doing violence to the disciplines, cultures, and art forms founded in natural virtue and the natural law. The Catholic Church is the home for anything that is true, good, beautiful, truly human, and receptive of the true God.

As the Book of the Apocalypse relates, however, all that comes from "the fearful and unbelieving and the abominable and murderers and whoremongers and sorcerers and idolaters and all liars" shall have no place in the heavenly city, but instead will be cast into the lake of fire to suffer forever the second death. On earth that heavenly city has its gates at the doors of the Catholic Church. Those who seek entrance into Heaven can do so only through entering the Catholic Church. And no more will the Catholic Church allow in the "fearful and unbelieving and the abominable and murderers and whoremongers and sorcerers and idolaters and all liars," than will Christ her King admit such filth into His Kingdom in Heaven.

There is no principle within either communism or capitalism, the two faces of materialism in modern economics, that mandates obedience to all ten of the Ten Commandments, to each of the Six Commandments of the Catholic Church, or to both of the two Great Commandments affirmed by Jesus Christ of loving God above all things and one's neighbor as oneself. The vast bulk of communist and capitalist theory is dismissive of such considerations as impertinent to the ends they seek. Almost the entirety of communist and capitalist practice is a violation of the majority, if not all, of the divinely revealed, ecclesially binding, and naturally established laws given for the protection, guidance, and perfection of man. Precious little would be left of either communism or capitalism as a viable system by which to order man's economic life, if all of what is offensive to God were to be removed. What few things in either system are not wholly repugnant to an authentic *sensus fidei* upon a very brief examination would be discovered to be generic principles found in practically every economic system, all of philosophy, and plain old common sense.

Furthermore, whereas philosophical truths from Greece, engineering from Rome, and musical principles developed in Christendom were brought into the Church by the faithful and in consonance with all else already present within the life of the Church, capitalism and communism came in the midst of a roiling storm of rebellion against the Faith and the faithful. The Church did not need to tear down buildings, to contradict truth, or to reinvent sound when accepting influences from outside of the Faith into the fold of Christ. Capitalism and then communism have destroyed society's commitment to a harmonious interaction between the Church and the state, to the family as the fundamental unit of society, and to the Faith as the ultimate means of man's ordering earthly life in obedience to and in hope for God's will to bring man to Heaven. It can not be demonstrated that any nation has ever embraced either capitalism or communism in such a way as to extend the freedom and exaltation of Holy Mother Church, to advance the cause of the Kingdom of Christ, and to bring men to Heaven.

Capitalism and communism *actively* disobey the Church in principle as well as in practice. The fact that there are materialists who do not desire to kill babies in the womb, divorce their wives in order to pursue adulterous affairs, and burn down convents filled with contemplatives, is a manifestation of laudable restraint on the part of many materialists who have yet to take their Godless principles to their logical conclusions. Capitalists and communists have been able to pursue such dastardly ends—and continue to do so—precisely because they have established nations with no reference to God and His law. True, not every communist or capitalist is an outright fiend, any more than every Catholic is prime material for canonization. However, there is nothing within communism or capitalism forbidding the fiend from being a fiend while remaining a materialist in good and law-abiding standing. Saints, on the other hand, must conform to a far higher standard than the license permitted by materialism:

I am the Lord thy God, who brought thee out of the land of Egypt, out of the house of bondage: thou shalt not have strange gods before me…

This prohibition would also apply to the idea of having *no* faith in the true God. Communism is in outright denial of the existence of God. It is hostile to the immemorial need of man to worship something other than himself. Capitalism does not require atheism, but its fervent indifferentism results in a practical atheism no less abominable than what happens in communist practice. Communists do what they do for the exaltation of the worker. Capitalists do what they do for the bottom line. Neither seeks to glorify God in all things, and in fact prefers to glorify God in nothing, essentially believing that God is nothing.

Thou shalt not take the name of the Lord thy God in vain.

Modernity, thy name is blasphemy. Our Lord is dishonored in His own Name by rock stars hubristically claiming more influence on mankind than our Savior Himself. He is dishonored in the deliberations of the European Union which desires to expunge His very memory from their falsified account of the history of Western civilization. He is dishonored in the Name of his Blessed Mother being attached to a play common in the game of American football. He is dishonored in the fact that using His Name as an epithet is a matter of protected speech when it comes to Hollywood films and television, but is a matter of violations of the same Constitutional principle when applied to the decorations appropriate to the celebration of His Birth. He is dishonored in the fact that His Name is utterly unknown in the communist world and so few Catholic missionaries are willing or able to enter to amend this foul state of affairs. By way of reparation here, let me say, ***Glory be to the Father, and to the Son, and to the Holy Ghost! As it was in the beginning, is now, and ever shall be, world without end. Amen. O most Sacred Heart of Jesus, have mercy on us! Immaculate Heart of Mary, pray for us now and at the hour of our death. Amen.***

Remember thou keep holy the Sabbath-day.

Part of the depravity that the French embraced in 1789 involved renaming the months of the year and the days of the week. Secularists ever since have had it in mind to ignore the sovereignty of God not only over human activity, but over time itself. The Lord's Day is no longer His, but merely another day to work for the workers' paradise. That same description applies in capitalist lands where 24/7 means access to frivolous consumption, immoral entertainment, and ceaseless labor. Once upon a time, the suggestion that Holy Days should be formal holidays would have been met with derisive laughter. Now after decades upon decades of apostasy under the tyranny of materialism, such a suggestion would be met with a puzzled frown—no one knows what a Holy Day is anymore.

Honor thy father and mother . . . that thou mayst live a long time, and it may be well with thee in the land, which the Lord thy God will give thee.

There is a new definition for the reward understood as part of this command. Rather than receiving the good that God intends, the modern child looks forward to the insurance policy that will pay out after he unplugs his dying father. Of course, mother and father should not be so shocked at such treatment from their surviving brood, given how their older brothers and sisters fared at the hands of the politicians, doctors, parents and grandparents who made it possible for the woman's "right" to choose to be exercised. The generation gap has guaranteed a world where children dismiss their parents as irrelevant and parents view their children as alien threats. Popular culture is riddled with examples of disrespect from the young directed toward the old, and of the old victimizing the young through actions of base selfishness. Divorce is no way to engender respect in one's children, nor is respect offered by children rejecting their parents mores and way of life. In the communist world, the perception of children as a threat takes on a very physical reality—children are set to spy on their parents so that the police can have yet more excuses to eliminate undesirables from the society.

Thou shalt not kill.

Among the undesirables so deemed by both communist and capitalist societies are the aforementioned infants in wombs, geriatrics in wheelchairs, and the injured on respirators. Billions of dollars exchange hands as a hideously misnamed "healthcare" system profits from its justifications to end life just begun, to declare life ended before death, and to assert an authority over such decisions to which judges and lawyers, governors and presidents, and even some bishops feel the need to submit. Gulags and concentration camps the world over have murdered in the name of the state. The American federal government and several state governments are allocating tens of billions of dollars to murder babies in the name of research for "healthcare". Euthanasia is increasingly accepted in many parts of the world, and inflicted involuntarily, as has been confessed by some of those guilty of murder under that guise of false compassion.

Thou shalt not commit adultery.

Divorce is legal in essentially every nation on earth. Fornication is an unremarkable commonplace among children, adolescents, and supposed adults. Psychologists insist that self-abuse is a "natural" part of childhood development. Sodomy has gained legal status in most of the Western world. Lawyers, websites, travel agencies, entertainment companies, and insurance firms profit from the decriminalization and tolerance of these heretofore forbidden activities. Divorce and fornication were part of the communists' agenda to dissolve the bonds that traditional morality once held on the psyches of the citizens. Immodesty and impurity are the life's blood of modern advertising, of the entertainment industry, the internet, literature, and clothing. Driving down a highway has become a veritably x-rated experience given what is brazenly displayed on billboards selling movies, casinos, TV shows, candy, toys, and political ideologies, among other things. Las Vegas sells bodies and bills itself as a "family destination".

Thou shalt not steal.

Communism could not have happened without theft on a scale unequaled in the history of mankind. Property taxes and other restrictions on property rights in the West amount to uncompensated confiscations of property, rendering claims of ownership by citizens laughable. Stop paying the property taxes on your house (before or after you finish paying off the mortgage, if ever) and you will discover who really owns your property. The attitude of many employees toward giving their employers eight hours of work for eight hours of pay betrays a larcenous heart at the center of capitalism. It is reflected in the attitude of those employers about their responsibility to compensate those employees for overtime and to offer the same loyalty to keep them employed that the employer expects from the employee to remain in his employment. Of course, neither the employee nor the employer wants to admit that everyone would be better off if more people were able to provide a living for themselves and their families without recourse to wage slavery. Employers rob employees of the same freedom to exercise economic freedom that the entrepreneur craves. Employees rob themselves by denying the desire to have such freedom, and fleeing from it on the rare occasions that it might be offered.

Thou shalt not bear false witness.

The propaganda machine of any nation violates this commandment with impunity. Often to do so they employ the expertise of professional liars who sell their wares on Madison Avenue. Kuwait hired a PR firm to convince the world to go to war on its behalf against Iraq. China sends museum exhibits of its ancient culture around the world to put a soft and pretty face on its ugly contemporary reality. The advertising budgets of corporations such as Proctor and Gamble, General Motors, and Coca Cola approach the size of the foreign reserves of some third world nations. Capitalists could not sell all that they sell without convincing people to buy things that they did not need and would not have wanted unless someone spent a lot of time and money to persuade them that life was diminished without yet another fashion to pursue until the next one comes along. No one should be subjected to the efforts of someone encouraging them to make purchases for the sake of making purchases any more than the world should be subjected to the spectacle of rogues from tyrannous regimes trying to convince us that they come in peace.

Thou shalt not covet thy neighbor's wife… [nor] his goods.

Envy makes the modern world of money go around. The very words "trophy wife" scream an intention to instill a sense of envy and the presence of envy prior to bagging the "trophy". It is a foul and demeaning fact that the notion of the "trophy wife" is part of the description of the man who has arrived at a certain high level of achievement while yet striving for further heights. Such a woman is merely a commodity procured along the way, likely to be replaced by a later model, very possibly an actual fashion model, when the mood strikes. Feminists are pleased that "trophy wife" has its mirror image in the sick expression "boy toy". The communist world seems less intent on such depravity given its loose understanding of the matrimonial bond right from its beginnings. What it lacks in envying wives, however, it makes up for in its penchant for envying the neighbors' goods. That neighbor might be the party member higher up in the politburo than oneself, or it might be the perks of the foreman at the factory whose equal status among the comrades is a bit more equal than the rest, or it might be the envy of an entire nation directed at the material wealth of an entire other nation reaping the benefits of keeping up with the Joneses. It has been said that the besetting sin of communism is envy while the besetting sin of capitalism is greed. An example of an envious man who lacked greed does not exist in the wild, but perhaps one day he will be produced in a genetic-engineering laboratory. What is certain is that neither the envious nor the greedy man understands the supreme virtue of charity.

It goes without saying that this wanton disregard for God's Ten Commandments results in an utter rejection of the Six Commandments of the Church and the two Great Commandments taught by Our Lord. Catholics do not endeavor to make excuses for communism, so nothing needs to be said about the foul fruits brought about by the errors of Marx; they are in no way compatible with the Faith. Many Catholics, however, insist that capitalism is capable of being grafted into a Catholic understanding of man's life in society. Fully two centuries have elapsed since capitalism began to be utilized on the national level around the world. It is this writer's contention that capitalism can not be shown, even in principle, to be neutral toward the Faith, and is in practice actively hostile to it.

Beyond that is the question of whether or not capitalism is friendly to, helpful for, and respectful of the faithful individual Catholic. Where is the evidence that capitalism, as such, has been useful as a tool to make men holy? What specifically capitalist principles and activities actually contribute to personal piety and the strength of the Church Militant? How can the capitalist fixation on the market, market share, and the bottom line be reconciled with the virtues of humility, simplicity, and charity? In what way can the desire for greater capital—money—as the driving force and ultimate good of capitalism be reconciled with the beatitude promised to the poor, and with the warning against the evil of loving money? And where, pray tell, are the people actually accomplishing such feats of sanctity in our midst today? It does not seem that the capitalist world is any more apt to produce a capitalist saint than the communist world will produce a communist saint—unless that saint is martyred by either capitalists or communists for knocking down the idols of materialism.

Father Smith
Sacerdos vagus
27 May 2005: The Second Day of Corpus Christi (St. Bede the Venerable)

Capitalism: An economic system designed for the maximizing of political power in the hands of those in favor of private theft.

Communism: A political system designed for the maximizing of economic power in the hands of those in favor of public theft.

Fascism: A system for the maximizing of power in the hands of those in favor of theft.

Anarchy: The power of theft.

Sin: The theft of power.

Dissolution of Church and State

Revolution vs. Evolution

I operate on this great republican principle, that the people will have virtue and intelligence to select men of virtue and wisdom. Is there no virtue among us? If there not be, we are in a wretched situation. No theoretical checks, no form of government can render us secure. To suppose that any form of government will secure liberty or happiness without any virtue in the people is a chimerical idea. If there be sufficient virtue and intelligence in the community, it will be exercised in the selection of these men; so that we do not depend on their virtue, or put our confidence in our rules, but in the people who are to choose them.—James Madison

Dr. Thomas E. Woods in *The Latin Mass,* Spring 2003 issue, makes a compelling argument that a fundamental difference separates what the United States effected through the war of 1776–1781 and the events in France *circa* 1789. The latter, according to Dr. Woods, was a revolution, the former an appeal to tradition. Dr. Woods avers that freemasonry produced the revolution, but had little effect on the proponents of tradition.

His assessment is correct in the particulars, but fails to see a broader connection between the Gallic rebels and the Yankee "traditionalists". True, the Americans did not seek to overthrow tradition in taxation, the penal code, or trade. They did, however, do the very things Dr. Woods described the French revolutionaries as having done, establishing "new governing structures, new provincial boundaries, a new 'religion'," albeit without the threat of the guillotine hanging over anyone's head. Pardon the pun.

The United States Constitution abolished the monarchy, erected a sovereign nation entirely disassociated from its mother country, and forbade a state religion. This last flies in the face of the natural law, the above statement from Madison, and the remarks of James Otis quoted by Dr. Woods: "There must be in every instance, a higher authority, *viz.* GOD" (emphasis in the original).

It is in the abandonment of a shared faith that America's revolution truly lies. Without common worship, virtue can not be agreed upon, rendering Madison's warning prophetic insofar as ours is a singularly vicious society. Without common worship, sovereignty rests not in God, but in the very legal positivism Dr. Woods quite correctly illustrates formed part of the founding fathers' rationale for resisting Britain, but was also operative in Revolutionary France, and is corrupting the American court system even now by way of jurists' declarations of the newfound 'rights' to murder babies in the womb and/or birth canal and for sodomites to wed with the blessing of the state. Without common worship, novelty and innovation become a phenomenon not only within liturgical experience, but in jurisprudence, economics, politics, and even science. Without God as the absolute guarantor of any human enterprise, disorder is inevitable.

An argument can be made that the United States Constitution intends to preserve tradition. This is best seen in the explicit reservation to the states of all powers that are not defined for the federal government. It is the violation of this fundamental principle, the encroachment of the central government on states' and individuals' rights, that constitutes the evolution of the American experiment from a defensible assertion of human rights in the face of tyranny, to the indefensible and at times demonic (cf. Roe vs. Wade) assertion of human willfulness over divine law.

It is a curious irony that many, who so stridently insist on federal protection of child murderers in the face of states that would pass laws limiting or eliminating the foul practice, are among the most vocal proponents of states' rights when said states wish to sanction the union of sodomites in blasphemous "marriages". Legal positivism destroys the very grounds for passing, enforcing, and interpreting the law. Brute force, either by militia or by majority, is the final arbiter of what is legal. This is impossible to avoid when the *good* is intentionally rejected as the measure of what is allowable and desirable in a society. The American Constitution appeals not to God as its *summum bonum*, but "the people of the United States" as sovereign, as lawgiver, as judge of man and men.

What is worst about the Constitution is not what it contains. The Constitution's primary fault lies in the absence of precisely that which James Madison insisted was necessary for the people who would implement it. As is so with an alarming proportion of our citizens, the Constitution ignores God and thus lacks virtue. It is powerless to prevent the very injustice which it ostensibly was crafted to alleviate. It is powerless to give our sovereign God the honor due Him according to justice.

A House Divided

Thomas Jefferson paraphrased Locke's enumeration of inalienable rights as "life, liberty, and the pursuit of happiness". The Establishment Clause of the First Amendment to the Constitution was meant to safeguard an individual's right to life, liberty, and the pursuit of happiness against the government's infringements on matters of religion. It is a cruel irony that this vital element in the Constitution has had exactly the *opposite* effect.

Abortion denies the right to life to the unborn citizen. Prohibitions against prayer in schools deny the right to liberty of religious expression to parents, students, and teachers. And the general disavowal of a place for God in the public discourse denies man's supreme *raison d'etre*, to know, love, and serve God in this life so as to be happy with Him forever in eternal life. Separation of the state from the Church has resulted in a nation ignorant of Christ and thus incapable of life, liberty, and happiness. For to know Christ is to be free (St. John 8:32), to know Him is to have life (St. John 17:3), and to know Him is to experience perfect beatitude (St. Matthew 5:12).

Two rulings from the Supreme Court in the year 2000 point out the glaring contradiction between faith as it is taught and faith as it is practiced. In virtually the same breath the majority of the justices claimed that the Constitution forbids prayer in public school football stadiums and allows babies to be impaled at birth. Our courts would rob our children of public expressions of faith and the right to life. We are setting a precedent by which future generations (if any survive our rapacious license) will be able to rationalize a denial not only of God and physical security, but of every guarantee that justice is anything but the arbitrary whim of those in power.

The United States of America has been called the most religious nation on earth. But how can we separate Church and state when we are the Church and we are the state? A house divided against itself must fall. What if a man in himself is divided?

Decisions of the Supreme Court have provided some indication of what many think the relationship between these two spheres of experience should be. A 'high wall', a term coined by Jefferson, characterizes the boundary cleaving the ecclesiastic and the political realms. Some have described the recent protections of freedom *for* religion as being freedom *from* religion.

Advocates of lowering the wall frequently point out that the Constitution's framers did not envision a public forum without a religious presence. It is clear that the early philosophers of American democracy took for granted a rather strong involvement of the Church in matters of state. Concurrently, the state was seen as a protector and endorser of religious life.

Modern interpretation of the Constitution denies that the Establishment Clause means more than an allowance for religious affairs to be conducted by individuals and groups within narrowly set bounds. The body politic can not accept (or reject) the idea of a spirit politic. Each must make these determinations on his own and then act according to conscience. The government is not permitted to impede or to assist this process.

These arguments for and against constitutional readings on freedom of religion miss an extraordinarily important point. Groups can define the scope of law, the reach of free expression of faith, and terms for interaction between moral and legal entities. It is impossible for an individual to demarcate where the soul ends and secular interests begin.

Put aside the legal questions stemming from the Constitution. Explain instead how a person determines for himself when he is being a man of faith and where he is exercising his rights as a citizen. What kind of integrity can be expected from a society of people able to separate love from justice?

It seems disingenuous to couch the debate on religious freedom in cultural terms. No one, not God Himself, can deny a man's faith. Whether or not a nation decides to have a large amount of religious freedom is not for the government to mandate. A nation has as much religious freedom as its citizens dare to exercise. Laws can neither restrict nor guarantee love.

Yet our society denies definitive good and evil. If there is neither good nor evil, there can be no virtue. If there is no virtue, there is no virtuous electorate. If there is no virtuous electorate, there will be nothing but panderers and demagogues to be elected by the selfish and the amoral. Injustice will be championed by Supreme Court justices.

You can not legislate morality, true, but you can hide behind laws to rationalize injustice. The Faith does not need a constitutional amendment. It only needs human hearts willing to believe. Between right and rights there is no separation.

An Ounce of Prevention

Where Dr. Woods is most unintentionally correct is in his assertion that the founding fathers desired to preserve tradition. What Dr. Woods fails to see is that the "tradition" in question was in no way *Catholic.* It did have freemasons, even more it had protestants, but above all it was secularist, which is much the same as saying protestant which is a short trek to freemasonry (basically the path from 1517 to 1717). The founding fathers, through the Constitution, carried on the denial of Catholic philosophy, theology, and morality begun in the "enlightenment" and ending all around us in a great apostasy.

Americans have a penchant for mimicking their "betters" across the pond. This is a time-honored weakness and insecurity within our national psyche. The old saw that America is a rush from barbarism to decadence without an intervening culture has caused untold hand-wringing among the European wannabes of the American "intelligentsia".

Having said this, the more down-to-earth among us have a snobbishness against snobbery. One of the worst things of which to be accused by a good ol' boy is the crime of putting on airs. One of the best ways to get elected by a populace of good ol' boys is for a multimillionaire to put on jeans and get photographed glad-handing at the union hall—a hall likely laid under siege by the millionaire's usurious ancestors against uppity union-card-carrying wage slaves.

We want wealth and all of its trappings, but none of its hierarchy. We want learning and all of its privileges, but none of its discipline. We want to have and eat the cake that Marie Antoinette offered the mob in vain—and we want the mob to bake the cake for us. *We want to be of the mob but not in the mob.*

Not so long ago, in the last decade of the last century of the last millennium, we impeached a president of the United States. One of the defenses offered for him was that the Europeans found little or nothing of note in his adulterous fornication. For the French, it was said innumerable times, a man's mistress is his wife's business and no one else's. Opponents of the Chief Executive were accused of voyeurism, political character assassination, and intellectual troglodytism.

Many of the same imperial defenders are now criticizing the current occupant of the Oval Office for his warmongering on the grounds that our friends abroad think ill of the effort. The very people who would pooh-pooh the moral rein that is the sentiment, "What would the neighbors think?" now insist that what the neighbors think should be what we think, even if the neighbors are not thinking so clearly. Even when the neighbors are moral troglodytes.

And here we come to the real peril engendered by the European penchant for revolution that gave us the twentieth century, the bloodiest century man has ever known. It was not the concentration camps. It was not the wholesale executions and the concentration camps. It was not the internal exiles. Europe's horror was none other than the European mind, indeed the loss thereof.

These past five-hundred years and more, the minds of Europe have embarked on the systematic dismantling of all that has made European culture. The Church, objective truth, and the affirmation of human rights in the context of a commonwealth of citizens obedient to God, have given way to atheism, skepticism, and the diminishment of man to a status of less worth than the average beast on the endangered species list. Refusing God, doubting reality, and glorifying nature while insisting that man is neither natural nor supernatural, Europe has set about the task of destroying itself.

This can be seen in the abysmally low birth rate on the continent. It is witnessed in the zeal for casting aside the sovereignty of nations in favor of a common currency on the way to a common law. And nowhere is it more in evidence than in the moribund state of the Church, whose history is denied by most Europeans, denounced by others, and despised by what passes for European thinkers. A day approaches when asked to define a European, one will find no individual who demonstrates the reality, no nationality that embodies its characteristics, and no belief that it ever existed. Soon, no one will know what Europe is, least of all the Europeans.

America is not far behind on this road to nowhere. Political elements within this country are conspiring to bring the Balkans to the Midwest. Whether by language, by customs, or by skin color, Americans are being cajoled, legislated, and seduced into believing that to be an American can mean an infinitude of things. The definition of America being offered derides, denies, and defies definition.

So long as one thing, one thought, does not inform a people of its identity, that people is no people. Europe grew from the unity of the Catholic Church. When that unity was cast aside in the protestant revolt of the sixteenth century, Europe began to unravel. Petty feuds between feudal lords grew into kinstrife between competing creeds. Rivalry about material wealth was warped into oppression based on the material origins of mankind. The Faith that transcends all racial and ethnic distinctions was banished in favor of the modern pastime of ethnic cleansing.

America's founding was more synthetic, less organic. It is hard to put one's finger on exactly what makes the *pluribus unum*. In fact, the loyalists of the Revolutionary War period, the Confederacy in the War Between the States, the conscientious objectors from both World Wars, and the protesters against the Vietnam War give stark expression to the fact that there has been plenty of *pluribus* in our history. One would be harder pressed to show where the abiding *unum* that is supposedly America subsists.

That America explicitly abstained from a creedal confession at its founding is the true source of the problem. The contemporary mania for separating the state from the Church to the point of persecuting the faithful is the fruit of the founders' original reticence. Many would say that the Constitution never intended that freedom of religion would become freedom from religion. Neither the framers nor the adherents to that position understand the law of unintended consequences, well described in the ancient saying, "The road to hell is paved with good intentions." It strains credulity to attempt to embrace the idea that the Constitution's explicit rejection of the true Faith and the true Church has a source in Heaven.

And what is more, it is absurd to believe that the masonic notion of separation of the state from the Church advanced by the freemasons at the Constitutional Convention was conceived as a means to advance the claims of Christ the King. It was masons who concocted the idea of a Godless state, masons who expunged God from the American Constitution, and masons who have influenced modern political structures from Philadelphia in 1776 to Paris in 1789 to Moscow in 1917 to the founding of the United Nations at San Francisco in 1948. It is only either willful blindness or ineptitude that would fail to see that masonic philosophy embodied in masonic documents crafted by masons would result in an entity entirely at odds with the will of God.

At some point Americans will need to come to terms with the fact that, as a nation, we began where Europe has ended, with a denial of God. Those who are not for Him are against Him. The American Constitution, in a pre-echo of post-modern European rebellion, gives God no place in the fabric of the national soul. At best He is ignored, but more often He is insulted. Such an attitude toward the greatest of all beings does not bode well for the treatment that can be expected toward the greatest of all created beings. Where God is disdained, one can have no hope that His creature will be reverenced.

Our current state was not the matter of a deliberate revolution occurring rapidly. We are the result of two-and-a-quarter centuries of inattention to the natural law, our Mother the Church, and God our Father. Independence Day is an annual and brutal irony. Yes, we are independent of Great Britain, but we are enslaved to a violent government, a consumerist economy, and sinful passions.

Perhaps the freemasons are not wholly to blame, but one can be forgiven his profound doubts that they are displeased. Dr. Woods' analysis is perceptive, but his conclusion is wrong. The Godless revolution of the French does have a common pedigree with the Godless Constitution of the United States of America: *apostasy from Christ and His Body the Catholic Church.*

Father Smith
4 June 2003, St. Francis of Naples: Iowa City, Iowa
26 February 2004, St. Caesarius of Nazianzus: Tustin, California

3 April, Jubilee Year—4th Monday of Lent

A Tale of Two Cities Revisited

Observers seem to be of the opinion that the city of God, New Jerusalem, is in need of urban renewal. Catholicism is accused of being all promise and no fulfillment. As in the days when Jesus walked among us in His earthly life, a sign is demanded to establish belief in the claims of the Kingdom of Heaven.

Christ's contemporaries were witnesses to miraculous signs and wonders. Jesus made the blind see, the lame walk, and the dead live. He turned water to wine and fed thousands with a few loaves. Ultimately, He was seen alive after His death by those who knew Him best. They went forth proclaiming this greatest sign as the basis for their firm faith.

We who are the inheritors of this mission of evangelizing are asked for a similar sign. People wonder where are the dead raised in our day. Prayers seem to go not only unanswered but unheard. There seems to be little of that original fervor left in the Church, when martyrs rather than bureaucrats reigned.

Before we are taken to task by our detractors, too many of whom claim to be Christians themselves, we should call to mind what Jesus actually said. He told us that we are to take up the cross each day and follow Him. We are to sell all, give to the poor, and follow Him. We are to lay down our fishing nets and follow Him.

When we do as He says, *i.e.* follow Him, He makes several other promises. He tells us that death will not conquer us. We are assured that the words we need to speak will be given us. And He warns us that persecutions, besides all other things, will be ours as well.

In the simplicity of our lives, by the prayer and love we share within the Church and outside of the Church, and through the Sacraments, particularly the Mass, we do the will of God and follow Christ. Lent is an opportunity to reflect on this ongoing reality and to remember what it means to be about our Father's business. The knowledge that this good work is being accomplished in us by the power of the Spirit of God results in the peace which this world can not give, in the joy known only by those who believe that they are truly God's children.

This is what it means to be a sign of contradiction to the worldliness of our times. When asked for a sign that the Kingdom is at hand we show the cross and ourselves on it. We proclaim the joy of those who are confident that sin and death are conquered. We respond to doubt as saints always have, by revealing in ourselves Jesus Christ and Him crucified.

Those who continue to disbelieve the cross seek a further sign. Jesus tells us that the sign of Jonah is what is forthcoming. Remember the repentance of the people of Nineveh. That is the sign we should offer to our friends who seek the glory before realizing the Way. God does indeed heal the sick and raise the dead. His primary work, however, is to forgive sins.

The common gift to those who are cured of both physical and spiritual infirmity is the gift of Faith. They believe that God does hear, and He responds with the grace of salvation. To see this glory the disbeliever must first renounce the blindness of his own sin. This sign will result in rejoicing in Heaven and in the heart of the forgiven sinner.

Some will dismiss all of this as pie in the sky. They will say that here and now is all that they seek. Their home is Babylon.

We should be critical of ourselves as we journey through Lent. We should ask ourselves where our faith is wanting. We should insist that our own hearts more fully embrace others in love.

But we should not yield to the criticisms of the world without demanding fair time. If indeed the promises of God and His Kingdom do not ring true to skeptics, we can ask whether or not the promises of this world are kept any better.

We live in a time of unparalleled prosperity. The United States is the most powerful nation ever, anywhere. Economic nirvana has been promised to those who believe in the profit motive, who call themselves consumers, who drive the engine of the economy by being in a state of perpetual desire.

What is the fruit of this faith? Do people have a sense of peace in building a bigger house and attendant mortgage? Are schools better places to learn now that moral doctrine has been replaced with metal detectors? Will families become closer as Mom and Dad spend more time at work, the children at daycare, and no one at the heavily mortgaged house? How happy will senior citizens be when Social Security is fully funded and they live the ends of their longer lives in very expensive nursing homes, never visited by their children and grandchildren who are out worshipping at the altar of eternal youth?

The promises of the world always wait for another day. You will be happy after you buy this product, after you get the promotion, after you graduate, after the kids leave the house, after the government increases your cola, after the Democrats/Republicans leave office. After tomorrow the good times and good ol' days will never end…

God's promises are now. We can love one another as brothers and sisters in Christ now. We can simplify our lives now. We can repent and forgive sins now. We can experience the joy of the saints in Heaven now—and forever.

It is curious how the most successful people according to the world's measures apostatize their faith once they have "made it". Ask the wealthy businessman what he will do with his fortune and frequently he will speak in terms of philanthropy. Ask the politician or athlete why he is retiring and more often than not it is to be able to spend more time with family. Ask the value-free artist why he creates and he will respond with idealism about a desire to express ephemeral, transcendent beauty or truth or fundamental reality. When the true believers from Babylon seek fulfillment, they don't talk about acquiring more wealth, power, or prestige; instead they seek things that are found only in New Jerusalem.

The Catholic who has embraced suffering, forgiveness, and mercy, does not seek wealth, power, and prestige. He seeks to share peace and joy, reconciliation and love. The worldly are ever after something they can't quite grasp now; the Catholic is satisfied so long as he has Christ.

Many are confused about the difference between Babylon and New Jerusalem because there seem to be a lot of similarities. Pain, sin, and death are common to both. The faithful of both cities seem inconsistent in their beliefs. A question provides a simple way to distinguish the one from the other: Where do you want to live forever?

If faith in God can not bring the promised peace of New Jerusalem into our midst, the citizens of Babylon who claim to be in possession of the secret of future happiness need to give the rest of us a sign that it is worth the wait.

Father Lawrence C. Smith
Jesus Christ, Prince of Peace Parish
Clinton, Iowa

Fanfani and Friends

Rambling reflections on a subject much too large for a mere book review

By all means, it is worth reading Amintore Fanfani's 1934 treatise, *Catholicism, Protestantism, and Capitalism* (republished in 2003 by IHS Press). However, it should not be undertaken without the firm resolution to be fair-minded. An additional requirement, then, is that one endeavor to examine Leo xiii's *Rerum Novarum,* Max Weber's *The Protestant Ethic and the Spirit of Capitalism,* Michael Novak's *The Catholic Ethic and the Spirit of Capitalism,* Pius xi's *Quadragesimo Anno,* and John Paul ii's *Centesimus Annus.* One would do well to include a healthy dose of Belloc, a sprinkling of Chesterton, and a helping of Father Vincent McNabb. Room should be made as well for Adam Smith, Edmund Burke, Milton Friedman, Karl Marx, and John Keynes. David Stockman, anyone? So many words to read, so little stomach to swallow them all. Ezechiel (3:1-3) had a much better diet.

This reviewer is trying to be fair, but finds it difficult, seeing how the various antagonists in the ongoing debate between the Faith and mammon stack the deck not only against one another, but against justice. The virtue of justice is expressed in the will to render each his due. The multitudinous champions of the legion of economic schools strive mightily to give their viewpoints due credit for all that is good in the world. They attempt to ascribe all that is ill to the adherents of competing philosophies, and they even give the devil his due by averring frequently that economic principles need not be drawn from the deposit of faith.

And here is where the grossest injustice is seen. Weber wants to show how the virtues of protestantism brought the world the wonders of capitalism. Novak would have us believe that capitalism is to be lauded as the firstfruits of Catholicism. Fanfani works at that most necessary and least accomplished of philosophical skills, making a distinction. Protestantism and capitalism share roots in a Catholic culture and the Catholic culture finds itself in the intolerable position of tolerating both protestantism and capitalism. This is far from an ideal situation, morally and economically.

Perhaps the strongest aspect of Fanfani's historical survey is pressing home the fact that one can not understand protestantism without reference to the Catholicism of which it is a set of heresies. He also does an admirable job of reminding the reader that capitalism grew out of deviations from Catholic norms of social justice, deviations stemming both from legal allowances and from sinful manipulation of markets by greedy merchants in tandem with eminently corruptible rulers (even, gasp, princes of the Church). Neither protestantism nor capitalism can serve to prove true the fallacy of evolution. Catholic doctrine did not evolve beyond itself to give the world a fitter set of religious dogmas manifested in the plethora of protestant sects. Capitalism does not represent the finest survivor of a pantheon of Catholic social and economic systems wherein inadequate material and financial methods gave way before the inexorable triumph of market forces. Protestantism is a rejection of Catholic truth; capitalism is Catholic social teaching gone awry.

Fanfani did not use terms quite so harsh. His analysis, however, makes clear his conviction that capitalism can not be described as a system or a spirit wholly in consonance with authentic Catholicism. Furthermore, to an extent much greater than either Weber or Novak, Fanfani is willing to admit that capitalism holds implications beyond its mere methodology. There is a moral element involved in any economic system. Fanfani remembers what so many have forgotten: economics is a subset of ethics, not a science unto itself. Economics is to be used to render justice, not to acquire things. And insofar as justice is pursued, the final end to be sought is the divine justice that offers man the mercy of the forgiveness of sins and the attainment of the Kingdom of Heaven. Capitalism goes much further down the road of encouraging sins than of renouncing them. Capitalism is infinitely more bent on the things of this world than it is conducive to the contemplation of that which is beyond this world.

Still, Fanfani falls prey to the same error that most commentators on capitalism have made. Capitalism is largely critiqued in terms of its effects on production, consumption, and the chimerical standard of a people's standard of living. (Novak devotes a large section of *The Catholic Ethic and the Spirit of Capitalism* to the question of how virtue can serve capitalism, but says little or nothing about how capitalism contributes to sanctity). Fanfani seems blind to the idea of applying to an economic model such statements as "Blessed are the poor in spirit, for theirs is the kingdom of heaven" (Mt.5:3); and "Son, remember that thou didst receive good things in thy lifetime… but now… thou art tormented" (Lk. 16:25); and "He that cometh from Heaven is above all" (Jn. 3:31). Has no one ever thought to make the social reign of Jesus Christ the King the lynchpin of his understanding of developing the fruits of the earth in obedience to the wonderful command, "Increase and multiply, and fill the earth, and subdue it, and rule over the fishes of the sea, and the fowls of the air, and all living creatures that move about upon the earth" (Gen. 1:28)?

Well, as a matter of fact, yes. Long after Adam made a botched mess of things, a tremendous man by the name of Benedict of Nursia put into practice a way to "love the Lord thy God with thy whole heart and with thy whole soul and with thy whole mind and with thy whole strength… [and] love thy neighbor as thyself" (Mk. 13:30-31). Under the marvelous banner of *Ora et Labora!* St. Benedict and his monks established a habit of discipline conducive to personal piety, communal fraternity and order, and, as a nice fringe benefit, the nurturing and developing of animal husbandry, agriculture, and the domestic arts. St. Benedict and his children that followed for centuries after knew and understood that if one seeks "first the Kingdom of God and His justice, all these things shall be added unto you" (Mt. 6:33). Pursuing the pearl of great price, beatitude in Heaven, the monastic communities in league with Catholic princes gave rise to the burgeoning civic centers of medieval Europe, preserved and extended the patrimony of learning all but lost elsewhere after the fall of the Western Roman Empire, and cultivated art, music, and architecture that has proved of permanent value regardless of the vicissitudes of history.

Some likely would object that a monastic model is hardly fitting for married couples and families, international trade, and technological advancement. One measure of the superiority of the monastic model to the current economic chaos is that the family, trade, and scientific discovery flourished as a result of what sound Catholic principles of economic life provided. It is telling that the modern world has made it next to impossible for authentic monastic communities to grow their own food, build their own chapels, and train their own novices.

The Catholic ideal allows man to improve his lot, both materially and spiritually. The economic models which have emerged since the abandonment of a strictly Catholic understanding of man and his call to holiness above all things, have led to the destruction not only of individual men's ability to own property and pursue private economies, but the Church has succumbed to a like impotence. Husbands and fathers are reduced to virtual serfdom, bound to mortgages, property taxes, and wage-slavery; dioceses manage multimillion-dollar usurious pension funds for priests; orders of religious women sell hospitals for hundreds of millions of dollars, and cease to care for the aged and infirm; and monks are reduced to producing computer graphics to support themselves. The twenty-first century has no prospects of producing a *Book of Kells*, Ambrosian Chant, or a *Summa Theologica*. It is all that most modern Church institutions can do to market their facilities as meeting centers, send religious as consultants to social service agencies, and rely on revenues from college football programs to fund the acquisition of big-name coaches who will attract star high school talent to improve the team which in turn will swell gate receipts giving rise to higher concession income resulting in the increase of football revenues…

Lest any others object that the above-mentioned chimera, the standard of living, was far lower in the days when monasticism and feudalism were *de rigueur*, keep in mind that the good life most desired was not to be found here on earth at all. It was not found in personal transportation, access to information, or employment at the expense of the family. Instead, the bulk of the population took pride in the beauty of the local cathedral, learned their catechism in keeping with their state in life, and worked in the home and its attendant fields without anxieties attached to the specter of unemployment, foreclosure, and bankruptcy. Those were the days when the days were spent wending one's way to Heaven, not through lines at Disneyland. None questioned the wisdom or truth of the words, "For what doth it profit a man, if he gain the whole world and suffer the loss of his soul? Or what exchange shall a man give for his soul? (Mt. 16:26)." Alas! there are souls among us who would find their answer in the New York Stock Exchange.

Yes, infant mortality was high in earlier centuries, but not as common as abortion is today. Yes, many died of injuries incurred in accidents, but not nearly so often nor as horrifically as the roughly fifty thousand who die each year in automobiles on this nation's highways. Yes, it was rare to find an adult who could read or write in the days when kings reigned, but the current state of "democratic" education for the masses can boast little better after all these years of trying and billions of dollars levied in taxes. "Nasty, brutish, and short," was the verdict pronounced on life before modernity by a wit of the modern age. Another talented mind nurtured in the enlightened ethos of the "post-Christian" era observed of his fellows, "The mass of men live lives of quiet desperation." The primary difference between these two assessments is that the objects of the first could understand their plight in the context of much better promised afterwards, a better that was hastened indeed by the brevity of the nastiness and brutishness. The objects of the latter assessment only grow more desperate as they come to believe that "this is as good as it gets."

But back to Fanfani…

He was surely aware that Pope Leo xiii in the encyclical *Rerum Novarum* offered solutions to the problems raised by capitalism. Pope Leo advocated a just wage, not as a goal, but as the means to assist workers to acquire property of their own and to become free of the bonds imposed by the factory system still in use even today, though now also applied to office complexes. Pope Pius xi issued his encyclical *Quadragesimo Anno* less than a half decade before Fanfani's *Catholicism, Protestantism, and Capitalism.* It was plain to the Pope as well as to experts and even to the common man that capitalism had produced grave ills far worse than were extant in Leo's day. War, depression, hyper-inflation, civic unrest, and the advocacy of even more Godless economic systems than capitalism, *i.e.,* socialism and communism, were in the ascendancy when Pius and Fanfani wrote. Both the Pope and the professor recognized the multitude of dangers facing the men of their day and spoke against them. None of those banes, veritable horsemen of the Apocalypse, has yet ceased to afflict the world.

What Fanfani did not address, but what lay at the heart of the Popes' messages, was that *all* of the principles, methods, and means employed in understanding and implementing man's economic life must be tributary to his ultimate need for salvation. Fanfani, Weber, Novak, and every one of the minds pursuing the discipline of economics from the modern standpoint ignore the fact that where numbers, commodities, and supply chains might be value neutral, the men who make them, the men who use them, and the men who labor to design them are moral agents. It is irrational to assume that any system that includes a human element is fool-proof, beyond sabotage, or an effective barrier against sin. It is not merely the case that where garbage goes in, garbage comes out. Man can take what was either good or neutral and make it bad; he can twist what was designed to create and use it for destruction; he can subvert that which is meant for the commonwealth to the increase of his personal wealth. In short, he can do practically anything except make what is bad into good, turn his ill will into justice, or exercise vice to the same effect as virtue.

Such, however, is exactly what capitalism attempts. Dealing in shortages is stock-in-trade for the shrewd businessman, where Christian charity dictates sharing with those who have not enough. Advertising does not blush at abusing the truth in order to move merchandise, where honesty demands that personal loss is preferable to committing fraud. Pride, lust, avarice, envy, gluttony, sloth, and anger motivate producers, distributors, and consumers alike; where the imitation of Christ is accomplished only by those who are humble, pure, generous, fraternal, temperate, diligent, and meek. What God instilled as attributes in His Prophets would never satiate the lust for profits in mammon.

Jesus impoverished Himself of His divinity. He was born a poor child, in a poor family whom our Faith names *Holy*. He lived His life among the poor, whom he called *blessed*. He died a poor man, literally deprived of the shirt on His back. He was interred in a borrowed tomb. The love which moved Him to suffer such is more than compensation for what the world would call lacks. This humility is the natural basis on which is built the glory revealed in His Resurrection.

Jesus Christ is the model for all that is Catholic. Any economic system that would beg acceptance by Catholics must seek compatibility with the person of Christ. No Catholic should be satisfied with an economic way of life that obscures, much less denies, Our Lord.

The herd of economists, past and present, who look to social salvation in capitalism look in vain. Economists inured to the excesses of capitalism at the expense of human dignity and divine law, especially as it regards usury, are willfully blind. Apologists for capitalism who champion it as better than socialism and communism have eyes in need of beam removal. Fanfani is a bit better than most in that he acknowledges some of the historical implications pointing to capitalism's dubious pedigree of heresy and avarice, of error and iniquity, of apostasy and vice. He, too, however, is senseless to capitalism's abject failure to render unto Caesar without stealing from God.

Capitalism is not a system based on a science whose principles work independently of the Faith. Capitalism is an economic system designed, managed, and used by men who countenance the sin of usury, who pursue wealth for its own sake, and who construct laws in society that diminish the place of the authentic worship of God. Capitalism can not be made to work among men who fear mortal sin in the soul more than death in the body, who woo Lady Poverty with a lover's heart, and who desire nothing more from this life than to live it in such a way as to glorify God now and thereby please Him enough to be rewarded to do so forever in Heaven.

Ut in omnibus glorificetur Deus.

Father Smith
Sacerdos vagus
30 June 2004: The Commemoration of St. Paul the Apostle

From the Roman Martyrology for the Thirtieth Day of June: At Rome, St. Lucina, a disciple of the Apostles, who relieved the necessities of the saints with her goods, visited the Christians detained in prison, buried the martyrs, and was laid by their side in a crypt which she herself had constructed…

Dear Editor (SeattleCatholic.com):

Here are just a few thoughts on the subject of taxation, broad in nature, applicable to the particulars of the conversation in question, but not restricted thereto:

1) Before Caesar receives his due, God must be given His due. Yes, Our Lord tells us to render unto Caesar that which is his. He also tells us to render unto God that which is *His*. What belongs to God is our whole heart, whole mind, whole soul, whole strength.

2) We are NEVER to participate in a known evil. Period. That is *absolutely* forbidden. Not only does St. Thomas Aquinas affirm this, but so also does St. Alphonsus Ligouri, St. Augustine, and the entire patrimony of the Church's moral theology.

3) Sovereign nations which elect to participate in an evil, with full knowledge and intent, are subject to correction by the Church. It has happened frequently in history that our Mother has had to place a monarch and/or nation under interdict due to violations of the law, either the natural law or divine law.

4) In a more Catholic era, a nation that imposed the murder of children as a burden to be supported through the taxation of its subjects or citizens would be judged to be in flagrant disobedience to God's law. That nation would be placed under interdict. With that having occurred, the subjects or citizens of that nation would be dispensed from offering support in material goods or labor to the wayward sovereign. Taxes would be expected to be withheld, as would any service in the military. Other Catholic princes would be permitted to assist the Church in removing the blameworthy parties from power.

5) To be specific to the question at hand, one writer suggested, in effect, that the bishops of the United States should find the government of the United States in breach of the moral order for its advocacy of child murder (or how about sodomy, or divorce, or usury). It would be appropriate, then, for them to place the nation under interdict. Part of the interdiction would be the withholding of the payment of taxes to the offending entity.

6) The fact that our bishops have not done so, nor has the Holy See under five popes in succession, leaves the faithful in a moral quandary. Should one contribute to the slaughter of innocents or not? The hierarchy is silent on the subject.

7) The trump card lies in the first seven words of the Preamble to the Constitution: *We, the People of the United States...* Ladies and gentlemen, the purveyors of government-funded child murder are not some amorphous "they" out there. The government of the United States of America is none other than the people thereof. Those who sanction child murder through election, legislation, and taxation, are you and I.

8) This nation was founded on the notion of self-determination in government. The Declaration of Independence lists a litany of grievances that included the unjust imposition of foreign laws on an unwilling populace. The effective tax rate was under ten percent. The king of England was charged with coercing a disenfranchised population through legislation passed by an unrepresentative governmental assembly.

9) Abortion in any form is foreign to the Kingdom of Heaven. Americans pay upwards of fifty percent of their annual income in taxes. The president, congress, and courts of the United States of America enforce laws allowing child murder in opposition to the will of a plurality of the citizens of this country. Thomas Jefferson, the main author of the Declaration of Independence, an influential thinker during the time of the drafting of the American Constitution, and the third president of the republic, suggested that a healthy democracy might need a revolution every twenty years or so. It is not unreasonable to posit that he would consider the obliteration in the womb of millions of human beings each year the proper matter of a citizen uprising.

10) The Constitution which enshrines the income tax also is interpreted by due authority, namely, the Supreme Court, to mandate a separation of the state from the Church, the allowance of sodomy, and, yes, the vacuuming, eviscerating, and scalding of infants in their mothers' wombs. No Catholic at all, under any circumstances, can be obliged to acquiesce to such blatant, arrogant, blasphemous

denials of our true sovereign, Jesus Christ the King of the universe. Those who elect to resist such injustice against themselves and against their Lord are on very firm moral ground, and the laws of the land by which they will be persecuted, far from binding any to obedience, will, in their rejection, be the instrument of the raising up of new martyrs for the Church.

To give the Lord our God the whole of our hearts, minds, souls, and strengths, includes our material possessions. First among those possessions in the social realm is our nation herself. One must ask, not whether blood money is due to Caesar for the extermination of "fetal tissue", but whether God will be pleased with the offering from us to Him of His slaughtered children before they have a chance at Baptism, the Faith, and life itself.

God bless you,

Father Lawrence C. Smith

Tustin, California

January 13, 2004—The Octave of the Epiphany of Our Lord (and His Baptism, too!)

P.S. One of the participants in this conversation stated that those in consecrated life are not subject to taxes. Two clarifications are in order: 1) religious men and women who labor for their communities and receive paychecks thereby do indeed have taxes withheld by the government; and 2) secular priests are considered to be "independent contractors" for the purposes of income taxes. Religious brothers and sisters and secular priests pay into the Social Security system and receive benefits from it. Additionally, every parish in the country incurs administrative and clerical costs in providing parishioners with tax statements each year. In effect, there is a tax on contributions to the Church in that it costs extra money to service the government regulations attached to the contributions. It is the matter of another letter to explain why it would be best if the faithful just offered their charitable contributions without seeking tax breaks after the fact. In short, let us just say that it is better to be rewarded by our heavenly Father than by Uncle Sam. LCS.[1]

1 Editors Note - While many churchmen and religious do volunteer to pay the "income" tax and Social Security/Medicare taxes, they are not required to, nor are most working Americans for that matter required to pay these "income taxes", which are in reality excise taxes on the excercise of a federal privilege. ObamaCare falls under this rubric as well. Please see www.losthorizons.

com and the book *Cracking the Code* for a fuller treatment of this subject.

Father Smith's Epistle to a Rich Young Man

Your question is not in the least bit obtuse. In fact, it is quite valid. A few thoughts that will, I hope, help to clarify things for you and perhaps others as well:

1) The Church has always advocated private property, which is one of the many reasons why she condemns communism.

2) So long as a successful businessman earns his money honestly, there is nothing wrong with him having lots of it—the caveat being that it is incredibly difficult to earn lots of money in the modern system without inflicting injustice on someone somewhere (beginning with oneself), but if one can manage that then…

3) One has the obligation in charity to give thanks to God by being generous with his fellow man. God has lifted up many saints and entrusted them with wealth, because He knew that they could be counted on to put material blessings to good use. The rich man must contend with that proportion problem between camels and needles' eyes, but if he navigates life well, with ample help from the grace of God, his sanctity will be enormous, of far greater worth than his bank balance.

4) Still, the bottom line is that holy poverty—not the impoverishment that comes from injustice, but voluntary poverty for the sake of the Kingdom of Heaven—is the Catholic norm. In this as in all things, Jesus is the model. Capitalism requires an inordinate attention to material things and is thus *very* dangerous to the soul. It is not impossible to be a holy businessman, but it is very perilous. The normal way to Heaven leads through the narrow gate.

5) Remember also that great wealth is allowed by way of what amounts to a dispensation. If one is burdened with the skills that make it possible to get on well in the world, then God permits one to make use of the skills, with the proviso that their fruits are then used, not for self-aggrandizement, but for the common good.

6) All wealth is kept in stewardship. No one "makes" wealth. Food comes from trees, shelter is built from the bones of the earth, clothing comes from the backs of animals. All of our raw materials are in the public domain. No one can really claim to own them. Each of us, however, must have what should be a considered a fair share to steward for the sake of pleasing God, enriching the society, and providing for our proper responsibilities according to one's state in life.

7) The problem with someone who has great wealth is a matter of asking "Why?" Why would someone feel the need to have more money than some nations possess? Why would someone feel the need to work in such a way that others are oppressed? Why would someone feel the need to control properties scattered around a nation or around the world? Why would someone feel the need to have hundreds if not thousands of other people subservient to him? If one can answer these questions in keeping with the virtues of faith, hope, and charity, then wealth can be the means to sanctity and thus to Heaven. It takes a fair amount of sanctity to begin with to come up with acceptable answers to such questions in keeping with the life of virtue. Someone with that kind of sanctity to begin with rarely has the urge to exercise it in the amassing of a fortune. It can be done, but instances of such are notable mostly for their rarity.

You will notice that the average rich saint spends quite a bit of energy in getting rid of his wealth. The average not-rich not-saint spends a lot of energy trying to figure out why it would be okay to get a lot of wealth. The rich saint expends himself on becoming holier, frequently by way of divesting himself of wealth. The normal sinner expends himself on getting along in and with the world, making sanctity an afterthought, if given any thought. Most of us putting sanctity at the forefront of our thoughts will find that being good before one becomes rich often precludes becoming rich. The sinner who becomes rich first rarely feels much desire to become holy after the fact. That in a nutshell illustrates the tension.

One could remain chaste while frequenting brothels, but that is an unwise habit to get into. One could remain faithful while reading heretical writings regularly, but that is imprudent. One can remain poor in spirit while being rich in pocketbook, but that is a risky business. Near occasions of sin constitute actual sins for most of us. The wiser route is to humbly acknowledge our weakness and not put the ourselves needlessly to the test—a test we are more than likely to fail.

> If one can be holy without wealth, why go to the bother of getting wealthy?
>
> If one can be holy without wealth, one can help other poor people to be holy without the bother of making them wealthy.
>
> The man who makes aid to the poor dependent on his wealth suggests that the poor themselves are incapable of charity.
>
> God makes sanctity sweet and easy—even the poor can attain it (Mt. 11:25-30).
>
> Great wealth coupled with great sanctity is difficult, not because God makes holiness hard, but because man makes wealth hard-hearted.

God bless you,
Father Smith

July 16, 2004: Our Lady of Mount Carmel

The Fate of False Infallibilities

Holy Mother Church is infallible. She is *truly* infallible. The bride of Christ is infallible because she preaches nothing but Christ, her Groom, Truth Incarnate, and Him crucified. Infallibility inheres in our Mother and Teacher; whenever she proclaims divine wisdom as it touches on the faith and morals of mankind, she is without flaw. She can not err in declaring what is required of man for his salvation, nor in explaining what is expected of man as he cooperates with grace in the project of obeying God's will. No stain of falsity taints the mystical Body of Christ as Peter guides the Church in knowing, loving, and serving Jesus Christ, the same yesterday, today, and forever. The gates of hell, the father of lies, the powers of the world can not prevail against the Barque of Peter, nor snatch away that which the hand of God the Father has claimed for His own, nor overcome those on whom the Son has sent the Spirit from the Father.

God has spoken His truth in Sacred Scripture. He can neither deceive nor be deceived. Nothing contained in the Bible is subject to human error. The Church is the authentic interpreter of God's word as it appears in the canon authoritatively delineated by the fathers of the Church and her solemn magisterium. What God has said to man in Holy Writ is true, expresses His will, and is given to the Church that she might make known divine revelation for the benefit of mankind. God does not, can not, and will not deny or contradict Himself. His Church does not, can not, and will not deny or contradict her Lord as she makes clear the meaning God has expressed through the Prophets, Apostles, and Evangelists.

Quod semper, quod ubique, quod omnibus creditum est! is the articulation by St. Vincent of Lerins of the means of being certain of Catholic truth. The *sensus fidei,* the sense of the faith, is the enduring gift of God to His people in which they are able to judge the vagaries of the world against the eternal and immutable truth of Christ (cf. 1 Corinthians 2:10-16). The *sensus Catholicus,* the catholicity of the members of the Body of Christ, is the indwelling of the Holy Ghost by which the

One Church is united in the One Faith given in the One Baptism through which the soul participates in the Cross of the One Lord, Jesus Christ (cf. Ephesians 4:1-31). The *sensus fidelium*, the sense of the faithful, is the assent of the steadfast children of the Church as they resist satan and sin, embrace the cross, and bear witness through sanctity to the omnipotence of divine charity overcoming the world, casting out the devil, and acknowledging God as Father (cf. St. John 16:25-33; St. Mark 8:34-38; and 1 Corinthians 13:1-13). What is always believed, everywhere, by all the faithful members of the flock as it has been handed down in tradition, taught by the authentic magisterium, and revealed by Sacred Scripture is safe and worthy of belief for all time. Nothing at dissonance with the immemorial teachings of the Church is true. All that the Church propounds to the faithful for their willing assent is true.

When in his capacity as universal shepherd under Christ, speaking to all the faithful with the intention of defining truth in the matter of faith or morals, the pope declares a teaching to be held by the Church with faithful obedience, that teaching is *ipso facto* infallible. God the Holy Ghost guarantees that nothing contrary to the Faith will ever be promulgated by the Church's magisterium. It is not the person of the Pope who enjoys this divine protection, but the formal and official teachings that flow solely from the papacy. By extension this charism of dogmatic inerrancy is shared by the full magisterium when convened under the pope in an ecumenical council *in which dogmatic statements are defined.* His Holiness is privileged by divine providence to be so endowed with the grace of infallibility insofar as he offers the faithful *only* that which has been transmitted through tradition; proceeds from the principles inherent in previous dogmas, traditions, or divine revelation; and/or adds nothing to or subtracts anything from those things which already belong to the patrimony of the Church in such wise that alien elements are introduced or essential elements are diminished.

Some would beg to differ that divine revelation, constant tradition, or the authentic magisterium are sources, examples, or guarantors of infallible truth. The modern world has become a parrot of Pontius Pilate, asking incessantly, "Truth? What is truth?" In fact, asking questions has entirely supplanted efforts made at arriving at *definitive* answers to questions. Strangely, however, modern man has placed a premium on certain authorities as the *de fide* sources of such provisional answers as will not offend the modernist's relativistic sensibilities. Modernity is absolutely certain that Holy Mother Church is incapable of defining absolute truth, while simultaneously asserting that self-admittedly limited secular institutions and disciplines can flawlessly lead man to the little truth of which he is temporarily capable of knowing.

American jurisprudence might claim for its battle cry, "*Credo nihil sed quod credo!*" Having denied the establishment of a state religion through the Constitution and erecting a positivist wall to separate the state from the Church through judicial fiat, modern America, indeed, the whole modern world, has made impossible any kind of shared belief. What "I" believe is all that is believable for me. "You" believe only those things credible to you. As a nation, "We" believe nothing; "we" believe *in* nothing. Our laws are predicated on the notion of creating domestic tranquility by allowing no one to say, do, or legislate anything offensive to anyone else.

What, pray tell, might qualify as speech, action, or law on which all might agree? Such agreement flows from a common faith. In what do Americans place their faith as a people? By Constitution, through litigation, and in law, Americans have agreed as a people to believe in nothing, to have faith in nothing, to be a people without a shared faith. What modern Americans are discovering is that they can say, do, and legislate nothing that will not offend someone.

Acknowledgement of this national paralysis is seen in areas as disparate as what one calls the period between the fourth Thursday in November and the first day of January, what is allowable in the content of broadcast entertainment, and what makes valid the distinction between a teen girl's right over her own body to terminate a pregnancy and her teen boyfriend's inability to stunt the growth of his body by the purchase and use of tobacco products. Political correctness corrects no one, but terrorizes everyone. It has no absolute measure of what makes a statement, an activity, or a political position "correct", but modernity is rife with people seeking to please the mandates of the politically correct. Not everyone is politically correct, but most everyone fears not being politically correct. Few people would admit to wanting to be politically correct, but even fewer people would dare the peril of being habitually incorrect.

There is no high priestess dictating what constitutes acceptable speech, behavior, and political activity, so when Americans fail to police themselves adequately through self-censorship and political pandering, the courts are petitioned to pronounce judgment on whether or not a given citizen or group of citizens have broken the sacred commandment, "Thou shalt not believe too boldly!" May a mother ascertain whether or not her daughter of thirteen has sought an abortion? The courts have said no. May school children invoke God as they pledge allegiance to the flag of their homeland? The courts have said no. May a town display images of Christ during the seasonal celebration of His birth? The courts have said no.

Americans through their courts have declared that they do not know where babies come from, therefore, tissue growths in women's wombs may be destroyed even as what appears to be an infant's head begins to emerge from the birth canal. Americans through their courts have declared that they do not know the difference between boys and girls, therefore, sodomy is permissible as an alternative "lifestyle", complete with insurance policies, employee benefits, and Disneyland holidays for the exclusive enjoyment of persons desirous of committing unnatural acts. Americans through their courts have declared that they do not know what private property is, therefore, cities restrict home "owners" in their choices of paint color for their houses, states tax citizens so that private corporations can build sports arenas for their own profit, and the federal government confiscates income from employees during their working years only to tax it again when the money is returned to retirees as a socialist pension.

No consensus exists among Americans about the moral law, the proper limits of government, and the justice of economic systems. Because Americans have no common set of *absolute* principles to which to appeal for resolution of conflicts, they have sullenly agreed to allow judges to serve as referees in the daily warfare that is the American body politic. How do judges judge? Constitutional law, juridical precedents, and common law philosophy require interpretation in their application. An individual judge or the Supreme Court justices all bring to their work personal weaknesses, political inclinations, and the *zeitgeist* surrounding all but perceived by few.

The air we breathe by which moral, political, and social convictions are voiced is a scientific methodology guided by a materialist philosophy. Empiricism governs how modern man sets about knowing. A relativistic subjectivism rules modern man's understanding of what is true and why he should act on truth in any given way. The here and now, the tangible, the measurable is the lowest common denominator on which the majority of men will agree as a shared context of life. Anything beyond the material world capable of empirical analysis is a matter of faith, and modern men have agreed that as a group we can believe nothing together. Faith is out of bounds; only what is knowable is admissible in the court of modern thought. Epistemology far more than theology is the metaphysical arena of exploration for modernity.

For a scientific age that is etymologically appropriate. "Science" is the search for knowledge, "epistemology" is the study of knowing and what is knowable. What does science know and how does the epistemologist know that it knows it?

Each scientific discovery is a veritable proclamation that what is known is that we were wrong about what we knew. Newton yielded to Einstein. The horse gave way before the horseless carriage, which in its turn is brought to bay by gridlock, a victim of its own success. The campfire was dimmed by radio, itself outshone by television, eclipsed now by the variety of entertainments available via computer. Medical science vacillates constantly about whether or not and how much wine, butter, and coffee are good for you.

Progress as measured by science is an evolution from the unknown into the less known. Scientific knowledge is an absurdly boastful assertion that nothing can be known fully, nothing can be known finally, and nothing can be known fundamentally. All of this would be woefully depressing were it not for the philosophic fact that proof of a universal negative is impossible. Thus, science can not know for certain that its claimed impossibilities are indeed impossible. Science declaring that faith in nothing is reasonable in deference to the effort to know something, is brought up short by the scientific and rational inability to demonstrate that God is part of the nothing that can be believed or is a kind of something that can not be known. Perhaps the man of faith is to be doubted for his lack of physical proof of the existence of the object of his faith, but the man of science is not to be believed when he insists that one take him on faith when he denies the capacity of the subject of faith to know something simply because science is self-admittedly agnostic on the matter. What is not known by science far exceeds what science knows for sure; what is not known by science is a matter of the inadequacy of scientific means to certain knowledge, not of the impossibility of certitude in knowledge.

Any decent, honest scientist admits this. As a thermometer has nothing to say about the height of the man whose temperature it is taking, science has nothing to say about the soul of the man that divines knowledge of the divine person who is the sole measure of man. It is not an insult to say of science that it is ignorant of the realm of spirit. It is the highest compliment to science to employ its tools in allowing the spirit of man to strive for true freedom. Man bound only to matter and only for death is in the bonds of slavery. Man striving to ken the fullness of truth is set free by the knowledge that a life in the spirit can be at least rationally posited. Science in denial of that possibility is in self-denial: science of itself can neither affirm nor reject faith, and in attempting to do either makes not only faith impossible, but science dies as well.

If man depends only on science for his knowledge of the world and of himself, then he will find himself trapped by science's inherent inability to know anything definitively. The paradox of science is that the first thing known must be the fact of ignorance. Unless an ultimate source and object of knowledge (God) exists, then science is reduced to being an ever-expanding arena of subjects for a never-ending increase of ignorance thereof. The key that unlocks this prison of pure reason is the Faith. Man electing to disregard faith is choosing to remain imprisoned in his senses, utterly unable to make ultimate sense out of what he perceives. Science might answer what, how, where, and when, but science knows nothing of who and why. In an exclusively material universe, there is no such thing as an "I" to be the subject of knowledge, there is no "Thou" to be the object of knowledge, there is no "We" to share knowledge (or faith, or hope, or love), and there is no purpose for the existence of knowledge nor for the seeking of knowledge.

So if faith in nothing is the mutual agreement of society, and knowledge of nothing is the ultimate verdict of science as to man's ability to judge his own purpose or *raison d'etre,* what, then, is man to do with himself during his very limited (spiritually, rationally, physically) time on earth? It would appear that modern man has fallen back on an ancient resolution to his quandary—eat, drink, and be merry, for tomorrow we die!

Modern man seeks solace in the marketplace. *Not* the marketplace of ideas—that would require knowledge or faith, of which he is entirely bereft, but the marketplace of money. Morning, noon, and night, twenty-four-seven, without respite for worship, family, or terrorist attack, modern America is admonished to labor for the almighty dollar. It is imperative to understand that the fruit of modern labor is *not* daily bread, but cash (although known all the same in 1960s parlance as "bread"). At the end of the day, on payday, in the endless days of retirement, the American laborer has not things made by his hands, crops from the ground he sowed, nor a patrimony for him to hand on to his sons and their sons; but a check, debts to diminish it, and taxes to remind him of the source of all "wealth".

Usury is the lifeblood of modern economics. Wealth is no longer measured in acreages, heads of cattle, or objects manufactured. Instead, liquid assets, interest payments, and stock options are the possessions of the modern materially endowed. No more is wealth threatened by plagues of locusts, marauding hordes, or droughts and floods. The bane of modern mammon is falling consumer confidence or tight money policy or protectionism among foreign competitors.

It is no little irony that in an age when human wealth is controlled by human decisions as has never happened in human history, man's economic security is fragile as never before. A man once knew how much he could expect an acre to yield, what a bushel would fetch at market, the amount he would owe in taxes, the habits of pestilence and vermin in his homeland, and that his son would have a stake on which to build his fortunes. Now a family must contend with employment decisions made in New York, tax policy made in Washington, market instability in Brazil, subsidies approved in Brussels, and promotional discounts out of Tokyo.

A thirty-year mortgage allows a family to pay for its home three times over. Property taxes permit them to rent from the government indefinitely. Loans against home equity provide liquidity for the family through the illusion of real estate generating income by just sitting there and appreciating in value for no apparent reason. The witch doctors of modern finance insist that all of this cash changing hands represents growing wealth, when in reality all that is happening is that more money is being printed. A house resting on its foundation is not working capital. It does not produce a crop. It can not give birth to garages, boat houses, or gazebos.

When Enron, K-Mart, and Global Crossing went belly-up, nothing tangible was destroyed. When the booming stock market of the 1990s went bust after 2000, a couple of trillion dollars vanished without a trace. When property values in big-city downtowns plunged, office space remained but developers and speculators skipped town with phantom profits while tenants paid real rents, cities paved real streets, and banks held real bad loans.

The modern economy is increasingly a matter of financial speculation, usurious lending, and conspicuous consumption to keep it all going. Money is used to breed money. The provision of unnecessary services provides employment for people whose livelihood depends on the misdirected industry of other people, and those other people must eat, wear, and upgrade all manner of goods that they do not need in order to pay their credit card debts, provide employment for other wage slaves, and give them something to do to take their minds off of their faithless, confusing, purposeless existence. An increase of wealth in the modern world is not an increase in crop yield, industrial production, or personal autonomy;

modern economics depend upon borrowing capacity, market manipulation, and financial policy by governments over which individuals have almost no control.

Modern man does not believe in God. He does not know why he exists. He will not look to the Church for answers. Instead, modern man places his social welfare in the hands of judges who make life and death decisions about morality; he desires a scientific measure to determine the good, the true, and the real by which life decisions are to be made; and he lives a life ruled by the vagaries of an economic system that no one understands, no one controls, and no one can escape. Modern man rejects the love and care of a provident God within the community of a faith-filled Church in favor of a universe judged by men who agree on nothing, know nothing of ultimate meaning, and erect lives built on the pursuit of things that have no lasting value.

An economy based on real property is almost immune from usury. An economy based on cash is an invitation to usury that becomes slavery to usury. A cashless economy, the boast of the prophets of future profits, devolves into a barter system where the commodities are not things grown, things built, or things traded, but the time, presence, and autonomy of *people*. What is the value of those people, the use of those people, the purpose of those people? To make things, to consume things, to be things that make and consume things that will decay or become obsolete, requiring more things to be made and consumed, which decay and become obsolete and require more things to be made and consumed.

Why? Because the market wants nothing other than consumption, consumables, and consumers. Because science knows nothing that can not be made or consumed. Because we the people have agreed to believe in nothing but what we can make and consume. We the people have built a world where nothing exists but consumption, the consumed, and consumers. What, then, does that make of the people? An existence of being made for consumption and consuming, and when all are consumed then comes the night, the nothing of which we have made of ourselves, that we know of ourselves, that we believe about the life we have given ourselves.

Such is the fate of those who know nothing of reason, of faith, or of God.

Father Smith

Sacerdos vagus 15 November 2003: St. Albert the Great

see Romans 6:23; Psalm 113:1-8; 3 Kings 18:17-40

Defining Distributism

Part 1: What it is not

Did you ever wonder how the Chicago Cubs baseball team has managed such consistent mediocrity for the better part of a century? Systematic futility is made, not born, and the primary locus of production for Northside-Chicago misplaced hope is none other than the capital of my home state, Des Moines, Iowa. The Iowa Cubs are the triple-A farm affiliate for the Chicago Cubs. A lot of the well-honed talent for disappointment experienced in the Friendly Confines was trained and perfected right here in Iowa.

Did you ever wonder who was the first person to receive the application of the principle that a bone-crunching "adjustment" of the back would lead to overall physical wellbeing? When you think about it, having somebody shove down hard with both hands on your spine is right up there with being the first guy to jump out of an airplane in flight or joining the first crew on a nuclear submarine spending six months underneath the arctic ice cap. Well, the first wise fools of chiropractic blazed their trail in my hometown, Davenport, Iowa.

Did you ever wonder where the likes of Pepsi or Froot Loops or Twinkies get the stuff that makes their products so enticingly sweet? Sugar gets a bad rap in the American diet, but corn syrup is used a whole lot more than plain old sugar to satisfy our collective sweet tooth. Few people realize just how complicated and industrial our food delivery system is, but if you ask the people of Cedar Rapids, Iowa, or Decatur, Illinois, they can attest that corn processing is right up there with steel mills and oil refineries for negative olfactory effect on local air quality. Not many places can boast a world-class corn processing operation, a huge beef by-products rendering plant, and a state-of-the-art chemical production facility within the city limits, but my current home in Clinton, Iowa, can.

So, if you wonder about how I come up with my peculiar take on the Chesterbelloc-inspired economic system of distributism, remember that mediocrity, medical adventurousness, and municipal stench are my birthright, mother's milk, and the air I breathe. But I blame neither heredity nor environment. I take full responsibility for the succeeding explanation of distributism.

Iowa will serve well to illustrate some of the aspects that help to define distributism. This is because Iowans both practice distributism and are ignorant of distributism. Iowa has an economy with a good cross-section of business, industry, and agriculture. And Iowa allows me to obey the writer's first commandment: *Write what you know!*

Let us be clear from the start about what we are not talking about when we talk about distributism. Distributism is not Walmart, it is not Social Security, it is not 9-to-5 on the factory floor. Distributism is certainly not capitalism, it is most definitely not socialism, and absolutely not communism. Distributism is not an answer, it is not a solution, it is not a *raison d'être*. Distributism is many things, but it is not most of the things with which we are familiar, distributism being mainly the things we find particularly special.

Well into the 1970s, the economy of Iowa was based on an interplay between family farms and the industry that supported them and grew from them. Most Iowans, for most of its history, have been farmers. Sometime in the latter half of the twentieth century that changed. Today, the biggest employers in the state are Hy-Vee Food Stores and John Deere Manufacturing. Mass employment is not distributism.

Winter in Iowa can see snowfalls of fifteen inches at a time, and wind-chill factors as low as fifty degrees below zero Fahrenheit. Summer in Iowa can begin in March and last into November (though April and October can be winter months), and temperatures can spend weeks at a time leaping toward one hundred degrees Fahrenheit. Oddly enough, such weather extremes do not keep Iowa from having one of the oldest populations in the country. Schools in Iowa consistently graduate over ninety-percent of their students, standardized test scores are among the highest in the nation, and the three state universities have world-class programs in a variety of disciplines. Notwithstanding all of this, Iowa experiences a severe brain drain each year as high school graduates flee the state to pursue work, education, and self-finding elsewhere. Population instability and demographic imbalance is not distributism.

People used to think that metropolitan Davenport (known as the "Quad-Cities" of Davenport and Bettendorf in Iowa, and Rock Island and Moline in Illinois) had a "recession-proof" economy. This was because the biggest employers in town made machines that harvest food. Since people always eat, it was figured that building food-plucking gadgets was as stable as being a doctor, mortician, or tax collector. The Quad-Cities lost twenty-thousand people during the farm crisis of the 1980s. Much of that population has been regained, but the manufacturing jobs were replaced by retail and service "industry" positions. Such reliance on factory labor and non-productive employment is not distributism.

Capitalism, socialism, and communism are the unholy trinity of materialism. By differing means they bring about the common end of asserting life on earth as the only life there is. Whether one is a "consumer" in capitalism, a "ward of the state" in socialism, or a "worker" in communism, one exists to get things, grant things, or make things. Things are the thing in materialism. Things contribute to distributism, but things are not the point of distributism.

The true distributist does not want to convince, coerce, or conspire for the cause of distributism. A distributist does not consider distributism to be much of a topic of conversation, much less the matter of crusades against other abstractions. There is no distributism in Heaven.

At present, it is very likely that you participate in quite a few activities that are at home in distributism. Equally likely is the probability that these activities are directed by something decidedly other than distributism. This is because the world around you is out of its mind. Insanity is not distributism.

So what is distributism? Please read *Defining Distributism, Part 2: What it is.* If you do not like what distributism is not, then I think you will really like what distributism is!

Part 2: What it is

John Steinbeck described a father preparing a son for distributism in the novella, *The Red Pony.* (For a wonderful paean to distributism in another Steinbeck work, read the one-page chapter thirteen of his epic masterpiece, *East of Eden.*)

There are some who will object that Steinbeck was a socialist in his early adulthood and probably never heard of distributism. That is quite possibly the case. But one need not understand the principles of counterpoint to enjoy "Row, Row, Row Your Boat". Steinbeck knew not Chesterton nor distributism, but he liked them both.

In *The Red Pony*, a father decides that his son is ready for greater responsibility. He sends the boy with a mare to a neighboring farm to have its stallion provide stud services. The pony that is born is to be the boy's responsibility—and property.

That father (and Steinbeck) has an intuitive understanding of distributism. Distributism works on the principle that someone has the right to own his own property—and does own it. This sounds simple, but the concentration of property in the hands of a minority of citizens common in capitalism (five percent of Americans own well over half of the liquid assets in the United States); the concentration of public lands and taxing authority possessed by the state in socialist systems (state and federal governments hold title to as much as one-third of several western states, and individual Americans pay as much as one-half of their income in local, state, and federal property and/or income taxes); and the concentration of agricultural and industrial means of production under direct government control inherent in communism (one hundred percent in theory, in excess of eighty percent in practice) are testimonies to how pervasive is the attack on private property throughout the world.

Distributism insists and assumes that ordinary people are able to feed, clothe, and shelter themselves. Furthermore, the distributist society expects that the food, clothing, and housing are direct products of the ordinary people who use them. Unlike the capitalist baron, a successful distributist would rarely desire, much less possess, more than one house. Unlike in the well-run socialist nanny state, it would be unusual for a man to ask a distributist government to employ him or to shoe his children. Unlike the omnipresent communist Rube Goldberg nightmare, distributists do not pretend to be able to determine in advance the size of a harvest, its price per bushel, or the number of dinners a family will eat at home in the next year.

Neither the warped "justice" of a few people owning everything, nor the twisted "fairness" of nobody owning anything occurs in distributism. The distributist system operates on the principle that each man has a right to his own things. He does not have a right to his neighbors' property. His neighbors collectively have no right to his property. Distributism allows for the possession and exchange of property, and asserts that a balance between the two is essential.

Family-sized portions are the norm in distributism. What a family needs to feed itself, produce a living, and make a home are the rights acknowledged by the distributist community. The family farm, the family business, and the family seat form the nucleus of activity among distributists. The family is both efficient cause and penultimate end of distributism (a discussion of its final cause and ultimate end comes in Parts 4 and 5).

Thus described, as being between causes and ends, distributism can be understood as an intermediate good. It comes from a good and tends toward perfection. Materialist economic systems are self-contained. Neither the faceless market, nor the nameless state, nor the heartless revolution look outside themselves for direction or justification. Materialism is its own reward (and ultimate punishment).

And thus another aspect of distributism is brought into relief. It is not an explanation nor an abstraction nor an absolute. Distributism is a means, a method, and a mood. It is not so much a way of life as it is a way to get out of the way of living one's life. It is not so much a set of instructions for what is required for the good life as it is acting on the conviction that life is good. It is not happiness as such, but it is how happy people choose to conduct their public and economic affairs.

Unhappy people do not make good distributists. By the same token, distributism will not and can not make anyone happy. Distributism understands what materialist economics does not: one eats to live, not lives to eat. Distributism is neither a point of departure nor a destination. It is eminently liminal, of and from the earth, but meant for the purpose of what lies beyond this life.

Iowa, my home, has some marvelously distributist elements in its persona. Each midsummer one can delight in hundreds of roadside stands, often manned by children, where fresh sweet corn is available. (I've seen a couple where the corn was free!) There are innumerable inns (disguised as bed-and-breakfasts) throughout the state, where guests and hosts share living quarters, meals, and pleasant company. And no state surpasses Iowa for the abundance of county fairs and *the* State Fair (they made a movie musical about it), where handcrafts, livestock, and produce are displayed by the men, women, and children—families—who labored on them.

Early Iowans (the state was admitted to the Union in 1846) never heard of distributism. All the same, the heavy emphasis on agriculture, small towns, and trades made Iowa much more the inheritor of the patrimony of medieval Europe (the vast majority of Iowa settlers were German, English, and Slavic) than the creature of the industrial revolution occurring as Iowa grew. Medieval Europe counted wealth in acres, whereas modern America counts wealth in stock shares. Most of Iowa for most of its history has stored its assets in silos before anything was in a bank. By contrast, only one Fortune 500 company is headquartered in Iowa.

This is not to say that Iowa is a distributist heaven. Iowa is just Iowa. It does serve, however, as a demonstration that distributism is not the pipe dream its critics believe it to be. Distributism might not be all around us, but we certainly have it within us. Distributism might not be here presently, but its roots run deep into our past. Distributism might not be probable, but our own experience shows us that distributism is definitely possible.

Part 3: What it looks like

Several subversive septuagenarians sat in my office one morning. These were pillars of our community, rocks upon which their families were built, grandmas to a woman. And they were talking revolution!

Some of the ladies had granddaughters who were causing them distress. Each had experienced the same offense in the midst of Sunday Mass. All wanted something done about it.

The beauty of their ire was that they had no desire for government intervention. They did not expect the priests to address the situation from the sanctuary. There was no outcry for a petition drive or legislation.

These grannies wanted action. They were going to do it themselves. They were going to sew some dresses!

What had happened was the ever-growing phenomenon of immodesty. My parishioners were weary of the weekly invitation to impurity being witnessed at Mass. But the women were astute enough about the local economy to know that few, if any, opportunities exist to buy actual dresses for girls. The gods of fashion don't allow that. My septuagenarian radicals also understood enough about young people and the feminine psyche to realize that a problem with vanity had a better chance at a solution through an appeal to beauty than through lecturing or criticizing.

Thus, the women thought of making some dresses for their granddaughters. Then they would "market" them as one-of-a-kind Grandma Originals for birthday and Christmas gifts. The *piece de resistance* was the decision to try to persuade the girls to learn to sew!

Time will tell whether or not the dresses are made or ever worn, but the distributist key is that our women did not surrender to the market. They did what they did, not to make a buck nor to spend a buck. They embarked on the project of making garments in order to clothe and adorn the human body!

But, Father, isn't that what all clothes are for?

In a word, no. Walmart sells clothes for a profit. Americans buy clothes because they can, and they buy them to make various meaningless statements about themselves. Third-world slaves make clothing to postpone death by starvation (after all, they are sewing, not sowing).

Obviously no economy restricts itself to the production and acquisition of clothing, but this serves as a good example of how distributism distinguishes itself. The distributist is motivated by a real human need, attempts the direct and personal satisfaction of that need, and is able to understand the need, the attempt, and the satisfaction. Distributism allows material goods to be used for human needs, toward human ends, on a human scale.

Chesterton mentions in *The Outline of Sanity* that one step toward distributism is to give one's custom to local, privately owned establishments. The final step of becoming a distributist is in being an establishment of that kind. In between these two steps is nothing.

Well, actually, not nothing, but less. The American committed to the distributist model needs to redefine his understanding of economics. His first step in that direction is to redefine his understanding of his own place in the economy. The very first step, then, is to demand to be freed of the inhuman label of "consumer".

Babies can not conceive of a difference between "need" and "want". When all one needs are dry diapers, mother's milk, and hugs and kisses, one's wants need not be denied. Not long into life, however, the child learns that there are lots of nice things to want. Temper tantrums ensue. The project of reaching adulthood includes distinguishing between needs and wants and learning how to sacrifice wants at need. Full maturity is learning to want only what is needed.

The consumer is in a perpetual state of immaturity. Our retail economy is predicated on businesses creating, not products, but artificial needs. These same businesses then offer the perfect product to satisfy the recent need. Of course, the businesses stay in business, not because they make such good products, but because they make such convincing pitches to the immature inability to know need from want.

A fully distributist economy has no consumers. Services are provided by the competent person to the person unable to perform the service himself, rather than a surly employee "helping" a lazy or harried consumer. Being cured of being a consumer entails the decision to go without as much as possible, refusing to rely on the work of wage slaves, the toxic beneficence of big business, or the smothering largesse of government. One can not make a national economy distributist over night, but one can certainly make his personal economy more distributist each day.

Economic activity in the distributist community would be poorer than in capitalism, but not impoverished as in communism, or stagnant as in socialism. What's more, the lessening of macro-economic activity would be balanced to a healthy degree by an increase in micro-economic activity. There might be fewer billions of dollars going overseas for cheap electronic products, but quite likely a greater number of musicians, actors, and other entertainers would find local audiences desirous of their talents. Even better, the populace at large would have incentive and opportunity to learn to sing, dance, and amuse themselves without binary or mechanical assistance. Fewer people would be celebrities, but most people would be able to offer positive contributions to the social, economic, and artistic life around their own homes.

It must be remembered and emphasized that poverty is relative. Distributists are not consigned to dearth, nor are they (as are capitalists) chained to an ever-growing demand for excess. The distributist economy can be maintained by the ordinary people in such wise that the level of technological infringement on normal life, the extent of international trade, and the quality and quantity of material goods are chosen variables, not the happenstance of the market or the arbitrary determination of the government.

But many will be unconvinced by these explanations. The beauty of distributism is that to a large extent I can do it without permission. Capitalist concentration of wealth, socialist taxation of income, and communist confiscation of property destroy fundamental freedom. As an illustration of this, I leave you with a question: "Considering all of the arguments against an individual's ability to establish a personal distributist economy, what does that say about the existence of true freedom of self-determination in modern America?"

Part 4: What it is for

Perhaps I will be vilified by my fellow distributists for saying so, but in the interest of honesty and full disclosure, I must reveal that distributism produces poverty. This more than anything else, I think, explains why distributism goes untried. Capitalism brazenly lusts after wealth. Socialism proudly passes the wealth around. Communism pretends there is no wealth. All three consider poverty an embarrassment, a failure, a sin. Distributism cultivates poverty.

Or, to put it positively and actually more accurately, poverty and a desire thereof produce distributism. Distributism then dutifully provides a structure wherein the poor can pursue their real love: the Kingdom of Heaven.

Distributism is not about things. It is about people. It is even more about each person. And most of all, it understands that social justice renders not only man his due, but God receives His due as well. Distributism recognizes that God is people, too.

The major activity of man is not economic, nor is man meant only to attend to his own concerns. Man is created in the image and likeness of God. That creation, that gift, is intended for the purpose of man's perfection through his knowledge of his origins and the revelation of his ultimate end. The distributist realizes that distributism is woefully inadequate to reach such a goal.

So distributism is about getting out of the way. Crops are planted to feed people, not to stock mega-supermarket shelves. Houses are built to keep the rain out and the coziness in, not to spark speculation about the neighbors' annual income. Clothes are made to draw attention away from nakedness and to permit natural movement, not to arouse baser instincts or prevent locomotion.

And man eats to live, not lives to eat. Man, not the mortgage or the tax collector, is the king of his castle. The man is not made by his clothes; a man is their maker and wearer.

Knowing this about himself, man is free to keep his economic concerns at the minimum they deserve. The whole point behind distributism is human freedom. Man is most free when he contemplates God.

That contemplation takes many forms. Perhaps its primary condition is silence. The distributist needs to be a man of silence. His ears should be attuned to his neighbor, to nature, and to the voice of God in prayer. Thus, distributism can use machinery at need, but will limit its use so as to limit its noise.

Contemplating God is a joyful reality. Angels and saints break into song because of their proximity to the divine. The good distributist will revel in his own shouts of exaltation and in the tunes he hears when his friends are moved in like manner. Distributism prefers melodies from the heart and out of the mouth, and so places a premium on opportunities for people to gather and serenade God, His creation, and each other. This might be Mass on Sunday, so the distributist society would restrict custom on the Lord's Day to allow everyone to worship. The observance might be secular, but the distributist government would not refuse God the opportunity to speak at the event. The family has frequent cause for celebration, and so God, as the central member of the family, would be a primary participant in the activity.

But life can not be an endless party. The healthy man will need time alone. He will need to cultivate silence with God. He will need to hone those skills, perfect those talents, and reflect on those insights that will be his gift of self to God and neighbor. A man who can not stand to spend time alone with himself should not inflict that company on anyone else.

Solitude is not a matter of inactivity. Much of the distributist's solitude is found in his daily work. Sweat equity and intellectual labor offer both an opportunity at individual effort and the chance to share one's labor and its fruit with others. Work in a distributist community is necessary and self-evidently so. The worker and his work are needed and properly valued by his peers.

Corollary to this is putting work in its place. This is perhaps at the heart of understanding distributism. Material goods are sought as means, not ends. The distributist labors so as to engage in what labor makes possible: prayer, solitude, silence, song, and communion. The distributist does not rest so that he can work harder, he works that he might have leisure to live.

Distributism is a means in a fallen world to seek what can not fall. It sees the world as fallen, but not irredeemable. Indeed, it is the reality of its redemption that shows it fallen. The distributist knows himself to be part of the world's fall. He also is certain that God has made each man to be a contributor to salvation. Distributism is an economic means for each man to participate in the salvation of all men.

This is, in a word, sanctity. Distributism does not sanctify, but the distributist craves sanctity. He uses distributism as a tool to arrange his life so that material needs contribute to spiritual imperatives. The distributist uses the things of this world in keeping with the laws of the world to come. The distributist need not *be* holy yet, but he needs to *want* to be holy now.

To ask a capitalist what he is doing is to invite the answer, "Making money." If one asks a socialist what he is doing, he will say something like, "Making a fair world for all." The communist asked that question will respond, "Making the workers' paradise." The only explanation for a distributist's motivation is, "Making my way to Heaven!"

He does this fully cognizant that the only things he makes are of this world with his own hands. The beauty of the distributist's awareness that lifts him above materialist despair, is his faith that the way to Heaven has been opened to him. It is open to all who are willing to leave all things behind and follow Christ. Distributism is the economic means to free oneself from the material chains of this world, to build up the treasured capital of the spiritual world, and thus be able to afford the Pearl of Great Price.

And here we come to the place whence all Chestertonian paradoxes emanate. For this wonderful Pearl is already paid for. The man who can afford the Pearl is he who understands that it is the gift of life given by Jesus Christ on the Cross. Faith in the Cross allows purchase without payment. It is the debt forgiven though the full price is paid.

Thus, distributism is indeed poverty, the poverty of complete self-emptying. It takes for its model and its motive force the cross of Calvary. **Not all Catholics are distributists, *but every distributist must be above and before all things, Catholic.*** No greater wealth exists in the universe!

Part 5: What it does

Jesus Christ was holy. People want to be like Jesus. Jesus Christ was merciful. People want to be like Jesus. Jesus Christ was loving. People want to be like Jesus. Jesus Christ was poor. People want to be different.

Oops.

Distributists need to believe, understand, and accept that distributism is different from the difference of the world. Imitating Christ, distributism is different from the world in its assumptions, its rationale, and its motivations. Distributists need to be prepared to think differently, to act differently, and to *be* different.

A big distributist difference is to cease desiring to *make* a difference. Distributism is not market manipulation, social engineering, or ushering in the reign of *ubermensch*. To be a distributist is not to embark on an evangelizing crusade. There is only one Gospel worthy of evangelizing others; Distributism is its servant, not its replacement.

This, I think, needs to mark the distributist's attitude. Distributism is how *I* live. I think it is *one* good way to live, even the best way, but surely it is not mandatory. After all, Jesus was not a distributist, but a mendicant.

Here lies an important distinction between distributism and materialist economics. Distributism humbly pursues a way of life, inviting and welcoming others to join in. Capitalism, socialism, and communism proudly export themselves. Where preaching does not work, they are not shy about exerting political force. Failing that, capitalism and communism will resort to gun-boat proselytizing.

Do not confuse humility with timidity. No one can pursue distributist freedom without a healthy ability to take risks and to be brave in resistance. A successful distributist might not convince any by his actions, nor persuade by his arguments, but he certainly will not shy away from a debate. Nor will he let the materialist draw him into a quarrel.

Fear not, friends! Simply because one's motivation is other than making a difference does not mean that being a distributist makes no difference. Distributism is not an exercise in futility. It remembers the admonition of Mother Teresa of Calcutta: "We are not called to be successful; we are called to be faithful!"

The faithful distributist will be different. That difference will have effects. Some no one will notice. Others can not but be noticed.

A few facts:

- the United States of America accounts for fully one-half of worldwide economic activity
- two-thirds of the American economy is retail-related
- about sixty-percent of all retail activity occurs during the season-formerly-known-as-Christmas
- most Americans claim to be Christians
- most American Christians celebrate the season-formerly-known-as-Christmas by going on an orgy of gross material consumption

If the Christians who desire distributism would refrain from insulting the honor of Christ with wanton greed, a great difference would occur. Advent, the traditional four-week period of penance before Christmas, would be spent in prayerful preparation, not on shopping frenzies. Christmas would be observed as a season extending well into January or even February, not an anticlimax ending abruptly and disappointingly on New Year's Day. Generosity to the poor rather than the overindulgence of the rich would mark the festivities commemorating the Incarnation of the holy, merciful, loving, *poor* Son of God.

And a lot less money would exchange hands!

Instead, the emphasis would be on piety directed to God and charity given to neighbor. Families would be brought together around the icon of the Holy Family of Jesus, Mary, and Joseph, rather than being driven apart to the mall, by depression, and in forgetfulness of the real gift of Christ at Christmas. Approaching the celebration for faith, not for profit, would profit the spiritual well-being of everyone concerned.

But bottom lines would suffer. Remember, though, that distributism is not motivated by making a difference. Being different at Christmas is meant for the purpose of acknowledging Christ's coming into the world to be its Savior. The cumulative weight of a lot of distributists being different might—or might not—result in other people realizing that something and someone has changed. Such a change no Christian could pretend would not be for the better.

Always keep in mind, however, that distributism is about life on a human scale. What the distributist does is quite hands on. *Why* he does it should be equally applicable to the individual. A good distributist motto could be: "Avoid solutions that require more work for others than is demanded of you." Improvements in moral character, diminishment of faults, and overall betterment of the person should be most immediately seen in the mirror of the soul.

At first, a distributist might feel all alone. This is not because distributism is permission to indulge in individualism. Quite to the contrary, family, community, and the Church are the primary context of human life, and thus of distributive life. Nonetheless, the initial distributist experience might be an article in a magazine or a site on the web or a work of the Chesterbelloc. Appetite thus whetted, the burgeoning distributist might be on fire to *do* something.

That is admirable and to be nurtured. But whether one's distributist community is a family, a farm co-op, or a monastery, one proceeds comfortable with the reality of remaining a minority. This is not defeatism. This is just the fulfillment of the distributist's dream: a world wherein a family can rule its own, not a family seeking to rule the world.

For some who are looking for the ideal of distributism there is a temptation to investigate scholarship on the subject. Others might visit various distributist communities scattered here or there. I am not much of an idealist. Realism makes more sense to me. Toward that end, I encourage you to read the most realistic description of a distributist personality that I know. You will find it—Surprise, surprise!—in a work of Chesterton. The story is *Manalive,* and the man living the distributist ethos to the hilt is Innocent Smith.

I like that name!

Father Smith
12 September 2002: The Holy Name of the Blessed Virgin Mary
Lunardi's Restaurant and Barnes and Noble Café, Davenport, Iowa

Where Does the Remnant Live?

Let not your heart be troubled. You believe in God: believe also in me. In my Father's house there are many mansions. If not, I would have told you: because I go to prepare a place for you. And if I go to prepare a place for you, I will come again and will take you to myself: that where I am, you also may be. And whither I go you know: and the way you know.—Jn. 14:1-4 (see chapters 13-17)

Parishioners of a certain age in towns where I served back in Iowa relate stories of their childhood during the Great Depression. Everyone was poor, but no one knew it, because they had plenty to eat from the farms where they lived, sturdy clothing made by their mothers, and simple yet comfortable homes built by their grandfathers in the days when their fathers could only watch or get in the way. The men that everybody knew were poor were the hobos. They did not call them "homeless" back then. "Bindlestiffs" or "vagabonds" or "bums", but not homeless. They had homes wherever they laid themselves down for the night after a day or three of riding the rails.

Hobos had quite a set of survival techniques. They could be day laborers if need be. They did not shun petty larceny when the opportunity presented itself. And they networked with a panache that would make a Harvard Business School honors student blush. This networking might be communicating where a particular sheriff was particularly careful about keeping the letter of the law, or places that had especially inviting wages for temporary workers, or the names and descriptions of their fellows who were not to be trusted to tell their real name, or share fairly around the campfire, or keep laws that only devils can imagine can be broken.

One other kind of networking in their repertoire was a kind of semaphore or sign language or secret code known only to the initiated. This involved marking houses along the rail lines where a man could be pretty sure of getting a good sandwich by asking politely. The families who lived in these places, with good and big hearts, did not always understand why it seemed that their doors received knocks so much more often than their neighbors' ever did. It turns out that the hobos had a system for leaving telltale signs, readable by other hobos, near the houses where they had found succor. Their fellows coming after looked out for those signs, and, finding them, allowed their more fortunate brothers and sisters yet more opportunities to exercise the virtue of charity by corporal works of mercy. Such benevolence—by both parties—has rarely been seen in the world since.

But I think that lately I have been privileged to participate in a renaissance of Depression-era social exchange. Several people have rung my doorbell in the very recent past. They are what moderns call "disadvantaged youth", ranging in age from fifteen to thirty years old. Perhaps I am being paranoid and/or cynical, but I think the last three are a direct result of my having been kind to the first one. The arcane symbol by which my house is designated as housing an easy mark remains obscure to me, as is, I am sure, its intended effect, but it has served its purpose of drawing these needy souls to my front door.

"Monique" is a black woman of thirty. She grew up in the Watts section of Los Angeles. Two children call her "Mom", but they call two different men "Dad"—if they ever see them. "Monique" wants to improve the conditions of her children's upbringing, and to better herself. She wants out of the *Novus Ordo*.

"Anita" is a fifteen-year-old girl of Latin descent from Compton. College is her goal in life at this point in her life. Anita did not know what Latin was when I offered to give her a blessing in our Mother Church's mother tongue. She wants out of the *Novus Ordo*.

"Darrell" is a Chicago native. In his mid-twenties, he describes himself, thumping the book in his pocket, as a Bible-believer. Darrell grew up in the African Methodist-Episcopal sect, fell into gang activity, escaped the gangs and eluded arrest, and now he wants out of the *Novus Ordo*.

"Tanya" is the granddaughter of a Navajo medicine man. She grew up on the reservation, joined the marines, had three children, and now, at twenty-three, Tanya wants more for herself, her babies, and her people. She wants out of the *Novus Ordo*.

Monique, Anita, Darrell, and Tanya did not find their way to my threshold in order to repent their past errors of beliefs contrary to the immemorial deposit of faith transmitted under the authority of St. Peter and his successors. None of them is in the least aware of what has gone on in the Body of Christ since the Second Ecumenical Council of the Vatican. The last thing that any of them expected was to be greeted by a Catholic priest. They were more confused than angry or disappointed at my explanation for why I considered their efforts to be counterproductive to their supposed goals. All that they wanted to do was to generate points for advancement in their organization by selling magazine subscriptions.

In other words, they all want out of the *Novus Ordo*.

Many of my readers perhaps share with Monique, Anita, Darrell, and Tanya a complete lack of understanding of what I am talking about. Setting aside my intentional and infuriating obscurity of expression, that lack of understanding is probably my gravest concern for the future of the Church as it is being approached by Catholics committed to her traditional Mass. God be praised for the traditional Mass, but if Catholics do not come to understand that the *Novus Ordo* is far more than merely the *Novus Ordo Missae*, there is a frightening possibility that the Faith will be destroyed even amongst the faithful who cling to true doctrine, unsullied Sacraments, and the belief that the mystical Body of Christ is the Catholic Church under His Vicar, the Pope.

When I resolved to cease celebrating the *Novus Ordo Missae,* there were hundreds of people whom I met willing to support me in pursuing my priestly ministry in keeping with the Church's constant patrimony. I was congratulated frequently for having "converted". I can not count the number of people who have assured me of their prayers, offered me material assistance, and thanked me for making myself available to bring the Sacraments and the Faith to hungry Catholics.

What seems to be misunderstood is the nature of what I left behind. Of course, I did not want to participate in Eucharistic sacrileges where Our Lord's Precious Blood was poured down the sink. No priest wants to stand idly by when a deacon preaches heresy during Sunday Mass. Neo-conservative and traditional Catholics alike can tell innumerable horror stories of abuses in marriage preparation, seminary training, and sex education in the schools. Legion is the name of the problems plaguing the Church Militant in modernist hands.

Modernism, however, goes far beyond just what takes place on Sunday in the sanctuary or in the sacristy. The *Novus Ordo* mentality, *i.e.* the heresy of modernism, has indeed given us a Mass devoid of continuity with the roots of our faith, dismissive of the rights of the faithful to receive the fullness of the Faith as it always has been taught, and designed to propagate disinformation in the name of dialogue, ecumenism, and empowerment. The modern hierarchy has been eager to implement a détente with the world in which a readily recognizable Catholic ritual for worship is replaced by a protestant-friendly, man-centered, committee-created fellowship meal.

All of this has happened in the context of a society imbued with *sixty years* of degraded morality, *a century and a half* of the deification of science, *two hundred years* of materialist economics, *four centuries* of atheistic philosophy, and *a half-millennium* of apostate and heretic "theology" assaulting the doctrines, rituals, practices, and authority of the Church. Add the two or so centuries necessary to prepare the ground of the protestant revolt and you are confronted with the reality that for *seven hundred years* the faithful have lived in a milieu actively hostile to everything holy. It began slowly, with both the Church and Catholic states opposing the attacks, but over the centuries the degradation has accelerated and the havens for orthodoxy have become fewer and more besieged.

The result of this *three-quarters-of-a-millennium* battle royale has been the codification in the laws of veritably every nation on earth of contraception, divorce, sodomy, abortion, and usury. Most Catholics committed to the immemorial traditions of the Church have no problem understanding that the *Novus Ordo Missae* is problematic, in part, because it does not pose a sufficient barrier to these crimes against God and His Church. These same Catholics, however, have neglected to realize that pursuing the traditional Sacraments, morality, and Mass of the Church requires that modernism in its *every* aspect be shunned. It is not enough to flee the modernist Mass. Modernist music, employment, politics, child-rearing, recreation, courtship, and education must also be absolutely rejected.

Absolutely.

Constantine the Great permitted the true Faith to come to a people who then were moved to examine everything about their way of life and to change that life in keeping with their new found gift of Catholic truth. Pagans approaching the Church for the Sacraments were initiated not only into a body of belief, but into a way of living out that belief. Hence, marriage practice changed, abortion and child exposure ended, the vomitoria were closed, sodomy was denounced, and, yes, oblations to the Caesar were forbidden. Prior to Constantine's official toleration of the Church, Catholics did not stand idly by and suspend certain elements of the practice of their faith until a favorable emperor seized power. They joyfully adhered to the Faith even though they were robbed of their goods, branded as traitors, and thrown to the lions.

This joyful adherence caused many pagans to ask how it was that these strange people were able to accomplish this amazing thing, and how it was they loved each other so. The pagans were not starving only for the truths that come from and lead to Heaven. The pagans also knew that life on earth had become unbearable. Catholics offered them *truth* that transformed the man in such wise that nothing was capable of diminishing the certitude that this life could indeed lead to eternal life. All that was necessary was for this life to be laid down in favor of that promised life, for one's friends, for one's enemies, and for the one God through His one Church.

Here is where Catholics of the modern day fall down. We know the Faith. We celebrate the Mass. We teach the truth. But we cling to this life. The suggestion that superhighways, condominiums, iras, movies, and sports teams can pose grave dangers to the sanctification of souls is met with skepticism and ridicule even among Catholics for whom traditional practices are otherwise habitual. A near rebellion arises among faithful Catholics when they are exhorted to trust that they need not succumb to the false dichotomy between the Republicans and Democrats, both of which champion materialism, contraception, divorce, sodomy, and, in most cases, abortion. It is not the mouths of lions that bring us terror, but the possibility of empty mouths, empty wallets, and empty churches.

Quite a few times in the past, the Church has risen above such perils. At Thabor, Chartreuse, Citeaux, and Mount Alverno, men and women have imitated the ark of Noah, the community of St. John the Baptist at the Jordan, and Our Lord Himself before He began His public ministry. From centuries past, the Carmelites, the Carthusians, the Cistercians, and the Franciscans offer the Church in our day a reminder and a model of how God takes His own from the world in order to prepare them for the task of transforming the world. Never in the history of the Church has the Kingdom of Heaven been advanced by men acquiescing to the ways of the world or making accommodations for the world within the Church or admitting that the world has any chance of overcoming the Church.

Our constant example has been one of boldly displaying the Faith as the great sign of contradiction.

So, indeed, Catholics following the traditions of the Church must refrain from participating in a ritual that is informed by worldly sensibilities. Yet more, however, the immemorial Mass presents the challenge to the faithful of receiving the graces flowing from Our Lord's pierced side and distributed from the Altar of the Cross, and conforming their lives in secular society to the death of Our Lord on Calvary. It does no good to strain at the camel of the *Novus Ordo Missae* only to swallow the twin camel of rock music, modern cinema, teen dating, the American Constitution, rising real estate values, the newest suv, and the stock portfolio that only Bill Gates would pity.

It is not only our in-laws still at the *Novus Ordo* parish we used to attend who stand in need of the fullness of Catholic truth. It is our boss at work. It is the banker holding our mortgage. It is the nice waitress at our favorite chain restaurant. It is the man in the Oval Office. It is the talk show host we almost always agree with. It is ourselves still wedded to modernism in our economics, our politics, our recreation, our understanding of history, and our neglect to be perfect as our heavenly Father is perfect, to be holy as God is holy, to love God with our whole heart, whole mind, whole soul, and whole strength. We must love God in our whole lives, not just during the hour spent on Sunday at the traditional Mass.

Anita received the fullest version of this tirade, though Monique, Darrell, and Tanya also got an earful. Each of them said they had not thought of things quite like this before. They were grateful that I took some time with them. I seriously doubt that any of them will be at my Mass this coming Sunday. But I have placed them in Our Lady's care with the prayer that she will bring them a tad bit closer to abandoning the *Novus Ordo* world where the *Novus Ordo Missae* is so much at home. If and when they leave that world, they will be homeless. Our task is to make sure that we have a home ready for them in which they, the Faith, and the traditional Mass and Sacraments feel absolutely at home.

But that can not happen unless and until we ourselves have utterly left the *Novus Ordo Missae* and the new world order for which it was concocted. We must have visible signs that our homes are places where the needy and hungry can receive their fill of what only the true Faith can provide. We must be easy marks, vulnerable to the lions, the scoundrels, and the pagan who wants a handout without realizing that his only satisfaction—and our only gift—is Christ and Him crucified.

No man can serve two masters. For either he will hate the one and love the other, or he will sustain the one and despise the other. You can not serve God and mammon. Therefore I say to you, be not solicitous for your life, what you shall eat, nor for your body, what you shall put on. Is not the life more than meat and the body more than raiment?...Be not solicitous, therefore, saying, 'What shall we eat?' or 'What shall we drink?' or 'Wherewith shall we be clothed?' For after all these things the heathen seek. For your Father knoweth that you have need of all these things. Seek ye therefore first the Kingdom of God and His justice: and all these things shall be added unto you. – Mt. 6:24-34

Father Smith, *Sacerdos vagus*
5 February 2004: St. Agatha

In Time of Advent

This therefore I say, brethren: the time is short. It remaineth that they also who have wives be as if they had none. And they that weep, as though they wept not. And they that rejoice, as if they rejoiced not. And they that buy, as though they possessed not. And they that use this world, as if they used it not. For the fashion of this world passeth away.—1 Cor. 7:29-31

Some have suggested that a legitimate expression of patriotism and love of country would be to spend lavishly on gifts during the "holiday" season. The minions of mammon are very concrete about what it means to be faithful to the service of their highest good. As of this writing, the prophets of the pursuit of profits are predicting an almost six percent increase in oblations to the almighty dollar this year over last year. Unemployment is down, the stock market is up, and interest rates are low as the year of consumption 2003 draws to a close. Hopes are high that 2004 will see a continuation of the American penchant for buying things they do not need from people who did not make them with money they do not have. The American economy is addicted to marketing, retailing, and credit. None seems to notice, much less care, that our "wealth" is founded on generating a sense of need out of uncontrolled desire; establishing riches on the principle of low profit margins for the producers of goods, high profit margins for the distributors of goods, and minimal wages for the workers who labor for no reason but to consume goods they can not afford; and everyone from governments at all levels to multinational corporations to individuals without incomes funding their excesses by borrowing and lending at usury.

If money makes the world go 'round, and the love of money is the root of all evil, and money can not buy happiness, then it is not unreasonable for the man of faith to consider how money—cold, hard cash—might be of value in the Kingdom not of this world and how money can be used, without being loved, and whether and what happiness can be had at no cost. Most of the world economy is spending the time from late November to late December spending money. It is eminently appropriate and morally necessary for the Catholic to examine what currency he is spending and on what he is spending it.

"Durable goods" are those wares in the economy expected to last three years or more. Census data in the United States tell us that it is common for people to move every five years or so. Treasury bills, mortgages, and young adults reach maturity after about thirty years. Mammon has definite expectations about how long its investments will perform and what kind of commitment it can expect from its thralls. Jesus Christ, the King of the universe, must deal with far greater uncertainty when it comes to ruling His subjects.

Lenten resolutions rarely last forty days. Advent does not even start before the debauchery of "holiday" celebrations is under way. The pristine soul washed clean of sin at Baptism is given infrequent and irregular opportunity to retrieve her original purity once First Confession and First Communion are made. Workers work five days out of seven, eight hours out of twenty-four, forty-four years out of seventy; but prayer and the life of faith receive maybe one hour out of the week, and most often just one or two hours—at Christmas and/or Easter—out of the whole year.

Stockholders, employers, and the tax man demand constant, increasing, and disproportionate returns on their investments. As a result of their demands being met, the world has hundreds of billionaires, thousands of millionaires, and billions whose countries are in debt for trillions of dollars. The world of cash and credit is awash in money and interest payments. Wealth as defined by consumer goods, consumer debt, and consumers consuming is growing worldwide. Yes, poverty still exists, but all the world is strongly resolved to convert everyone to the rolls of employees, taxpayers, and mortgage holders. The gospel according to mammon is alive and well and spreading to the ends of the earth.

God, however, has a really hard time convincing anyone to labor in His vineyard with an eye toward increasing in sanctity and inheriting an everlasting reign in the Kingdom of Heaven. This is not only a matter of fewer people believing in God, fewer believers going to church, and fewer Sacraments being offered by

God's true Church shepherded by St. Peter's successor the Pope. It is a sad reality that even those who go to Mass, receive absolution in the Sacrament of Penance, and strive to obey the moral law do nothing to conform their personal economics to the Christian ideal of holy poverty. The faithful do even less by way of efforts to convert the world's economy in the direction of divine justice and charity.

Perhaps the most distressing and egregious example of the dearth of fidelity in the faithful is the participation by Catholics in the frenzy of "holiday" activities during the season of Advent. Rather than a quiet, prayerful, and sacrificial time of penance and preparation for our Savior's coming at Christmas, Advent has become a period of undisguised greed, shameless consumption, and scandalous inattention to the spiritual life. Catholic parishes throw Christmas parties before a week of Advent is completed. Catholic families spend huge sums of money on one another with but the slightest nod in the direction of the child Jesus on Christmas Day, and totally ignoring its Octave, relegating Epiphany to an afterthought, and forgetting Candlemas and the Purification in the rush towards (Saint) Valentine's Day. One shudders in revulsion and dismay in contemplating the number of sacrilegious communions made on December 24th and 25th in "honor" of Jesus on His Birthday.

It has been pointed out to this writer for years that parishes and families are constrained by schedules beyond their control, that school pageants and concerts need to take place before the vacation period, that families are best able to travel before Christmas in order to be together. The problem is not that exceptions need to be made in unusual circumstances. The problem is that the worldly considerations of shopping, sales, and schedules rule the entirety of our culture's approach to Advent. The problem is that *nothing* is done to celebrate Our Lord's birth once the 25th has come and gone. The problem is the utter unwillingness of individual Catholics, Catholic families, and Catholic parishes to make sacrifices so as to give God the honor which is His due as He deserves and in the way the Church, not the secular society, shows Him homage.

No effort is being made by Catholics to *change* the worldly disgrace that has been heaped upon the celebration of Christmas. Instead, Catholics have changed to conform to the world's calendar and customs. This is entirely unnecessary. There is nothing to keep a parish from celebrating its Christmas festival on the Saturday nearest the feast of the Epiphany. There is no reason that a family can not have its gathering for Christmas on the Feast of the Holy Family—a Sunday. There is really good cause for an individual Catholic to take advantage of the

Feast of Our Lady's Purification as a time of reflection on how well his Advent resolutions have taken hold, *and* what Lenten resolutions might be in order to build on them.

Where unique circumstances present themselves, then allowances can be made. The Sabbath was made for man, not man for the Sabbath. An impending death, military service, a baby on the way, employment by the fire department, or some other situation impossible to change might make it necessary to move Christmas festivities into Advent. But the wealth of opportunities provided by the Season of Christmas renders such necessity the exception, not the rule. In fact, observing Advent and Christmas according to the practice of the Church allows far more time for preparation and celebration, costs far less, and honors Our Lord with poverty and simplicity rather than insulting Him with greed and excess.

How should Advent be spent? Like Lent, but with a difference. Penance and mortification are common to both Advent and Lent. Prayer and fasting are appropriate to each of the seasons. The distinction between them lies in how God's grace is at work in the faithful.

Advent is the time to make ready for Christ to live with us. Lent is the time to make us ready to die with Christ. Advent makes Lent possible, Lent makes salvation possible. Advent is the time when eternity approaches earth. Lent is the time when time reaches consummation in Christ's eternal Sacrifice to the Father. Advent leads to Christ's life in time on earth. Lent leads to Christ's eternal life in Heaven. The Cross—through the Mass, penance, and mortification—is the bridge connecting Advent and Lent, Christ and His Church, man and God.

Each of the Church's penitential seasons is a dying to the world with the goal of attaining new life in Christ. As life in Christ is absolutely different from life in the world, the life of the Catholic should be different having been immersed in the grace of the penitential seasons. This Advent should begin holier than last Advent and end holier than it began. Next Lent is the platform on which to build the better Lent that will come a year later. Last Advent or Lent might well be my *last* Advent or Lent, so I should make each Advent and Lent the best season of my life until that time.

These considerations are not just liturgical niceties and the rantings of a rubrical purist. Advent each year is a microcosm of the whole life of faith. As our annual Advent disciplines are proximate preparation for the commemoration of our Savior's Incarnation, we spend our whole life from birth to death preparing for Our Lord's Second Coming and our final Judgment.

It is hardly to be expected that the man incapable of four weeks of vigil while awaiting Christ's Birth will be able to sustain an effort requiring seventy years or more. If we would not hope in vain to be ready to meet Our Lord when we come to judgment, then we must be ready to labor now in anticipation of celebrating His coming among us in the flesh. Jesus humbled Himself to share His glory with the faithful; we who desire to receive that glory must first join Him in humility. It is ours to choose whether our humbling will be our choice for a time on earth, or God's Judgment against us for all eternity. Or to put it in mammon's language, "you can pays me now or you can pays me later, but youse gonna pay".

"Christmas comes but once a year," says the sappy, secular song. Jesus has promised that he who welcomes Him in his heart will receive the Father and the Son as guests forever. Christ approaches even now; let us use this Advent as the time when we go out to meet Him. But to meet Him we must seek Him where He lives: in poverty, simplicity, and humility. The pure of heart, they who seek only God and utterly reject the world, will see God face to face and be made at home with Him forever in Heaven.

Father Smith
Sacerdos vagus

1 December 2003: The First Monday of Advent
Vinyamar, Tustin, California

see St. Luke 16:8–16

The Two Faces of the City of Man

Heads, I win: There is no sin in the world.
Why should anyone respect the laws which have you as their source
if you will not respect the laws which have God as their source?

Freedom of the press is ensconced in the Bill of Rights amended to the Constitution of the United States of America, guaranteeing citizens' activity in the marketplace of ideas without undue government interference. Notwithstanding the license some have taken to indulge in obscenity, incendiary polemics, and demagoguery, Americans hold sacred the right to print, broadcast, or transmit whatever is of moment, of interest, or of profit to society. The power of the word both to reflect and to shape reality is acknowledged as a fundamental principle of this and most democracies.

Children frequently are introduced to the concept of press freedom by way of examining the elements of journalistic reporting and storytelling. The "who-what-where-when" complex of questions is presented to students to help them learn the skills of observation and the rules of rhetoric and articulation. So deeply ingrained in our social psyche is this approach to understanding our world that the products of such analysis are assumed to be accurate, self-evident, and incontrovertible. If it appears in print, on the air, or referenced at an official website, then it must be true. Violations of this trust can result in public shaming, lawsuits, and even incarceration.

Untrammeled freedom to express in public whatever is on one's mind is predicated on the notion that either truth is the subject being propagated or the object being sought. It is no accident that such is the national attitude in the United States, given that this is a decidedly materialist culture, devoted to the advancement of science as final arbiter of reality, and dedicated to empiricism and technology as the means to explore, comprehend, and subdue the natural world. Truth as concrete reality is a primary good, hence, the expression of ideas consonant with or desirous of truth serve the good. A free press can not (and may not) hurt anyone, because truth is its matter and the truth ultimately is good to know and to share. Thus, lies and liars receive no protection under the principle of a free press.

But is a half-truth true?

America is rife with sources of information concerning "who-what-where-when" things happen in society. Raw data inundate our every day. How, however, is one to sort through and organize all of the facts, distinguish the falsehoods therefrom, and then determine the nature of the truth being espoused and one's response thereto?

Or more simply put, *why do things happen?*

It is the policy of reputable disseminators of information to restrict themselves to reporting verifiable, objective matters in the body of their stories. In other words, "who-what-where-when" is all that is considered—just the facts, ma'am. Speculation is not deemed appropriate in a reportorial venue.

Why is considered under the heading of editorials and opinions. Theoretically, everyone can agree on the facts, or at least on establishing a means to determine their veracity. What requires further thrashing out is explaining their origins, their ramifications, and their relative importance.

As an aside, it is curious how much of newspapers, the broadcast media, and the internet is given over to advertisements. If truth is the ultimate goal of the press, one wonders what truth is held dearest by commercial interests. Those eager to point out that making money in homage to the almighty dollar is the major motivator of business would do well to ask whence comes the profit made by capitalists, and what motivates the customers of said capitalists to agree to supply them with so much capital. Who can be most trusted with discerning truth: manipulators of the market, or those in the market so manipulated? How can one be sure that a free press is free from manipulation?

But that aside aside, the content of the media—whether print, broadcast, or electronic—conveys a certain image of the world. There is crime in the streets, corruption in government, and concupiscence in the population. What sells newspapers, boosts ratings, and generates website hits is the sensational, the intense, and the violent. What drives disagreements in specific controversies far exceeds the attention given whatever general principles on which parties agree that could provide a context for conflict resolution. Pornography is peddled, high culture is applauded, and Americana is celebrated—indiscriminately and in fairly equal amounts.

Why does all of this get ink, air time, and downloads?

Because businesses make money that way. Or because that's what the public wants. Or because the government is oppressive. Or because our schools are inadequate. Or because that's the way of the world.

But *why?*

What no one seems willing to admit is that the press is free to report any fact and to editorialize any explanation—except that mankind is wallowing in *sin.*

Imagine this as the beginning of a newspaper article: "Two men were convicted today of committing the sin of theft by robbing a bank . . ." Or this for the lead story on the evening news: "A new poll released today indicates that Americans consider the *sin* of adultery to be much more harmful to society than the *sin* of fornication. . . " Or a website with this on its home page: "Earn the highest possible returns on usurious investments in the Third World by taking advantage of loopholes in the tax code explained by our trained professionals . . ."

It will be pointed out that bank robbery is defined as a felony, not as a sin. That not everyone agrees that fornication is immoral. That one man's sin of usury is another man's just return on a capital investment.

But *why?*

Are there no media executives who understand and accept the moral law? Is there no audience among the God-fearing who desire a no-holds-barred approach to describing the state of the world? Would the government persecute this kind of press freedom?

An odd self-censorship is operative in America. No laws forbid describing illegal or immoral behavior as sins. The Establishment Clause applies to government (and schools and public squares and the politically correct), but not to media outlets. Yet the public forum is utterly devoid of a daily accounting of world events from the perspective of the Faith. The descriptions of reality ignore God, thus explanations, blame, and solutions for the ills of the world ignore God.

But *why?*

The aforementioned Establishment Clause is interpreted in such a manner that the muzzle intended for government is self-imposed on the citizenry. Obeying the law of unintended consequences, our sinful elimination of God from the workings of government has resulted in the elimination of God in the workings of American life, including the expression of truth through the press. Fittingly, we neither admit the sin that removed Our Lord from our Constitution, nor the sins riddling our hearts. The Constitution is silent on the subject of God and the government is silent on the subject of God. We the people are the government, silent on the subject of God in our laws, our press, and in our understanding of the truth.

So long as God's sovereignty is denied by our nation, our facts will be half-truths at best, and wholly useless toward attaining our supposed goals of life, liberty, and happiness. We deny life to the unborn, the ill, and the old. We are enslaved to bodily appetites, oppressed by one another's greed, and impotent to understand why. We have more money, more gadgets, and more health than any other civilization in history, and our whole economy is predicated on the idea that it is not enough, that better things will replace these things, that satisfaction and contentment with a sufficiency is impossible.

Without God, neither we nor the world make sense. If there is no God defining sin as an offense against His Majesty, then there is no sin, we all are good, and our world is filled with the fruits of our goodness...?!?! Or if it is true, as the newspapers sometimes imply, that bad things happen now and then, then the denial of God and His absolute goodness operative in the world leaves one wondering about the wisdom of giving selfish, shortsighted, and sometimes silly people like us the right to say, print, or believe whatever we want. How can one account for evil in the world without a God forbidding it, or for good in the world without a God mandating it, or for truth in the world without a God revealing it?

There are those who would tell us that all that is necessary is the "who-what-where-when" approach to reality. Therein, in the material, tangible, objective world, lies truth and our ability to recognize it and to agree on it. No more can be reasonably expected in a pluralistic and free society.

So much, then, for a free press. The only purpose for having a free press is to allow the free exchange of *ideas.* These ideas can be tolerated so long as they pursue truth. Ideas can not be measured by, contained in, or subjected to instruments designed for empirical evaluation. If the only truth acknowledged is material, there is no need for free speech, free press, or free religion. All that is necessary then would be scientists, recording devices, and no-nonsense news readers to give us just the *facts*—a town crier would do the trick.

But if ideas are *good* and what makes them good is their *truth*, then God *must* be acknowledged. This acknowledgement must be in the citizenry, in the press, and, yes, in the Constitution. Or put another way, God must be loved with one's *whole* heart, *whole* mind, *whole* soul, and *whole* strength. Denial of our obligation to obey this greatest Commandment accounts for our denial of the second greatest Commandment, to love our neighbors as ourselves. Evidence of this two-fold denial is in each day's news.

Denying God and neighbor, *why* should anyone believe in democracy and democratic rights? *Why* should citizens obey the laws of the land? *Why* should the government allow the press, the citizenry, or the faithful any freedom at all?

Sin confessed tells us *who* is wrong: the sinner. Sin confessed tells us *what* is wrong: offending God. Sin confessed tells us *where* it leads: hell. Sin confessed tells us *when* the remedy will come: with repentance. And the final mystery is revealed in why repentance is possible: because Christ Jesus loves us unto death, even death on the Cross.

Perhaps this makes no sense to empiricists and leaves them unsatisfied. To the world immersed in the senses and the nonsense of sin, grace is unfathomable. This world, our culture, is self-admittedly attached to satisfying perpetually insatiable appetites. Those who insist on nothing but physical existence as the meaning of life have the whole of their physical lives to pursue such happiness. At the end of this life, they will come to an end of happiness, and they will discover to their eternal horror that they forfeited their liberty when they exercised their "right" to be "free" from God. In the parlance of Madison Avenue, you can have it all—but you can't take it with you. C.S. Lewis put it very aptly when he wrote, "In the end there are two kinds of people: those who say to God, 'Thy will be done', and those to whom God says, '*Thy* will be done.'"

Will someone please explain how the First Amendment obeys the First Commandment?

Tails, you lose: There is no grace in the home.

What makes you think that tomorrow will fulfill your present hopes any better than your present has fulfilled the hopes of yesterday?

Modernity has expelled God from the body politic. This should not surprise anyone. God has also been made unwelcome in his own house, the Church. This should not surprise anyone. Most people have kept God out of their houses. Jesus could find no room in the inn, but at least Mary and Joseph were able to give Him a home in Nazareth. The modern world has made Our Lord homeless again.

Since the Second Vatican Council there has been an ongoing and explicit effort to render mundane the Church's approach to worship, to ecclesial structure, and to activity in the world. Stencils, statues, steeples, organs, and communion rails have been removed from old church buildings or eliminated in the design of new buildings. Priests forego vestments in the sanctuary, Roman collars on the street (much less cassocks), and formal titles of address. Rock music, laymen, and protestants have entered the sanctuary, while priests, altar boys, and the Blessed Sacrament have left the sanctuary. Bishops' conferences speak out vociferously on the subjects of Third World debt, aids, and refugees, but have very little to say to heterodox clergy, disobedient religious communities, or the laity absent from Sunday Mass, meeting with equally dismal results in their efforts to convert the ways of the world and to correct wayward Catholics.

At the same time that priests refuse to wear priestly garb, lay "ministers" don albs and perform functions proper to the clerical state. Houses with "cathedral" ceilings are popular just as church buildings are constructed without vaults, arches, or acoustics. Homilies must not be given with references to "political" matters, but parishes must give parishioners irs-mandated contribution records, observe ADA requirements for building construction and renovation, and at times participate in insurance programs that fund contraception and abortion.

Two recent Popes have addressed the United Nations, a body advocating abortion, contraception, and the masonic ideal of Church-state separation within a globalist governmental system, without taking the un to task for propagating error and immorality. Bishops in Germany make regular and bellicose demands for open communion with protestants. Canadian bishops have mounted but tepid opposition to their government's imminent codification in federal law of sodomite unions. Not one bishop in the United States has yet disavowed the usccb's (informal) declaration that Jews need not acknowledge Jesus Christ for salvation. Liturgical innovations and abuses such as Communion on the hand, altar girls, and extraordinary ministers of the Eucharist remain exceptions *de jure* but are habitual *de facto*.

Many, most, Catholics perceive none of these things as problematic, heretical, or of much importance. In fact, it is the tenor of the times that the Church has not gone far enough fast enough down this road of ecumenism, lay empowerment, and dialogue with the world. Any urge to criticize the Church on these issues is motivated by a desire for more of the same and for more radical changes in keeping with the times.

There are members of the Church who laud the Church's direction as progressive, if perhaps pusillanimous, and at times too attached to tradition. Overtures by the Church toward the world, some think, will allow the Gospel to be spread where the Church's past rigidity and reaction made her incomprehensible, if not repugnant, to non-Catholics. By listening to the world, so goes this reasoning, the Church is opening up a two-way communication by which Our Lord will be heard by people and in ways never before possible.

Certainly the world is being heard more by the Church. The Second Vatican Council's declarations on religious liberty and ecumenism, and the post-conciliar Mass are permeated with American sensibilities, modernist philosophy, and protestant spirituality. It has yet to be seen how the United States, the World Council of Churches, or academia have embraced Christ as King, transubstantiation, and objective truth as expressed by St. Thomas Aquinas.

But what of ordinary Catholics? They have at last been "empowered" to bring their gifts to liturgy, church governance, and ministry in the community. No longer is Father's the only voice in the parish, or Sister's the only voice in the school. The laity have come of age. What affect has this had on Catholics at home?

Declining attendance at Sunday liturgy is a well-documented phenomenon in the post-conciliar Church. The "Table of the Lord" has ever fewer people dining at it. They are sleeping in, golfing, playing soccer, shopping, doing the household chores left over from the work week. Although the people who are at Sunday liturgy do not understand that it is supposed to be a *sacrifice*, for the *expiation* of man's sins, to *satisfy* divine justice, it is claimed that their qualitative participation in liturgy is deeper, better, and more understood than before the Council. It is lamentable that so many miss Sunday liturgy, but it is not a mortal sin, so we are told.

Sunday dinner is a rare occurrence in an increasing number of homes, as are family meals during the week. Mom is tired, the kids are at the mall, and Dad is watching football. Or during the week, Mom and Dad are working, Junior is at the library, and Julie is at soccer practice. When the family gets together for "quality" time or at the holidays, the fact that the television is going, the in-laws do not speak to each other, and much of the food was catered, elicits but a passing nostalgia from the grown-ups about how much things have changed (for the better, for worse, who knows?) since they were kids. It is lamentable that families are together so rarely, so briefly, but there is nothing wrong with two-income households, electronic entertainment, and families with only one or two children, so we are told.

That families eat together infrequently does not bespeak of impending starvation. Americans are sedentary, eat junk food, and eat too much. They do not persevere in exercise regimens, diets, or refraining from fast food. Although they eat alone, on the road, and not nutritiously, Americans eat very often, and while growing fatter Americans seem to miss neither their meals nor their families.

Fewer and fewer Catholics go to Sunday Mass. More and more Catholics go to Communion at every Mass they attend. Fewer and fewer Catholics go to Confession. More and more Catholics are confused about what constitutes a mortal sin. Sunday Mass is likely a cesspool of sacrileges being committed.

An odd phenomenon has resulted from this morass of inattention, misinformation, and lies. On the one hand, the lack of good Confessions has resulted in a spiritual tapeworm in the body of Christ. Our Lord is being consumed, but his graces are refused by unrepentant sinners. Spiritual nourishment can not come to those attached to mortal sin. Starvation threatens in the midst of plenty.

On the other hand, many are becoming puffed up with pride, spiritually obese from an inflated sense of self. No longer is Holy Eucharist an incredible mercy from God to man, but the nonchalant conclusion to an over-familiar experience. Communion is seen as something "owed" to those who attend Mass, rather than the astounding offer of God's grace to unworthy men. Those who "minister" do so with a sense of entitlement, instead of recognizing that only rarely and in unusual circumstances should the laity enter the sanctuary, and *never* touch the Blessed Sacrament. God's offer of His Eucharistic graces so often received unworthily has resulted in the diminishment of pious humility, and a surfeit of profane hubris.

Immense efforts are expended to recruit lay "ministers" for the Mass, or for "ministry formation" programs. More and more laity are sought for work in the sanctuary and the chancery, but much less is done to draw the absent laity back to the pews. Still less energy is devoted to filling seminaries with men called to the priesthood.

Thus, Father is not in his place as the head of the household. Women step in to fill the paternal role and leave the maternal role unfilled, ill-defined, and unappreciated. It is a scandal that such descriptions can be used to describe both modern Catholic homes and parishes. If it is the estimation of some that women as mothers have not received their due recognition from the Church and in society, will that recognition be more forthcoming when women devalue maternity and succumb to the same milieu productive of and caused by insensitive, competitive, promiscuous men? Will the forces that viciously drove men from the family farm and family business be revealed as somehow benign in driving mothers from the family hearth?

The spiritual reality in the Church where Father is absent from and/or marginal in the family, mother is bent on replacing Father, and both are indifferent to the presence and rearing of children is reflected in the contraceptive mentality embraced by married Catholics. The institutional Church appears to be undisturbed by empty pews, closed parishes, sold hospitals, foundering schools, shrinking seminaries, abandoned confessionals, and invalid conjugal bonds. Likewise, Catholic parents live in ever bigger houses with ever fewer children, just like their non-Catholic counterparts. Parish halls, gathering spaces, and office buildings are being built by parishes that have closed their schools, convents, and sodalities. Catholic couples boast of homes that accommodate as many cars as children, use contraception with no more qualms than their pagan neighbors, and divorce at the same rate as their protestant friends.

In the average Catholic home in America there is no holy water, no statue of Our Lady, no Crucifix. The Rosary is not a family devotion. Grace is not said before or after the rare family meals. What is present is the spirit of the world. Electronic equipment brings in pornography over the air and online, conversation does not avoid the indelicate or immodest, and purity is an unknown concept from a disregarded past.

America is a new world wherein God may be denied, the Church may be denied, and children may be denied. There is an oft-repeated litany among parents today who have denied their children conception, birth, and an intact, two-parent home. Modern parents insist that children are not respectful, lack discipline and direction, yet can think for themselves and make good decisions. These same parents deprive their children of the guidance of Mother Church in matters of respect, discipline, and moral choices. Parents and children both have calculated that this equation adds up to pleasing the God they gave themselves permission to deny. He, they think, would never deny them their heavenly reward.

The Kingdom of Heaven welcomes the humble, the contrite, and the pious. Prayer and praise constitute the joy of the saints. God's children are those that accept their need for the Cross of Christ, and bear their own crosses with Him in obedience to our Father.

The modern world is proud, brazen, and blasphemous. Men of the world seek pleasure, convenience, and wealth. Man on earth has wrought a world of barren marriages and orphaned children, where death reigns, mercy is unknown, and justice is reduced to brute force.

Whether or not a particular individual in the world is judged by God to merit the Kingdom of Heaven is in the providence of God alone. Each of us, however, is effecting now the raw material out of which our eternity will be made and judged damned or saved by God. One may be forgiven for honestly wondering if those who like modernity, license, and the cult of man can ever learn to like unchanging truth, self-sacrifice, and the eternal reign of Christ the King.

Modernity has shown repeatedly an antipathy for the full message of the Gospel. What sign can these times give us that they believe, speak, and live the truth? The Church has many members willing to be thoroughly worldly; dare we think the world will ever return the favor and return home to the Church by returning the Church to the home?

Father Smith, *Sacerdos vagus*
26 October 2003: The Solemnity of Christ the King

A culture has no place in liturgy and the faith, if liturgy and the faith have no place in that culture.

The Feast of Saint Barnabas the Apostle

I could begin a homily about St. Barnabas by talking of the fact that he was the fifteenth Apostle. Remember, there were the original twelve, then St. Matthias, St. Paul, and, lastly, St. Barnabas. But I am not going to talk about that.

We could explore his missionary activity from Cyprus to Jerusalem and back to Cyprus, with many stops all around and in between. St. Barnabas was a companion with St. Paul on many journeys throughout the ancient world, a tremendous advocate for the Faith in the early Church. But I am not going to talk about that.

Instead, let's look at martyrdom, both in the sense of St. Barnabas specifically, and the martyrs in general. Obviously, all the martyrs sacrificed their lives with, and for, Christ. But there are practically as many ways of dying a martyr's death as there are martyrs who have died. There are, however, several very important things that all of the martyrs share, and which we would do well to imitate in our own lives, even if a violent death is not asked of us in giving witness to the Faith.

Here I am going to offer Father Smith's "Five Acts of Dying to Self." These are five things that every martyr, indeed, every Catholic who desires sanctity, encounters as part of bearing witness to Christ and Him crucified. All Catholics are called to embody these actions, but these actions do not always result in a bloody martyrdom. These actions require the grace of the Holy Spirit, by which any Catholic can accomplish them; actual martyrdom requires not only the willingness of the martyr, but the assistance of his oppressors. These "Five Acts of Dying to Self" can work whether or not we have anyone nearby ready to ill-treat us for the sake of the Faith.

First, to die to self, one must love the life God has given him. The gift of self to God is not a matter of some worthless thing being offered as an insult back to the original giver. No, life is a precious gift from God, of such great moment that God counts it worth His trouble to send His Son to redeem mankind. This is not because we are so wonderful in ourselves, but because human life comes from God in the first place. It is not that we first loved God, but that He has first loved us. Because of His love, we can love what He loves. The lives that we offer to God are of infinite value because of God's love, Christ's Cross, and the Spirit's gifts.

Second, having learned the love of self that flows from the first great Commandment to love God above all things, and which is the predicate of the second great Commandment to love our neighbors, to die to self one must accept the necessity of death. This comes both from acknowledging our own sinfulness and the death which sins deserve and, far more, the realization that it is not our own life which we crave, but the divine life which alone is capable of satisfying us. Paradoxically, once one understands how tremendous is the gift of human life, one comes to a deeper understanding of the source of that life, God Himself. We love our human life, but we love the Giver of that life all the more. And as God has given us that life, we seek to do the same. Made in His image and likeness, we imitate His generous giving. God gives us human life with the promise that divine life will follow; we offer our human life in faith that He will keep His promise and bestow on us far more. He will bestow on us divine life.

Third, knowing that the divine life is our ultimate desire, to die to self requires that we learn to deny the self. Human life, the pleasures of this world, and the beauty of creation cannot fulfill man's true desires. The comforts we seek, the ease we pursue, the luxuries with which we surround ourselves are ultimately, in the words of St. Paul, just so much rubbish. At best created beings point beyond themselves to the Creator. At worst, creatures can become obstacles that first obscure and then prevent the vision of God for which they, and we, are made. At their best and at their worst, creatures must be eschewed by him who would know and possess God and only God. Once the sign reveals the reality, the sign passes away. Once the veil is removed, it is no longer perceived. Once love is embraced, faith which points to it and hope which seeks it out are consumed in glory. This creation is passing away, and the man who would die to himself allows the passing glories of the world to pass him by.

Fourth, the self denial that is capable of resisting the temptation to comfort and luxury and even licit pleasures bears fruit in a further willingness to take on suffering. Ours is to take up our crosses each day and follow Christ. The cross is not only about dying and death, it also is about suffering. There is no cross without suffering, no Golgotha until a *Via Dolorosa*, no passion bereft of pain. We must keep in mind that to embrace the cross is to embrace all of Christ's Passion, which will of necessity include intense suffering. It is typical of us Americans to flee from pain, but that flight is not compatible with discipleship. Perhaps it will help if we remember that although suffering hurts, it is not fatal, and it is supposed to hurt. When the cross brings pain, there is nothing wrong. The cross entails a sacrifice not only of life, but of well-being and of physical peace. This presents maybe the hardest challenge in the project of sanctity. The idea of losing one's life is approachable by many; it is while the life is being lost that many of us draw back in fear. Christ's words bring comfort: "Do not fear the world. I have overcome the world!" This world includes pain and suffering, thus, we need not fear them in Christ.

Fifth, having learned to love the life that God has given, desiring all the more the life of God from whom our lives proceed, releasing our claim to comfort in this life, and embracing the suffering by which salvation is signified as a contradiction to the world, at last we say to God, "Lord, I don't care!" This is not apathy, but a holy indifference. We acknowledge that God, His life and love, is our only need. As such we do not care at all what else comes, so long as by it God is received. There is no joy to which we cling, no pain from which we recoil on our way to union with Christ and Him crucified. At the same time, there is no joy that we will lack nor pain that can harm us so long as we are in communion with Christ and Him crucified. We are ultimately indifferent to all things, caring only for the Creator of all things. If we have Our Lord, nothing else can move us, nothing else will overwhelm us.

Jesus in the Beatitudes tells us, "Blessed are the pure of heart, for they shall see God!" It is this vision of God that provides the motivation for dying to self. The soul who wants to see God, wants to see only God. In that search for God in this life on earth, all things are set aside that do not lead directly to God. And once the vision of God is approached, all other things fade away. The mission of the Apostles and martyrs is to bear witness to Christ and Him crucified. That is our mission as well. The successful saint is he who accepts nothing but the vision of Christ in himself, and having that glimpse of Jesus, shows nothing but Christ to the world.

One can not give what one does not have. To bear witness to Christ, one must have experience of Christ. The fundamental way of knowing Christ is to know Him in the Eucharist, in the Breaking of the Bread—which is another way of saying to know Him crucified. What the Apostles and martyrs show to the world is Christ on the Cross in their hearts. That is all they can see, so that is all they can show.

To the extent that the vision of God is our sole desire here on earth, we will be rewarded with that vision. Through a glass darkly at present, Jesus is revealing Himself to us in our lives, in our suffering, and in our death to sin and self. On the Last Day, God will reveal Himself in the fullness of glory, the sight of which is our whole Faith, whole Hope, and whole Love. In that vision we will have life and have it abundantly. We who have died to self on earth will live in Christ forever in Heaven.

Father Smith
Prince of Peace, Clinton, Iowa

15 November 2001: Saint Albert the Great: Albertus Magnus

See Wisdom 7:22-8:1 & Lk. 17:20-25

St. Albert the Great was very, very smart. One could argue that he was the smartest man alive for at least part of his life. Certainly he was one of the top ten minds of the 13th century in Europe.

This aspect of the person of St. Albert reminds me of something that Jesus said. In the Gospel of St. Matthew, chapter eleven, he calls out, "Father, Lord of Heaven and earth, to you I offer praise, for what you have hidden from the learned and the clever, you have revealed to the merest children!" St. Albert definitely qualifies as being among "the learned and the clever". Does this mean, then, that he is among those from whom the mysteries of God have been hidden?

By no means! Jesus tells us that those who are like little children are those who appreciate and enter the Kingdom of Heaven. St. Albert, though a brilliant man, maintained that childlike quality that alone is able to grasp the inner life of those in whom the Holy Spirit dwells.

It is important to make a distinction between "childlike" and "childish". St. Albert, as is the case with all who attain the Kingdom of Heaven, cultivated a childlike trust and love of God. There is a contrary attitude among those who wish to seem sophisticated and wise—that is, learned and clever—that really is childish, even though they desire to appear worldly and mature.

Think of it this way: childlike wonder, trust, and love is evident in the son who goes up to his father and says, "Daddy, why is the sky blue?" This child is amazed at what he sees, really wants to understand it better, and is convinced that his Dad is the person who can tell him the truth. This child expects and believes that his Dad knows everything and is happy to receive the wisdom that his Dad will pass on to him.

There are childish people who approach their parents with skepticism and cynicism. They ask questions like, "Okay, Dad, can God make a rock too big for Him to lift?" This sort of child doesn't really want an answer—he thinks he already knows it all. He already has dismissed the existence of God. His real goal is to put Dad in his place. He doesn't think his Dad knows everything—in fact, he is more convinced that his Dad knows nothing.

Childlike people look around them and are awestruck at how wonderful creation is. They delight in its beauty. For them, the whole world points to a God who loves, who brings joy, who makes Himself known through everything there is. Such childlike people are certain that God is to be experienced through the things that God has made. They eagerly seek out more of His creatures, not to glory in the art, but to catch a glimpse of the exquisite vision of the Artist.

The Book of Wisdom tells us that it is through His Wisdom that God has endowed His creation with knowledge of His love. Wisdom pervades all that God has made. Those who seek to perceive this gift become wise themselves, reflecting the glory of God in their own lives. St. Albert understood this. He sought deeper and deeper into the natural sciences, not to make a god out of nature, but to see more clearly how nature reveals the maker who is God. St. Albert was convinced that the more one knows of the natural order, the more one's faith is confirmed that it is God who has ordered all things.

Childish sorts figure they know not only better, but they know best. Ironically, the word "science" comes from a Latin word that means "to know". Our modern science, falsely divorced from faith, insists that ultimately we can not know. Each scientific discovery reveals not that there is a point to their searching, but that there is ever more that is unknown and unknowable. It is an endless quest that results in a sense of futility.

Quasi-scientists deny that God exists, and thus deny that there is a principle that gives order to the universe. They end up by denying the very means that they have of understanding their own discipline. Without God there is no order. Without order there can be no predictability, only randomness. If all is primarily random, then science can not make any definitive statements about the universe that it seeks to explain.

If the universe can not be explained, then mankind and the individual life have no explanation, no meaning, no purpose by which to set one's goals. No one can understand the universe, his neighbor, himself. A universe where people believe like this explains things like war, school shootings, lonely grandparents, unwanted children, and unredeemed death.

St. Albert and all good scientists realize that God has made Himself known in all creation. Rather than deny that science has an authentic relationship to faith, the good scientist allows science to confirm his faith in a God who loves His creation so much that He is present everywhere in it. The wisdom that pervades all things is a sign of God who has made all things. The goal of science is to gather knowledge that leads to wisdom that believes in God and returns His love.

We live in an age of science. Often science sounds like a god. Things are condemned if they do not "obey the laws of science". Appeals are made to believe something because "that's what science tells us". Scientists begin to sound like pagan priests as they arbitrate for the "uninitiated" what it means to be a human being, what the purpose of life is, where life comes from, how it is to be lived.

Because of this fawning on science, we would do well to follow the lead of St. Albert the Great. He understood that science is for something. It is meant to guide us to God. It does not end in a dispassionate objectivity, but results in a passionate love for creation, a joyous experience of God's highest creation, man, and an intimate unity with God the Creator.

Too often we let our science get ahead of us and control us. Our wealth, technology, and medicine frequently surpass our ability to understand them. We lose sight of what they are for and the fact that we actually create and control them, not they us. In our rush to make things that more and more imitate human beings, we have made human beings to imitate things. Voice synthesizers replace talking on the front porch, eating in the car replaces dining with the family in the dining room, internet sites replace sharing a hug after a long absence.

What's worse, however, is reducing human beings to numbers in measurements of productivity based on units manufactured. Names are lost amid the cacophony of PINS and Social Security numbers and passwords for the PCS so common in homes and offices. We are on the threshold of using technology to manufacture human bodies for the express purpose of using them as replacement parts for other human beings.

Before us are three options. One is that which we seem to be choosing right now, to hurtle down the road of gadgetry, technology, and false convenience. Our machines will become more and more human and our people will be more and more dehumanized. Science as it is so often practiced today offers no reason why this should not be. This is because such is a moral issue and moral issues can only be resolved by an appeal to absolute truth, but absolute truth relies on the existence of an absolute God and this bad science denies the existence of God.

Another option is to flee the monster of science which we have created. We can, as the Amish do, throw out novelties because we do not understand them and it is hard to control them. This risks the error of condemning certain creatures as inherently evil. Such would be a denial of our longstanding Catholic perception of the divine acclamation concerning creation: "And God looked on all that he created and called it Very Good!" The Manichaeans, the Zoroastrians, and the Puritans had an unhealthy disdain for the material world. King David in the Psalms, St. Francis in the "Canticle of the Sun", and St. Albert in championing the study of the natural sciences would strenuously beg to differ with that kind of attitude. The God who has revealed Himself through Jesus Christ, His Incarnate Son, seems to like the idea of being united with the material world.

The third option, the correct option, is to embrace the intellect which is truly a gift from God. We are to use this intellect in such a way that the objects of its study help us better to appreciate the God who made all things. We are to enjoy these creations and rejoice in the love of their Creator. Using them to excess, as modernity would have us do, ends in the destruction of the relationship between men and the world, between humans and each other, between man and God revealed in Jesus Christ. To reject their use entirely, as overly spiritual philosophies would suggest, results in the diminishment of the human, contempt for the nature of which man is a part, and a denial of God's own word calling all creation good.

It is for us to use restraint and to utterly reject those things of science which are bent on destruction. We must take time to understand the complicated things that science discovers, eschewing their use until we are morally fit to control them instead of being overwhelmed by them. We need to support one another in times of sacrifice and self-denial—such as Advent, Lent, and all Fridays—when we voluntarily set aside our material wealth in order to appreciate better the tremendous spiritual blessings to which the earth and all it contains is pointing us. To celebrate with one another, in our parish community, in the secular society, and within the eternal Church that Jesus is Emmanuel, God-with-us.

He has chosen to be with us as the transcendent Creator of all, as immanent in all creation, united with us in the Blessed Sacrament wherein the Body-Blood-Soul-Divinity of Jesus Christ makes the new creation a marriage between earth and Heaven. The Kingdom of Heaven is not to be seen with the eyes of a telescope or microscope, to be declared present there in the stars or there in the test tube. The Kingdom of Heaven is in our midst, surrounding us, within our hearts, uniting us with God who loves us, now and forever.

Father Smith
Jesus Christ, Prince of Peace Parish
Clinton, Iowa

P.S. The answer to the question, "Can God create a rock so heavy that he can't lift it?" is "Purple and isosceles!" This is a contradictory, nonsensical question. It is akin to asking, "Should a circle have four corners or five?" Having said this, however, there is someone who can make a rock too heavy for God to lift: man. Each individual has the power to make of his God-given heart a stony deadness which God, respecting the free will of all men, can do nothing about. Not until the sinner lifts his stony heart to God is God able to give him instead a heart of flesh, bursting with divine love. God can not thwart Himself, but man can refuse and reject the power of God—rejecting love and life in the bargain.

Saint Joseph the Worker

Jesus Christ, Our Lord and Savior, chose to be born of the immaculate flesh of the Blessed Virgin Mary. God from God, the eternal Word begotten of the Father before all ages, Jesus took on the burden of mortality, dwelling in the flesh as a man among men. The Second Person of the Most Holy Trinity deigned in perfect humility to be received in the womb of His glorious Mother, who obediently cooperated in the divine plan of salvation at the message of the Archangel Gabriel. God's Holy Spirit overshadowed the Virgin, Christ was conceived, and the Word became man. His dwelling place among us was Nazareth, the home of a descendant of David, the chaste spouse of the Mother of God, Joseph.

Jesus learned from Joseph to work honestly, to hearken to God in silence, and to rejoice in God's bounty in the midst of material poverty. The hands that lifted a dead girl from sleep, whose touch gave sight to the blind, whose strength cleansed His Father's house of thieves, sought never to create wealth or to indulge in frivolous comforts or to assert the desires of the flesh over the will of God. Joseph instilled in Jesus an awareness that sufficiency is a greater bounty than plenty, that God is heard best when all else is silent, that the craft of man imitating God's act of creation builds an edifice not of perishable matter but of imperishable spirit.

Jesus was mistaken for "the carpenter's son". The people around Him are to be excused if in looking on Jesus they recognized in Him more of His Foster-father than of God the Father. In merely natural terms it is likely that His physical mannerisms resembled the man responsible for teaching Him what it means to be a child of God. We hear His mother's influence in Gethsemani when He submitted to the will of God: "Not my will, Father, but your will be done!" (Lk. 1:38). We "hear" Joseph echoed in the silence of Christ before Pilate (Jn. 19:9).

But, of course, in all things Jesus came only to do the will of Him who sent Him. Jesus had work to do: to enkindle a flame upon the earth, to preach the good news to the lost sheep of Israel, to give sight to the blind, to overcome the world, to lay down His life for His friends. Joseph's work ethic proves invaluable in accomplishing God's plan of salvation.

From the very first, both the Blessed Virgin and St. Joseph sought to obey God. They submitted to Him the firstfruits of their loving obedience as prescribed in the law. It was their constant care to raise Jesus to be a man of righteousness and holiness.

Modernity needs to learn from the example of St. Joseph in imitation of the humble willingness of Our Lord. The work of the hands of St. Joseph was directed by his knowledge that they served the greater purpose of performing the work of faith. He did not labor as a carpenter for its own sake, but for the sake of his wife, their Child, and his obedience to God.

Jesus spoke and did those things which gave glory, not to Himself, but to His Father. Both Jesus and Joseph knew that the dignity of work comes not from the raw act of labor, but from the end to which it is directed. Work meant merely for monetary or egoistic gain is impoverishing and demeaning to the laborer. Work done at the direction of God and for His glory alone bears fruit that nourishes the laborer in this life and unto eternal life.

Faith makes it possible for man to order his priorities properly. By faith man knows that his ultimate end is union with God; by reason man knows that all natural activities must then be placed at the service of this supernatural goal. By love is accomplished the task of submitting what reason teaches to the direction of what faith promises in the confident hope that God will perfect the work He has begun in man and in which man is called to cooperate.

It is impossible to describe the scandal and shame in which the faithlessness of modern society now wallows. Lacking faith, man has disordered his world such that work is no longer placed in the service of a greater end, but is become an end in itself. The family, once the beneficiary of work, has become the prime victim of *employment*. Where once rest was considered the appropriate reward for ample work well done, leisure is now confused with sloth. Once play was the province of children in neighborhoods, but now it is hyper-organized by adults enrolling children in leagues for athletic activities requiring hundreds of dollars' worth of fees and equipment, long hours practicing, and travel between cities and across states.

Far from enfleshing the words of Isaiah repeated by Christ proclaiming liberty to slaves, the modern approach to work does not embolden the freedom of the children of God, but results in invisible chains and monstrous burdens. The arena where the faithful are permitted to exercise devotion to God is shrinking. The social stigma attached to seeking treasure that does not rust or rot is becoming harsher. The fruit borne of labor without reference to God is wicked, violent, and deadly. And rest, peace, and silence are being banished from the face of the earth.

Jesus tells us that we can not serve both God and mammon. That He chose to be born in poverty and raised in the house of the simple worker Joseph, tells us that God places a premium on work done by those satisfied with a minimum of worldly wealth and receptive of the bountiful grace of Christ. That so many of us would be hard pressed to describe our jobs as being in harmony with serving God alone tells us whom we actually serve.

Modern economics, modern employment, and modern desires do not include a place for God. St. Joseph gives us an example of what happens when God receives pride of place in the human heart: "If anyone loves me, he will keep my word, and my Father will love him, and we will come to him, and will make our abode with him" (Jn. 14:23). In the hearts of the Blessed Virgin Mary and St. Joseph, Jesus found great love. In the home of Nazareth the Father's will was obeyed by all; the Son was the center of the life they shared; and the Holy Spirit filled their hearts with a passion for prayer, the willingness to sacrifice, and the power to live as children of God—on earth, laboring in the Lord's vineyard, and in Heaven, resting forever in the bosom of the Father.

Jesus comes to dwell with us, Body-Blood-Soul-Divinity, in the Mass. Of His fullness, grace upon grace, we are privileged to receive. We are called to set aside even that work which does not interfere with God's will in order to obey His Son's command to eat His Body and to drink His Blood, that we might have abundant life. At Mass we have a momentary foretaste of that life with Christ no longer obscured by the trammels of mortal life. At Mass we can see—and taste—the fruit of the work of God's salvation in us. No longer do we eat the fruit of the tree of knowledge and receive death. We eat of the fruit of the Tree of Life—Jesus crucified— and receive knowledge of God!

St. Joseph the worker reminds us to honor honest work. More than that, however, he illustrates that the laborer is to be valued more than his labor. Still more, St. Joseph guides us to the realization that Christ is the focus of all our efforts on earth. In Christ we are given a Mediator by whom God the Father is offered the work of our hands, the love of our hearts, and the whole of our lives. Jesus Christ takes away the sins of the world that those who believe in Him and in His cross can find a dwelling place in His Father's house—as He dwells among us so shall we dwell with Him, now and forever.

Father Smith

Jesus Christ, Prince of Peace Parish
Clinton, Iowa

21 June 2001—Feast of Saint Aloysius Gonzaga

I knew that the Church has a heart and that such a heart appeared to be aflame with love. I knew that one love drove the members of the Church to action, that if this love were extinguished, the Apostles would have proclaimed the Gospel no longer, the Martyrs would have shed their blood no more . . . Then, nearly ecstatic with the supreme joy in my soul, I proclaimed: "O Jesus, my love, at last I have found my calling: my call is love. Certainly, I have found my proper place in the Church, and you gave me that very place, my God. In the heart of the Church, my Mother, I will be love, and thus I will be all things as my desire finds its direction."
—St. Thérèse of Lisieux

Love! Then do what you will.—St. Augustine of Hippo

Love is not an emotion. I often find myself telling this to people (myself among them) who are struggling with the virtue of charity. They nod their heads and mumble agreement. Their mouths say, "Yes, yes, yes!" but their eyes say, "Say what?!"

Most people think that love is an emotion, a feeling, a reaction to a person. When we think of the people we love or of being in love, we think of lumps in our throats, of flutters in the stomach, a skip in our step. We call that love. This is simply incorrect. There is a huge difference between love and the emotions.

Think about it this way: emotions are reactions to circumstances in life. Getting cut off in traffic makes you angry, finding a twenty-dollar bill that you forgot in a suit jacket makes you happy, hearing of the death of an old friend makes you sad. These are appropriate responses to things outside of you. What you feel corresponds to what has happened.

Love is the fulfillment of *commands* from God. That is not the same thing as an emotion. Fulfilling the command is not a reaction to an external event. Love is an act of the will in obedience to the source of all love, God.

God says, "Love with all your heart, mind, soul, and strength!" That is a command. Your emotions don't work that way. If I order you right now to have emotions, nothing will happen. Watch: be happy! Now stop. Now I order you to be sad! Now stop. Now I order you to be angry. Now stop. Now be happy again!

See. No one can order you to have an emotion. Emotions happen from the outside in. It is not for nothing that we call them feelings. Emotions work in the mind the way nerves work in your skin. If I slap you across the face, you feel pain. If I dump a bucket of water on you, you will feel wet. If I turn the air conditioning off, you will feel warm.

When people are mean to us, we feel angry. When a dog jumps up and starts barking at us, we feel fear. When a friend calls on the telephone, we feel happy. These emotions are like the pain, the wet, and the warmth. We feel them because something outside of us affects us and it is registered inside of us.

Now, we might feel something and not react to it. I might hold my anger in traffic and not honk my horn at the person who cut me off. You might just stand there and let me punch you in the mouth. You might not complain if the temperature rises without the air conditioning turned on. Our reaction doesn't change the feeling. The feeling is there. We have no control over it. We have total control over what we do with it.

God tells us to love. All the time. Not just when we feel like it or when it feels good or when we feel motivated. We are to love with all that we have and all that we are: heart, mind, soul, and strength. Love is not something from the outside in, but from the inside out.

God has first loved us. He writes his law, the law of love, on our hearts. We are able to obey His law of love, not because there are nice people around, or because we will get a reward for it, or because we feel good today, but because God the Holy Spirit dwells in us. He has made us His temple. He has made us living vessels of love. The Kingdom of Heaven—of *Love*—is within us!

Because of that love inside of us, we can give the love away. We can give that love back to God with our whole heart, mind, soul, and strength, and to our neighbor as Jesus has loved us. We can offer ourselves on the cross out of love, not because we need to, or because we are forced to, or because someone else has asked for it or deserves it. We love as God loves, because God is within us. God has *chosen.* We love because we *choose* to love. It is done on purpose, not as a reaction, but as a gift. Just like God's love to us is a gift in the first place.

Loving actions are not themselves love. St. Paul tells us that we can preach, move mountains, and offer our bodies to be tortured, but without love, those actions are noisy gongs gaining nothing and being nothing. The love that is patient, kind, pleased with the good, forbearing, and eternal is the motive force that makes all loving actions worthwhile. We do not love by doing good things; we do good things by the power of love. As God has loved us first and makes it possible for us to return His love and pass it on to others, our own love makes it possible for us to perform the mighty works of God, the acts of faith, the signs of the Kingdom that Jesus has promised us.

The greatest sign of love is life. He who loves lives. God is love and God is life. He who dwells in love dwells in God and shall dwell with him forever. The living are able to feel. This is where love and emotions come together. Because God has loved us we can love in return. Because we love we are alive. Because we are alive we can feel. Because we feel we can be angry or sad or frightened or joyful or delighted. The person who does not love is not alive, has no feeling. He is hardhearted and lacks compassion.

Love is not an emotion. It is the condition for all of the emotions. Without love all the emotions die. Without love the human person is dead. We see the living dead around us (and in the mirror) when we see hatred present and mercy missing, when there are hungry people in the midst of plenty, when faith is denied to those desperately in need of knowing God. Our lack of love can kill both the body and our souls.

The living love of Christ was moved to action by everything around Him. The merciless hatred of the Scribes and Pharisees moved Jesus to anger as He denounced them in public. The hunger of the multitudes in the desert places moved Jesus to pity, so He fed them with the five loaves and two fish. The faithless sinning of mankind moved Jesus to compassion as He obeyed his Father, ascended the Cross, and said, "Forgive them, Father; they know not what they do!"

All things are not love, but love is all things. Love can do all things: it can be joyful, sorrowful, angry, playful, and awesome. These things without love either die or destroy their victims. Love is the blank slate, the *tabula rasa*, the white page on which all being is writ. Love is the grounds for life, the grounds for acquittal from sin, the grounds surrounding the royal court of the King of

Heaven. The capacity for emotion is not the prerequisite of love; love is the necessity that allows emotions to be shared.

Love does not feel good. Love does not feel bad. Love feels—and it is good that it feels, that it is not dead to pain or joy. Love does not feel right. Love does not feel wrong. Love *is* right at all times in all circumstances for all people. Love utterly rejects, renounces, and refuses wrong—*i.e.* , sin—at all times in all circumstances for all people.

God dwelling in our hearts gives us the command to love. We are to love our enemies, lay down our lives for our friends, and proclaim the Gospel—not because our enemies are nice, or because we owe our friends, or because anyone asks to hear the Gospel. We do these things simply because the will of God is writ upon our hearts. God loves. We love. It has nothing to do with you or me or with circumstances. Love is not about us; love is all about God. Because God loves and God dwells in our hearts, we love—completely, constantly, and unto the end of our lives!

Love is not accidental to God. Love is of the essence of God. It is His very nature, like water being wet, sugar being sweet, and fire being hot. Love is all that God does. As water would not be water if it were dry, God would not be God if He were not love. In accepting the Lord of love into our hearts, we become like Him. We take on love. In taking on love we are embracing the divine nature. We become one with God in response to Christ's becoming one with us. God became man that man might become God! That is why receiving Christ in the Sacraments, especially at Mass, is so important. Jesus is how the love of God lives in us and we in Him.

Jesus shows the greatest love by going to the Cross for us. He did not sin. He, as the Second Person of the Most Holy Trinity, is not mortal. He did not need to die. But because He loves us, He chose to give us Himself—His love, His mercy, His life—on the Cross. He did this so that we in turn could imitate Him in whose image and likeness we are intended by God. We are to choose the cross, to choose life, to choose love for God through our obedience, and love for our neighbor through our compassion.

St. Aloysius is a wonderful example of this obedience and compassion. He was a wealthy nobleman who put aside his fortune in order to obey God and join the Jesuits in poverty. He was a healthy young man who imperiled his health by assisting victims of the plague. He chose to follow Jesus to the cross and die in service to his brothers who could not help themselves.

St. Aloysius is noted for purity, innocence, and charity. He accused himself of being a sinner. This accusation was not believed by his contemporaries and strikes us as being rather improbable. What St. Aloysius understood that we lesser folk need to heed is that the love shown us by Christ is willing to take on all of the infirmities of the beloved. St. Aloysius not only took on the burden of the physical debilitation of the plague, but he did penance not only for his own sins, but for the sins of all of the people whom he loved. In this he was a true imitator of Christ, who for our sake took on the burden of all of our sins and carried them to the Cross.

God is love. God is omnipotent. Love is omnipotent. In receiving and accepting God's love, by *obeying* His command to love, we participate in the all-powerful divine will. Our obedience to the command to love with our whole heart, whole mind, whole soul, and whole strength is the source, means, and goal of our free will.

Human freedom depends on the obedience that is possible *only* through love. Without loving obedience from God within the heart, man is reduced to reacting to the power of the world. Unless he is set free by love, man is a slave to hunger, cold, fear, lust, anger, hatred, pride, oppression, greed, injustice—in a word, man becomes a slave to sin. Without love man merely reacts to all things, but he is able to do nothing and to gain nothing—except sin, *i.e.* , he is a clanging cymbal reduced to being nothing.

No power in the universe can conquer you if you love. Because God is love, your desire to love shares in His unconquerable power. Nothing can overcome God, nothing can overcome His love—God Himself can not keep you from loving, for God is love and He will never deny Himself. If you love, God will never deny you.

Love is the power from God to act rather than to react. It is the union of being and will that makes all things possible. Love is the difference between the lifeless pursuit of the appetites common both to animals and the faithless; and the power over death manifested on the Cross—where love, obedience, and life are bound together in perfect *communion.*

It is on the Cross that we *see* love perfected. It is an act of the will, not of necessity. It is an act of the heart, not a reaction of the body. It is the power of love bringing life where all is dead, compassion winning over hatred, and mercy consummating all justice. Let us approach the Altar of God and receive this tremendous Sacrament of love. Let us offer it in union with Jesus in this Mass on earth, that we might come to share in the life of which it is the sole means to receive the bliss of Heaven…

Father Smith
Jesus Christ, Prince of Peace Parish

Put me as a seal upon thy heart, as a seal upon thy arm: for love is strong as death, jealousy as hard as hell. The lamps thereof are fire and flames. Many waters can not quench charity, neither can the floods drown it: if a man should give all the substance of his house for love, he shall despise it as nothing!—Canticle of Canticles 8:6-7

Introduction to *Distributist Perspectives Volume I*

Chicago is my hometown. Not in the sense that I was born there and can claim lifelong residency. In fact, I lived there but five years during and after college and visit now but briefly every two years or so. Chicago can claim, however, to be the context where I started growing up and reached my majority, if not my maturity. Alas! that process continues to madden my friends and family even now.

No, Chicago is my hometown not because *I* am from there, but because I found *home* there. Not *a* home, mind you, but all the elements that constitute home for us transients living on this sad rock of earth.

In Chicago are neighborhoods every bit as parochial as the smallest European hamlet. One can find art as sublime as anything wrought by man's imagination at any time. Chicago's reputation for crime, in the courthouse as much as in the courtroom, towers as tall as its skyscrapers. The cooks who cook home-cooked meals there might have made a journey across time zones, through war zones, or braved no-parking zones to find the cozy hearth where dinner is enjoyed. Whether prairie, ocean, or desert says *home* to you, Chicago can be your home for as long as you are looking for one.

One can even recognize a bit of Davenport, Iowa, my birthplace, in Chicago. In the Loop one might see a chiropractor's office—a product of the science developed in the 19th century by a Davenport man. Under an El platform, one might dream of the romance of trains that radiate from Chicago to all points of the compass, heading west thanks to the first railroad bridge across the Mississippi at a site near Rock Island, Illinois—opposite Davenport. On a summer afternoon in Lincoln Park, one might delight in the scent of fresh-mown grass, cut, perhaps, by a tractor built by John Deere's company—headquartered next door to Davenport in Moline, Illinois. There is a lot in Chicago to remind you of somewhere else, practically anywhere else.

Decades of planning and improvement have caused this phenomenon. Hogs are not butchered there these days, *pace tanti viri* Carl Sandburg. State Street, that great street, has been revitalized according to the principle by which Carson's and Field's were melded into conglomerates whose interests extend far beyond the shores of Lake Michigan. And, as is so typical of 21st-century American metropolises, more "Chicagoans" live in the 'burbs than between Evanston and Calumet City and Oak Park and the Lake. Chicago today has better air, better water, better paving (if not better traffic), and better race relations than a century ago.

One thing about Chicago most certainly is not better. Chicago is not very good at being *Chicago.* It can do a passable impression of New York. There are hints of Paris about it in the springtime. Beijing can be seen peeking out of portions of the near-south side. But the *je ne sais quois* that makes a city unmistakably itself is being lost in Chicago—and everywhere else.

The fact that behemoths like Chicago are finding their identities submerged by the multinational juggernaut of modern economics is the surest sign that the hydra of materialism—capitalism, socialism, and communism—is every bit as virulent and deadly as described by Pope Leo xiii and all other clear thinkers. Man's peril is revealed by the destruction of the great no less than the small.

The "global village" creates not a small world, but a hideously misshapen, cancerous, ravenous grotesque posing as Main Street. A world shrunken to the size of a town would be suffocating; a town swollen to the size of a planet is the stuff of nightmares. Who wants an elephant-sized amoeba in his intestine, or a potted Sequoia in the living room? What is sorely needed is a sense of proper proportion, indeed, a sane and human perspective.

Elsewhere than in the essay included in this collection, G.K. Chesterton says that the madness of the mathematician is the attempt to draw a map of the universe—to scale. More sane is the artist's effort merely to render reality in a picture. The eight writers in this collection paint pictures of the human project from a variety of perspectives. No one of them is complete, and taken together they are hardly exhaustive of the many facets through which man sees and is seen by the world around him. But their sketches give good glimpses of who man is and what he might be, warts and all. It must be kept in mind that capturing the "warts" is far easier than encompassing the "all".

Man is more than man knows. His knowledge of the universe is only partial, and his knowledge of that part of the universe which is himself is even smaller. We see as through a glass, darkly. Only God is far enough away from man to be able to get the proper perspective so as to know all of man. God is the true artist who alone has a mirror big enough to hold up to His creation, by which man, the greatest of His creations, is rightly seen.

Thus, if man is to know anything of himself, he must seek a God's-eye view. Any intellectual endeavor trying to grasp the truth of man, any science seeking knowledge of man that omits mention of man made in the divine image is doomed from the start. At best the intellect will grasp the body and miss the spirit, the science will find itself knowing more of ignorance than of truth. In both cases, the part that is known will be neither the larger nor the better part.

There is all the difference in the world between the doctor performing an autopsy and the cadaver that is its victim. Modern man examines man the corpse and learns deadly things. There is a place for autopsies, namely, learning which things are deadly to life; however, an autopsy is a woefully bad way to learn about how to live. A more wholesome desire is to contemplate human *life* and the final causes that make it worth living.

George Maxwell, Hilaire Belloc, G.K. Chesterton, Eric Gill, Harold Robbins, Arthur J. Penty, Harold J. Massingham, and Commander Herbert Shove lived in times of unprecedented social trauma. Their essays in this collection reflect an effort to shine a light into the morass that the unbridled greed of capitalism and the reactionary socialism of their day had created, threatening to destroy completely the humanity of man. These men and many of their contemporaries saw dark days ahead.

Darker than anything they could have imagined has been our past, which was their future. Men of the late nineteenth and early twentieth centuries could not have envisioned the madhouse that modernity has become. Theirs was a world where beauty still had a place, man was yet believed to be at the pinnacle of creation, and God was held by most men to be Lord over all. Sanity was taken for granted almost as much as was common sense. Unnoticed at the time was the peril to common sense posed by the economic attack being waged against the common man.

The recent report from the field of psychology that rest makes some people sick underlines the point made by George Maxwell in "*The Truth About Work*". That point, in short, is that work must come to an end because work is not an end in itself. Contemporary workers, nonetheless, have been conditioned to the reality that work is their life. Malaise, both physical and psychological, is setting in among some workers on their days off or holidays because the end of work seems to them to be the end of life. This is because the insane economic situation trapping mankind has made work the end, i.e. , the purpose, of life. Retirement is no longer about resting but has become an excuse to find (or has created the necessity of finding) a new and different job.

Life has not always ended thus. One who is intent "On Knowing the Past"—the title of Belloc's contribution to this collection—will find that once upon a time oppressed people were seen by themselves and by their oppressors as unfortunate. Modern man, almost wholly ignorant of the history that was necessary to make him, now applauds the wage slave as the dawning of a new economic day. "Full employment" is a statistical fantasy, but, all the same, employment is everyone's dream. It does not occur to employees that something better has ever existed for the ordinary man's living than to provide extraordinarily wealthy men with their wealth.

A serf might not have known where his next meal was coming from, but he knew his origin in the Creator and his final destination of Judgment Day. Wage slaves are assured of three hots and a cot, as prison inmates describe such a plight, but have almost totally abandoned belief in a transcendent goal for man. Serfs obedient to the Faith and wage slaves submissive to the almighty dollar would agree, for wildly different reasons, on one thing: the serf is better off dead. The smug wage slave does not realize that his peak salary signifies his highest accomplishment. His life insurance policy and 401(k), however, leave him, after death, worth significantly more to the taxman than at any time in his working life.

"Economies of scale" is the catchphrase that rationalizes this vision of disposable people, worth more in their absence than in their presence. It is embodied in the trend toward larger and larger corporations with fewer and fewer employees. Hordes of men are vital to the conglomerate, but any given man is entirely expendable.

There is a colossal contradiction between the ideal in the law where each man is held sacred and the practical life of economics where any man can be disposed of at will. In the name of individual children, we herd them into ever-larger schools, while demanding smaller class sizes, overpaying teachers who insist they are poorly paid, and seeking to slash education budgets—for schools that should not exist in the first place. In the name of customer service, we build ever larger "big box" retail stores, whose corporate headquarters are far from the customer, who is himself subjected to survey-tested, market-driven, mass-distributed merchandise tailored to his individual tastes. In the name of more efficient government, we pay for it with a tax code that requires a multibillion-dollar industry to decipher it each year; we enslave "citizens" for forty percent of the year to pay their tax burden; and we, the people, habitually elect the kind of person who thinks this state of affairs needs only repairing, not replacing. Chesterton was able to wax humorous and ironic about this, laughing before he was driven to weep in his essay "*On Organization and Efficiency*".

This laughable lunacy caught Eric Gill's attention in his speech "*Painting and the Public*". The fact that a modern employee is actually penalized if he thinks without permission, indeed, if he thinks at all, would not have surprised Mr. Gill. We have come to a pass where workmanship is exiled to the domain of the very wealthy or the rather eccentric. The average American eats food processed by adm and served by McDonald's; he lives in a house gift-wrapped in materials from Alcoa and sold by Century 21; he wears clothes slave-manufactured by Nike and peddled at Walmart; and he pays for all these "quality" products with the wages begrudged him by gm or money lent him at usury by Bank of America. It would be the work of a doctoral dissertation to describe how we came from the art of the artisan to the product of the production line—and called it "good".

In our day no less than in that of Harold Robbins, "nothing has been done at all" to remedy the perverse economic and moral situation in which the world languishes. It is the unwillingness of many men, and the inability of most, to recognize the dire straits of materialist economics that make a cure not just unlikely, but impossible. Robbins' essay, "*The Buttress of Freedom*", ends with the diagnosis that man formerly enjoyed a more evenly distributed economic power, but that political power was exercised almost exclusively by the rich. Modern man enjoys an even more distorted distribution of economic power amid a mere chimera of political power for the mass of men. What political power the common man now has is employed to ensure that he remains an employee—with his vigorous consent.

Arthur J. Penty wrote what amounts to the distributist "Declaration of Independence" just before he died in 1937. *"Distributism: A Manifesto"* is a clarion call exhorting men who would not be slaves to throw off their shackles, all too often self-imposed. The specific points of the Manifesto are testimony to the fact that much of the enslavement of wage slaves is intellectual, moral, and spiritual. Wrong thinking throughout society has resulted in one part of society, the wealthy, oppressing and exploiting the other part of society, the working and middle classes—with the explicit permission of the oppressed.

Certainly there is a necessity to plainly lay down the nature of the grievances held by those who wish human freedom against those intent upon human bondage. Missing, however, is sufficient and explicit reference to the role played by God and the Faith in effecting man's freedom. The greatest slavery is not to matter, but to sin. Both the American Declaration of Independence and the distributist *Manifesto* suffer from the failure to insist on God's part not only as the origin of freedom, but as *the object of freedom.* Unless and until man desires freedom not for his own sake nor for the sake of freedom, but for the glory of God alone, he will find that his most fervent efforts move him all the farther from both goals—both the one he wrongly pursues and the one he was created to attain.

Materialists of all stripes, whether they are the oppressed or the oppressor, have acquiesced to a common system. It is not until someone is able to insist that he desires something entirely different that a difference will be made in how life is lived. To quote from Harold J. Massingham's essay, "*And his Mental Exodus*": "Become different from your enemy; do not, under another name, manifest him in yourself." It is not systems that need to change, but the hearts of men that need to be converted through the love of God, by the Love who is God.

Captain Herbert Shove begins his essay, *The Growth of Industrialism*, with a quote from Pope Leo xiii's encyclical Rerum Novarum. This is a terrific point of departure. Captain Shove recognizes that in the wholesale departure from a commerce governed by a Catholic ethos lies the ills of materialism. Industrialism as such is not the problem. Machines and industry are no worse than the men running them. The problem is the materialist indifference, which almost inevitably grows into hostility, to the Faith. Men without a moral compass will make a mess of whatever they touch, no matter how good the material with which they work.

Perhaps it is because I am a priest that I am fervent in my hope that distributism can find a home in our lives. Perhaps it is because I am a priest that I am not at all sanguine about the potential in contemporary society for making the profound changes which distributism would demand of it. The man of faith knows nothing if not the wonder of the hand of God at work in the world. The man of faith is painfully aware of how hard-won true repentance must be. Hope and realism meet on the Cross of Christ.

And that, of course, is the *crux* of the matter. Man is God's mirror. The works of man, therefore, must be godly, for their only proper object is divine. The ultimate success, wherein man achieves union with the divine, is the obedience of Christ crucified. The will of God and its reflection in man, the artistry of God and its perfection in man, are united on the Cross. It is there that the two orders, Creator and the created, are made one, the one bringing the other to the fulfillment for which it was made. Distributism must be above all other things an effort to order human living according to that which it is called to imitate: the living God.

Conversations about distributism with trained and professional economists invariably slide into other subjects, as the "experts" despair of ever making clear to the distributist that he is not being practical, that he is ignorant of the incredible complexity of the mechanics of economics, that normal people do not desire the good sought by distributism. Distributists, we are told *ad nauseam,* do not understand the facts. There are technical elements within economics that distributism simply can not address.

With all due respect to economists who merely know more: Poppycock! They might know more, but they surely do not know better. Faith informs both distributism and the distributist who endeavors to implement it. The love of money, the root of all evil, informs materialist economics and, all too often, its practitioners. A wise judge can overcome his worst errors of fact, but a corrupt judge does all the more evil as his facts improve. One would be hard pressed to demonstrate that the practical ends of materialism demonstrate anything other than the final degradation of the human person.

Distributism has as its ultimate goal the elevation of the human person from his fallen state into union with God. It is certainly possible to argue about whether or not distributism is fitted to attain this goal. The difference between distributism and materialism is that the distributist will defer to a superior means to his exalted end, whereas, obviously, the materialist will cling to his money until his bitter end.

This conversation is finally one of morality. St. John Vianney said, "The eyes of the world see no further than this life, while the eyes of faith see deep into eternity." The perspective proper to man is not one that focuses upon himself, for in such a case he will find himself blind, seeing neither himself in his myopia nor the world in his disdain.

Man's proper perspective is one of seeking God; and in seeking Him, finding Him; and in finding Him, seeing Him; and in seeing Him, being able at last to see himself as he is meant to be: *In action like an angel, in apprehension how like a god! The beauty of the world! The paragon of animals!* In short, man will see himself at last in Heaven. Materialism ends in this world. Distributism seeks life in a world that will never end. That is, indeed, the long view, and one of a better—the best— home!

Father Smith
September 2003

Crickhollow, Newton, Iowa

The Economy of Salvation

How the Son of God Employs Fathers in the Work of Building the Kingdom of God

> *Therefore I say to you, be not solicitous for your life, what you shall eat, nor for the body, what you shall put on. Is not the life more than meat and the body more than raiment? Behold the birds of the air, for they neither sow, nor do they reap, nor do they gather into barns: and your heavenly Father feedeth them. Are not you of much more value than they?... Consider the lilies of the field, how they grow: they labor not, neither do they spin. But I say to you that not even Solomon in all his glory was arrayed as one of these. And if the grass of the field, which is today and tomorrow cast into the oven, God doth so clothe, how much more you, O ye of little faith! Be not solicitous, therefore, saying, What shall we eat: or, What shall we drink: or, Wherewith shall we be clothed. For after all these things do the heathens seek. For your Father knoweth that you have need of all these things. Seek ye therefore first the Kingdom of God and His justice: and all these things shall be added unto you.—Mt. 6:25-33*

Introduction: Una Voce

Catholics are not supposed to be protestants. This should be a painfully obvious statement, particularly in regard to ecclesial governance, theology, and morality. But, although many are uncomfortable in the period since the Second Council of the Vatican with the lines that are being blurred between Rome and the rest of those claiming belief in Christ, none seems to take exception to an issue of far longer standing and perhaps even more deeply ingrained in Western man's collective psyche. Whether or not Catholics and protestants should share administrative structures, forms of worship, and proscriptions on certain behaviors, all tend to agree that the way men make a living is pretty much the same, differences of faith notwithstanding. No matter what it might mean to seek the Bread of Life in Holy Communion, daily bread is a common need met by practically all moderns of any or no faith by means of *capitalism*.

The assumption that Catholics and protestants do not and need not have differences of approach to understanding man's pursuit of sustenance on earth is seriously flawed. First and foremost must be recognized the fact that there is no single voice that can define just what it means to be authentically protestant. This leaves the door open for "protestant" economic practices profoundly at variance not only with Catholicism, but with other forms of protestantism. The Amish sheep farmer and the Calvinist manufacturer will have very little to claim for mutual principles guiding their respective decisions on pursuing a livelihood, exercising worship, and declarations on the nature of sin. Curiously enough, the Amish farmer can find at least a limited affinity with the detachment of St. Francis of Assisi, while the Calvinist industrialist would take no exception to the work ethic of St. Joseph.

At the very root of the protestant understanding of the human person in *whatever* aspect of mortal experience is being discussed, is the assertion of the right of the individual to determine his own course. This is not merely a matter of Martin Luther parting ways with the Holy See, but of, for example, the aforementioned Amish being "divorced" by the followers of Menno Simon, or John Wesley finding the retooled faith of Elizabeth I too confining, or the leaders of Anglicans throughout the Third World vilifying Gene Robinson of New Hampshire. In addition to this shared protestant penchant for seeking communion apart from one another, they share another, rather ironic pedigree. ***All protestants can look to the Catholic Church as their origin.***

Amintore Fanfani in his 1934 treatise, *Catholicism, Protestantism, and Capitalism*, spells out very well how Catholics tolerated, then pursued, and then mandated practices that brought the world what became modern capitalism. In the same vein, it was from a unified Catholic culture and ethos that the protestant multiplicity arose. This simultaneous set of departures by Catholics from Catholic ethics of economics, orthodoxy in doctrine, and adherence to ecclesial order did more than produce rival claimants to the name "Christian". Divergent understandings of faith and how it is played out in daily life also produced a dichotomy between Catholics and protestants not only of what is permissible, but of what is *meritorious* in man's economic activities. It is not possible to make a final determination of which activities in modern economics would be acceptable to all protestants, but it is very easy to demonstrate how often modernity veers from definitive Catholic teaching on ethics, morals, and justice.

One can not overemphasize how crucial to questions of social and economic justice is the inability among protestants to clearly define what is forbidden, what is allowed, and what is virtuous, in the human person. Multitudinous opinions on these issues carry ramifications far beyond who becomes rich or who remains poor. These are life and death realities. Men sharing mores and a worldview will meet with certain difficulty and probable failure in offering their fellows a fair opportunity to produce food, shelter, and clothing. Men without a common set of truths out of which to pursue their livelihoods guarantee that many men will exploit other men, *and the exploited will have no principle by which to correct their oppressors.* Appeals to sentimentality and emotionalism will be made on the one hand, and on the other will be violent struggles to take for the deprived what they perceive was stolen by the privileged. Neither sentiment nor violence is a basis for a rational resolution to social injustice, and neither emotionalism nor strife can be the basis for an ongoing effort to preserve civilization.

Where no protestant is able to speak for all protestants about what constitutes fundamental departures from an "orthodox" *sine qua non*, the Cicar of Christ on earth, the Pope, holds an Office whose responsibilities include teaching definitively what is authentic to the Gospel, what is required for salvation, and what will lead to damnation. It is the matter of a wholly other work to describe how this aspect of papal authority has been muted in regards to economic matters. What is of importance here is to acknowledge the power of the papacy to provide a consistent and coherent body of doctrines useful in man's daily life, *and* to outline several of the most egregious ways in which modern capitalism violates Catholic dogma, natural law, and the divine will. This capacity to articulate for all believers what is of the Faith and that which is antithetical thereto is an inherent and irreconcilable difference between the Catholic Church and protestant sects. The failure of Popes to fully exercise this capacity coupled with the protestant impotence to agree with one another about matters of truth has resulted in the extraordinary economic and social injustices rampant in the modern capitalist world.

Pride, lust, avarice, gluttony, envy, anger, and sloth are the seven deadly sins. They feed off of and lead toward each other. In a variety of ways, capitalism encourages men to cultivate these sins. Protestants have no agreed-upon set of principles to counter capitalism's claims of the legitimacy of various vices at work in man's economic life. Catholicism has defined over the centuries many principles that clearly condemn fundamental activities within capitalism that nonetheless have become commonplace in the average man's daily experience.

Humility is not an attribute of a capitalistic society. No one strives through capitalism to be the least important, the most serving, or the greatest in generosity as expressions of success. *If you've got it, flaunt it* is far more indicative of the capitalist ideal. It is telling that modern capitalism has replaced the charitable hospital run by women religious vowed to poverty with the multibillion-dollar healthcare conglomerate; eliminated the family farm of a hundred acres or less in favor of agri-industry behemoths with properties counted in the millions of acres; and created fortunes of staggering size for speculators who produce nothing but stock portfolios. America's three largest private fortunes, Microsoft, Walmart, and Berkshire-Hathaway, were unapologetically accomplished—and continue to grow—by way of the caprices of Wall Street. This has been done through an intentional disparity between the value of what they "produce" versus the going rate of their stock certificates. An identical understanding of such ephemeral "wealth" is what funds pension funds, mutual funds, and the Social Security "trust" fund.

Once upon a time, to know one's place meant to contribute to the order of society, to benefit from the stability of society, and to offer tangible and necessary goods to society. Capitalistic pride has resulted in a society predicated on markets whose primary trait is chaos, workers who can not predict where they will live or how they will make a living ten years into the future, and labor whose fruits are intended to become obsolete within the time-frame of an ever-quickening business cycle so as to require the purchase of other equally short-lived "services" or commodities of dubious worth in producing good citizens, happy people, or sanctity. All of this is done by the mechanisms of and in enslavement to the sin of usury. Jesus Christ said, *Take my yoke upon you and learn from me, for I am meek and humble of heart, and ye shall find rest for your souls, for my yoke is sweet and my burden is light* (Mt.11:25-30).

It hardly needs to be pointed out that the modern world is awash in the filth of carnality. Within living memory popular culture once forbade the use of the four-letter expletive referent to the eternal condemnation of the immortal soul.

As things stand at the beginning of the twenty-first century, there are media easily available even to children wherein no word is censored, no action is veiled, no violence disdained, no depravity beyond bounds, and no irreverence rebuked. The internet is predominately an information superhighway for access to immorality. Billboards, advertisements in magazines, television programs, motion pictures, radio broadcasts, sporting events, and political fundraisers have become venues for squalor that would make Caligula blush—or drool. Jesus Christ said, *Babylon the great is fallen, is fallen: and is become the habitation of devils and the hold of every unclean spirit and hateful bird: because all nations have drunk of the wine of wrath of her fornication; and the kings of the earth have committed fornication with her; and the merchants of the earth have been made rich by the power of her delicacies* (Apocalypse 18:2-3).

Houses have gotten larger while families have grown smaller. Cars have lower gas mileages just as the price of oil is perceived as poised to set new highs. Corporate executives in the United States have salaries several hundred times greater than their average employees; those average employees make in six months what some Third World garment makers earn in ten years fabricating the clothes worn by Americans—jet-setters and laborers alike. Lotteries, riverboat casinos, and the city of Las Vegas attest to the insatiable desire of Americans to get something for little or nothing, constant failure notwithstanding. The oft-lamented phenomenon of grade inflation in academics is a subtler version of the American craving for ever more, gained honestly or not. Greed breeds injustice as well as ever greater insensitivity to one's own unjust wants. Those who have less do not care whether or not they have enough, they just want more. It does not occur to the avaricious that their unhappiness is caused by being unhappy over what they do not have, rather than being grateful for what they do have. If enough is not enough, more will never be enough. Jesus Christ said, *remember that thou didst receive good things in thy lifetime, and likewise Lazarus evil things; but now he is comforted and thou art tormented* (St. Luke 16:25).

Compare such phrases as "super-sized", "all-you-can-eat", "we never close", "no-risk trial period", "make thousands part-time", "earn a degree on your weekends", and "two-for-one" with Jesus Christ saying "enter through the narrow gate"; "these demons can be cast out only with prayer and fasting"; "he who saves his life shall lose it"; "better to enter paradise lame than to be cast into Gehenna with both feet"; "from those who are given much, much is expected"; "go, sell all that you have, give to the poor, and come, follow me"; and "it is easier for a camel to pass through the eye of a needle than for a rich man to enter the Kingdom of Heaven". The 401(k), double coupon days, and the frequent need for garage sales are testimonies to the insecurity of modern men, disbelieving that He who upholds the sparrows and counts the hairs on heads will also feed His children (the Bread of Life) today, house them (in His many mansions) tomorrow, and clothe them (in His glory) forever. Somehow, Providence is not enough for those intent upon eating, drinking, and making merry today, for tomorrow they die. This spiritual malaise is not unrelated to America's ongoing weight problem. Yet ignored today, as it was by the original example to whom it was applied, are the words of Jesus Christ in the parable, *Fool, this very night thy soul shall be demanded of you! And whose shall those things be which thou hast provided?* (St. Luke 12:20)

When the Browns are having trouble keeping up with the Joneses, visa is happy to *lend* a helping hand—repaid at the rate of an arm and a leg. When daughter is in anguish over her lack of the latest fashions, Mom is more than willing (with the help of MasterCard) to remedy the situation with a day-trip to the mall. When Junior is cut from the team, Dad demands (with the backing of American Express) that he prepare for next season at the local health club. When the current administration learns from intelligence sources that a banana republic's dictator might be developing the bomb, the citizenry is pleased to mortgage themselves and their grandchildren to yet another weapons system. When someone shouts that he deserves the same things as the next man, the faithful ear might catch the intense whisper of Jesus Christ saying, *None is good but God. (Mt. 19:17)*

Union and management do not negotiate, they posture. The customer service department renders less service than it gives and receives customer abuse. Advertising has given us "cola wars", "price wars", and "The Battle of the Network Stars". It matters not whether the preservation of the family, customer satisfaction, or promotional bragging rights are on the line, winning is everything, the only thing, and, most of all, *my* thing. To prevail, to vanquish, to overwhelm in the name of merely material gain is a perilous dismissal of Jesus Christ's warning that *whoever is angry with thy brother is in danger of the judgment… and whoever shall say, 'Thou fool!' shall be in danger of hell fire.* (Mt. 5:21, 22)

Don't feel like making dinner? The microwave will do it for you. Don't want to think about the paper due tomorrow? Spend your evening instead arranging your address book with the new software your Dad just bought. Want to go for a walk? You have to drive ten miles to the trail just built along the old railroad right-of-way. Don't want to feel guilty about how self-serving your life is? Then just forget that Jesus Christ told St. Martha, *One thing only is needful, and Mary hath chosen the best part, which will not be taken away from her.* (Lk. 10:42)

In addition to the seven deadly sins, capitalism makes room as well for the four sins that cry to Heaven for vengeance. Murder, sodomy, defrauding the laborer, and oppressing the widow and the orphan have their places on Wall Street, not to mention Main Street. Abortion feathers the nests of doctors, employs activists, and motivates career politicians under the cover of federal law. Municipal, state, and federal governments have sanctioned perversion, mandating that privileges heretofore reserved to Matrimony be given to perpetrators of unnatural acts—with a significant financial incentive involved through taxes, expenditure of disposable income, and the sale of pornography. Obligatory Social Security payments, auto insurance, and non-cash employee benefits take money from the pockets of the poor and middle class, expose them to double taxation, reward obscenely wealthy conglomerates, reduce the buying power of the populace, and subject the common man to a wage slavery from which his paycheck deductions offer no opportunity of escape. Wage slavery effectively creates orphans by wrenching *both* the father and the mother from the home (an injustice which should be visited upon neither sex), exposes children to unfit surrogate parents through the public school system, and contributes to the breakup of the family with the devastation of divorce, which disproportionately harms women and children. As the final insult added to these injuries, usurious loans, property taxes, and unstable employment render home ownership either an impossible pipe dream or a cruel delusion for the majority of moderns.

There is not space here to go into all the details of how modern capitalism thrives on the hubris, concupiscence, appetite, greed, jealousy, hate, and despair native to unredeemed man. Suffice it to say that looking out for number one, being liberated and uninhibited, getting the most toys, being first on the block, taking the last cookie, tasting the sweetness of revenge, and grabbing the gusto are predicated on a worldview that champions material acquisition, while being dismissive of or hostile to a spiritual reality superior to merely physical concerns. Billions are invested, trillions exchanged, and incalculable losses incurred based on an exclusively this-worldly understanding of man's ultimate purpose.

Is that, then, the last word on what should occupy the space between the womb and the tomb? Heavens no! God has *much* more to say to man than Madison Avenue might offer. Our Lord gets His word out through His vicar, through His clergy, and through His sons who head the families where He is made at home.

Feed My Sheep!: How the Holy Father and the Bishops can help Jesus save the world.

> From Paragraph 83 of Leo XIII's *Rerum Novarum*: "… let them not cease to impress upon men of all ranks the principles of Christian living as found in the Gospel; by all means in their power let them strive for the well-being of people; and especially let them aim both to preserve in themselves and to arouse in others, in the highest equally as well as in the lowest, the mistress and queen of the virtues, Charity. Certainly, the well-being which is so longed for is chiefly to be expected from an abundant outpouring of charity; of Christian charity, We mean, which is in epitome the law of the Gospel, and which, always ready to sacrifice itself for the benefit of others, is man's surest antidote against the insolence of the world and immoderate love of self, the divine office and features of this virtue being described by the Apostle Paul in these words: 'Charity is patient, is kind… seeketh not her own… beareth with all things… endureth all things'" (1 Cor. 13:4-7).

Jesus Christ came not to be served, but to serve. His mystical body, the Catholic Church, continues His work. It is not the place of the Church to change economics; it is the place of the Church to announce the Good News of salvation. Those who hear the Good News will live lives according to its mandates. It is not for the world to dictate how the Gospel is to be tolerated in men's lives, but for the Gospel to mold a world in keeping with the obligations that lead to eternal life. His Holiness the Pope and the bishops in union with him have the charge from God Himself to offer food to His flock in such a way as to free them to do the work of building up the Kingdom of Heaven. God's law, the natural law, and the laws of the Church are not intended to restrict the citizens subject to Christ the King, but to provide for them a context in which to exercise the freedom of the sons of God.

Toward that end, the hierarchy of the Church would do well to refrain from offering yet another encyclical letter on social justice or a pastoral letter on human rights or, heaven forfend, a blue-ribbon committee to study the problem with secular and religious leaders. Instead, what the Church and the world need to hear is the Good News, the Gospel of Jesus Christ—and to hear that the leaders of the Church are taking it seriously. This is to say that as *spiritual* leaders they set the tone for the conversation. It is not so much an estimation of the state of things at present that requires exposition, but a constant iteration of eternal things put before the minds of men. Our work in this passing world must ever be directed by a desire to live in the world that will never end.

Jesus Christ, the same yesterday, today, and forever, is the patrimony of the Church. His birth in Bethlehem forms the basis for our understanding of how a life pleasing to God looks. Jesus was born a poor child, in poor circumstances to a poor family. He lived His life among poor people and proclaimed the Good News that the poor are *blessed!* Jesus died a criminal's death literally lacking the shirt on His back.

In that death, His crucifixion on Calvary Hill, Jesus empties Himself of all human dignity, of creaturely life, of the honor due Him as God. He is left with absolutely nothing. The very torments of hell become His sole possession. During His teaching ministry He stressed that it is *only* through the Cross that God's will is accomplished, that life is preserved, and that the sinner shows himself a true disciple.

Consummating all creation on Good Friday, Jesus then takes up His life again on Easter Sunday. He enters into his Father's glory on Ascension Thursday. One day—soon, let us pray—He will return in that glory to judge the living and the dead. Those who would go on living are commanded to do as the Lord of Life has done: to lay down this life; to reject the allurements of the world, the flesh, and the devil; and to trust in the providence of God to provide *all* that is needed; food, shelter, clothing, and life itself.

The Pope is the successor to St. Peter and the bishops are the successors to the other Apostles. As the original Twelve went forth to the ends of the earth and proclaimed the Kingship of Christ crucified and risen, each succeeding generation of the magisterium is charged with carrying on the labor of spreading the Gospel. Jesus did not wield a kingship shaped of things of this world. The princes of the Church, although also stewards of material goods, have as their primary authority the power of binding and loosing on earth and in Heaven. Their sons and daughters in the clergy and laity stand in profound want of the voice of Christ calling mankind to sanctity in every aspect of earthly life. As such, the preaching task, far more than cares of administration, is at the heart of the role of shepherd given to the Pope and the bishops in communion with him.

Christendom was not the matter of a wonderful economic policy put in place that then supported nice people who ended up becoming holy. The Social Reign of Christ the King was pursued in the daily life of countless Martyrs, Confessors, and Virgins, who through their tireless witness to Christ and Him crucified gave birth to a society predicated on perfecting man through the grace of God mediated through the Sacraments of the Church. Our bishops would do well to remember this as efforts are made to confront a world grown Godless once more. The world will not be met and defeated on its terms, but by bringing to bear the power of grace, the gift of the Sacraments, and the wealth of divine charity shared among the children of God. Truly the best service that the hierarchy could offer the Church is not to dictate what we are to do, but to articulate *why* the Church exists on earth: *Jesus Christ is Lord of all! He has given us an example of holy poverty. He has promised a reward to those who sacrifice all with Him. And He commands all to love as He loves, unto death, to new life, forever and ever. Amen!*

I won't charge a royalty if they use those lines in their sermons.

Do this in memory of me! The role of the parish priest in Christ's work in the world.

> From Paragraph 77 of Leo XIII's *Rerum Novarum*: "It is clear, however, that moral and religious perfection ought to be regarded as their principal goal, and their social organization as such ought above all to be directed completely by this goal… Therefore, having taken their principles from God, let those associations provide ample opportunity for religious instruction so that individual members may understand their duties to God, that they may well know what to believe, what to hope for, and what to do for eternal salvation, and that with special care they may be fortified against erroneous opinions and various forms of corruption. Let the worker be exhorted to the worship of God and the pursuit of piety, especially to religious observance of Sundays and Holy Days. Let him learn to reverence and love the Church, the common Mother of all, and likewise to observe her precepts and to frequent her Sacraments, which are the divine means for purifying the soul from the stains of sin and for attaining sanctity."

On the subject of sermons, but two words are necessary for the faithful to hear from their priests in the pulpit in order to understand how best to conform their economic lives to their faith: ***Go home!*** Where will we find the means to transform the world from the den of mammon to the house of God? ***Go home!*** How can we make a difference in such a large economy to bring greater justice to bear on our economics? ***Go home!*** Who is responsible for ensuring that the Gospel is at the heart of how we make decisions that affect our material well being? **Go home!**

Perhaps the most devastating aspect of the ills wrought on the world by a worldly understanding of economics is the ongoing and accelerating destruction of the family. Parishes throughout the world, it is sad to say, are contributing to this phenomenon. Whether it is the extraordinary expense of the physical plants that are being built, or the immense size of staffs doing work of dubious worth, or a chaos of activities that demand the presence of parishioners at meetings, fund-raisers, and, every now and then, Mass, the parish has become a true burden to the average family. Add to all of this the dizzying array of events attached to the few remaining and barely Catholic schools, and it becomes evident that the family spends more time at work, at school, and at socializing than with one another.

An irony in this age of lay "empowerment" is that the activities of the Church have become tied up with a physical location. The parish hall, the rectory, and the school have replaced the front porch, the back yard, and the kitchen as the places where most Catholics engage one another. Since parishes are so rarely neighborhood realities in the twenty-first century, the *only* time that parishioners see one another is on Sunday. Thus, coffee-and-doughnuts hour becomes the primary context for the majority of the laity to learn to love their fellows sufficiently to sell all and give to the poor, to lay down their lives for their friends, and to take up their crosses each day and follow Jesus.

Father needs to tell everybody to just **Go home!**

The parish should not become a surrogate living room. Prayer and glorifying God should be the emphasis when the parish priest is exhorting his parishioners to greater efforts at sanctity, not appeals for capital campaigns, or selling candy for new school computers, or raffling off cars or cash to beef up the endowment. ***Father should not encourage consumerism and materialism in the name of advancing the work of God.*** The parish priest should set the tone that the children of God in their parish family live in a house devoted to *prayer.* Anyone can show hospitality in his own home. The unique role of the Church is to bring the people together to receive from God what He has to offer—Christ crucified—and to offer in return humble thanks, joyful praise, and reverent awe.

Then, when everybody does ***Go home!*** the fruits of the gifts of God can be shared. It is in the home that the lessons learned in the Church are applied. We are here, not to buy more things or to have "better" things or to earn more to have more things. The tone set by the parish priest will go a long way toward reminding parishioners that, as Christ's Kingdom is not of this world, His flock is laboring for a reign not of this world. But if the parish is caught up in frenetic activity, material acquisition, and misplaced priorities that neglect the spiritual altogether, then when it comes to personal decisions on purchases, employment, and investment, it is not to be expected that suddenly a flock whose shepherds have never guided them in a sense of holy poverty and focus on God, will suddenly insist that their houses, cars, home-entertainment systems, Disneyland vacations, and usurious credit cards will reflect a desire to imitate Jesus.

Insofar as the parishioners are at the church, they will be in need of their priests being at the altar, in the confessional, and on their knees. It is absurd to think that the lay faithful at work in the world will, on the whole, be more spiritually centered and fervent than their priests are. Like fathers, like sons. Parish priests who set an example of worldly anxiety, committee-driven decision making, and material avarice will have a parish full of worried, tired, and unsatisfied—and unsatisfiable—basket cases. The priest who leads in prayer, who demonstrates a desire for sanctity, who joys in holy poverty sets a standard for his people that, if they strive to meet it, will result in a peace that this world can not give.

Father Pastor is not an administrator. He is not a businessman. He is not an employer. Father is ordained *in persona Christi* to offer the Holy Sacrifice of the Mass, to forgive sins, and to mediate grace to a sinful world. The priest who makes prayer, penance, and service in love of God above all things and neighbor above himself will go far toward helping his people escape the trap set by the world. As Dorothy Day said, "The less one takes from Caesar, the less one must render to Caesar!" The parish priest can offer a tremendous gift to his parishioners by modeling for them and exhorting them to a life given to laying up treasures in Heaven, where neither rust, moth, nor thief—nor inflation—can diminish them.

... as Christ also loved the Church and delivered Himself up for it.: Holy fathers at home.

> From Paragraphs 18-21 of Leo XIII's *Rerum Novarum:* "Rights of this kind which reside in individuals are seen to have much greater validity when viewed as fitted into and connected with the obligations of human beings in family life… No law of man can abolish the natural and primeval right of marriage, or in any way set aside the chief purpose of matrimony established in the beginning by the authority of God: 'Increase and multiply' (Genesis 1:28). Behold, therefore, the family, or rather the society of the household, a very small society indeed, but a true one, and older than any polity! For that reason it must have certain rights and duties of its own entirely independent of the State… As already noted, the family, like the State, is by the same token a society in the strictest sense of the term, and it is governed by its own proper authority, namely, by that of the father… To desire, therefore, that the civil power should enter arbitrarily into the privacy of homes is a great and pernicious error… Paternal authority is such that it can neither be abolished or absorbed by the State, because it has the same origin in common with that of man's own life… Inasmuch as socialists, therefore, disregard care by parents and in its place introduce care by the State, they act *against natural justice* and dissolve the structure of the home."

It is in the home that the freedom of the sons of God is exercised by the laity. At work the boss is in charge. In government, nobody, everybody, and somebody else is in charge. And even in these days of frowning on clericalism, when it comes to being on the parish grounds, Father or the oligarchy running things with him is in charge, not the average parishioner. But even in this benighted age, a man's home is still his castle. No one can keep a father from exercising paternal service to his little flock, the family, in perfect conformity with the teachings of the Church, the message of the Gospel, and the example of Our Lord.

Husband-fathers hold a priestly role in the home. They are nourished by sound teachings, strengthened by sacramental grace, and encouraged by their priests' examples to guide their families in emulating the Holy Family of Jesus, Mary, and Joseph. Dad is the go-to man responsible for insisting that the family's home is a house of prayer. That Jesus is the primary member of the family. That the honor due to mother and father flows from placing God the Father at the head of the family and obedience to Him in all things as the fundamental rule of the house. The Fourth Commandment is dependent on adherence to the First Commandment.

Fathers are given to families for leadership. Of utmost importance is their leadership in striving for Heaven. The Dad should lead the family daily Rosary. The Dad should gather the family to go to frequent Confession. The Dad should prepare the family at home in prayer on Sunday and Holy Days before heading to church for Mass. The Dad should be insistent on having time each day to nurture his own spiritual life in private prayer, as well as making time in the family's schedule for retreats, pilgrimages, and pursuing the corporal and spiritual works of mercy. The Dad should speak frequently to his children about the vocation to which God is calling them, and he should cleave faithfully to his wife as they together fulfill their vocation as parents and spouses.

Embracing such spiritual disciplines will bear fruit in filial piety, love of God, and confidence in His promise of salvation. A family led in this way will not want television polluting their home. They will hold popular music, material acquisitiveness, immodesty, profane language, and irreverence in utter disdain. Christmas will be preceded by a holy Advent bent on the penitential preparation for receiving God's Son into their midst, not a feeding frenzy at the trough of mammon to fuel a bloated economy. Such a family will be bound together so strongly that the children growing up will not have an uncontrollable urge to leave home, but will instead understand that their family is always their home, and the next generation will be lovingly received into the bosom of a group of people who know themselves, who know who they are as a family, and who know a well-founded hope for achieving their ultimate goal of living together forever in Heaven.

Before the revolution is mounted to sweep away the excesses of capitalism and make the world safe for whatever it is a revolution of that kind would deem worthwhile, it must be considered what kind of men are making things change. *Good men will help make changes for the better, bad men will make changes for the worse, and men without a sense of good and bad and insistent that no one else should impose such sentiments on others will be the most evil.* Too much time is lost, too much breath is wasted, and too much energy dissipated waiting for the "system" to change. Beyond the fact that no "system" has a will to change and is entirely at the behest of its human creators and users, is the fact that only a fool would leave something as important as his immortal soul—and his family's immortal souls—in the hands of bureaucrats, politicians, and "market forces".

True power lies in each man governing his own affairs in keeping with the universal call to holiness. The Browns have no control over whether or not the Joneses will cooperate in building the Kingdom of Heaven, but both the Browns and the Joneses have absolute control over what happens in their respective homes. The key to transforming the world is to transform the individual soul and then the family. It is the father within the family who must decide the direction such a transformation takes. There is no coincidence in the fact that the destruction of the family began not with forcing women into the workplace, or putting children in compulsory public schools, or taxing income and nonproductive real estate, but *in removing the father from the family farm or the family trade.* Much of the cure to what ails us is dependent on returning the father to his proper place at the head of the family and in the home.

Pride is at work among those who ignore the essential work of making families holy under the headship of the father. The mindset that sees such efforts as inconsequential encourages the very problems attacking the family. Strong families are not a by-product of good economics or social theory. Mankind must strengthen the family or all economics will be a matter of slavery and the community will be that of inmates in prisons. It is not a waste of time or a distraction to begin the task of correcting the imbalances in macro-economics by focusing on the domestic economy.

Setting priorities is not one of modernity's strong suits, hence, it is forgotten that the macro-economy exists to support the home economy, and the home economy exists to support the needs of the body in service to spiritual perfection. Families are not made for work, but work is meant to nurture the family. Prayer is not intended to sustain man in his daily life of toil, but his daily life of toil makes sense only as a means to sustain the effort to attain eternal life. We do not work all day and grudgingly give a little time to prayer at infrequent intervals. We pray each day and throughout the day, taking time periodically to do the work that makes prayer possible. People incapable of ordering their lives toward the eternal will find themselves laboring for that which is ephemeral, dehumanizing, and, ultimately, deadly.

So, the father in a family must be keenly aware of his responsibility to guide his little flock to good pastures. Where he interacts on a community level, it will be with the desire and understanding that public efforts are intended for the preservation and enrichment of his family and all families. The common good is not merely a matter of what is good for all, but seeks to gain what is good for each. A collection of people inattentive to being good at home will not accomplish any good together. Conversely, a society of strong families has a firm foundation on which to increase justice, peace, and, in proper proportion, prosperity.

Conclusion: A (very) few practical considerations

> From Paragraphs 80 and 82 of Leo XIII's *Rerum Novarum*: "Through past events we can, without temerity, foresee the future. Age presses hard upon age, but there are wondrous similarities in history, governed as it is by the providence of God, who guides and directs the continuity and the chain of events in accordance with that purpose which He set before Himself in creating the human race… And since religion alone, as We said in the beginning, can remove the evil, root and branch, let all reflect upon this: First and foremost, Christian morals must be re-established, without which even the weapons of prudence, which are considered especially effective, will be of no avail to secure well-being."

Everybody likes concrete suggestions for solutions to problems. Here are a few suggestions for the Catholic who desires to serve God more than mammon: Believe what Jesus teaches through His Church, pray fervently and constantly, and spend more time at home than you spend anywhere else. These will likely be thought too vague and general by most people. It is an indication of our collective paucity of imagination and the decline of the *sensus Catholicus* that such simplicity is thought to be too little to be effective. The lack of a simple life, of simple desires, of simple work is what has gotten us into the morass where now we live. We have forgotten that searching the depths of the Wisdom of God is denied to the learned and clever, but revealed to the merest children, of whom is made the Kingdom of Heaven. In its typical penchant for contrariness, modernity also balks at explanations that require thought, study, and discipline. Sometimes you can't win for losing.

Sigh… To be a bit more specific, then, a suggestion for the hierarchy to take to heart: Declare a Holy Year to celebrate the primary truths of Catholic faith. Begin in Advent with an emphasis on *Emmanuel,* God with us, particularly in His Real Presence in the Blessed Sacrament of the Altar. Encourage the faithful to bring the reality of Our Lord's loving abiding with us to the end of time from the Church to the home out into the world. Celebrate the Christmas mystery around the sacred mysteries of the Mass and throughout the entirety of the Christmas season right up to the feast of the Presentation.

Continue the Holy Year observance with an emphasis on Our Lord's Sacrifice at Calvary. Shift the focus in the Mass from Our Lord being with us, to his salvific action in our midst. Approach Lent having received the awe-inspiring gift of Christ in the Incarnation with the intent of returning that gift through sacrifice, penance, and mortification. Allow the Lenten disciplines to be an expression of the willingness to love as Jesus loves, to obey the Father as Jesus obeys Him, and to offer all in sacrifice along with the perfect holocaust of Good Friday.

From Easter through the time after Pentecost is an opportunity to emphasize in the Mass how the Cross accomplishes the forgiveness of sins, and how the gifts of the Holy Ghost bear fruit in the hearts, minds, souls, and bodies of those who conform themselves entirely to Jesus. It is during this period of the year that witness is given by the faithful to the world that indeed the Lord Jesus saves and that real hope is present that fallen man can rise above his miserable state in the world and dare to claim unity with God Himself! The glory of God in Christ is present in the Mass where the work of salvation goes on unceasingly and bears fruit in the Body of Christ bringing His offer of eternal life to the whole world.

Once the hierarchy has declared this Holy Year, the parish priest has an outline for the work ahead of him in the local community. In addition to observing the universal Church's celebration of the Holy Year, the parish priest can use it as an opportunity to make permanent changes in the spiritual lives of his flock. One simple yet profoundly significant gesture would be to change the parish's fiscal year to reflect the liturgical year. This would allow all of the parish's material labors to refer back to their spiritual bases and more readily reflect the truer goals of parish activities.

Thus, the period of Advent and Christmas would become a time to focus the parish on examining how they go about their work, examining themselves for adherence to lives that are receptive of Christ in all things. As the calendar year comes to an end, and the liturgical year begins, the world becomes quieter, darker, and more introspective. This is a great context for whatever might be necessary by way of preparing the parish for appeals to support the material needs of the parish and broader community. Christmas, then, becomes a time to rejoice in what God has given, rather than in offering more of the same of what the world calls wealth. The parish should never descend into being self-serving, but should always be on the lookout for how better to be of service in assisting one another to be holy, providing for the poor, *and making converts to the Faith to join the parish in its service.* The new year should be the time the parish renews its resolve to be holy as God is holy, to be perfect as the Father is perfect, and to be compassionate as the Lord is compassionate.

That resolve becomes the basis for the Lenten sacrifices that follow shortly after the Christmas Season. Sacrificial giving, both in terms of the corporal and spiritual works of mercy, prayer, and material goods, can form part of the parish's collective taking up of the cross with Jesus. If indeed it is necessary to ask for money beyond what is offered in the weekly collection (and this need should be examined for its underlying cause, for such need should be rare), then Lent lends the proper focus for why to give, how much to give, and how to make use of what is given. Far more than parish needs, however, the priest should encourage and guide his people toward finding needs outside of their immediate community, so as to broaden the scope of the true mission of the Church to preach the Gospel, offer the Sacraments, *and save souls.*

In the time of Easter and after Pentecost this work of seeking souls to bring to Christ's salvation becomes the heart of the life of the parish. Having recognized the immensity of the gift of Christ at Christmas and rallying the parish to offer themselves with Him at Lent, the parish then can burst forth from their "Upper Room" and live out what they believe and what they have promised. This will bear fruit in the homes of the parish, in the sacramental life of the community, and in their willingness to give witness to the desire of the Church to bring Christ to the whole world. These efforts flow much more soundly from the liturgical calendar than from a fiscal calendar or a school calendar, and the parish thus gives a far stronger message about their priorities built on God and His providence rather than the arbitrary dictates of man.

Lastly, and mostly, this will to receive Christ, to unite His body more firmly to Him as the Head, *and* ***never to rest until every soul on earth is a member of His Body,*** finds its most far reaching effects in the homes of the faithful. Individual souls, not parishes or dioceses or episcopal conferences are given salvation. Those individuals are born to, raised in, and learn from families in the home.

Most learning should be in the home. Mothers and fathers are the first and primary teachers of children. Collective education in the modern world is nothing short of abominable. Those who insist that somehow other people's children will benefit from being subjected to the indifference and neglect which the average parent inflicts on his children, the hostility to good sense and morals in school bureaucracies, and the outright Godlessness of most curricula, probably claim never to have inhaled, that they never look at the pictures but only read the articles, and always obey the speed limit. In a world where second-hand cigarette smoke is attacked with a vengeance not seen since the Salem witch hunts, it is obscene to suggest that any parent should allow his child's body, mind, and soul to be exposed to the filth spread among children in schools, the warped philosophy among teachers, and the malignancy of the government entities that set school policy.

Fathers can do little that would be more beneficial for their families than to establish the home as the locus for *all* activities. If at all possible, he should work for the family's sustenance from the home. The mother should be the primary caretaker of the home. And the children should receive instruction, play, and learn to pray in the home. The family should do nothing elsewhere that it does not do in the home.

There is an especially important lesson that fathers and mothers should endeavor with all their skill, imagination, and prayer to impart on their children as they introduce the little ones to the wonders of life, the responsibilities of being in a family, and the joys of serving and loving God with one's whole heart, mind, soul, and strength. Children should have an understanding from a very early age *that to live differently from the Catholic ideal is abnormal, self-destructive, and against common sense as well as deleterious to a saintly life.* The child raised in a Catholic home should understand that God comes first, that the Church is a generous Mother, that the family is a tremendous gift always to be treasured, and that the things of this world are subservient to the needs of supporting the family, becoming holy, and obeying God. Modern man needs to teach his children the life lesson that modern life has gone horribly awry. The Catholic family needs to revive the tradition of proclaiming Jesus Christ as sovereign King—so that generations to come will not find that to be an extraordinary assertion, but the truest and happiest statement of simple fact.

Perseverance

No matter how the night oppresses, I
will always make my way back home to Dawn;
regardless how the dark might make me cry
in pain, through pain to Day I press anon.
Undaunted by the wounds of mounting years
and heedless of my ever waning youth,
no ancient terror nor my childish fears
shall stop my search for Heaven's deathless truth.
Although assail'd by sins' temptations fierce
when naught seems hidden but the help of grace,
the veil that veils the nations I shall pierce
until at last I see God's holy Face.
Take this to be the declaration for
my part 'gainst hell in righteous, ruthless war.

Do not think I have come to bring peace on earth; I have not come to bring peace, but a sword! – Mt. 10:34 —see also Eph. 6:10-20

Now the whole parable and purpose of these last pages, and indeed of all these pages, is this: to assert that we must instantly begin all over again, and begin at the other end. I begin with a little girl's hair. That I know is a good thing at any rate. Whatever else is evil, the pride of a good mother in the beauty of her daughter is good. It is one of those adamantine tendernesses which are the touchstones of every age and race. If other things are against it, other things must go down. If landlords and laws and sciences are against it, landlords and laws and sciences must go down. With the red hair of one she-urchin in the gutter I will set fire to all modern civilization. Because she should have clean hair, she should not have an unclean home; because she should not have an unclean home, she should have a free and leisured mother; because she should have a free and leisured mother, she should not have an usurious landlord; because there should not be an usurious landlord, there should be a redistribution of property; because there should be a redistribution of property, there shall be a revolution. That little urchin with the gold-red hair, whom I have just watched toddling past my house, she shall not be lopped and lamed and altered; her hair shall not be cut short like a convict's; no, all the kingdoms of the earth shall be hacked about and mutilated to suit her. She is the human and sacred image; all around her the social fabric shall sway and split and fall; the pillars of society shall be shaken, and the roofs of the ages come rushing down; and not one hair of her head shall be harmed.

– G.K. Chesterton, *What's Wrong with the World*

Why, even the hairs of your head are all numbered, therefore, fear not!—Lk. 12:7

Father Smith, *Sacerdos vagus*
10 August 2004: The Feast of St. Lawrence

Sensus Catholicus with Father Smith

I confess, Father—I am bored because I am boring. How can I lead my family in pursuing the faith with greater zeal, while spending more time at home and making it the place where we grow in knowledge and love of God and each other?—Bored in the Lower Peninsula

Dear Bored and all Readers,
I call my answer to this vital question:

In Love with Lady Poverty

Music is always an ensemble experience. It requires a composer, a composition, a performer, an instrument, and an audience. Composer, performer, and audience must accomplish the distinct yet interrelated tasks of composing, performing, and listening. To attain their goals as creator, interpreter, and appreciator, composer, performer, and audience share a common responsibility: *to practice.*

In addition to the human participants in this artistic enterprise, two indispensable inanimate objects are employed, a piece of music and a musical instrument. The piece of music's quality will reflect the skill of the composer, while the quality of the performance depends to a fair degree on the excellence (or lack thereof) of the instrument. Thus, a fourth human agent is introduced into the equation, that of instrument maker. Three of the four human agents, composer, performer, and instrument maker, rely on the competence of the other two for their overall success. At the same time, an outstanding effort by one or two of these three can be rendered utterly futile if the work of even one of his fellows is wanting in polish. The performer to a great extent can compensate for his collaborators' shortcomings, but a good listener will recognize an enfeebled composition or an inferior instrument even when a virtuoso attempts to overcome such imperfections.

Practice is absolutely necessary for each of the human members of this ensemble. Composers must master music theory. Performers must master their instruments. Instrument makers must master the skills of design and craftsmanship according to the demands of their specialties. The audience must have a sense of the philosophical significance of music, the attributes of good musicianship in live performance, and the aesthetic qualities which make certain sounds and not others pleasing to the ear. With so many potential pitfalls, it is little wonder that some musical experiences are little more than grating. The greater wonder is that any music is ever executed expressive of beauty, truth, and goodness at all.

Besides mere competency of skills, there are two other essentials to an edifying musical endeavor. The lesser, 'tho' of immense importance, is a passion for the art. Composer, performer, instrument maker, and audience need to care about what they are doing. Indifference is deadly to art. Commercialism represents a passionate interest—in money—but is fatally indifferent to transcendence. Good art is indifferent to material return, but is passionately devoted to an immanent experience of the attempt to express transcendent reality.

Most vital to this complex dynamic is a unity of vision regarding *meaning*. All parties to this group effort must have an identical understanding of what they are doing. A shared aesthetic is absolutely necessary for composer, performer, instrument maker, and audience all to be satisfied. Each will be frustrated if his fellows seek an end divergent from his own. Bach would be appalled at the idea of his compositions rendered on the kazoo. Stradivarius would cringe at the notion of one his instruments in the hands of a high school marching band. Toscanini would be insulted to be asked to accompany the rides at an amusement park. No one would pay for tickets to hear Muzak performed by an all-flute orchestra staffed by the local biker gang.

This consideration of *meaning* in the artistic venture is directed not only by what (the composition) is performed, by how (the instrument) it is performed, and by whom (the performer) it is performed, but, more than all of the above, by *why* it is performed. Here thought must be given to the aspirations of each member of the ensemble in question. *Why* do composers compose, performers perform, instrument makers make, and listeners listen? What is being communicated, who is to say it, how does he say it, and for whom is it a valuable statement?

Composers must have something to say. Performers must have the power of speech by which to say it. Instrument makers must be able to fashion suitable voice boxes. Audiences must be in possession of the faculty of understanding abstract speech. Fail at any one of these and virtual silence—even unmeaning and gibberish—is the result.

God the most holy Trinity, Father, Son, and Holy Ghost, is the single instance of this artistic endeavor perfectly accomplished. The Father conceives the Word from all eternity. The Son is that Word, eternally uttered by the Father. The Holy Ghost is the very uttering of the Word by the Father for all eternity. The Father is Who says, the Son is What is said, and the Holy Ghost is the eternal Saying—and God the Trinity, Father, Son, and Holy Ghost, is the eternal Audience among whom is shared the Conception, the Word, and the Utterance. All else is mere, pale, and wildly inadequate analogue. Creation mutters the thundering proclamation of its Creator: god is!

"Good art is indifferent to material return, but is passionately devoted to an immanent experience of the attempt to express transcendent reality." God is the Artist *par excellence*, and as such pursues this very goal. The Incarnation of the Second Person of the Most Holy Trinity in the womb of His Blessed Mother, the Virgin Mary, is the immanent encounter of *the* Transcendent: God Himself. Not only does God become one with man, but men meet God man-to-Man/God. God does precisely what St. Paul describes in the Second Epistle to the Corinthians: He does not desire what is ours; He desires *us*. And in the same vein, He does not offer what is His; He gives *himself!*

And here—at long last—we come to a love affair with Lady Poverty.

Poverty is the mode in which God speaks to man: Jesus took on the form of a slave. Poverty is what God has to say to man: Jesus became obedient. Poverty is the enfleshment of the Word of God: even unto death, death on the Cross. From His poor birth in a cave, into the poor family of Mary and Joseph, among the poor people of Nazareth and Galilee, unto His poor death on Calvary, Jesus manifested the will of God as an embracing of humility. Even more than the acknowledgement by the great saints of their inherent lowliness before the Lord, the Incarnation is God's own *choosing* to be humbled, and by that choice to exalt those who admit the utter humility of their being.

If indeed the *perfect* musical dynamic is Father-Son-Holy Ghost Conceiving, Being, and Uttering *the* Word for all eternity, then the best analogue of that reality in creation, short of the Incarnation itself, is the heart of the saint in submission, begging to be a vessel in which this sublime truth might be made manifest among men. Who better to compose this *magnum opus* than the Father, what better medium to express it than the Son, how better to render their perfection than the Holy Ghost? Thus, the saint gives his mind and will to the Father to believe and to know the truth—*Ecce Ancilla Domini!* He offers through, with, and in Christ the voice given him by the Father to proclaim the truth—*Fiat mihi secundum verbum tuum!* And in the power of the Holy Ghost, his heart bears and his lips proclaim nothing but the Sign of the Cross on which hung the Savior of the world—*Magnificat anima mea Dominum!*

Caritas, charity, love is at the core of all of this. Love of God above all things is the greatest Commandment, followed by love of neighbor as the self. The Cross, to be taken up daily in pursuit of Christ, is *the* Way to His Truth that Life is won thereby. Essential to a life lived on the cross in obedience to loving God through neighbor as self, is the willingness, eagerness, and selflessness that is found *only* in holy poverty.

Those who love God love only God and God's. They will keep nothing that is not acceptable to God. They will seek nothing that does not lead to God. They will love nothing that does not allow for love of God. For them who would have the love of God, nothing is loveable apart from God.

Holy poverty is the cross by which the soul is crucified to the world and the world to the soul. Holy poverty is the humbling of the heart admitting an absolute need for God's mercy, grace, and love. Holy poverty is the gift, the only gift, of the child of God to his brothers hungry for what the world is powerless to provide. Holy poverty is the condition necessary, the space required, within the heart, mind, soul, and strength of the man who would dare to invite the Lord of lords to be the Guest abiding with him forever.

Holy poverty is the amazing symphony whose first chord is *Fiat lux!* Holy poverty is the unparalleled virtuoso who alone can perform such a work unto its final cadence, *Consummatum est!* for He was with the Composer from the very start, *In principio erat Verbum!* And holy poverty alone has cultivated an appreciative ear who can tell the difference between a Judgment upon a *Dies irae, dies illa*, and the commendation, *Euge serve bone, et fidelis!*

In other words, vulgar in the best sense, to be poor is to *give.* God *gives.* He gives creation as Creator. He gives to creation by way of grace. He gives in creation as its Savior.

Impoverishment is *not* the same as being poor. The impoverished are victims, the oppressed. The blessed poor *will* their poverty. They either sell all and give, or they take up a daily and chosen cross, or they give their last two cents from want never having known a surplus.

Modern men discerning the compatibility of modern economics—in the home or in the nation-state—with eternal truth, would do well to reflect on this. Materialism in its three dominant forms of capitalism, socialism, and communism do *not* give. Capitalism *takes* as much as is arbitrarily deemed legal. Socialism *takes* whatever the caprices of a ruling elite deem necessary. Communism *takes* everything. One might say that pure capitalism is heartless, pure socialism is mindless, and pure communism is soulless. That leaves nothing but the strength of men to render some kind of worship, and the strength of the masses subject to materialism, i.e. , the world, the flesh, and the devil, is then compelled to serve the minority of men who are strong.

The Catholic ideal is to *give* all—heart, mind, soul, and strength—to the invisible God, and to do so through the visible brother. It is no accident that Holy Scripture frames all of this in terms of love. This is not a matter of balancing consumption and production. This is not an issue of supply and demand. This is not an equation seeking abstract justice. Bookkeepers, bean counters, and statisticians are not needed when the only sum in use is *all.* Saints do not count the cost because the price is beyond calculation: infinite love.

What God has demonstrated, time and again, throughout salvation history, is a will toward *communion.* Communion is like conception—either it is or it is not. God is emphatic about His covenant as an all-or-nothing proposition. Everything short of Catholicism, everything short of the Cross, leaves something outside the offering of all to God. For some the market is Godless. Some would have a Godless government. Still others limit God even in their religions. *Only* in Catholicism is Christ *all* in all.

Anyone who would bring the Faith from the Mass to the capitol to the market and to the home, must first desire the truth of the Mass above the state and mammon and even the hearth. He who has God, has all. He who has all without God, has nothing. Seek ye *first* the Kingdom of God and *His* justice, and all other things shall be added unto you.

Wife and husband, parents and children, present things and future things must be relinquished. The passing things of this world must be reckoned dung. The world and all its wonders are to be forfeited for the one needful thing: contemplation of Christ and him *crucified.*

The Cross! The Cross! The Cross!

Until and unless the Cross is loved, Christ is yet distant. If Christ is distant, one can not please His Father. If the Father is not pleased, hell, not Heaven, is man's final home.

Short of active persecution, lacking calumny and dispossession of goods, denied the gift of martyrdom, far the majority of Catholics, especially in the Western world, have only what was rejected by the sad, rich, young man—*poverty* for the sake of the Kingdom. Most of us must embrace the cross by humbly, obediently, and, finally, joyfully, wooing Lady Poverty. To gain salvation is to love Jesus; to love Jesus is to love His cross; to love His cross means, for most of us, to *love* Lady Poverty.

How does one love Lady Poverty, love the cross, love Jesus? One *wills* it! Love is *never* describable as "falling" in love. One *falls* into mud, into sin, into perdition. Love elevates, exalts, and excels. To fall is to become less. To love is to be *made* more.

We are loved by God, even unto death, death on the Cross. The Cross is the way God *chose* to love us. We must choose to love even as we are loved, for it is not that we loved God, but that God first loved us. What pleases our beloved is the Cross. To please Him is not to *take* what we want, but to *give* what satisfies Him. Perfect satisfaction is given God the Father by God the Son giving Himself on the Tree of the Cross. We can do no better than that, and, for most of us, *willed* poverty is the most direct way to accomplish it.

This is a love song. The very theme of love comes from the Mind of God. *The* Word of this song is the Son of God. The Melody in which it is sung is the Spirit of God. And the beloved delighting in this exquisite performance is the Blessed Trinity.

Sit down. This is important: *the instrument on which this sublime masterpiece is performed is the human soul, crafted by God, perfected through holy poverty, premiered in the concert hall of the cross, and, after the intermission of death, an endless encore is given in Heaven!*

"Stop, Father!" the critics complain. "This is all lovely and poetic—but you were asked to be *practical!*"

Ladies and gentlemen, Bored in the Lower Peninsula and everywhere else, **Faith must come first!** You need to *believe* that ***God is!*** That Jesus died and l*ives!* That the Cross is *the* means to glory! That Bethlehem, Nazareth, and Calvary are not anomalies, but the *norm* of those who belong to Christ.

Folks, do you or do you not trust, believe, and love Jesus Christ, the Incarnate Second Person of the Most Holy Trinity, the Head whose Body is the Catholic Church?

If so, then love His poverty, love His humility, love His Cross! Love of Christ can not depend on *feeling* good about suffering and death. Loving Christ *must* acknowledge the necessity of *willing* the good of suffering and death.

Too often, I am afraid, husbands and wives "love" one another more according to their feelings than in accord with the will—not of blood, not of flesh, not of the will of man, *but born of God!* To be a child of God is to do His will. His will is that adoption comes through Baptism. Baptism is a participation in the Cross of Christ, whose Flesh and Blood, real Food and Drink, bring eternal life. Love of husbands and wives reflects God's love as revealed in Christ Jesus. To love Him and His cross is to *believe* Him when He says to take up a daily cross, to give to the poor, and to render heart-mind-soul-strength to God, and the leftovers to Caesar. Nobody *feels* like doing this—it hurts—*unless and until they WILL to do it!*

And, much like childbirth for both the mother and the child, once the pain is endured, it is forgotten in the glory of living.

Marriage based on the passions rather than on *the* Passion is demeaning to both parties. St. Paul tells us to love the husband by obedience, and to love the wife through total sacrifice. Is it conceivable that Christ loves His Bride less than St. Paul instructs mere mortals to love one another? Is it anything short of blasphemy to suggest that a bride owes her husband more than the human soul owes her Lord? Bride and groom are one, ergo, the poverty of Christ the Groom as Head must be shared in a mutual offering of poverty from the Bride, the Body of Christ, the Church and her members.

The passions must give way to the Passion of Christ. His Passion is not for the satisfaction of carnal appetites. Jesus thirsts and hungers for souls. The faithful Catholic, then, must learn to crave what our Savior craves. To do this means to believe Him when He tells us that the Cross is obligatory. Holy poverty is an encounter with the Cross in which Jesus is present to crucify worldly wants in the soul, and to raise to new life souls intent upon nothing but the Bread of Life.

Bored people are full—of things, of debts, of themselves. Boredom is the result of unworthy appetites filled beyond capacity. For the bored worldling, nothing entices, nothing excites, nothing satisfies because he wants for nothing.

Holy poverty cleanses the palate and makes room in the heart for an infinite hunger. This hunger can only be satisfied by Christ and Him crucified. Souls hungry for Christ burn with a zeal to receive Him, and in receiving Him they desire yet more. Thanks be to God, this infinite hunger has at its disposal the infinite satisfaction of the Cross, wherefrom is harvested the Fruit of the Tree of Life, the Body of Christ, whereby man has hope of the never-ending satiation of all desire in the Beatific Vision.

Anyone whose passion is aflame for Lady Poverty does not stand idly by while others ignore her. He wants his queen spoken fair by all. He wishes her delights to be shared by all. He demands that her loveliness be acknowledged by all.

Lady Poverty is realized as this fairest maiden in the revelation of the love of God by Christ crucified. To love God is to love His Son. The Son shows His love by dying on the Cross. The Cross is embraced by releasing one's own claims on the wealth of this world in favor of obtaining the Pearl of incalculable price. Lady Poverty is loveable because she helps us to love Christ. We love Christ because He first loves us. He loves us because He is God and God is Love and the love of God the Father-Son-Holy Ghost is an abundance surpassing the capacity of all creation to contain. Such love is a spendthrift, scoffs at mere gold, and laughs cash unto scorn. The lover of God, in imitation of his beloved Lord, paupers himself in order to give no less than everything so as to share far more than all.

God Himself gives Himself, not for lands or jewels or "precious" metals. His only want is the human heart, mind, soul, and strength. Salvation comes to those who seek a fair exchange with God: of self for Self, of all time for all eternity, of passing life for endless life. This is not a project for businessmen or for thrill seekers or for the timid. Only *lovers* need apply.

What a long answer to a short question of fifty words or less. And I still have not told you how to do it. But I have told you what to do: Love the Lord thy God with thy whole soul, with thy whole heart, with thy whole mind, and with thy whole strength; and love thy neighbor as thyself! As well, I have told you *why* to do it: Not that we first loved God, but that God has first loved us. If you *believe* that He loves, then *act* on His love.

God is in love with poverty: the poor, the poor in spirit, the humble, the meek, the pure, the persecuted, and the self-sacrificing friend. Before anything else is attempted in the spiritual life, one must first take God at His word: that He loves us, forgives us, and will never abandon us. When that truth is all in all for us, then life begins. Our souls, our homes, our work, our nation, our world will be directed toward only those things reflective of the divine will that every knee in Heaven, on the earth, and under the earth bow and proclaim that the Lord Jesus Christ is in the glory of God the Father. Amen!

Lovers of Lady Poverty ruthlessly remove whatever comfort or luxury or seeming necessity is not in keeping with such homage. Lady Poverty's lovers delight in whatever cross, sacrifice, or inconvenience allows them to offer such homage. All wealth blushes before the splendor of Lady Poverty, and no dearth is noticed in the Presence of the Lord whose beloved is Lady Poverty.

Are people in love ever bored?

God bless you,
Father Smith

In Love with Lady Poverty

In Heaven's vaults for all to see I keep
a gem of gold and one of silver hue;
the lesser gilds the treasures dreamers reap
while greater gleams the jewel where all comes true.
Poor Solomon the king wore naught but rags
where beggared minds thought glory was revealed;
each guest who visits me goes home and brags
of bedclothes spun from lilies of the field.
In love with Lady Poverty I gain
a wealth unmeasured but by mortal tears
of joy that taste as sweet as summer rain
on youth that grows the finer with the years.
The only thing which I would count as loss
is life or death without our Savior's Cross.

27-28 September 2004
Sts. Cosmas and Damian, and St. Wenceslaus
Demiceli's Ristorante, Garden Grove, California; and Vinyamar, Tustin, CAf

For us as Catholics, the Distributive State (i.e. , the State in which there are as many owners as possible) is not something which we discuss, but something we have to propagate and institute. No advance in social thought or social action is possible if we are seeking to prove to ourselves as a theory what we should be trying to realize as a fact.

—Father Vincent McNabb, OP, *The Church and the Land*

Part Three

Preface to Volume III: Three Months of Christmas and the Holy Rosary

21 November 2009: The Presentation of the Blessed Virgin Mary, the Mother of God

Today is the Feast of the Presentation of the Blessed Virgin Mary to God in the Holy Temple in Jerusalem. Our Lady is like Our Lord in all things, including in this anticipation of the Mystery of His Presentation roughly twelve years before the first Christmas. Just as Jesus is offered by His parents on earth to His Father in Heaven within the sacred precincts of the house of God, so also Mary is offered by her parents on earth to Our Father in Heaven within the sacred precincts of the house of God. Saint Joachim and Saint Anne presented Mary to God in an action that prefigures the Presentation of the Son of God by the Blessed Virgin Mother of God and Saint Joseph. In each instance, the child is given to God with no reservations, holding nothing back, desirous of nothing other than that God receive not only the best from His creatures, but that God receive everything His creatures have to offer. Mary is given to God wholly and entirely, Jesus is given to God wholly and entirely. Saints Joachim and Anne had nothing better to give to God than the Immaculate Conception, so they rendered her to Him with the love of their whole hearts, whole souls, whole minds, and whole strength. Mary and Joseph had nothing better to give God than the Son of God, so they rendered Him to Him with the love of their whole hearts, whole souls, whole minds, and whole strength.

The result of the perfect offering by a creature to his Creator is simply *life*. After the gift of Our Lady was given by Saints Joachim and Anne to God, Our Lord blessed them with the fulfillment of His salvific will that God become a man in the life-giving womb of the Mother of God, the daughter of Saints Joachim and Anne, the Blessed Virgin Mary. Saints Joachim and Anne gave their child to the Father, and the Father gave His child to their child. Several years later this exchange was repeated in a far greater way. Now the Mother of God and the foster-father of God gave their child to God, and the Father blessed that gift with the bestowal of eternal life on them who would accept the Son as truly sent by the Father. The gift of Saints Joachim and Anne led to the life of man shared with God in the Incarnation of the Second Person of the Most Holy and Blessed Trinity. The gift of Mary and Joseph led to the life of God shared with man in the Crucifixion and Resurrection of the Son of God. The Presentation of Mary and the Presentation of Jesus are part of an unfathomable and eternal gift exchange—man is graced to be the sustenance of life for God in time, and man is graced to be sustained in the life of God for eternity. In that sense, in the sense of an exchange of gifts, the life of faith on earth and the eternal life of Heaven are an experience of a permanent Christmas.

Advent and Lent present to us Mysteries overflowing with revelations of life in the midst of death. Jesus is born, beginning His visible life on earth, in the depths of lifeless winter. Jesus rises to new and eternal life in His glorified body, having died the death on the threshold of the dawn of life in the season of spring. All of the life of Jesus is a manifestation of the Mystery of the Cross, the great Sign of Contradiction. He begins life in the dead of winter; He dies on the cusp of spring wherein life bursts forth anew. But, too, Jesus enters His life on earth having abdicated His claims to the glory of Heaven, beginning His life with us in an act of Sacrifice, dying, as it were, to His almighty power as the Son of God in order to become a helpless child of man. Then at the end of this earthly life Jesus introduces the sublime treasure of the Bread of Life, His very Body and Blood, to the astonished Apostles on Holy Thursday, inaugurating the tremendous acts of His immolation and death on the Cross with the offering of unending life to His friends.

In the life of the Blessed Virgin Mary, we see echoes and pre-echoes of the transcendent will of God that life overcome death by death. Mary is the only child of a couple thought by all to be incapable of childbearing, first because of barrenness, and then because of advanced age. God brings forth the life of His supreme creature from a womb thought to be lifeless. Later God outdoes Himself by bringing forth the life of God manifested in man by the prodigy of a virgin conceiving and bearing a son, the Son of God. God reveals life to the eyes of faith where the faithless see only death. Mary is the instrument of the Sign of Contradiction, the instrument of the Cross, in her every thought, word, and deed. She thinks and knows herself to be the lowliest of creatures, yet she believes on the word of the angel that she is to be the very Mother of God, while still remaining a virgin! She knows that the hour of Jesus is not yet come, but on her word, Our Lord performs His first miracle, making the savorless water yield splendid wine! Mary is the Cause of Our Joy, bearing the Son of God in the flesh; Mary is the Mother of Sorrows, offering her Son Body-Blood-Soul-and-Divinity on the Cross. Mary is the daughter of God who is the Mother of God. Mary is the Mother of God who is the Spouse of God. Mary is the Spouse of God who is the Handmaid of the Lord. Mary is the Handmaid of the Lord who is the Queen of Heaven and earth. Mary is the Queen of Heaven and earth, Commander of the hosts of Heaven and Mistress of the saints from earth, who is at the same time the gentle Mother of the Church. Mary is the Mother of Mercy whom God has ordained from all eternity to be the instrument by which the head of the serpent is forever crushed underfoot!

At the heart of the reconciliation effected by the Sign of Contradiction which is the Cross, which is the life of Mary, which is the life of Jesus, is the meeting between mercy and truth, the kiss shared by justice and peace. The truth of man's condemnation is met by the mercy of God manifested on the Cross of Christ. The justice of the divine wrath is satisfied by the peace of God poured out from the outstretched arms of Jesus on Calvary. It is true that man deserves damnation because of Adam, but the Mother of Mercy, Mary, has been found acceptable among the orphans of Adam and Eve to receive and to dispense the infinite clemency of the Father. It would be just for God to destroy the world forever in retribution for the unspeakable offenses thrust in His face by his human creatures, but the Queen of Peace has sued for terms with the offended majesty and won for man, not a Judge, but a Savior. The courtship of truth and mercy has flowered in the nuptials of justice and peace, and from this union life springs forth both divine and human from the womb of the blessed Mother of God. In Mary truth can not deny mercy, nor can justice reject peace, for in Mary the creature is like unto her Creator in all things, and the Creator well pleased in His handiwork loves her and desires her to be in perfect communion with Him. Life is the result, the life of the Son of God in time on earth, and the life of the Kingdom of God forever in Heaven.

Alas! In time not all have been willing to be a part of what our Blessed Mother so perfectly accomplishes in her heart, soul, mind, and body. Rather than offering themselves wholly and entirely as Mary is offered wholly and entirely in the love commanded by God, most men have chosen instead to retain all claims to their own so-called right to nefarious and false freedom. From Adam and Eve, through Cain, down to the apostasy among the Jews fought so valiantly by the Machabees, men have demanded to be ruled by lies, yielding to a merciless thirst for each other's blood. They have denied all justice, warring instead on all that is good, true, beautiful, weak, and poor. Tyranny beyond description has been the realm established by man under satan in foul opposition to the freedom of the sons of God willed by Our Father, offered by His Son, received in the power of the Holy Ghost by any man willing to set aside the frauds of the world, the deceits of the flesh, and the lies of the devil. But the mass of men have lived lives wholly and entirely in pursuit of the selfish desires of their depraved hearts, and instead of bearing fruit in the divine life whose perfection is the Son of God born from the womb of the Blessed Virgin Mary, these fiends do the works of death. Life not given wholly and entirely to God is dead and deadly.

What follows are four examples of the deadly works of men divorced from the example of the Blessed Virgin Mary and the life of Christ manifesting the will of God…

1517, 1536, 1587: Martin Luther had been an Augustinian priest before apostasizing, marrying a disgraced nun, and dying a broken man. Henry VIII of England had been a Catholic monarch defending the one true Faith before he succumbed to the passions of the flesh, submitted his will to the tyranny of pride, and destroyed faith in the realm he had been consecrated to protect and increase. Between Luther the wretch and Henry the cad, an unholy communion existed from which there issued a foul daughter, Elizabeth I. This person was physically deformed, morally degenerate, and spiritually defunct. These *facts* have not prevented the British people, who followed her in apostasy and heresy, from dubbing her "the virgin queen", in blasphemous mockery of the Blessed Virgin Mary, Queen of Heaven and earth. Among Elizabeth's uncounted travesties of justice was the sin of regicide. Frightened that her status as an illegitimate daughter of Henry VIII would result in Mary Stuart successfully asserting her authentic claim to the English throne, Elizabeth had Mary executed to consolidate her tyranny and to put an end to any hope of restoring England to the Catholic Faith. Elizabeth's descent into heresy led directly to the crime of murder, and the especially reprehensible crime of regicide, the killing of the legal monarch.

1517, 1717, 1789: Martin Luther had been an Augustinian priest before apostasizing, marrying a disgraced nun, and dying a broken man. France had been a Catholic nation, indeed, the oldest of Catholic nations, honored with the title, *The Eldest Daughter of the Church*, producing saints, emperors, and a thoroughly Catholic culture over the course of almost one thousand years. Then France abandoned her faith in Jesus Christ and in her Mother the Catholic Church and embarked on the madness that culminated in the Reign of Terror. Luther and France consorted in an unholy communion wherein the evil men of freemasonry were spawned to the destruction of the kingdom. Having thrown off allegiance to the Pope in the sixteenth century, Luther and his spiritual offspring endeavored in the eighteenth century to divest themselves of loyalty to the Church herself, denying not only the Head but also the Body. The result was the mob. Revolution swept across France from the 1780s,through the nineteenth century, and continues to this day. Millions of men were slaughtered in the name of liberty. Millions of women were violated in the name of equality. Millions of children were denied access to the grace of the Faith, and thus denied salvation, in the name of fraternity. One man in particular was the victim of this debauched frenzy of hatred, his Royal Highness Louis XVI. The headless mob set about beheading the populace, reaching the climax of its bloodlust in regicide, beheading the king as if he were just one other commoner among the millions of commoners so treated.

1517, 1848, 1917: Martin Luther had been an Augustinian priest before apostasizing, marrying a disgraced nun, and dying a broken man. Karl Marx had been the son of a Jew before the family made a sham conversion to a sham sect, Methodism. Living off the income from his family's comfortable bourgeois holdings, Marx wrote ridiculous tracts in opposition to private property, the bourgeois culture, and faith in God. Luther and Marx conspired across the centuries in the person of Vladimir Lenin to produce the world's first communist government. That government was founded on the graves of the Russian royal family of Czar Nicolas II. In the name of freedom, Luther, Marx, and Lenin seized all property from the serfs and the aristocracy for the sole use of the government. In the name of a better life, Luther, Marx, and Lenin systematically starved various segments of the population of the Soviet Union over the course of thirty years. In the name of religious liberty and atheism, Luther, Marx, and Lenin imposed a government with a satanist, Lenin himself, at its head. Luther was not satisfied with denying papal authority that he screeched during the sixteenth century. From 1517 on his evil brood of philosophical descendants thought it insufficient to jettison the principle of a unified church organization, the position championed by the denizens of freemasonry beginning in 1717. Their ideal was not realized until the revolutions in Russia in 1917, when the very idea of God was expunged from politcal theory, from cultural institutions, from the very minds of the subjects of the new order of things. And, yet again, this revolt against truth was accomplished and crowned with regicide, this time not a Cathoic head of state being dethroned, but a schismatic. All the same, the people had determined to have no king, no caesar, other than themselves—and the evil men leading them in such determinations.

1517, 1776, 2009: Martin Luther had been an Augustinian priest before apostasizing, marrying a disgraced nun, and dying a broken man. George Washington, Benjamin Franklin, and Thomas Jefferson had been subjects of the crown of Great Britain. With the mandate of a very small minority of the colonial population of North America, Washington, Franklin, and Jefferson were among a vanguard of rebels who presumed to declare war on their king. That revolution, begun in 1776, continues unabated to this day. Whether overthrowing their own revolutionary ideal of resisting taxation without representation when Washington led U.S. government troops against American citizens staging a tax revolt; or overthrowing the ideal of liberty from unwanted sovereigns when Lincoln led the largest *war-time* slaughter of American citizens in American history (that number pales in comparison to the millions killed in the once-peaceful womb); or overthrowing the ideal of freedom for all regardless of ethnic background when Franklin Roosevelt interned tens of thousands of citizens for the crime of having ancestors from Japan—in all of these and many other instances, the principle of denying the past, improvising principles in the present, and rewriting history when future events make the past inconvenient has been an essential element in the American experiment. As with the Luther-inspired rebels in England, the Luther-inspired rebels in France, and the Luther-inspired rebels in Russia, the Luther-inspired rebels in Washington, d.c., and their subject peoples continue the commission of the crime of regicide even to the present hour. Elizabeth I killed one queen. The mob in Paris killed one king and one queen. The Soviet communists killed one czar, his czarina, and their children. You will notice that the numbers involved have increased with the centuries. Keep in mind that the self-appointed monarch of the United States of America is *We the People*...That being the case, regicide in these United States can not be limited to a man, to a man and his wife, or to a man and his wife and their children. The "royal family", so to speak, in the United States at present numbers something over three hundred million souls. Daily, the regicide involves four thousand infant heirs to the throne, stretching back in legal precedent thirty-six years now, and between fifty and one hundred million executions depending on how one interprets the data. In addition, countless thousands of monarchs are slaughtered by family members for the crime of age, illness, or injury. Beyond all of that are the other millions of monarchs of America who have lost the will to reign, and have abdicated their thrones voluntarily by sacrificing themselves on the altar of self-murder. Indeed, all of these regicides are a type of suicide, for when one is the king and one kills the king, one is committing suicide. Americans must at some point wake up to the idea that they are following a truly suicidal path.

Elizabeth killed the queen in the hope of remaining the queen; she died childless, the murdered queen's son inherited the throne, and the grandson of that king was deposed within three years of being crowned, and England has had no sovereign monarch ever since. Indeed, within a century of Elizabeth's death, England ceased to be, subsumed in the modern concoction known as the United Kingdom of England, Scotland, Wales, and Northern Ireland, a.k.a., Great Britain. The kingdom of England is dead. Long live the Parliament.

The mob killed the king and the queen in the hope of usurping their power and receiving the favored treatment once reserved for the royals. Instead, the mob unleashed the reign of terror on itself, murdering untold millions of commoners in their rage against the throne. After the riots of the revolution became too much to stomach, the French welcomed an emperor to bring peace to its lands, and to bring war to the whole of Europe. The First Republic did not last. The Napoleanic Empire did not last. The Second Republic did not last. The Third Republic did not last. The Fourth Republic did not last. The Fifth Republic will not last. The French killed France, and the French are now busy going about the work of contracepting the French out of existence.

Communists declared God dead. As of this writing, God is very much alive, but communism is ashamed to call itself by name, even though its corpse continues to haunt the modern world. When the Soviets killed the czar, Russia lost its identity, its history, its very name. The thing called Russia today is a doppelganger, an imposter, a figment. Russia, like England and France, is gone, never to return.

France, England, and Russia owed their establishment to the Catholic Faith and to the institutions and authority of the Catholic Church. When they cast aside their obedience to the Vicar of Christ, then the Church of Christ, and then the Father of Christ, France, England, and Russia committed corporate suicide. The United States of America never acknowledged God as sovereign. The United States of America has never accepted Christ as King. The United States of America has never professed Catholicism as the true Faith by which the laws and customs of this society are to be directed. In the absolute denial of the God of life, the United States of America is a stillbirth, never born, never alive. Contraception, abortion, euthanasia, suicide, and sodomy are the policies of the death wish that is America. That the government of the United States of America and the governments of its constituitive states *mandate* the adovcacy for, the subsidizing of, and the acquiesence to the abominations of contraception, abortion, euthanasia, suicide, and sodomy is not surprising—he who overthrows Christ as king elects death as master. Death rules the United States of America. If you doubt that fact, ask the African slaves brought to these shores, or the American Indians confined on reservations, or the innumerable families destroyed by easy divorce, or the babies slaughtered legally by their mothers, or the unspeakable number of souls languishing in hell even now because they put being an American above, before, and instead of being Catholic. England killed its king, and England is no more. France killed its king, and France is no more. Russia killed its king, and Russia is no more. America is killing its kings, one family, one fornication, one sodomizing, one contraception, one suicide, one infant, one citizen, and one soul at a time—and it is only a matter of time before there are no more Americans left for Americans to kill.

Such is what comes of keeping all for oneself, rather than giving one's all to God as Saint Joachim and Saint Anne gave Mary to God, and as our Blessed Mother and Saint Joseph gave Jesus to God. He who gives all to God, gains life. He who keeps all for himself, buys death.

Last week I warned you that this week's sermon would be decidedly negative. In that same vein, then, we conclude with the eighth of our reflections on the connections between Advent and Lent, between the Crib and the cross, between Christmas and Easter. There will be, however, one bright ray of hope at the very end even though we are considering *8) Herod—Judas:* Herod was not the king of the Jews. Herod was not even a legitimate Jew. Herod was a puppet of the hated Roman overlords. Herod knew this. The Jews knew this.

The Romans knew this. Only the Romans liked that state of affairs, and, indeed, on a political level, only the Romans benefitted from that state of affairs. Herod desired to legitimize his rule as much as possible, for reasons of vanity as much as for reasons of social order. It galled Herod to know that everyone knew that he was not only not the legitimate ruler of Israel, but that all of his supposed power was actually in the keeping of the Romans. Thus, when word began to circulate that a true King of the Jews was born, Herod wasted no time in attempting to shore up his grip on power. Kings are meant to enforce justice, so it is not surprising that a false king utilized injustice in his exercise of power. Herod sought to kill the newborn King of the Jews, unjustly, and did so by ordering the murder of dozens of other innocents in an act of depravity aggravating the inherent injustice. Herod failed. The murders instigated by Herod resulted in the slain boys being exalted to the altar of God as martyrs in the cause of divine justice. The kingdom Herod sought to maintain by murder ceased to exist less than seventy years after Herod's abomination. And the King whose blood Herod lusted after was indeed shed, but that did Herod no good, for Herod was a lying murderer denied entrance to the Kingom where no lies nor lovers of lies nor murderers are admitted. In other words, Herod showed himself a minion of the father of lies and the first murderer, the devil, and so won for himself, not a crown of glory, but eternal bondage in the servitude of the damned. Even now the King whom Herod would deny reigns and shall reign forever and ever. Satan, however, has other minions. As Herod sought the Blood of Christ at the beginning of the life of Jesus, so, too, did Judas seek the Blood of Christ at the end of the mortal life of Jesus. Where Herod was an illegitimate king, Jesus had raised Judas to be a true prince, willing for the Iscariot a seat from which to judge the twelve tribes of Israel. Judas was among the number God had called to be His instruments to proclaim the Good News of salvation to the ends of the earth. The love of Christ did not motivate Judas. Receiving an everlasting reward did not motivate Judas. Seeing the victory of God over satan did not motivate Judas. Instead, Judas denied justice and all that is owed to God, seeking for himself the satisfaction of his pride, the indulgence of his own will, the attainment of thirty pieces of silver. Judas gained thirty pieces of silver, inadequate for the purchase of the world, much less the acquisition of one's soul. From Judas neither Judas nor God was given justice. Rather we understand whence Judas received his orders and to whom he gave his allegiance when we remember the name Jesus gave the traitor: *son of perdition.* Judas did not reign with God the Father in Heaven, but descended to the infernal throne of his father in hell. Herod's treachery was a part of the destruction of Israel, whose king he desired to be. Judas' treachery did not result in the destruction of the Kingdom of Heaven, whose King Judas refused to serve. The treachery of Judas led directly to the destruction of the kingdom whose king can claim Judas as son, the kingdom of the damned, the kingdom of hell, the kingdom of perdition, whose lord is satan, whose son is Judas. Judas killed himself, committed suicide, and deprived his father of an heir—the kingdom of hell is at an end, not so much because Judas and satan have conspired in their own defeat, but because Jesus Christ, born of Mary, has overcome the world, the flesh, and the devil, sitteth at the Right Hand of the Father, and of His Kingdom there shall be no end!

20 November 2009: Saint Felix of Valois

All Saints House, Silver Cliff, Wisconsin

Addendum—Three deaths of abominators separated from the mercy of God:

Judas (betrayer of God the Son): suicide by hanging, wherein his bowels burst asunder

Arius (heretic priest and cause of massive apostasy): bowels burst asunder before desecrating a church with his presence

Luther (heretic monk and cause of massive apostasy): lifelong dyspepsia and constipation

Mob coups through salvation history—A genealogy

Let him who would understand these presents hearken to the Word of the Gospel of Jesus Christ according to St. Matthew, chapter the first, verses one through sixteen; according to St. Luke, chapter the third, verses twenty-three through thirty-eight; according to St. John, chapter the first, verses one through eighteen; and of the same beloved disciple, chapter the eighth, verses thirty through fifty-nine.

Heed ye also the testimony of the Prophet Isaias, in whose mouth the Lord God hath been pleased to place the prophecy of the reign of the Messias thus:

Her time is near at hand, and her days shall not be prolonged. For the Lord will have mercy on Jacob, and will choose out of Israel, and will make them rest upon their own ground: and the stranger shall be joined with them, and shall adhere to the house of Jacob. And the people shall take them, and bring them into their place: and the house of Israel shall possess them in the land of the Lord for servants and handmaids: and they shall make them captives that had taken them, and shall subdue their oppressors. And it shall come to pass in that day, that when God shall give thee rest from thy labor, and from thy vexation, and from the hard bondage, wherewith thou didst serve before, thou shalt take up this parable against the king of Babylon, and shalt say: How is the oppressor come to nothing? the tribute hath ceased? The Lord hath broken the staff of the wicked, the rod of the rulers, that struck the people in wrath with an incurable wound, that brought nations under in fury, that persecuted in a cruel manner. How art thou fallen from heaven, O Lucifer, who didst rise in the morning? How art thou fallen to the earth, that didst wound the nations? And thou saidst in thy heart: I will ascend into Heaven, I will exalt my throne above the stars of God, I will sit in the mountain of the Covenant, in the sides of the north: I will ascend above the height of the clouds, I will be like the Most High. But yet thou shalt be brought down to hell, into the depth of the pit…

Behold the Lord shall lay waste the earth, and shall strip it, and shall afflict the face thereof, and scatter abroad the inhabitants thereof. And it shall be as with the people, so with the priest: and as with the servant, so with his master: as with the handmaid, so with her mistress: as with the buyer, so with the seller: as with the lender, so with the borrower: as with him that calleth for his money, so with him that oweth. With desolation shall the earth be laid waste, and it shall be utterly spoiled: for the Lord hath spoken this word. The earth mourned, and faded away, and is weakened: the world faded away, the height of the people of the earth is weakened. And the earth is infected by the inhabitants thereof: because they have transgressed the laws, they have changed the ordinance, they have broken the everlasting covenant.

Therefore shall a curse devour the earth, and the inhabitants thereof shall sin: and therefore they that dwell therein shall be mad, and few men shall be left. The vintage hath mourned, the vine hath languished away, all the merry-hearted have sighed. The mirth of timbrels hath ceased, the noise of them that rejoice is ended, the melody of the harp is silent. They shall not drink wine with a song: the drink shall be bitter to them that drink it. The city of vanity is broken down, every house is shut up, no man cometh in.

There shall be a crying for wine in the streets: all mirth is forsaken: the joy of the earth is gone away. Desolation is left in the city, and calamity shall oppress the gates. For it shall be thus in the midst of the earth, in the midst of the people, as if a few olives, that remain, should be shaken out of the olive tree: or grapes, when the vintage is ended. These shall lift up their voice, and shall give praise: when the Lord shall be glorified, they shall make a joyful noise from the sea. Therefore glorify ye the Lord in instruction: the Name of the Lord God of Israel in the islands of the sea.

From the ends of the earth we have heard praises, the glory of the Just One. And I said: My secret to myself, my secret to myself, woe is me: the prevaricators have prevaricated, and with the prevarication of transgressors they have prevaricated. Fear, and the pit, and the snare are upon thee, O thou inhabitant of the earth. And it shall come to pass, that he that shall flee from the noise of the fear, shall fall into the pit: and he that shall rid himself out of the pit, shall be taken in the snare: for the flood-gates from on high are opened, and the foundations of the earth shall be shaken. With breaking shall the earth be broken, with crushing shall the earth be crushed, with trembling shall the earth be moved. With shaking shall the earth be shaken as a drunken man, and shall be removed as the tent of one night: and the iniquity thereof shall be heavy upon it, and it shall fall, and not rise again.

And it shall come to pass, that in that day the Lord shall visit upon the host of Heaven on high, and upon the kings of the earth, on the earth. And they shall be gathered together as in the gathering of one bundle into the pit, and they shall be shut up there in prison: and after many days they shall be visited. And the moon shall blush, and the sun shall be ashamed, when the Lord of hosts shall reign in mount Sion, and in Jerusalem, and shall be glorified in the sight of His ancients.

Thus saith the Lord.

God is.
God is the Omnipotent, Omniscient, Omnipresent Creator of all.
God is the King of the universe.
God is absolutely just in the exercise of his sovereignty over His creation.
God is Unending, Uncreated, and Unchanging.
God is forever as he has ever been: Almighty, Sovereign, and Perfect.
God is.

Lucifer was.
Lucifer was created as an exquisite angel of light by God.
Lucifer was offered the choice to honor God as his Creator.

Lucifer in his unspeakable pride denied the sovereignty of the almighty.

Lucifer became an angel of darkness, a demon.

Lucifer, in rejecting the rule of God, sought to establish his own rule in God's creation.

Lucifer failed.

In his rejection of the sovereignty of God, his attempt at dominion, and his failure thereat, Lucifer became the enemy of God, the personal manifestation of evil itself, satan.

Satan and his legions of fallen angels refused God's just sovereignty and embraced instead the injustice of anarchy, for where God is not acknowledged as Lord, none can rule in His stead.

God is.

God is Father, Son, and Holy Ghost.

God the Father through God the Son in the power of God the Holy Ghost wills to create man.

God the Father wills to create man.

God the Son is the Word through whom man is created.

God the Holy Ghost is the vivifying power by whom man lives.

God is.

Adam was created by God in the divine image and likeness.

Adam was set as sovereign king by God over God's creation in the Garden of Eden.

Eve was given to Adam to be his queen and to share in his rule.

satan in the guise of a serpent deceived Eve.

Adam hearkened to Eve, fell prey to satan's deceit, and embraced the pride of the fallen, losing sovereignty, kingship, and kingdom.

satan rebelled against God.

Eve rebelled against God and against Adam.

Adam rebelled against God, against justice, and against himself.

Adam and Eve rejected the just rule of God, in which Adam was sovereign beneath the sovereignty of God, and entered into the anarchy of the dominion of satan in the world.

Subjected to the rule of satan, Adam and Eve ruled neither creation nor themselves.

God is.

God is merciful.

God in His mercy assured Adam and Eve, even as He sent them into exile, that a victorious enemy of their enemy would come one day.

God in His mercy spared Noah.

God in His mercy made a covenant with Abraham.

God in His mercy called Moses His friend.

God in His mercy gave Himself to Israel to bring them justice, to give them order, to be their King.

God is.

Israel, in its faithlessness, demanded to have a man as king like all the nations of men had kings.

Samuel reminded Israel that they had God as their King.

Israel insisted that they wanted a man for a king.

Samuel warned them that men as kings would be oppressors, unjust, and disordered.

Israel rejected God as King, and begged for a man to be their king.

God is.

God chose Saul to be king over Israel.

God was displeased with Saul's faithless injustice.

God raised up David to be a king after His own heart.

God called David His son.

God promised that the line of David will never end.

God is.

The sons of David were faithless.

The sons of David worshipped idols.

The sons of David refused to keep their covenant with God.

The sons of David oppressed Israel.

The sons of David were defeated by Assyria.

The sons of David lost Jerusalem and were sent into exile in Babylon.

The sons of David returned to Jerusalem, only to return to faithlessness.

God is.

God in His providence from all eternity chose a remnant out of Israel.

God chose a righteous Daughter of Sion of the house of David from among the faithful remnant of Israel to be the bearer of glad tidings to His people.

God formed this Daughter from the very womb to be sinless, to be pure, to be full of His grace.

God in the fullness of time sent forth the Archangel Gabriel unto the Blessed Virgin Mary to proclaim to her the presence of the Lord.

God the Holy Ghost, pleased to hear her humble submission as the handmaid of the Lord, overshadowed her, and thus she conceived in her inviolate womb the very Son of God!

God is.

Jesus Christ is God.

Jesus Christ is Lord.

Jesus Christ is the Son of God and the Son of Mary.

Jesus Christ is the King of Kings.

Jesus Christ is the King of the Jews.

Jesus Christ is the Savior of the world.

Jesus Christ was condemned to die on the Cross by the Jews, who shrieked, "Crucify him!...We have no king but Caesar!"

God is.

God heard Adam reject Him as King and cast him out of Eden.

God saw the wickedness of Noah's time and sent the flood to erase man from the earth.

God was stayed in His anger at Aaron and all Israel by Moses who pleaded that He spare them for their faithlessness in the desert.

God condemned Saul for his unrighteousness and took the kingship from his house and established the house of David forever.

God sent His Son Jesus Christ to restore kingship to Israel, only to hear the foul words, "We have no king but Caesar!"; Israel is dispossessed of priest, prophet, and king until the will of God is fulfilled just before the Son of Man, Jesus Christ, the King of Kings, returns.

God is.

Jesus Christ is risen!

Jesus Christ has given the Keys to the Kingdom of Heaven to His Vicar on earth, St. Peter.

Jesus Christ has guided His Flock, His Body, His Bride, the Church, the Barque of Peter through the Holy Ghost from the time of Linus through Sixtus II through Siricius through Leo I through Gregory I through Leo IX through Gregory VII through Pius V through Pius X, and shall unto the end of time.

Jesus Christ has commanded the Good News of the Kingdom of Heaven now at hand be proclaimed through the Office of His Vicar wielding the Keys of Peter to bind and loose on earth and in Heaven.

Jesus Christ has promised Peter that the devil desirous of him shall not have him, that the gates of hell assailing him shall not prevail, that the Church has in him a rock foundation.

God is.

God maintains His children on the way where apostasy would lead them astray.

God upholds His truth where heresy would deny Him.

God preserves His Church in sanctifying grace where schism would kill the life given by the Holy Ghost.

God is the Lord of history, even and especially where His sovereignty is rejected by the world.

God exercises his sovereignty in history through His Church, given to man that all men might come to know God and Jesus Christ whom He sent.

God is.

St. Peter anointed Charlemagne to succeed Constantine the Great in governing the nations in the Name of Christ.

St. Peter received the willing acquiescence of Edward, Louis, Henry, Stephen, Wenceslaus, Helen, Cunegunda, Margaret, Elizabeth, Bridget and numerous others to be anointed and to reign in the Name of Christ.

St. Peter has been pleased to raise King Edward, King Louis, King Henry, King Stephen, King Wenceslaus, Queen Helen, Queen Cunegunda, Queen Margaret, Queen Elizabeth, Queen Bridget, and numerous others of the royal state to the Altar of God.

St. Peter enjoyed no less than a thousand years from Constantine until Charles

V an unquestioned acknowledgement that the Christian state is in service to the Kingdom of Christ.

St. Peter was defended by Catholic monarchs from the heretics following the errors of Mahomet.

St. Peter was supported in orthodoxy against the schismatics adhering to the rebellion of Photius.

St. Peter has never been defeated in his defense of the sovereignty of Christ the King before the assaults of the world, the flesh, and the devil.

God is.

God the Son is present in the world in His Body the Catholic Church.

God the Son rules through His Body the Catholic Church.

God the Son has chosen nothing other than the Catholic Church to be His bride.

God the Son has no sheep in His Flock who do not belong to the Catholic Church.

God the Son does not know anyone who is not a member of His Body, who is not a child of His Bride, who is not within the Fold of the Catholic Church.

God is.

Martin Luther rejected St. Peter as the Vicar of Christ on earth.

Henry VIII rejected St. Peter as the vicar of Christ on earth.

George Washington rejected the Body of Christ as the only legitimate context for the rule of men on earth.

Napoleon Bonaparte rejected the Body of Christ as the only legitimate context for the rule of men on earth.

Karl Marx, Vladimir Lenin, Josef Stalin, Mao Zedong, and Fidel Castro rejected God as Sovereign of the universe.

The United Nations Charter, The United States Supreme Court, and the European Union Constitution reject God as Sovereign of the universe.

Not one nation on earth in the 21st century, including the Vatican City State, demands that Jesus Christ be recognized as sovereign King of all nations.

God is.

God was rejected as King by satan.

God was rejected as King by Adam.

God was rejected as King by Israel.
God was rejected as King by the heretic Mahomet.
God was rejected as King by the schismatic Photius.
God was rejected as King by the apostate Henry.
God was rejected as King by the modernist Washington.
God was rejected as King by the atheist Marx.
God was rejected as King by the secularist UN, EU, and US Supreme Court.
But God still is I AM!

'tho' demons deny Him, ***God is.***
'tho' pagans are ignorant of Him, ***God is.***
'tho' Jews refuse Him, ***God is.***
'tho' Mohammedans blaspheme His Son, ***God is.***
'tho' Photians rebel against His Son's Vicar, ***God is.***
'tho' protestants revolt against His Truth, ***God is.***
'tho' democracies dethrone Him, ***God is.***
'tho' communists and socialists denounce Him, ***God is.***
'tho' modernity desires to do without Him, ***God is.***

There is no justice without God.
There is no rule without God.
There is no order without God.
There is no truth without God.
There is no freedom without God.
There is no authority without God.
There is no sovereignty where God is not King.

Jesus Christ must be King.
Jesus Christ must be Lord.
Jesus Christ must be the only Name by which men are saved.

Jesus Christ must be the name at which every knee in Heaven, on earth, and under the earth bends.

Jesus Christ must be the Head and his Body must be the Church.

Jesus Christ must be the Living Bread come down from Heaven, without which none comes to Heaven, with which the soul comes to eternal life.

Jesus Christ must be all in all,

For Jesus Christ is God.

Where Jesus Christ is not acknowledged as God,

Where the Body of Christ the Church is not acknowledged as His Bride,

Where the successor of St. Peter is not acknowledged as His Vicar,

There is no faith, no justice, no order;

There satan wields dominion over the lesser creatures rebelling against God;

There sin and death hold sway without any hope of an overthrow of their tyranny;

There man forfeits all claim to kingship, sonship, and sovereignty, succumbing instead to the everlasting anarchy of the torment of satan.

God is.

Is He recognized by the UN, the EU, or the US as sovereign over all?

Is He deferred to by science?

Is He the goal of economics?

Is He honored by false religions separated in any way from the Catholic Church?

Is He, acknowledged as Father, Son, and Holy Ghost, the central resident in every home on earth?

Is He worshipped in spirit and in truth through the Holy Sacrifice of the Mass on every altar in the world by the authentic priesthood of Jesus Christ?

Is He given Honor, Glory, and kingship through Catholic sovereigns, over Catholic nations, under the Roman Pontiff serving as Vicar of Jesus Christ until He comes again to judge the living and the dead?

Is He your Lord, your God, your King, now and forever?

Regardless of your answer

God is.

Psalm 84

Lord, Thou hast blessed Thy land; Thou hast turned away the captivity of Jacob.

Thou hast forgiven the iniquity of thy people: Thou hast covered all their sins.

Thou hast mitigated all Thy anger: Thou hast turned away from the wrath of Thy indignation.

Convert us, O God our Savior: and turn off Thy anger from us.

Wilt Thou be angry with us forever? Or wilt Thou extend thy wrath from generation to generation?

Thou wilt turn, O God, and bring us to life: and Thy people shall rejoice in thee.

Shew us, O Lord, Thy mercy; and grant us Thy salvation.

I will hear what the Lord God will speak in me: for He will speak peace unto His people.

And unto His saints: and unto them that are converted to the heart.

Surely His salvation is near to them that fear Him: that glory may dwell in our land.

Mercy and truth have met each other: justice and peace have kissed.

Truth is sprung out of the earth: and justice hath looked down from Heaven.

For the Lord will give goodness: and our earth shall yield her fruit.

Justice shall walk before Him: and shall set his steps in the way.

Glory be to the Father, and to the Son, and to the Holy Ghost! As it was in the beginning, is now and ever shall be, world without end. Amen.

Wandering Back from the Desert

Finding our lost Sensus Catholicus

Father ~

Thank you. There are so very many sites and sources available that discuss "Tradition," that knowing which ones are best is difficult. If there are any you would be comfortable suggesting please do so.

On the same subject any direction on how best to re-educate our misled minds would be helpful. I suppose it is our own "re-education camp" but Catholic instead of communist.

Question about purity and chastity—the homeschooling group is planning a Prom for high school aged kids. We have no intention of participating as we are confident that this is inappropriate for our 10th grader. The question arises, though, about when it is appropriate. What advice is offered by the church Fathers and saints? I do not even know where to begin looking for the answers. We can keep following our parental instincts for now but that will not work into their twenties.

Please keep us in your prayers,
KV November 2005

Several Preludes

6 November 2002: St. Felix of Tunis

Dear A –,

This is actually the second letter I've written you from Amsterdam. The first, penned yesterday, was consumed in flames. While in the midst of working on the third and last page, I inadvertently allowed the other two to fall into a small candle on the table where I was writing. What was left of the paper was insufficient for the task of filling a dust pan, much less being capable of conveying any meaning to you.

There is a candle at this table, but I'm keeping my eye on it—and the letter away from it.

At present I am at lunch at a small café called Frenzi. It is a quiet place, so I assume the Dutch word means something other than the same sounds made in English. So I hope. It is possible that Frenzi waits 'til the night to be frenzied. I'll not be here long enough to find out.

Amsterdam is experiencing my presence due to the fact that I am too nice for my own good. This trip is being made at the behest of my older sister, who is a resident of the city and, as of late last year, a citizen of the Netherlands. She cajoled and harangued my father and stepmother, my brother and his wife and son, and me to make a family visit together. Were I truly the ogre many impugn me to be, I would have told my sister *et al* that I wished not to waste the time, money, or patience such a trip costs. Alas! I, too, fall victim to the temptation to be nice at any cost. Grinning and bearing it can be offered as a mortification… Can't it?

Bearing it in part means enduring the Godlessness that is Holland, Europe, and all the Western world. Really there is no difference between American agnosticism (atheism in practice) and Dutch disbelief ("humanism" being the current euphemism). What is different here from home (or my unreal and unreasonable facsimile thereof in Clinton) is that Europeans long ago abandoned any pretence of faith. The Dutch were early, vocal, and belligerent apostates. They've been at undoing the divine for nigh on a half millennium.

So I don't like this place.

Don't get me wrong, though. The people are friendly, the streets clean and safe, my hotel quaint and charming. They know how to cook, to entertain, and to build. The one thing they will not do is worship something other than man and man's. This is not a pleasant place for a priest.

But as I said, the Dutch really don't differ from Americans in this. In fact, the Dutch possess a certain almost-refreshing honesty. They really reject God, and that is that. Americans cling to an hypocrisy wherein one is not sure which they believe: their Sunday words or their Monday-through-Saturday actions. One is not sure, but one has strong suspicions. I know where I stand with the Dutch. I suspect that Americans in general and my parishioners in particular can not stand, would not bear the fullness of our faith.

My father is rather Dutch. Obviously not in genealogy, but in ideology. He and I had a somewhat lengthy conversation last night in a pub not far from the infamous Amsterdam red light district. Dad listens politely, disagrees, and then dismisses. He then asks for further clarification of my views with a view toward incorporating them in a novel he's writing. Truth for him is not something to be sought, found, held, and made war over; but a mater for dialogue, dialogue, dialogue, and then denial. Not denial of the terms of the debate or of one position instead of another, but of the existence, perceptibility, and acceptability of truth itself.

That's my Dad. Imagine a whole nation founded on that notion. You need not imagine it. You live in it. Some have called the era of Christendom the age of faith. The enlightenment is misnamed the age of reason. Modernity is lamented as the age of anxiety. The post-modern world (please ask no one for a definition of it—there isn't one) might be "christened" (bad pun, I know) the age of doubt, or better, the age of confusion.

Wisdom was once the virtue of holding one's tongue until knowing something true and truly worth saying. Modern wisdom, such as it is, is the presumption to declare one's ignorance a universal phenomenon. Not universal in the sense that one humbly admits to fundamental ignorance in need of knowing; but one proclaims one's ignorance as indicative of an ontological reality in man, indeed, the universe. It is a laughable pride. Someone admitting his own ignorance should not have the cheek to presume he is equipped to judge another's knowledge. It would be folly to allow him to speak. It would be a greater folly to agree with him. Such is the folly of our time.

But what else would one expect from the ignorant?

It just occurred to me how one might have described the progression (regression, really) from faith through rationalism through anxiety through confusion. Ancient man applied capital punishment for both murder and blasphemy. Modern man executes only for murder. Post-modern humanity aborts the unborn. Ancient man waged war for God and country. Modern man fought for empire and/or democracy. Post-modern humanity euthanizes the old and weak. Ancient man rejoiced in the birth of a son. Modern man labored in the science of medicine to reduce infant mortality. Post-modern humanity seeks to reduce human populations and maximize plant and animal populations. Ancient man believed in a provident God profoundly concerned with man on earth. Modern man grew amazed at man's ability to place man and earth in a cosmic context. Post-modern humanity thinks man a plague, believes the universe indifferent to him, and wants to colonize other planets once earth is outgrown.

In short, ancient man discovered man loveable by virtue of a loving God.

Modern man discovered powers in man once attributable only to God.

Post-modern humanity is discovering that without God, impotence and death reign.

Post-modern humanity has nothing to live for. It has abandoned modern man's willingness to embrace causes to die for. And it has rejected ancient man's zeal for truth worth killing for. Man without passion is reduced to a lifeless humanity. Man without Christ's Passion does not merit the name man, for without God there is no image of the divine, no transcendence, no mind beyond the animal's refusal to die but ignorant of why life is lived.

All of this stems from denying absolute truth. Without truth, one can not know sin. Ignorant of sin, man will not beg mercy and redemption. All that is left is sin's wages: death. Truth's opposite is the lie. Man is in the midst of denying truth, embracing sin, and demanding death. God gives His Son to be our truth, to give us Sacramental grace, and to show the way of the Cross, the Tree of Life. One would look far these days to find many (any?) who believe this. But after all, Jesus Himself asked, "When the Son of Man returns, will He find any faith upon the earth?" If the Son of God finds it necessary to have to search for faith, how much more must my sin-riddled eyes make that search. Pray God that the light of faith shines in me, in you, in the visible Church on the last day. That day, at today's sunset, is yet one day the nearer. Maranatha!

God bless you, (signed) Father Smith

P.S.—One final thought: The Church condemned as mortal sins euthanasia, suicide, and abortion. Today, apostate mankind would make euthanasia mercy, suicide an illness, and abortion a human (woman's) right. Where faith teaches that murder is *always* wrong, modernity would have us believe that it is permissible to murder a sick person, one's own person, or what society deems a non-person.

All of this murder of real human beings in the name of man, of being humane, of "advancing" humanity beyond religious "restrictions". Religious restrictions which taught life are abandoned in favor of ever more available access to death. Some progress, huh? LCS.

6 November 2002: St. Felix of Tunis

Dear J –,

Here in the midst of Amsterdam I sit on a barstool within the Balmoral Pub. I drink a Beamish Stout. Chesterton is the literary fare. Other than my thoughts and Chesterton's words, English is not spoken here.

It is perhaps unfair to expect my mother tongue to be available to nurse me in this foreign land. But I stopped here because the bright sign outside promised English and Scottish ales, stouts, and lagers. Imagine my surprise when on my entering I saw a dozen-and-a-half oriental faces staring at me in neither English nor Dutch. Evidently, the Balmoral dining room is available to let for private parties. The only room in the inn is at the bar.

I *never* sit at bars. But never is now no more. Was it ever possible for man? With man, yes; with God, no.

So, by God's grace I sit at the bar, imbibing Beamish, brooding indoors in consonance with the North Sea drizzle outdoors. This simply must be of God because God knows I would not choose such circumstances as these. A good philosopher would point out that my own free will brought me here: I chose to take this ill-starred family trip, I chose to take the walk tonight, I chose to take the turns that took me to the Balmoral.

But I, too, am a philosopher. I am but an efficient cause within God's providence. He it is who has arranged the universe for me to be able to participate in this evening. Without Him, I would be busy not being rather than idly being in Amsterdam. Final causes trump efficient causes every time. Of such is Judgment Day made.

This night is doomed to fall short.

One nice thing about the Dutch: they still smoke. When I order my second pint, I will stoke my pipe and banish the two bartenders' infernal cigarette fumes. Pipes have far greater capacity for making a smoke-filled room full than do cancer sticks. And pipes smell much better.

At times mind-reading would be a handy skill. I wonder what the locals make of a tall, black, fountain-pen wielding, bright red-and-white argyle sweat-er-vest wearing, Roman Catholic priest drinking stout and puffing a pipe. In England, people asked. In Holland, people stare. I'm in a bad mood. I smile broadly to them.

The world has really changed (for the worse) since Chesterton. Gilbert found an excuse for delight in the midst of rather drear circumstances. He was a better man than I, but my world is far worse than his. It's not so much that there is less delight, but so much more that is dreary. By the time I get past the drear and am ready for delight, it's time for bed.

It probably is my own fault. I should just find a nice cell, pray my Office, study St. Thomas, celebrate the real Mass, and prepare my soul for the aforementioned Day of Judgment. My paranoia insists that I am not allowed this because the cosmos is designed to send me towards odd pubs and away from peace and quiet. After all, *my* plan would keep me out of everyone's way. Obviously the universe is not constructed to minimize my adverse impact, but to maximize its capacity to irritate me. The silver lining to my cloudy Day of Judgment is that if I endure this earthly travail with a modicum of patience, my salvation will have been wrought not by an heroic sanctity, but by an ironic absurdity.

O.K. It's time for a new Beamish. At this point the bar has received a half dozen authentic English speakers. Real English speakers. With accents and everything. And one of them just bought a cigar. You can do that here. Beamish. Cigars. Pipes. Life ain't all bad, I guess.

Aside from our *ad nauseam* and *ad infinitum* discussion about the imminent dissolution of the inviolable, indefectible, immemorial Church, my angst includes the fact that the world and I don't get along. NewChurch is no Church, but outside of a Church there is only the salvation of a pipe and a pint, inane conversation, and traveling from one mass-produced culture to its twin two or more time zones distant. *You* can form a rock band. I can only crawl under a rock. And I bruise so easily.

Chesterton had God, the Mass, and the last hurrah of Empire. We have humanism, fellowship meals, and the internet. This is so not fair. What's worse is that I *know* that where we are isn't the best place we've been. In this ignorance would have been bliss: unknowing of transubstantiation, one could be impressed by digital communications; but once one has been given God, what else could possibly satisfy?

When I get back to the States I have to start making decisions. I can't keep on as I have been. (By the way, *Iota Unum* is not conducive to calm.) Soon, quite soon, I must decide which of the forks I will take: *Novus Ordo* and modernity, with attendant "respectability"; or Tradition and calumny, ignominy, and, quite probably, infamy.

Cheery thoughts, no?

I can't be sure, but I bet that the neo-Catholics are ecstatic about the November election results. I don't blame them—the alternative would be worse. Their fault lies in not realizing that the Republican victory is still a victory for the Revolution. Not not realizing, but not admitting. You heard it here first! Abortion will remain legal, income taxes and property taxes will not be repealed, and consumerism will be no less in evidence. Were I wrong about this, I would be convinced that a change had occurred and a celebration would be in order. As it is, I am in mourning.

You won't get this letter until I return, so I need not worry that I brought you down tonight. Anyway, you might have plenty of reason to be down without my help. At any rate, I am praying, for you, our families and friends, the Church. I am confident that you're doing the same. Thanks.

In Christ and Mary, (signed) *LCS.*

10 November 2002: St. Andrew Avellino

Dear F –,

From amidst the native scents of Amsterdam—monosodium glutamate, gorgonzola, jalapeno, and the Colonel's original recipe—I send you greetings! Few times in your life will you receive letters penned by a Roman Catholic priest in a protestant country, buffeted by North-Sea rains, dining on northern Mediterranean cuisine, wielding an authentic ink-well filled fountain pen. I am nothing if not odd. Nay, a walking, writing contradiction.

No pride do I take in this. The Tin Man wanted a heart, the Scarecrow brains, the Cowardly Lion—you guessed it!—courage, and Dorothy her home. Father Smith begs belonging, a communion of faith, yes, a Church. It is my growing conviction that what Vatican II gave us was not a renewed Church, but a denuded church. Much of my time in this Godless, or should I say gods-filled, land has been spent ruminating on this reality.

Sometimes I wish that I were a drunkard. Inebriated oblivion would solve nothing, but neither would it feel anything. Twenty-four-seven sobriety can be painful. Even on holiday I am haunted by the ghost of ecclesiologies past.

Four days ago I stumbled into a 19th-century neo-gothic church run by the Jesuits. It was striking in its ornamentation and untouched by the liturgical revolution—except for the obligatory Cranmer table blighting the sanctuary. *But*, the literature in the narthex promised not one, but *two* Latin Masses each Sunday. Today is Sunday. I came to Mass.

After a passable schola chanted a prelude, what did I hear? The prayers at the foot of the altar? No. The asperges beginning an unannounced High Mass? No. Directions for all to kneel as we prayed the Holy Rosary in preparation for the Sacrifice? No. Our presider proclaimed welcome to visitors. We were instructed that Mass would be conducted in Latin…According to the prescriptions of the Second Vatican Council.

Now, for Jesuits this is pretty impressive. For *Dutch* Jesuits this is astounding. So if one must endure the *Novus Ordo Missae* yet again, this was a less-than-abominable instance. Still, *Novus Ordo* is protestant, Latin notwithstanding.

These last five days I have written seventy manuscript pages explaining why protestantism is concomitant with damnation. Catholic Apologetics International, the apostolate of Robert Sungenis, has tentatively agreed to run it on their web page. They might change their minds after they read it. I'm pretty direct. You'll see the e-mail version of it before you get this letter, so you can judge for yourself.

But, anyway, I am not particularly pleased with protestantism in any form at present. It is safe to say that protestantism in any form, most particularly the *Novus Ordo* variety, will be the recipient of increasing vitriol from my pen. Protestantism has no redeeming value to it, but much that invites perdition.

This position is not held by my family. The trip to Amsterdam of which I am now victim is the brain-child (a bastard, really) of my sister, a resident and a *citizen* of this benighted sovereign state. Big Sis wanted us to get together, reconnect, and strengthen family bonds.

Mind you, my parents divorced nineteen years ago. My Dad and stepmother will have been married eighteen years at Thanksgiving. My older brother (my only sibling not making this trip) speaks to us on average twice a year from his home in Kansas City. My younger brother, his wife, and their child (but not his illegitimate son by another woman in Illinois) live in Georgia. And, as I said, my big sister is now a Dutch citizen (this does, by the way, entail renouncing American citizenship).

I, on the other hand, live within fifty miles of our home town, my address is published in an international directory, I am in frequent contact with friends from my siblings' childhood, and I practice the Faith given each of us at birth. Guess who is considered the outsider in our family dynamic?

Early this afternoon I had a *tete-a-tete,* (that's Dutch for "come to Jesus" talk) with my sister. Gently I expressed my sense that our family does not share a common set of values. I intimated that this state of affairs causes me discomfort and concern.

My sister, the modernist, explained that my ego is the problem, that the Roman Catholic Church is *not* intended by God, that we all worship the same God and should accept one another unreservedly, and that if I love my family I will embrace them and their beliefs uncritically. I have lived to experience a live advertisement for apostasy and syncretism! The World Council of Churches has an unpaid spokesperson on staff in my family.

As happens with my neo-Catholic friends in the clergy, my modernist family tells me that I am the source of division, that *I* lack charity (my sister uses the English "love"—I doubt she knows the Dutch for *caritas*), and that *I* am abandoning *them.* By wanting to be what we all claim we are, *I* am on the infamous trajectory of schism.

Several times my sister insisted that reason and faith are incompatible. She understands faith as a feeling, and feeling as superior to words. Dogmas and definitions are mere words, unrelated to the deeper reality of Christ. Jesus did not come to correct, teach, and to redeem, but to share compassion indiscriminately. This compassion evidently extends to everyone and everything except the Church that claims Him as her Founder!

When I pointed out to my sister that her broad-minded, all-inclusive principle of Christianity required me to reject my own "feelings" on the subject, she declared that our conversation was useless because I was not "open" and had already made up my mind. Telling her that she and the whole family had already made up *their* minds and rejected traditional Roman Catholicism brought the accusation that I was judgemental and believed Mohammedans and Hindus were all going to hell. I expressed my fear that I have no idea what will keep my *family* from hell.

The long and the short of it is that I am pilloried for not changing to please my family, but they have no qualms or desires referent to changing to please God. It's supposed to make me feel better to make them feel better for a few years on earth, even though I have reasonable fears that their temporarily feeling better will result in eternal misery. You might also note that no concern is given by my sensitive, compassionate family to how their son and brother the Roman Catholic priest feels about all of this.

MELODRAMA ALERT

F—, the devil in the form of my sister *begged* me to forsake the immemorial Faith. I was pleaded to embrace what they embrace: indifferentism, syncretism, and apostasy. Satan at least offered Jesus worldly power. My family offered me nothing except that *they* would feel better. In the spirit of the age, I ask, "What's in it for *me*?!"

Modernism can not appeal to reason. It destroys faith. And it negates natural relationships such as filial devotion, patriotism, and the honor of keeping an oath. Given that NewChurch would have me become a modernist, what in the name of all that is good and true do I gain from abandoning the Faith of my Fathers?

What makes my sister think that by embracing a self-centered philosophy, I will pay *more* attention to *her* immortal soul than I do now?

Yours in Christ's peace, (signed) *LCS.*

Sweeter than Revenge — A Rationale for this Writing

Revenge is mine, and I will repay them, saith the Lord! (Deuteronomy 32:35). Only fools presume to take to themselves divine prerogatives. Well, so does satan. Oh, yes, and also sinners. Okay, it happens all the time. But neither the preceding title nor the succeeding paragraphs should be construed to convict yours truly of falling into presumption on this particular occasion. Although a catalogue of grievances will be described herein and a day of satisfaction thereof predicted, vengeance is far from the meaning or desire informing this effort. Mercy given is mercy received; may all mine enemies receive through me a superabundance of what God has granted me so copiously. *Et dimitte nobis debita nostra sicut et nos dimittimus debitoribus nostris!* A fine prayer when prayed in the spirit in which it was taught; a horrible self-cursing when it is offered but lip service, while like service to neighbor is denied.

For nearly a half-decade as of this writing, the question has nagged and gnawed this writer of just why so many, nigh on all, of the adults of the generations immediately before and immediately after Vatican II succumbed so readily to the ethos of the modern age and the modernists' errors. *Instantaneous* is not too strong an adjective to describe the reception offered by the clergy and lay faithful to the concoction brewed by the hierarchy in Rome from 1962-1965, bringing to fruition within the Church the attempts to subvert the Body of Christ dating from at least the fourteenth century, through the protestant rebellion, festering in the erudite ignorance spawned by the age of "enlightenment", rabidly descending into the violence of the revolutions yet blighting the modern world, and exploding in a mass apostasy with the dawn of the twenty-first century. An historical analysis is sufficient to explain the heavy forces at work for more than a half-millennium eroding the *sensus fidei* within the Church, resulting in a daily onslaught on average Catholics against orthodox doctrine, pious practice, ritual integrity, economic justice, and political order. That there was scattered resistance beginning even before the end of the Second Council of the Vatican is the exception which proves the rule that virtually every Catholic on earth embraced the departures to the Faith embodied by the "spirit" of Vatican II. It is not surprising that some of the faithful and clergy recoiled at the admonitions to walk away from the Faith of the Fathers of the Church. What still boggles this mind is that there was not a wholesale series of personal refusals to acknowledge the legitimacy of such a project; indeed, there was, rather, a general capitulation to that which had been formally condemned by the Church up to and including the very year in which the Council began. In other words, we know why so many were weakened by modernism, but how does any given individual account for his own participation in the debacle?

Turnabout is fair play, they say. In the interests of equal time, time has been spent by this writer prior to penning these thoughts thinking about the questions addressed to those of us born since the Council as to why some of us evince a "nostalgia" for the bad old days rampant before the Council. None has explained to my satisfaction the why of my elders' behavior giving succor to the enemies of the Church. It would be refreshing and informative if what follows were to result in a reflection on the part of the generation now becoming septuagenarians of the part they played in bringing to pass what Pope Paul VI termed an "autodemolition of the Church", what Pope John Paul II described as a "silent apostasy", and what Pope Benedict XVI (when he was Joseph Cardinal Ratzinger) has lamented as "the dictatorship of relativism". Perhaps if the generation of adults now entering middle age are able to articulate how they have come to insist on the entirety of the traditions of the Faith, their elders might find the words necessary to make a rational explanation for how they came to believe that those traditions are entirely expendable. Besides, it is easier for me to say what is on my mind than for me to be able to oblige another to make what is on his mind make sense to me.

The Way We Were When We Were In, Not Of, the World

Women used to be able to walk down the streets of New York City. Alone. At night. Safely. Within living memory! Lest this strike some as a bit farfetched, let us not forget that there are yet cities on the earth where this is still the case. Cities are not inherently dangerous. It is a peculiarly modern scourge that "city" is now synonymous with "savagery". Not only is this a modern peculiarity, it is a modern oxymoron, for "city" and "civilization"—that is, "civilized"—are of a piece. It takes man to order, build, and govern a city. It is beastly to live in environs where one might be killed, dispossessed of home, and/or starved by one's own kind. The city is meant to be a place where man is safe to live, to raise a family, and to pass on that safety, posterity, and sense of home. And, as well, a city should be a place with streets on which it is safe to walk.

Men used to be able to provide for their families. At home. Without a job. Alongside their wives and children. Within living memory! The context for what is now an otherworldly notion used to be called the *family farm.* On the farm, food was grown. A house was built. Clothes were sewn. By the people who ate them, lived in them, and wore them. Taxes, multinational corporations, and *ennui* did not conspire to destroy this bucolic lifestyle. It is a testimony to the depravity of modernity that the family farm has been abandoned by family farmers *en masse* in favor of cities where women can not walk the streets safely. Imagine how awful modernity must have made the farm in order for the modern city to be preferable to it. Imagine what modernity must have made of the modern farmer's mind for the modern city to be preferable to the family farm. Shudder for a few moments while contemplating the fact that quite a few of the men who yet labor on the farm *commute* to their jobs from cities!

Children used to be able to grow up knowing that Mom was in the kitchen and Dad was in the fields. And the girls did not mind learning housekeeping from Mom. And the boys did not mind learning Dad's trade. And Mom and Dad expected that their flesh and blood would find nothing extraordinary in such lessons. Within living memory! Homeschooling did not always mean that a curriculum concocted by "experts" who never met their victims, I mean, students, was inflicted on youngsters within their residences instead of behind barred windows in an institutional setting easily mistaken for a penitentiary. Homeschooling used to mean that the home was where the best and most important life lessons were learned: the Faith, how to grow up to be honorable like Mom and Dad, the skills of socializing with older and younger children, showing respect to elders, and, yes, ABCs. And in those instances where a good case could be made that such lessons were better assimilated away from home, the locales where it occurred were not dens of iniquity devoted to undermining the home and the authority of the parents, but to complementing the wisdom already begun to be imparted by the first and best teachers of children, their Moms and Dads.

Not everyone needs to live in cities. Not everyone needs to live on farms. Not everyone is able to be homeschooled. Once upon a time, however, a man and his family were not destroyed, were in fact nurtured, by the circumstances involved in realizing the combination of God's will, personal choice, and social norm by which a man's life was ordered. Part of the dismay of the people born since the mid-60s is that life now resembles more a life sentence than the first gift given by God. Home is a place to escape to be out with friends, out in the world, never to return when one has grown up. School is literally an armed encampment, complete with guards, firearms, surveillance cameras, body searches, and doors and windows secured *from the outside!* The farm is a wilderness never visited by tourists who instead frequent zoos for trees, also known as city and national parks. The city is a jungle about which movies are made with titles such as *Escape from New York.* No one should be surprised that two, almost three, generations raised under these conditions will not desire to stay at home, in school, or near the other people subjected to such oppression. People given the grace of the Faith might well demand other, better alternatives.

How has the Church responded to these challenges inflicted by the world? By closing schools. By closing parishes in rural communities. By opening its colleges to teachers who instill in their guinea pigs, I mean, students, the mores of a world that is emphatically urban, decidedly materialistic, and wholly un-Catholic. Prelates of the Church are on record endorsing candidates for public office who are hostile to support for Catholic education, the definition of the natural family, and the maintenance of morality in keeping with the Ten Commandments, the Commandments of the Church, and the Two Great Commandments. When children of the Church ask her for guidance, they are told to find the answers in "dialogue" with false religions, in organizations devoted to erecting a society divorced from reference to the true God and His true Church, and in looking within their own hearts, which are self-admittedly confused and frightened. Sanctifying grace seems to be the one remedy unpalatable to the snake oil salesmen prescribing ecumenism, academic freedom, and secularism as the cures for what ails the world.

And people wonder why some of us beg to differ?!?

The Family that Stays Together...Does not Exist

Human history has yet to witness the spectacle of the formation of the B.A.B.I.E.S. Union—Babies Amalgamated to Banish Infant Exploitation Soon. (*Please* chortle at that—it took me five minutes to come up with it.) Children are not banding together demanding that mothers and fathers present countenances above the cradle every bit as adorable as those within the crib. There are no court cases, yet, where plaintiffs well under the age of reason are suing their guardians for alienation of affection committed after being tucked in for the night. Toddlers are not seeking personal injury lawyers to pursue damages for pain and emotional suffering due to being laughed at when falling after the first step, being slobbered over by the puppies who thought they were from the same litter, and being dressed in Grandma's idea of cool or hip or cuter than Mildred's grandkids up the street.

At the same time, thus far mankind has been spared the indignity of mothers and/or fathers placing liens against newborns' future earnings to compensate for duress endured for the nine months prior to delivery. There is still no legal precedent set for empty-nesters to recover expenses, good names, or non-grey hairs lost during their offspring's teen years. Grandparents are afforded a certain satisfaction at what affects their spoiling of their grandchildren will produce on their children, but something is lacking in the fact that so much time elapses between youthful infractions and the poetic justice effected when the chicks' chicks come home to roost. At most, and worst, parents of grown children are able to sport bumper stickers on their Airstreams declaring, "We're spending our children's inheritance!" To which said children are reduced to two words in reply: Nursing Home.

There is a modicum of the natural law yet in force, a modicum of natural affection still present in homes. Children can still be prevailed upon to sign Mothers' Day cards and ask Dad for an advance on the allowance. Mothers still write and sign Fathers' Day cards for their children and offer the only hugs worth having this side of Heaven. Even the media pay tribute to these almost indestructible truths of human nature with TV specials, movies, and sales at the malls occurring like clockwork. Ma Bell is never so happy as when Ma is made so happy with all the telephone calls—long distance—she receives on Mothers' Day.

Don't get too teary-eyed just yet.

Modern jurisprudence has given credence to creatures known as "wrongful life" suits. Persons *not* murdered by their parents litigate against their parents and/or doctors for *not* being butchered *in utero,* during delivery, or after birth. Somehow courts have discovered that justice does not deny fault being attached to those who would spare a fellow human being the fate of death. Life is now defined as the fate worse than death. I hesitate to ask the following question for fear that some fiend will seek to answer it with action: What would be proper compensation for an aggrieved party when the end sought but denied was death, and how can money be considered a fair compensation under such circumstances?

Parents are not suing ungrateful children for misspent lives. Instead, parents are suing to have children murdered before they leave the womb so as to afford the parents the opportunity to further misspend their lives. It may be the case that the only defense against a wrongful life suit is to ensure that the chip-off-the-old-block goes to the incinerator before he whines in court for having been taken to the woodshed once too often. This dynamic begs the question, of course, of how a child can sue after birth to punish his parents for not killing him, but no recourse is required to be offered the child murdered before birth who might plead to be allowed to continue living. Children are granted a right to demand to have been murdered by their parents, and parents are granted a right to murder their children. Just in case any are wondering, such "rights" are never granted, absolutely denied, and forever called abominations by God.

Should unhappy children come to term, they then must come to terms with their parents unhappy with being each other's spouses. Not only must the children cope with their parents' constant bickering. Not only must the children cope with their parents' divvying up who gets whom for which holidays. Not only must the children cope with determining which of their parents is more to blame for the disaster which has become all of their lives. But the children must also come to cope with what it means when the Church declares that after twenty-one years, Mr. and Mrs. Jones were never married, although there were no diriment impediments, they were married in the church, and had received instruction from a priest. The Church has done little to come to terms with the dissonance presented between its former absolute prohibition against divorce, and its current requirement that civil divorce be procured before an annulment may be pursued. As well, the Church has not come to terms with the ubiquitous assumption that annulment is just a fancy Catholic word for divorce.

And do not even get me started about the fact that bishops in this country stated publicly during the last election cycle that pro-murder presidential candidates may be supported if they also wanted to balance the budget and grant tax relief, conclude the war in Iraq, and respect the "rights" of sodomites—stances taken by each of the major political parties' candidates. When he was Joseph Cardinal Ratzinger, Pope Benedict XVI opined that such candidates could be licitly offered Catholic support so long as they were advanced for their opinions not in opposition to the Faith, rather than for their convictions which held the Faith in contempt. As if Hitler could be supported for his policy of getting the currency stabilized as long as he was not endorsed for his desire to find a "final solution"!

Some young adults of the Vietnam era burned buildings, shot people, and blew up cars in opposition to Nixon's continuation of Johnson's prolongation of the French's interference in Indochina. Today we are told by no less a personage than the President of the United States, echoed by his Attorney General, and parroted by his appointee for Chief Justice of the Supreme Court—both (supposedly) Catholics, no less—that child murder is the law of the land, that they will do nothing to repeal that law, that they will enforce that law. Our bishops utter a not a peep to decry such a foul policy. The Pope blathers on about "healthy secularity". Laws are passed to make peaceful abortion-protesting a federal crime on par with mob activity, and the college students of the eighties were vilified by their aging hippy parents for their apathy exhibited during their years in college. Those same parents, now grandparents, reap huge investment dividends from the stock market fantasy world created in the nineties, by the people who derided the evil of the espousal of Gordon Gecko's creed from the eighties, "Greed is good!" Now all of these people are profiting from the smoke and mirrors of the "expanding" economy based on home equity. Morality, politics, and finance are now run by the minds that brought us this morass.

Happy people do not express their happiness in ways that result in the death of others. Healthy people do not define happiness as whatever one's passions dictate. Holy people do not get addicted to drugs, rid themselves of their families, and elect known fiends to high public office. It is now the case that a man who staunchly defended sanctity, declared his desire to cooperate fully with the teachings of the Church in ordering society, and recognized Christ as Sovereign King of the universe and the Blessed Virgin Mary as the Queen of Heaven and earth would stand absolutely no chance of being elected to any statewide or national office. On the other hand, child murderers, advocates of sodomy, divorced people, the greedy, and false religionists may broadcast their errors and win decisive election victories, not in spite of, but because of their hellish philosophies, habits, and gods. ***Are we to believe that no one is to take exception to this wretched, obscene, unspeakably offensive status quo?!?***

Partial, Passive, and Stupefied Apathy

Mass attendance is at an all-time low, hovering in the single-digit percentages among Catholics in various large cities around the world. Catholics are not going to confession in droves. Outright denial of the sanctity of the marriage bond and its primary purpose of raising up children for the glory of God—taking the forms of fornication, cohabitation, contraception, adultery, and divorce—among Catholics, mirrors that of pagans, Jews, and protestants, with some protestants and Jews showing more respect for the institution than some Catholics. Convents, monasteries, novitiates, seminaries, and rectories were emptied in the 1970s and 1980s almost as quickly as divorce courts wrecked families. Many of the few persons who present themselves for preparation for the Sacrament of Holy Matrimony have not been Confirmed. Perhaps millions of souls avail themselves of regular "healing" and "anointing" Masses, but precious few priests make themselves available to attend the dying with the Last Sacraments of Confession and Viaticum immediately prior to the death of a Catholic. Baptisms, however, continue at a brisk pace, albeit without the full exorcisms and ceremonies of the ancient rite.

Did everyone who went to Mass in the old days hate it? Was Jansenism the only motivation that Catholics found for seeking God's mercy? Is "serial monogamy" really preferable to "till death do we part"? Perhaps it was the case that such singularly unhappy professed men and women Religious and secular priests were responsible for the hundreds of millions of lay faithful growing up to despise the entirety of the patrimony taught them by such malcontents? Is Confirmation a hard concept or merely a concept not adequately considered, engaged, and utilized by the bishops bestowing the Sacrament? What is so odious about the idea of being prayed for, prayed over, before death, and thereby being prayed into Heaven by the power of a Sacrament? Is it superstitious, outdated, or triumphalistic to perform "an outward sign, instituted by Christ, to impart grace"?

If we are to assume as correct the estimation of the adults of the generations immediately before and after Vatican II that the ways of the Church needed wholesale jettisoning, it does not follow that they are the best judges of what should replace what was jettisoned. They were by their own reckoning the victims of a systemic malady imposing guilt, unjustly deriding their fellows, and warping the Word of God. Acknowledging that the perpetrators of such a heinous set of offenses stand in profound need of correction, does it not also follow that their followers may well know what is wrong, but be utterly unequipped to define what is right?

Of course, such a supposition accounts for the penchant of those folks looking to protestants, secularists, and even atheists for a cure. But what are protestants if not disaffected Catholics from an earlier era, secularists but timid men unwilling to make statements of faith in aught but material gain, and atheists but the antithesis of Catholics, making absolute claims no more provable nor certain of assuring happiness than anything proclaimed by any Saint or Pope or Council? If the *one* Church is not right, why is belief in the *one* God right? If many churches can be right, why can not the many gods of the pagans be right? If the many gods of the pagans are right, why may I not worship a god whom none but I recognize and call good that which all but I recognize as bad?

There are explicit statements from various quarters of the magisterium, up to and including Popes John Paul II and Benedict XVI, asserting the rights of the secular to remain secular, of the Jews to remain Jews, of the protestants to remain protestant, and the schismatic eastern churches to remain in schism. How is it, then, that a Catholic faithful to immemorial Catholic tradition is to be taken to task for remaining Catholic? Talmudic Judaism, masonic secularism, and heterodox Christianity need not change at all, but Catholics must change all?!? This is not merely unfair, this is absurd! Beyond its absurdity lies an utter unnecessity: **Jesus Christ is the same yesterday, today, and forever, and so is His Body, the Catholic Church!** None who clings to Christ needs to repent his beliefs, to apologize for his beliefs, or to change his beliefs. **The obedience demanded of the Catholic is permanent, therefore, the Church to which he offers his obedience must be permanent in her teaching, in her practices, and in her rituals!**

The Lion Lies Down with the Lamb

There will be no protests, no sit-ins, no catchy sophomoric slogans. The ruling elite need fear no purges, no pogroms, no re-education centers after they are deposed, for none among their loyal sons will depose them. It might prove necessary to declare a few anathemas, define some as excommunicant, and condemn certain heresies and heterodoxies, but before any of that occurs, in keeping with genuine Catholic tradition there will be opportunity for explanation, retraction, and repentance. In all likelihood, before anything of the sort is to happen, not a few will find themselves posing silent opposition to wayward hierarchs while destitute on the street, behind bars, or even on death row. Perish the thought, but it is not unthinkable, that some faithful children of Holy Mother Church might find themselves in such straits on the word of the very shepherds given them by Christ to guard them from the wolves.

It is true that the period from two centuries or so before the Council until now has been one of unparalleled material increase around the world. Also true is the fact that in countries once considered thoroughly protestant, Catholics now can confidently aspire to lead in finance, politics, and entertainment. This rush by Catholics to seek acceptance by the prevailing non-Catholic powers in the world ignores the words of Jesus, "What doth it profit a man to gain the whole world but to lose his very soul?" A desire to bring a Catholic influence into the workings of the world is self-defeating if success is bought at the price of Catholics being admitted to the halls of power only on the condition that they never mention the Faith, the immutable laws of God, and the necessity of all men to be Catholic if they are to be saved. Catholics attempting to influence the world while downplaying Catholicism are so many noisy gongs, fruitless trees, and lights under bushel baskets.

The era of Christendom was a period in which the Church offered the world a coherent order that protected the family, nurtured the Faith, and glorified God. Since the protestant revolt, the world has inflicted on the Church, with the appalling cooperation of some members of the Body of Christ, an environment where murder is encouraged, abominations are defended in law, the family is ridiculed, the Faith is attacked, and God Himself is denied. Any imperfections present during Christendom, and heaven knows there were many, could be identified, critiqued, and corrected by an objective measure in keeping with an existent ideal. Modernity champions the rule of personal whim and preference, claiming that no absolute measure of right and wrong exists, and then proceeds to assail the faithful for committing the unforgivable sin of pursuing perfection. Christendom can be taken to task for frequently failing its ideal, although innumerable saints stand as witness to the fact that perfection is attainable. It is not possible for modernity to point to the perfect modern, for there is no ideal for which to strive, no measure by which the masses can imitate the successful few, no highest good that stands in judgement of evil or as the goal of lesser goods.

At some point it will become clear that some Catholics will not participate in denuded worship, false ecumenism, Americanism, masonry, immorality, usury, or the "spirit" of Vatican II—not refraining from some of those things or many of those things or most of those things, but *refusing every single one of them without exception and in their entirety.* Modernism would suggest that some kind of generation gap is operative, but years have nothing to do with this. Some folks old, some folks young, some folks in between, and all of them children of the Kingdom of Heaven, will adhere to that which Catholics everywhere at all times and in *toto* have believed since Jesus breathed the Holy Ghost upon the Apostles and the Blessed Mother in the Upper Room. Look not for revolution, but for return, a return to what the Church has always been, has always believed, has always taught. Fear not that the return will be a return to the violence and fears of the revolution, but instead look for a renewal of the ancient messages, "*Noli timere*!" and "*Laudate Dominum*!" and "*Jubilate Deo, omnis terra*!" and "*Pax vobiscum*!" and "*Gloria in excelsis Deo!*" proclaimed by Prophets, sung by Angels, and assured by God Himself.

If indeed the Vatican II generation had reason to be displeased with their forebears, then far more have the succeeding generations since the Council cause to express dissatisfaction with the ruined patrimony offered them as an excuse for the one, true Faith of Jesus Christ in His Church. Rather than following the lead of the post-Vatican II generation and running the risk of furthering their faults, the Church at large must put in practice once again the tools guaranteed by God to foster the faith: prayer, mortification, and the Sacraments. To very loosely paraphrase G.K. Chesterton—Catholics before the Council had not tried prayer, mortification, and the Sacraments in keeping with immemorial tradition and found them wanting, but Catholics before and since the Council have abandoned tradition and left themselves in want of the sanctifying grace available only in prayer, mortification, and the Sacraments. The Church does not need a new generation of young turks to come along and disrupt the status quo. What the Church needs is the constancy of every generation to desire, defend, and disseminate the Truth to all nations, Baptizing them in the Name of the Father and of the Son and of the Holy Ghost. What worked on a Sunday almost two-thousand years ago and every day since then will continue to work until the end of time when dawns the endless Day of the Kingdom of Heaven.

Father Smith.

29 September 2005
St. Michael the Archangel
Holy Family House, Silver Cliff, Wisconsin

Conjugal Fidelity
Against ecumenism

Thy twin I heard give voice to pretty things
much as art thou so often wont to do,
but more akin they were to cobra stings
than sweetness sipped by none ‘til thee I knew.
There is a double of the wonder shown
upon thy face within the gilded morn,
yet like the weeds where roses once were grown
is dawn beside the beauty thou hast borne.
Should any fiend or ever cad presume
to lay a hand on thee and thus decide
himself to be a not unworthy groom,
I soon will prove his fault a suicide.
In love the fool can not be fooled, nor I
mistake eternal Truth for satan’s lie.

Father Smith

28 September 2005
St. Wenceslaus
Holy Family House, Silver Cliff, Wisconsin

A Matter of Dialogue

Those who are led by the Holy Ghost have true ideas; that is why so many ignorant people are wiser than the learned. The Holy Ghost is light and strength. When we are led by a God of strength and light, we cannot go astray.

To the man who gives himself up to the Holy Ghost, there seems to be no world; to the world there is no God.

O Jesus! To know Thee is to love Thee! Did we but know how our Lord loves us, we should die of joy!—St. Jean-Marie Baptiste Vianney

DePaul University used to employ an Australian soccer coach. In addition to his duties on the field, this Aussie also taught a course titled, "Theories and Techniques of Coaching". I took that course during my junior year to satisfy the physical education requirement of my degree.

Many priests from Ireland have provided sacramental ministry in the United States. More than a decade ago a diocese in one of the southern states sponsored a seminarian from Ireland to study for the priesthood in order to serve in America after ordination. That man attended seminary with me, being ordained a year or two before me.

For several years my home diocese employed a religious sister in the religious education office, charging her with the task of overseeing parish efforts in adult education. This sister grew up in England. She and I met while I worked in the same office cataloging the electronic media owned by the continuing education department of the diocese.

The untutored ear hearing the speech of an Australian, an Irishman, and an Englishwoman frequently falls into the error of labeling all of the sounds as "British accents". I have heard the same mistake in reference to persons from South Africa as well. In fact, I must confess that at times all of those accents sound alike to me, too. Given that each of the locales producing those accents was once part of the British Empire, it is not odd that there are similarities in the way they speak English. However, to say that Australians, Irish, and English share a common British imperial heritage is far, far different from saying that they are the same thing. Only someone utterly unfamiliar with their distinct qualities could possibly mistake any one of those accents for any other of them. No real Brit could ever commit such a heinous error as thinking the mother tongue is the same on the Emerald Isle as it is Down Under or in Merrie Olde England.

Long before familiarity breeds contempt it brings recognition. To recognize something is to know it. When something is intimately known, it can be loved. Contempt comes not from close proximity, but from taking for granted a knowledge which is neither thorough nor fully possessed. To truly know something, to really grasp it, to be perfectly familiar with it is to participate in the divine act of loving one's own, what belongs to one by right of ownership, through a mutual sharing, or from the grace of receiving a gift.

Love of what is owned, shared, or given and received leads to a greater knowledge of the beloved. That increase of knowledge will result in a concomitant magnification of love, flowering in further knowledge, gaining yet more knowledge of love in the beloved *ad infinitum*. Familiarity is the basis of boundless love and knowledge of the beloved. And when something is loved it is loved for what it is, not for what it is not. Thus, true love depends upon being familiar with what the beloved is, and on knowing well what it is not.

So, when one is familiar with English, when one knows the varieties of accents with which it is spoken, one comes to a deeper love of the language expressed in countless inflections, innumerable variations, a myriad of dialects. The more there is to know the more there is to love. Professor Higgins from G.B. Shaw's *Pygmalion*, made yet more famous by the musical *My Fair Lady*, forgot knowledge and love and fell into contempt by taking for granted that he had heard all that English accents had to say to him. His life completely changed—for the better—when he discovered how contemptible was his prideful erudition and how attractive the fiery humility of Eliza Doolittle. In short order, their unfamiliar linguistic worlds collided, but contempt gave way to a common language based on a mutual understanding of the intimacy that grows when the unknown at last is known. That intimate knowledge allows its possessors to live *together* happily ever after.

Faith is a language. Faith is a gift. Faith is an action. It is a common tongue which can bear a plethora of accents. It requires a sensitive ear to detect the subtle distinctions between various voices. It demands an innate capacity wed to diligent study. Faith only makes sense when it is understood as a communication, not of knowledge, but of love, yet a love that rejoices in knowing ever more how to communicate love to the beloved. The fundamental communication of love is the mutual desire to live happily ever after together—*forever.*

But one Word is adequate to convey this loving communication. Only one Mouth has ever uttered that Word. There is only one Voice with the power to sound that Word spoken by that Mouth. Jesus Christ is the Logos, the Word. His

Father for all eternity has savored the meaning of the Word. In the Holy Ghost the Truth of the Word is articulated by His Father perfectly, fully, ceaselessly. Love is the Word spoken. Love is why the Word is spoken. Love is the Motivation of the speech, the Content of the utterance, and the Sound of the voice.

Faith is the conviction given by God, the grace given by God, the communication given by God that the love of the Most Blessed Trinity is meant to be shared by the creatures made in the divine image and likeness. That love is intended to be returned to God in kind and to be shared among His creatures. Faith is the evidence of the truth of the extraordinary hope given to man that he may live with God in beatitude forever. Faith is the substance within the human heart by which the invisible God is perceived, in which the divine Mystery is made known, for which God became man for the salvation of sinners. It is the gift of faith with which God declares to man, "I love you!"

Through the gift of faith, man is able to respond to God's sublime question, "Do you believe me?" God does not so much ask if man believes in Him, although that sentiment is indeed implied by the question. Still less is God interested in how much man knows *about* God, for although greater knowledge can lead to a closer relationship with God, human knowledge is ever inadequate to the comprehension of the divine totality, and man's mind is not sufficient either to express human being or to encompass the fullness of the divine. God's gift of faith to man is the divine declaration of God to man, "I love you!" That same gift results in man's ability to respond to God's question, "Do you believe me?" with a resounding "Yes! I love you, too!"

Without the grace of faith, man is incapable of making a response of "Yes!" to God. Instead, man will direct his love away from the Creator toward creatures, seeking not the one true God, but pursuing countless false gods. The false god allah does not love man enough to be a man. The false gods of nature do not love man enough to preserve man from eternal death. The false god almighty dollar does not love man enough to bring order, direction, and reason to bear on the conduct of life on earth. The false gods of science do not love man enough to teach certain knowledge of human being or comprehension of divine being to the soul engaged in the act of learning. The false gods that deny Jesus Christ, the one true God, do not love man enough to tell him the full truth about the Creator's love for His creation and His incredible love for man himself, a love willing to die for the beloved. Lacking faith in the loving God, man is reduced to a hopeless state surrounded by uncreated creatures, insatiable appetites, irrational philosophy, ultimate purposelessness, and unredeemed oblivion. Faithless man is alone in cold space, alone in his interactions with his fellow man, and alone in absolute separation from God now and forever.

With the grace of faith, man is given someone to talk to, something to say, and the power of speech. Faith brings about the communion of the divine with the human. Through that communion, each man is given the means to union with all men. Another way of saying this is that faith is the condition by which love of God is known by man, the love of God dwells within the hearts of men, and the love of God is shared by each man with all men. Set above the mute beasts, the man of faith can say who he is, how he is to live, and the purpose for which he exists. Faith teaches each man and all men what it means to be created in the image and likeness of God, how that creation is to be repaired, then preserved, and the eternal love sustaining that effort in time unto a perfection known only outside of time. Faith is the revelation, experience, and expression of love: God tells man He loves him, man thus knows God's love, and God receives back from man the love He gave man in the beginning.

As with every language, faith is learned best by immersion and in childhood. Accent, colloquialisms, and humor can be neither taught nor learned. They are received in and make sense only in context. Nuance and subtlety can not be reduced to ink on paper, inflection and drawl do not translate into theories, facial expression and hand gestures find no substitutes or explanations in a thesaurus or dictionary. It is true that describing just what all of this is is impossible. The native speaker of a language nonetheless immediately knows an imposter, a technician, a foreigner when he hears one.

Catholics embracing the traditions of the Faith must not make the horridly protestant mistake of thinking that fidelity finds its ultimate authority in a document, that orthodoxy can be divorced from ancient and constant usage, and/or that understanding sanctity depends more on expert testimony than on the actual experience of saints living in a state of grace. *Catholic* Faith is not just who speaks. *Catholic* Faith is not just what is said. *Catholic* Faith is not the babble common to pagans as well as to atheists. *Catholic* Faith is the Living God, living in the Mystical Body, alive with members living true to the example of Christ crucified. *Catholic* Faith is the Word of God given to the Church of God, teaching Him to the creatures of God with authority and power stemming from the perfect and unchanging truth of the Word. *Catholic* Faith is the immutable Truth of God alive in time. *Catholic* Faith is the discourse between Heaven and earth, the exchange shared by eternity with time, the common life in the Holy Spirit uniting the sons of God through the Son of God with God the Father.

Deprogramming from the Cult of Man

The sun never hides his light for fear of inconveniencing the owls.

My child, we must not be afraid of doing good, even if it costs us something.

If you are afraid of other people's opinion, you should not have become a Christian.—St. Jean-Marie Baptiste Vianney

Anyone seeking a Catholic "re-education camp" need not look very far. It can be found in Nazareth. It is frequented by the likes of Saints Basil, Macrina, and Peter of Sebaste; Saints Benedict and Scholastica; St. Bernard and his beloved Blessed Humbeline; St. Thérèse and the other Martins of Lisieux; and Saints Peter and Andrew, Sts, James and John, and Saints Simon, Thaddeus, and James. It is nestled on Elm Street, on Main Street, on the street where you live. In a word, Catholic reeducation—deprogramming from the cult of man—occurs in the *family.*

Much like, in fact, exactly as we learn language from our parents and older siblings, we learn the grammar and syntax of the Faith in the home. Our first home is, of course, the house of God of prayer, the Church, reflecting the many mansions of our Father's House in Heaven. This primary Home of the faithful gives form to the houses in which the faithful make their homes on earth. At our mothers' knees on Main Streets we learn to speak lovingly with the voice of angels as heard from Our Mother living at the end of the Via Della Conciliazione in Rome. Our mothers speak our Mother's tongue, and we learn in the homes of our fathers the Faith of the Fathers. Mother Church is at home in the domestic church; our fathers' homes on earth are the thresholds of our Father's house in Heaven.

Go home!

Orphans of Adam and Eve, in but not of the world, are adrift and hopeless when charity grows cold in their hearts and the light of faith is dimmed by sin gnawing their souls. It is only when the entirety of the ways of the world, the flesh, and the devil are abandoned utterly that those orphans find true sonship in Christ within the bosom of Holy Mother Church in service to God the Father. Faith is a family affair. Families belong in the home. The home is where the Sacred and Immaculate Hearts dwell, where God's will is perfectly obeyed, where charity is above all, hope encourages all, and faith in Christ is all in all hearts, souls, minds, and bodies.

The Catholic family must engage the larger society around them as a context, not as a goal. Society exists for and from families, not families for and from societies. The first society, in time and in primacy, is the family. The family is the society *par excellence*, chosen by God to be the context for His Incarnation, the image expressed by His Church, and the revelation of His glory in Heaven. The perfect society is that where a father reigns, a mother's heart loves, and children obey. The Holy Family of Jesus, Mary, and Joseph embodies this perfection. Christendom of Holy Mother Church beneath the Holy Father the Pope with faithful sons obediently ruling the state presents this ideal to the world. God the Father, the Blessed Virgin Mary the Mother of God the Son, and the saints of God live as a family society in the unsullied peace in the Kingdom of Heaven.

Within the family, then, is learned the speech of the Faith known as the *sensus Catholicus*. The sense of the Catholic—that which faithful subjects perceive and the power of the faithful to perceive what is authentically of God—is not first a matter of study, but observation. The Bride of Christ contemplates her Groom. The children of the Church imitate their Mother Mary in imitating Christ. Families look to the saints beneath their Queen to see how the will of God is to be expressed. Mothers and fathers express God's will to their children by example in action so that the Word of God is lived not only as a vague desire or empty speech, but as acts bearing eternal significance. Baby's first catechism is not a published text, but a living witness.

This experience of the family in small is identical to the experience of the Body of Christ the Church at large. Before the words of the Gospel were written down, the Word who is the Gospel came down from Heaven and became flesh. Ere Apostle or martyr gave testimony to the Cross of Calvary, Calvary was given in spirit and truth on Maundy Thursday at the First Mass, the Last Supper. The Empty Tomb was seen first, then recorded; the Lord ascended as a model to be repeated, not as a story to be deconstructed; and the Holy Ghost descended in tongues of fire; enflaming tongues to exhort men to live the Gospel, not to pay lip service to the Gospel or to render it a dead letter in ink on paper couched in legalese. The Word became flesh, not print, and those who believe the Word disdain the deadly letter of the law in favor of the living Spirit who writes on hearts, enkindles love, and dwells in earthly temples destined for Heaven.

Advent and Lent are central to doing justice to the ways of God, the Way of Christ. They are those times of penance when the faithful shed yet more of the world—permanently—in order to more purely put on the new man, Jesus Christ. The beginning of wisdom is the fear of the Lord. Faithfulness begins by shunning the world, the flesh, and the devil for fear of losing the Lord. Advent and Lent provide regular, extended, and focused opportunities to examine one's life, to discard what offends God, and to seek greater fidelity by atoning one's sins, aiding one's neighbors, and serving God above all in charity.

Perfect charity casts out all fear. Hence, as the world, the flesh, and the devil are increasingly rejected, there is an increase in confidence that God loves us more than satan can hate us. Love is sufficient not only to overcome the world with and in Christ, but to please God by cooperation with His grace. What is more, through that cooperation with grace which separates man from slavery to sin and satan, there is made a real union between God and man in divine charity.

In that divine charity, each man loving God above all things recognizes the joy and beauty of obeying the law of love for his fellow man. The first locus of obedience to the divine commandment of charity for neighbor is for the neighbors in the family: husband, wife, and children. Wisdom begins with fear of the Lord. Fear finds its end in charity. Charity begins in the home. If men are to fear the Lord, love the Lord, and have charity for their neighbors, then their efforts must begin in their homes on earth, with the hope of Heaven as their motivation, sustenance, and end for every thought, word, and deed.

Before the Hebrews came to the Promised Land, they wandered forty years in the desert. Jesus spent forty days in the desert in anticipation of His public ministry, consummated on the Cross. Catholics spend four weeks in darkness deepening before the dawn of Christ at Christmas, and forty days of fasting before the Lamb who was slain brings the eternal Feast of Himself to man through Calvary at Easter. Noah's forty-day ordeal, Moses' twice-forty-day vigil, and the forty hours of Christ in the tomb are all types of the Church, the Body of Christ, fulfilling that wanted in Christ's Cross on Good Friday: the full participation of heart, soul, mind, and strength of each man in the obedience to God the Father wrought by God the Son on Golgotha, and rendered in spirit and truth through the worship offered by the sons of God in Holy Mother Church.

Two-year-olds do not improve their vocabulary by conversations with other toddlers. Babbling infant gibberish can neither be the goal of the baby nor a source of permanent satisfaction for his parents. Proper to the state of childhood and to the task of childrearing by adults is the effort of guiding the child in putting aside the things of childhood in order to embrace the fullness of manhood. Children must have exposure to and interaction with their elders in order to reach a healthy maturity. Grownups must strive to draw the child out of immaturity toward full stature, lest the charm of childhood degrade into an endless adolescence.

Analogous to the forty days riding out the flood by Noah, the forty years the Israelites spent in the desert, and the forty days of temptation endured by Our Lord, is the period of maturation experienced by the growing child. That which is inadequate or in error is rejected. The insufficiencies of peers are recognized and a better way is embraced. Preparation is made for a task of profoundly different kind and extraordinarily greater degree. All men, the chosen people, and the Son of Man serve in due measure to demonstrate to each person the will of God apart from self-will; the election which constitutes God's vocation offered to the faithful; and the concord of heart, soul, mind, and strength between the Father and His obedient Only-Begotten Son and the sons obedient in the Father's adoption.

Furthermore, the Church offers twice each year an opportunity for her faithful sons to go out from the world like Noah, to heed the call of God like Moses, and to offer an acceptable holocaust to the Lord as Jesus. Advent and Lent represent times of growth for the children of God in imitation of their elders who have gone before them. The penitential seasons are a casting aside of the filth of the world as Noah faithfully accomplished, like the infant must come to discard his diapers. They are an acknowledgment that God desires more and other from man than man can hope to attain on his own, as Moses convinced the reluctant Hebrews to believe, like the boy who realizes that his father offers more by way of life's lessons than his playmates can conceive. Violet is the color donned by both kings and penitents: Christ the King performing perfect penance for His subjects; growing children enduring discipline as they set about acquiring skills and knowledge that will serve them in the day of their coming of age and inheritance; and the mourning mortification of the flock of Christ as they are prepared to receive their Shepherd and to reign with their King.

All of this growth takes place in the context of the family. This peculiar family is in but not of the world, called to go forth from it *and* to bear glad tidings to it. Within this family the junior members contemplate and imitate the example of their elders in obedience to the image they receive from their Father taught them by their Mother. These children of this family seek to jettison the deadly habits of their fellows outside of the family, while begging further communion for themselves and their fellows with the family members who have reached the fullness of maturity. Each member of this family heeds the head of the family, hearkens to His Word, and faithfully repeats Him in perfect harmony with the Spirit in which the Word is communicated by the Head. Nothing is desired or grasped which is not in consonance with the family's way of life, mode of speech, and understanding of itself. Everyone in the family believes that everyone of the family must look, sound, and act according to the Beauty, Truth, and Goodness whose very being is at home in the Head of the family whence all else proceeds.

In Plain Language, Please

Jesus Christ was not afraid of being laughed at.
—St. Jean-Marie Baptiste Vianney

Whenever God has revealed His will for man it has been in the context of a society. Eden provides the first example of this, where God's first commandment to His creatures made in His image and likeness, "Be fruitful and multiply!" is given after He has declared that, "It is not good for man to be alone." After the Fall, Noah is saved with his family, Abraham is offered a great people as the fruit of his fidelity, Moses leads that people in receiving God's Covenant, David is the king of that people wherein the Covenant will reach perfection, and that perfection is the Incarnation of God, Christ the King, within the Holy Family with Mary and Joseph at Bethlehem, the King's city, and Nazareth, the prophesied home of the Messiah of God. It is not good for man to be alone, and the men faithful to God discover that they are never abandoned in doing God's will. God wills that ultimate fidelity depends on him dwelling with His people, taking on flesh to share all with them, and exchanging life for life—giving immortality to mortality. Perfect fidelity to the will of God is best expressed in the communion given the name *Emmanuel*, God-with-Us. It is not good for man to be alone without his family or without his fellow man or without his God. Jesus Christ comes into the world truly God and truly man among men, within a family, to form a family, a holy people, a peculiar nation, a people set apart as inheritors of the Kingdom of Heaven and the house of God.

"My Father's house," as Jesus puts it, "is a house of prayer". It can be understood also in reference to the eternal dwelling place of God in Heaven. And, too, it can be interpreted by extension to mean the royal family of God, more ancient than the pharaohs, infinitely more powerful than the Carolingians, of unutterably greater nobility than Plantagenet, Romanov, or Hapsburg. God has formed a family for Himself not of foundlings, nor of bastards, nor of stepchildren. The children of God beneath the Son of God are heirs in Christ and heirs with Christ, younger brothers and sisters of the King, princes and princesses of the Kingdom of Heaven. God's children are full members of His family, full relations through His Spirit and water, sharing with Jesus Christ God as Father and Mary as Mother.

Royal families are sacred, the king receiving crown and anointing from the Church. To be sacred is to be lifted above and away from the mundane. Rule is weightier than service, for the ruler below God must not only govern his subjects, but is himself subject to God's rule. Nobles in God's royal family must learn not only the rule of inferiors and dependents, but also self-rule. Indeed, ungovernable is the people ruled by the man who can not govern himself. The first task of the faithful in attaining reign in the Kingdom of Heaven is to do what neither satan nor faithless sinners do, namely, *serve.*

Jesus shows this by his example in his divine infancy, his obedience through his minority, and his self-abnegation on the cross. The deeds of Christ are echoed in the words of Christ: *If you would be greatest in the Kingdom of Heaven you must deny yourself and serve the least; he who humbles himself will be exalted; the Son of Man came not to be served but to serve.* This theme of service informs the prayers addressed by the Son to the Father: *Thy Kingdom come, Thy will be done; Not my will, Father, but Thy will be done; Father, into Thy hands I commend my spirit!*

The Catholic echoes this service through his willingness to submit to the divinely ordained rule of the parents in the home. He manifests obedient humility by voluntary acts of mortification encouraged by the Church originating in the penitential seasons of Advent and Lent and renewed on a daily basis throughout the year. Each Catholic learns the life common to all Catholics through denying self, dying to self, and dedicating self to the Cross as the Tree of Life whose fruit is the Bread of Life, Jesus Christ.

This means, then, that the Catholic on his way to sanctity disavows the Godless ways of the world. The Cross renders one dead to self, dead to the world, and alive in Christ Jesus. He who has tasted the Bread of Life finds no savor in the banquets of the world, the flesh, and the devil. Fasting from the false feasts of mammon leaves one hungry for the real Food and real Drink of Christ's Body and Blood. The poverty of the Kingdom of Heaven reduces the riches of the nations to rags. There is no room in the human mouth for gluttony where the human heart has an insatiable desire for grace. No satisfaction is had in pursuing appetites, fashion, and passions; but overabundance of wealth is possessed by those whose desire for glory is fulfilled in Christ's Passion. As the saying goes, no less true for being old: to have everything in the world without Christ is to have nothing; to have nothing in the world but Christ is to have everything.

The progression of acquiring an authentic *sensus Catholicus* begins with the renunciation in toto of the world, the flesh, the devil, and one's very self. It continues with the cultivation within the family at home of those habits conducive to a life of sacrifice, service, and sanctity. At its height the *sensus Catholicus* leads the faithful soul in a fervent zeal to avoid evil, to do good, and to lay down one's life for love of enemy, for love of friend, and for love of God. *Anything* not in keeping with this ultimate goal of self-immolation for, with, and in Christ is utterly rejected. All of life is directed by the Catholic sense of what is holy, simple, and charitable. *Sensus Catholicus* will be uninterested in the curiosities presented by fashion, it will be repulsed by the suggestion that anything is preferable to the will of God, and blank mystification is the response *sensus Catholicus* offers when worldly wisdom is proffered as sufficient for understanding the world. Where the true *sensus Catholicus* is cultivated the human person increasingly seeks mortification, rejoices in the opportunity to aid a fellow in need, and is indifferent to either material dearth or wealth so long as spiritual good is received through prayer, the Sacraments, and charity above all.

St. Paul admonishes, "'Go out from among them and be ye separate,' saith the Lord, 'and touch not the unclean thing. And I will receive you. And I will be a Father to you and you shall be my sons and daughters, saith the Lord almighty'" (2 Corinthians 6:17-18 referencing Isaias 52:11 and Jeremias 31:9). The *sensus Catholicus* motivates the faithful to go out, to be set apart, to be a holy nation separate from the people insistent on walking in the darkness of the ways of the world. This going out can be understood on several levels. It is the physical going out necessitated by the avoidance of occasions of sin. There is the social going out wherein families seek others who are seeking sanctity as their basis and forum for recreation, culture, and trade. Most profoundly is the spiritual going out whereby the children of the Church hunger for the Sacraments rather than for the allure of the world, nourish sanctifying grace within their souls instead of feeding the appetites of the flesh, and obey the commandments of Christ leading to the humility of the Cross rather than succumbing to the tyranny of satan which brings nothing but shame disguised as glory.

Sensus Catholicus is the living expression of the will intent upon the beatitude, *"Beati mundo corde, quoniam ipsi Deum videbunt!"* Blessed are the pure of heart, for they shall see God! It is the faculty by which the profane is recognized and rejected, the sacred is acknowledged and accepted, and the desire for God and His will manifested in the Cross becomes the single measure by which thoughts, words, and deeds are deemed of worth by the faithful soul. The communion of saints shares the *sensus Catholicus* as the common sense of Catholics, judging right from wrong, willing always the good, and doing all for charity toward neighbor solely for the sake of God. Such common sense for the Catholic flows from the grace of faith received in Baptism by which the faithful participate in the Cross of Christ consummated in the Mass in Holy Communion. Faith enlightens the mind, then, so that learning reinforces the supernatural powers inherent in the soul within the state of grace. This is the language of the Kingdom of Heaven, communicating charity through the Cross of Calvary between the Persons of the Blessed Trinity and the persons redeemed by the will of the Father through the Passion of the Son in the power of the Holy Ghost. The *sensus Catholicus* knows that the will of the Father is the absolute law of the universe, that only the Son has perfectly obeyed that will, and that the Holy Ghost brings adopted sons to the Father through the Son so that they can obey, be redeemed, and share in the reign of Christ Jesus to the glory of God the Father.

The Syntax of Sanctity

The saints never complained.

The saints were so completely dead to themselves that they cared very little whether others agreed with them or not.

Our Lord is never found in pomp, pleasure, or luxury, but in lowliness and humiliation. —St. Jean-Marie Baptiste Vianney

Exclusive conformity to God's plan of salvation is the work of the *sensus Catholicus* in the life of the faithful. Through the *sensus Catholicus* the faithful know what is sinful, denounce it, and avoid it. What is more, the *sensus Catholicus* spurs the faithful to seek the holy, to ask the grace to embrace it, and to strive ever more to conform to the example of Christ and Him crucified. Persons growing in the *sensus Catholicus* resonate with the truths taught by the Church, distinguish licit activities from the traps of the world, and increasingly act on the conviction that Heaven, not earth, is their true home.

As such, Heaven's citizens, not hell's denizens nor the world's inmates, form the society sought through the *sensus Catholicus.* The child baptized into the true Faith is received into a communion of persons who know their true identity, who know how to act from the truth of their being, and who know that such fidelity results in final and perfect union with the Author of their being and of each of their faithful acts. It is by the *sensus Catholicus* that such knowledge is communicated, understood, and put into action.

Humility is the means by which the saint is able to say his first words, addressing God as Father and the Virgin Mary as Mother, much like the baby learns to say "Daddy" and "Mommy". It is the saint's priest within the Church where he first understands spiritual paternity *in persona Christi* and spiritual maternity from *Mater Ecclesia.* His family at home gives flesh to the spiritual reality present in Heaven. At each stage of growth the saint comes to a deeper realization of the infinitude of God and the peace that grows from serving God in obedience to the superiors God has placed over him. Each saint knows that every saint not only starts at the bottom, but profoundly wishes to remain last and least, in favor of giving God all glory and esteeming His glory in all things and all persons above and before the self.

St. Jean-Marie Baptiste Vianney, the Curé of Ars, repeating Saint Augustine, teaches us that humility is the first virtue, humility is the second virtue, and humility is the third virtue. He also likens humility in relation to all the virtues as the chain is to the Rosary beads: remove the chain and all the beads scatter; remove humility and all the virtues fall away. Humility is the foundation on which base the edifice of sanctity is built. Without humility nothing can rise from the ground, all crashes to the ground, for humility *is* the ground, the *humus,* which gives firmness and support and stability to all above it—one gets nowhere until beginning in humility. The human, made from *humus*, must remain grounded in humility if he is to rise above his earthly state and aspire to the heights of Heaven. The vaults of Heaven are exceedingly exalted, and the tower that reaches them must be tremendously tall, but the tower is only as secure as its foundations are deep. Humility is the deepest foundation possible, capable of scaling the highest of pinnacles, Heaven itself.

This truth flows from the fact that its fullness is revealed by the will of God. The Second Person of the Most Blessed Trinity, God the Son, dwells on high with the Father in the Holy Ghost within eternal glory. Taking on flesh from the Blessed Virgin Mary in the power of the Holy Ghost, Jesus Christ, the Word of

God the Father, descended to earth. In the world, but not of the world, He came unto his own but His own owned Him not, crucifying Him on the Tree of the Cross. Dying indeed, Jesus descended into hell, vanquishing satan and freeing the captive souls. He rose again from the dead on the third day, returning to the earth in body and soul perfectly united to His divinity. Forty days later, Jesus ascended to the Right Hand of his Father in Heaven, whence He shall come to judge all, casting the damned into hell, and bringing the saved with Him to dwell in Heaven forever. Thus, Jesus knows the way from Heaven, has trod the Way of Sorrows to hell, and gives Himself to be the Way to conquer hell, transcend the world, and gain the reign of Heaven.

Saints humbly acknowledge the sinfulness which merits hell. Humility prompts them to serve God's Kingdom faithfully on earth. Heaven is the reward won by God's grace for the humble. Humility can be heard from the lives of saints saying things like "Christ must increase and I must decrease" (St. John the Baptist); "Silver and gold I have none, but what I have I give thee: in the name of Jesus Christ of Nazareth, arise and walk!" (St. Peter); "To me, the least of all the saints, is given this grace, to preach among the gentiles the unsearchable riches of Christ" (St. Paul); "Neither dost thou fear God, seeing thou art under the same condemnation? And we indeed justly: for we receive the due reward for our deeds, but this man hath done no evil" (St. Dismas); "Behold the Handmaid of the Lord: be it done in me according to thy word" (the Mother of God).

Humility focuses the eyes of the faithful so that they pierce the dross of this world now ending, so as to perceive the splendor of the world that will never end. Lives lived according to an authentic *sensus Catholicus* not only look different to those observing them from the outside, but they see differently from within this worldview. To be made in the image and likeness of God means more than appearing to be like God, but really knowing as God knows, understanding as God understands, and judging as God judges. This is to esteem the world not by worldly reckonings, but according to the measure of the Kingdom of Heaven.

Thus, the faithless enter each day as a burden of further toil in the employ of oppressors for the acquisition of wealth of the meanest and most fleeting kind. Each day is one day fewer before the end of days in death. Any day is doomed to repeat the vanity of every newless day under the age-old sun. Faithless life is a horror of dread for the hateful sameness (with which he has grown all too familiar) inflicted on man by himself, and a terror of the hopeless unknown awaiting him (which newness he finds anything but lovable) after the horrible dread passes into oblivion. At best man is left to divert himself with unsatisfying pleasures of painful brevity; at worst he is left to imagine what pleasure is from the depths of either rank deprivation or disgusted satiety.

Faith built on humility, on the other hand, brings the lens of the *sensus Catholicus* to bear on man's daily life. He labors faithfully alongside a Master who imposes a sweet yoke and an easy burden, bearing the bulk of the bitter and the harshness Himself. The fruits of his labor withstand moth, rust, and thief, perduring forever. The dawning day is a summons for which he keeps faithful vigil, leaping into each day with the vigor and zeal with which he hopes to answer the Trumpet call on the Last Day bidding him to rise to final Judgement. On the dawn of the Last Day, the saints will not beg another hour of the sleep of death before arising to endless life in Christ. Each day, then, the faithful soul on earth keeping company with the saints in Heaven goes forth to answer his Lord's call, whatever it might be, whenever it might come, however it must be accomplished, whoever gives voice to it, because the humble are eager to obey the Lord who loves them. Days of grace pass swiftly bringing ever greater and more wondrous experiences of the breadth and depths and heights of the love of God in Christ Jesus.

From this humble will to serve the Lord with fervent zeal results the supreme sign of sanctity recognized by and expressed through the *sensus Catholicus*: taking up the cross each day and following Jesus. To proud sophisticates this is the height of absurdity. To men ignorant of God through and in Jesus Christ, this is an unspeakable scandal. But to those who believe, faithful children of God, souls given by grace the *sensus Catholicus,* this is the very stuff of beatitude. It is the poor, the meek, the sorrowful, the hungry and thirsty, the merciful, the pure, the peaceful, and the persecuted who know beatitude; and they come to poverty, humility, sorrow, want, mercy, purity, peace, and persecution through the cross with Jesus.

Learned through the *sensus Catholicus* is the inadequacy of bodily health, material wealth, or social standing to provide the heart's truest desires. The faithful do not deprive their loved ones of food, shelter, and clothing; but they refuse food, shelter, and clothing divorced from the charity perfected on the Cross. The poor, the pure, and the persecuted have nothing from the world and can offer the world nothing of its own. The poor, the pure, and the persecuted pray for an increase of unworldly blessings, and this they share with the world, with the prayer that the world will not remain self-satisfied, satisfied with selfishness, nor satisfied until Christ Jesus is all in all.

Humility, zeal, and the cross are commanded by the Lord: "Go, sell all, give to the poor, store thus treasure in Heaven, and follow me!" "He who hates his life will save it." "Unless the grain of wheat falls to the ground and dies, it remains just a grain of wheat." "He who humbles himself will be exalted." "Love the Lord your God with your whole heart, with your whole soul, with your whole mind, and with your whole strength! . . . Love your neighbor as yourself!" The foolishness of God is greater than the wisdom of men, righteousness must surpass religious legalism, and God's measure exceeds the comprehension of men. Absurdity and scandal are accusations from fools and egoists. Charity expressed with humble zeal in self-sacrifice is the means accepted by the wise who would learn the sublime truths from the mouth of God, taught by his Word, understood only in the Spirit with whom He deigns to grace man with a share in divine and eternal life.

What is the Matter of the Kingdom not of this World?

Nothing is so contrary to charity as pride.

When two things are to be done, we may choose the one which is least pleasant.

Pure souls shall form a circle around the Lord. The purer we have been on earth, the nearer we shall be to him in heaven.

—St. Jean-Marie Baptiste Vianney

Prepositions are vital parts of speech. The question is not, "What is the matter with the Kingdom not of this world?" Asked that way, it is of a piece with the addled mentality of those who find things like "faith", "large families", and "God" to be problems. One gets the answers to questions in the mode in which the questions are asked. If you define "faith", "large families", and "God" as problems, you will get problematic solutions galore, but precious little understanding of the objects of your inquiries. There is nothing the matter with the Kingdom of Heaven—unless one desires perdition—but there is matter of which the Kingdom of Heaven is possessed on earth, territory claimed by its rightful King. It is most legitimate to ask what that matter is, akin to taking a survey of land so that its rightful owner may lay claim and build the home in which he will house his family.

Bread and wine are essential elements of the Kingdom of Heaven on earth. Bread strengthens the body and wine gladdens the heart. Bread and wine also are the apt matter for confecting the Sacrament of the Body and Blood of our Lord Jesus Christ, from which gushes forth the infinite mercy of His Most Sacred

Heart. God has willed that nature and supernature depend on the humble grain and fruit of the vine for the sustenance of man on earth unto eternal life. The nexus of mortal and divine life is found by the grace of God in the humble elements by which is offered the Sacrifice of the Mass. Life depends on proximity to sustenance. The *sensus Catholicus* seeks places where food for the body grows from the earth and food for the soul comes down from Heaven.

Eating and drinking are unique among human activities. They are reflections of the divine will for man's ultimate beatitude. On the Altar of the Cross, Christ spread out the Food and Drink of His Body and Blood in order to nourish His Flock that they might avoid a death wherein no hunger is sated, no thirst is quenched, and no suffering ceases. The life given and gained on the Cross bestows on the faithful a sustenance wherein hunger, not satisfaction, ends. God's life grants a fulfillment where thirst, not quenching, is exhausted.

Eating and drinking are a cooperative venture between God, His creation, each man, and all men. Unlike angels, who need no material sustenance, and unlike animals and plants, that have no will to exert in seeking sustenance, man is called to cooperate with God in the care of the bounty of the earth, to cooperate with the natural order God has willed for creation, and to cooperate with his fellows in cultivating and distributing the fruits of God's grace, nature's largesse, and man's toil. In this activity, man's natural and supernatural essence is brought into play. He must receive the grace of humility to acknowledge his absolute dependence on God. He must use his innate reason to bring forth from the soil, the sea, and the countryside the material necessities for human existence. And he must act on the virtue of charity by which the overwhelming excess of nature is to be shared with all mankind, none burdened with too much, none plagued by too little.

Sowing and harvesting are apt metaphors for God's work among men. He offers man the privilege of accomplishing the divine will. He includes man in the fruits of a labor which man does not merit nor can he effect on his own. He expresses a wondrous mystery wherein the supernatural and the natural are brought together within the heart of man by way of the hands of man submitting to God and ruling over nature. God gives man satisfaction both in the hopes running high when the seed is sown and in the pleasant toil that comes with those hopes brought to fruition. When the harvest is complete, it becomes the basis for further hope and greater joy in the plantings and yields yet to be. Rest is possible, labor is rewarded, and peace reigns within and without man's soul.

The wedding feast is a fitting description of Christ's Kingdom. Union occurs between bodies and souls. Bounty is shared joyfully and fearlessly. Fruitfulness is celebrated for the blessings of the past and the promise of the future. Humility is received by the groom and authority is acknowledged by the bride. The wedding feast flows from all that has gone before and is meant to be a harbinger of what is to come. It provides a symbol of the life that is to be shared henceforth permanently.

Christ's Cross, the labor of the vineyard, the joy of the harvest, and the bliss of the wedding feast are intimately united in the Mass. The seeds of Faith are sown in the lessons and the Gospel, and brought to fruit in the *Credo*. Thanksgiving for the harvest is rendered in the Offertory. Angelic ecstasies are heard in the *Sanctus.* And the consummation of all of it occurs in the immolation of the Lamb who, under the forms of bread and wine, makes Himself the Food and Drink by which His Bride is made a Mother, her many children become the sons of His Father, and His Spirit is poured forth so that death is thrown down and the Kingdom of Life begins His reign on earth as it is in Heaven.

Faith is best served by seeking living arrangements conducive to participating in this reality. People should live where food grows. The growing of food is meant to nourish the body in its task of providing a venue where the soul may be conformed to God in Christ. Perfect conformity to Christ is had only in communion with Him in the Mass. Thus, the ideal to which the *sensus Catholicus* is drawn is a rural setting in imitation of Moses on Mount Sinai, Jesus on the Mount of Quarantine, eremitic solitaries, monastic foundations, and mystics bent on contemplating the divine, where livelihood is not divorced from the land and the Mass is available daily and the other Sacraments on a regular basis. This should be a Catholic community in which the constant rites, teachings, and habits of the Church are the exclusive offering presented to the faithful by the priest.

A brief digression on the subject of Latin: Latin does not demand or guarantee a true *sensus Catholicus.* A language in itself is a natural phenomenon, not expressive as such of the divine will. The *sensus Catholicus,* however, has its genesis in the Latin-speaking ancient world, where Latin was the *lingua franca* and then became the tongue of erudition and worship. The *sensus Catholicus* is not native to Latin, but Latin is native to the *sensus Catholicus.* Speaking Latin does not lead to the *sensus Catholicus,* but the *sensus Catholicus* insists on Latin as the language first spoken by our Mother the Church to the world, the language in which she has served the nations as teacher beneath Christ the divine teacher, and the precious speech spoken to God in the exquisite prayer of the immemorial Mass. The Church, absent hearers with an authentic *sensus Catholicus,* is perceived as speaking vernacular tongues with an accent, lacking idiomatic ease, and in poor translations. It is the sound of Shakespeare rendered in Mandarin Chinese. Grace from God, however, brings those vernacular speakers to the bosom of their Mother where they can learn her language and speak as native sons without need of dictionary, interpreter, or repeatedly redacted documents. Worldly error can be embraced and expressed by Latin, powerless in itself to correct heresy and immorality. The *sensus Catholicus,* however, trains the heart to love God, trains the tongue to speak God's truth, and trains the will to obey God's commands in all things at all times for all men. Latin is the language by which Holy Mother Church teaches the nations; the Holy Ghost teaches the children of the Church by the *sensus Catholicus* to distinguish truth from error in any language.

Catholics gathered around the Mass, in a rural setting dedicated wholeheartedly to sanctity and truth, will understand their responsibility to do their utmost to live saintly lives *for the sake of the salvation of their neighbors.* Peter Maurin once said that a good society is a society where it is easy to be good. Catholics in families and parishes must make it their constant care to be good so that their beloved neighbors have a good society to which to conform, rather than a hellish chaos from which to escape. Peer pressure among the saints is a matter of competing to raise one's fellows to higher levels of sanctity than oneself. This can not be done by depraved souls, who can only drag others down to their debased level, but is accomplished by saints in service to sanctity, or rather, reformed sinners aiding their brothers to avoid their former sins.

Left behind by reformed sinners in the extended Advent and Lent of the life of faith on earth are all the old ways of the world: media filth disguised as entertainment, avarice in the name of making a living, envy for the sake of social status, machines substituting for human relations, and pride trumpeted at the expense of humble faith, hope, and charity. In other words, the *sensus Catholicus* revolts against modern pipelines from hell such as television, radio, movies, the internet, and video games. The faithful will have nothing to do with lies in the newspapers, pornography from periodicals, or blasphemy pretending to be literature. Convenience does not rule the daily life of the would-be saint, nor will he succumb to the seduction of social acceptance—human respect—at the cost of pleasing God. One of the primary signs of a healthy *sensus Catholicus* in operation is the ability to define, demonstrate, and denounce the usury rampant in modern economic life since the destruction of Christendom in the protestant revolt.

Rather than internet insipidity, printed insanity, or recorded confusion, modern Catholics should have access to what Catholics have had since Our Lord walked the earth: instruction from the priest, converse with other faithful Catholics, and study commensurate with one's state in life. No Catholic home should lack the daily habit of the Rosary. If daily Mass is unavailable, then following the prayers and lessons in a hand missal such as *The St. Andrew Daily Missal* is invaluable. Alongside that should be daily readings from Dom Prosper Guéranger's *The Liturgical Year.* Great edification and indulgences come from pious reading of the Holy Bible—if a family reads one chapter of the Gospels each day, they will read the inspired life of Christ four times every year. Guiding their understanding of the Sacred Scriptures must include the Church Fathers, such as St. Thomas Aquinas' stupendous *Catena Aurea*, and a solid catechism such as *The Catechism of the Council of Trent.* Also of assistance in comprehending the Word of God is contemplating them who know him best, His saints. References such as Butler's *Lives of the Saints, The Roman Martyrology,* and Jacobus de Voragine's *The Golden Legend* are indispensable. Great saints who describe the effort necessary for beatitude include St. Francis de Sales in his *Introduction to the Devout Life,* and St. Thérèse the Little Flower in her autobiography, *The Story of a Soul.* Magisterial declarations of dogmatic weight particularly applicable to this period of history are Leo XIII's *Rerum Novarum,* St. Pius X's *Pascendi Domenici Gregis* and *Lamentabili Sane,* and Pius XI's *Quas Primas.* Recreational reading with Catholic novelists provides both rest and instruction. Three of the many available are Louis de Wohl's *Lay Siege to heaven,* Monsignor Robert Hugh Benson's *Come Rack, Come Rope,* and G.K. Chesterton's *Manalive.* Enormously more exists, but need not be mentioned unless one has mastered already all of which he is now aware. Part of the *sensus Catholicus* is knowing when to stop, and realizing that gluttony can be spiritual and intellectual, as well as physical. The Kingdom of Heaven contains the best cooperators with God, not necessarily the best and the brightest, the bestsellers, or the best read of the world's luminaries.

Immersion is key to learning, understanding, and expressing both faith and language. The child must set aside baby talk, the student must put down his dictionary, and the immigrant must forget his mother tongue if fluency is ever to come in language. Likewise, the Catholic must reject the world's views, the ways of worldly life, and the world's tyranny over man's understanding of spiritual matters if the sinner is ever to become a saint. Naturalized citizens are always living in two countries; if their children are ever to be true citizens of the new country, the parents must release all family ties to the old country, including language. No one insistent on remaining a citizen of the world will ever be a citizen of the Kingdom of Heaven. There is no dual citizenship. The former worldling who loves poverty, who craves the cross, who forgets himself in his constant thoughts of God and neighbor has received the *sensus Catholicus* and is on his way to living now in the world in consonance with the world without end. God loves him, he knows this, and he knows how to answer God's question, "Do you believe me?" in thought, word, and deed with all of his heart, all of his soul, all of his mind, all of his strength, and with all of his family within God's family in the Church, until he dwells forever with God and his family in Heaven.

Current Events: The White Man's Burden

Christian Europe: Anno Domini 313-1517, R.I.P. Christendom was brought to the brink of extinction by the introduction of an alien competitor, for reasons of greed, by unscrupulous men. It succumbed to its fitter rival, which has no natural enemies (only supernatural enemies), and was driven from its habitat by the encroachments of aggressive, urban, and industrial human society; the victim of evolution, natural selection, and its own excessive success.

Encroached upon by foreign powers
bent on conquest of a weaker foe,
a fading native people cowers,
adding shame to fill their cup of woe.

Through feast and famine long enduring
kings this way of life had freely trod,
their wives' and children's rights ensuring
for the honor of their home and God.

But now the end is surely nearing
of their liberty and right to rule
themselves without the pain of fearing
unjust death or bondage yet more cruel.

In lust for land and love of money
hordes are on the march and bound the main,
'tho' bitter proves the milk and honey
flowing in the wake of lucre's gain.

This tortured realm is seized by violence
wrought by both the victor and the lost;
unrighteous anger yields to silence
as defeat in winning's deadly cost.

The progress of the modern onslaught
whelms indigenous societies,
and leaves their ancient cultures untaught
in their homes or universities.

United Nations high commissions
take a pause in mercy's just pursuit,
while Brussels fails to see conditions
that the Hague demands for filing suit.
From neither Hollywood nor Greenpeace
issue any statements to decry
the base refusal to bring surcease
to these victims of the System's lie.

An army daily growing greater
sweeps across this land where few are born;
destruction coming soon or later
matters not when none are left to mourn

the final hour, 'tho' far from finest,
when the whimper, not the bang, is heard
that sets the sun which once shone brightest
on the realms where Europe spread the Word.

Father Smith
12 November 2005: Pope St. Martin I
Holy Family House, Silver Cliff, Wisconsin

Re-establishing Christendom III: In the Church

Where Christ is King

A Prelude

Laws must transcend the man if they are to be just; law must transcend men if there is to be justice. It serves no one well to be ruled by a bully. Equally inadequate is the anarchy of despotism wherein all must obey, but none need admit responsibility. Man wants neither the tyrant nor the bureaucrat for his liege and lord. But democracy ill-used is no improvement. My daily life is a gauntlet in which I am pummeled in the one moment by the sinner who tells me that my "paternalistic" Catholic morality impinges on his personal sovereignty; and in the neighboring moment by the "paternalistic" hierarchy of said Church waxing silently eloquent on matters such as the obligation of Sunday Mass attendance, the prohibition against contraception, or the advisability of sending one's children to Catholic schools. My superiors have charged me with leading a flock in such wise that the flock goes nowhere it would rather not.

In this ethos of absurdity there is no separation of Church and state. Our government insists that children are powerless to resist tobacco corporations' manipulative marketing of their legal products, and then proceeds to tax those companies to the point of socialist takeover in order to fund, among other things, education programs for children. *Kids, if you want textbooks and lab supplies, get some adult to smoke another pack today!*

These same children are deemed impotent before their baser urges and are given, free of charge, medications and devices that encourage them, through a false sense of security, to engage in behaviors perilous to their bodies, minds, and souls, as well as to our society. Our children are admonished, at taxpayer expense, to just say "No!" to drugs, to eat healthy snacks, and to get regular exercise; but their government-sponsored cheerleaders surrender before the "insurmountable" obstacle of pubescent hormones. There are no programs for clean needle exchanges in schools for adolescent heroin addicts, no playground giveaways of Twinkies for toddlers with too much of a sweet tooth, no subsidized purchases of remote controls for teenaged couch potatoes, even though there is an epidemic of drug abuse, obesity, and illiteracy among America's youth. But "safe sex" courses, condom distribution, and abortion counseling are available in schools from Watts, L.A., to Washington, D.C., to address the problems associated with "underage" fornication.

Behind the curtain of license, disguised as liberty, where our inconsistent minders keep their dirty secrets, is an unwillingness to submit the individual to a higher law. Not the law of other individuals or groups of individuals, but a law untouched by fickle appetites, the fads of the day, or the fancies of philosophers. Our wayward world lacks leaders who would offer men the blessing of the natural law.

It is telling that modernity claims that man is opposed to nature in his technology and economy of life. Simultaneously it is the modern vogue to insist that man is incapable of contact with any objective supernatural reality. Man is a fiend at enmity with mother nature, and a fool for believing that he might somehow transcend this world. Such is the Gospel according to evolutionary biology and the "new" "theology".

G.K. Chesterton famously warned that to deny the supernatural is not to assert the natural, but to descend into the unnatural. Hence the importance of the natural law. It is the bridge between the ultimate law of God and the laws of men meant to reflect it. The natural law prevents the despair that would come from the conviction that man is utterly divorced from the divine, and the tyranny of man asserting himself as God.

St. Paul makes use of the natural law when he tells the pagan Romans that none can plead ignorance when it comes to righteous living. Jeremias prophesies that the Lord will write His law on every heart, so that God Himself will see to it that all men can know Him. In the Apocalypse, St. John sees the revelation of God's will that all nations enter into the New Jerusalem.

Ancient Rome, modern America, and every creature made in the image and likeness of God have the benefit of God's truth available to them. We are no more ignorant than the pagans of antiquity, no more willful than exiled Israel, no more persecuted than the saints have ever been. The rule of law is the birthright of all men.

What is curious about man, rather than animals, vegetables, and minerals, is that he can choose which law will rule him. Man either will be a law unto himself, in which case he will be a subject in the kingdom of chaos; or he will subject himself to God's law, manifested in the natural law and expressed in the justice of human laws, in which case he will reign in the Kingdom of Heaven.

It would be most odd if man elected to live in chaos, but odder still if he rejects the current chaos and follows the narrow way. Chesterton also said, "Whatever occurs to me as ridiculous has always occurred to somebody else as wise." Wouldn't it be wonderfully ridiculous if everybody decided to let God rule not only the universe, but everyone in it?

> *The Only Ruler by Which Rulers are Measured*
>
> *My Kingdom is not of this world. If my Kingdom were of this world, my servants would certainly strive that I should not be delivered to the Jews: but now my Kingdom is not from hence... Thou sayest I am a king. For this was I born, and for this I came into the world: that I should give testimony to the truth. Every one that is of the truth heareth my voice... Thou shouldst not have any power against me, unless it were given thee from above. Therefore, he that hath delivered me to thee hath the greater sin.—St. John 18:36, 37; 19:11*

Sin is a grammatical error on the metaphysical plane where "can" is mis-defined as "may". Modernity is a morass in which willful misrepresentation of the nature of things is made public policy, the basis of personal morals, and the ethos of the men responsible for the governance of the Church. It is essentially a reversion to the barbarism of "might makes right", the "law of the jungle", and the "survival of the fittest". Good manners, common sense, and any appreciation for the dignity of the *imago Dei* in man recoil at pursuing life predicated on such an understanding. As well, the solemn magisterium condemns it in the *Syllabus of Modern Errors* of Pope Blessed Pius IX, A.D. 1864: Proposition declared in error

—"Right consists in physical fact; all the duties of men are an empty name, and all human deeds have the force of right."

All authority is from God. The exercise of that authority may not transgress the bounds observed by God Himself. In the flesh He came into the world to give testimony to the truth. The Son deferred to the Father. The Holy Ghost gives nothing but that given by the Son in obedience to the Father. The law as given by the Father, to its smallest letter, is fulfilled by the Son, not destroyed by Him, not changed by Him, not improved by Him, not evolved by Him, not superseded by Him, not ignored by Him, not contradicted by Him, not denied by Him, not updated by Him, not modernized by Him. The Son is the supreme lawgiver, and the law He gives and upholds is the immutable law of God the Father. The Father and the Son are one; the law they love is one. Those who claim to love the Father and the Son love that law.

Under the Son, obedient to the Father, men entrusted with rule on earth, either temporal or spiritual, exercise authority with the same freedom enjoyed by the Son. They are free to teach the law to the nations as witnessed by the Son. They are free to enforce the law as judged by the Son. They are free to forgive infractions against the law in keeping with the mercy of the Son. In short, they may know and proclaim the truth, and in that knowledge and proclamation, they are free.

A "right" to false worship is as nonsensical as asserting a "right" to theft. In the moral law, freedom and license are distinct. In the usage of English, "may" and "can" are distinct. In conscience, grace received and grace refused are distinct. No one is "free" to reject God anymore than one is "free" to commit grand theft auto—ask souls in hell or prisoners in the penitentiary if their acts manifest freedom. The power to do is not the same as permission to do— satan rebelled in fact and, by definition, in disobedience; he did not assert his freedom, but reduced his freedom to nothing. The citizen committing a crime, the soul committing a sin, the angel committing rebellion, forfeit their freedom.

At the same time, the police officer abetting a crime, the parent leaving a child unbaptized and in ignorance of the Faith, and the bishop placing the ways of the world over the rights of the Kingdom of Heaven are guilty of disobedience to the divine law. Remaining silent in the face of crime, refusing to adhere to the practice of the Faith in the home, or permitting the freedom and exaltation of Holy Mother Church to go undefended are to submit oneself and one's charges to the tyranny of mob rule, enslavement to sin, and imprisonment in the clutches of the devil. Government, families, and prelates are instituted by God to do battle against the world, the flesh, and satan. Infidelity to the mission of truth, sanctity, and humble assent to the will of God by nations, individuals, or hierarchs of the Church is damnable disobedience. To stand by while the Divine Majesty is offended is to be condemned to the same punishment meted out to those who actively revolt against the Lord of all creation.

No authority is given anyone on any level to impose personal whim on his subjects. Since it is from God that all authority derives, the Pope, the bishops, and the pastors of the Church, parents, and government officials, exercise their authority, not for their own sakes, but for the sake of giving God all glory. In this they imitate Christ, who Himself gave nothing of His own, but only that willed by His Father. The Father has all authority, bequeaths it to His Son, who, through the Holy Ghost, bestows it on those who believe in Him. Faith in Christ is shown in being obedient to the word of Christ as given by those who have themselves obediently received His word.

"Divine right" of kings separated from Christ *the* King is no more valid in a sovereign nation than in the Catholic Church. Secular rulers, be they legislators, executives, or courts may not create laws that break God's law. St. Peter teaches us that we must obey God above men. What the first Pope infallibly observed binds all of his successors. Neither may the prince of this world, nor princes in the world, nor the princes of the Church disregard the precepts binding on all men given by God in nature, revealed by God through the Prophets and Scriptures, and willed by God by the Church.

Thus the protestations of those who would embrace every single teaching of every single bishop because the bishop or the council or the pope propagated the teaching are not necessarily championing true justice. Nor is justice advanced by observing the travesties enacted by parliaments or enforced by heads of states or expanded by judicial fiat. One is bound in obedience, but that obedience belongs finally to God and must be in service to His truth. Obedience that does not serve truth is not of God and is therefore unjust. Bishops who demand obedience to themselves when they are disobedient to the truth, and thus to God, are doing injustice to their subjects. Secular authorities who mandate the protection of persons committing sins that cry to Heaven for vengeance call down the wrath of God on themselves and on their depraved subjects. The faithful who offer obedience without discerning it as being tributary to the truth suffer injustice for themselves, deprive their leaders of proper respect, and deny God His due. Obedience without truth is ultimately oppression.

Truth itself comes from God and is unchanging. Innovation can not be equated with ultimate truth. Truth is preserved and nurtured through tradition, that which is handed down to posterity having been firmly rooted in eternal truth. Without roots in eternal truth, tradition withers and becomes no more than personal whim. No one can be obliged to obedience based on whim, for arbitrary will is bound to the subjective nature of man without reference to God. Obedience is owed to God alone, and personal whim denies Him His due. Whim can not be a vehicle by which the faithful are confirmed in sanctity; no one is made holy by obeying caprice.

The faithful are called to make a permanent commitment of obedience to the truth; the truth to which they commit their obedience must be permanent.

Any demand of obedience based on whim, arbitrary will, caprice, innovation, or novelty is itself disobedience. Such things can not give God his own because they are not of God. They assert human will over divine will. Subjects of those in authority who seek novelty and newness for their own sakes participate not in the sanctifying of their lives, but in the injustice of rebellion against God. Proper authority seeks only to honor God, doing so by handing down only that which God has deigned to reveal as His will.

There is no obligation for the faithful of the Church or citizens of a state to obey anything that is not consonant with the tradition handed down by the will of God. Subjects need not justify disobeying novelties, rather, it is the innovators who must demonstrate that they are not introducing contradictions to tradition, either secular or ecclesial. It is not necessary for something to be bad for the faithful to balk at receiving it; all that is needed is for the innovation to be foreign to tradition and alien to the revealed Word and will of God. One would have an extraordinarily difficult time explaining how anything describable as an "innovation", "novelty", or "change" can be construed as consonant with immemorial, unchanging, divine Truth.

Obedience binds *only* to tradition in scripture, doctrine, and practice. If the faithful are presented with teachings, examples, or documents that do not reflect fidelity to God through the unchanging patrimony of the Church, then they are free to ignore the innovations. This holds whether the context of the innovation is in man's secular relations or within the workings of Holy Mother Church. Those who are so gifted may be obliged to present questions for clarification to those in authority. Any who are confused should not suffer any qualms about doing what the Church has always done, in all places, by all the faithful, of all times. What has always saved, will always save. Doubts arise only when deviations are offered in the place of definitions. When the shifting sands of time encroach, the faithful are always safe in planting their feet firmly on the solid rock of the timeless Faith.

For more than a half of a millennium, man has suffered from the ill effects of ignoring this truth. Where authority is abused, tyranny reigns. As men in authority wander further afield from seeking the Kingdom of God and His justice, the affects of their meanderings become ever more apparent in lawlessness. This is not a matter of law being renounced in principle. Rare are the times more subservient to the law than those in which respect for law wanes, as is the case today. The problem is not a lack of law, nor of laws being broken, nor of legal authority being rejected. Modernity, in both secular and ecclesial realms, suffers from too many laws, from conflicting laws, and from a bewildering array of jurisdictions interpreting laws. Hyper-legislation, regulation, and litigation are the marks of tyranny, not of a free society. The opposite of the rule of law is not only the lawlessness of anarchy, but also the lawlessness of the *over* rule of law. Sanctity produces fewer laws. Sinfulness produces the police state. Suburban charity would be more at home in a prison cell than in a monk's cell.

The project of re-establishing Christendom is an effort that requires a sober appraisal of the mess that confronts us. Beyond that and more important is the obligation to be mindful of the theological virtues. The *Faith* that gives us confidence in the power of Christ and Him crucified, able to overcome the world and to set us free from the power of the world, the flesh, and the devil. The *Hope* that sustains the faithful in all times and places is that he who trusts in the Lord will never be confounded. This Hope produces a willingness to lose all—wealth, family, life itself—so long as a place in Heaven is obtained thereby. The *Charity* that comes from God, is manifested on the Cross, and compels the labors of the Church to bring all men through the power of the Holy Ghost into the sheepfold of Christ to the glory of God the Father. Amen!

What Was, Is, and Never Should Have Been

The idols of the gentiles are silver and gold, the work of men's hands. They have a mouth, but they speak not. They have eyes, but they see not. They have ears, but they hear not. Neither is there any breath in their mouths. Let them that make them be like to them, and every one that trusteth in them.—Psalm 134:15-18

Our antecedents in the economy of salvation do not comprise a golden age of fidelity, courage, and nobility. Contemplating this is a sobering thought when one realizes as well that we have in many ways declined from the days of old. Still more disturbing is the consideration of what such a state of affairs bodes for the future. The example of Our Lord, Our Lady, and the saints of the Church offer hope to the fallen, but honesty demands as well the admission that the majority of men given those wonderful models availed themselves not of the good that was available. Examining our own consciences, individually and collectively, will result in the confession that we most often resemble not the extraordinary few who sought and attained perfection, but the ordinary many who denied perfection's existence or ignored its summons to sanctity.

Adam and Eve made a god of their desire to eat that which was pleasing to see, to know that which was forbidden, and to obtain divinity for themselves at the behest of a liar accusing the true God, the God who is Truth, of lying. The ancient pagans, before and after Abraham, made gods of their bellies and whatever other parts of their bodies voiced loud demands. Abraham's descendants, the Jews, made gods of golden calves, of demons that ate babies, and of the law that was intended to bring them closer to the Lawgiver Himself, God. Men of every age have woven from whole cloth notions of the divine based on rejecting the truth of Christ, reflecting the politics of a particular epoch in history, or attached to the persona of a single man whose teachings and worship died with him. The love of money, St. Paul tells us, is the root of all evil, and the love of money has moved the hearts of sons to patricide, prompted nations to commit genocide, and resulted, on one notable occasion, in deicide. On American money is the famous quote, ironically rooted in Holy Scripture, "In God We Trust"; begging the question of whether the statement is referent to the divine or is a proclamation of faith writ upon the very object of faith. Passing rare are the men and nations willing to spend all—time, money, life—in the effort to render God his due and thereby receive a due reward from God.

Men must have worship or go mad. There is a peril in this part of our nature in that false worship leads to madness as well. Man without the divine falls lower than the beasts. his heart will be of stone. His mind will become a desert. His world will increasingly be a place filled with despair at the prospect that there is nothing but the world, nothing beyond the world, nothing better than the world, nothing for which the world was made, nothing but nothing. Men who believe in nothing, that is, men who place their trust in anything other than the true God, will countenance consuming other men (for instance, in the medicines derived from fetal tissue), killing their own children (in the name of mercy, convenience, or scientific "progress"), or enslaving men in the industry of manufacturing death (birth control pills, nuclear weapons, and hospitals with euthanasia policies come to mind). Civilization depends on the true Faith in the true God. Absent that truth, barbarism will rain terror on the weak, the enemy, the friend, the family, the self.

True worship of God allows man from his knees in awe, humility, and love, to aspire beyond himself, raised by the divine mercy to legitimately lay claim to a share in the divine stature. Proud man, ignorant man, deceived man reduced to the worship of creatures is stunted, diminished by the effort to stoop below himself to be united to that which is beneath him. Worshipping man does men no good, for it is beneath human dignity to mistake the image of God for God Himself. But the man of God knows that he bears the image of God, that he has heard the Word of God, that he can see God in authentic worship, that he can taste God therein, and that God wills him to be His son and to imitate Him in charity, sanctity, and perfection. God became man that man might become God; and men who do not make their own gods will be made divine by God.

Knowing who God is guarantees a rule of law founded on justice and capable of mercy; the laws by which men are governed reveal the divine source, or lack thereof, of the laws. When law derives from individual men, the point of a gun, or the balance in a checking account, be sure that injustice reigns over all. Likewise, do not seek justice in a land where the lawgiver is worshipped in wood, stone, or gold—be they wampum, statues, or traded in a commodity exchange. Gods made from men, from force, from building materials, or from money can not produce or preserve a healthy, happy, holy society. Paper gods are no improvement.

The paper to which reference is here made is not the brightly colored swaths on which a large variety of masonic, read demonic, symbols are depicted with which worship is conducted at various cathedrals of mammon present in every city from coast to coast. Paper in this context is another display of masonic, read demonic, influence on the world bereft of Jesus Christ and His Body, the Catholic Church. At Philadelphia in 1789, at San Francisco in 1945, and at Brussels in 2004, documents on paper were fashioned to serve as the gods ruling the lives of billions of men. These pieces of paper were invested with authority, power, and absolute sovereignty over individuals, families, and even nations. Principles present in the universe, found solely in ink on paper, lacking any reference to absolute truth, objective reality, or the true God, govern the daily affairs of the world's teeming masses without any higher authority to which to appeal against the injustices thus wrought, absent any immutable means to interpret the meanings of the words expressed by the dead or dying men who crafted the new gods, and in denial—often violently—of any right, rule, or reign other than that effected by the unthought rendered in blue-black dye across a surface of decaying tree pulp.

False gods wrought in the image and likeness of their worshippers are no better than their makers. The makers of false gods can not be made better by worshipping their falsity. Gods so created are neither divine nor human, but misshapen, misbegotten, misnamed fonts of lies. The ultimate source of false gods is satan in hell. The ultimate destination of the men foolish enough to place their trust in false gods is to place themselves under the rule of satan in hell. Before this life ends and perdition begins, the worshippers of false gods bring a little bit of hell to the experience of all on earth. Lies, injustice, and oppression—the eternal state of hell—become under the regime paying homage to false gods the policy of nations and the state of human being within them. Man making gods descends into inhumanity, failing both at making real gods and at making a world fit for man. If one makes a false god, one will become what one has made: absolutely untrue, wholly wrong, forever impotent. Or in the words of King David, deaf, dumb, blind, unfeeling, and dead, fit for nothing but burning, like so much paper. The fires of hell blaze amazingly hot from all of the wooden idols cast into the flames; imagine how much hotter will be the conflagration when the billions of reams of modern gods are added to the furnace!

Among the first of the pantheon of perdition to be immolated should be the one ratified by the United States of America in 1789. The anthem to anarchy which is the American Constitution is a false god that obediently decrees the nothing desired by its makers: nothing of obedience to the true God, nothing other than the whims of the men who wield actual power, nothing capable of effecting true happiness for the unhappy men doomed to live under its thralldom. Certainly one of the great tragedies resulting from that travesty against justice which is the governing document of this nation, is the fact that so many of our benighted citizens are convinced that the injustices caused by the use of this Constitution can be remedied by the Constitution. This is simply impossible, given the fact that the men who interpret the Constitution are insistent on creating positive law out of whole cloth, applying the law in self-contradictory ways, and interpreting the Constitution in light of elements completely absent from the Constitution.

For instance, one may read the Constitution paragraph by paragraph, from Preamble to the 27th Amendment, translated into any of seventy-two languages, backwards and upside-down and standing on one's head, and one will find absolutely nothing instructing the government to be hostile to the Church. Words to that effect simply do not appear in the document. However, beginning with Thomas Jefferson, hallucinators have perceived in the Constitution a *high wall* between the Church and the state, they have discerned a prohibition from uttering the very word *God* in public schools, they have beheld a national interest in questioning whether or not a man of the Faith is fit to serve as a Supreme Court Justice, a Cabinet Secretary, or President of the United States. A cleric uttering opinions on electoral matters from his pulpit will call down the wrath of the government, which will promptly destroy that cleric's legal status within a recognized church, subjecting him to ruinous taxation and the probable dissolution of his apostolate (that is, if said cleric is pusillanimous enough to believe his ministry is dependent on the provision of the almighty dollar rather than on the providence of almighty God).

While one is vainly searching the Constitution for the words "separation of church and state", one will not be distracted by allusions to or definitions of powers possessed by the federal government to coerce the various states to remain within the Union. The Constitution is not cluttered with references to a taxing authority that results in financial penalties levied against states seeking independence from Washington, d.c. None of the austere majesty of the framers' original language is obscured by untidy details of how one or more of the three branches of the federal government is empowered to imprison state legislators or executives should any of them be so bold as to declare a sovereign state free of the tyranny wielded by the denizens infesting the masonic metropolis on the Potomac between Maryland and Virginia. Even though Abraham Lincoln managed to do so, ordinary citizens endowed with normal powers of perception are entirely incapable of locating within the text of the Constitution any delineation of powers proper to the federal government as a whole, or the executive in particular, permitting the use of live ammunition against citizens guilty of the imagined felony of wishing to imitate the founders' love of freedom by divesting themselves of an odious overlord. One is able, however, to read in the Constitution a clear description of how human chattel are to be treated under the laws of the nation; the definitive statement that powers not explicitly given to the federal government are reserved to the states and/or individuals; and that the Establishment Clause specifically limits *federal* actions, not states' or individuals'.

This proclivity to see that which is invisible and to overlook that which is obvious extends to a Constitutional issue of more modern import. *Insane* would be among the adjectives (along with *dishonest*, *demonic*, and *disgusting*) appropriate to attach to the attempt to suggest that the framers of the Constitution envisioned infanticide as one of the rights threatened by George iii for which the new document was the proper guarantor. Murdering babies, either in utero or during or shortly after birth, was decidedly not a desire expressed by any of the persons responsible for establishing the governing structures of this nation. To the extent that property rights are recognized by the Constitution—and the 2005 Supreme Court decision in the case of *Kelo et al v. City of New London* calls into question whether or not the government does recognize the existence of private property—it is surely not the case that the framers thought that the exercise of property rights included the right to commit murder, nor that the rights could be construed as to mean that unborn human beings could be defined as property, nor that the right to own human beings could be denied without recourse to Civil War—oops!

Here is seen how the hallucinations involved in constitutional law lead to the depravity and insanity of the modern world. A nation without a professed belief in God need not believe in His prohibition of murder. A nation without a professed belief in God need not believe that it is bound by the same rules which it asserts must be obeyed by other sovereign nations. A nation without a professed belief in God can term one set of human beings property, another set free, and use force to prevent the protection of human beings who are in peril of being destroyed as property, and use force also to confiscate the property of subjects acting within the law to protect their property rights from usurpation by the federal government acting outside of the bounds of constitutional law. One need not make sense when one denies the very Author of reason, but neither should anyone who agrees to place power in the hands of such men expect justice, security, or reasonability in government or public life.

A nation without a professed belief in God will say that human beings may be owned, then that human beings may not be owned, then that human beings may be owned again. Owned human beings may be killed without due process of law, owned human beings may be freed from their servitude by the denial of laws which made their servitude legal, owned human beings may be killed while others, seeking to save them, may be prosecuted under law for their efforts. The President may cite partisans of an unapologetically religious bent advocating force against other citizens in his effort to enforce the freeing of legally held human property, descending to butchering citizens by the tens of thousands in order to effect his will; but citizens who peaceably invoke the protection of the Mother of God for the children of God in peril of being murdered in their mothers' wombs are descended upon by the subordinates of the Chief Executive in the name of protecting other citizens' "right" to dispose of human property under cover of a phantom principle pretended to be in the Constitution. This nation was established with the explicit right of citizens to hold other human beings as property. This nation was almost obliterated by the struggle to deny that right, and this nation now demands the right of citizens to murder human beings declared property under law. The Constitution has been invoked—by Congress, by the Supreme Court, and by the President—to assert, enforce, and impose each of those positions.

All of those positions can not be right. The Constitution which is used to support each of these positions can not be entirely right. However one determines the rightness or wrongness of those positions and the Constitution, the measure must be something other than, higher than, better than the Constitution. Among the citizens subject to the Constitution is not the best place to seek a judge of the Constitution, seeing that they are the ones who made the Constitution, with all of its flaws and self-contradictions in the first place. Beyond that fact is the fact that the citizens are the subjects, not the judges of the Constitution. Adding to the difficulty is the fact that the judges of the Constitution in the courts are themselves taken from the citizenry, appointed by executives taken from the citizenry, and confirmed by legislators taken from—and all answerable to—the citizenry. The citizens made the Constitution, the citizens must obey the Constitution, the Constitution is authoritatively interpreted by persons put in place by the citizens, those interpreters may be removed by the citizens at will, making the citizens the judges of the judges of the Constitution which is meant to stand as judge over the operations of the nation. Who is in charge when everyone is in charge? No one! Hence, the statement earlier that the Constitution is an anthem to anarchy.

It is profoundly to be hoped that a Catholic reading this would, out of an authentic *sensus Catholicus,* protest, "Well, of course, the Church is the corrective to this abysmal state of affairs." Profoundly to be hoped as well is that no Catholic with an authentic *sensus Catholicus* is unaware that obedience to the separation of Church and state is not very much in evidence in the modern structures and statements of the visible Church. Within the Church, the state's desire for a divorce is granted by way of members of the Church behaving, not as men of the Faith, but as men of the world. Paradoxically, the closer churchmen come to the world, the greater is the divide between the state and the Church, precisely the evil intended by the masons. Where men of the Church parrot the truisms of false worship, demanding religious liberty, separation of the state from the Church, and the brotherhood of man devoid of a relationship to the Son of God, there is less and less influence of grace on the workings of the world, and more and more insistence on moral license, moral depravity, and moral destruction. Satan and his masonic minions have discovered that the best way to separate the state from the Church is to co-opt the men of the Church into the ways of the world, familiarity of the members of the Church with the world thus breeding contempt within those members of the Church for the Church, esteeming the world all along.

So, the men of the Church allying themselves with the men of the world, the flesh, and satan, succumb in like manner to the affliction of seeing things that are not there and being blind to reality and to truth. Such churchmen see resemblances between Catholicism and the enemies of the Faith, which prompted our Savior to warn them, "I never knew you! Depart from me, you that work iniquity!" These blind guides somehow can see truth in denials of the Truth by them who adhere to the errors of Mahomet, the Talmud, or the Declaration of the Rights of Man. But they are powerless to see the sense of the Word of God proclaiming, "I am the Truth!" or his Apostle declaring, "What concourse hath Christ with Belial?" or His Vicar commanding "That in all things God may be honored through Jesus Christ, to whom is glory and empire forever and ever, amen!"

In the spirit of the age, the defenders of Vatican II advance its spirit. They enjoin the members of the Church to join the world in joy and hope. Dignity in worship is tenuous, but the dignity of humanity is sacrosanct, regardless of the indignities perpetrated against men of the Faith, the laws of the Faith, or the object of the Faith, Jesus Christ. Our age is one in which the light of men is diminished in its power to be certain of the truth of the Word of God. The Pastoral Council claims as its Flock all of mankind in the spirit of brotherhood without reference to God the Son, and obliges none of mankind to be made part of the Flock in the power of the Holy Spirit and water making men sons of God in the Body of Christ, the Church. There exists a right to disbelieve in the Church, even though its unity, sanctity, catholicity, and apostolicity are articles of the only faith that saves. The members of the Church who hold this mindset would have the whole Church refuse to assert her right to teach all nations and Baptize them in the name of the Father, and of the Son, and of the Holy Ghost.

Because of this spirit omnipresent in the texts of the documents of Vatican II, in the minds of the prelates authoritatively interpreting Vatican II, and the loyal adherents to Vatican II among the laity, immemorial rites, doctrines, and practices of the Church are called into question. There is felt a need to apologize for actions by faithful sons of the Church from the past. At present there is but an apologetic admission of the legitimacy of the claims of the Church to be the repository of authority to teach the Gospel to all the world. Appeals are made at the very highest levels of the Church to the work and policies of masonic institutions as the sole and best means to peace in the world. Princes of the Church publicly pray with heretics, make concessions to the unreasonable and unjust demands of schismatics, and invoke the false gods of false religions. And all the while, many otherwise well-meaning Catholics refuse to see the extent of the damage caused by this sorry state of affairs, or to admit their own complicity in it by making excuses for the inexcusable, or to realize that where they attack the loyal sons of the Church who rise to her defense against lies and calumny, they are making themselves enemies of the Church, of truth, of Our Lord and Savior Jesus Christ.

No one is a friend of the Church, of the truth, or of Our Lord and Savior Jesus Christ who is able to construe the meaning of *Sacrosanctum concilium* to require the composition of a new Mass. That document did in no way mandate a vernacular Mass. There is no obligation by the Church or her faithful contained in the first of the texts from Vatican ii to believe that *Quo primum* is abrogated, that the immemorial Mass is no longer the Roman rite, or that any rite other than the Latin rite codified at Trent, ratified by Pope St. Gregory the Great, and descended from Apostolic usage binds the faithful or must be celebrated by the clergy. *Sacrosanctum concilium* does not say these things, nor do any of the succeeding fifteen documents from the 2nd Vatican Council. Anyone who says otherwise is either illiterate, mentally deficient, or a liar. The possibility also exists that such an assertion stems from the ignorance rooted in the failure to actually read the documents of the 2nd Vatican Council which supposedly give rise to the spirit of that Council. However one comes to such erroneous conclusions, one can blame one's own inadequacy, the brazen disobedience so in evidence after the Council, or the woeful combination of human sin in tandem with satanic rebellion; but one can not blame the Council itself—except insofar as the Council fathers irresponsibly failed to anathematize any who would so rashly undermine the *sensus fidei* and endeavor to redirect the *sensus fidelium* into paths of the world demonstrably in error and at odds with the truth of Christ in the Church of Christ.

Outside of the Church of Christ there is no salvation. Vatican II, for all its legion flaws, did not deny this. Nothing in the 1962-1965 Council condemns the Catholic who adheres to the teaching of Pope Leo iii and the 1215 statement of the Fourth Lateran Council, "There is but one universal Church of the faithful, outside of which no one at all is saved." At the end of the twentieth century, the Church did not forbid belief in what she believed at the beginning of the fourteenth century, when she infallibly taught through Pope Boniface viii's Bull, *Unam Sanctam,* "We declare, say, define, and pronounce that it is absolutely necessary for the salvation of every human creature to be subject to the Roman Pontiff." The Roman Pontiff on the papal throne in 1441, Eugene IV, echoed this truth in his Bull, *Cantate Domino*, saying, "The most Holy Roman Church firmly believes, professes, and preaches that none of those existing outside the Catholic Church, not only pagans, but also Jews and heretics and schismatics, can have a share in life eternal; but that they will go into the eternal fire which was prepared for the devil and his angels, unless before death they are joined with her; and that so important is the unity of this ecclesiastical body that only those remaining within this unity can profit by the Sacraments of the Church unto salvation, and they alone can receive an eternal recompense for their fasts, their almsgivings, their other works of Christian piety, and the duties of a Christian soldier. No one, let his almsgiving be as great as it may, no one, even if he pour out his blood for the Name of Christ, can be saved, unless he remain within the bosom and the unity of the Catholic Church." No more did Vatican ii warn the faithful against those earlier Vicars of Christ in this dogmatic teaching than they themselves departed from the very first Vicar of Christ, Pope St. Peter, who insisted that Jesus Christ is "the stone which was rejected by you the builders, which is become the head of the corner; neither is there salvation in any other; for there is no other Name under Heaven given to men, whereby we must be saved."

This divine Savior is the Head of which the Catholic Church is His One, Holy, and Apostolic Body. Any separated from the Body are separated from the Head. No one loves the Head who does not love the Body. Vatican II said nothing to render this truth false. Still operative at the time of the Council was the Oath Against Modernism, taken by every successor of the Apostles present at Vatican

11. Also still in force was the Creed of the Council of Trent, to which all repenting schismatics and heretics had to agree before being readmitted to the life of grace they forfeited after Baptism. The Oath Against Modernism says in part,

> "...Thirdly, I believe with equally firm faith that the Church, the guardian and teacher of the revealed word, was personally instituted by the real and historical Christ, when He lived among us, and that the Church was built upon Peter, the prince of the apostolic hierarchy, and his successors for the duration of time. Fourthly, I sincerely hold that the doctrine of faith was handed down to us from the Apostles through the orthodox Fathers in exactly the same meaning and always in the same purport. Therefore, I entirely reject the heretical misrepresentation that dogmas evolve and change from one meaning to another different from the one which the Church held previously. I also condemn every error according to which, in place of the divine deposit which has been given the Spouse of Christ to be carefully guarded by her, there is put a philosophical figment or product of a human conscience that has gradually been developed by human effort and will continue to develop indefinitely... I also condemn and reject the opinion of those who say that a well-educated Christian assumes a dual personality—that of a believer and at the same time of a historian; as if it were permissible for a historian to hold things that contradict the faith of the believer, or to establish premises which, provided there be no direct denial of dogmas, would lead to the conclusion that dogmas are either false or doubtful...I firmly hold, then, and shall hold to my dying breath, the belief of the Fathers in the charism of truth, which certainly is, was, and always will be in the succession of the episcopacy from the Apostles. The purpose of that is, then, not that dogma may be tailored according to what seems better and more suited to the culture of each age; rather, that the absolute and immutable truth preached by the Apostles from the beginning may never be believed to be different, may never be understood in any other way.

> I promise that I shall keep all these articles faithfully, entirely, and sincerely, and guard them inviolate, in no way deviating from them in teaching or in any way in word or in writing. Thus I promise, thus I swear, so help me God.

This vow is very much in keeping with the Creed assigned by Trent to those professing faith in Christ and His Church, saying in part,

> I resolutely accept and embrace the apostolic and ecclesiastical traditions and the other practices and regulations of the same Church. In like manner I accept Sacred Scripture according to the meaning which has been held by Holy Mother Church and to which she now holds. It is her prerogative to pass judgement on the true meaning and interpretation of Sacred Scripture. And I will never accept or interpret it in a manner different from the unanimous agreement of the Fathers.
>
> I also acknowledge that there are truly and properly seven Sacraments of the New Law, instituted by Jesus Christ Our Lord, and that they are necessary for the salvation of the human race, although it is not necessary for each individual to receive them all. I acknowledge that the seven Sacraments are: Baptism, Confirmation, Eucharist, Penance, Extreme Unction, Holy Orders, and Matrimony; and that they confer grace; and that of the seven, Baptism, Confirmation, and Holy Orders can not be repeated without committing a sacrilege. I also accept and acknowledge the customary and approved rites of the Catholic Church in the solemn administration of these Sacraments. I embrace and accept each and every article on original sin and justification declared and defined in the most holy Council of Trent…
>
> I acknowledge the holy, Catholic, and apostolic Roman Church as the Mother and Teacher of all churches; and I promise and swear true obedience to the Roman Pontiff, Vicar of Christ and successor of Blessed Peter, Prince of the Apostles.
>
> I unhesitatingly accept and profess all the doctrines, especially those concerning the primacy of the Roman Pontiff

> and his infallible teaching authority, handed down, defined, and explained by the sacred canons and ecumenical councils and especially those of the most holy Council of Trent and of the ecumenical Vatican Council. And at the same time I condemn, reject, and anathematize everything that is contrary to those propositions that have been condemned, rejected and anathematized by the Church. I, N., promise, vow, and swear that, with God's help, I shall most constantly hold and profess this true Catholic Faith, outside which no one can be saved and which I now freely profess and truly hold. With the help of God, I shall profess it whole and unblemished to my dying breath; and to the best of my ability, I shall see to it that my subjects or those entrusted to me by virtue of my state in life shall hold it, teach it, and preach it. So help me God and His holy Gospel.

Oaths worded in this spirit do not admit of easy denial. It is the sense of the Church that a vow thus made is binding unto death. The letter and the spirit of these oaths were still in force throughout the entirety of the Second Vatican Council. When one endeavors to make sense of the conciliar documents on religious liberty, the Constitution of the Church and the World, and the Dogmatic Constitution on the Church regarding the identity, mission, and nature of the Body of Christ, it is imperative, obligatory, of the Faith that one does so reaching no conclusion other than that the Mystical Body of Christ is the Catholic Church, beneath the successor to Peter, the Pope, and membership in which is absolutely necessary for salvation. Variant interpretations, ambiguous verbs, and philosophical obfuscations must give pride of place to clarity. The Mystical Body of Christ and the Catholic Church beneath the Pope are identical, to say one is to say the other, to say anything other is to deny this truth. Unless one is in communion with the Body of Christ under the Pope at the moment of one's death, one is damned forever. Good manners, prudence, and charity demand that one assumes that the fathers at Vatican ii understood this, believed this, and meant to teach this. Those who teach otherwise in the name of the Council fathers, if incorrect in their estimation of the Council fathers' fidelity, are guilty of a serious sin of slanderous dishonesty. Those who teach otherwise in the name of the Council fathers, if correct in their estimation of the Council fathers' infidelity, must admit that the fathers violated their solemn oath, that they taught error, and that they are not to be followed or obeyed in their error.

When Cowardice is king

Bullies on playgrounds and overindulgent grandmothers share a common trait: they make it difficult for the boy to grow up. The bully does not want the boy to grow up, because the grown man beats up bullies. Overindulgent grandmothers do not want the boy to grow up, because property-owning husbands and fathers will look elsewhere than cookies, hugs, and pinched cheeks to satisfy their needs. Some boys do not wish to grow up because they are afraid of bloody noses or frightened by the prospect of long nights of worry about providing for the family. Good boys look forward to overcoming the bully and outgrowing the desire to be spoiled, because it offers the opportunity to put might in the service of right, and to make a return to the past for the future good being made in the present. Bad boys never get over their fears of bullies or their attachment to grandmothers' apron strings. A real man thanks the bully for being part of what made him stronger, and thanks the grandmother for providing the good times that must, and have, come to an end to make way for yet better times.

Cowardly men afraid of bullies recoil at the prospect of imitating the manly resistance mounted by the early settlers of the frontier at the western reaches of the newly founded United States. Men such as Shay and Bradford took up arms against overweening governments, both state and national. Unequal taxation, prosecution for crimes at far removes from the residences of the accused, and lack of representation of taxpayers in the electoral process were hallmarks of the governments administered by the two men named George on either side of the Atlantic Ocean at the end of the eighteenth century, George of the house of Hanover in London and George Washington in New York. Where George III of Great Britain was branded a tyrant for such policies, George Washington is venerated as the Father of the United States. Revolution against the sovereign Crown of Britain is a badge of honor borne by the men led by Washington the revolutionary from 1776 until 1781. George Washington the President pursued as treasonous felons the men who resisted him in arms from the mid 1780s until the early 1790s. The first and last sitting President of the United States to lead men in battle wielded force against his fellow citizens asserting the same rights that Washington himself championed in his cause against his rightful king. Washington not only set the precedent by which later presidents limited themselves to two terms in office, but also established the principle of using the armed force of the federal government against American citizens repeated by Lincoln in the nineteenth century, by Roosevelt in the middle of the twentieth century against the citizens of Japanese descent, and by Clinton at the end of the twentieth century at Ruby Ridge, Idaho, and at Waco, Texas.

It is the shame of cowards to yield to the claims of might as right. Apologists for America, right or wrong, cowardly assert that abuses of governmental power, by officials of the United States, are always expressions of liberty and justice. They would have all citizens forget the example offered by innumerable heroes throughout American history who resisted the injustices cloaked by assertions of legal authority, constitutional allowance, or political expediency. A government founded in the wake of armed rebellion should not be surprised that the citizens who own such as a birthright might find cause to take up arms against the descendants of the rebellion. Cowardice rather than inherent error forbids the examination of the possibility that armed resistance might be appropriate in some cases, even used against the instruments and officials of a sovereign government. Even when that government is defined as being "we the people".

Oftimes it is the case that mere bullets and explosives provide insufficient firepower. When that is the reality confronting the man of honor, he must bring out the big guns. This usually means fighting courageously by doing *nothing.* Not the nothing in evidence when cowards lament wrongs in which they are participating because they are told the law requires them to do so. Not the nothing of making excuses for the abuses of power by the men in charge based on the fact that they are the men in charge and they have power, so they are excused by their craven subjects begging pardon for not being properly subservient. Not the nothing of attacking other victims of the bully state who have decided to stand up to the bully—and to the allies of the bully evolving from victims into bullies in their own right. No, there are far better ways for doing nothing than these.

For instance, there is the story of the nothing done by Saint Maurice and his companions. "[He] was the commander of a legion in the Roman Army called the Theban Legion, because it had been recruited in the Thebaid in upper Egypt. This legion was composed of 6,666 men, every one of whom was a Catholic. They were noble, holy and devout soldiers. They were ordered by the Roman Emperor Maximian to sacrifice to pagan gods. They all refused. The Emperor first killed every tenth man. But still the legion would not give in. Again, he killed every tenth man. But the valiant regiment held out. Finally, when asked once more to sacrifice to the gods, Maurice in the name of his soldiers, replied, 'O Caesar, we are your soldiers. But we are also the soldiers of Jesus Christ. From you, we receive our pay. But from Him, we receive eternal life. To you, we owe service. But to Him, we owe obedience. We are ready to follow you against the barbarians, but we are also ready to suffer death rather than renounce our faith.' They were then all slaughtered. Saint Maurice knelt down and was beheaded" (from the website of Saint Benedict Center, Richmond, New Hampshire, www.catholicism.org).

Nothing also was done by Saint Thomas More when confronted with the ill will of his benefactor, King Henry viii of England. Commanded by the king to urge his suit to divorce Queen Catherine, the Chancellor of the Realm, Lord Thomas, did nothing. Ordered to take the loyalty oath imposed on the Catholic citizens of the nation in which the primacy of the papacy was denied, Sir Thomas the nobleman did nothing. Beseeched by wife, family, and friends to refrain from resisting the royal schism, the man of integrity, Thomas More, did nothing. Led to the gibbet by force of an unjust decree of death, Saint Thomas did nothing, except stretch his neck, forgive his tormentors, and obey almighty God.

Of course, history has never seen such a spectacle of heroically doing nothing as was displayed in the Praetorium, along the *Via Dolorosa*, and on Calvary. Caesar sentenced God to death, and Jesus said nothing in His defense. The chosen people of God spat on the face of God, and Jesus offered nothing of resistance to their hatred. The King and Queen of Heaven and earth suffered excruciating punishment for their blaspheming subjects, and they held nothing back of mercy, forbearance, and love. Theirs is the model for all true subjects of earthly kings and faithful children of Holy Mother Church.

Compare the nothing employed by the Theban Legion, St. Thomas More, and the Son of God and His Mother, with the nothing done to end abortion by supposedly pro-life politicians in legislative and executive branches at both the state and federal levels. Not all nothings are created equal. When a saint utilizes the weakness of God and seemingly does nothing in the face of his persecutors, Heaven is moved to move men of the earth to the Faith. Whole families, cities, and nations have thus been won for the true Church by the blood of the martyrs. When men of the world plead worldly prudence, or faith in a paper god, or hope that the ways of tyrants will change given enough time and patience, in the name of love of country, death comes to bodies and souls and their efforts to accomplish justice without condemning the perpetrators of injustice come to nothing. The power of God creates all from nothing, but the powers of the world bring themselves, their slaves, and their works to nothing. Cooperating with evil is no way to end evil, doing less evil than one's neighbor will not end evil, being afraid to be good abets evil. The only means to destroy evil is to have nothing to do with it and to do nothing but good.

In the context of modern America, this means denouncing all political parties and candidates that in any way whatsoever allow for the commission of murder under cover of constitutional law. Good people will not permit bad people to sully their homes with the sound of foul opinions advocating the "rights" of baby killers, abominators, and home wreckers. None but a fool would offer money to one's oppressors for the sake of financing further oppression, thus decent folk will not fund indecent fiends marketing immodesty, inculcating indifference to God, and calumniating Catholicism. Standing up to the bully that is the modern world means being unafraid of being unpopular, risking material dearth, enduring political marginalization, physical attack, *and even being called names.*

New heroes of the Faith will need to take stock of the fact that *absolutely all of the world's governments since the revolting protestants, opportunistic politicians, and faithless Catholics destroyed Christendom have predicated their laws on a denial of God and His Church.* When coming to grips with what is left for a man of the Faith to embrace in modern society, the inescapable conclusion he must reach is nothing. Salvation is not to be had from the mores of the world, nor from the size of one's stock portfolio, nor from the most recent version of tyranny posing as democracy, nor from religions confessing belief that God does not know what truth is, nor from going along to get along. Salvation comes from adhering to nothing but the Catholic Faith, from doing nothing but imitating the example of Our Lord and Our Lady, and desiring nothing but to love God the Father with one's whole heart, whole soul, whole mind, whole strength, and one's neighbor as one's self for the sake of divine charity. Nothing else is enough. We must give to the world nothing but the conviction that we owe God our all.

All that we have to give God that He finds acceptable is what He has given us in the first place. It is not that we have loved God, but that He has first loved us. We did not choose Christ, but He has chosen us. The love and election of the Lord is manifested in the deposit of the faith taught by Jesus, guaranteed by the Holy Ghost, recorded in Sacred Scriptures, transmitted through the Apostles, preserved in Church tradition, authoritatively interpreted by the magisterium, and given flesh in the lives of the faithful. This deposit is not some of these things, nor most of these things, nor any of these things that suits an individual's fancy. To love the Lord our God with our whole heart, whole soul, whole mind, and whole strength means to love the whole of the body of truth He has given us in each and every way He has revealed His will throughout history. Love of God with the whole of one's being will be expressed in freely assenting to the truth as authentically taught by the Church *and* in bringing that truth to bear in one's activities in the world.

Surely the first to believe and accept this approach to our faith must be the shepherds of Our Lord's flock, the Pope and the bishops in union with him. Alas! such is not always the case. All too often the Church has seen the spectacle of wayward shepherds joining their wayward flocks in waywardness. This is a matter of the blind leading the blind. More absurd, and yet more tragic, is the phenomenon of injustice wherein the sighted allow themselves to be led by the blind. It is the singular shame of the Church during the era since the protestant revolt, slowly at first but now with alarming abandon, to have her sons within the hierarchy acquiescing to the world in matters of finance, mimicking the laity in matters of morality, imitating despotic kings in their notions of rule, accepting the doubts of science applied to the Faith, and forgetting that attaining the Kingdom of Heaven is the one task of the Church, prelates, priests, and people alike. This writer once wrote:

> Bishops are taken to task on a regular basis for their various shortcomings, imagined or real. This has been true in the Church since St. Paul had to remind St. Peter of orthodox teaching concerning dietary practices. Good bishops respond to corrections, either from their brothers in the episcopate or from members of the flock, with humility and, when warranted, with contrition. Bad bishops respond with rationalizations, obfuscation, and legalese. St. Peter modeled the proper contrition of a good bishop. The English hierarchy at the time of Henry VIII, excepting St. John Fisher, saved their miters, if not their souls. That is not the goal of a good bishop of the Roman Catholic Church, but, in their cases, being Roman Catholic was a temporary condition.
>
> It is a common fallacy to attribute the infallibility and indefectibility of the Church (and the offices by which dogma is guarded and propagated) to the persons of the men who hold

magisterial positions. The fractured logic runs something to the effect that if the Church is perfect and indefectible in all her teaching, then the men who lead her must as well be without flaw in their intent and impeccable in the execution of their duties. Such a mistaken understanding stands the colloquial GIGO principle (Garbage In, Garbage Out) on its head, producing the POPES principle: "Peter's Office Produces Errorless Shepherds", as if merely donning the papal tiara affects the man who is Pope in such wise that nothing he says or does is capable of denying the font of authority symbolized by the crown (a crown now lamentably on display in a museum, rather than gracing the pontifical pate).

It must be mentioned, as well, that the converse of this flawed mindset is equally false. Petrine authority does not effect impeccability in the person of the Pope, nor do the Pope's human frailties translate into a diminishment of the papacy. The majesty of the Vicar of Christ is not dependent on the occupant of the throne; occupying the throne does not confer upon its holder personal sanctity or inability to sin. The man who is Pope sacrifices much, but not his free will.

Properly understood, the relationship of office to man is one in which the man must conform to his office, which is itself a gift in conformity with divine providence. The papacy does not bend to the Pope, but the Pope must bow to the immemorial deposit of truth endowed and entrusted to the papacy. Insofar as he does this, the Pope exercises infallibility. Where he fails at this, the Pope is reduced to being a noisy gong, a clanging cymbal, profiting nothing and being nothing, profiting no one and harming each one. Truth and the papacy remain, a Pope's waywardness, willfulness, or even wantonness notwithstanding.

Infallibility attaches not to *papal* teaching but to papal *teachings.* It is not the action of the Pope speaking which is infallible, but the content of the truth propounded which is without possibility of error. Only the Pope may so propound an infallible truth, but a Pope's propounding can not make an error true. Infallibility rests less in the sounds that come from the mouth than in the reflected sheen from the eternal Word living in the heart of the papacy at the heart of the Church. It is profoundly to be hoped that the heart of the Pope welcomes the divine light to make His home in him.

This writer was asked to rethink something preached in a recent homily. At that time he referred to the current crisis in the Church as, "a crisis not of leadership, but of 'followship'." Others suggested that such is not the case. It is, these gentle critics insisted, bishops and the Pope refusing to lead or leading ineluctably astray that has resulted in the shipwreck experienced since Vatican II. Our hierarchy can not be excused for following the flock, for in so doing they lead the flock to disaster. Their fault is not in being over-willing to cultivate public opinion, but in being too willing to eschew, silence, and resist their role as shepherds, teachers, and fathers.

None of this runs counter to the statement from the sermon in question. Indeed, seeking to follow the flock is to lead them astray. One more step, however, completes the explanation for how the Church has come to this pass: *The magisterium has been unwilling to* ***lead*** *the faithful AND unwilling to* ***follow*** *Tradition.*

It is this unwillingness to defer to Tradition that has brought about the woeful circumstance of shepherds who will not guide, guard, or govern. Failure to "bow to the immemorial deposit of Truth endowed and entrusted to the papacy," at the head of the magisterium, is a matter of the shepherds giving poor example to the flock. The flock does not follow the shepherds for two reasons: the shepherds do not lead—the flock—and the shepherds do not follow—Christ. These hirelings drink the milk and wear the wool, but do not walk the walk. They insist on obedience from their inferiors, but give but token obedience to Christ the Good Shepherd. Choosing not to follow His lead, the shepherds have led all the sheep astray. They manifest a dereliction of duty and gross pride.

Obedience in proper proportion is lacking. The episcopal office is due the obedience of its holders, receiving from them

> their willingness to conform to divine truth. Bishops in turn can expect to receive the grace of office, the power to preach the truth, and the obedience of their flock due to those whose charge is not to feed on but to feed the sheep. When the bishops submit in unwavering obedience to God's truth as mediated through the episcopal office, then the laity are safe in obeying the bishops. Disobedient bishops are a danger to themselves and to the souls in their care.
>
> If bishops deny obedience to the truth, their flock is obliged to avoid the direction of their wayward shepherds. If truth is the common object of episcopal and lay obedience, then obedience will neither be overstated by bishops leading in error, nor understated by laity demanding error. Truth as the common object of obedience allows the laity to follow the magisterium with confidence, and the magisterium to exercise the virtue of humility, the authority of office, and service to God alone.

Pope Leo XIII expressed a similar sentiment in paragraph 15 of his 1881 encyclical letter, *Diuturnum illud*, thus:

> "The one only reason which men have for not obeying is when anything is demanded of them which is openly repugnant to the natural or divine law, for it is equally unlawful to command and to do anything in which the law of nature or the will of God is violated. If, therefore, it should happen to any one to be compelled to prefer one or the other, *viz.*, to disregard either the commands of God or those of rulers, he must obey Jesus Christ ...And yet there is no reason why those who so behave themselves should be accused of refusing obedience; for if the will of rulers is opposed to the will and the laws of God, they themselves exceed the bounds of their own power and pervert justice; nor can their authority then be valid, which, when there is no justice, is null."

Not exhausting the subject, Pope Leo also said in *Libertas praestantissimum of 1888:*

From Paragraph 6: "This subject is often discussed by the Angelic Doctor in his demonstration that the possibility of sinning is not freedom, but slavery. It will suffice to quote his subtle commentary on the words of Our Lord: 'Whosoever committeth sin is the servant of sin' (John 8:34). 'Everything,' he says, 'is that which belongs to it naturally. When, therefore, it acts through a power outside itself, it does not act of itself, but through another, that is, as a slave. But man is by nature rational. When, therefore, he acts according to reason, he acts of himself and according to his free will; and this is liberty. Whereas, when he sins, he acts in opposition to reason, is moved by another, and is the victim of foreign misapprehensions. Therefore, "Whosoever committeth sin is the servant of sin".'...the wise man alone is free; and by the term 'wise man' was meant, as is well known, the man trained to live in accordance with his nature, that is, in justice and virtue."

From Paragraph 13: "...obedience is greatly ennobled when subjected to an authority which is the most just and supreme of all. But where the power to command is wanting, or where a law is enacted contrary to reason, or to the eternal law, or to some ordinance of God, obedience is unlawful, lest, while obeying man, we become disobedient to God ...all being free to live according to law and right reason; and in this, as We have shown, true liberty really consists."

From Paragraph 24: "There can be no doubt that truth alone should imbue the minds of men, for in it are found the well-being, the end and perfection of every intelligent nature; and therefore nothing but truth should be taught both to the ignorant and to the educated, so as to bring knowledge to those who have it not, and to preserve it in those who possess it. For this reason it is plainly the duty of all who teach to banish error from the mind, and by sure safeguards to close the entry to all false convictions. From this it follows, as is evident, that the liberty of which We have been speaking [liberty of teaching, a.k.a. academic freedom] is greatly opposed to reason, and tends to pervert men's minds as it claims for itself the right of teaching

> whatever it pleases—a liberty which the state cannot grant without failing in its duty."
>
> From Paragraph 30: "But when anything is commanded which is plainly at variance with the will of God, there is a wide departure from this divinely constituted order, and at the same time a direct conflict with divine authority; therefore, it is right not to obey."

Or, as this writer has repeated innumerable times, *disobedience to the disobedient is obedience.*

The penchant shown by Popes and prelates since the Second Vatican Council to display affection for modern errors is lamentable, to be sure. No less disturbing is the willingness of so many lesser clerics and lay faithful to accept this misplaced devotion to contemporary unthought. Religious liberty, academic freedom, universal salvation, wholly secular states, and adulterated worship are just a few of the legion un-Catholic positions taken by the Catholic hierarchy for more than a half-century now. But regardless of the frequency with which such positions are maintained, or the exalted state of the men maintaining them, no one is bound to assent to them, for they are against the letter of the Faith and against the spirit of the Faith. In most instances they do not even follow the letter of Vatican ii, but indeed represent the infamous "spirit" of the Council which seemingly is comprised of nothing other than denials of the philosophy, theology, and practice of the Church from earlier eras.

Do not lay hands on the Lord's anointed! Although a strong argument can be made that secular matters at times require the use of force to bring justice to the oppressed, such can not be the case where the justice of God in the Church is in question. *Never, never, never* may the primacy of Peter, the apostolic succession of the episcopate, or the sovereignty of Holy Mother Church be challenged. *Never.* Where error, abuse of power, or capitulation to the world is in evidence among the hierarchy, even the Pope himself, the proper response of the faithful Catholic is the aforementioned *nothing.* Nothing may be said or done to call into doubt the legitimacy of the Petrine office. Nothing may be said or done which gives encouragement to the enemies of the Church, those within or those without the sheepfold. Nothing may be said or done expressive of despair that anyone but God the Holy Ghost guides the Mystical Body of Christ always in keeping with the providence of God the Father.

As well, then, nothing may be said or done supportive of what hierarchs say and do in opposition to immemorial truths and traditions given them for the teaching of the nations. Nothing may be said or done acquiescing to the ethos of the world infecting men of the Church. Nothing may be said or done confirming children in the sense that the Church herself is as fungible, as evolving, as unstable as the media circuses, the bread and circuses, the madhouse which modern science, politics, and pseudo-philosophy declare is the state of reality. Nothing may be said or done in denial of that which Catholics have believed unanimously, ubiquitously, and unchangingly. Nothing may be left unsaid or undone to demonstrate absolute fidelity to the entirety of the Deposit of faith, regardless of who might be in disagreement, no matter the sanctions threatened for such fidelity, in spite of any hardships incurred as part of taking up the cross of Christ each day and following Him to Calvary and thence to the bliss and joy promised His faithful on the Last and Endless Day.

Kings of realms may not oppress their subjects. Presidents of nations may not give license to their subjects to commit immorality. Popes may not impose error on their subjects. The fact that most people will accept oppression, throw themselves into sin, and embrace error does not change reality. There is no authority, secular or spiritual, to legitimate wrong as right. None has the right to be wrong. Or, in the words of the already quoted Pope Leo XIII, error has no rights. Justice means rendering each his due. Obedience is an act of justice. Disobeying God is the supreme act of injustice. To obey any man of any state of whatever power in rebellion against the will of God is unjust, unloving, and damnable. Not only the tyrants who dictate such repugnant actions will be punished by the supreme Judge on Judgement Day, but their subjects who willingly—willfully—submitted themselves to that injustice will be subject to that punishment. He who aids a prophet because he is a prophet receives a prophet's reward; he who cowardly aids the faithless by being faithless will receive the punishment reserved for the faithless coward.

In other words, follow Peter, not Judas.

Where's a mythic hero when you need one?

Posterity is grateful that history has not universally practiced the politics of expedience. Though our common human heritage is filled with its share of Iscariots, Benedict Arnolds, and Vichy governments, our patrimony has seen better. We are the beneficiaries of innumerable profiles in courage from antiquity to the very present.

Were it not for the boldness of the likes of Constantine, the pre-Revolutionary French, and the Americans during Britain's finest hour, the world might well be run by pagan monarchic nazis. Of course, no serious historian would suggest that Constantine's embrace of Christianity, French affection for Benjamin Franklin, or the lend-lease policy of Depression-plagued America were purely altruistic actions. They were, however, unorthodox and risky commitments to causes that were anything but ventures assured of success.

Constantine sought not salvation, but allies in his struggles to advance imperial interests. In fact, his first act in favor of the Church was not official sanctioning, but mere decriminalization. The aristocratic French sought less to aid democracy than to harm their neighbors across the Channel. They would have been horrified to realize—as they did too late—the ramifications of anti-monarchical sentiment in their own kingdom. Most Americans sought little more than jobs from the New Deal Administration. Many Congressmen and Senators used anti-war sentiment quite effectively to thwart Roosevelt's attempts to expand assistance to America's European friends.

Giving realism its due, however, does not diminish the significance of these (and other) historic advocacies of the underdog. Prudence dictated that Christianity should be shunned as a disruptive element in the Roman Empire. The British could not be allowed to lose their New World colonies because of the risk to the territories claimed by every European power. Conventional wisdom was that the United States preferred dealing with its own economic disaster rather than with the military catastrophe brewing far away. None of these assessments was false, but all proved wanting when placed in the scale of political, philosophical, and strategic genius.

Iscariot, Arnold, and the Vichy were shrewd. In the short term they might have seemed vindicated. Christ died. The British remained a threat to America for more than a third of a century after the Declaration of Independence. Hitler conquered more of Europe than any Caesar, Charlemagne, or Napoleon.

Those whose measure is shrewdness might well have predicted the Goths, the Reign of Terror, and the Cold War. It is not likely, though, that minds perceptive enough to understand the reality of absolute personal deity, of the ascendance of personal freedom, of the right to political self-determination were themselves blind to the eventuality of being transcended by the ideals they championed.

All that is left of Rome's empire is her Church. France saw her own revolution descend to anarchy and then into the eventual dictatorship of Napoleon, establishing a stable republican government only in the twentieth century. The tangible loss of national innocence in the United States during the Cold War period has yet to reveal a concomitant gain.

We are the inheritors of these treasures amassed through history. All too often, unfortunately, we behave, not like our pioneering forebears, but like the spoiled scions of Old Money. We make our fortunes, not the old-fashioned way of earning, but by the newfangled obsession with the lottery.

There is a monumental difference between the perils braved by our adventurous ancestors and the wagers made by our greedy selves. Risk in the past involved hands-on interaction with the land, with ideals, with human beings. Today's corporate warrior speculates in other peoples' money, in the stock market, in copyright law, and in virtual realty.

The stuff of which greatness is made requires an ability to identify the good desired, the fortitude to confront risk, and the willingness to bear the cost entailed. Far from being alien to human nature, this dynamic is constitutive of human history. What we ignore to our mortal peril is that the other half of this equation is quiescence in the face of necessity, complacency with the status quo, and cowardice before unknown hardship. One would look long, perhaps in vain, to find leaders in our country whose standard is that of greatness rather than sameness. It seems the fatal flaw of democracy is that the leaders are drawn from the led.

November's first Tuesday is little more than two months distant. Instead of voting for candidates who pledge more of the same or a return to a golden age that never was, it is time for American citizens to take on the mantle placed on them by representative democracy.

It is not enough to vote—campaigns need workers. It is not enough to campaign—ballots need candidates. It is not enough to run—citizens need leaders.

Leading means to do what others will not. To get out in front. To take chances. To be ready to vindicate truth and righteousness, though all the world be arrayed against you.

Our votes are not meant for the winners, but for the best. Our ideals our not meant to be palatable, but to be true. Our goal is not meant to keep us where we are, but to lead us on to where only the bold, the great, and the selfless can find the way.

History, my friends, is a harsh judge, but not the harshest.

The preceding paragraphs might have been written in 2004. They were not. It was the presidential election of 2000 that prompted those thoughts. Their author, yours truly, is not at all satisfied with them. He yet labored under the delusion that the system in place provided a remedy for the system in place. He was wrong. When the 2004 presidential elections came along, he understood things better. Here is a sample of what he said:

America's Politics of Perdition

> Your Eminence,
>
> It is difficult to fully express my gratitude to you for your recent clarification of the principles involved for men of good will seeking to cast votes in popular elections according to the moral guidance offered by the Church. As you are well aware, the situation in the United States is quite volatile. Your explanation provided the Episcopal Conference an excellent means to navigate these perilous waters. I convey here my personal thanks for the invaluable assistance your wise words represent. Solomon himself would have been hard pressed to state so clearly the absolute prohibition of supporting candidates known to hold problematic positions *viz.* the moral law; while making the fine distinction that a voter may in conscience decry said candidate's shortcomings, yet support him all the same in favor of other meritorious ideas, policies, and accomplishments. Brilliant, Your Eminence, exquisitely brilliant!
>
> Your Grace will be pleased to know that I have employed what I wish to flatter you by calling "Ratzinger's Rationale" to another matter of governance vital to the Church in the United States. On the principle, almost along the lines of that called "double effect" most often invoked in medical ethics, that good may be pursued separate from the evil known to be attached to it, so acutely articulated by Your Eminence, I have sent a set of recommendations to the Congregation for Bishops in the Holy See regarding vacant sees in the United States facing pressing

pastoral needs. Your splendid proposition has given exactly the foundation needed to calm those who might find my suggestions challenging.

His Eminence Bernard Cardinal Law and their Excellencies Archbishop Rembert Weakland and Bishop Anthony O'Connell head the list of names which this Nunciature urges the Holy See to consider as appointments for ordinaries in a number of dioceses in the United States. Given their proven track record as shepherds with profound pastoral sensitivity, administrative competence, and total dedication to the vision of His Holiness Pope John Paul II and Vatican II, issues of age, past legal inconveniences, and any misgivings within popular opinion can easily be resolved with an appeal to "Ratzinger's Rationale". These worthy prelates are not being put forward in order to endorse any views they might have on seminary formation, celibate chastity, or personnel policies not quite in line with accepted practice in the rest of the Church; but because they have tremendous skills, talents, and experience sorely required in shepherdless local churches who would welcome pastors of souls with their histories of affection for the People of God, dedication to the service of humanity, and commitment to preserving and extending the new Springtime of faith of which they have been such prominent promoters.

Again, Your Eminence, thank you for the wisdom that you shared which resulted in this felicitous resolution to certain pastoral difficulties begging my attention. You are an inspiration to us lesser sons of the Church. With gratitude and fraternal warmth, I remain

Yours in Christ,
Archbishop Gabriel Montalvo, JCD
Papal Nuncio to the United States of America

Ahem.

None would seek justification in any way to defend a decision so obtuse, mindless, and insulting as appointing as bishops, known perpetrators of immoral acts or those who tolerated such while in former positions of authority. There is no fear that Cardinal Law, Archbishop Weakland, or Bishop O'Connell will ever head dioceses again. Of course, in the case of Cardinal Law, his "demotion" involves the burden of administering one of the four major basilicas of the city of Rome.

This willingness to brave a storm of criticism in such public and visible matters of scandal and outrage is not possessed only by the apparatus ruling the Holy See. Citizens of the United States are more than willing to turn their self-blinded eyes to the morally reprehensible records of the two men currently vying for the presidency. Sad to say, Catholics are among those who see less evil, hear less evil, speak less evil, and call it good.

It is never ever permissible to do evil. Good may not under any circumstances be the excuse for committing an evil act. Bad means can not lead to good ends.

During the present electoral contest, however, a refrain is recurring ad nauseam encouraging Catholics to vote on the basis of choosing "the lesser evil". Others have pointed out long before this writer was ever born that the lesser of two evils is still evil. Wishful thinking, good intentions, and "nice" people can not change reality or alter the path that leads to hell. Good is that which is all good; evil is so because of whatever defect it possesses, however small.

President Bush allows babies to be murdered for stem-cell research, after rapes, as a response to incest, and if a mother's life purportedly is at risk. Senator Kerry accepts all of that, adding to the President's list child murder at the discretion of a woman's choice for whatever reason or none. Senator Kerry wants states to regulate sodomite unions. So does President Bush. The current Chief Executive is of the opinion that the Constitution is properly interpreted to mean that laws offensive to the will of God may be passed according to the will of the people. Senator Kerry concurs. Senator Kerry is also a self-admitted participant in committing atrocities during time of war. President Bush has made public confession to alcohol abuse, immaturity, and irresponsibility leading to brushes with the law.

Baby killing, sodomy, and faithlessness are evil. Murder and unnatural acts cry to Heaven for vengeance. To have no God violates the true God's First Commandment to His chosen people, and denies the greatest Commandment articulated by His Son, Our Lord and Savior, Jesus Christ: *Thou shalt love the Lord thy God with thy whole heart, with thy whole soul, with they whole mind, and with thy whole strength!*

Practically everyone retches at the idea of placing perverts in the role of shepherd and guardian over children's bodies and souls. The same people, absurdly, can stomach as rulers men who countenance children being scalded, vacuumed, and rent limb from limb—by their mothers! Catholics who would not have sodomites as bishops would elect as president men who defend the "rights" of sodomites to "marry", to commit their abominations, to broadcast their foul propaganda in public, to insinuate depravity in school curricula, and to adopt helpless children to be subjected to degenerate environments as their only homes. Bishops are vilified for "hiding" behind laws and lawyers to escape criminal and/or financial liability for their dioceses' (mis)management of abuse cases; but the populace continues to reelect to office the very lawyers who concoct laws so offensive to the sense of justice of all parties involved; the abused, the accused, and the confused prelates in the middle of it all.

Hackles rise among apologists for this sick state of affairs as they protest by way of demanding, "What are we supposed to do—waste our votes on third-party candidates?" To this a reasonable response would be, "Do whatever you want. It's a free country, isn't it? Vote third party, write in a name, don't vote at all. Vote for whomever you think *best*. Isn't that what it means to have *free* elections?"

Freedom does not, however, inhere in knowingly establishing in power men who will use that power to encourage the slaughter of infants, the abandonment of the conjugal bond, and the deposing of Christ as Sovereign King. To patiently endure such a regime imposed by force of arms could lead to heroic sanctity. To lend one's agreement, financial support, and labor to efforts informed by such abominations is disgraceful. It is hard to decide which is most despicable: philosophies and policies founded in base iniquity, the men who promulgate them, or the people who accede to them.

No compliment to a political system is offered when to vote for a competent, qualified, and moral candidate is described as a "waste". Not much freedom remains to those who accept the dictates of a two-headed cabal, the Replutocrats and the Demoblicans, in the name of liberty. It is a waste, as the expression of representative government, to offer political franchise and universal suffrage to a "citizenry" blindly willing to receive what most of them consider to be options between one *evil* and a lesser *evil*. Bring back the days of smoke-filled rooms, machine politics, and "bought" elections—they were more honest, less hypocritical manifestations of the truth tacitly admitted by those adhering to the lesser-evil doctrine for choosing leaders of the "free" world. It has not been explained how this dearth of choices is materially or substantially different from Soviet Politburo operations rubber-stamped in popular elections.

Modern man bemoans the "restrictions" on his free will that require deference to the will of God. Our Lord offers perfect freedom in choosing His will, but most men reject that in order to effect their own wills. Democratic politics force men to choose between two equally foul options, and mindless voters agree to impose on themselves what they *know* to be unjust. God offers eternal life where democracy offers tyranny—and God's people choose… tyranny! *This* is what modern man calls freedom?!?

Judgement Day will bring the revelation of each heart's content based not on whether his candidates won elections, but on whether the candidates for whom he voted should have won elections in order to bring obedience to God's will to bear on the governance of peoples. Worthy is the soul whose every righteous candidate lost every election; woe to the soul whose compromise candidates won every election by being willing to offend God by gross injustice inflicted in the name of law. A nation with almost 300 million inhabitants incapable of finding for a leader even one man true to Christ, His Kingdom, and His Church has little hope of preserving itself against the inevitable assaults that will beset it from within. If the lesser of two evils is the best that can be offered by a nation's citizens, then much, much worse than the present evil will be their collective future.

The mindset of *choosing*, as opposed to *enduring* evil, led to the election of Hitler and the Nazis on their promises of economic stability, restored national prestige, and military security. A world war was necessary to replace that vision of world order with the New World Order being brought into existence in the 21st century. Some improvement. The politics of compromise, willing to endorse the lesser of two evils, resulted in the enshrinement in the United States Constitution of the legal fact that dark-skinned persons were to be counted as three-fifths of a person rather than being ignored as non-persons. The War Between the States was fought, civil unrest in the mid-twentieth century was inflicted, and continuing disparity in economics and political power is tolerated as the consequences of the Constitution's other fatal flaw (the truly fatal flaw was excising Christ as King from the national identity). The cynical political reasoning that it is expedient that one man die for the sake of the people bore ill fruit in deicide. That decision drew the battle lines between Heaven and hell that ushered in the war being fought even now and unto the end of time.

Jesus Christ is the victor in that war. All that remains for man is for each man to choose the side on which he will battle. *Every* thought, word, and deed—and vote—in this earthly life is a declaration for or against Jesus Christ and eternal life. In this battle with powers and principalities, not flesh and blood, flesh and blood lends aid either to satan or to Saint Michael. It beggars belief to imagine that evil—rationalized, chosen, and willed—to any degree will be welcomed by Saint Michael in his efforts in obedience to God almighty.

Be ye holy as I the Lord your God am holy! (Leviticus 19:2). Be ye therefore perfect, as your Father in Heaven is perfect! (St. Matthew 5:48). Love the Lord thy God with thy whole heart, with thy whole soul, with thy whole mind, and with thy whole strength! (St. Mark 13:30).

These **commands** from God leave no room for philosophies in denial of Him, provide no wiggle room for politicians who would rather avoid Him, and offer no room for compromise to the people of a nation who prefer to accept a lesser evil instead of Him and only Him. Decision 2004 is before us. Choose a side.

Father Smith
Sacerdos vagus
6 September 2004: St. Zachary the Prophet

Contrary to false political ideologies protesting otherwise, the modern men of the Church have bound themselves intimately to the men of the world in the state. Separation of Church and state is observed in its constant breaching insofar as the men willing to be false to the freedom and exaltation of Holy Mother Church pursue liberty in keeping with the world, the flesh, and the devil. In the same year, six months earlier, as the above was written, the Holy See issued a statement from Pope John Paul II that resulted in this writer feeling compelled to object by saying the following:

The Exaltation of the Absurd

His Holiness, Pope John Paul II, is reported by the Zenit News Service (23 February 2004) as advocating, "an adequate separation of church and state so that citizens, regardless of their religion, can make their contribution to society." He is quoted as saying, "In fulfilling this task, the clear distinction between the civil and religious spheres allows each of these sectors to exercise its proper responsibilities effectively, with mutual respect and in complete freedom of conscience… In a pluralistic society the secularity of the state allows for communication between the different spiritual dimensions and the nation... The church and the state, therefore, are not rivals but partners: In healthy dialogue with each other they can encourage integral human development and social harmony."

The story goes on to relate that the Pope perceives a positive sign in the Turkish Constitution that recognizes "freedom of conscience, as well as freedom of religion, worship and instruction...These constitutional guarantees, once they have become part of ordinary legislation and therefore of the living fabric of society, permit all citizens regardless of religious belief or affiliation to make their contribution to the building up of Turkish society... The nation is thus able to benefit from the hope and the moral qualities that draw their strength from the deeply held religious convictions of the people." It is the desire of the Pope that such a progressive stance will bring the juridical recognition of the Church, presumably not only in Turkey, but in all nations.

Setting aside the critical problem of the fact that "distinction" and "separation" are entirely different—*separate*—words with very different—*distinct*—meanings, rendering it impossible to make use of them interchangeably as His Holiness endeavored to do in the statement quoted by Zenit, it must be pointed out that the Pope's own argument eliminates his desired goal, namely, of establishing religious pluralism as normative to society and guaranteed by secularism. Religious freedom is *not* a goal of secularism. Increasingly secular states invariably experience a *lessening* of religious tolerance, a *diminishment* of the influence of authentic morality on the public mores, and the *removal* of a place for God and His Church from official policy, national objectives, and cultural identity.

As a case in point, one needs look no further than the poster child of national secularism enshrining the chimera of religious freedom, the United States of America. The Constitution of this country *explicitly* denies pride of place to the Body of Christ, the Catholic Church, and any other religious organization, within the philosophy, structures, or mechanisms of the government. The Church is forbidden to comment from the pulpit on political issues on pain of losing the all-important tax-free status afforded the pusillanimous who prefer legitimacy in the city of man rather than citizenship in the city of God. Sodomy has been endorsed as a protected "right" by the Supreme Court of the United States, the Supreme Court of the State of Massachusetts, and the mayors of San Francisco and Chicago, as well as the two most prominent candidates for the nomination of the Democrat party for President. The current Republican President thinks sodomite marriage unacceptable, but is on record as wishing to codify laws in favor of sodomite "civil unions". Contraception, divorce, abortion, and usury are commonplace to the point of being unremarkable in the minds of most Americans.

Looking further afield one sees that France has passed a law criminalizing the wearing of religious symbols and apparel in public places, such as Mohammedan women wearing veils, Jews wearing yarmulkes, and Christians wearing large crucifixes. The French have the cheeky temerity to suggest that this law is a protection of the rights of Mohammedan women against the tyranny and injustice of Mohammedan religious practice. Soviet Russia was as secular a country as could have been conceived, and its secularism perdures in the post-Soviet era. The result of this ongoing secularist bent is that the Russian government outlawed almost every religious group in the world from seeking members within its borders, excepting only the Russian Orthodox Church and a few small religious entities that pose little threat to the monolithic status quo.

Closer to hand, our neighbors to the north in Canada are in the process of making a "hate crime" out of public opposition to "gay rights", and leaders in that nation are so bold as to aver that abortion and homosexuality are Canadian values that must be given every legal support imaginable. Secularist, Marxist, and masonic regimes in Cuba, Mexico, and Nicaragua have a disturbing habit of seizing Church property, imprisoning clergy, and executing bishops. Secularism and pluralism in Haiti have resulted in the spectacle of a country that holds voodoo as its national religion being presided over by a former Catholic priest who just happens to be in sympathy with communism.

Secularism has not made the Mohammedan minority in India or the hindu minority in Pakistan any safer. Catholics in Northern Ireland do not benefit, religiously or economically, from the enlightened secularist policies of England. The Dalai Lama is in exile precisely because the Red Chinese are quite indiscriminate in their application of nonsectarian values toward Buddhists, Catholics, or their fellow atheists who dare seek for man the rights already denied to God.

"Religious freedom" can not stand up even in the abstract because of that pesky law of non-contradiction forbidding a statement and its opposite to be simultaneously true. A nation committed to offering human sacrifices for the appeasement of the gods can hardly be expected to be tolerant of a group of people in its midst who insist on the absolute sanctity of human life. One can not say as statements of absolute truth both that men must always be killed and that men must never be killed.

Lest any demur that human sacrifice is an extreme example unbefitting a sober argument, please remember that the slaughter of innocents is very much a concrete issue regarding religious beliefs as they touch on the subject of abortion. How, pray tell, can one nation respect the religious beliefs of two sets of people, one of which literally celebrates the scalding, evisceration, and impaling of infants, and the other of which is convinced that such barbarity cries to Heaven for vengeance?

But even if the theoretical notion of religious liberty could be sensibly and sanely maintained, which it can not be, actual human experience across several centuries, around the world, and among billions of people demonstrates that it simply does not work. The practical result of religious liberty is the freedom to not practice religion becoming the prohibition of religious practice ultimately leading to the persecution of religious practitioners. Religious persecution by the religious is at least logically consistent: error has no rights. Religious persecution by those claiming to champion religious freedom adds to the injury of injustice the insult of illogic, hypocrisy, and rank dishonesty.

Perhaps the most absurd aspect of the Pope's statement, however, is that there simply is no reason within the concept of religious liberty binding on all of its advocates to explain *why* religious liberty should be offered to anyone at all. Some secularists are atheists. Most would probably describe themselves as agnostics. A secularist calling himself a religionist is a walking, talking oxymoron. A religionist calling himself a secularist is an apostate.

It would seem that the desire of a secularist approach to the problem of sectarian discord is predicated on the fact that religious strife stems from religious disagreement. What happens, then, when the secularists disagree? An answer to that question can be found in the history books on the subject of World Wars I and II; in the contemporary media describing the conflicts in Iraq, the Korean peninsula, and the Ivory Coast; and in the revealed word of God almighty in the Book of the Apocalypse, chapter eighteen.

The Pope making his appeal to the government in Turkey begs the question of why a diplomat from a Mohammedan country, about to join the economic organization of Europe with stated policies offensive to Christian morality, should listen at all to the head of the Catholic Church. Secularist man is satisfied that he can solve all of mankind's problems without recourse to the divine, faith, or the Church. That is the *definition* of secularism; it is thoroughly opposed to the truths, morality, and worship native to religion.

What ails man is not that there are too many religions fighting over what is good, in need of a secularist referee to bring deluded simpletons to their senses. What ails man is the unwillingness of the hierarchy and members of the Catholic Church to fight for the *one* Faith, *one* Baptism, and *one* Lord as revealed to and taught by His *one* Church, wherein true peace can be shared, real hope is offered for the relief of mortal woes, and the love of God is experienced with the confidence that He will judge, not referee, with justice and mercy on the Last Day. How his Holiness expects a conglomeration of unbelieving, immoral, and money-grubbing bureaucrats to do what the Church seems unwilling at present to attempt admits of no rational explanation.

Father Smith,
Sacerdos vagus
25 February 2004: Ash Wednesday

The Bottom Line

Rarely if ever is it pointed out that Caesar must join his subjects in rendering unto God that which is God's. God does not receive His due from those who are ignorant of His identity, His will for the moral life, or the necessity of worshipping Him in *His* Spirit and in *His* Truth. Obscuring the law of God, silencing the mention of the Name of Jesus, and confusing the sheep of His Flock are acts of disobedience and injustice. Men who deny the existence of God, who deny the divinity of Jesus and/or the divine Maternity of His Mother, Mary, or who deny the primacy of His Vicar on earth commit blasphemy against the Divine Majesty. First among men in offering God all glory, honor, and kingship are the members of the hierarchy of the Catholic Church beneath the successor of St. Peter, the Pope in Rome. It is for them to ensure that Caesar is not remiss in his duty to render God's to God, including the children He claims through His merciful love. Rendering unto Caesar ultimately is rendering unto God, for Caesar owes God what everyone owes God—*everything.* Caesar, too, is commanded to love the Lord God with his whole heart, whole soul, whole mind, and whole strength, and lead his whole nation—the neighbors he is commanded to love as himself—in doing the same. As Saint Ambrose so wisely put it, "The grandest title of an emperor is to be a son of the Church; the emperor is in the Church, not over her." This sentiment applies to presidents, prime ministers, and potentates of every stripe with equal force.

A story is told of John Cardinal Newman after his conversion to the one, true Faith. Conversing with one of his former fellows in the heresy of Anglicanism, the Cardinal failed to convince his companion of the necessity of belonging to the Catholic Church for salvation. That man responded instead by saying, "With all due respect, Your Eminence, you worship God your way, and I will worship God my way." To which the prince of the Church replied, "No, sir. You worship God your way and I will worship God *His* way." This is in the category of stories that if it did not happen, it should have. Regardless of whether or not the incident happened in fact, it is in fact the truth.

Much space has been taken up in these pages with quotes. There seems yet room for at least one more:

From the *New Advent Catholic Encyclopedia*: "Religious Indifferentism"
(which includes the public praise of false religions)

II. Restricted Indifferentism

In distinction from this absolute Indifferentism, a restricted form of the error admits the necessity of religion on account, chiefly, of its salutary influence on human life. But it holds that all religions are equally worthy and profitable to man, and equally pleasing to God. The classic advocate of this theory is Rousseau, who maintains, in his *Emile*, that God looks only to the sincerity of intention, and that everybody can serve Him by remaining in the religion in which he has been brought up, or by changing it at will for any other that pleases him more (*Emile*, III). This doctrine is widely advocated today on the grounds that, beyond the truth of God's existence, we can attain to no certain religious knowledge; and that, since God has left us thus in uncertainty, He will be pleased with whatever form of worship we sincerely offer Him. The full reply to this error consists in the proof that God has vouchsafed to man a supernatural revelation, embodying a definite religion, which He desires that all should embrace and practice. Without appealing to this fact, however, a little consideration suffices to lay bare the inherent absurdity of this doctrine. All religions, indeed, may be said to contain some

> measure of truth; and God may accept the imperfect worship of ignorant sincerity. But it is injurious to God, who is truth itself, to assert that truth and falsehood are indifferent in His sight. Since various religions are in disagreement, it follows that, wherever they conflict, if one possesses the truth the others are in error. The constituent elements of a religion are beliefs to be held by the intellect, precepts to be observed, and a form of worship to be practiced. Now—to confine ourselves to the great religions of the world—Judaism, Mohammedanism, Christianity, and the religions of India and the Orient, are in direct antagonism by their respective creeds, moral codes, and cults. To say that all these irreconcilable beliefs and cults are equally pleasing to God is to say that the divine being has no predilection for truth over error; that the true and the false are alike congenial to His nature. Again, to hold that truth and falsehood equally satisfy and perfect the human intellect is to deny that reason has a native bent towards, and affinity for, truth. If we deny this we deny that any trust is to be placed in our reason. Turn to the ethical side of the question. Here again there is conflict over almost all the great moral issues. Let an illustration or two suffice. Mohammedanism approves polygamy; Christianity uncompromisingly condemns it as immoral. If these two teachers are equally trustworthy guides of life, then there is no such thing as fixed moral values at all. If the [unmentionable acts of obscene worship] are as pure in the sight of God as the austere worship that was conducted in the temple of Jerusalem, then we must hold the deity to be destitute of all moral attributes, in which case there would be no grounds for religion at all. The fact is that this type of Indifferentism, though verbally acknowledging the excellence and utility of religion, nevertheless, when pressed by logic, recoils into absolute Indifferentism. "All religions are equally good" comes to mean, at bottom, that religion is good for nothing.

We might all be wrong, but, my modern(ist) friends, we are not all right.

But what are we to do when the Vicar of Christ and the successors to the Apostles under him refuse, or are reluctant to acknowledge, this simple truth.

Nothing. If you are not a bishop or the Pope, do not pass judgement on those who attempt to be Catholic in ways different from yours. Pray for them. Explain to them if they ask. Do not join them in their errors. You need not declare them in error to refuse to accept their errors. Preach and live the Truth. Correct your brother's errors and leave the judgement of his soul to God.

There is but one magisterium in the Catholic Church. It is comprised of the Pope and the bishops in communion with him. The rest of us need to be very cautious about demanding of others a justification for how they are attempting to be faithful. Certainly we might ask our fellows to explain their choices to us with an eye toward greater fidelity in our own hearts. We must, however, steadfastly resist the temptation to insist that others make themselves make sense to us and satisfy our demands for orthodoxy.

Should one find himself in the position of being questioned by a member of the hierarchy, it is incumbent upon him to offer the clearest, truest, and most Catholic explanation within one's means to provide. In these trying times one may discover that the layman or simple cleric has a better grasp of Catholic orthodoxy than a prelate. If that is indeed the case, all that can be done is to respectfully disagree with him, pray for him, *and offer no disrespect of him in public or in private.*

Catholicism is an offering of the grace of God to sinful men. That is all that a faithful Catholic is able to embrace and to transmit. Catholicism is fundamentally for things: for Christ, his Church, her Sacraments, their grace, and the salvation it affords. Protestantism is an erroneous fundamentalism that is *against* things: Christ's One Church, His Vicar of that Church on earth, her seven Sacraments, the actions that flow from the grace of faith, and a definitive body of Truth proclaimed authoritatively by the Vicar of Christ, through the Church, in perfect imitation of her Lord. The Catholic faithful to tradition will spurn anything that smacks of protestantism and will cleave humbly to the life of sanctity in keeping with the Cross, the Sacraments, and the Truth.

Be Catholic. Pray. Do penance. Mortify the flesh. Reject all of the ways of the world. Go to Confession. Assist at Mass.

Catholics are not protestants. They are not protestants in some blanket denial of the authority and existence of the papacy. They are not protestants in an inconsistent acknowledgement of the papal office and some jurisdiction without any reference to a universal ministry. They are not protestants in pursuing an allegiance with the world divorced from continuity with the Church's own history.

They are not protestants in the finding by individuals of an ability on their own authority to declare other authorities null.

Church laws are given by God, through the magisterium, with the intent of offering souls the means to their salvation. They are the vehicles of attaining the freedom of the sons of God. Children of the Church who obey what they should, as they should are not in fetters, but are at liberty to realize the life of sanctity. Although they will proclaim the Kingdom of Heaven to all in earshot, they will at root be asserting only their own witness to the grace of God at work in them. This is legitimately understood as implying their conviction that all might licitly follow their example, but it can not be construed to mean that any others are required to imitate that example.

For those who desire a more forceful warning leveled at the hierarchy, take comfort in these words of St. Augustine of Hippo:

> *Excerpted from Treatise 45 on the Gospel of St. John*
>
> "...[T]he Lord has spoken to us in similitudes of His flock, and of the door, by which the sheepfold is to be entered. Let the pagans therefore say, "We lead good lives!" If they do not enter by the door, what does it profit them in which they glory? A good life is profitable to man if it leads to life everlasting, but if he is not to have life everlasting, what shall his good life profit him? Because they can not be said to live well, who either through blindness are ignorant of the very end of all good living, or through pride despise the same. But no man has a true and certain hope of living forever, unless he acknowledge the life which is Christ, and enter by the door into the sheepfold.
>
> Such men as these, therefore, for the most part, try to persuade men to live well, and yet not to be Christians. They wish to climb up another way, to steal and to kill; not, like the Good Shepherd, to keep and to save. And so there have been certain philosophers, holding many subtle discussions upon the virtues and the vices; dividing, defining, reasoning out very clever arguments, filling volumes, airing their own wisdom with loud trumpets; who would even dare to say to others: "Follow us; keep to

> our sect, if you would live happily." But they did not enter by the door; they wished to destroy, to slay, and to kill.
>
> What shall I say of these men? Behold, the Pharisees themselves were wont to read of Christ, and, in that very reading, their voices re-echoed Christ, they hoped for His coming, and yet did not recognize Him while He was with them. They boasted that they themselves were among the seers, that is, among the wise, but they denied Christ, and entered not in by the door. Therefore, also would they, if they chanced to lead them away to slay and to kill them, not to deliver them. So much for them. Let us look to those who glory in the Name of Christ himself, and see whether they by chance are entering in by the door. For there are countless numbers who not only boast that they are seers, but would have it appear that they are enlightened by Christ; yet they are heretics."

For those who desire words of comfort for our beloved shepherds, the Pope and all the bishops in union with him, offer these words of St. Augustine of Hippo:

> "Pray for us who live in so precarious a state, as it were between the teeth of furious wolves. These wandering sheep, obstinate sheep, are offended because we run after them, as if their wandering made them cease to be ours. 'Why dost thou call us?' they say; 'why dost thou pursue us?' But the very reason of our cries and our anguish is that they are running to their ruin. 'If I am lost, if I die, what is it to thee? What dost thou want with me?' What I want is to call thee back from thy wandering; what I desire is to snatch thee from death. 'But what if I will to wander? What if I will to be lost?' Thou willest to wander? Thou willest to be lost? How much more earnestly do I wish it not! Yea, I dare say it, I am importunate; for I hear the Apostle saying: "Preach the word: be instant in season and out of season." In season, when they are willing; out of season when they are unwilling. Yes then, I am importunate: thou willest to perish, I will it not. And He wills it not, who threatened the shepherds saying: "That which was driven away you have not brought again, neither have you

sought that which was lost." Am I to fear thee more than Him? I fear thee not; the tribunal of Donatus cannot take the place of Christ's judgement seat, before which all appear. Whether thou will it or not, I shall call back the wandering sheep, I shall seek the lost sheep. The thorns may tear me; but however narrow the opening may be, it shall not check my pursuit. I will beat every bush, as long as the Lord gives me strength; so only I can get to thee wherever thou strivest to perish."

For those who might be asked advice from hierarchs on how they should proceed, suggest these words of St. Augustine of Hippo:

> "Who could love us more than God does? Nevertheless God makes use of fear in order to save us, although He teaches us with sweetness. When the Father of the family wanted guests for his banquet, did he not send his servants to the highways and hedges, to compel all they met to come in? This banquet is the unity of Christ's Body. If, then, the divine goodness has willed that, at the fitting time, the faith of Christian kings should recognize this power of the Church, let the heretics brought back from the by-ways, and schismatics forced into their enclosures, consider not the constraint they suffer, but the banquet of the Lord to which they would not otherwise have attained. Does not the shepherd sometimes use threats and sometimes blows, to win back to the master's fold the sheep that have been enticed out of it? Severity that springs from love is preferable to deceitful gentleness. He who binds the delirious man, and wakes up the sleeper from his lethargy, molests them both, but for their good. If a house were on the point of falling, and our cries could not induce those within it to come out, would it not be cruelty not to save them by force in spite of themselves? And that, even if we could snatch only one from death, because the rest, seeing it, obstinately hastened their own destruction, as the Donatists do, who in their madness commit suicide to obtain the crown of martyrdom. No one can become good in spite of himself; nevertheless, the rigorous laws of which they complain, bring

> deliverance not only to individuals, but to whole cities, by freeing them from the bonds of untruth and causing them to see the truth, which the violence of the deceits of the schismatics had hidden from their eyes. Far from complaining, their gratitude is now boundless and their joy complete; their feasts and their chants are unceasing."

Catholic Citizens of heaven and Earth

Give your secular rulers the gift of loyal subjects whose first loyalty is the Kingdom of God. Give the Pope the spiritual gift of being a member of his flock who loves his predecessors, their teachings, and the Truth no less than the filial affection offered the current Holy Father. Give God the gift of loving Him more than father and mother, wife and child, one's very life and self. Love Him with whole heart, whole soul, whole mind, and whole strength. Offer whatever is left over to your secular rulers.

Make it clear to the government that you understand that citizens do not exist for the sake of the state, but that the state exists for the sake of the salvation of citizens according to the will of God. Obeying that will results in living the Faith in such a way that approval by one's bishop or the Pope does not become the ultimate goal, but supporting the hierarchy in the goal of winning approval in individuals, the society, and the Church at large of only those things which preserve the Faith in its entirety. Obedience does not necessarily lead to sanctity, as is seen all too painfully in the experience of the Germans obeying the Nazis, the United States Supreme Court obeying the political pressures that brought *Roe vs. Wade* to the docket, and the average penitent having obeyed his passions between visits to the confessional. Bellies make lousy gods, but so does force, and so does the faceless mob. Obedience does not lead to sanctity, but sanctity demands obedience to the font of holiness, God Himself. He has commanded; "Be ye holy as I the Lord thy God am holy!...Love the Lord thy God with thy whole heart, with thy whole soul, with thy whole mind, and with thy whole strength...If you love me, you will keep my commands...My command to you is this: love one another as I have loved you...There is no greater love than that a man lay down his life for his friends..."

If your parents tell you to play in traffic, disobey them. If your president tells you to kill your children with surgery, devices, or chemicals, disobey him. If your priests or Pope tell you that what the Church used to say is wrong and that you must now follow them in following the ways of the world, disobey them. God did not say, "Be ye obedient because I the Lord thy God am obedient." God said, "Be ye holy as I the Lord thy God am holy." His Son followed that teaching faithfully when He declared, "If you love me, keep my commands." And the Father and the Son both teach and command, as we are able to understand through the power of the Holy Ghost, that we are to love the Lord Our God with our *whole* hearts, *whole* souls, *whole* minds, and *whole* strength. Sanctity does not come from obedience—just ask the Watergate burglars, the Nazis at Nuremberg, or Adam and Eve after Eden if you don't understand that. Obedience comes from sanctity— as is proved by the words, *Fiat mihi secundum verbum tuum,* and *Fiat voluntas tua sicut in caelo et in terra,* and *non sicut ego volo, sed sicut tu.*

If you don't understand Latin, just realize that sanctity is what Our Lady obediently gave the Father, sanctity is what the Son taught us to give the Father in obedience, and sanctity is the obedient gift of the Son to the Father. Our Lady and Our Lord did not obediently become holy. Their holiness demanded obedience. Those who are holy obey proper authority. One can be obedient without being holy. The holy can not remain holy without obedience, but obedience without sanctity leaves one in servile obedience to the unholy. Our Lady and Our Lord are holy, and thus they obeyed. Our task is to seek their sanctity, and thus obey as they obeyed. If we begin with obedience without acknowledging the sovereignty of sanctity, we will be enslaved. Obedience without sanctity is servitude. Sanctity with obedience is freedom.

We can not obey if we are not holy. We must not obey anything that does not lead to our holiness. Nothing is holy that rejects the perfect, eternal, unchanging will of God as it is expressed through the perfect, everlasting, unchanging teachings of the Church. This is true regardless of who you are to obey, be it your parents, your president, your priests, or your Pope. Your parents, your president, your priests, and your Pope must also obey God. If your parents, your president, your priests, or your Pope disobey God, then you disobey your parents, your president, your priests, or your Pope. Disobeying the disobedient is a true manifestation of obedience to God.

Humility is sane, it is in touch with reality, it is honest. To be humble is to know that God is above all, not only above you, but above your parents, your president, your priests, and your Pope. If you are humble you will not insanely obey the insanity of parents who tell you that making money is the most important part of life, or the insanity of your president who says that we must be friends with the enemies of God, or the insanity of your priests who say that you must obey your bishops who agree with your parents and your president, or the insanity of your Pope who says that the only insane thing would be to call all of this insane. The humble person is like the boy who told the emperor he had no new clothes, indeed, no clothes at all. The humble person is the honest person. He will say, "The world, the flesh, and the devil are wrong, liars, and evil. The Church is not now, never was, and never will be in error. What she has taught from the time of Jesus is what I will believe until the day I die. No matter who disagrees with this, be he my father, father of the country, father pastor, or the Holy Father, I will shun his lies and embrace Jesus Christ, the way, the truth, and the life." Or as a humble woman in my acquaintance once told me, "I will leave the Catholic Church when Jesus Christ leaves the Catholic Church."

The Sabbath was made for man, not man for the Sabbath. Obedience was made for sanctity, not sanctity for obedience. The Catholic papacy is to lead all men of the world to the Catholic Church, not to lead the Catholic papacy and the Catholic Church into the ways of the world. It is that simple. That is the simple truth. Follow no one who is going anywhere other than to the Cross of Christ, the Gate of the Kingdom of Heaven, the Tree of life, the Sign borne by the Groom and the Bride sealing their hearts in perfect love on earth, unto perfect and eternal life in Heaven.

Christendom is not of this world, but dwells within: in the human heart, in the family, and in the nation. It is in the world, but not of the world. Christendom is the Kingdom by which Heaven reveals its reign at hand. Christendom is the Catholic Church within every nation where souls acknowledge the absolute sovereignty of Christ the King. There is no divine right of kings except they exercise their rule as regents of the only rightful King, who is Himself divine.

Re-establishing Christendom requires humility. The lay faithful must humbly attend to their responsibilities in the world, seeking to bring sanctity to the world through their fidelity to the Church, fretting and obsessing less on the human weakness manifested by the shepherds of the Flock of Christ, and insisting more on the sanctity by which God's power will operate throughout the Body of Christ to preserve the Church against her enemies from within and without. Those shepherds must humbly bring sanctity to bear on their reception of divine Truth and their assent to the Deposit of Faith as they teach the nations, administer the Sacraments to the faithful, and rule and judge souls in keeping with the justice which finds its perfection in mercy. It is for the men of the world to set aside their demonic pride and respond to the graces present in their midst through their neighbors already of Christ's Flock, offered through the instruction of Christ's chosen shepherds, and rejected at peril of eternal perdition subject to the prince of the world, satan, who desires to wield his infernal rule in despite of God on earth and absolutely separated from God in hell. Humility is manifested in the poor in spirit. Christendom is the Kingdom of Heaven present on earth. It is through the humility of the poor in spirit that Christendom will reign supreme on earth in consonance with God's promise that the humble will reign in His Kingdom.

Fear not the world, for Jesus has overcome the world! Powers and Principalities are arrayed against us, but God is for us, and none can overcome Him. Even now the head of the serpent is beneath the foot of Our Lady; we who dwell beneath the protection of her mantle will share in her victory, in which she has full share in the victory of Christ, *victor mundi.*

Father Smith

25 September 2005
Nineteenth Sunday after Pentecost
Holy Family House, Silver Cliff, Wisconsin

Defining our Terms

Ground Rules for Useful Dialogue

1. Introduction

Heaven is a Kingdom. The King of Heaven is Jesus Christ, the Second Person of the Most Holy Trinity, the Son of God. The Queen of Heaven is the Blessed Virgin Mary, immaculately conceived, absolutely free from sin, so that she would be worthy to obey the will of God the Father to bear the Son of God as His Mother, conceiving Him in her pure womb by the power of the Holy Ghost. Heaven is the house of God whose many mansions are the home of His children conceived not by blood or by flesh or the will of man, but according to the will of God by water and the Holy Ghost. Heaven's Kingdom is not of this world. Heaven's King reigns not over realms and lands, but in the hearts of the blessed who believe in Him and obey His commands. Sovereignty from Heaven is the eternal rule begun for us in time. Heaven's reign is at hand.

Where Heaven's rule holds sway on earth, men come to know that earth offers them no abiding place. Nations are loved insofar as they provide a context for heeding the sovereignty of the eternal King, Jesus Christ. Countrymen are acknowledged as brothers regardless of their ethnic roots so long as they recognize a common sonship in Jesus Christ as children of God the Father. The peace wrought by this unity is the work of the Holy Ghost within the Body of Christ, His Bride the Catholic Church, Mother of the faithful sons of God. This peaceful unity is in this world, not of this world, and lasts beyond the end of this world.

That which is done by men in this world, by which they obey, cooperate with, and wield divine authority, must ever reflect the law God has established in creation, written on human hearts, and taught his Church. Man's free will is effective only when he chooses life, rejects the unnatural, and dedicates himself wholeheartedly to the charity by which he was created, in which he is nurtured, and for which he is willed by God. Fidelity to this humble obedience is manifested in worship of God in spirit and truth; filial piety to family, neighbor, and country; and willingness to sacrifice everything in favor of the good as given by God alone.

Each man begins his mortal life of service to the goal of God's gift of eternal life within a family. Within the family lives the charity ordained by God to be the work of life on earth and the condition for endless life in Heaven. As God gives love excepting none of His being in commitment to the unbreakable bond He wills for His children, husbands and wives, in union with their children must offer themselves to, and for, one another with the intention of never abandoning them whom God has willed to be the recipients of His abundant love. Man and woman are given to one another for the purpose of raising up children for the glory of God. Husbands and wives give themselves unto death for the sake of the love of God expressed in the family He has made for Himself to share His deathless joy in Heaven.

Societies depend upon the sanctity of the family for their stability, prosperity, and continuation. Societies depend upon the sanctity of the family for their *raison d'etre,* guiding principle, and ultimate purpose. As the family is in small, so will the society be at large. Every element of family life is ordered toward the end of aiding its members attain eternal life. Every aspect of society is ordered toward the end of aiding families in their work of rendering God His due, and thus attaining eternal life. *The just society is that society which offers the family an environment conducive to giving God all to which He justly lays a claim: the hearts, souls, minds, and strength of the creatures made in His image and likeness.*

Jesus Christ is the only Name given to men by which divine justice is accomplished. He fulfills all justice by His perfect act of mercy on the Cross of Calvary. God can not deny Himself; Jesus Christ is the truth of God incarnate who offers His Father all glory, denying Him nothing of His Body, Blood, Soul, and Divinity in thought, word, or deed. Each faithful soul who acknowledges the Word made flesh on earth will be acknowledged by the Word before the Throne of His Father in Heaven. That grace-filled heart will find himself made the dwelling place of the Father and the Son in the Holy Ghost, and will discover a place for himself in the many mansions of his Father's house in Heaven.

The first abode of the Father and the Son in the Holy Ghost on earth was the inviolate womb of the Blessed Virgin Mary. Full of grace from the instant she was made the Immaculate Conception, the Mother of God is the proof *par excellence* of the divine will to live forever with His creatures. Mary demonstrated her perfect discipleship to her divine Son by her humble acquiescence to the Father's will that she be His Son's Mother, by her confident intercession resulting in His first public miracle, and by her steadfast witness to His immolation on the Altar of the Cross. God the Father rewarded her extraordinary fidelity by willing her presence among the college of the Apostles when they received the gifts of the Holy Ghost at Pentecost, by her following His Son to glory enthroned in Heaven, and by the fulfillment of her prophetic word received in Holy Scripture, *All generations shall call me blessed!* Lesser sons of God need not despair of salvation for the Queen of Saints goes before them treading the Way of Christ wherever He is found: at Bethlehem, in Nazareth, on the streets of Galilee, atop Calvary, upon Heaven's highest throne.

God's adopted sons are not left orphaned. Standing in place of Mary, the Mother of God and Mother of the faithful sons of God, is Holy Mother Church. Standing in place of Heaven's King is His Vicar the Pope. On earth the children of God are given a womb as Jesus received His from the Blessed Virgin Mary; the waters of Baptism and the power of the Holy Ghost conceiving divine life united to human flesh in imitation of the Word being made man when Christ was conceived at the sound of His Mother's *Fiat!* On earth the children of God are given a shepherd to guard and guide them on the way of the Cross to the Pastures of Heaven as St. Peter and his successors faithfully obey the command of the Good Shepherd, "Feed my lambs!" The sheep are fed in obedience to His word that, "My Flesh is real Food and my Blood is real Drink!" The faithful sheep thus fed at the hands of their obedient shepherds are promised life abundant, eternal, and divine.

What follows in the next several pages is a brief elaboration on this outline of truths firmly embraced by the Catholic Church. Dialogue depends on mutual intelligibility. Two parties incapable of understanding *both* stances are not engaged in dialogue, but in babbling gibberish. Dialogue's goal is not further dialogue; dialogue's goal is *Truth.* Conflicting accounts of the truth can not result in resolution through compromise—a little error shared by both sides does not generate a little truth, but a whole lot more error. Not until error is identified, admitted, and corrected can resolution be reached. Not until there is a clear exposition of principles can the truth or falsity of those principles be established. Where firmly embraced principles contradict one another, the parties can *never* be reconciled—it is the condition of war between truth and lies, Heaven and hell, Christ and Belial. Those in error should not seek resolution or reconciliation, but repentance. At the risk of committing a foolish and egregious sin of presumption, this writer offers here a sketch of the contribution of the Catholic Church to the dialogue by which is further articulated that revealed by God to be His unchanging truth.

2. Peace among nations depends on unity within the true Faith

Truth does not change. Jesus Christ is the Truth. Jesus Christ is the same yesterday, today, and forever.

Forms of government may change. Whether monarchical, republican, aristocratic, tribal, or directly democratic, all can prove effective in the task of exercising authority for the common good of society and the good of individuals within families. Principles of justice can not change, for all authority is from God and its legitimacy depends on obedience to His immutable law founded in charity. A nation increases its domestic tranquility and peace beyond its borders as it increases its fidelity to the divine law expressed in the natural law, taught in ecclesial law, and ensconced in civil law. Hostile nations might deem a righteous nation fair game for attack, but a righteous nation poses no threat to its neighbors. Nations at peace are nations of justice. More important than defining the parameters of a just war is establishing the conditions of a just peace. War is invariably an assault on justice destroying peace, but peace must be understood as more than merely the absence of war. True peace is restored when war ends and justice reigns. Cessation of hostility and resumption of social order must involve an element of mercy.

Justice between nations resulting in peace among nations must obey the dictum, "One can not give what one does not have." A just peace can not be offered by unjust nations. A just peace offered by a just nation will not be accepted by an unjust nation. A just nation will, however, seek peace in the name of justice by offering mercy to its unjust opponent. As war so often leads to acts of injustice on both sides, mercy extended by one side might well accomplish justice for all sides.

It is rare in this world for nations to conceive of security in terms of mercy. Many would aver that the harsh reality of the world is that neighbors are not to be trusted. True peace transcending the mere absence of war is barely believed in as a theory and considered unrealistic, unlikely, and unfeasible in practice. Justice established by force of arms is man's typical problem-solving technique; mercy as the best realization of justice is thought impossible for man. Nonetheless, what man finds impossible is found by men of the Faith to be possible with, indeed commanded by, God.

Jesus Christ in saving individual men from the ravages of sin and death makes it possible for groups of men to do as He has done, namely, to effect justice by rendering mercy. The Cross of Christ is both the realization of perfect justice and the means of perfecting justice. On Calvary Jesus satisfies the requirements of man's debt of sin, making atonement to God. By that same Cross, each man and thereby every nation is offered the power to give God His due, to honor the rights of other men, and to safeguard the peace craved by the nations.

Bereft of faith in Jesus Christ, unjust nations and individuals will scoff at the notion of mercy as being an expression of weakness. The power of God given in Christ crucified exposes the weakness of the ways of the world for what they are: illusions of strength masking an absolute impotence. The just man and the just nation imitating Christ can make an offer of justice to an unjust foe by way of mercy. The foe has the power to reject that mercy, thus refusing justice and prolonging war; but justice for the merciful is not at the mercy of the unjust. Justice received depends on the measure by which justice is offered; the mercy given as the justice desired to be received; and the final appeal to the Judge who does not measure with the weights of the unjust world, but with the Justice whose perfection is Mercy from beyond the world. That otherworldly justice bestows a peace which the world does not know, will not have, and can not give.

3. The Natural Law must inform moral acts

Truth does not change. Jesus Christ is the Truth. Jesus Christ is the same yesterday, today, and forever.

Justice as the condition of peace is a matter of submission to the law. There is but one law operative in the universe, the will of God the Father, God the Son, and God the Holy Ghost. Divine law has as its highest expression the will to charity. God has willed that His law of charity be manifested in three ways: throughout creation by the natural law, among His children of His adoption under ecclesial law, and within the society governed by civil law. Based as they are in divine truth, which can not be self-contradictory, the natural law, ecclesial law, and civil law must never deny divine law, and, by extension, may not reject one another.

Peace as the fruit of justice properly rendered in mercy will flourish in societies where the single divine law and its three manifestations in creation are observed by all subjects. Divine law and the natural law are wholly independent of human will and are absolutely incapable of change. Ecclesial law and civil law embody many aspects of the immutable divine law and the natural law, but also include elements indicative of man's changing conditions in time. These changing manifestations of man's relationship to the divine law and the natural law within ecclesial law and civil law may *never* contradict, deny, or reject that which is immutably decreed by God. Breaking God's immutable law is an injustice against His Divine Majesty, an assault on the rights of fellow men, disruptive of the peace of society, contributory to the conditions of war, and an obstacle to human freedom.

Mankind beset by the ravages of war, the peril of crime, the dishonor of enemies, the betrayal of loved ones, and the constant threat of death is not free. Freedom in truth must be in consonance with the Truth given by God. Ecclesial law and civil law in harmony with divine law and the natural law are meant to be guarantors of human freedom and means to perfect human freedom. God's ultimate law of charity is not about what may not be done, but is a command of what *must* be done. The perfection of laws on earth in the Church and in the state is the establishment of a context in which mortal life is released from the bonds of mortality and given the freedom of immortal life.

Thus, the laws of the Church and of the state will protect the sanctity of life. They will safeguard the conduct of that life in matters of economics. Weak persons will themselves be protected by the law from the loss of property and other rights. Interactions between persons physically, emotionally, spiritually, and politically will have definitions in Church and state laws by which the natural law is acknowledged and divine law is obeyed. In short, the goal of ecclesial law and of civil law is to effect, to the greatest extent possible, a state of justice on earth in keeping with the perfection of that justice reflecting the will of God in Heaven.

Citizens of earthly kingdoms, then, will seek to live in time as nearly as possible to life as experienced in eternity. Law-abiding subjects of the Kingdom of Heaven in the world endeavor to ensure that the will of man embraces his natural state as the creature made in the image and likeness of God *willed by God for the purpose of receiving supernatural life.* G.K. Chesterton once said that the rejection of the supernatural yields not the natural, but the unnatural. Also true is that the rejection of the natural gains not the infinitude of the supernatural, but the utter and unending naught of the unnatural. The most natural thing for man is to live a life in time predicated on, sustained by, and destined for an eternal supernatural life.

Ecclesial law is the nexus where the will of man expressed in civil law and the will of God inherent in creation as the natural law are given direction toward the fulfillment of divine law. As Jesus Christ unites in Himself His human will to His divine will in obedience to the supreme law of charity, willing even death on the Cross for the sake of friends thus set free from slavery to sin and death, so also His Body the Church unites the desires and needs of man within the confines of creation to the intent of God for man's salvation. It is through the Church that the state is able to find purpose for its just governance of the natural life of men. It is in the Church that the natural state of men offered in the context of secular society is transformed to be apt matter for inclusion in the supernatural Kingdom of Heaven. Christ the Head and His Body the Church reveal the sacrifice of love which God wills for the world in order to forgive the condemnation justice demands in favor of the salvation mercy merits.

Civil law, then, is at its best when men recognize the divine prerogatives writ large across creation and taught to the last iota by the Church. The nation that is just understands that it is not over the Church, but within the Church. It brings to bear on matters of governance, a fidelity to the highest law of God by way of establishing order in society based on the natural law and submissive to ecclesial law. The just nation seeking peace recognizes the source of all justice and peace within the Cross of Jesus Christ, who offers His mercy to the nations through the mediation of His Body the Church. There is no peace without justice, no justice without mercy, no mercy without the Church, no Church without the Cross, and no Cross without Jesus Christ, in whom Heaven and earth, the supernatural and the natural, and God and man are made one.

4. Society depends on holy families

Truth does not change. Jesus Christ is the Truth. Jesus Christ is the same yesterday, today, and forever.

Society at one with the Church at one with her Lord, in whom the supernatural and the natural are mutually given in mercy perfecting justice bringing peace, is built on and exists for the human family. Husband and wife given to one another for the sake of raising up children for the glory of God form the family, which constitutes the fundamental unit of society. The first society is the family, and the family does not exist unless and until a union occurs in which natural life can be generated, increased, and offered for supernatural life. No more than the family can society be described in terms of atomism and individualism. By definition, all human society begins with a union of bodies, souls, and God's will for their beatitude. Removing any of these three elements—the natural, the supernatural, or divine providence—results in the complete destruction of the society, whether the society of the family or the society of the nation. Holy families ensure the health of society; the healthy society establishes the conditions by which families are most able to attain sanctity.

Jesus Christ gives Himself in an unbreakable bond to His Bride the Church. No more than life can continue with the head separated from the body can the will of Christ be gainsaid that life in Him is dependent upon union with him through His Bride the Church. There is no life apart from Christ, and there is no union with Christ apart from His Bride the Church, bone of His bone, flesh of His flesh, enlivened by the Spirit He shares in perfect charity with His Father. As the Blessed Virgin Mary, although a mere creature, brings forth the only-begotten Son of God in the order of the flesh she shares with Him, so also the Church imitates Our Lady in Maternity bearing countless sons of God's adoption through the power of water and the Holy Ghost. The union of Christ and His Bride is for the purpose of raising up children of the Father in the love of the Holy Ghost. Jesus bears his Cross as the Sign of the reality of this union, as the means by which this union is consummated, and as the ultimate expression of the identity of the offspring born from and belonging to this union. The union of Christ the Groom and His Bride the Church, entered by Baptism in water and the Holy Ghost, is absolutely experienced in the offering of Christ Body, Blood, Soul, and Divinity immolated on the Altar and received by God the Father and all the faithful through the hands of the priest consecrated *in persona Christi* in Holy Communion with the Blessed Sacrament.

Man and woman reflect in Holy Matrimony the union whose perfection is Christ the Groom with His Bride the Church. The Cross of Christ informs the whole of the life of husband and wife. At Baptism, each suffers death with Christ, where sin is rejected and destroyed, rising to a new life of grace. The Cross is fully received at the Sacrifice of the Mass where an acceptable holocaust is received by the Father from the Son and offered by Him through His priest for and to those baptized in His Cross. Again, in the vows of Holy Matrimony, the Cross is taken up by man and woman, who lay down lives of separation and take up a life of union devoted to the communion shared within the family, the Communion of Saints worshipping God alone, and the Holy Communion of the Mass wherein the orphans of Adam and Eve call on God as *Father* in Spirit and in Truth within the bosom of their Mother the Church by whom the Father receives perfect Sacrifice and praise and in whom the Father is pleased to call sons those whom His Son is pleased to call *brothers.*

God and man in Christ, Christ and His Church, and husband and wife are absolutely unbreakable bonds established for the freedom of the sons of God in keeping with the will of God. Human happiness on earth and man's salvation in Heaven depend upon the integrity of these bonds. If these bonds are deemed irrelevant, unbinding, or nonexistent, then there can be said to be nothing of permanence given to man. There can be no justice in a society where the unity of God and man, Christ and His Church, or man and wife can be called into question; for if faith in God given by Christ and hope in God shared by the faithful, who believe in His Resurrection from the dead, and charity of and from God experienced by man and woman imitating Christ and the Church, do not last forever, then nothing had by man for a time in the world is of any value whatsoever. A heart convinced of this utter futility of worldly things bereft of faith, hope, and charity for the things of Heaven can never know peace, will never have peace, and is powerless to share peace. The society rejecting God and man in Christ, Christ and His Church, or husband and wife, will be divided against itself, against its neighbors, and against God. It will have no hope for the peace of the Kingdom of Heaven, but will find itself in the grip of the hell that is war in this life and damnation in the afterlife.

5. Poverty of spirit brings prosperity transcending material goods

Truth does not change. Jesus Christ is the Truth. Jesus Christ is the same yesterday, today, and forever.

Faith in God given by Christ and *Hope* in God shared by the faithful who believe in His Resurrection from the dead and *Charity* of and for God experienced by man and woman imitating Christ and the Church are the bulwark against the despair that destroys peace, foments war, and dissolves societies. Faith, Hope, and Charity flow from, are united on, and bear fruit by the power of the Cross. Faith is belief in Jesus Christ, Son of God and Son of Mary by the power of the Holy Ghost, risen from the dead. Hope is the confidence that Christ's victory over the world by His Cross will be fully shared by the faithful on the last and endless

Day. Charity is the gift of God's life given on Calvary's Altar and returned to Him in humility, contrition, and obedience on the Altar at Mass. These three, Faith, Hope, and Charity, endure inseparable from one another, perfected on the Cross. Only that which is united in Faith, Hope, and Charity can be transformed from ephemera doomed for destruction with the end of time into heirs of the Kingdom of Heaven given glory forever. Even now men can read the signs of the times, judge the tree by its fruit, and discern the spirits to determine whether they are directing their use of things in this world toward the wilderness where sin-laden goats shall perish, or in the footsteps of the Good Shepherd toward the pastures where His sheep will find their mansions in their Father's house in Heaven.

It is the Cross by which Sign Christ knows His sheep and His sheep know their Shepherd. His sheep judge the things of this world to be rubbish, of no worth in comparison to the human soul, an unnecessary encumbrance for those who prefer to sell all, give to the poor, store treasure thus in Heaven, and follow the Good Shepherd even unto death, death on the Cross. To be too busy about many things is to neglect the one needful thing and risk rejecting and losing the better part. When seeking the presence of Christ's Church bringing the Cross lifted high into the world to transform the world, one finds his object in seeing unity, sanctity, catholicity, and apostolicity. The signs of the Cross at work bearing fruit in the Church confronting the world are the faithful being *poor, persecuted, pure, and prayerful.*

The Kingdom of Heaven is at war with the world. But just as Jesus Christ came to bring a peace unlike that given by the world, so, too, the sword He wields refusing the peace of the world has a potency unlike and far greater than the weapons wielded by the world. Jesus Christ reigns upon the highest Throne, crowned in glory, bearing the scepter of royalty whose lineage brooks no rival. In Christ Jesus sword, throne, crown, scepter, and victory are one. *The reign of Christ is established on His Cross.*

His loyal subjects, then, obey His commands by dwelling within the bounds of His realm. Jesus is the Prince of Peace, the Seat of Mercy, and the Lord of Love. By the Cross the Prince of Peace casts down and thrusts out the prince of the world, satan. By the Cross the just Judge forgives the debt of the slaves in bondage to the world, the flesh, and the devil. By the Cross charity reigns over all, is in all, and conquers all. The Cross is the chasm dividing hell from Heaven, it is the winnowing fan that distinguishes the tares from the wheat, and it is the gate barring wolves from the fold and the mark separating the goats from the sheep.

The condemnation consumed by those guilty of the Blood of the Lord is heard in the cries of, *Crucify him! Crucify him!* The salvation won for those washed in the merciful Blood of the Lamb is declared in the witness of the Centurion, *Surely, this man was the Son of God!* The Kingdom of Heaven is beset by violence, and the tide of blood shed in the violence of the Cross bears away to the Kingdom of Heaven the faithful subjects who bear the cross with their triumphant King.

Persecution is the cross embraced in the face of oppressors. Purity is the beatitude of the heart made wholly open to the will of God. Prayer is the labor of the Holy Ghost on behalf of the inarticulate children of God ignorant of what to say to their heavenly Father. The signs of the Cross at work as the Church confronts the world in being persecuted, pure, and prayerful are a matter of a faithful acceptance of what others have to offer. Humility is the condition for all virtues—as St. Jean-Marie Vianney says, "The first virtue is humility. The second virtue is humility. And the third virtue is humility." He also says that humility "is like the chain of the Rosary: remove it and all the beads, all the virtues fall away." It is through humility that the faithful are able to endure persecution, to practice purity, and to pray ceaselessly. Persecution, purity, and prayer are gifts from outside oneself; humility is the gift *of* oneself, insignificant as it is, little as it might be, worthless as it seems, but given wholly and selflessly.

Poverty—of spirit and of material goods—is a means of receiving and increasing the virtue of humility. The materially poor can always give more of themselves. The materially wealthy but poor in spirit can always give more things in order to give more fully of themselves. Humility is always in the company of poverty. This is most perfectly seen in the humility of Jesus in the poverty of the manger, the humility of Jesus in the poverty of the wine-less wedding feast, the humility of Jesus amongst the poverty of the 5,000 in the desert, the humility of Jesus accepting the poverty of Golgotha, and the humility of Jesus in the poverty of a borrowed tomb.

Jesus teaches that the humble will be exalted. Thus, His humility exalts man in a union with his Creator. The humility of Jesus responds to the intercession of His Mother with an overabundance of wine. The Son of God humbly feeds a multitude a miraculous feast, knowing that most of them will shortly walk away in angry disbelief. No greater degradation and humiliation has ever been or ever shall be than Christ dying, and no greater glory ever revealed than in His empty tomb. That glory will be seen forever by the humble who become like children, the humbly pure of heart, and the humble who confess their guilt in hope of hearing the wondrous judgement, *This day thou shalt be with me in Paradise!* The seed that humbly falls to the ground losing life shall gain a life bearing fruit thirty, sixty, and a hundredfold.

That is true wealth. The truly wealthy on earth labor for the treasure of Heaven, selling all, giving it away, and gaining Heaven thereby. Neither rust nor moth nor mortality can touch the jewels possessed by the meanest pauper of Heaven. Nothing the world holds can compare with the least object of Heaven. The glory of the world wrought in gold is the stuff which the blessed tread underfoot in the New Jerusalem.

Poverty for the sake of the Kingdom of Heaven, like Faith, Hope, and Charity, is an act of the will. It is an offer of the bounty received from God rendered back to God out of obedience, trust, and love. The more that one receives in gifts from God, the more one is required to offer in gift to God. From those who are given much, much is expected. This holds in the natural world no less than in the supernatural.

Cleverness of serpents (worldly wisdom) yields in a union with the innocence of doves (God's wisdom) within holy poverty. Holy poverty does not seek the increase of the wealth available to be secured by rich people, but establishes a society wherein the wealth of all, rich and poor, is made secure. Therein the widow fears no foreclosure. No orphan is condemned to the streets. Laborers receive a wage sufficient to allow them to purchase real property through thrift and industry. Not only is usury forbidden, but the usurer is punished. Humility expressed in poverty is the desire for more wealth created for sharing with people in love of God and one another, rather than for more wealthy people in love with money.

A useful lesson to be learned in youth and taken to heart into old age is the principle that one gets the answers to the questions one asks. Answers are only as good as the questions to which they respond. Hence, if one asks the question, "How rich can I be and still get to Heaven?" one will learn much about now hard it is to acquire wealth, retain wealth, and let go of wealth on the way to the grave, but precious little about attaining the kingdom of Heaven.

If, on the other hand, one asks Our Lord Jesus what must be done to enter the Kingdom of Heaven, he will hear the very useful, practical, and attainable answer given the rich young man: *Go, sell all you have, give to the poor, thus store up treasure in Heaven, and come, follow me!* That rich young man, Lazarus' oppressor Dives, and the doomed silo builder failed to learn the lesson which Christ would teach His own: narrow is the way of salvation, needles' eyes do not admit camels, and the whole of the world is insufficient compensation for one soul.

True peace is not found in hoarding riches or in lacking riches. True peace comes either from giving riches from the motivation of heartfelt charity, or from the richness borne by the soul who leaves all behind—wife, husband, mother, father, sister, brother, children, property—in order to seek and find Jesus. When the Good Shepherd claims His sheep looking to be found by Him, they share a peace which this world can not give, alien to the wealthy, and undesired by the avaricious whether wealthy or poor.

The blessed poor who inherit the Kingdom of Heaven know like St. Paul how to cope with either a sufficiency or with want. The poor in spirit who are materially wealthy do not measure their worth in property, and neither do the materially poor count their blessings by way of what they lack. Holy poverty understands that lacking the grace of humility either riches can be a curse, as with King Midas; or poverty can be a curse, as John Steinbeck put it, "You who handled poverty badly will handle wealth equally badly." It is in neither the possession nor in the lack that blessing lies, but in the heart filled with a desire which only the love of Christ can satisfy.

Curiously, both holy poverty and material greed manifest insatiable appetites. The billionaire is ever after more money, and the pauper saint is in constant want of grace. If he is true to his craving, the billionaire will come to his deathbed still desiring money, but arriving at a place where money is not to be had and buys less happiness than it could on earth. The saint faithful to his vocation anticipates the Day of Judgement knowing that the grandest expectations of the blessed will be infinitely surpassed in the reward announced with the glorious words of the just Judge: *Come, you blessed of my Father, into the Kingdom prepared for you from the foundation of the world!* The saint in Christ is where infinite need is met by inexhaustible largesse.

6. Jesus Christ is King of All

Jesus Christ is the single possession of the sheep of His Flock. He is their true wealth, their only desire. As the saying goes, to have everything but God is to have nothing, but to have nothing but God is to have everything. To see Jesus Christ is to see the Father. To believe in Jesus Christ without yet seeing Him is to receive a greater blessing. To see Jesus Christ for all eternity is the very definition of Heaven. In that Vision is all the glory of the universe, and it belongs to everyone whom the Father claims as His own, and to anyone who claims Jesus Christ as his all.

Eternal life in Heaven begins with mortal life on earth. Human life is meant to be nurtured in the family. Jesus Christ is the bond by which husbands and wives tenaciously cling to one another in their mutual attachment to the love of Christ. For the sake of the love from and of God, mothers and fathers offer themselves wholeheartedly to their children that they might grow up to know, love, and serve God now and be happy with Him forever. Jesus Christ is the love shared in Holy Matrimony, Jesus Christ is the love given by parents to children, Jesus Christ is the love from God the Father returned to Him by the children adopted by Him in Jesus Christ through water and the Holy Ghost.

Written on the very heart of every creature made in the image and likeness of God is His eternal law. God's will for perfect charity is manifest in the natural law, taught by ecclesial law, and meant to be realized in civil law. Jesus Christ is the Word through whom creation is made. Jesus Christ is the Truth taught by His Church for the salvation of souls. Jesus Christ is the Sovereign before whom every knee must bend in Heaven, on earth, and under the earth. The only justice, order, and rule possible comes from, is guided by, and submits to Jesus Christ.

In Him is found the only source of peace. Nations separated from Christ through sin, heresy, schism, apostasy, or ignorance can not share Christ with one another. Incapable of sharing Christ, they are incapable of conceiving true peace, desiring to share true peace, or experiencing true peace within their borders or with foreigners. Such nations are doomed to war. The world not only wars against Christ and His Kingdom, but is ever beset by strife in homes, on the streets, and across battlefields.

But the nation who accepts Jesus Christ as Sovereign King will seek peace and find it. His peace will be offered by His subjects to other nations. His peace will inform the righteous laws enacted by His subjects who rule in His Name. Families will share His peace within homes shielded from injustice by the nation founded on Jesus Christ. Jesus Christ will be the one treasure pursued by those families, defended by their nation, and prodigally spread by them throughout the world.

Any attempt to pursue peace, rule, or prosperity without being submissive to Jesus Christ in keeping with divine law, the natural law, and ecclesial law will end in a denial of Jesus Christ. Witting or no, men who do not submit to the rule of Christ will find themselves ruled by the antichrist. Antichrists will rise up to pervert human strivings so that war will be desired more than peace, depravity will gain legal standing, the family will be attacked in law, and prosperity will be defined in terms of material objects whose worth, pleasure, and possession can not last. These men can provide no mercy, only tyranny; no justice, only brute force; no charity, only worse than bestial passions; and no true joy in this life, only despair at the end of life. Life without Christ is faithless, hopeless, loveless, and brief.

Jesus Christ *is* life. He promises abundant life. He has pledged us complete joy. He has vowed never to abandon us, in life, at death, forever. Jesus Christ can be trusted to fulfill His word, for it is true. *Truth does not change. Jesus Christ is the Truth. Jesus Christ is the same yesterday, today, and forever.*

7. The Blessed Virgin Mary is the perfect model of humanity restored to the image and likeness of God

From the instant of her Immaculate Conception, the Blessed Virgin Mary was destined by God for perfect discipleship in His Son. Our Lady is the perfect vessel chosen by God to bear Him whom the heavens can not contain. Jesus Christ willed that the perfect tabernacle to be filled with Him in grace would be His mother Mary. Scripture proclaims that all generations will call her blessed for the singular call given her by God. She never once failed to heed the Father's call, to obey her Son's commands, to offer the love of the Holy Ghost.

No treasure compares with the bounty of receiving Christ in one's heart. No Christian ever received the fullness of Christ Jesus—Body, Blood, Soul, and Divinity—as completely as the Blessed Virgin Mary. Our Lady was created for Our Lord in a unique way far above the purpose for which any of His other creatures were brought into being. Her humble acknowledgement of this wondrous truth left no room in her heart for anything other than fulfilling His will to be perfect as God is perfect, to go to the Cross with the Son, and to receive the very life and love of God within her from the Holy Ghost. The Blessed Mother desired nothing of worldly wealth, accepting instead only the riches brought by Heaven.

Receiving that treasure, Our Lord Jesus Christ, Our Lady proceeded to nurture and guard that infinite wealth through her chaste marriage with St. Joseph. Each marriage is made for the purpose of raising up children to the glory of God. The marriage of the Virgin Mary and St. Joseph accomplished the sublime task of raising up the only-begotten Son of God for His glory.

Within the Holy Family at Nazareth, the will of God informed every thought, word, and deed. Jesus Christ stood at the center of the Holy Family, the position He should have in every family. Our Lady was the dutiful mother, laboring to keep a house where Jesus Christ could feel at home; every wife and mother's responsibility. St. Joseph toiled by hand to provide materially for his family, aware of the awesome burden of fostering God's child and being accountable to Him for the quality of his performance; thoughts which should be at the forefront of the minds of every husband and father under God. Mary and Joseph looked to the just laws given by God, revealed by His holy people, and administered by the state not as onerous obstacles, but as helps to obeying God and thus pleasing Him. Our Lady and her most chaste spouse were not lawyers seeking loopholes to avoid the law. They were children who loved everything given them by their Father: life, each other, the law, their Son, and His love.

The love of Jesus Christ was what prompted His Mother to share her flesh with the Word of God. In the flesh given Him by His mother, our Lord Jesus bore the Cross by which He consummated the saving act wherein the mercy of God is given to men. When men receive mercy from God, they can share it with one another. On that mercy ultimate justice depends. Where justice is served through mercy, peace can reign, God is obeyed, families are safe, Christ is received, and He receives all glory, honor, and kingship as is His due.

Jesus Christ never abandons His own. His Mother Mary never abandoned her Son. She heard the angel's word and conceived her Lord by the power of the Holy Ghost. Angels watched over the birth of Jesus as Mary nursed Him at her breast in the stable. It was at Mary's word that Jesus deigned to work His first public miracle. She followed Him at each step along the way of the Cross. Her mother's Heart shared His torment unto death on Calvary. Mary's faith received the reward of seeing her Son raised from the dead. And at Pentecost she was on hand as once again the power of the Holy Ghost descended upon the earth.

For just as Our Lady never abandoned her firstborn son, she ever stands by those adopted by the Father through water and the Holy Ghost. So, as she was on hand when Jesus was born, she stood at the foot of the Cross when His pierced side gushed forth the life-giving fount of Blood and Water giving birth to the infant Church. Our Lady was there when her Son miraculously appeared in the Upper Room and breathed on the newborn Church, commissioning them to know peace, to love, and to show mercy through the forgiveness of sins. And on the great Day of Pentecost, the Mother of God saw the Church burst out into the world to proclaim the Good News of salvation in the power of the Holy Ghost, just as she had seen her Son go into the towns of Galilee teaching, healing, and forgiving.

Where Jesus is, there also is Our Lady, our Queen, our Mother. Christ's faithful may never deny Him, His Father, or His Mother. The children of God claimed by the Father are not half-brothers in Christ. No, His Father is our Father; His Mother is our mother. We share the same humanity He received from His mother. We are privileged to participate in the divinity He shares with His Father in the Holy Ghost.

Blest is she who believed the promises of the Lord! Mary believed because she recognized the truth when it was presented to her. She understood that the truth proclaimed in the law and the prophets was to be fulfilled *in her!* The truth proclaimed through the ages does not change. Mary gave the Truth the name foretold for Him by the angel: *Jesus, the Lord saves. Jesus is the truth. Jesus does not change. The salvation of Our Lord is the same yesterday, today, and forever.*

8. The Pope is God's guarantee of success

Jesus did not establish one means of salvation on Pentecost, a different one a millennium-and-a-half later, another one a half-century ago, and yet a further one to be announced by a sect waiting to be incorporated in Geneva or New York. Salvation comes from the Cross. The Cross is received through water Baptism. Baptism is ordered toward the participation in Calvary which is the Mass. The Mass is offered only by Christ's Church, and His Church is governed, at His command, by the Pope. Salvation does not come to those who deny God. Salvation does not come to those who deny the Son of God, Jesus Christ crucified. Salvation does not come to those who deny the Mother of God. Salvation does not come to those who deny the son of the Father appointed to be the Vicar of the Son and His Mother's defender.

Salvation is had by those who receive what St. Peter and his successors offer as their only wealth, neither silver nor gold, but the Name of Jesus Christ. In His Name they feed His Flock His Body and Blood immolated on the Cross in the Mass. In His Name they teach the nations and Baptize in the Name of the Father, and of the Son, and of the Holy Ghost. In His Name they cast out demons, heal the sick, and raise the dead. In His Name they are willing to lay down their lives for their friends, to love their enemies, and to rejoice when they are tortured for the sake of the Name of Jesus Christ.

The flock entrusted to St. Peter and his successors benefits from this unwavering embrace of the Cross by the example it offers for the sanctity in and of the family. Christ lays down His life for His sheep, St. Peter lays down his life for

Christ's Flock. Husbands lay down their lives for their wives and children. The Bride of Christ the Church obeys her Lord in all things for the sake of the Flock. The faithful of the Church obey the Vicar of Christ for the sake of their salvation. Wives obey their husbands in the task of bringing sanctity to the whole family. The love of husbands must stop at nothing, even death, to provide for their families. The obedience of wives must express the humility of Mary, not the pride of Eve, so that their husbands will receive due support in obeying God for the salvation of the whole family.

The Pope has nothing to teach except the sacrificial love and the humble obedience of the Cross that lead to salvation. Every dogma, all the history, and each ritual of the Church is for the salvation of souls, the highest law of the Church. Salvation can not be offered by the Church in any way that makes salvation impossible. This means that the Church may *never* violate the divine law or the natural law, and she must resist civil laws where human will is given precedence over divine will. The laws of the Church support the freedom of the sons of God, not the lawless license of the orphans of Eden.

With that in mind, God has given the Church under the Pope to the world to be *the* supranational institution bringing the peace of Christ to the world. The keys to the Kingdom of Heaven by which the Pope binds and looses, unlock the treasure of God's mercy in the Sacraments, particularly in the Sacrament of Penance. Individuals receiving the mercy of God are made able to move nations to share that mercy with one another. The mercy which bridges the gap between God and man and between individuals also has the power to bring nations together. The bond of peace wrought by justice perfected in mercy unites God and His children and brothers in Christ, and can establish harmony between nations. And just as no confusion of persons occurs where the peace of Christ reigns between God and the human soul and between individuals thus reconciled, national identity is preserved where Christ is given kingship. Sovereign nations are preserved from war, defended from injustice, and freed from fear when Jesus Christ is their King. The strife between nations passes, but the nations themselves are free and can flourish.

They will flourish by enacting laws which respect divine law and the natural law, and which reinforce ecclesial law. Justice in law, within these states, will provide a safe context in which families can nurture the graces given by God and increase the material well-being of society in keeping with the supreme law of charity. Through this charity individuals, families, and all of society will be bound more closely together in the Faith which Jesus Christ has commanded His Body the Church to teach the nations. Those who believe and are Baptized will be among the multitudes processing into New Jerusalem on the Last Day. They will discover that their endless life in the Kingdom of Heaven began when they determined to live in the Kingdom at hand among the nations of the world.

Christ's Gospel of salvation is all that the Church under the Pope has to offer the world. To avoid sin and to do good, to be Baptized and consume the Body and Blood of the Lord, to confess our sins, to venerate Our Lady and the saints, and to worship God through the immolation of Christ in the Mass are the lessons taught by Jesus, passed down in the tradition of his Church, and mandated by Christ through his Vicars' binding and loosing. The Pope can not change this. St. Paul could not change it. An angel of light has no power to change it. To attempt to alter the immutable is to be subject to anathema. The teachings of the Church authoritatively declared by the Pope can not change because they are true. *Truth does not change. The teachings of the Church are the teachings of Christ, the unchanging Truth. Christ and His teachings through His Church are the same yesterday, today, and forever.*

9. Conclusion

It is, of course, the case that many beg to differ with the Church's steadfast teachings. Not only is the content of her truth challenged, but the very constancy of her faith in Jesus Christ and His truth is attacked. The only thing that comes close to equaling the unchangeable nature of truth is the willful rejection of that Truth from antiquity through modernity. From satan before Eden to secularists seeking utopia, some things never change. What does change constantly, however, are the grounds cited for refusing submission to Christ and His Church.

Some hackles rise at the suggestion that the Church is the proper agent for protecting national sovereignty, improving international relations, and securing world peace; but many of those same people demand such a role for the Godless United Nations. Holy Mother Church's age-old insistence on the inviolability of the matrimonial bond is met with ridicule among the sophisticates who in the same breath lambaste marriage as an outdated institution while bellowing that its privileged position in society should be extended to fornicators and deviants. The Church would have her members have large families with many children who learn respect for and life lessons from their parents. Worldly people are shocked by couples with more than two children and subject parents to hostile inquiries from agents of the state who wish to teach perversion to children, Worldly people depict parents as bumbling idiots in the media, exalt youth as the *sine qua non* of popular culture, and foam at the mouth when efforts are made to protect children from parents and strangers who would boil, dismember, or impale them during the first nine months of their lives. Love of neighbor and the proper use of material things guides the Catholic, providing a foundation for understanding the meaning and purpose of life; angst-ridden worldlings declare life meaningless and purposeless, despair of man's perfection, and love money with all their heartless, soulless, mindless impotence in the face of unavoidable death.

Dialogue demands truth as the object of discussion. The world lukewarm to, in denial of, or ignorant about Jesus Christ and His Church guided by His Vicar, is in error. Catholics have nothing to gain from lending credence to error. The Church can forgive error, she can correct error, and often she must denounce the purveyors of error, but listening to error in dialogue is a matter of enduring so much gibberish. Before dialogue can begin, both parties must agree on the existence, the nature, and the accessibility of truth. Those who deny the truths of the Catholic Church have nothing to say to her. The Catholic Church will continue proclaiming the Truth of Jesus Christ and Him crucified without compromise until He returns to claim for Himself the people who have kept His faith unalloyed, unapologetically, and unashamed.

Little difference in practice is found in the various sources of error and the futility of engaging them in dialogue. If a man is certain that niggers, kikes, and spics are subhuman, rational conversation with him is impossible. If a woman is convinced that two mothers are better for her children, after she divorces their father for refusing to let her kill their unborn brother, reasoned discourse can not occur with her. If a group of people decide that they are infallible in declaring that Jesus turned water into grape juice but that the Pope is mistaken when he thinks he devours real Flesh and real Blood every day, it is madness to engage them in theological debate. If a Catholic believes that getting to Heaven does not depend upon being in communion with the Pope, only a fool would try to persuade him through speech that it makes sense for him to remain Catholic or for him to attempt to convince others to convert to Catholicism. As the world brazenly preaches the gospel that Mohammed, the Buddha, Caiaphas, Madeleine Murray-O'Hare, and Pope St. Pius x all believed in the same deity, the argumentative powers of Socrates are inadequate to communicate truth to the souls steeped in self-delusion. It is passing strange that irreconcilable differences between a husband and wife are readily construed to be absolutely insurmountable obstacles to successful resolution of marital conflict, but few to none balk at the notion that thousands, millions, and billions have hope of finding common ground by spewing mutually contradictory, dishonest, twisted, hostile, and morally reprehensible ravings at one another.

Teaching, correcting, and reprimanding—not dialogue—is what God expects of his Church. The world has a right to clear enunciations of the truth, regardless of how often or how much the world rebels against such. The salvation of countless souls depends on the Church wasting no more time in fruitless babble, and wasting no time in coming to rededicate herself to preaching the truth to every nation, in season and out, when convenient and inconvenient, even at the risk of losing her tax-free status, the modern form of martyrdom. Indeed, very harsh will be the judgement on Catholics who did not feed those hungry for the Truth, quench those thirsty for the waters of life, clothe with sanctity those living in naked sin, heal those members of the Body of Christ crippled by heresy, and visit with the true Presence of Christ the lonely dying facing imminent judgement. Dialogue must end, and the ensuing silence must be filled with one voice, once and for all declaring one truth: **the same yesterday, today, and forever, Jesus Christ is Lord!**

Father Smith
Sacerdos vagus

17 July 2005
Ninth Sunday after Pentecost (St. Alexis)
Travelers Inn, Missoula, Montana

Regnum Christi

A Handbook for Citizens of the Kingdom of Heaven in Exile

Welcome, child of God!

You have just been baptized, washed clean of the stain of Original Sin, snatched from the clutches of the enemy satan, and are now a member of the Body of Christ, the Catholic Church, thereby becoming an adopted Son of God the Father through water and the Holy Spirit. During the days and years ahead as you mature into the full stature of the New Man, Jesus Christ, whom you have put on through this marvelous Sacrament, you will be assisted by extraordinary graces from your Father in Heaven. Our Queen and Blessed Mother Mary will be at your side at all times to intercede with her divine Son on your behalf.

Already you have been assigned a Guardian Angel to accompany you all the days of your life, watching out for your stumbling feet, protecting your toes from stubbing, and steering you clear of questionable persons and places. A large number, too great to be counted in fact, of witnesses go before you in a cloud of glory and surrounding you with the love of God. Many of them, you will discover, are special friends chosen for you by God to offer you particular example, encouragement, and, as needed, correction and chastening. Remember, if you ever have any questions or difficulties, God the Holy Ghost, the Third Person of the Most Blessed Trinity and your divine Advocate, is available at all times, day and night, with a bounty of Fear of the Lord, Piety, Fortitude, Knowledge, Understanding,

Counsel, and Wisdom to aid you in absolutely every task before you as you faithfully work out your salvation with fear and trembling in the firm hope of attaining the perfection of the charity that casts out all fear.

Jesus Christ, our Sovereign King, has waged war on your behalf, destroying sin, conquering death, and casting out the prince of the world, satan. Our Holy Mother Church, for whose freedom and exaltation your daily prayers will be offered, has mediated to you the graces of the triumph of the Cross of Christ. These graces fortify the Church Militant as its members continue the battle bringing to consummation at the end of time the victorious strife engaged by Heaven over hell. You are the beneficiary, along with the many other members of the Body of Christ, of these graces. Use them well and go forward to your share in the struggle by which you will gain a portion of the eternal reign of Christ the King!

This manual is offered to you as a general guide for how life is conducted in the Kingdom of Heaven as it pertains to its loyal subjects in exile in but never of the world. It is strongly recommended that you make frequent use of the information contained herein until you are thoroughly familiar with the traditions, teachings, and practices common to the worshippers of God in spirit and truth. Most of our newest citizens discover that the new life in Christ they have embraced is so different from their old ways of sin and death that they simply must forget all that they once knew about conducting life in the world, and essentially begin from scratch. As well, it is regrettable that not a few fall victim to pride, believing that somehow their old ways were sufficient or, God forbid—and He does forbid—even better than the habits of sanctity instilled in the hearts, souls, minds, and bodies of the true children of God. What is described below is not just better than your old life in bondage to sin, in peril of death, and oppressed by satan, but it is *wholly* different. And, remember, when God says be holy as He is holy, He means to be *wholly* holy as He is holy, with your *whole* heart, *whole* soul, *whole* mind, and *whole* strength. Keep in mind that God is the Author of all, including language, so when He says something, He means it— as He said it, He means it, and because He meant it, He says it.

The world, of which you now have repented, is not your friend. It is not slightly damaged and in need of just a few repairs. There is *nothing* of the world that is desirable for possession within the Kingdom of Heaven. This world is passing, destined for judgement in fire, and slated for utter replacement. Anything and anyone attached to the world will suffer the same fate. As a new child of God, you have begun the tremendous work of ensuring that you, your loved ones, and

all of your endowments are preserved from destruction so that God the Father has the joy at the end of time of looking on you and calling you a beloved son in whom He is well pleased. You will discover that such an experience will bring you joy as well, and, indeed, immense pleasure.

Specific instructions on dogmas, doctrines, and the devotional life of the Church are contained in the catechism issued through the authority of Mother Church (that from Trent is especially informative), and, thus, none of that will be treated herein. Instead, this brief survey is intended to provide general principles necessary to navigate the treacherous waters besetting the Barque of St. Peter. The manual is divided into three categories subdivided into three sections each with each of the sections offering three points to remember—the Kingdom of Heaven *really* likes trinities. The schema for the manual is as follows:

Part I: The Body

A. Section 1: Food
   1. Why to eat
   2. How to find food to eat
   3. With whom to eat

B. Section 2: Shelter
   1. Where to live
   2. How to provide a house
   3. What goes inside a house

C. Section 3: Clothing
   1. Modesty
   2. Simplicity
   3. Utility

Part II: The Mind

A. Section 1: Science
   1. The nature of knowledge
   2. The knowledge of nature
   3. The limits of empiricism

B. Section 2: Philosophy
   1. The law of non-contradiction
   2. Defining terms of debates
   3. Where philosophy ends

C. Section 3: Theology
    1. Revelation
    2. The magisterium
    3. The queen of the sciences

Part III: The Soul

A. Section 1: Free Will
    1. *Imago Dei*
    2. Obedience
    3. Sin as slavery

B. Section 2: Body and Soul
    1. The body aiding the soul
    2. The soul aiding the body
    3. Body and soul in enmity

C. Section 3: Life and Death
    1. Life is an absolute, but life on earth is not
    2. *Avoid evil!* is absolute—*Do the good!* is relative.
    3. Reward and punishment

Little time or study will be necessary to realize that this is far from an exhaustive treatment of the subjects in question. Primary to the effort at hand is to demonstrate the clear separation between those who are of the world and those who are of the Kingdom of Heaven. Ruled by the King who declares, "Let your yes mean yes and your no mean no," the Kingdom of Heaven should not be expected to admit of any ambiguity about what properly belongs to it and that which is foreign to it. The world is a wasteland of black, white, and grey, admixed, confused, and dreary. The Kingdom of Heaven is the domain of Light Himself, brilliant, filled with the vision of glory and the glory of the vision, and pleasing to Him in Whom there is no darkness, Who paves in gold, and Who created the rainbow as the first sign of His mercy.

Part I: The Body

Section 1: Food

We eat because we are hungry, not because we are bored. We eat to live, not live to eat. We eat to celebrate a worthy event, refraining from making eating the event which is celebrated. We eat enough to keep the body strong, and a strong body is capable of abstaining from kinds of food and certain times of eating in order to contribute to the strengthening of one's character. We eat what is put before us, grateful for plenty and uncomplaining in dearth; we do not cause dearth by refusing to eat what is put before us, and we shun plenty when it becomes a temptation to gluttony.

Food grows on trees, from the ground, beneath the sea, in the woods, and within mothers' breasts. Common sense dictates that as one proceeds through life one arranges things in such a way that trees, the earth, water, countryside, and loving companions are ever nearby. It also makes sense that each man would have at least a modicum of knowledge of how to extract sustenance from the land and sea. There is nothing inherently evil or erroneous about supermarkets—except for the unfortunate misconception that such is the locale wherein milk, bread, and eggs are *produced*. Restaurants can be delightful venues for the abovementioned celebration of worthy events, but they are woefully inadequate as replacements for the kitchen hearth and the taste and feel of meals made from scratch by the hands of wives and mothers. In the same way that food should be moderated in the amounts in which it is consumed, moderation should also mark the frequency with which meals are pursued in restaurants and foraged in their entirety from supermarket chains. Kitchen gardens should be employed, at least to some extent, in stocking kitchen cupboards, and kitchen stoves should be employed daily to lade kitchen tables.

The only thing worse than preparing food that one does not like is to eat food with persons one does not like. Avoiding either of these ills is a matter of charity. One learns to like whatever food is available by remembering that unavailable food is the worst kind of food. Likewise, one must learn to like one's family remembering that eternity is a long time to be apart from them—if you wish to not spend time with them on earth, you will spend eternity being separated from them in hell. Such is not the worst incentive for finding it within one's heart to enjoy simple food and the simple company of one's flesh and blood. There is certainly a problem when eating many meals with persons unrelated is preferable to dining with one's own family. If this problem should arise, the solution is not a matter of getting more new friends, but of developing a new attitude about the old family. Love of neighbor is the second Great Commandment, after love of God, which is accomplished in large part through the love of neighbor. The first neighbors one ever meets are in one's family. Charity begins in the home, and charity is fed, in large measure, through the happy meals spent in the company of neighbors.

Fast food, junk food, and comfort food should strike healthy ears as being unpalatable. Among oxymorons, fast food is one of the most nonsensical—fast food is no food at all. Edibles should not include anything with the modifier junk attached to them—we are what we eat, so imagine what comes from eating junk food. Sympathetic ears, warm hugs, reassuring smiles, the sight of home, and true words bring emotional comfort. The only food that brings comfort is that which relieves one after having had a diet of fast food, and the comfort is merely physical, not emotional. Inanimate objects can not bring emotional or intellectual satisfaction to the mind or soul.

There is a penchant in modernity for labeling things: certain speech as politically incorrect, certain people as belonging to various nonexistent ethnic groups, and certain foods as natural, artificial, organic, and/or all of the above, which last designation might stem from belonging to ethnic groups whom political correctness forbids naming by name. For anyone concerned about whence his food comes, there is a simple remedy—simple, mind you, not necessarily easy—a simple remedy available in the act of growing one's food oneself. Then pesticides, insecticides, and herbicides can be applied to the point of suicide at one's own discretion—or not! Barring residency in nations other than this one, one need never worry about *Made in China* appearing on the produce produced in one's own backyard. And, thus far at least, the government is not interested in regulating, restricting, or registering the fruit of private labor accomplished on private property for use in the private sector.

In each and all of these considerations, the citizen of the Kingdom of Heaven is liberated by a sense of freedom, a sense of the possible, and good old-fashioned common sense. There is no room in the Kingdom of Heaven for those who fall into the ways of the world simply because that's what everyone is doing. Most of the world is either dying of starvation or from the effects of overeating. Unnatural death is decidedly *not* one of the results of living obedient to the mores and customs of the saints.

Central to this truth is the fact that the saints realize, and actually believe, that the body *is* subject death. Worldlings have a bad habit of doing deadly things in denial of the fact that death will take them all. Citizens of the Kingdom of Heaven understand that death of the body is not the worst thing that can happen to a person. Death of the soul in hell is the worst thing that can happen to a person. Thus, saints-in-the-making are insistent on living responsibly in this world acknowledging that this world is ending—without them. The soul destined for

Heaven lives apart from this passing world, leaves behind the trammels of this world in death, and is no more of the world in eternity than it was in time. Fear of death motivates worshippers of the body; fear of displeasing the Lord motivates the worshippers of Christ in spirit and truth. Fearing death, death becomes the final judgement; fearing God, God rewards the faithful with eternal life.

Section 2: Shelter

Houses generally are built of wood, stone, brick, or in combinations thereof. Houses generally are built on lots slightly bigger than the houses themselves, allowing in most instances space for but a modest yard. Houses generally are built to ward the ill-effects of the elements, to provide security for the dwellers therein, and to promote a sense of happiness and wellbeing.

As well, houses generally are built for the occupants to use for, on average these days, five years. Houses generally are built for the profit of developers, construction companies, and banks. Houses generally are built at a cost that results in the buyer spending thirty years paying off the principal (two or three times over at least) and the interest. Houses generally are built with the idea in mind that the debtor will leverage his debt into a larger house one day and/or borrowing power for greater indebtedness as the years go by. Houses generally are built as part of the engine driving a boom economy; houses generally are not built when the economy goes bust.

Another way in which houses generally are not built is by their occupants. Most home "owners" do not know the first thing about drywall and laying foundations. Houses generally are not built for the use of people who will do much more with them than sleep in them and argue over them in divorce proceedings. Houses generally are built for use by people who spend a third of the day at work or school, an eighth of their waking hours in various modes of transportation, a quarter of the day in some kind of "recreational" activity more often than not involving inordinate attention being given to lights dancing across a screen of some sort, and the bulk of any remaining time complaining about all of the things that need to be done around the house that never seem to get done. Additionally, these people who have mortgaged themselves to an enormous debt for the house, who work ridiculously long hours to service the debt for the house and to meet life's other pressing needs, and who point to their "dream home" with great pride and a sense of accomplishment long before the bank surrenders title to them—these people go to malls, amusement parks, and wilderness areas because home is so boring.

Some people in human history have had the novel idea of building houses in the country. There they build their dream homes themselves, according to their specific needs and abilities, not according to a developer's set of variations on a theme. These houses are situated on land that is ample enough to offer an acreage for growing food, space for children to run about, and for untamed environs where animals, creeks, and curious humans can roam about unfettered.

Houses built under these conditions are not subject to a tyranny known in the United States of America as the *property tax*. Productive land might well have a levy placed on the produce, but none of the inhabitants of places where such houses are welcome would dare think that land can be taxed just for being landed on by a house and family. A house constructed in these circumstances is considered the property of its builder, who is not to be reduced to being the renting tenant of a government entity in perpetuity.

And as the property of their builders, these houses are at the disposal of said builders. If one of them would like to add a room, he may do so without consulting the local owners' association. If one of them would like to drain a marsh so as to plant corn, he may do so without asking the permission of a government bureaucrat in charge of wetlands, deserts, and the oppression of citizens. If one of them would like to stay in the house his whole life and hand it down to his eldest son to hand to his eldest son, then he may do so without worrying that the exercise of the absurdity of eminent domain will result in his back forty becoming the fast lane on the new highway to MegaMallUSA. If one of them would like to build his house in such a way that it would require his three older boys to take turns carrying Grandma up and down three flights of stairs to and from her bedroom each day, he may do so and his sons should thank him in his dotage for teaching them to honor their elders and to be conscientious in performing the corporal works of mercy.

Boredom is not allowed in houses built to these specifications. The land needs care. The buildings need maintenance. The people need not look far to see the next thing that needs doing. One of the delightful things that will need doing on a regular basis will be the spontaneous decision, over which no one has veto authority except one's own common sense, to do absolutely nothing right now.

What is allowed in these houses and their environs is their full use. Hunting and fishing require no permits. Campfires can not be forbidden. Cottage industry is entirely unregulated. The castle's king, the husband/father, has no royal oversight commission empowered by his fellow kings from their neighboring castles, nor does he exercise such interference in their domains.

There are historians who can tell tales of a time when the peasantry abode in such circumstances. It will be pointed out that vermin frequently shared space with families, much like the lice that run through third grade classrooms in our day or the legendary sewer rats of New York City terrorizing the inattentive, or the gads of termites fumigated every five years in posh suburban homes near Los Angeles. It is a fact that the average medieval peasant lived in what would now be called a hovel, resembling in most respects the public housing available in big cities throughout the United States—with the major difference being that the medieval peasant owned his hovel and could not be put out of it. Marauding hordes might beset a medieval village from time to time, true, but there was never a knight on every street corner inspecting each passing donkey cart for hemlock or eye-of-newt—gang graffiti, the highway patrol, and home (in)security systems attest to a different reality in the twenty-first century. Peasants were indeed bound to the land, but they also knew nothing of RIFS, outsourcing, or Chapter 11 reorganization.

Modernity is rather unimaginative. Suggestions that our society might return to the medieval understanding of property rights are met with an instantaneous dismissal as if such would mean a return to medieval understanding of indoor plumbing. The medieval man would not have balked at all of the modern notions of "home improvement", indoor plumbing being a prime example thereof. It is very sad that modern man thinks that not owning, not using, and not building his own home is an improvement. Such modern ideas of "progress" are, to any but the modern mind, unimaginable.

Exile was among the worst of nightmares for the medieval man. To lose one's home, family, and friends was to lose one's identity, one's very self. The little boy, growing up in the modern suburban dream home, dreams of the day when he can finally escape and be on his own in an apartment in the big city. The little girl, growing up in the modern dream home in the big city, dreams of the day when she can finally have a family in the suburbs. The woman, commuting from the suburban dream home to her office tower downtown, dreams of the promotion, coupled with alimony, that will allow her to move her two children and herself to a condo uptown. The man out of work and living in an apartment complex has dreams of selling his suburban dream home so as to move the ex and the two kids to a cheaper place and ease his support payments. When one has no home, one likely will have no family, no friends, and no sense of self to lose.

This world is a dream world inhabited by impotent dreamers plagued with nightmares. The Kingdom of Heaven deals with reality. Citizens of the Kingdom of Heaven do not look forward to the day when their address will change, but to the endless day where nothing changes. They do not live in fear fanned by mortgages, real estate values, and interest-rate fluctuations. Confidence is the hallmark of these citizens, but not confidence in the phantom market and its invisible hand guided by its nameless manipulators; rather, they are confident in the God who saves. Worldlings are taught that salvation inheres in saving the almighty dollar, a god who must be saved but who saves no one. The Kingdom of Heaven is ruled by the King who spends Himself endlessly, without diminishment, enriching His subjects, making them wealthy enough to live in mansions on streets paved in gold, within walls of pearl, whose very being is light and life! Now *that's* something to look forward to, to prepare for, to promise one's children!

Section 3: Clothing

Several subversive septuagenarians sat in the office of a young priest one morning. These were pillars of their community, rocks upon which their families were built, grandmas to a woman. And they were talking revolution!

Some of the ladies had granddaughters who were causing them distress. Each had experienced the same offense in the midst of Sunday Mass. All wanted something done about it.

The beauty of their ire was that they had no desire for government intervention. They did not expect the priests to address the situation from the sanctuary. There was no outcry for a petition drive or legislation.

These grannies wanted action. They were going to do it themselves. They were going to *sew some dresses!*

What had happened was the ever-growing phenomenon of immodesty. These parishioners were weary of the weekly invitation to impurity being witnessed at Mass. But the women were astute enough about the local economy to know that few if any opportunities exist to buy actual dresses for girls. The gods of fashion don't allow that. The septuagenarian radicals also understood enough about young people and the feminine psyche to realize that a problem with vanity had a better chance at a solution through an appeal to beauty than through lecturing or criticizing.

Thus, the women thought of making some dresses for their granddaughters. Then they would market them as one-of-a-kind Grandma Originals for birthday and Christmas gifts. The *piece de resistance* was the decision to try to persuade the girls to learn to sew!

Walmart sells clothes for a profit. Americans buy clothes because they can and to make various meaningless statements about themselves. Third-world slaves make clothing to postpone death by starvation (after all, they are sewing, not sowing). This dynamic, operative almost universally in the world, results in clothes that leave their wearers little better than nude, and worse, without shame for their nakedness. Rather than adorning the body in accord with a clean mind, a pure heart, and a spotless soul, clothing, according to the world's standards, is a matter of exciting the passions, enflaming the baser instincts, and is pleasing only to the denizens of hell with naught but ill regard for the citizens of Heaven.

Said citizens of that Kingdom don apparel conforming to principles markedly other than those observed by the worldly. Here are three principles that encompass much of what is to be expressed in the clothes worn by the man who wears, but is not made by, the clothes:

1. It is impossible to overdress
2. Ditch-digging clothes may not be worn to a formal dinner, but formal-wear can be used in digging ditches.
3. Women are not men, men are not women, and people are not animals.

When in doubt, don't—don't dress down, that is. Dressing up is nothing ever to be ashamed of. Jesus tells a parable of a wedding guest who gets thrown out of the celebratory feast. His fashion *faux pas* was not a matter of sartorial perfection carried to excess. Also keep in mind that a lack of clothing was part of the degradation to which Our Lord was subjected on Calvary—only the shameless ignore their own nakedness or would inflict it on others. Saints in the Kingdom of Heaven do not worry that the sanctity with which they clothe their souls is "too much" for the occasion of coming into the presence of the Lord of the universe. Citizens of the Kingdom of Heaven in exile upon the earth should dress physically in keeping with the inner spiritual reality given them in being clothed with Christ in Baptism. Their Baptismal garment of purest white is the primary garb for daily wear and tear throughout earthly life unto eternal life.

"Isn't this impractical?" some might ask. No. The lower is always inadequate to accomplish the higher, but the higher transcends and encompasses the lower. Thus, God can take on humanity, the Church can dwell in the world, and modest clothing can be used in the midst of strenuous work, mundane activities, and worldly venues. Immodest clothing, however, becomes an occasion of sin for others on the street, distracts from important efforts attempted in daily life, and often threatens physical health in the accomplishment of manual labor—skin cancer, fallen arches, and amputated limbs being among the hazards of dressing inadequately for the harsh conditions of some physical exertions.

Dressing up and dressing well do not mean dressing like a fool. Dangling baubles, gaudy makeup, and bizarre hairstyles are unbecoming to feminine beauty. Foppish accoutrement, feminine adornment, and bizarre hairstyles are unmanly. Clothes should hide nakedness, protect from the elements, and adorn the physical image of God; they are not for strange ornamentation, drawing attention to themselves, or impeding locomotion. Clothing should be worn in sufficient quantity to prevent wandering eyes from leading wandering minds into impure thoughts. In fact, the best clothes are those clothes which permit the beholder to see them without imagining the wearer without them, while at the same time allowing both the beholder and the wearer to forget that they are worn at all.

Part II: The Mind

Section 1: Science

The air we breathe by which moral, political, and social convictions are voiced is a scientific methodology guided by a materialist philosophy. Empiricism governs how modern man sets about knowing. A relativistic subjectivism rules modern man's understanding of what is true and why he should act on truth in any given way. The here and now, the tangible, the measurable is the lowest common denominator on which the majority of men will agree as a shared context of life. Anything beyond the material world capable of empirical analysis is a matter of faith, and modern men have agreed that as a group we can believe nothing together. Faith is out of bounds; only what is knowable is admissible in the court of modern thought. Epistemology far more than theology is the metaphysical arena of exploration for modernity. For a scientific age that is etymologically appropriate. Science is the search for knowledge. Epistemology is the study of knowing and what is knowable. What does science know, and how does the epistemologist know that it knows it?

Each scientific discovery is a veritable proclamation that what is known is that we were wrong about what we knew. Newton yielded to Einstein. The horse gave way before the horseless carriage, which in its turn is brought to bay by gridlock, a victim of its own success. The campfire was dimmed by radio, itself outshone by television, eclipsed now by the variety of entertainments available via computer. Medical science vacillates constantly about whether or not and how much wine, butter, and coffee are good for you.

Progress as measured by science is an evolution from the unknown into the less-known. Scientific knowledge is an absurdly boastful assertion that nothing can be known fully, nothing can be known finally, and nothing can be known fundamentally. All of this would be woefully depressing were it not for the philosophic fact that proof of a universal negative is impossible. Thus, science can not know for certain that its claimed impossibilities are indeed impossible. Science declaring that faith in nothing is reasonable in deference to the effort to know something, is brought up short by the scientific and rational inability to demonstrate that God is part of the nothing that can be believed or is a kind of something that can not be known. Perhaps the man of faith is to be doubted for his lack of physical proof of the existence of the object of his faith, but the man of science is not to be believed when he insists that one take him on faith when he denies the capacity of the subject of faith to know something simply because science is self-admittedly agnostic on the matter. What is not known by science far exceeds what science knows for sure; what is not known by science is a matter of the inadequacy of scientific means to certain knowledge, not of the impossibility of certitude in knowledge.

Any decent, honest scientist admits this. As a thermometer has nothing to say about the height of the man whose temperature it is taking, science has nothing to say about the soul of the man that divines knowledge of the divine Person who is the sole measure of man. It is not an insult to say of science that it is ignorant of the realm of spirit. It is the highest compliment to science to employ its tools in allowing the spirit of man to strive for true freedom. Man bound only to matter and only for death is in the bonds of slavery. Man striving to ken the fullness of truth is set free by the knowledge that a life in the spirit can be at least rationally posited. Science in denial of that possibility is in self-denial: science of itself can neither affirm nor reject faith, and in attempting to do either makes not only faith impossible, but science dies as well.

If man depends only on science for his knowledge of the world and of himself, then he will find himself trapped by science's inherent inability to know anything definitively. The paradox of science is that the first thing known must be the fact of ignorance. Unless an ultimate source and object of knowledge (God) exists, then science is reduced to being an ever-expanding arena of subjects for a never-ending increase of ignorance thereof. The key that unlocks this prison of pure reason is the Faith. Man electing to disregard faith is choosing to remain imprisoned in his senses, utterly unable to make ultimate sense out of what he perceives. Science might answer what, how, where, and when, but science knows nothing of who and why. In an exclusively material universe, there is no such thing as an I to be the subject of knowledge, there is no Thou to be the object of knowledge, there is no We to share knowledge (or faith, or hope, or love), and there is no purpose for the existence of knowledge nor for the seeking of knowledge.

Children of God look around them and are awestruck at how wonderful creation is. They delight in its beauty. For them, the whole world points to a God who loves, who brings joy, who makes Himself known through everything there is. Such childlike people are certain that God is to be experienced through the things that God has made. They eagerly seek out more of His creatures, not to glory in the art, but to catch a glimpse of the exquisite vision of the Artist.

The Book of Wisdom tells us that it is through His Wisdom that God has endowed his creation with knowledge of His love. Wisdom pervades all that God has made. Those who seek to perceive this gift become wise themselves, reflecting the glory of God in their own lives. Many saints understood this. They sought deeper and deeper into the natural sciences, not to make a god out of nature, but to see more clearly how nature reveals the maker who is God. Saints are convinced that the more one knows of the natural order, the more one's faith is confirmed that it is God who has ordered all things.

All good scientists realize that God has made Himself known in all creation. Rather than deny that science has an authentic relationship to faith, the good scientist allows science to confirm his faith in a God who loves His creation so much that He is present everywhere in it. The wisdom that pervades all things is a sign of God who has made all things. The goal of science is to gather knowledge that leads to wisdom that believes in God and returns His love.

We live in an age of science. Often science sounds like a god. Things are condemned if they do not "obey the laws of science." Appeals are made to believe something because "that's what science tells us." Scientists begin to sound like pagan priests as they arbitrate for the uninitiated what it means to be a human being, what the purpose of life is, where life comes from, how it is to be lived.

Because of this fawning on science, we would do well to follow the lead of saints like St. Albert the Great. He understood that science is for something. It is meant to guide us better to God. It does not end in a dispassionate objectivity, but results in a passionate love for creation, a joyous experience of God's highest creation, man, and an intimate unity with God the Creator.

Too often we let our science get ahead of us and control us. Our wealth, technology, and medicine frequently surpass our ability to understand them. We lose sight of what they are for and the fact that we actually create and control them, not they us. In our rush to make things that more and more imitate human beings, we have made human beings to imitate things. Voice synthesizers replace talking on the front porch, eating in the car replaces dining with the family in the dining room, internet sites replace sharing a hug after a long absence.

What's worse, however, is reducing human beings to numbers in measurements of productivity based on units manufactured. Names are lost amid the cacophony of PINs and Social Security numbers and passwords for the PCs so common in homes and offices. We are on the threshold of using technology to manufacture human bodies for the express purpose of using them as replacement parts for other human beings.

Before us are three options. One is that which we seem to be choosing right now, to hurtle down the road of gadgetry, technology, and false convenience. Our machines will become more and more human and our people will be more and more dehumanized. Science as it is mainly practiced today offers no reason why this should not be. This is because such is a moral issue and moral issues can only be resolved by an appeal to absolute truth and absolute truth relies on the existence of an absolute God and this bad science denies the existence of God.

Another option is to flee the monster of science which we have created. We can, as the Amish do, throw out novelties because we do not understand them and it is hard to control them. This risks the error of condemning certain creatures as inherently evil. Such would be a denial of our longstanding Catholic perception of the divine acclamation concerning creation: "And God looked on all that He created and called it VERY GOOD!" The Manichees, the Zoastrians, and the Puritans had an unhealthy disdain for the material world. King David in the Psalms, St. Francis in the *Canticle of the Sun*, and St. Albert in championing the study of the natural sciences would strenuously beg to differ with that kind of attitude. The God who has revealed Himself through Jesus Christ, His Incarnate Son, seems to like the idea of being united with the material world.

The third option, the correct option, is to embrace the intellect which is truly a gift from God. We are to use this intellect in such a way that the objects of its study help us better to appreciate the God who made all things. We are to enjoy these creations and rejoice in the love of their Creator. Using them to excess, as modernity would have us do, ends in the destruction of the relationship between men and the world, between humans and each other, between man and God revealed in Jesus Christ. To reject their use entirely, as overly spiritual philosophies would suggest, results in the diminishment of the human, contempt for the nature of which man is a part, and a denial of God's own word calling all creation good.

It is for us to use restraint. To reject utterly those things of science which are bent on destruction. To take our time in understanding the complicated things which science discovers, eschewing their use until we are morally fit to control them instead of being overwhelmed by them. To support one another in times of sacrifice and self-denial—such as Advent, Lent, and all Fridays—when we voluntarily set aside our material wealth in order to appreciate better the tremendous spiritual blessings to which the earth and all it contains is pointing us. To celebrate with one another, in our parish community, in the secular society, and within the eternal Church that Jesus is Emmanuel, God-with-us.

He has chosen to be with us as the transcendent Creator of all, as immanent in all creation, united with us in the Blessed Sacrament wherein the Body-Blood-Soul-Divinity of Jesus Christ makes the new creation a marriage between earth and Heaven. The Kingdom of Heaven is not to be seen with the eyes of a telescope or microscope, to be declared present there in the stars or there in the test tube. The Kingdom of Heaven is in our midst, surrounding us, within our hearts, uniting us with God who loves us, now and forever.

Section 2: Philosophy

A thing can not be and not be at the same time. The same statement can not be true and untrue at the same time. God, Truth Himself, can not contradict Himself, being the same yesterday, today, and forever. These statements are the ABCs of philosophy. Until they are learned, understood, and acknowledged, no further love of wisdom can be sought, for no wisdom can exist where there is no truth, and the denial of these principles results in the annihilation of the ability of the human mind to embrace truth. Of course, the inability of so many in the world to pursue wisdom with any hope of success is a direct product of their refusal to cultivate a deep and abiding Fear of the Lord—the beginning of Wisdom—within their hearts.

Among men purporting to possess the powers of the modern intellect, something of a contradiction in terms itself, there is a penchant for denying absolute truth altogether. Grey is the color of their true love's truth. Rather than being a perspective on reality and a view of the world, this is tantamount to a self-indictment of blindness, at least of being blind to color, and, thus, blind to much if not all of reality, truth, and wisdom.

"You must learn to love the grey!" is something of a national anthem for this ilk. However, contrary to these connoisseurs of contradiction, black and white, right and wrong, good and evil do exist. The confusion rampant in the world is due in part because black and white have been confused one for the other, resulting in this grey that so many would have us "love". God's very first act of creation is to separate: light from dark, earth from sky, sea from earth. In other words, creation is the divine declaration, "This is not that!"

Such is the fundament of being. Remember the theological construction: the Father is not the Son, the Son is not the Spirit, the Spirit is not the Father; each is wholly God. They are one, distinct, and whole, while not being separate, confused, or identical. Categories and the power to discern them constitute the first activity of the intellect. If indeed there are difficult decisions to be made in the moral life, they lie in the realm of what to do about nuclear weapons, how to feed so many hungry people, and what one is to do when approached by a beggar who smells of alcohol. Citizens of the Kingdom, on the other hand, have no trouble discerning the wisdom in admitting the truth that Sunday Mass is always to be attended, cohabitation is never appropriate, abortion is an abomination, sodomy is unnatural and forbidden, self-abuse is never licit, materialism is a sin, divorce is a failure, and charity must be above all.

If one would use colors as a metaphor for reality, black and white as well as grey are insufficient. God paints across the spectrum. A grey world leaves all indistinct and unrecognizable. A world of nothing but black and white would be two-dimensional and no more real than a photographic negative. Reality corresponds to the rainbow: there are distinctions between the colors, they are united in white light, they can be distinguished by the prism, they are visible to the eye, they can combine to create new and marvelous hues, and they have gradations beyond the power of human retinas or tongues to discern and describe. All the colors mixed indiscriminately is grey (which is not good); all the colors extinguished is black (which is nothingness); all the colors have their origin in light himself (who is the only Good, from whom all good things come). Such light was seen at the

Transfiguration of Our Lord, where he appeared in dazzling white; such light is the reward of those who walk in the light of faith on earth and attain the glory of God's Kingdom in Heaven. On the other hand, the Left hand, is grey, the color of the goats, the tares, and the sound of weeping, wailing and the gnashing of teeth.

Good philosophers recognize the fact that the three paragraphs immediately above are chock full of the sort of statements that of necessity spill over into theology. Wisdom is the object of truth, truth the object of knowledge, and the senses the initial means to knowledge in time. However, such knowledge is itself provisional and incomplete, and the truth built on it can not lead to ultimate perception of reality, nor can the wisdom flowering from it in itself teach more than one creature can teach another.

Absolute and ultimate knowledge can come to creatures only from their Creator, who reveals greater truths beyond His creation within His creation, and in so doing displays the indescribable Wisdom guiding it all. Those who would deny this must also deny their ability to know anything more than this world, and must admit that their knowledge, truth, and wisdom shall end in the death of this world. Citizens of the Kingdom of Heaven delight in the Wisdom of God who delights in the sons of men in this passing world and in the world that will never end.

But back to things more philosophical. The nation of the United States of America prides itself on being God-free. Normally this is expressed as having religious liberty as one of the rights guaranteed by its government to its citizens—begging the question of who is doing the guaranteeing if the government is made by the citizens—and is meant to protect the citizens, but the Constitution is designed to defend the liberties of the citizens from an overweening government by government mechanisms. If the citizens are powerful enough to enforce laws against the encroachments of an unjust government, then why is it necessary to have the government issue guarantees against itself? If the government comprised of the citizens is powerful enough to oppress the citizens, then who are the citizens powerful enough to overcome the government when it runs amok against the citizens, against itself? What is the use of a God who requires Godless men to defend Him on behalf of "believers" who trust that justice can be had from princes dedicated to excluding trust in God in governance?

That is a sample of the "order" typical in the world. There are many unpleasant implications to philosophy in rank rejection of its ultimate end in theology. For instance, freedom of the press is ensconced in the Bill of Rights amended to the Constitution of the United States of America, guaranteeing citizens' activity in the marketplace of ideas without undue government interference. Notwithstanding the license some have taken to indulge in obscenity, incendiary polemics, and demagoguery, Americans hold sacred the right to print, broadcast, or transmit whatever is of moment, of interest, or of profit to society. The power of the word both to reflect and to shape reality is acknowledged as a fundamental principle of this and most democracies.

Children frequently are introduced to the concept of press freedom by way of examining the elements of journalistic reporting and storytelling. The "who-what-where-when" complex of questions is presented to students to help them learn the skills of observation and the rules of rhetoric and articulation. So deeply ingrained in our social psyche is this approach to understanding our world that the products of such analysis are assumed to be accurate, self-evident, and incontrovertible. If it appears in print, on the air, or referenced at an official website, then it must be true. Violations of this trust can result in public shaming, lawsuits, and even incarceration.

Untrammeled freedom to express in public whatever is on one's mind is predicated on the notion that either truth is the subject being propagated or the object being sought. It is no accident that such is the national attitude in the United States, given that this is a decidedly materialist culture, devoted to the advancement of science as final arbiter of reality, and dedicated to empiricism and technology as the means to explore, comprehend, and subdue the natural world. Truth as concrete reality is a primary good, hence, the expression of ideas consonant with or desirous of truth serve the good. A free press can not (and *may* not) hurt anyone, because truth is its matter and the truth ultimately is good to know and to share. Thus, lies and liars receive no protection under the principle of a free press.

But is a half-truth true?

America is rife with sources of information concerning "who-what-where-when" things happen in society. Raw data inundate our every day. How, however, is one to sort through and organize all of the facts, distinguish the falsehoods therefrom, and then determine the nature of the truth being espoused and one's response thereto?

Or more simply put, *why* do things happen?

It is the policy of reputable disseminators of information to restrict themselves to reporting verifiable, objective matters in the body of their stories. In other words, "who-what-where-when" is all that is considered—just the facts, ma'am. Speculation is not deemed appropriate in a reportorial venue.

Why is considered under the heading of editorials and opinions. Theoretically, everyone can agree on the facts, or at least on establishing a means to determine their veracity. What requires further thrashing out is explaining their origins, their ramifications, and their relative importance.

As an aside, it is curious how much of newspapers, the broadcast media, and the internet is given over to advertisements. If truth is the ultimate goal of the press, one wonders what truth is held dearest by commercial interests. Those eager to point out that making money in homage to the almighty dollar is the major motivator of business would do well to ask whence comes the profit made by capitalists, and what motivates the customers of said capitalists to agree to supply them with so much capital. Who can be most trusted with discerning truth: manipulators of the market, or those in the market so manipulated? How can one be sure that a free press is free from manipulation?

But that aside aside, the content of the media—whether print, broadcast, or electronic—conveys a certain image of the world. There is crime in the streets, corruption in government, and concupiscence in the population. What sells newspapers, boosts ratings, and generates website hits is the sensational, the intense, and the violent. What drives disagreements in specific controversies far exceeds the attention given whatever general principles on which parties agree that could provide a context for conflict resolution. Pornography is peddled, high culture is applauded, and Americana is celebrated—indiscriminately and in fairly equal amounts.

Why does all of this get ink, air time, and downloaded?

Because businesses make money that way. Or because that's what the public wants. Or because the government is oppressive. Or because our schools are inadequate. Or because that's the way of the world.

But *why?*

What no one seems willing to admit is that the press is free to report any fact and to editorialize any explanation—except that mankind is wallowing in *sin.*

Imagine this as the beginning of a newspaper article: "Two men were convicted today of committing the *sin* of theft by robbing a bank..." Or this for the lead story on the evening news: "A new poll released today indicates that Americans consider the *sin* of adultery to be much more harmful to society than the *sin* of fornication..." Or a website with this on its home page: "Earn the highest possible returns on *usurious* investments in the Third World by taking advantage of loopholes in the tax code explained by our trained professionals..."

It will be pointed out that bank robbery is defined as a felony, not as a sin. That not everyone agrees that fornication is immoral. That one man's sin of usury is another man's just return on a capital investment.

But *why?*

Are there no media executives who understand and accept the moral law? Is there no audience among the God-fearing who desire a no-holds-barred approach to describing the state of the world? Would the government persecute this kind of press freedom?

An odd self-censorship is operative in America. No laws forbid describing illegal or immoral behavior as sins. The Establishment Clause applies to government (and schools and public squares and the politically correct), but not to media outlets. Yet the public forum is utterly devoid of a daily accounting of world events from the perspective of the Faith. The descriptions of reality ignore God, thus explanations, blame, and solutions for the ills of the world ignore God.

But *why?*

The aforementioned Establishment Clause is interpreted in such wise that the muzzle intended for government is self-imposed on the citizenry. Obeying the law of unintended consequences, our sinful elimination of God from the workings of government has resulted in the elimination of God in the workings of American life, including the expression of truth through the press. Fittingly, we neither admit the sin that removed Our Lord from our Constitution, nor the sins riddling our hearts. The Constitution is silent on the subject of God, the government is silent on the subject of God. We the people are the government, silent on the subject of God in their laws, in their press, and in their understanding of the truth.

So long as God's sovereignty is denied by a nation, its facts will be half-truths at best, and wholly useless toward attaining the goals of life, liberty, and happiness. Life is denied to the unborn, the ill, and the old. Enslavement is the norm, in bondage to bodily appetites, oppressed by greed, and impotent to understand why. America has more money, more gadgets, and more health than any other civilization in history, and its whole economy is predicated on the idea that it is not enough, that better things will replace these things, that satisfaction and contentment with a sufficiency is impossible.

Without God, neither the individual man nor the world of men make sense. If there is no God defining sin as an offense against His Majesty, then there is no sin, all are good, and the world is filled with the fruits of man's goodness...?!?! Or if it is true, as the newspapers sometimes imply, that bad things happen now and then, then the denial of God and His absolute goodness operative in the world leaves one wondering about the wisdom of giving selfish, shortsighted, and sometimes silly people like Americans the right to say, print, or believe whatever they want. How can one account for evil in the world without a God forbidding it, or for good in the world without a God mandating it, or for truth in the world without a God revealing it?

There are those who would say that all that is necessary is the "who-what-where-when" approach to reality. Therein, in the material, tangible, objective world, lies truth and the ability to recognize it and to agree on it. No more can be reasonably expected in a pluralistic and free society.

So much, then, for a free press. The only purpose for having a free press is to allow the free exchange of *ideas*. These ideas can be tolerated so long as they pursue truth. Ideas can not be measured by, contained in, or subjected to instruments designed for empirical evaluation. If the only truth acknowledged is material, there is no need for free speech, free press, or free religion. All that is necessary then would be scientists, recording devices, and no-nonsense news readers to give us just the *facts*—a town crier would do the trick.

But if ideas are *good* and what makes them good is their *truth*, then God *must* be acknowledged. This acknowledgement must be in the citizenry, in the press, and, yes, in the Constitution. Or put another way, God must be loved with one's *whole* heart, *whole* mind, *whole* soul, and *whole* strength. Denial of the obligation to obey this greatest Commandment accounts for the denial of the second greatest Commandment, to love the neighbor as the self. Evidence of this two-fold denial is in each day's news.

Denying God and neighbor, *why* should anyone believe in democracy and democratic rights? *Why* should citizens obey the laws of the land? *Why* should the government allow the press, the citizenry, or the faithful any freedom at all?

Sin confessed explains *who* is wrong: the sinner. Sin confessed explains *what* is wrong: offending God. Sin confessed explains *where* it leads: hell. Sin confessed explains *when* the remedy will come: with repentance. And the final mystery is revealed in *why* repentance is possible: because Christ Jesus loves man unto death, even death on the Cross.

Perhaps this makes no sense to empiricists and leaves them unsatisfied. To the world immersed in the senses and the nonsense of sin, grace is unfathomable. This world, its culture, is self-admittedly attached to satisfying perpetually insatiable appetites. Those who insist on nothing but physical existence as the meaning of life have the whole of their physical lives to pursue such happiness. At the end of this life, they will come to an end of happiness, and they will discover to their eternal horror that they forfeited their liberty when they exercised their "right" to be "free" from God. In the parlance of Madison Avenue, you can have it all—but you can't take it with you. C.S. Lewis put it very aptly when he wrote, "In the end there are two kinds of people: those who say to God, 'Thy will be done', and those to whom God says, '*Thy* will be done.'"

While someone endeavors—in vain—to explain how the First Amendment obeys the First Commandment, citizens of the Kingdom of Heaven who hold temporary citizenship in modern nation states, such as the United States of America, will continue to seek the ways of wisdom founded on truth borne on rational knowledge of the created world revealing the existence of its Creator. Skeptics will abound, to be sure, within this world, but, embracing the spirit of the age just this once, the faithful are permitted a skepticism of skepticism. If men can doubt God, then men of God can doubt men. Time will tell whose faith proves to be most trustworthy, and which philosophy is revealed to have been most wise.

Section Three: Theology

Were a three-year-old child to engage a game of hide-and-seek with a sadistic thirty-year-old, electing to be *it* while his older companion sought a hiding place, the toddler would be utterly incapable of winning should the other *hide* by hopping in his car and driving a thousand miles away. In a like manner, *Deus Absconditus* does not exist. God is not hiding. God is not hidden away in the human subconscious. God is not a Gnostic secret waiting for the eager adept to be initiated into the sublimities of hidden knowledge. If God were truly hiding, then there is no way at all for man to so much as to conceive of His existence—it would be a poor God who could not hide Himself sufficiently to prevent human speculation from proposing Him as at least in consonance with human reason. If God were merely the hidden mysteries of the universe, the natural phenomena, laws, and principles governing the uncreated cosmos, then He would not be God the Creator, but the god creation. If God were but the prize won by human effort at grasping the unknown in tandem with other men already successful in such endeavors, then the being subject to such seizure would hardly be the divine omnipotence, but would more aptly be describable as a singularly impotent commodity.

The only way that man can conceive of the existence of God is for God to *will* such a conception in the mind of man. Our very desire to know of God is of God. The practically universal craving of man to know the divine is itself obedience to the divine will. Man's search for purpose, order, and comprehension is a product of the plan, consummation, and truth by which divine Wisdom designed the universe and all its contents including man. A God hiding Himself unsuccessfully, a God whose hiding is describable in terms of human discovery, a God whose hiddeness is a matter of being ubiquitous in His supposed creation would be as irrational, impossible, and discernible as the circle with five corners the reader is now asked to imagine as he finishes reading this paragraph.

None of this is sufficient to prove that God *does* exist. It all merely means that if God does exist and he preferred us not to know it, we not only would not, but could not know it. There are only two explanations for man's ability to conceive of the existence of God: A) God does exist and He wills human knowledge of that fact; or B) God does not exist and human speculation about that idea is either a delusion, or an insanity, or an error, or a deception. Again, it can not be maintained that God exists desiring that man have no inkling of that truth, while asserting that somehow man on his own, unaided by and against the will of God, has stumbled onto the secret. Theology is not so much seeking to answer whether or not God exists, as addressing the issue of whether or not man is mad for positing a being possessing the attributes of "God". Philosophically it is not unreasonable to assume that God does not exist, but one is left then with no means of explaining matters of ultimate purpose, the final cause of all things, and why any given man should bother getting up in the morning. Once one allows for the existence of God, the only question is, *What does He want?*

This question can be answered only when one first believes that God Himself has revealed that He is, who He is, and why He has allowed man access to this singular piece of knowledge otherwise utterly hidden from all creatures in the material world. Painful is the obviousness that multitudes of men down the miserable millennia have assumed and asserted various affirmations that they indeed know that, who, and why God is and wants. The quandary before men and each man, then, is determining which one is right or is the insanity defense the only other option—for although it is tenable that all ideas of God might be mistaken, if any is right, it can be only one of them. Remember: *A thing can not be and not be at the same time. The same statement can not be true and untrue at the same time. God, Truth Himself, can not contradict Himself, being the same yesterday, today and forever.* If God exists, He does not change, He does not change His mind, and He does not change His will for men varying from time to time, place to place, and culture to culture. Of course, if you persist in the insistence that God does not exist and man is master of all, consider these lines:

If man unbound
you would pursue
regardless of
the good and true

then you may not
deny my will
is free to break
Thou shalt not kill!. . .you.

Adhering to such sentiments is a diriment impediment to citizenship in the Kingdom of Heaven.

If indeed God exists, and that means that only one God exists, and the human-project depends on finding the one avenue to such knowledge, then that one avenue would be the one teaching that God exists, only one God exists, and human salvation is impossible without entering upon the Way teaching this truth. For if God exists, He must be true, and the path to God must be a path of truth. That true path must teach as true the truths that God exists, only one God exists, and but one way to the one God exists. Any suggestion otherwise would be untrue, ungodly, and unuseful for human salvation.

There is no lack of false religions purporting to satisfy the demands of reason in their application of the tenets of their ersatz faiths. When it comes down to it, all of the false faiths in all of the false gods fail due to a lack of interest—false gods just are not that interested in the real needs of mankind. The false god allah does not love man enough to be a man. The false gods of nature do not love man enough to preserve man from eternal death. The false god almighty dollar does not love man enough to bring order, direction, and reason to bear on the conduct of life on earth. The false gods of science do not love man enough to teach certain knowledge of human being or comprehension of divine being to the soul engaged in the act of learning. The false gods that deny Jesus Christ, the one true God, do not love man enough to tell him the full truth about the Creator's love for His creation and His incredible love for man himself, a love willing to die for the beloved. Lacking faith in the loving God, man is reduced to a hopeless state surrounded by uncreated creatures, insatiable appetites, irrational philosophy, ultimate purposelessness, and unredeemed oblivion. Faithless man is alone in cold space, alone in his interactions with his fellow man, and alone in absolute separation from God now and forever.

Jews no longer have priest, prophet, or king to guide them—truth can not be had in an ununified conglomeration of folks whose number simultaneously includes Judas Iscariot, Simon Wiesenthal, Karl Marx, Groucho Marx, Sammy Davis, Jr., the Rothschild family, and many of the original funders and founders of the communist revolution in Russia, all without a means of determining a consistent measure of what constitutes membership in the group or a mechanism for expelling those who fall short of that measure. Protestantism is more a matter of posturing than of positing truth, the defining element of those sects being an attitude of denying anything proclaimed by the Catholic Church, including in some instances the divinity of Christ, the existence of God, and the historicity of Jesus. Mohammed had to reject Christ's claims about Himself and Judaism's prophecies about the Messiah in order to make Islam make sense; he wanted it both ways: to claim continuity with the truth and to introduce novelties that contradict ancient wisdom. That is the time-honored practice of all heretics. Schismatics follow suit by denying the claims of authority of the one true Church, only to set up authority in opposition to the Bride of Christ, although utterly incapable of establishing *bona fides* better than "Thou art Peter and on this rock I shall build my Church!"

Within the true Church Jesus has been betrayed by individuals time and again, just as He was after the Last Supper. This fact no more disqualifies the truths of her claims than the foul treachery of Judas disqualifies Jesus as Savior of mankind. The one Head shares with His one Body the privilege of suffering every indignity for the sake of obedience to God the Father, up to and including the inconstancy of brothers and hatred from those given the most love. Mother Church says with her Lord and Savior Jesus Christ the words of Psalm 54:

> Cast down, O Lord, and divide their tongues; for I have seen iniquity and contradiction in the city. Day and night shall iniquity surround it upon its walls: and in the midst thereof are labour and injustice. And usury and deceit have not departed from its streets. For if my enemy had reviled me, I would verily

> have borne with it. And if he that hated me had spoken great things against me, I would perhaps have hidden myself from him. But thou a man of one mind, my guide, and my familiar, who didst take sweetmeats together with me: in the house of God we walked with consent. Let death come upon them, and let them go down alive into hell. For there is wickedness in their dwellings: in the midst of them. But I have cried to God: and the Lord will save me. Evening and morning, and at noon I will speak and declare: and He shall hear my voice. He shall redeem my soul in peace from them that draw near to me: for among many they were with me. God shall hear, and the eternal shall humble them. For there is no change with them, and they have not feared God: He hath stretched forth His hand to repay. They have defiled His covenant, they are divided by the wrath of His countenance, and His heart hath drawn near. His words are smoother than oil, and the same are darts. Cast thy care upon the Lord, and He shall sustain thee: He shall not suffer the just to waver forever. But thou, O God, shalt bring them down into the pit of destruction. bloody and deceitful men shall not live out half their days; but I will trust in thee, O Lord.

Because she is so intimately united to her Lord, Holy Mother Church clings to all that He has given for all time. She reflects the immutability of her divine Master in her faithful adherence to the Deposit of Faith entrusted to her and guaranteed by the power of the Holy Ghost. An illustration of this conviction can be seen in this excerpt from the papal oath of office:

> I vow to change nothing of the received Tradition, and nothing thereof I have found before me guarded by my God-pleasing predecessors, to encroach upon, to alter, or to permit any innovation therein;
>
> To the contrary, with glowing affection as her truly faithful student and successor, I vow to safeguard reverently the passed-on good, with my whole strength and utmost effort;
>
> To cleanse all that is in contradiction to the canonical order, should such appear;

> To guard the Holy Canons and Decrees of our Popes as if they were the divine ordinances of Heaven, because I am conscious of Thee, whose place I take through the Grace of God, whose vicarship I possess with Thy support, being subject to the severest accounting before Thy divine Tribunal over all that I shall confess;
>
> I swear to God almighty and Our Savior Jesus Christ that I will keep whatever has been revealed through Christ and His successors and whatever the first councils and my predecessors have defined and declared.
>
> I will keep without sacrifice to itself the discipline and the rite of the Church. I will put outside the Church whoever dares to go against this oath, may it be somebody else or I.
>
> If I should undertake to act in anything of contrary sense, or should permit that it will be executed, Thou willst not be merciful to me on the dreadful Day of divine Justice.
>
> Accordingly, without exclusion, We subject to severest excommunication anyone—be it ourselves or be it another—who would dare to undertake anything new in contradiction to this constituted evangelic Tradition and the purity of the Orthodox faith and the Christian religion, or would seek to change anything by his opposing efforts, or would agree with those who undertake such a blasphemous venture.

The progression of authority bestowing knowledge of the will of God and handing down the tenets of the Faith in obedience predates the Church, being the image of the relationship of the Father and the Son. The Father has all authority, bequeaths it to His Son, who, through the Holy Ghost, bestows it on those who believe in Him. Faith in Christ is shown in being obedient to the word of Christ as given by those who have themselves obediently received His word.

Misunderstanding this progression and the obedience that proceeds therefrom is a typical attribute of modern men in the Church. There is a fallacious assumption that infallibility in the papacy is a function of the person of the pope, attaching to his every utterance, action, and written sentiment. By extension this presumption is given to individual bishops, congregations of the Holy See, and conferences of bishops, so that each organ of the institutional Church is invested with an authority that Christ Himself never exercised.

For remember the words of Jesus: "You did not choose me, but I chose you…" (John 15:16). Authority is given to no one to create from whole cloth statements in the Name of God. The faithful can not and should not understand the offices held by those in authority to grant their holders the exercise of that authority in their own right. It is only in obedience to God and in harmony with His truth that ecclesial authority may be wielded. This authority is vested in the persons who hold office, but it is not personal authority—it is official authority. It is unjust, disobedient, and sinful to attempt to usurp that authority to accomplish personal gain, be it monetary, political, or philosophical.

The question for the faithful is, "Do you accept the gift the Father reveals through his Son's Church?" The infallibility of the Holy Ghost-guaranteed Church is not in question; the disciple of Christ is being tested in faith. It is not a matter of the worthiness of the Pope, but the proper obedience of the Christian.

Such obedience is not blind. The teaching from the Father through the Son is the gift of knowledge given in the Holy Ghost. The teacher, the Vicar of Christ, in obedience to the Father, is guaranteed infallibility by the Holy Ghost, who imparts prudence, wisdom, and counsel as well. The faithful of the flock of Christ, seeking the Father's will, are given the gift of understanding by the Holy Ghost. The theological virtue of Faith confirms the disciple in his certitude, the virtue of Hope spurs him on to further sanctity, and the virtue of Charity unites the soul to the Source of all knowledge, truth, and love, the Most Holy Trinity. Thus the faithful recognize the divine origin of the Church's infallible teaching.

Receiving the teaching of the Church is not a matter of mindlessness on the part of the faithful. They are recipients, but not absolutely passive ones. By their own personal attempts at sanctity they increase their openness to the teachings of the Church. At the same time they become better able to discern that which contradicts her truths.

This serves them both in terms of avoiding sin and error in the world, and in recognizing falsehood when it is presented as truth from God. St. John (1 John 4:1-6) admonishes the faithful to test all the spirits, reject the spirit of error, and to listen only to God. St. Peter (2 Peter 2:1-3) warns that false prophets and teachers will rise to lead astray the unwary, enticing them to sin, heresy, and unbelief. Our Lord Himself (St. Luke 12:49-59) proclaims that the truth will divide the good from the evil, and that men have the capacity for discerning that which is good, and of ordering their lives in accordance with the good, so as to achieve salvation.

Power to know right from wrong, good from evil, truth from falsehood is both a natural and a supernatural endowment. Man can know from his senses, from experience, and from reason truth as it pertains to the material world, and those aspects of the spiritual world proper to man. Sin, however, darkens the intellect, dimming human understanding not only of things from beyond this world, but even of objects perceptible to the senses and engaged by reason. Supernatural faith restores and improves man's ability to know the natural, to perceive the supernatural, and ultimately to find union with the divine. The discipline of theology engages man's reason as the vehicle for created beings in time coming to know their Creator dwelling in eternity, by virtue of that Creator having dwelt in time, perduring in time through His grace-mediating Body the Church, and bringing that Body through the travails of time into the rest and peace of eternity.

A hierarchy of being exists in the universe, with God at its summit and inanimate nature at the bottom. In the same vein, the relative position of man's activities can be placed in a hierarchy, those having as object mere matter being the lowest, those having the divine as their supreme object being the highest. Thus the sciences can be ranked in a like manner: organic chemistry ranks higher than inorganic, chemistry has precedence over physics, and physics is above geology. Theology as the science, the ascertainment of knowledge, of God is supreme over all sciences, the ultimate knowledge available to man, indeed, the pinnacle of all knowledge. All other sciences find a proper place within theology.

Lesser sciences exclude and/or are ignorant of that which is above them. By the same token, lesser sciences benefit from greater clarity beneath the light shed on them from above by the greater sciences. Geology can teach much, but teaches much better when the truths of physics are applied to it. All of the natural and human sciences have much to offer man, but they are perfected only when illumined with the light available solely through true theology. In the end, without theology the lesser sciences are left in the dark regarding ultimate things, the question of purpose for being, and explanations for how man is to engage the universe if nothing distinguishes him within the universe from those elements of it which do not reason. Theology is the only science able to offer a reason to reason for asking questions, seeking their answers, and judging truth from error. In a word, theology is the only science that has any faith that there is hope that charity exists to provide man with a response to his desperate ***Why?***

Part III: The Soul

Section 1: Free Will

Man is made in the image and likeness of God. This means not only that one looks like God in the spirit, but that one looks like God in how he perceives the world. It is not merely a matter of how one is seen, but of how one sees; not just of how one looks, but of that for which one seeks. It is the nature of the search, the means by which one searches, and the goal for which one searches. *Imago Dei* is man's being AND action—just like God!!!

Man must see with the eyes of the Lord. The son resembles the father not only in how he looks to the world, but in his worldview. To have our Father's eyes is not just to look like Him, but to see like Him, to learn to recognize what the Father reveals as good and true. That is the gift of the sons of God in the Faith: to see even as they are seen.

At the center of this vision is the Cross of Christ. Faithful citizens of Heaven do not look at the Cross as do the faithless, with despair. They look on the cross and see man's greatest and only Hope. This is the Love that all saints experience in bearing all for Christ.

Confusing "freedom" with "license" is a common mistake. People take license to do things they are not free to do. Free will in angels and man is the power to choose to obey God, something denied all other beings. Animals, vegetables, and minerals must obey God by virtue of their very being. They have no choice in the matter. They obey perforce. Angelic and human freedom inheres in the freedom to choose to obey God. The license taken to reject obedience results in the utter loss of freedom.

God built man with free will in order for him to make use of it in obedience to Him. Man is "hard-wired" to freely obey God. That is the way free will is meant to be used. Abuse of the power man has as a rational creature results in the freedom being destroyed, the being had from God being destroyed, for God has created man to be free only by obeying Him. When men disobey God, they destroy their freedom and, if unrepentant, destroy the creation God has made them to be as free children of His love.

Willing evil is absolutely forbidden. A little evil chanced for the good always diminishes the moral agent. As St. Thomas says, *Bonum est ex integra causa, malum ex quocumque defectu.* A little evil does no good.

Some fools think that evil is allowed to exist in order to *create* free will. Ouch! NO! NO! NO!

Free will is not a choice between good and evil. Free will is the choice between God and nothing—and God, not the devil, temptation, or human pride, creates. Eek! To suggest that the defining attribute of man as a material/spiritual being is the work of evil is, is—is evil!

Indeed, God creates *ex nihilo*, but though He creates from nothing, He most certainly does not create for nothing. To be or not to be is not the question; to be good or to not-be good—that is the question! The damned deny God's will toward being good, but their being evil does not undo His original act of creation. To be evil is to not-be good, but it is not to be nothing. The damned may want to be nothing in opposition to God's will that they be good, but in attempting to deny God's will that they be good, they still do not get the nothing that they want, they only get to not-be good. Neither God's will nor their will is done! That is the essence, the being of evil. It is a slavery, an impotence, in which both divine omnipotence and creaturely free will are rejected.

Neither God nor man can create nothing. Man can choose nothing, but this perversion of his free will in opposition to God's will does not gain nothing, it becomes evil. What damned men are left with, then, is not the nothing of denying God, but the condemnation to being evil. God does not ratify the rebellious soul's disobedience with oblivion, for God can not deny Himself, or His act of creation. God forever upholds His original creation, but the denial of the good of that creation becomes the eternal experience of evil for the damned soul. Demons and damned souls can choose to not-be good, but they can not choose to not be.

Destruction of a creature is not an expression of freedom, but of slavery. To use a creature for something other than its created end is to bring ultimate destruction to that creature. The misused, the abused, the destroyed are not free, but are damned. Here is how Pope Leo XIII put it (*Libertas praestantissimum of 1888)*, explaining how St. Thomas Aquinas put it:

> From Paragraph 6: "This subject is often discussed by the Angelic Doctor in his demonstration that the possibility of sinning is not freedom, but slavery. It will suffice to quote his subtle commentary on the words of Our Lord: 'Whosoever committeth sin is the servant of sin' (John 8:34). 'Everything,' he says, 'is that which belongs to it naturally. When, therefore, it acts through a power outside itself, it does not act of itself, but

> through another, that is, as a slave. But man is by nature rational. When, therefore, he acts according to reason, he acts of himself and according to his free will; and this is liberty. Whereas, when he sins, he acts in opposition to reason, is moved by another, and is the victim of foreign misapprehensions. Therefore, "Whosoever committeth sin is the servant of sin".'...the wise man alone is free; and by the term 'wise man' was meant, as is well known, the man trained to live in accordance with his nature, that is, in justice and virtue.
>
> From Paragraph 13: "...obedience is greatly ennobled when subjected to an authority which is the most just and supreme of all. But where the power to command is wanting, or where a law is enacted contrary to reason, or to the eternal law, or to some ordinance of God, obedience is unlawful, lest, while obeying man, we become disobedient to God...all being free to live according to law and right reason; and in this, as We have shown, true liberty really consists."

In short, freedom comes from God. To be free means to incline one's being toward God. The *only* expression of freedom is choosing to be as God has created man to be, namely, to be good. To choose to be other than good is not freedom, but is the slavery of being evil. The evil are not free. Only the holy are truly free as God, sanctity itself, is free. Freedom in angels and humans is part of their reflection of the being of God. Being holy, being good, as God is good and holy is the only means to preserve and exercise freedom. To be holy as God is holy is to be free; to be free requires being holy as God is holy.

Section 2: Body and Soul

Life comes in many different forms. Some life is bodily without a rational soul. Some life is bodily with a rational soul. Some life is spiritual without a body. Here is a brief schema of what life exists in the universe:

Life: The Owner's Manual

Standard Equipment
Carbon, protein, and water
in every son and daughter,
'tho' some, to be fair,
don't need much air.

Most make use of light
but not always for sight
'cause it's also good,
say the plants, for food.

And whether one is fruit or meat
you'll want a modicum of heat,
for if you get too hot or cold
you'll not get very old.

Available Options
A most marvelous thing
is a flock taking wing,
but more miraculous still
is the thrush's trill.

How to make their own glow
some worms and flies know;
another secret delight
is the bumblebee's flight.

Spiders and beavers build
but none of them gild;
the ants do lots of work,
but sloths have none to shirk.

Wise seem the eyes of owls
and sad the coyote's howls,

but neither can tell
the ill from the well.

Deluxe Models (Limited Editions)
Angels we have heard on high
but they lack tongues to speak and wings to fly;
the Cherubim and Seraphim
only want to be with ***Him.***

Demons are what angels won't
by being what the angels don't:
on primrose paths they chose to trod
the way to death—away from God.

Neither spirit nor flesh is man
'tho' in Eden from both (and God) he ran;
unique his terrible call:
to be a soul-in-body all.

Human beings are persons of both flesh and spirit. Men do not possess bodies and souls, men *are* bodies and souls, embodied spirits. A body without a soul is a corpse. A soul without a body is a ghost. Corpses and ghosts are what come of an erroneous understanding of human being—and acting on it.

Action flows from being. The works of the flesh are material; those of the human soul are spiritual. Whether good or not, in either the material or spiritual realm, depends on the will responding to reason based on knowledge of reality. Body and soul are meant to work together to effect the overall good of the whole person. Sometimes it is necessary for the body to sacrifice a measure of well-being for the higher good as directed by spiritual considerations. It is *never* acceptable to sacrifice a spiritual good in favor of a merely physical advantage. Since the works of the flesh are material, they pass away; spiritual actions, on the other hand, have eternal ramifications. Thus, temporary material deprivation is desirable when permanent spiritual improvement is thereby possible.

Fasting from food, sleep, and speech stretch the endurance of the body. They also increase the power of the will to endure the struggle to avoid all evil and to do only good. Giving into the body's weakness destroys both body and soul. Overcoming that weakness is a path to preserving body and soul unto eternal glory.

Brother Ass, as St. Francis referred to his body of flesh, is to the soul what Cain was to Abel. The body is of the species of blessings generally labeled as "mixed". It is in essence good, being made by God and worthy to house the souls of the Blessed Mother and the Son of God. However, the body is also the locus of the fiercest of the battles in the world since the Fall of Adam and Eve, the war each man must wage against himself. The body is to be nourished and nurtured, not coddled; it is to be treasured as a gift from God, not prized in itself; and it is to be discarded in death in favor of the glorification that will belong to the saints on the Last Day.

Catholic citizens in heaven and on earth are not Manicheans, Puritans, or Zoroastrians. The material world is not coeval with the spiritual world. The material world is not evil as such. The material world is not an end in itself, itself doomed in its present state to come to an end. Matter need not be feared, may not be worshipped, and should not be ignored as a legitimate means of engaging the larger reality in consonance with the will of its Creator. Creation is not the revelation of a glorious god, but is the revelation in small pointing to the infinite glory of God.

Physical eyes, ears, noses, mouths, and fingers are utterly incapable of grasping that truth without the guidance of reason directed toward spiritual truth. Truth, Beauty, and Goodness die without a rational soul to perceive them. There are no connoisseurs of music among the hawks eating sparrows in mid-warble. No judgement is forthcoming from a celestial tribunal, to weigh the arguments of the sun, that its rights are infringed upon by the nightly encroachments mounted by the moon. There is no reason for nature to be found within nature; any mind desiring such must look outside of nature, beyond the natural mind, and beg admittance to knowledge of the supernatural.

In time, this journey is impossible for the body to take. It is endeavored only in the spirit, and only insofar as spiritual truth is sought and grasped. That search and that embrace can succeed only when the human soul is infused with divine grace. Grace from God sufficient for salvation may be obtained nowhere except in the Sacraments of the Catholic Church, predicated on the Cross of Christ engaged in Baptism and consummated in the Sacrifice of the Mass. Walking the path of grace on the way to the Kingdom of Heaven, the citizen of the Kingdom of Heaven in exile in the world is given the light of the Faith by which to see with a sight capable of piercing the veil that covers the peoples. He is given understanding upon hearing the truth of the Word of God with a charity that prevents him from becoming a noisy gong or a clanging cymbal. Sweetness beyond all telling is tasted when God Himself is made Food for the journey, as the Lord Jesus in the Blessed Sacrament of the altar descends onto tongues hungry for the Bread of Life.

All is seen clearer when the eyes of the soul illumine the eyes of the body. Every truth is perceptible to the ear trained to detect divine Wisdom through the cacophony of worldly imbecility. Satisfaction is unending for the appetite desirous of consuming *Panis Angelicus.* And the beauty present in the world, the delight in human creativity, and the savor of simple natural blessings is immensely increased for the man who, by grace, is able to properly value them. Those who treasure the gifts of God in the world are not those who amass worldly treasures. No, the real lovers of creation's blessings are those who see them for what they are, know their true worth, and enjoy them as means, not ends, to good from God which is invisible to the world, beyond the comprehension of the worldly, and finally perfected in the world that will never end.

Adam's Fall resulted in a divorce occurring within man of the body and soul. They are rendered enemies of one another by Original Sin. And the war between Heaven and hell has as its most vital battleground the human person, where body and soul are enlisted either as agents of satan or members of the Church Militant destined for victory in Christ Jesus. Sharing in His victory, the human person must die to himself, taking on the cross with Christ, and willing the defeat of the world, the flesh, and the devil in his own soul through the thoughts, words, and deeds of time being given in their entirety to God. The whole heart, whole soul, whole mind, and whole strength of man lives or dies dependent on the choice for or against God. Either the soul comes to grief by obeying the passions of the body, or the body comes to glory by obeying the deep desire of the soul to share in the Passion of Christ with and in the Body of Christ. If body and soul do not win this battle together under the direction of spiritual truth and goodness, then both body and soul will be lost. It is not either-or, but all-or-nothing. Body and soul are designed to be one—warring for all eternity with the damned if obedient to the father of lies; in perfect peace forever if obedient with Jesus to the holy will of God the Father.

Section 3: Life and Death

Life comes from God, who is truth. Death is the domain of the devil, the father of lies. The Spirit of God informs the law of God, and leads to life. Satan twists the letter of the law in such a way as to make it deadly to its adherents. Without charity, the greatest divine attribute, the law is a dead letter. Hatred is the heartless desire of satan and his minions, bringing a message of death to those who hearken to him. To cling to life is to embrace all truth in Jesus Christ. Death comes to those who receive the dead letter of the lies told by the world, the flesh, and the devil. Alas! even some who purport to be members of the body of Christ have accepted lies over the truth, to wit:We, the People who are Church in Corinth, Galatia, and Ephesus, in solidarity with one another and with all oppressed by poverty, injustice, and the sins of society, who are seeking peace and harmony with every sister and brother in whom God's salvation is being worked out by the creator's very act of creation, and his coming among humankind as a sharer in the grace belonging to all the world, send greetings to our fellow-worker Paul who once was Saul.

> We are pained, dear Paul, by the tone of the two or three letters (we lost track of the exact number) that you sent to Corinth and each of those received by Church in Galatia and Church in Ephesus. We are grieved at the name-calling, referring to Church in Galatia as *stupid* and yourself as a *fool*, expressing a horrible lack of self-esteem and a patriarchal condescension to the People of God who share with you a common baptismal priesthood. We are especially saddened at your rigid and culture-bound insensitivity to the gifts that women can bring to the ministry of teaching, Proclaiming at the Table of the Word, and bringing God's maternal qualities to the Table of Fellowship we all share with our brother Jesus.
>
> And beloved Paul! think of the hurt felt by our Jewish and Greek friends when they heard of your reactionary remarks concerning them. Peter showed so much more understanding and progressive thinking in his efforts to reconcile our current practice with the venerable and ancient customs of the Temple and Table of the Chosen People. We must show restraint in remarking on your old-fashioned ideas about those who worship God

in the divine multiplicity or graven in the materials of creation. To be frank, yet always gentle, friend Paul, you are guilty of the sin of inhospitality—and would have us bring that sin to the Table of God!

Our disappointment is all the more heartfelt because of the openness you seemed to show on your visits. You never raised your voice. You reprimanded no one. You appeared willing to accept Church in all its diverse and rich expression of love for humankind and the cosmic creator. We are confused, wondering which is the *real* Paul, the warm companion who walked with us, or the harsh and aloof man of his letters. We wonder if even Paul knows his real self. Is there still some of the old Saul in him, unable to fully embrace the becoming and evolutionary newness to which God calls us all?

But we know there is hope, Paul! As you so beautifully said yourself, there are only three things, faith, hope, and love, and the *greatest* of these is love! We know the person capable of such tremendous empathy will ultimately see that love reveals that all are one. We who are Church will love like Jesus and embrace everyone in love: slave or free, Jew or Greek, woman and her co-worker man! No human experience or expression of love can ever be excluded from our worship of God, who is love manifested by humankind. Please, Paul, pray on this and accept our gift of love. We look forward to receiving the gift of love becoming Paul!

Before we close we ask you to reflect as well on the difficult, and dare we say, obscure things you wrote concerning the place of Jesus in the universe, marriage relationships, and the afterlife. Very few of us have any appreciation of your ideas and how the God of our various understandings would permit them to be true. Even fewer of us agree with you. It seems to us that Jesus places much more importance on the here and now and making this life peaceful and agreeable to all. Jesus was a uniter, not a divider! Let us dialogue on these issues and reach consensus. But if we do not come to share a consensus, may our ongoing dialogue become a mutual offer of non-judgemental acceptance.

> Send our greetings with a big hug to Sosthenes, Timothy, and all the women and men empowered to be Church for you. May God who maternally gives life to creation, who shares in the pain of humankind, and who is the blesser of all with the spark of divinity grant you grace and love. Peace, Paul. :)

The foulest lies, and the most woefully effective, are those that tell most of the truth, mostly truth, admixed with error. Man is inherently drawn to the truth. Where the truth is used as a disguise for a lie, there is a deadly peril for those men incapable of distinguishing truth from falsehood, all too often succumbing to the fatal mistake of accepting the lie as truth, accepting truth as compatible with lies. There is no life to be had for them so cursed with credulity lacking the assent of the will to the grace of the true Faith.

Among the most pernicious of lies clinging to truth is the twisted logic resulting in the exaltation of earthly life as an end in itself. Creation is good, as declared by the mouth of God in His very act of creating it. However, it is most evil to believe that creatures are good in themselves without reference to their Creator and refusing use of them according to the will of Him who made all things. Life is good, but life on earth is meant for more than just the earth. All creatures are given to men for the purpose of man's use of them in working out his salvation with fear and trembling, not with arrogance and presumption. A life lived on earth for nothing beyond the earth will come to a disastrous end with the end of the world. Only the lives willing to release their hold on the earth will discover a far better life beyond the beauty of this world, beyond the comprehension of man to imagine, beyond simply food, shelter, and clothing, instead being nourished on the very life of God, housed in divine mansions, and clothed in glory.

Do the good! and *Avoid evil!* are the two moral imperatives given to the faithful through the natural law, the magisterium, and the divine law meant for the salvation of man. Through obedience to this dual admonition to seek sanctity and reject sin, the faithful cooperate with God's plan of salvation. In His plan God's activity is creation and redemption. Man's activity results in God's creation either being damned or glorified. What a man *does* is his contribution to the project of establishing what he *is* for all eternity. Each of the two moral imperatives must be engaged in man's life in the world. "Do the good," is a relative command. "Avoid evil," is an absolute command. Between birth and death man is given ample opportunity to obey these commands and thus be saved. Free will gives him the power to choose, but the power is dependent on the choice. Man's free will is increased in choosing righteousness; it is diminished when he chooses sin. The saint is truly, fully, and eternally free as a son and heir of God. The sinner dies in perpetual slavery, bound forever to his sin, entirely incapable of asserting his will to happiness, which he falsely sought by disobedience to God on earth. A man is able to do only so much good. His responsibility is limited by his very being. God alone can do all good. Man participates in the infinite goodness of God. It is divine grace and mercy which deigns to extend the infinite good of God to the finite man. Doing but a little good is rewarded with endless beatitude. In giving God His due, man receives infinitely more than is his due from God. There is *never* an instance in which evil may be done. No sin is ever permissible, and none can be attributed to the divine will or imputed to the person of God. Sin belongs utterly to the world. Each man's sins are uniquely his own. Although God gives the saved full portion of His life beyond their just desserts, the perdition of the damned is solely his own work and the fruit of his own demerits. Grace in its very being is a sharing in love; sin and its wages, death, are confined to the guilty soul and makes impossible any communion on earth or in Heaven. Being, in keeping, with the divine will, is inherently good. God's original creation received His benediction six times before he declared His work *Very good!* (cf. Genesis 1:1-31). This truth has been confused by many to mean that good attaches to the human person regardless of how he exercises his free will. It is a commonplace to hear a man's sins related with the summary judgement, "But he's a good person." Man may have begun good, but original sin, concupiscence, and sinful actions disfigure that goodness in time and, potentially, destroy it for all eternity. Allied to the separation between life and death pertinent to the final disposition of the human person are the signs manifesting whether or not the soul is choosing life. Death is evinced by an existential despair enveloping a person. Life is manifested in a confident hope in the face of all that occurs until eternal life is received. A simple way of describing this dynamic would be:

1) The secularist laments a man's "early" death as "dying before his time"; the Catholic acknowledging John 12:24, understands that a man must die before his eternity.

2) The worldly die as if no life awaits: in despair. The Catholic lives as if no death awaits: in hope.

3) It is the will of God that man redeemed dies just in time.

Eye has not seen nor ear heard nor human mind conceived of the delights of Heaven. God's mercy in the world also extends to sparing men a full appreciation of the horrors of hell. It should be evident, however, to men of reason that delight is to be preferred to horror, in whatever degree, of whatever kind, for whatever duration. Faithless souls see pain, hardship, and deprivation in the world only as horrors to be avoided. Faithful souls see pain, hardship, and deprivation as the delights of those privileged to share in God's mercy through the Cross of Jesus Christ. Only the true Faith is efficacious in bestowing the power to see beyond appearances into the deeper truths veiled to physical sight by concupiscence. Too late will faithless souls discover their error when finding not only were they utterly incapable of avoiding all pain, hardship, and deprivation on earth, but that such faithless cravenness results in pain, hardship, and deprivation as their lot for all of eternity. Great is the joy of the faithful soul who discovers that the little consolations, the little consolation, he received in his pain, hardship, and deprivation on earth bear fruit in an eternity of bliss, complete joy, and abundant life.

All the books of all the world throughout all of time are inadequate to the task of describing the fullness of the life of Christ. All the books of all the world throughout all of time are inadequate to the task of describing the life in Christ meant to be lived by the members of the Body of Christ. This brief excursus humbly acknowledges its laughable lack. As well, however, it is to be profoundly desired in prayer that it might serve as some small aid to souls eager to embark on the wonderful labor of bearing the Lord's sweet yoke and light burden. May He who began the good work of salvation in you bring it to perfection, and with mutual sentiments of charity solicitous for the salvation of all of our fellows, *Oremus pro invicem!*

Father Smith

19 November 2005
St. Elizabeth of Hungary
Holy Family House, Silver Cliff, Wisconsin

A Sure Thing

What madman, fiend, or fool would dare believe
that e'er the strife between the sun and clouds
besetting earth with frequent cause to grieve,
where life itself seems draped in deadly shrouds,
will come to resolution in a night
of tempest winter-wrought beneath the noon,
and quelling hope as if a summer blight
assailed the stars and made the moon to swoon?
But lunatics, the damned, and addled brains
would think it sense such nonsense fit to tell,
as if the fire of dawn is quenched by rains
or birth is daunted by the tolling bell.
No more than counting after one begins
can satan aught but lose what Jesus wins.

Father Smith.
21 November 2005: The Presentation of the Blessed Virgin Mary
Holy Family House, Silver Cliff, Wisconsin

My sheep hear my voice. And I know them: and they follow me. And I give them life everlasting: and they shall not perish forever. And no man shall pluck them out of my hand. That which my Father hath given me is greater than all: and no one can snatch them out of the Father's hand. I and the Father are one.—St. John 10: 27-29

These things I have spoken to you, that in me you may have peace. In the world you shall have distress. But have confidence. I have overcome the world.—St. John 16:33

If This, Then That...

Dignitatis Humanae says, "The Vatican Council declares that the human person has a right to religious freedom. Freedom of this kind means that all men should be immune from coercion on the part of individuals, social groups, and every human power, so that, within due limits, nobody is forced to act against his convictions nor is anyone to be restrained from acting in accordance with his convictions in religious matters in private or in public, alone or in associations with others. The Council further declares that the right to religious freedom is based on the very dignity of the human person as known through the revealed word of God and by reason itself. This right of the human person to religious freedom must be given such recognition in the constitutional order of society as will make it a civil right." (see Paragraphs 2-5, 6-7; this principle is reiterated in the *Catechism of the Catholic Church,* Paragraph 2106)

Canon 1311 of the 1983 Code says, "The Church has an innate and proper right to coerce offending members of the Christian faithful by means of penal sanctions."

As regards Catholics who would practice the immemorial Tradition, discipline, and Sacraments as they stood prior to 1962, it would seem, then, that either the canon does not apply to them, given the force of the statement from the Council, and all sanctions they have suffered these past thirty or more years are unjust; or coercion to bring into line other members of the Body of Christ wherein the Church of Christ subsists (see *Lumen Gentium* 8) would be in order.

If it be argued that Photians and protestants are not subject to papal authority, then one of two conclusions is necessary: either they are not, in fact, members of the Body of Christ, and therefore are denied access to salvation; or communion with the Holy See is not necessary for salvation.

If it be argued that membership in the Body of Christ is not necessary for salvation, then sanctions such as suspensions and excommunications applied to Catholics adhering to immemorial tradition are meaningless and null.

If it be argued that Photians and protestants are somehow in communion with the Holy See but need not obey its mandates, then it must be explained how traditionalists who acknowledge the authority and validity of the Holy See are excluded from communion therewith; as well is necessary an explanation of how disobedience to due authority by Photians and protestants does not impede salvation.

If it be argued that subjects of the Holy See are bound to obedience to the Holy See for the sake of salvation, but those who are not subject to its authority are not so bound, then what is being said is that the means to salvation are not absolute but relative, changing for each man according to circumstance. If one law does not bind all for the sake of salvation, then none can say what is necessary for any individual's salvation.

If it be argued that the Holy See is competent to teach the necessary means to salvation, then said teachings must be made clear to all *and observed by all.*

Canon 1313 states, "If a law is changed after an offense has been committed, the law which is more favorable to the accused is to be applied." If the ceaseless teaching of the Church, *Extra ecclesiam nulla salus,* has been changed such that Photians and protestants can gain access to salvation outside of the Roman Catholic Church, then this changed law, according to the principle expressed in the new canon, must apply, as well, to subjects of the Holy See, particularly those who incurred sanctions before 1983.

If the laws pertaining to salvation can change from time to time, then they can be construed to apply in different ways from man to man; likewise, if the laws of salvation given by God, taught by Christ, and endowed by the Holy Ghost upon the Church are eternal, immutable, and irrevocable, then they apply to all men at all times.

Either *Dignitatis Humanae* allows for all men to seek God in whatever way conscience dictates, which includes the immemorial doctrines, practices, and Sacraments of the Roman Catholic Church; or all are bound to obedience to the Holy See, whose authority is given by God solely for the purpose of handing down the Deposit of Faith without novelty, innovation, or deviation.

Father Smith

7 December 2002
Feast of St. Ambrose
Prince of Peace Parish, Clinton, Iowa

"For us as Catholics, the Distributive State (i.e., the State in which there are as many owners as possible) is not something which we discuss, but something we have to propagate and institute. No advance in social thought or social action is possible if we are seeking to prove to ourselves as a theory what we should be trying to realize as a fact." —Father Vincent McNabb, OP, The Church and the Land